North [illegible] Blue Book

2017-2019

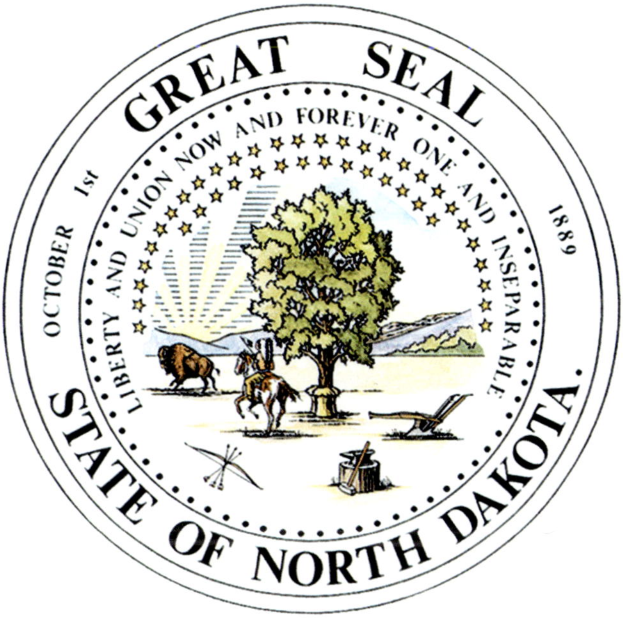

October 2017

Compiled by
DEDICATED VOLUNTEERS

Published by
SECRETARY OF STATE
ALVIN A. JAEGER

Editorial Notes and Acknowledgments

The *2017-2019 North Dakota Blue Book* traces its lineage back to 1887. This 32nd edition continues the tradition by presenting a review of the state's social, economic, environmental, cultural, and political status.

Published under the authority of the territorial legislature, the 1887 and 1889 books, produced by Mandan attorney, Theodore K. Long, reflect their purpose in the title – *Long's Legislative Handbook and Rules of the Legislative Assembly of the Territory of Dakota*. These early books were intended primarily to provide information to legislators.

Following statehood, a series of North Dakota books under the name *Legislative Manual* appeared biennially from 1889 through 1919, with the exception of 1915 and 1917. The earliest contained contents similar to Long's handbooks. Beginning with the 1897 edition, the books, bound in hard blue covers, offered historical, statistical, and political information. See the "North Dakota Blue Books" chart in these introductory pages for a history of publication dates.

The first volume carrying the title *North Dakota Blue Book* appeared in 1942. Until release of the 1995 edition, specific legislative authorization and appropriation was used to publish the Blue Books. In 1995, Secretary of State Alvin A. Jaeger began publishing the Blue Book using funds appropriated to his office and has continued to do so. The book was printed with spiral comb binding to make photocopying easier and changed to a book style perfect binding in 2003. This book and the 11 immediate past editions are important companions to each other in presenting a complete story of the state's history. Copies of recent editions are available through the State Historical Society of North Dakota Museum Store at the North Dakota Heritage Center at 701-328-2822. Digital versions of all books are available on the Digital Horizons website at http://digitalhorizonsonline.org. A digital version of this edition is also available at https://sos.nd.gov.

The Secretary of State thanks the many state employees and private citizens from across the state who spent untold volunteer hours writing documents, compiling information, completing data entry, providing photographs, proofreading, and editing. Without the assistance of these dedicated individuals, the production of the *North Dakota Blue Book* would not be possible. The list of contributors to the 2017-2019 edition follows these acknowledgments.

The 1995 and 1999-2001 *Blue Books* have been recognized with "Notable Document" Awards from the North Dakota Library Association. The 2007-2009 edition received national recognition from the National Conference of State Legislatures in the category of Citizen's Guide.

While every effort by authors and editors of the *2017-2019 North Dakota Blue Book* has been made to provide accurate information, errors and oversights naturally occur. Please provide comments regarding discrepancies or errors to:

Secretary of State
600 East Boulevard Avenue, Dept. 108
Bismarck, ND 58505-0500

Call: 701-328-3664
Fax: 701-328-2992
Email: sos@nd.gov

Copies of the *2017-2019 North Dakota Blue Book* may be purchased at:
State Historical Society of North Dakota Museum Store
North Dakota Heritage Center
612 East Boulevard Avenue
Bismarck, ND 58505

Call: 701-328-2822

Alternate formats of this publication are available upon request.
Call 701-328-2900 or the North Dakota Relay System at 800-366-6888.

Cataloging in Publication
North Dakota blue book. — 1942- .—
[Bismarck, N.D. :s.n.]
v. :ill. ; 23-24 cm.
Frequency varies.
Issue for 2017-2019 has title: North Dakota Blue Book
Issued by the North Dakota Secretary of State
ISSN 0191-0612 = North Dakota blue book

1. North Dakota—Registers. 2. North Dakota—Politics and government—Periodicals.
I. North Dakota Department of State. II. Title: North Dakota Blue Book.

JK6430.N6 353.9'784'002 56-129

ISBN 978-0-9742898-6-1

North Dakota Blue Books

Legislative Manual	Printer	Secretary of State
1889-1890	*Bismarck Daily Tribune* State Printers & Binders	
1897	*Bismarck Tribune* State Printers & Binders	
1899*	*Bismarck Tribune* State Printers & Binders	
1901*	*Bismarck Tribune* State Printers & Binders	
1903	*Bismarck Tribune* State Printers & Binders	
1905*	*Bismarck Tribune* State Printers & Binders	
1907*	*Bismarck Tribune* State Printers & Binders	Alfred Blaisdell**
1909*	*Bismarck Tribune* State Printers & Binders	Alfred Blaisdell**
1911*	*Bismarck Tribune* State Printers & Binders	Patrick D. Norton**
1913*	*Bismarck Tribune* State Printers & Binders	Thomas Hall
1919*	*Bismarck Tribune* State Printers & Binders	Thomas Hall

* Outside book cover reads North Dakota Blue Book, inside title is Legislative Manual

** Secretary of State's name does not appear on the books until 1907

Manual for the State of North Dakota	Editor	Printer	Secretary of State
1926	Charles Liessman (Deputy Secretary of State)	Allied Printing, Fargo	Robert Byrne
1930	Charles Liessman	Knight Printing, Fargo	Robert Byrne
1932	Charles Liessman	Bismarck Tribune	Robert Byrne

North Dakota Blue Book	Editor	Printer	Secretary of State
1942	G.A. Gilbertson (Deputy Secretary of State)	Bismarck Printing Co.	Herman Thorson
1954		*Bismarck Tribune*	Thomas Hall
1961		*Bismarck Tribune*	Ben Meier
1973	Jay Bryant		Ben Meier
1981	Jay Bryant	Kaye's Printing, Fargo	Ben Meier
1889-1989 North Dakota Centennial Blue Book	Curtis Eriksmoen	Kaye's Printing, Fargo	Ben Meier
1995-1997	Volunteer Editorial Board	Quality Printing, Bismarck	Alvin A. Jaeger
1997-1999	Volunteer Editorial Board	United Printing, Bismarck	Alvin A. Jaeger
1999-2001	Volunteer Editorial Board	The Printers, Bismarck	Alvin A. Jaeger
2001-2003	Volunteer Editorial Board	Quality Printing, Bismarck	Alvin A. Jaeger
2003-2005	Volunteer Editorial Board	Quality Printing, Bismarck	Alvin A. Jaeger
2005-2007	Volunteer Editorial Board	Richtman's Printing, Bismarck	Alvin A. Jaeger
2007-2009	Volunteer Editorial Board	Richtman's Printing, Bismarck	Alvin A. Jaeger
2009-2011	Volunteer Editorial Board	Image Printing, Bismarck	Alvin A. Jaeger
2011-2013	Volunteer Editorial Board	Image Printing, Bismarck	Alvin A. Jaeger
2013-2015	Volunteer Editorial Board	Image Printing, Bismarck	Alvin A. Jaeger
2015-2017	Volunteer Editorial Board	Image Printing, Bismarck	Alvin A. Jaeger
2017-2019	Volunteer Editorial Board	Image Printing, Bismarck	Alvin A. Jaeger

State of
North Dakota
Office of the Governor

Doug Burgum
Governor

Greetings from the Office of the Governor!

North Dakota has a fascinating history and a compelling story to tell. From the Native American tribes who flourished on the prairie to the homesteaders who established our state's agricultural roots, to the entrepreneurs leading the way into the 21st century economy, we have always been an aspirational people. We dream big and work hard.

Today, we recognize the fruits of that hard work in our vibrant communities, our thriving economy and our growing population. We take pride in the rich cultural heritage passed down from our ancestors, the industriousness of our strong energy sector and the innovative efforts of our educators. Ours is a history filled with pioneering spirit – a spirt we carry forward with respect for the past, gratitude for the present and inspiration for the future.

The Blue Book is a treasure trove of information about all things North Dakota, offering a wealth of facts on state government, politics, history, culture and the unique qualities and attractions that make our state a special place to live and visit.This edition of the Blue Book shines the spotlight on "Pride of Dakota," a program that has promoted and enhanced the marketing of North Dakota businesses, services and homegrown products since 1985. Readers also will find a new chapter commemorating the 100th anniversary of the United States' entry into World War I and the significant impact it had on North Dakota.

Other chapters celebrate the talents and accomplishments of North Dakotans from various walks of life. A chapter on tribal-state relationships features the 2016 inductees into the North Dakota Native American Hall of Honor, located in our world-class North Dakota Heritage Center & State Museum. Recognition also is rightly given to the 50th anniversary of the North Dakota Council on the Arts and the national athletics championships won by our colleges and universities – sources of pride and inspiration for all North Dakotans.

Deepest gratitude goes to the authors, editors and other volunteers who contributed countless hours to producing the North Dakota Blue Book, a tremendous resource for residents and non-residents alike. Thank you for your hard work and dedication, and for the love of North Dakota that shines through the pages of this delightful book.

Curiosity is the key to unlocking our potential. Let the North Dakota Blue Book ignite yours, and enjoy the journey!

Regards,

Doug Burgum
Governor

ALVIN A. JAEGER
SECRETARY OF STATE

HOME PAGE www.nd.gov/sos

PHONE (701) 328-2900
FAX (701) 328-2992

E-MAIL sos@nd.gov

SECRETARY OF STATE
STATE OF NORTH DAKOTA
600 EAST BOULEVARD AVENUE DEPT 108
BISMARCK ND 58505-0500

Dear Reader,

The publication of the *North Dakota Blue Book 2017-2019* represents the twelfth consecutive biennial edition published by the Secretary of State's office. The sequence began with the 1995 edition, which covered the six year information gap between it and the Centennial edition published in 1989 when North Dakota celebrated its 100th birthday. In comparison, only twenty editions were published in the 106 years between statehood in 1889 and 1995.

As with the other eleven editions, this publication was created with the help of faithful volunteers. Over fifty individuals contributed their research and writing skills to this edition. The group included librarians, historians, agency personnel, and others who are committed and passionate about the preservation of valuable North Dakota history.

A highlight of this edition is the story of Pride of Dakota, a marketing program under the state's Department of Agriculture. Since 1985, it has promoted and enhanced the marketing of North Dakota businesses, products and services. In addition, along with information about energy, education, agriculture, elections, state officials, legislators, etc., this edition includes a chapter dedicated to World War I and the 100th Anniversary of that event, a chapter recognizing the 50th anniversary of the North Dakota Council of the Arts, and a listing of the national championships won by the state's universities and colleges athletic teams.

I believe this book is unique because it covers information about North Dakota not readily available in any other single resource. It is an indispensable source for research and for gaining general knowledge of the state. In addition, each of the individual biennial editions beginning in 1995 contains selected information not published in any of the others.

Because of that, I am pleased that (beginning with the 1919) the editions of the *Blue* Book are digitally available online through the Secretary of State's website at sos.nd.gov. A valuable feature is the ability to search each book individually or all books collectively. Bound copies also continue to be available for viewing and research at the North Dakota State Library in Bismarck, the State Archives, all state university libraries, and several municipal libraries throughout the state.

I am grateful for everyone who made this publication a reality. In particular, I thank Kim Shaw, my executive assistant, the staff of Clearwater Communications, and the members of the editorial board – Marlene Anderson, Shari Mosser, Sarah Walker, Dana Schaar Jahner, and Kim Shaw. Their editing skills, insight, dedication, and understanding of the significance of the *Blue Book,* and its role in preserving the history of North Dakota, is what makes this publication a reality.

As with the previous editions, I am confident the state's fascinating history and its exciting future will prompt your interest to learn more about this wonderful state that we call home – North Dakota.

Sincerely,

Al Jaeger
Secretary of State

A Brief Word About the Origin of the Term 'Blue Book'

The *Merriam-Webster Online Dictionary* offers four contemporary definitions of "blue book:"

1. a register especially of socially prominent persons
2. a book of specialized information often published under government auspices
3. a blue-covered booklet used for writing examinations
4. a periodically issued price list (as of used cars)

With respect to the *North Dakota Blue Book*, the term "blue book" refers to a compendium of information about the state's political, economic, social, cultural, and environmental history and current status. Most states regularly produce a "blue book."

To determine where the term "blue book" originated, look to our English ancestors. In the 1800s, the British government printed reams of reports from Parliamentary committees and royal commissions. These documents became commonly known as "blue books" because of their blue paper covers. These "blue books" were generally loaded with testimonies, figures, and facts. Their purpose was to provide the public with government information, legal, political, or commercial, and to assist policymakers with decision making. The term "blue book" later came to mean any report published and distributed by the British Parliament.

On the Covers

The cover of the *2017-2019 North Dakota Blue Book* highlights North Dakota's agricultural heritage and one of the state's top industries. In the foreground, stalks of wheat await harvest and represent North Dakota's chief agricultural commodity. In the background, a red barn stands steadfast on the farmstead, providing shelter, storage, and a beacon on the prairie.

The back cover pays homage to the book's feature chapter "Pride of Dakota," which highlights the program that has promoted and enhanced the marketing of North Dakota businesses, products, and services since 1985. Pictured are Kaye (Quanbeck) Effertz and John Sandbakken, North Dakota Department of Agriculture marketing specialists who were featured in a 1988 *Bismarck Tribune* article about the program.

Chapter Title Photographs

2017 marks the 100th anniversary of the United States' entry into World War I. The images presented at the beginning of each chapter give readers a glimpse into the State Historical Society of North Dakota's extensive collection of World War I posters.

During World War I, the posters were used as communication devices. They could be easily displayed and seen by whole communities and resonated with all ages and education levels. Used to sell bonds, recruit forces, encourage conservation of resources, increase production of agricultural and industrial goods, and mobilize public opinion of the war, the different imagery and coloring evoked feelings of national pride, fear of the opposing forces, and a need to work together.

During this time, curator Melvin Gilmore actively worked to collect these posters for the State Historical Society of North Dakota. Gilmore saw a need for collecting these documents, even going so far as trading duplicate American posters with European dealers to obtain foreign posters for the collection.

The collection, MSS 10935, resides in the North Dakota Archives. It is one of the largest collections of World War I posters in the country. Consisting of 921 individual images, with some from foreign countries, the images display used and unused poster art or poster propaganda reflecting the war from around the world.

Blue Book Contributors and Photography

Foreword: Doug Burgum, Governor; Alvin A. Jaeger, Secretary of State

Chapter Title Pages Photos: Jim Davis, Head of Reference; Sarah Walker, Reference Specialist, State Historical Society of North Dakota

2017-2019 Blue Book Committee Members: Marlene Anderson, Director of Library Services, Bismarck State College; Kylah Aull, Library and Records Services Manager, North Dakota Legislative Council; Annie Bennett, Communication Specialist, Clearwater Communications; Kylie Blanchard, Communication Specialist, Clearwater Communications; Jesse Bradley, Communications Manager, North Dakota Department of Commerce; Jim Davis, Head of Reference, State Historical Society of North Dakota; Helen Hanley, Executive Assistant to the Commissioner, North Dakota Indian Affairs Commission; Ned Kruger, Geologist, North Dakota Geological Survey; Shari Mosser, Librarian, North Dakota State Library; Michelle Mielke, Public Information Specialist, North Dakota Department of Agriculture; Mike Noone, Natural Resource Economist, North Dakota State Water Commission; Dana Schaar Jahner, Vice President, Clearwater Communications; Kim Shaw, Executive Assistant, North Dakota Secretary of State; Ted Smith, Law Librarian, North Dakota Supreme Court Library; Sarah Walker, Reference Specialist, State Historical Society of North Dakota; Dale Wetzel, Public Information Specialist, North Dakota Department of Instruction

2017-2019 Blue Book Editorial Committee Members: Marlene Anderson, Director of Library Services, Bismarck State College; Kylie Blanchard, Communication Specialist, Clearwater Communications; Shari Mosser, Librarian, North Dakota State Library; Dana Schaar Jahner, Vice President, Clearwater Communications; Kim Shaw, Executive Assistant, North Dakota Secretary of State; Sarah Walker, Reference Specialist, State Historical Society of North Dakota

Chapter 1 – Pride of Dakota: Michelle Mielke, Public Information Specialist, North Dakota Department of Agriculture
Photo Credits: page 1, State Historical Society of North Dakota (SHSND) 10935 P139; page 2, North Dakota Department of Agriculture (NDDA); page 4, NDDA; page 5, NDDA; page 6, *Bismarck Tribune*; page 7, SHSND 31580; page 8, SHSND 31580; page 9, NDDA; page 10, SHSND 31580; page 11, SHSND 31580; page 12, (top) NDDA and (bottom) SHSND 31580; page 13, SHSND 31580; page 14, SHSND 31580; page 15, NDDA; page 16, (top) Roger Johnson, National Farmers Union, and (bottom) NDDA; page 17, NDDA; page 18, NDDA; page 23, The Barn Guy; page 24, Lighthouse Soy Candles; page 25, PEAR'D; page 26, Mikey's Country Candy; page 27, Vitality Inc.; page 28, Ashley Beth Pottery; page 29, HIT Inc.; page 30, Prairie Rose Organic Seed; page 31, RSVP Dakota Store; page 32, Mattie Richardson; page 33, Buffalo Gals Mercantile; page 34, Maple River Winery; page 35, Nourished by Nature; page 36, Rilos + MiMi; page 38, NDDA

Chapter 2 – North Dakota Almanac: Jim Davis, Head of Reference, State Historical Society of North Dakota; Eric Jensen, Deputy Public Information Officer, West North Dakota National Guard; Kevin Kirkey, Site Supervisor, North Dakota Parks and Recreation Department; Beth Gigante Klingenstein, Executive Director, North Dakota Council of the Arts; Shari Mosser, Librarian, North Dakota State Library; Kathy McGhan, Administrative Manager, International Peace Garden; Michelle Mielke, Public Information Specialist, North Dakota Department of Agriculture; Mike Nowatzki, Communications Director, Office of the Governor; Karen Olsen, Program Director, Kids Count; Diane M. Rogness, Historical Sites Manager, State Historical Society of North Dakota; Beth Feldner, Marketing Director, North Dakota State Fair; Jamie Olsen, Communications, North Dakota Department of Transportation; Kim Schmidt, Public and Media Relations Manager, Department of Commerce-Tourism Division; Pearl Schneider, Administrative Assistant, North Dakota Parks and Recreation Department; Laura Thomas, Park Ranger, Theodore Roosevelt National Park; Sarah Walker, Reference Specialist, State Historical Society of North Dakota; Annie Bennett, Communications Specialist, Clearwater Communications; Kylie Blanchard, Communications Specialist, Clearwater Communications
Photo Credits: page 39, SHSND 10935 P076; page 40, SHSND978-02 J66j; page 41, Shutter Stock 64051492; pages 43-47, North Dakota Secretary of State; page 48, North Dakota Parks and Recreation Department; page 49, North Dakota Game and Fish Department; page 50, (top) North Dakota Forest Service and (bottom) North Dakota Secretary of State; pages 51-53, North Dakota Secretary of State; page 54, North Dakota Museum of Art; pages 55-59, North Dakota Secretary of State; page 60, Lewis and Clark Fort Mandan Foundation; page 62, Castle McLaughlin, Peabody Museum of Archaeology and Ethnology, Harvard University; page 63, North Dakota Tourism; page 70, Chris Hawley Architects/Facility Management; pages 77-120, North Dakota Office of the Governor; page 122, Sgt. Ashley Johlfs, North Dakota National Guard; page 125, Clearwater Communications; page 126, Tessie Jones Photography; page 127, Phyne Photography; pages 134-136, North Dakota Tourism; page 137, State Historical Society of North Dakota; page 138, North Dakota Parks and Recreation Department; pages 139-140, North Dakota Tourism

Chapter 3 – Federal-State Relationships: Shari Mosser, Librarian, North Dakota State Library; Kari Knudson, Chief Deputy Clerk, U.S. District Court-North Dakota; Ted Smith, Law Librarian, North Dakota Supreme Court Law Library; Bob Wefald, Chairman, *USNS CITY OF BISMARCK* (T-EPF-9)
Photo Credits: page 145, SHSND 10935 P062; page 150, *Minot Daily News*; pages 164-170, North Dakota Federal Courts

Chapter 4 – Judicial Branch: Sally Holewa, State Court Administrator, North Dakota Supreme Court; Ted Smith, Law Librarian, North Dakota Supreme Court Law Library
Photo Credits: page 171, SHSND 10935 P020; pages 175-179, North Dakota Supreme Court; page 184, North Dakota Supreme Court

Chapter 5 – Executive Branch: Kim Shaw, Executive Assistant, North Dakota

Secretary of State; Annie Bennett, Communications Specialist, Clearwater Communications
Photo Credits: page 205, SHSND 10935 P023

Chapter 6 – Legislative Branch: Dustin Assel, Counsel; Kylah E. Aull, Library and Records Services Manager; Justin J. Blasy, Legislative Services Specialist II; John Bjornson, Legal Division Director; Jennifer S. N. Clark, Counsel; Andrea Cooper, Lead Legislative Services Specialist; Kyle W. Forster, Information Technology Manager; Courtney Hartleib, Legislative Services Specialist I; Christopher S. Joseph, Counsel; Donavan D. Klein, Administrative Unit Supervisor; Allen H. Knudson, Legislative Budget Analyst and Auditor; Samantha E. Kramer, Counsel; Claire Ness, Counsel; Brad Metz, Legislative Services Specialist II; Kayla Seifert, Legislative Services Specialist I; Jim W. Smith, Director; Robert Tallman, Legislative Services Specialist I; Emily L. Thompson, Counsel; Lori Ziegler, Legislative Administrative Officer, North Dakota Legislative Council; Arik Spencer, Executive Vice President, North Dakota Motor Carriers Association
Photo Credits: page 319, SHSND 10935 P014; pages 326-372, Don Anderson Photography; page 373, North Dakota Secretary of State

Chapter 7 – Tribal-State Relationships: Claudia Berg, Director, State Historical Society of North Dakota; Kylie Blanchard, Communication Specialist, Clearwater Communications; Scott Davis, Executive Director, North Dakota Indian Affairs Commission; Lorraine Davis, Executive Director, Native American Development Center; Helen Hanley, Executive Assistant to the Commissioner, North Dakota Indian Affairs Commission; Bradley Hawk, Indian Health Systems Administrator, North Dakota Indian Affairs Commission; Kimberly Jondahl, Director of Communications and Education, State Historical Society of North Dakota; Cheryl Ann Kary, Ph.D, Executive Director, Sacred Pipe Resource Center; Stacey LaCompte, Executive Director, North Dakota Indian Business Alliance
Photo Credits: page 411, SHSND 10935 P281; pages 414-420, State Historical Society of North Dakota; page 422, North Dakota Tourism; page 426, North Dakota Tourism; pages 432-433, North Dakota Indian Business Alliance; page 442, North Dakota Tourism

Chapter 8 – Elections: John Arnold, State Election Director, North Dakota Secretary of State; Lee Ann Oliver, Elections Specialist, North Dakota Secretary of State; Kim Shaw, Executive Assistant, North Dakota Secretary of State
Photo Credits: page 443, SHSND 10935 P177; page 454, North Dakota Association of Counties

Chapter 9 – Education: Marlene Anderson, Director of Library Services, Bismarck State College; Chris Erickson, Public Affairs Manager, North Dakota University System; Wayne Kutzer, State Director and Executive Officer, North Dakota Department of Career and Technical Education; Dale Wetzel, Public Information Specialist, North Dakota Department of Instruction
Photo Credits: page 455, SHSND 10935 P140; page 470, North Dakota University System

Chapter 10 – Agriculture: Michelle Mielke, Public Information Specialist, North Dakota Department of Agriculture
Photo Credits: page 487, SHSND 10935 P134; page 488, U.S. Government, Public Domain; page 489, www.globalhemp.com; pages 491-492, North Dakota Department of Agriculture (NDDA); page 494, Jamie Edwards, 2016 Pilot Producer; pages 496-497, NDDA; page 498, NDSU Langdon Research Extension Center; pages 499-500, NDDA; page 502, Midwest Dairy Association; page 508, Courtesy of Journal Communications Inc./Steve Woit

Chapter 11 – Natural Resources: Mike Noone, Natural Resource Economist, North Dakota State Water Commission; Craig Bihrle, Communications Supervisor, North Dakota Game and Fish Department; Sandra Johnson, Conservation Biologist, North Dakota Game and Fish Department
Photo Credits: page 509, SHSND 10935 P115; pages 510-511, Dan Brothers, Meteorologist, North Dakota State Water Commission; page 522, North Dakota Game and Fish Department

Chapter 12 – Energy: Jesse Bradley, Communications Manager, North Dakota Department of Commerce; Ned Kruger, Geologist, North Dakota Geological Survey
Photo Credits: page 523, SHSND 10935 P114; pages 525-526, Brothers & Company; page 528, Dakota Spirit AgEnergy; page 530, North Dakota Tourism; page 532, Brothers & Company; page 536, North Dakota Tourism

Chapter 13 – North Dakota During World War I: Jim Davis, Head of Reference, State Historical Society of North Dakota; Perry Hornbacher, Professor of History, Bismarck State College; Sarah Walker, Reference Specialist, State Historical Society of North Dakota
Photo Credits: page 537, SHSND 10935 P217; page 541, SHSND 00044-00014; page 542, SHSND 11086-30-02; page 544, SHSND E0071-00001; page 547, SHSND 10064-00134; page 548, SHSND 10935 P086; page 558, SHSND A4633-00001

Coordination and Formatting: Kim Shaw, Executive Assistant, North Dakota Secretary of State; Robin Pursley, Graphic Designer, Clearwater Communications; Dana Schaar Jahner, Vice President, Clearwater Communications

Indexing: Robin Pursley, Graphic Designer, Clearwater Communications; Dana Schaar Jahner, Vice President, Clearwater Communications

Editing, Proofreading, and Marketing: Kim Shaw, Executive Assistant, North Dakota Secretary of State; Annie Bennett, Communication Specialist, Clearwater Communications; Kylie Blanchard, Communication Specialist, Clearwater Communications; Dana Schaar Jahner, Vice President, Clearwater Communications

Table of Contents

Chapter One

Pride of Dakota

Pride of Dakota

Since 1985, Pride of Dakota has promoted and enhanced the marketing of North Dakota businesses, products, and services. It was launched with a mere 20 companies and has since grown to more than 500, ranging in size from "mom-and-pop" operations to large companies with more than 100 employees.

Membership is open to businesses whose products are created, produced, processed, or manufactured in North Dakota. Members include food and beverage companies, manufacturers, publishers, artisans, gift manufacturers, and service providers. Associate members, such as commodity groups, government agencies, educational institutions, and retailers, also support the program.

Pride of Dakota's goal is to provide local business owners the business development resources and marketing opportunities they need to be successful.

Beginnings

Several people had a part in the events leading up to the creation of Pride of Dakota. North Dakota businessman Harold Fettig suggested to State Representative Bruce Laughlin that the Legislature fund a state product labeling program in the 1980s.

Representative Laughlin, along with Representatives Kent, O'Connell, Larson, and Lindgren, sponsored House Concurrent Resolution 3049 in March 1985 requesting the development and promotion of a North Dakota product label by the North Dakota Department of Agriculture (NDDA) and use of the slogan "Buy North Dakota Products" on all literature and items printed with state funds.

Commissioner of Agriculture Kent Jones led the NDDA when Pride of Dakota began. Becky Jones Mahlum shared her father's perspective on the program, "My dad had a dream that North Dakota farmers and ranchers could market directly the things they grew and raised. He didn't like that the only real option at the time was for them to sell their commodities to the same place they bought their seeds. He wanted to give them the marketing tools to begin setting up their own businesses."

The resolution read as follows:

Buy North Dakota Products
A concurrent resolution requesting the development and promotion of a North Dakota Product Label by the Department of Agriculture and requesting use of the slogan "Buy North Dakota Products" on all literature and items printed with state funds.
WHEREAS, North Dakota is a major producer of many grains and other agricultural products; and
WHEREAS, the consumer may not be aware of the number of products raised, processed, and packaged in North Dakota; and
WHEREAS, there is a need for domestic efforts to make consumers more aware of nutritional values of the products raised in North Dakota;
NOW, THEREFORE, BE IT RESOLVED BY THE HOUSE OF REPRESENTATIVES OF THE STATE OF NORTH DAKOTA, THE SENATE CONCURRING THEREIN:
That the North Dakota Department of Agriculture, in cooperation with the various commodity groups, retail associations, and food producers in North Dakota, develop a North Dakota product label and plan promotion efforts to showcase North Dakota-made products;
BE IT FURTHER RESOLVED, that the slogan "Buy North Dakota Products" be displayed on all literature and items printed with state funds.

With the resolution in place, the idea for the Pride of Dakota program itself came from Commissioner of Agriculture H. Kent Jones, who had seen a similar idea in Minnesota that year.

Jones asked a small group of North Dakota businesses and NDDA's marketing staff to develop an identifiable state brand that would designate products as "made in North Dakota." The steering committee was asked to make North Dakota consumers aware of the many products produced and processed within the state.

The steering committee formed the North Dakota Products Council (NDPC), which was guided by the NDDA. Its purpose was "to increase the sale of North Dakota produced and/or manufactured products by increasing public and retail awareness of those products." It was hoped the NDPC would run the program, like a trade group.

NDPC board members and their respective businesses at the time included Jesse Harrold, Dakota Candy; Alec Zorn, Dakota Brands; Sylvia Benser, Prairie Products; Jack Bernabucci, Coca-Cola Bottling of Jamestown; and Bob Thornberg, Dawn Enterprises of Walhalla. Advisory board members and their respective businesses at the time were Lloyd Schmidt, Red River Valley Potato Growers Association; John Sandbakken, NDDA; Bill Patrie, Economic Development Commission; Dean McIlroy, North Dakota Agricultural Products Utilization Committee; and Judi Adams, NDPC.

In total, the program started with the following 20 active members.

1. Crystal Pure Water Inc. (Fran Gilliss)
2. Thermal-Line (Al Leingang)
3. Koerner's Old Style Mustard (Marvin Koerner)
4. Papa's Greenhouse (David Pearce)
5. Dakota Coach Inc. (Diane Cowdrey)
6. Doeling's Dairy (Gene Doeling)
7. Quality Boneless Beef Co. (Thomas Blakeway)
8. Slick Products (Larry and Don Silbernagel)
9. Golden Sunshine Distributors Inc. (Dennis Zeiszler)
10. Larson's Super Value (Rich Rohrer)
11. Dakota Sun Products (Jesse Harrold)
12. Window World Inc. (Ron Voeller)
13. Cloverdale Foods Co. (Lori Schlosser)
14. Roman Meal Milling (Bob Manuel)
15. Dawn Enterprises (Bob Thornberg)
16. Candee-Saueressig Inc. (Mylo Candee)
17. Prairie Products (Stephen and Sylvia Benser)
18. Coca-Cola Bottling Co. of Jamestown (J.R. Bernabucci)
19. Dakota Brand (Alec Zorn)
20. Knoefler Honey Farms (Reuben Lehmann Jr.)

Original businesses that are still a part of the Pride of Dakota family include Papa's Granola, originally Papa's Greenhouse (David Pearce), and Cloverdale Foods Co. (Scott Russell).

The name "Pride of Dakota" was coined by Mylo Candee of Candee-Saueressig Advertising. Bob Saueressig of the same agency designed the original logo.

The original Pride of Dakota logo from the late 1980s.

NDPC had financial difficulties and dissolved over a dispute regarding the ownership of and payment for the logo. The NDDA took over both the program and the logo, with the NDPC becoming an advisory board. A *Bismarck Tribune* editorial at the time said this of the move, "Running the campaign as a private venture by the NDPC – a group of contributing businesses – was an admirable attempt. But like similar councils in other states, the North Dakota group found it simply didn't have the financial strength to operate on its own."

Legislation was sponsored in support of the program in 1987 by Representatives Bruce Laughlin and Bruce Larson and Senator Dan Wogsland. House Bill 1516 provided an appropriation of $5,000 to the commissioner of agriculture for administration of the Pride of Dakota logo promotion program for the biennium beginning July 1, 1987, and ending June 30, 1989. The bill passed overwhelmingly and was signed by Governor George Sinner.

Early Push

The program started out with a focus on food. Commissioner Jones reached out to some of the larger food companies such as Cloverdale and Fettig's Frozen Dough Products to ask if they would help lead the group. They willingly agreed and would later serve as mentors to businesses just starting in the program.

John Sandbakken and Kaye (Quanbeck) Effertz, former NDDA marketing specialists working in the Pride of Dakota program, said they "pounded the pavement" traveling the state with Pride of Dakota displays in the back of their car. They set up in different locations throughout North Dakota to talk to people about the program. In 1988 alone, they crisscrossed 11,600 miles across the state. Their message was to let people know which products were made in North Dakota, to encourage them to look for the products in stores, and to ultimately purchase the products. They emphasized to people the more North Dakota products they purchased, the greater benefit to the state. Overall, the message was "North Dakota first."

Kaye Effertz standing in front of the display she used to help promote Pride of Dakota.

Sandbakken said it was a tough sell, because with limited funding for the program – $5,000 from the Legislature and money collected from dues – they couldn't promise a lot for membership. The benefits for members at the time included the ability to use the logo on their products and to participate in Pride of Dakota

Kaye Effertz and John Sandbakken were featured in a 1988 Bismarck Tribune *article about the program.*

promotions. It also provided members an opportunity to network with other North Dakota companies, large and small. Sandbakken and Effertz said they had passion for the program and convinced businesses to sign up because it was a good thing to be a part of and to promote the state of North Dakota.

Membership dues were based on a business's number of employees, ranging from $50 to $250. Associate memberships cost $50 and were typically purchased by organizations such as commodity groups, who wanted to support the program. Sandbakken said they spoke to various groups to create awareness of the program and recruit companies to join. They did not have a lot of money to do anything else in terms of paid promotions, and the focus was getting businesses to join and use the logo.

After a successful pilot program in Bismarck's Dan's Supermarket stores, a Pride of Dakota grocery store promotion featuring North Dakota products in grocery flyers was expanded. Dan's Supermarket featured North Dakota products in their store flyer that was mailed to consumers throughout Bismarck/Mandan and the surrounding area. Sandbakken had connections with some grocery warehouses, having previously worked for Nash Finch. After the Dan's Supermarket promotion, several promotions were arranged that were conducted in stores across North Dakota supplied by the Nash Finch warehouses in Minot and Fargo, plus Super Valu warehouses in Fargo and Bismarck. The promotions were very successful. A hand-drawn flyer showed the impact that buying North Dakota products had on North Dakota individuals and companies. Items like shelf talkers (printed signs) in stores were also used to highlight Pride of Dakota products.

A hand-drawn flyer touted the benefits of buying North Dakota products.

Grocery store promotions continued to raise North Dakotans' awareness of the program. A series of promotions called "A Taste of Dakota" were held at major grocery stores across North Dakota. Pride of Dakota companies sampled and sold their products to customers right in the store. The event was promoted through television commercials, newspapers, signs, and news stories. As a result of the promotions, some participating members started selling their products to the store.

Page 6 □ Wednesday, January 31, 1990 □ The Bismarck Tribune □ Food

Buy North Dakota First!

Look for North Dakota Products in your local retail outlets.

For more information contact the North Dakota Department of Agriculture
Sarah Vogel, Commissioner
224-2231

Cloverdale Foods Co.
Meat Processor & Full Food Distributors
Mandan, ND 58554

North Dakota Mill & Elevator
"Quality Millers Of North Dakota Wheat Since 1922."

Silver Crest Bakery
"Fresh Every Sunrise"
New Rockford, ND 58356

Dakota Ink Designs
"Pen & Ink Stationery & Cards with nostalgia Prairie Designs."

The top portion of a Pride of Dakota Month newspaper ad from the **Bismarck Tribune** ***in 1990. The full page ad included more businesses and contact information below.***

Governor George Sinner declared January 1987 as the first Pride of Dakota Month. It was changed to March in 1991. Some of the activities during the early years included distributing a press release, showcasing the product display at several locations, conducting a Pride of Dakota label contest at schools, putting on a Pride of Dakota lunch for legislators, and offering in-store promotions in grocery stores.

In 1988, Pride of Dakota became a presence at the North Dakota State Fair. NDDA sponsored booths with Pride of Dakota companies showcasing their products. It started with just a table or two, but has since expanded to more than 20 vendors showcasing and selling their products under a large tent. One memorable year included boxer Virgil Hill, a North Dakota native, making an appearance and signing autographs. At the fair, $1 lunches featuring North Dakota products are typically served, and a food contest is held in which taste-testers vote for their favorites. Proceeds are donated to the North Dakota FFA.

Some of the Pride of Dakota projects for the 1989-1991 biennium included:

- Grocery store promotions.
- Pilot projects with restaurants to highlight North Dakota products on the menu.
- A cook-off/recipe contest.
- A buffet of North Dakota products for legislators.

A booth from one of the first years the Pride of Dakota Day at the State Fair was held. Behind the table are (left to right): Kaye Effertz, Commissioner of Agriculture Sarah Vogel, Ellen Crawford, and John Sandbakken.

- Public service announcements and billboard campaigns.
- Pride of Dakota Day at the State Fair.
- Booths at ag expos.
- Pride of Dakota materials distribution.
- A marketing seminar to enhance business skills for members and nonmembers.

State Fair attendees taste test varieties of kuchen as part of a Pride of Dakota Day at the State Fair food contest in 2010.

Legislators and legislative staff enjoyed a Pride of Dakota buffet in 1989.

The restaurant promotion involved promoting Pride of Dakota products on the menus of various restaurants in order to create a greater consumer awareness of North Dakota's products and to encourage North Dakota restaurant managers to buy North Dakota products when possible. The Pride of Dakota menu items were offered as specials and, as an extra incentive, Pride of Dakota gift packs were given away in each restaurant. Restaurants participating during 1989 included The Grainery of Fargo, Wagon Masters in Jamestown, and Caspar's East 40 in Bismarck.

A Pride of Dakota buffet for legislators and legislative staff in 1989 allowed them to taste North Dakota products and created a greater consumer awareness of the quality products North Dakota produces. The menu included local meats, pasta, salsa, snack items, soup, potatoes, condiments and sauces, beans, beverages, breads/buns, dairy products, and much more.

An early 1990s photo shows Page Public School fourth graders and their teacher, Jan L. Moen, posing with their collection of labels.

Getting Children Involved

The Pride of Dakota program got children involved early in its history. In the late 1980s, the NDDA distributed lesson plans about entrepreneurship for fourth- to eighth-grade classrooms. The materials included current members and products of the Pride of Dakota program.

Some of the activities that were available in the lesson plans included:

- North Dakota map searches for company locations.
- Worldwide map searches for company distribution areas.
- Crossword puzzles using company clues.
- Word searches.
- Preparation of timelines.
- Logo creation and advertisement development for a new company.

In 1990, a label contest was started for fourth graders in participating schools across North Dakota. Children were encouraged to collect Pride of Dakota labels during a specific timeframe with the incentive of potentially winning an Apple computer for their school as the grand prize. At that time, not all schools had computers, and the prize was highly desired. Other prizes included savings bonds and gift certificates. The promotion was a huge success the first year with nearly 500,000 labels submitted, exceeding all expectations. Small communities rallied around the contest, getting everyone in town to collect and submit labels. The first year's grand prize winner was Betty Spenst's fourth-grade class at Kensal Public School. With just five students, the class turned in 18,833 labels with the help of the entire community. The promotion greatly raised brand recognition and also highlighted the amount of sales for North Dakota companies.

Commissioner of Agriculture Sarah Vogel: "I've been a Pride of Dakota fan since its creation by Commissioner Kent Jones and I still am. My home is filled with Pride of Dakota products, and my relatives have grown to expect Pride of Dakota products for Christmas. I always try to serve Pride of Dakota products at gatherings at my home. As I look back at the period between 1989 and 1996 when I served as commissioner, I am proud of the exponential growth of the Pride of Dakota program. I learned a lot from these companies: they were creative, they were resourceful, and they were optimistic. They had to navigate complex challenges to see their visions become reality. The citizens of the state of North Dakota should be very proud of members of the Pride of Dakota program and support them as much as possible. Pride of Dakota is not just a 'feel good' labeling program; it is an effective and tested grassroots-driven economic development program."

Expanding the Program

By 1989, the Pride of Dakota program had just over 100 members. In the early 1990s, the program got a boost when the Legislature increased funding for the program, establishing an appropriation of $150,000 per biennium.

Arts and crafts companies were added into the Pride of Dakota membership in the early 1990s. By 1991, members totaled 145, and a membership directory was published to help consumers find their favorite products and services. That directory listed 64 food products companies, 38 manufacturing and printing companies, 23 crafters, and 23 associate members. The directory continues to exist today, although now it is online at www.prideofdakota.com.

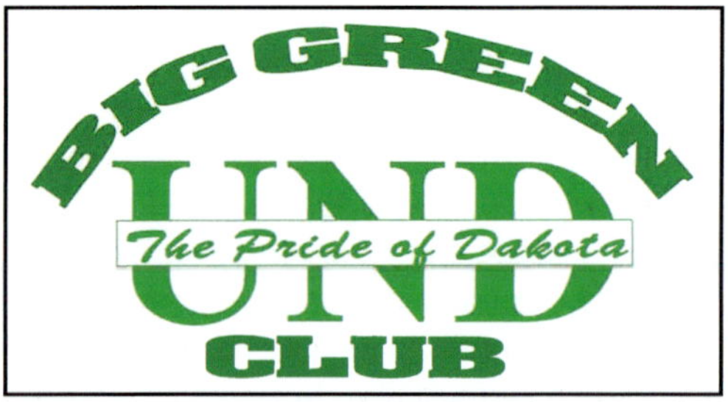

The Big Green Club bumper sticker from the early 1990s.

A partnership with the University of North Dakota (UND) in 1991 and 1992 allowed the school's athletic booster club, the "Big Green Club," to use the words "The Pride of Dakota" in their advertising. UND used the phrase for multiple things, including hockey season ticket flyers, basketball season ticket flyers, schedule posters, scholarship brochures, a statewide billboard campaign, programs, and media guides. The promotion worked well to help the Big Green Club gain an identity in their inaugural year and generated an enormous amount of publicity for the Pride of Dakota group. The partnership did not continue, however, as UND redesigned the Big Green Club logo and chose not to incorporate the Pride of Dakota trademark.

The cover of the Best of the Midwest Food Show program in 1990.

The early 1990s also brought new opportunities for Pride of Dakota companies, such as trade shows and fancy food shows. One such show was the Best of the Midwest Food Show in Denver in September 1990. Fifty-five companies selling everything from lefse to pizza to pasta presented their products to approximately 225 buyers. Buyers represented brokers, wholesale, retail, restaurant, and food service companies from the Denver area. The Pride of Dakota program provided part of the funds necessary to attend the show, covering the booth and pre-show promotions. Companies were able to secure grants from the North Dakota Agricultural Products Utilization Commission (APUC) to cover travel. According to a report on the effort, companies felt the promotion was very beneficial and that North Dakota companies were able to get good exposure at the Denver market.

Pride of Dakota companies participated in many such shows throughout the 1990s and into the mid-2000s, including some organized by the NDDA within the state and others offered out of state. The Pride of Dakota Wholesale Gift Show was an in-state show attended by local buyers. It was held in different cities throughout the state, such as Mandan and Fargo. One out-of-state show popular with Pride of Dakota members was the Minneapolis Gift Mart. Pride of Dakota members that attended were pleased with the new sales and valuable contacts made there. The cost to attend was subsidized by the Pride of Dakota program.

In 1991, the NDDA commissioned UND's Social Science Research Institute (SSRI) to conduct a consumer survey about the Pride of Dakota program. The survey included questions about consumers' recognition of the Pride of Dakota logo and program awareness. Fifty-nine percent of the respondents were aware of the Pride of Dakota program, and 12 percent were not sure. Respondents were also asked if a logo identifying North Dakota products would have an effect on their purchase decision, and 79 percent said it would influence them to purchase products manufactured or processed in North Dakota.

In 1991, NDDA was able to secure Phil Jackson, a North Dakota native, former NBA star, and then head coach of the Chicago Bulls, to do a public service announcement. The announcement aired on television across North Dakota.

"Hi! I'm Phil Jackson, head coach of the Chicago Bulls and proud native of North Dakota. Every team plays its best when it has the home court advantage. You can give our home state of North Dakota that same advantage when you buy North Dakota first. Look for the Pride of Dakota emblem, your guarantee of quality. Be part of the winning team – buy North Dakota products."

According to Sandbakken, Jackson readily agreed to donate his time to the making of the announcement. Jackson was filmed at the Bulls training facility in Deerfield, Illinois, and final production work was done by Meyer Broadcasting of Bismarck.

Pride of Dakota continued the use of celebrity endorsements in 1992 when they brought Phil Hansen, a North Dakota native and defensive lineman for the Buffalo Bills, to Bismarck during Pride of Dakota Day at the KFYR Agri-International. He signed autographs while attendees sampled Pride of Dakota foods, learned about North Dakota companies, and signed up to win prizes. Fifty-six Pride of Dakota businesses participated in the event, which was designed to develop increased consumer awareness about Pride of Dakota companies and organizations.

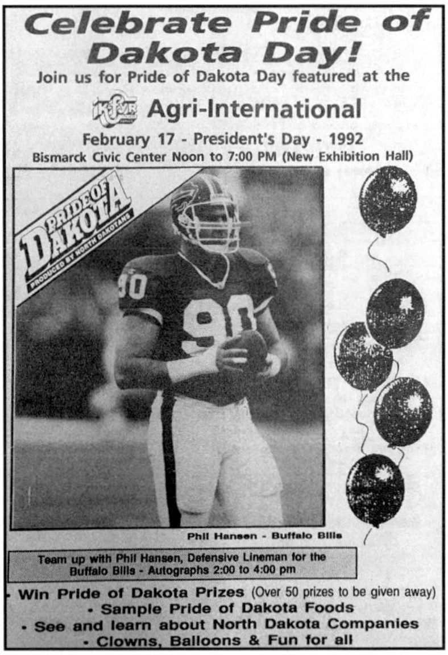

A newspaper advertisement for Pride of Dakota Day at the KFYR Agri-International.

In 1993, the first Pride of Dakota Holiday Showcase was held in Fargo. It featured 75 Pride of Dakota businesses, live entertainment, cooking and decorating demonstrations, drawings, prizes, and more. A Christmas tree decorating contest was also held, with the trees later being donated to charity. It did much better than expected, with 10,000 people attending in two days, according to Sandbakken. He remembers companies did not know what to expect, with it being the first showcase ever. "Some companies sold out of products the first half day, and many drove across North Dakota that evening to pick up more products for day two," he said. "One company sold $13,000 worth of lefse!"

Showcases quickly became popular, and soon more locations were added. Bismarck added a showcase in 1994, Minot in 1997, and Grand Forks in 2002. These four Holiday Showcases now collectively attract more than 35,000 customers annually.

A late-1990s Holiday Showcase in Minot.

In 2000, Pride of Dakota members ran a Dakota Store at the Norsk Hostfest in Minot. The space allowed up to 30 members to display their items, and various Pride of Dakota owners took turns operating the store. This promotion continued through 2004.

Harvest Showcases in the fall were added in Dickinson in 2009 and in Williston in 2011. The Dickinson event continues while Williston's ended after a five-year run.

Shoppers enjoy samples at a 2013 Pride of Dakota Holiday Showcase in Bismarck.

Not surprisingly in a rural state, the showcases are not only a commercial event, but a social one as well. Friends and families often get together and travel considerable distances to spend the day sampling and buying Pride of Dakota products. The members themselves also look forward to getting together.

"Pride of Dakota is giving me the opportunity to meet with other North Dakota makers and grow through their knowledge and experience," said Ashley Norberg of

Agriculture Commissioner Roger Johnson: "I've always viewed the Pride of Dakota program as a wonderful opportunity for especially small agriculturally related businesses to get a helping hand with their marketing and promotions. The members of Pride of Dakota always treated me, the marketing staff, and one another as family. I know it made a meaningful difference to many companies – a perfect example of government at its best!"

Ashley Beth Pottery. "It has also opened my business up to markets I had not had the opportunity pursue yet. It has been great to learn from makers with more experience and then meet and grow along with the newly emerging makers."

Krista Ulrich from Designs by Krista Marie explains, "The Holiday Showcase is a large part of my annual income. Not only have I made amazing friends through the program, but I have made wonderful business connections that have allowed my business to continue to thrive."

The Pride of Dakota School Lunch Day started in March 2002 during Pride of Dakota Month. It celebrated its 15th anniversary in 2016 with 60,472 students from 237 North Dakota schools participating. The NDDA supplies posters and other promotional materials to participating schools, as well as sample menus prepared by the North Dakota Department of Public Instruction. Each school or school district

Agriculture Commissioner Doug Goehring enjoys lunch with Mary Stark Elementary students in Mandan during the 2016 Pride of Dakota School Lunch Day.

decides on its own menu. For example, the 2016 menu for Fargo Public Schools included a Cloverdale hotdog (Mandan) on a Pan-O-Gold bun (Fargo), French fries from Cavendish Farms (Jamestown), and SunGold Foods Snackwave Trailmix (Fargo) with honey roasted sunflower kernels and soynuts. Many districts continue to serve North Dakota foods all year long. As stated on its website, the Fargo Public Schools Nutrition Services utilizes North Dakota products to serve more than 1.5 million breakfast and lunch meals each school year. The program helps young people understand where their food comes from and how to make healthy food choices. It also demonstrates to school administrators and school lunch directors that North Dakota companies can supply many of their menu needs, and it shows North Dakota companies that school lunch programs can be an important market for their products.

Members continued to take part in opportunities such as Pride of Dakota Day at the North Dakota State Fair, the Pride of Dakota Holiday Showcases, the Wholesale Gift Show, Minneapolis Gift Mart, the National Restaurant Show, and other wholesale food and gift shows.

Breaking Into Cyberspace

In the early days of the program, members relied on word of mouth. As the internet and social media came into existence and started flourishing, it had an enormous impact on the world of promotion, marketing, and sales. Pride of Dakota members could now easily reach customers across the nation and around the world.

An advertisement placed in the 2016 North Dakota Travel Guide.

Pride of Dakota members use the program's website – www.prideofdakota.com – to advertise and market their products and services. The website also helps members keep up with program activities. In addition to the website, Pride of Dakota members and customers can keep up with the program's activities through its accounts on Facebook, Twitter, and YouTube.

The NDDA provided benefits such as weekly emails with marketing and management ideas, an online message board, a newsletter, marketing seminars, promotion of the program at events such as Marketplace of Ideas, a membership directory, point-of-purchase materials, the coordination of a Pride of Dakota advisory council, promotion during Pride of Dakota Month, grants to help Pride of Dakota companies attend other shows to promote their products, mentoring services, and a business expansion program.

The current Pride of Dakota logo.

Brand Recognition

Customers increasingly look for the distinctive Pride of Dakota logo. The original logo was replaced in 2000 with a more modern design created by Kranzler-Kingsley Advertising of Bismarck (now KK Bold). The blue, white, and gold oval logo bears the name Pride of Dakota and in smaller letters the phrase "North Dakota originals." The emblem can be found on label stickers, placards, shelf talkers, and other promotional materials available to members, many of whom have the logo directly printed on their product labels and brochures.

By 2006, 79 percent of North Dakotans were familiar with the Pride of Dakota program, according to a study conducted by UND's Bureau of Governmental Affairs and commissioned by the NDDA. The study included questions about consumers' recognition of the program logo and general program awareness. Of the consumers who had heard of Pride of Dakota, 88 percent had purchased a Pride of Dakota product. Consumers said origin of production factored first in their reason to purchase a Pride of Dakota product.

Agriculture Commissioner Doug Goehring: "The Pride of Dakota program has grown considerably over the last several years due to the hard work of our member companies, the efforts of our business development staff, and the patronage of thousands of loyal customers. This program serves as an important marketing tool for North Dakota companies that are competing in more conventional and traditional retail markets with unique products and services that possess a little of their own personality. There is a great amount of joy, pride, and intimate knowledge that goes in to every product or service our members are providing."

"It went from an idea to a strong brand," Sandbakken said. "The branding has definitely grown and created brand awareness. If you see the logo or hear the words, you know instantly."

"By using the Pride of Dakota logo in advertising and on individual products, people recognize 'made in North Dakota' and in turn appreciate having a local business carrying those unique food and gift products," said Deb Lee of RSVP Dakota Store.

"Pride of Dakota has meant brand recognition – people instantly equate Pride of Dakota with caring and quality," said Katy Kassian of Buffalo Gals Mercantile.

Membership Today

Today, the Pride of Dakota program provides more than 500 local business owners the business development resources and marketing opportunities they need to be successful.

To qualify for Pride of Dakota membership, a company must be physically located in North Dakota or manufacture or produce its products in North Dakota. Only products that were produced, processed, or originated in North Dakota or are significantly altered by input of labor, process, or intellectual content in North Dakota qualify as Pride of Dakota products. For items to be considered Pride of Dakota products, they must be made or assembled by an owner or employee of the company or by a company volunteer.

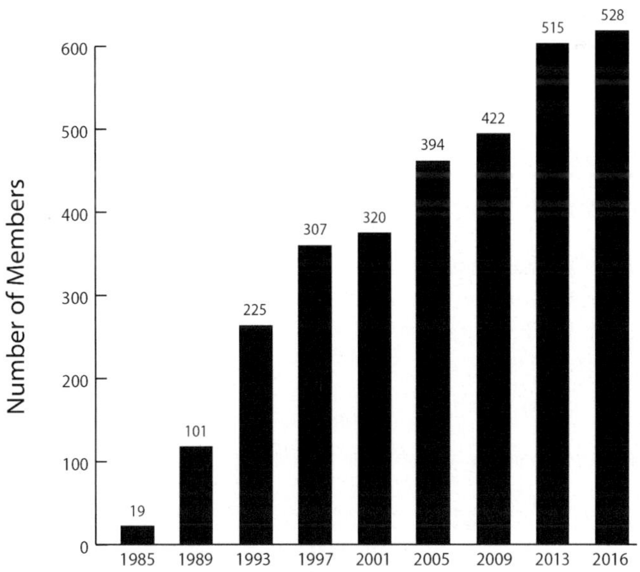

Membership totals by selected year.

The benefits Pride of Dakota members enjoy include:

- Advertising – The Pride of Dakota program places advertising on behalf of all members to increase awareness of the program and promote events. It also participates in other promotions that benefit its members. One such promotion is the opportunity to take part in a rotating panel of business-related organizations on a local AM radio station. Pride of Dakota companies are chosen at random to spend the hour being interviewed. Resource-type people and groups are also occasionally brought in as guests to provide information to business owners.

- Email Updates – Emails on marketing and business topics, along with vendor opportunities, are sent out periodically to all Pride of Dakota members.

- Export Assistance – For companies interested in exporting, Pride of Dakota provides consulting and programs for assistance and market research.

- Logo Usage – All Pride of Dakota members may use the Pride of Dakota logo on their packaging, marketing materials, websites, and other published materials. Members can also purchase Pride of Dakota stickers to place on their products.

- Networking Opportunities – Networking gives Pride of Dakota members the opportunity to learn from the experiences and successes of other member companies and to develop mutually beneficial business relationships.

- Newsletter – The quarterly, electronic newsletter highlights upcoming projects, marketing, and business development opportunities, feature stories on member companies, a calendar of events, and more.

- Point-of-Purchase Materials – Shelf talkers, shelf tags, and stickers featuring the Pride of Dakota logo are available for members to purchase.

- Pride of Dakota Month – March is Pride of Dakota Month. Promotions and materials elevate the awareness of the program. Pride of Dakota members and retail stores carrying their products receive signage announcing they support North Dakota businesses. Several retail stores typically offer in-store promotions, hold Pride of Dakota sales, offer samples of Pride of Dakota products, and more. The program is advertised more heavily, and contests are held on social media.

- Pride of Dakota School Lunch Day – Hundreds of school lunchrooms around the state feature North Dakota wheat, beef, durum, beans, sunflowers, pork, and other commodities on their menus during the annual

Pride of Dakota School Lunch Day, typically held in late September or early October.

- Reduced Rate Cooperative Advertising – Pride of Dakota offers member companies discounts on advertising in local and regional publications as part of program promotions.

- Retail Store Promotion Program – The Retail Store Promotion Program offers free benefits to North Dakota retail stores that carry Pride of Dakota products. Participating retailers have a profile page on the Pride of Dakota website and are linked to each profile page of the companies whose products they carry. Retail stores also have access to Pride of Dakota point-of-purchase materials and can apply for the Retail Store Grant to help fund events featuring North Dakota products. For the first 20 years, Pride of Dakota focused its efforts on production and manufacturing. With the introduction of the Pride of Dakota Retail Store Promotion Program in 2004, the NDDA expanded the Pride of Dakota vision into the retail sector. Currently, 210 retail establishments statewide belong to this program.

- Seminars/Workshops – Each year, the NDDA offers training and resources on business and marketing topics, one-on-one consultations with experts, and networking opportunities with other entrepreneurs. Past topics have included advertising, packaging, labeling, trademarks, logos, business planning, marketing, social media, brand building, funding opportunities, and more.

- Social Networking – Pride of Dakota works to increase awareness of the program and individual member companies through its social media channels. Currently, the program utilizes Facebook, Twitter, and YouTube.

- Trade Show Assistance – Pride of Dakota provides financial assistance to members attending regional, national, and international trade shows. The program enables Pride of Dakota members to receive financial assistance for attending either a wholesale or a retail trade show outside North Dakota.

- Vendor Opportunities – At the popular Harvest and Holiday Showcases, along with a number of other one-day events, Pride of Dakota members can set up a booth and sell their products to thousands of shoppers. A Harvest Showcase is held in Dickinson during the fall, and Holiday Showcases are held in Grand Forks, Minot, Fargo, and Bismarck during the winter. Pride of Dakota Days are held at the State Capitol in the spring and fall, and thousands of visitors stop by the Pride of Dakota tent at the North Dakota State Fair.

- Website – The Pride of Dakota website provides every member company with its own profile page to share information about its operation, products, or services. Members can also use the website to register for Pride of Dakota events, renew membership, and purchase materials.

These benefits have proven profitable in many different ways for members of the Pride of Dakota program. Membership dues actually remain the same today as they were in 1985 based on the business's number of employees, ranging from $50-$250.

"Pride of Dakota has provided valuable training on everything from product pricing to laws for food products. My businesses aside, I believe that Pride of Dakota is a fabulous resource for our rural state. I believe that many businesses would not have become what they are, or even been inspired to start, had it not been for the Pride of Dakota program," said Katy Kassian of Buffalo Gals Mercantile.

At the end of 2016, membership totaled 528 and was divided among several different categories with Artisans & Gifts and Food & Beverages comprising the largest numbers.

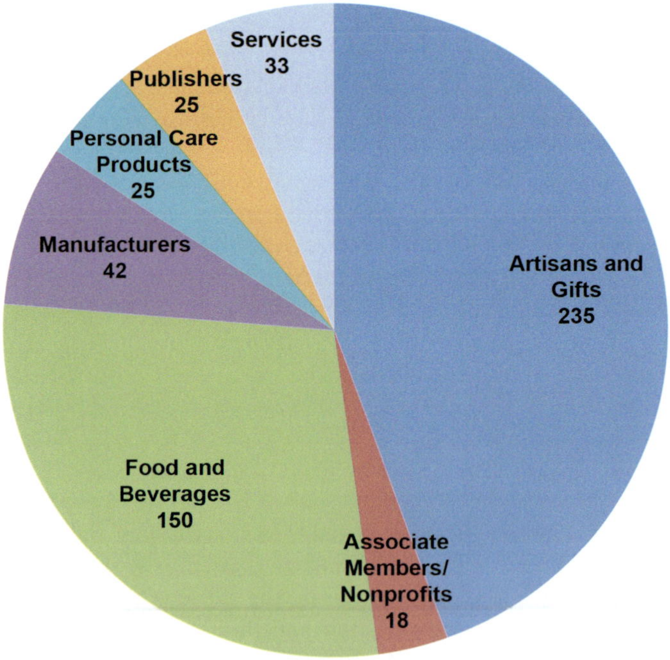

Membership by category (data from the end of 2016).

Member Profiles

A number of current Pride of Dakota members, identified by the NDDA based on completion of a member survey in late 2016, are profiled below. Information about all members is available at www.prideofdakota.com.

The Barn Guy

Owner: Cary Piatz
Established: 2005
Location: Bismarck
Category: Artisans & Gifts
Member Since: March 1, 2006

History: Cary Piatz grew up on a farm, playing with toy barns his grandpa made for him. After his grandpa was unable to make the barns, Cary inherited the art. He started by making simple barns for his family and friends. As time went on, he began to add more details, making his barns more realistic. He has been making barns in his spare time for more than 20 years and enjoys woodworking.

Products/Services: The Barn Guy offers a wide selection of wooden toy barns, fences, and feeders. Products come in different sizes, colors, and types of woods. Custom orders are also available.

POD Membership: The business owners joined Pride of Dakota in order to market their products as made in North Dakota. They have taken advantage of networking and vendor opportunities in the program and have expanded since they joined. They sell their products both within North Dakota and across several states. They have calls throughout the year and people who specifically look for their products.

Barns await finishing touches in Cary's workshop.

Lighthouse Soy Candles

Owners: Chad and Jamie Tollefson
Established: 2008
Location: Cavalier
Category: Artisans & Gifts
Member Since: July 1, 2008

History: Lighthouse Soy Candles was created in 2008 to supplement the Tollefson's income so one of them could remain at home to raise their children. They started with a hand-poured soy candle line and then added a bath line a year later.

Products/Services: Lighthouse Soy Candles provides a variety of soy candle products and soy bath and body products. They offer hand-poured soy candles in containers, pillars, votives, and soy wax melts. Their candles can be ordered in 50-60 scents and in about 10 different containers. Lighthouse Soy Candles also offers home and catalog shows, fundraisers, and wholesale opportunities.

POD Membership: The business owners joined Pride of Dakota for assistance in expanding their business. They have taken advantage of logo usage, networking, point-of-purchase materials, seminars/workshops, trade show assistance, and vendor opportunities in the program. They have expanded their business since joining Pride of Dakota and now sell their products within the state, across the United States, and internationally.

The Tollefson Family: Chad and Jamie with Allisyn, Brian, and Samantha.

PEAR'D

Owners: Lacey Heid and Rachel Neumiller
Established: 2013
Location: Bismarck
Category: Artisans & Gifts
Member Since: July 15, 2015

History: Rachel Neumiller and Lacey Heid learned how to sew from their mother, who learned from her mother. It is in their blood to create, and PEAR'D is an expression of that. They love to find fabric that's modern and unique, while using functional pattern designs to create products.

Products/Services: PEAR'D creates and sews zippered pouches, market bags, and kid and adult aprons. They also teach sewing classes on their own through Modern Textiles in Fargo and through Bismarck State College.

POD Membership: The business owners joined Pride of Dakota to market their products as made in North Dakota. They have taken advantage of logo usage and vendor opportunities in the program. They have expanded their business since they joined Pride of Dakota and sell their products within the state, across the United States, and internationally. When asked what Pride of Dakota has meant to their business, Rachel said, "We know North Dakota is full of talented small business owners, and we're grateful to be part of that community. Pride of Dakota has been a great way to further share our love of North Dakota and connect with local makers."

L to R: Rachel Neumiller and Lacey Heid, the owners of PEAR'D.

Mikey's Country Candy

Owners: Lesli Getzlaff and Sharon Brauer
Established: 1988 by original owner Mikell "Mikey" Wilkens; purchased in 2014 by current owners
Location: Burlington
Category: Food & Beverages
Member Since: September 1, 2009

History: Mikell "Mikey" Wilkens, the original owner of Mikey's Country Candy, was newly married to a farmer, learning to milk cows and adjusting to living on a farm. She experimented a lot and came up with a butter toffee recipe similar to the Almond Roca she enjoyed eating in her native Seattle. She named it Dakota Crunch. She made small orders for friends and sold them at craft shows. Eventually, her husband remodeled their garage into a kitchen in order to expand. She officially opened her doors on November 1, 1988. She sold the business to Cindy Yale and Nyla Sorenson in 2009. In 2014, sisters Sharon Brauer and Lesli Getzlaff purchased the business. They continue to use the original recipes that Mikey used, along with some new recipes of their own. The best known are Dot's Pretzel candy bars. Dot asked Lesli if she could come up with a candy using her broken pretzels, and they turned it into the number one selling product.

Products/Services: Signature items include Dakota Crunch, Dot's Pretzel candy bars, chokecherry creams, turtles, Dakota salted nut roll, cashew clusters, prairie chips (chocolate dipped potato chips), milk chocolate and white chocolate candy bars with sunflower seeds, and solid dark chocolate candy bars.

POD Membership: The business owners joined Pride of Dakota to market their products as made in North Dakota. They have taken advantage of logo usage and vendor opportunities in the program. They have expanded their business since they joined Pride of Dakota and sell their products across several states. They said they have found that people want products made in North Dakota, and Pride of Dakota has helped promote that.

Original owner Mikey Wilkens (center) with current owners Sharon Brauer (left) and Lesli Getzlaff (right) at a Bismarck Pride of Dakota show. Mikey is pointing to a picture of their Dakota Crunch toffee that was featured in **Food Network** *magazine representing North Dakota.*

Vitality Inc.

Owner: Dean Aasand
Established: 2001
Location: Carrington
Category: Personal Care Products
Member Since: October 1, 1999

History: At first, Dean Aasand just bought a couple of emus because he wanted to raise something. The business started when Dean and JoAnna Stinar of Morning Star Ranch joined together to produce products.

Products/Services: Vitality provides a complete line of emu oil-based products, including hand lotions, facial moisturizers, lip balm, pain relief lotion, skincare, cream, and pure emu oil. Emu oil protects, moisturizes, and improves skin conditions and reduces pain and inflammation of sore muscles and joints.

POD Membership: The business owners joined Pride of Dakota for assistance in expanding their business. They have taken advantage of logo usage, networking, vendor opportunities, and the retail store promotion program. They have expanded their business since they joined Pride of Dakota and sell their products within the state and across the United States.

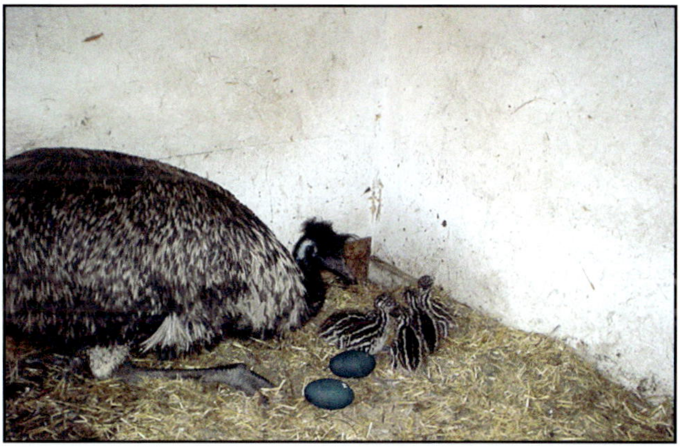

A male emu with emu eggs and chicks on the Morning Star Ranch. Under farm management, emu eggs are normally incubated and hatched in an incubator. Occasionally, a male emu is given the opportunity to incubate and hatch the last few eggs of a laying season like they do in the wild living in Australia.

Ashley Beth Pottery

Owner: Ashley Nordberg
Established: 2015
Location: Fargo
Category: Artisans & Gifts
Member Since: August 16, 2016

History: Childhood passions shaped Ashley Nordberg's future. She loved being outside as a kid, getting dirty, experimenting, and combining all sorts of mediums. She never touched clay until college, and according to her, it's pretty much been a love story since. Ashley graduated from Minnesota State University Moorhead in 2012 with a bachelor's degree in ceramics and an understudy in art education. She worked as a professional art framer for two and a half years while keeping her passion of creating as work on the side until summer 2015, when she took the plunge into full-time artist and stay-at-home mom. She works out of a home studio, where she does her wheel throwing, hand building, and runs electric and gas kilns with her husband.

Products/Services: Ashley Beth Pottery makes original, handmade pieces of both functional and decorative pottery. Her work has a vintage feminine inspiration, with some woodland creatures and storybook imaging along the way. Functionally, she makes cups, mugs, plates, bowls, and pitchers. For decorative work, she makes wall sconces, planters, and vases, as well as a ceramic jewelry line. She incorporates floral patterns, textures from buttons, lace, and other sewing materials, as well as hand-drawn images of forest creatures.

POD Membership: The business owners joined Pride of Dakota to market their products as made in North Dakota and for assistance getting started as a business and help in expanding. They also were looking to connect with other local makers and business owners. They have taken advantage of networking and vendor opportunities in the Pride of Dakota program. They have expanded their business since they joined Pride of Dakota and sell their products within the state, across the United States, and internationally. Pride of Dakota allowed Ashley to meet with other North Dakota makers and grow through their knowledge and experience. It also opened her business to markets she had not had the opportunity to pursue.

Mugs awaiting completion in the Ashley Beth Pottery studio.

HIT Inc.

Contact: Dee Grosz
Established: HIT Inc. was established in 1979 as an agency to work with people with developmental disabilities in residential and vocational programs. West River Produce, their commercially licensed kitchen, was started later as part of the vocational program.
Location: Mandan
Category: Manufacturers
Member Since: October 1, 2007

History: HIT Inc. was started in 1979 by several parents of children with developmental disabilities to provide housing and vocational opportunities in the Bismarck-Mandan area. The agency has grown in the past 38 years and now supports more than 150 people with developmental disabilities and their families in private homes, group homes, and apartment settings, as well as in vocational pursuits throughout Bismarck and Mandan. HIT also offers brain injury services, infant development services, and West River Head Start. HIT employs more than 500 people in these pursuits.

A few HIT clients working at West River Produce, HIT's commercially licensed kitchen.

Products/Services: HIT provides employment for adults with disabilities and operates several small businesses that produce North Dakota products. West River Produce, HIT's licensed kitchen, produces fruit pizza, veggie pizza, fresh fruit and vegetable trays, snack mixes, boxed lunches, cookies, and more. In addition, West River Production makes the Wrap-It-Game, a popular outdoor game that involves players trying to beat each other in tossing a bolo ball at a set of ladders. They also make gift crates with a brand of North Dakota and a buffalo on each side.

POD Membership: The business owners joined Pride of Dakota to market their products as made in North Dakota. They have taken advantage of point-of-purchase materials, seminars/workshops, and vendor opportunities in the program. They have expanded the business since joining Pride of Dakota and sell their products within the state. When asked what Pride of Dakota has meant to their business, Laura Kourajian, HIT vice president for community services, said, "Pride of Dakota is the single most effective thing we have done to grow our small business, giving us access to vendor shows that have expanded our visibility in our community."

Prairie Road Organic Seed

Owner: Dan and Theresa Podoll
Established: 1997
Location: Fullerton
Category: Food & Beverages
Member Since: March 1, 2012

History: All of the seed that is sold by Dan and Theresa Podoll is grown on their farm near Fullerton, which has been certified organic since 1977. They began producing certified organic vegetable seed for organic seed companies in 1997. A number of their varieties were actually bred on their farm; the rest are heirlooms. Many of the varieties bred on their farm gained popularity, and they decided they should be packaging their own seed and marketing them to growers and gardeners in the region. They now market seed under their own label, Prairie Road Organic Seed. All of their seed is open-pollinated, and they conduct ongoing selection work to further adapt the varieties to northern growing conditions and to improve the seeds' appearance, taste, and performance.

Products/Services: Prairie Road Organic Seed is a wholesaler and retailer of certified organic vegetable seeds that are bred, selected, and adapted to perform well under northern growing conditions and short seasons.

POD Membership: The business owners joined Pride of Dakota to market their products as made in North Dakota and for assistance getting started as a business. They have taken advantage of logo usage, networking, reduced rate cooperative advertising, seminars/workshops, trade show assistance, and vendor opportunities in the program. They have expanded their business since they joined Pride of Dakota and sell their products within the state and across the United States. The Pride of Dakota program has provided their business with priceless exposure to a targeted customer base of people interested in supporting North Dakota businesses.

One of the Podoll's gardens.

RSVP Dakota Store

Manager: Deb Lee
Established: 2009
Location: Jamestown
Category: Services
Member Since: December 1, 2011, as current business (also joined in mid-1990s as earlier business)

History: Deb Lee started selling North Dakota products with a business partner at a candy store in the mall in Jamestown in 1990. They developed the Gifts Dakota Style catalog featuring Pride of Dakota gifts and food items. They closed the store in 2000 and sold the catalog business to what would eventually become Home Sweet Home in Minot. In 2005, Deb started a seasonal store with business partners, and in 2009, it went year-round as a social enterprise – the RSVP Dakota Store. Currently, the store is a 501(c)(3) nonprofit, and it supports a community volunteer center in Jamestown.

A view inside the RSVP Dakota Store.

Products/Services: RSVP Dakota Store is a year-round retail store in Jamestown that features North Dakota food, gifts, and an exclusive line of t-shirts. Customized gift and food assortments are available for conference speakers, silent auctions, customer base, and everything else. The store opens in the summer at the Frontier Village in Jamestown and is run by volunteers.

POD Membership: The business owners joined Pride of Dakota to market their products as made in North Dakota. They have taken advantage of networking, point-of-purchase materials, the retail store promotion program, and vendor opportunities. The business has expanded since they joined Pride of Dakota, and they sell their products both within the state and across several states. The Pride of Dakota Showcases have helped people recognize the offerings made in North Dakota and appreciate having a local business carry those unique food and gift products.

Mattie Richardson, ND's Teen Author

Owner: Mattie Richardson
Established: Started writing in 2007 and publishing in 2009
Location: Sheldon
Category: Publishers
Member Since: April 1, 2015

History: Mattie Richardson started writing her first book, *Appaloosy*, when she was 13 years old. She published it at age 16 and printed 100 copies. She continued writing and publishing, and currently has five published books and has sold thousands of copies. She sells the books online and in multiple states. She hopes her business will continue to grow and has plans to include different genres, such as nonfiction, graphic novels, and compilations. She also plans to create and sell illustrations from her books; products from her books such as postcards, posters, bookmarks, and t-shirts; and possibly audiobooks. She is a speaker and regularly speaks to schools and other organizations about writing and inspiring others to reach their full potential.

Products/Services: All five of her published books are carefully crafted historical fiction novels that aim to entertain while teaching readers about American history. She is also a speaker who presents at schools and events.

POD Membership: The business owners joined Pride of Dakota to market their products as made in North Dakota and for assistance getting started as a business. They have taken advantage of vendor opportunities in the program. They have expanded their business since joining Pride of Dakota and sell their products both within the state and across several states. When asked what Pride of Dakota has meant to her business, Mattie said, "Pride of Dakota gives me opportunities that I otherwise wouldn't have had. It helps people understand that I am local, and so they will give my products a chance. It lets people know that my products exist and gives them the chance to meet and interact with me."

Author Mattie Richardson signs a copy of one of her books.

Buffalo Gals Mercantile

Owner: Katy Kassian
Established: 2010
Location: Regan
Category: Artisans & Gifts
Member Since: September 1, 2010

History: Katy Kassian has always done something to supplement income on the farm, whether baking, sewing, or photography. She started baking biscotti and was working with another Pride of Dakota member, Jo Khalifa at MoJoRoast. They started talking about potatoes that Katy was going to harvest, and Jo offered her some bags to use for gathering them. As Katy started looking more closely at the colorful bags, she decided they couldn't be used for potatoes and gave them a new life as upcycled hats and other items.

Owner Katy Kassian holding up some of her homemade biscotti.

Products/Services: Buffalo Gals Mercantile is home of the original Sakhat™. They also make unique, hand-crafted burlap handbags, as well as vintage-inspired aprons, novelties, and homemade biscotti.

POD Membership: The business owners joined Pride of Dakota to market their products as made in North Dakota and for the instant name recognition associated with Pride of Dakota. They also were looking for classes and resources. They have taken advantage of networking, point-of-purchase materials, seminars/workshops, trade show assistance, and vendor opportunities. They have expanded their business since they joined Pride of Dakota and sell their products both within the state and across the United States. When asked what Pride of Dakota has meant to her business, Katy said, "Pride of Dakota has meant brand recognition - people instantly equate Pride of Dakota with caring and quality. Over the years, Pride of Dakota has opened many opportunities to me."

Maple River Winery

Owner: Greg Kempel
Established: 2002
Location: Casselton
Category: Food & Beverages
Member Since: September 1, 2002

History: Greg Kempel's goal in 2001 was to make about 1,000 bottles of wine for friends, neighbors, and relatives. That number soon grew to be a lot more. The Kempels handcraft each wine every year with farm fresh fruit harvested by local people. Today, their winery and distillery uses close to 100,000 pounds of North Dakota fruit.

Owner Greg Kempel and his family outside their winery.

Products/Services: Maple River Winery has been producing award-winning wines with locally harvested fruits since 2002. In 2010, their Strawberry Rhubarb Wine was named the Best Fruit Wine at the International Wine Competition. They have a year-round tasting room and also offer online ordering and shipping of the wines and Pride of Dakota products.

POD Membership: The business owners joined Pride of Dakota because a good friend was a member and had praised the program. They have taken advantage of export assistance, logo usage, networking, point-of-purchase materials, the retail store promotion program, seminars/workshops, trade show assistance, and vendor opportunities in the program. They have expanded their business since joining Pride of Dakota and sell their products both within the state and across the United States. When asked what Pride of Dakota has meant to his business, Greg said, "Our North Dakota winery has been successful because of marketing outside of North Dakota. We could not have done this without the staff at Pride of Dakota."

Nourished by Nature

Owner: Paul Brown
Established: 2013
Location: Bismarck
Category: Food & Beverages
Member Since: May 1, 2014

History: Nourished by Nature was developed by the Brown family in 2013. The Browns had been selling grass-finished and pasture-raised products for years but noticed an increase in demand, so they decided to start their direct-marketing business. Now, people have the opportunity to buy Nourished by Nature products throughout North Dakota.

Products/Services: Nourished by Nature offers locally-raised, grass-finished beef and lamb, pastured pork, free-range eggs, and a wide variety of garden produce. Their livestock are humanely raised in a natural setting without the use of GMOs, synthetic hormones, or antibiotics. Nourished by Nature products are available through various farmers markets and online.

POD Membership: The business owners joined Pride of Dakota to market their products as made in North Dakota. They have taken advantage of networking and vendor opportunities in the program. They have expanded their business since they joined Pride of Dakota and sell their products within the state. When asked what Pride of Dakota has meant to his business, Paul said, "Pride of Dakota has given us great exposure through being listed on the website and through the Holiday Showcase."

Cattle grazing on the Brown ranch.

Rilos + MiMi

Owner: Christy Remmick
Established: 2012
Location: Devils Lake
Category: Artisans & Gifts
Member Since: December 1, 2014

History: Rilos and Mimi are nicknames for owner Christy Remmick's identical twin daughters, Riley and Emersyn, given to them by their big brother, Hunter. Founded in 2012 and funded by sales of used items on eBay, Rilos + MiMi now offers products in several retail stores in the country.

Products/Services: Rilos + MiMi designs and creates modern bags and accessories for people of all ages.

POD Membership: The business owners joined Pride of Dakota to market their products as made in North Dakota and to showcase their products to North Dakota customers. They have taken advantage of networking and vendor opportunities in the program. They have expanded their business since they joined Pride of Dakota and sell their products within the state, across the United States, and internationally. When asked what Pride of Dakota has meant to her business, Christy said, "Pride of Dakota has given me the opportunity to market my products as made in North Dakota and to also reach more customers in North Dakota through website mentions and being able to participate in vendor shows."

Christy's children and a friend help mail some orders, both to North Dakota retailers that carry Rilos + MiMi products and online customers.

Impact in North Dakota

For many communities across North Dakota, having a Pride of Dakota company in the area means not only pride but opportunity. These companies bring business and networking opportunities, help expand the local economy, provide employment, and draw tourists to the area.

When asked about what their businesses have meant to the local community and the state, Pride of Dakota members said:

"We created an economic opportunity by purchasing fruit from area residents, as well as bringing tourists from all over the world."
– Greg Kempel, Maple River Winery

"Our local community has been impacted greatly since we purchased Amberland Foods. We employ several people with disabilities within the community. It gives them meaningful paid work." – Tiffany Kearns, Amberland Foods

"Rilos + MiMi does a few give-back events, including sponsoring a youth fishing clinic for the last two years in Devils Lake. We also donate several items to local charity auctions throughout the year." – Christy Remmick, Rilos + MiMi

"It has added not only a unique product, but has brought in a lot of tourism – many people from out-of-state come to our tasting room."
– Susan Ruud, Prairie Rose Meadery

"Shoppers come to town for our little store, and I hope that trickles to other businesses and eating establishments." – Kristy Llerenas, A Touch of Honey

"We speak all over the world about our farming and ranching practices and host thousands of people on our ranch every year. We expose them to how we manage our ranch and furthermore value-add the products that we raise."
– Paul Brown, Nourished by Nature

A *Bismarck Tribune* editorial from the late 1980s foresaw the potential of the program with this statement:

"We think that, properly promoted, it [the Pride of Dakota program] has a lot of potential yet to improve sales of North Dakota products, especially agricultural. People in this state are proud of their productivity and will support efforts to increase it."

The Pride of Dakota program has lived up to that prediction, from its humble beginnings with a couple dozen members to serving more than 500 members and becoming a widely recognized brand in the state and beyond.

A field of North Dakota flax.

Buffalo in the North Dakota Badlands.

Chapter Two

North Dakota Almanac

North Dakota
Origin of the Name

On March 2, 1861, President James Buchanan signed the bill creating the Dakota Territory, which originally included the area covered today by both Dakotas as well as much of Montana and Wyoming. The name was taken from that of the Dakota or Sioux Indian Tribe. Beginning about 1877, efforts were made to bring Dakota into the Union as both a single state and as two states. The latter was successful, and on November 2, 1889, both North and South Dakota were admitted.

Since President Benjamin Harrison went to great lengths to obscure the order in which the statehood proclamations were signed, the exact order in which the two states entered is unknown. However, because of alphabetical position, North Dakota is often considered as the 39th state.

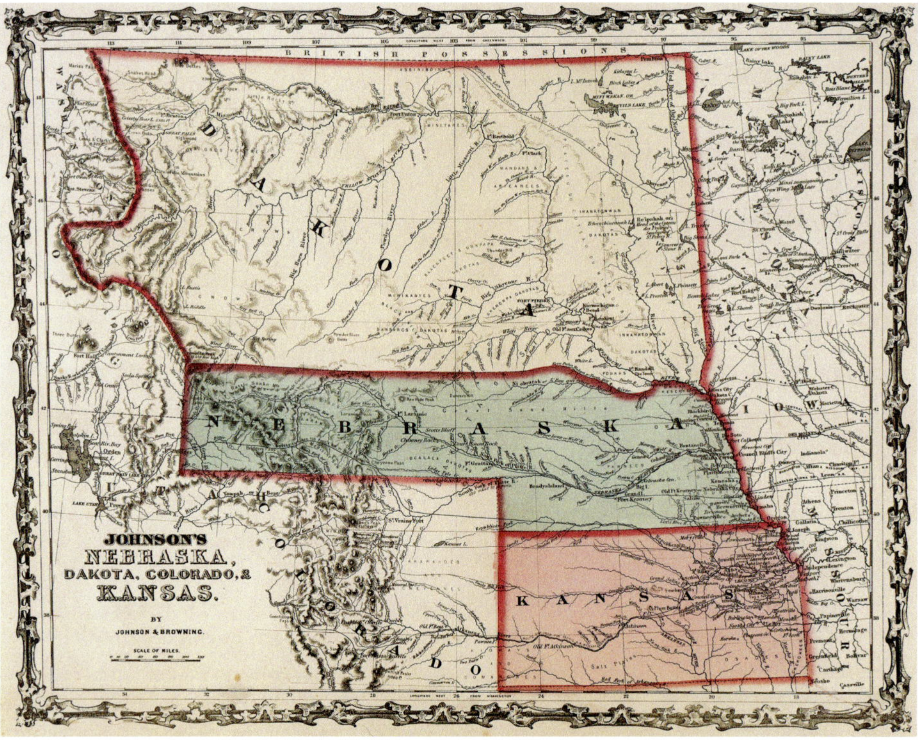

This 1862 Dakota Territory map by Johnson and Browning includes part of the present states of Montana and Wyoming. It shows numerous Indian tribes and their homelands, but the new territorial capital at Yankton is not located on the map. The eastern boundary of Dakota Territory is in the general area, but not quite tied to the Red River of the North.

Nicknames

Peace Garden State – The International Peace Garden straddles the international boundary between North Dakota and the Canadian province of Manitoba. In 1956, the North Dakota Motor Vehicle Department, on its own initiative, placed the words "Peace Garden State" on license plates. The name proved so popular that it was formally adopted by the 1957 Legislature (North Dakota Century Code [NDCC], Section 39-04-12).

Flickertail State – Flickertail refers to the Richardson ground squirrel, which is abundant in North Dakota. The animal flicks or jerks its tail in a characteristic manner while running or just before entering its burrow. On December 15, 1889, during the first session of the North Dakota Legislature, Representative Frank Thompson from Cass County introduced the following resolution in the House:

Whereas, The Spirmophilus Richardsoni, or flicker-tail gopher, is a creature endemic to this land of the Dakotas; therefore be it Resolved, That we, the house of representatives of the state of North Dakota, do by this resolution christen every child born or who may hereafter be born within the boundaries of this state with the name "Flickertail," which christened name shall be applied in the same manner as the word "Sucker" is applied to children born in Illinois, "Wolverine" to those born in Michigan, "Badger" to those born in Wisconsin, etc.

A flickertail peering out of his home.

The resolution was adopted and, for 10 minutes, North Dakota stood dubbed "the Flickertail state." It was then reconsidered and all mention of it was expunged from the House Journal. In 1953, the Legislative Assembly defeated Senate Bill (S.B.) 134 that would have adopted the Flickertail facsimile as the official emblem of the state.

Roughrider State – This name originated in a state-supported tourism promotion of the 1960s and 1970s. It refers to the First U.S. Volunteer Cavalry, which Theodore Roosevelt organized to fight in the Spanish-American War. In fact, the "Roughriders," which included several North Dakota cowboys, fought dismounted in Cuba due to logistical problems. In both 1971 (H.B. 1383) and 1973 (H.B. 1443), the Legislative Assembly defeated bills intended to change the words "Peace Garden State" on state license plates to "Roughrider Country."

Dakota – An attempt to drop the word "North" from the state name was defeated by the 1947 Legislative Assembly (House Concurrent Resolution [H.C.R.] J). Again in 1989, the Legislature rejected two resolutions (Senate Concurrent Resolutions [S.C.R.] 4031 and 4032) intended to rename the state "Dakota."

Great Seal of North Dakota

From the time of its ratification in 1889, North Dakota's Constitution has always contained the same detailed description of the state's Great Seal. Now found in Section Two of Article XI (titled General Provisions), the description of the Great Seal was initially located in Section Two of Article XVII (titled Miscellaneous) in the 1889 version of the Constitution. Some of the wording contained in the Constitution's description is the same as that used for the territorial seal approved on January 3, 1863, by the Legislative Assembly of the Territory of Dakota.

The description reads as follows: A tree in the open field, the trunk of which is surrounded by three bundles of wheat; on the right a plow, anvil and sledge; on the left, a bow crossed with three arrows, and an Indian on horseback pursuing a buffalo toward the setting sun; the foliage of the tree arched by a half circle of 42 stars, surrounded by the motto "Liberty and Union Now and Forever, One and Inseparable;" the words "Great Seal" at the top; the words "State of North Dakota" at the bottom; "October 1st" on the left and "1889" on the right.

Research has failed to reveal the reasons the selected symbols were chosen. As a result, various theories have been advanced over the years. For example, the tree has been identified as an American Elm. However, the American Elm was not adopted as the state's official tree until 1947. The three bundles of wheat could represent the three branches of government – executive, legislative, and judicial. The plow, anvil, and sledge may make reference to the agricultural background of the state and to its strong work ethic. The bow and arrows, buffalo, Indian on horseback, and setting sun could be reminders of an integral segment in the history of the northern plains. The motto is a quote by Daniel Webster.

Although North Dakota became the 39th state, the seal has 42 stars across the top. Since it was not known at statehood as to which "number" North Dakota would be, it is assumed that the stars represent the 42 states that would comprise the Union by the end of 1889.

While the content has generally been true to the description, the design of the Great Seal itself has varied through the years. The first known design is found in the *1887 Blue Book*. There were designs with slight variations from its predecessor in at least 1899, 1907, 1909, 1911, 1913, 1919, 1926, 1929, 1973, and 1987. In the spring of 1987, then-Secretary of State Ben Meier commissioned Dickinson artist Lili Stewart to create a new design. That design was approved on September 17, 1987, and is still used today.

Since statehood, the Secretary of State has been charged with the custody of the Great Seal. The first legislation related to the Great Seal was passed by the First Legislative Assembly in 1890 (S.B. 23). Nevertheless, relatively few changes in the law were made through the years. A major change was made in 1975 which

North Dakota's seal is shown here in three presentations.

prohibited the use of the Great Seal in advertising and for commercial purposes. An exception was passed in 1985 (effective until June 30, 1991) allowing the use of the Great Seal for approved commercial purposes as a part of North Dakota's Centennial Celebration. Otherwise, for many years the use of the Great Seal was largely dependent on numerous opinions issued by the Attorney General.

To more clearly define the acceptable uses of the Great Seal and to end the dependency on the opinions, S.B. 2448 was passed by the 1995 Legislative Assembly. The bill gave the Secretary of State greater flexibility and authority in carrying out the custodial responsibilities related to the Great Seal. In addition, it specifically prohibited the use of the Great Seal for political purposes. The existing law was also amended to allow the Great Seal to be reproduced, with the concurrence of the Secretary of State, on items offered for sale as gifts and souvenirs by the State Historical Society and the Parks and Recreation Department.

The bronze likeness of the Great Seal in the Capitol's Memorial Hall was dedicated in a ceremony held on February 22, 2006. It measures six feet across and weighs 440 pounds. The Capitol Grounds Planning Commission undertook the project to coincide with the 117th anniversary of the Enabling Act, which allowed North Dakota, South Dakota, Montana, and Washington to join the Union as individual states. The seal and its commemorative 570-pound plaque were made by Metal Arts Company, a Mandan foundry. The seal, plaque, and installation cost approximately $48,000.

State Motto

"Liberty and Union Now and Forever, One and Inseparable" is the state motto (North Dakota Constitution Article XI, Section 2).

The motto of Dakota Territory was "Liberty and Union, One and Inseparable, Now and Forever." This language was suggested by Dr. Joseph Ward of Yankton, South Dakota, who was quoting from Daniel Webster's *Reply to Hayne*. However, the motto used for the Territory had two of the phrases reversed; when North Dakota became a state, that error was corrected.

State Latin Motto

A state Latin motto was adopted by the 62nd Legislative Assembly in 2011, creating a new section to Chapter 54-02 of the North Dakota Century Code.

"Serit ut alteri saeclo prosit." "One sows for the benefit of another age."

A State Creed

(Never Officially Adopted)

We believe in North Dakota, in the beauty of her skies, and in the glory of her prairies.

We believe in the People of North Dakota, in their strength of Body and Mind, in their High Sense of Right, and in their Desire to establish a Great Commonwealth wherein the things that count for Human Welfare shall be first.

We believe that by Thought and Act we can magnify our State and the Life of our People, bind the East and the West, the North and the South by Roadways, Communication and Good Will, and give our Sons and Daughters the Opportunity to Work at Useful Tasks within our borders.

We pledge to those seeking new homes the Hand of Hospitality and extend to them a Welcome to our Commonwealth where they may find Peace and Happiness.

We pledge that the freedom our Fathers won here and elsewhere shall continue as the Heritage of our Children.

We, as a People, because of growing Intelligence and a Nobler Outlook, seek Unity of Purpose; we desire to lead a Richer Common Life, and hope to render a Larger Service to the State and the Nation.

(This state creed, written by Frank L. McVey, former president of the University of North Dakota, is first found in the *1926 Manual for the State of North Dakota*.)

The State Flag

On January 21, 1911, Representative Colonel John H. Fraine introduced H.B. 152 designating an official flag for the state of North Dakota (1911 S.L., ch. 283). The legislation specifically required that the flag conform to the color, form, and size of the regimental flag carried by the North Dakota Infantry in the Spanish-American War in 1898 and Philippine Island Insurrection in 1899; the only exception was the name "North Dakota" placed on the scroll below the eagle. On March 3, 1911, the Legislative Assembly adopted the North Dakota state flag. North Dakota Century Code Section 54-02-02 describes the state flag in detail.

In 1951, S.B. 156 established the North Dakota State Flag Commission to consider changes to the flag (1951 S.L., ch. 303). The commission concluded the flag "too closely resembled the coat of arms of the United States and that the flag was not symbolic of North Dakota." The commission's conclusions were widely challenged and its suggested changes rejected. S.B. 265 was introduced during the 1953 session and contained the recommendations of the flag commission. That legislation was defeated.

In 2011, H.B. 1097 established design and color codes for the flag. The State Historical Society is required to provide to the public a description in writing of the flag, and any flags purchased by a state entity or a political subdivision must substantially meet the requirements of this section.

Although there are requests for information regarding a 39-star flag for North Dakota, such a flag never existed. North Dakota was the 39th state to be admitted to the Union. It entered at the same time as three other states, and a separate flag was never made for North Dakota.

State Coat of Arms and the Governor's Flag

In 1957, the Legislative Assembly passed H.B. 822, sponsored by Representatives Clifford Lindberg and Gillman Olson, to create the North Dakota coat of arms (1957 S.L., ch. 330). When the Governor is using the coat of arms as a flag, there must be a white star placed in each of the four corners (North Dakota Century Code Section 54-41-04). The North Dakota coat of arms was displayed for the first time by the National Guard at Camp Grafton on June 16, 1957.

54-41-02 Significant elements of coat of arms – The colors of yellow, gold, and green are indicative of the great agricultural state of North Dakota and has particular reference to ripening grain and the abundant grazing areas. The Indian arrowhead forms the shield of the coat of arms and symbolizes the "Sioux State." The three stars denote the trinity of government: legislative, executive, and judicial. Each star in the bend is given the heraldic value of thirteen, which signifies the thirteen original colonies of the United States, and the cumulative numerical value of the three stars indicates that North Dakota was the 39th state admitted to the Union. The stars also allude to the history of the territory under three foreign flags. Three stars are borne upon the coat of arms of Meriwether Lewis of the Lewis and Clark expedition and also on the coat of arms of Lord Selkirk, head of the first permanent settlement in this state. The fleur-de-lis alludes to LaVerendrye, a French explorer who was the first known white man to visit the territory of this state. The blue and gold wreath in the crest reflects the history of the territory as part of the Louisiana Purchase. The crest, which shall constitute the military crest of the state of North Dakota, is a motif taken from the state seal, and to the Sioux Indian tribes, signifies mighty warriors.

State Coat of Arms

54-41-03 Authorized use – The coat of arms of this state may be used in a manner consistent with the respect and dignity due a state coat of arms and its symbolic values by the following persons, organizations, and agencies:

1. The governor of North Dakota

2. The North Dakota National Guard

3. Departments and agencies of the state of North Dakota

4. North Dakota veterans organizations

5. Officially recognized North Dakota educational institutions, systems, or divisions

6. Recognized North Dakota patriotic organizations

Constitution of North Dakota

The Constitution of North Dakota was adopted on October 1, 1889, with a vote of 27,441 to 8,107. As of July 2017, the North Dakota Constitution has 20,148 words.

State Flower

(North Dakota Century Code Section 54-02-03)

Wild Prairie Rose (Rosa Blanda or Arkansana) – The flower has been identified as Rosa Pratincula in species.

Created by: 1907 S.L., ch. 231, S.B. 134
Sponsored by: Senator Louis B. Hanna

The flower sports five bright pink petals with a tight cluster of yellow stamens in the center. The wild prairie rose grows along roadsides, in pastures, and in native meadows.

State Bird

(North Dakota Century Code Section 54-02-06)

Western Meadowlark (Sturnella Neglecta)

Created by: 1947 S.L., ch. 329, H.B. 270

Sponsored by: Representatives John Halcrow, Alexandar Dalzell, Freeman M. Einarson, Palmer Levin, Leo E. Callahan, Daniel Power, Arthur W. Benno, Winfield M. Smart, Walter Bubel

Approximately the size of a robin, the meadowlark sports a yellow breast with a black bib over its mottled brown body. These song birds are found from Wisconsin to Texas and westward to the Pacific.

State Tree

(North Dakota Century Code Section 54-02-05)

American Elm
(Ulmus Americana)

Created by: 1947 S.L., ch. 329, H.B. 270
Sponsored by: Representatives John Halcrow, Alexandar Dalzell, Freeman M. Einarson, Palmer Levin, Leo E. Callahan, Daniel Power, Arthur W. Benno, Winfield M. Smart, Walter Bubel

Common across the state, the American Elm can reach 120 feet or taller. The tallest American Elm in the state has been recorded by the North Dakota Forest Service at 82 feet.

State Insect

(North Dakota Century Code Section 54-02)

Convergent Lady Beetle
(Hippodamia Convergens)

Created by: 2011 S.L., ch. 54-02, H.B. 1219

Sponsored by: Representatives Glen Froseth, Patrick Hatlestad, Gary Kreidt; Senator Karen Krebsbach

The convergent lady beetle is commonly known as a ladybug. A group of second graders from Kenmare lobbied for this legislation.

State Fruit

(North Dakota Century Code Section 54-02-17)

Chokecherry (Prunus Virginiana)

Created by: 2007 S.L. ch. 452, S.B. 2145
Sponsored by: Senators Stanley Lyson, Nicholas Hacker; Representatives Patrick Hatlestad, Gary Sukut

Mentioned by Lewis and Clark in their journals and long a staple of the Native Americans on the Northern Plains, the chokecherry is a thicket forming shrub or small tree and is a valuable habitat for birds and small game animals. The fruit, which is deep red and relatively small in size, is somewhat bitter tasting when taken from the plant but is prized for making jams, wines, and syrups.

The designation was spearheaded by the sixth grade class at Rickard Elementary School in Williston, which lobbied for a state fruit beginning in February 2006.

State Song

(North Dakota Century Code Section 54-02-04)

***North Dakota Hymn* with words by James W. Foley and music by Dr. C. S. Putnam**

Created by: 1947 S.L., ch. 327, H.B. 130
Sponsored by: Representatives Kenneth Fitch, Charles Yirchott, Clair Brickner, John Brady, Arthur Johnson

In 1926, Minnie J. Nielson, North Dakota Superintendent of Public Instruction, asked Poet Laureate James Foley of Bismarck to write the lyrics for a song about North Dakota. Foley created a poem that could be sung to the tune, *The Austrian Hymn*. Dr. C. S. Putnam, conductor of the North Dakota Agricultural College Band in Fargo, arranged music for Foley's work. The first public presentation of the *North Dakota Hymn* was in the Bismarck City Auditorium in 1927.

The *North Dakota Hymn* is found on the following pages.

2

North Dakota Hymn

MIXED VOICES

Words by
JAMES W. FOLEY

Music by
Dr. C. S. PUTNAM

3
sea; North Da - ko - ta, North Da - ko - ta,
ways_ North Da - ko - ta, North Da - ko - ta,
skies. North Da - ko - ta, North Da - ko - ta,
song; North Da - ko - ta, North Da - ko - ta,
Here we pledge our-selves to thee. North Da - ko - ta,
We will serve thee all our days. North Da - ko - ta,
Brave the Soul that in thee lies. North Da - ko - ta,
In our hearts for - ev - er long. North Da - ko - ta,
North Da - ko - ta, Here we pledge our-selves to thee.
North Da - ko - ta, We will serve thee all our days.
North Da - ko - ta, Brave the Soul that in thee lies.
North Da - ko - ta, In our hearts for - ev - er long.
North Dakota Hymn 2 Mixed V.

State Art Museum

(North Dakota Century Code Section 54-02-11)

Established in 1972 at the University of North Dakota in Grand Forks, the state's first professional art gallery researches, records, collects, and exhibits North Dakota's visual art history. Gallery leadership in the development of cultural life through art was recognized by the Legislative Assembly. In the fall of 1996, the State Board of Higher Education transferred ownership of the gallery to a private, nonprofit organization – the Friends of the Museum of Art.

The University of North Dakota Art Galleries were known as the State Art Gallery until the 2003 Legislative Assembly changed the name to North Dakota Art Museum.

Created by:	1981 S.L., ch. 519, S.B. 2359
Sponsored by:	Senator Evan Lips; Representatives Jim Gerl, Michael Unhjem

Amended by:	2003 S.L., ch. 456, S.B. 2318
Sponsored by:	Senators Duaine C. Espegard, Linda Christiansen, Ray Holmberg; Representative Eliot Glassheim

State Fossil

(North Dakota Century Code Section 54-02-08)

Teredo-bored Petrified Wood

Created by: 1967 S.L., ch. 378, H.B. 933
Sponsored by: Representative Wayne Sanstead

The Teredo was a worm-shaped mollusk related to clams, mussels, and oysters. It burrowed its way through sequoias and other trees growing near warm-water swamps in North Dakota 60 to 80 million years ago. As the trees in the mineral rich water petrified, some of the wood was replaced by silica and quartz, thereby preserving evidence of the Teredo. North Dakota was not represented in the Smithsonian Institution's mineral collection. Naming of the Teredo-bored petrified wood as the state fossil remedied that situation and promoted the fossil to tourists, geologists, and rockhounds.

State Fish

Northern Pike (Esox Lucius)

Created by: 1969 S.L., p. 1385, S.C.R. 21
Sponsored by: Senators Frank Wenstrom, Robert Chesrown, John Decker, Guy Larson

North Dakota waters have yielded mammoth size Northern Pike, resulting in a national sports fishing reputation for the state.

Official Academy of Science

North Dakota Academy of Science (originally at the University of North Dakota, moved to North Dakota State University in 1989)

Created by: 1959 S.L., p. 920, H.C.R. "X"
Sponsored by: Senators George Longmire, George Saumur

The purpose of the academy is to promote and conduct scientific research and disseminate scientific knowledge. Toward that end, the North Dakota Science Research Foundation raises funds and distributes grants on behalf of the academy.

State March

(North Dakota Century Code Section 54-02-09)

Flickertail March

Created by: 1989 S.L., ch. 628, H.B. 1671
Sponsored by: Representative Harold Trautman

In 1975, the Legislative Assembly passed H.B. 1160, which designated James D. Ployhar's *Spirit of the Land* as the official state march (1975 S.L., ch. 462). Ployhar had been commissioned by the North Dakota Band Directors Association to compose a march appropriate for official state functions. *Spirit of the Land* was played in the Capitol's Memorial Hall by the Jamestown High School Band on the day the bill passed the House of Representatives in February 1975. Once designated as the state march, *Spirit of the Land* was sent to a publisher. The title happened to be nearly identical to that of another march. As a result, the publisher requested a new title be selected. Ployhar agreed to *Flickertail March*. In 1989, the Legislative Assembly approved the change.

Official Salmon Derby

Trophy Takers Salmon Club's Blackjaw Fever Salmon Derby

Created by: 1989 S.L., ch. 892, S.C.R. 4038
Sponsored by: Senator Joe Keller; Representatives Bob O'Shea, Lyle Hanson, Clarence Martin

The Blackjaw Fever Salmon Derby annually brings in contestants from many states and North Dakota communities to Lake Sakakawea. To recognize the economic impact of the derby and its role in promoting tourism through sport fishing, the Legislative Assembly made this designation.

Sports Hall of Fame

Created by: 1993 S.L., ch. 737, S.C.R. 4030
Sponsored by: Senators David E. Nething, Dale Marks; Representatives Lyle L. Hanson, John M. Howard, Joe Kroeber, Terry M. Wanzek

To honor persons who worked to promote and develop athletics in North Dakota, the Legislative Assembly established the Sports Hall of Fame in Jamestown.

Official High School Hockey Flag

Created by: 1977 S.L., p. 1438, H.C.R. 3035
Sponsored by: Representative Earl Strinden

The 1976 Bicentennial state high school hockey tournament displayed an official flag that became the North Dakota state high school hockey flag. It recognized the growing popularity of the sport.

State Beverage

(North Dakota Century Code Section 54-02-12)

Milk

Created by: 1983 S.L., ch. 548, H.B. 1301
Sponsored by: Representatives Leslie Gullickson, Brynhild Haugland, Charles Mertens; Senators Francis Barth, Pete Naaden

By official designation, the Legislative Assembly recognized the importance of North Dakota's dairy industry.

Agricultural Hall of Fame

Created by: 1997 S.L., ch. 70, H.B. 1362
Sponsored by: Representatives Gereld F. Gerntholz, Robert Huether, Leland Sabby; Senators Larry J. Robinson, Terry M. Wanzek

Established to recognize individuals who have made outstanding contributions to the state's agricultural industry, the Agricultural Hall of Fame is officially located at the North Dakota Winter Show in Valley City.

State Grass

(North Dakota Century Code Section 54-02-10)

Western Wheatgrass (Agropyron Smithii)

Created by: 1977 S.L., ch. 475, S.B. 2444
Sponsored by: Senators Kenneth Morgan, Robert Albers, Francis Barth

Western Wheatgrass, a tough native prairie grass, once covered nearly all of the state. The North Dakota Chapter of the Society for Range Management called for adopting an official state grass. Western Wheatgrass was selected for its adaptability to soil conditions, its performance record for hay and pasture, and its role in range management as a species found in all the state's counties.

State Dance

(North Dakota Century Code Section 54-02-16)

Square Dance

Created by:	1995 S.L., ch. 492, H.B. 1412
Sponsored by:	Representatives Ben Tollefson, Bob Martinson, Clara Sue Price, RaeAnn Kelsch; Senators Terry M. Wanzek, Corliss Mushik

The 1995 Legislative Assembly designated the square dance as the official American folk dance of North Dakota.

Fort Mandan and Lewis and Clark Interpretive Center

Created by:	1995 S.L., ch. 493, S.C.R. 4029
Sponsored: by:	Senator Layton W. Freborg; Representatives Jeff W. Delzer, Albert "Mick" Grosz

The 1995 Legislative Assembly designated Fort Mandan and the Lewis and Clark Interpretive Center as the official Lewis and Clark Bicentennial Project for North Dakota.

State Language
(North Dakota Century Code Section 54-02-13)

English

Created by: 1987 S.L., ch. 619, S.B. 2096
Sponsored by: Senators Harvey Tallackson, Pete Naaden, Earl Kelly; Representatives Rosemarie Myrdal, Orville Schindler

North Dakota joined other states in a nationwide movement to make English the official language. Opposition came from organizations and persons fearing loss of foreign and native language or diminished access to diversity of other cultures. Supporters acknowledged the measure and legalized what was already in practice. The designation made official the common bond that allows for communication and conduct of business.

State Railroad Museum
(North Dakota Century Code Section 54-02-14)

Mandan Railroad Museum

Created by: 1989 S.L., ch. 629, S.B. 2496
Sponsored by: Senators Corliss Mushik, Walter Meyer; Representatives Dan Ulmer, Jim Gerl, Dick Tokach

Selection of the Mandan Railroad Museum, established in 1972, reflects the importance of Mandan as a railroad town. Since 1989 was the state's centennial year, legislators also recognized the influence of railroads in North Dakota history.

First Nations Day
(North Dakota Century Code Section 01-03-13)

Created by: 2003 S.L., S.B. 2410
Sponsored by: Senators Dennis Bercier, April Fairfield, Ronald Nichols, David O'Connell, Harvey D. Tallackson; Representative Merle Boucher

To recognize the indigenous peoples of the State of North Dakota and their contributions to the state and to the United States, the governor shall issue a proclamation each year designating the Friday before the second Monday in October as First Nations Day.

Honorary Equine

(North Dakota Century Code Section 54-02-15)

Nokota Horse

Created by: 1993 S.L., ch. 504, S.B. 2498
Sponsored by: Senator Pete Naaden

The Nokota breed may well be those distinct horses descended from Sioux Chief Sitting Bull's war ponies. Some still run wild in Theodore Roosevelt National Park.

North Dakota Governors

✔ Biographies and photos of North Dakota governors can be found in the *2001-2003 North Dakota Blue Book.*

Aerial shot of the North Dakota state capitol grounds.

North Dakota State Capitol and Grounds

State Capitol

North Dakota's present capitol is, like many of the state's residents, a child of the Great Depression of the 1930s. It was designed and built after fire destroyed the original capitol on December 28, 1930. Hard-pressed for cash, the 1931 Legislative Assembly scraped together funds from a number of sources: insurance, income from the sale and rental of land assigned to capitol development since statehood, and a decades-old capitol building fund. Then legislators placed a $2 million limit on expenditures for the new building.

The three-member Board of State Capitol Commissioners charged with overseeing construction sorted through a series of proposals offered by architects from throughout the country before selecting Chicago architects John A. Holabird and John W. Root to design the building. To fulfill a statutory requirement that North Dakota architects participate in the design process, William F. Kurke of Fargo and Joseph Bell DeRemer of Grand Forks were designated as associates to the Chicago firm.

The selection of Holabird & Root probably related to the firm's long experience with tall, office-style structures, a building style which found favor with the commissioners after visits to Lincoln, Nebraska, and Baton Rouge, Louisiana, where skyscraper capitol projects were nearing completion. The final design combined a 19-story tower, intended to house the executive and judicial branches of government, with a legislative wing, fronted by a columned memorial hall. The tower, in both massing and details, closely resembled another Holabird & Root project, the Ramsey County Courthouse-St. Paul City Hall, then being built in St. Paul, Minnesota.

Historically, capitols have offered an opportunity for states to show off their culture and development through the lavish use of art in the form of paintings and sculpture. The spending limit imposed by the legislative assembly made this almost impossible for the Bismarck building. The architect's selection of Moderne architecture and its companion decorative form, Art Deco, both focused largely on geometric shapes, offering opportunities for inexpensive decoration. To save money, this style was limited to the legislative wing and the lower two floors of the tower. More than half of the tower's interior was left unfinished in 1934. Later the area was decorated by Depression-era federal agencies which utilized the space as the 1930s progressed.

Ironically, the first state capitol, originally that of the Dakota Territory, built in 1883-1884 with additions in 1893-1894 and again in 1903-1904, was similarly bereft of decorative features and for the same reasons: legislatively-imposed spending limits. To stretch their decorating budget, the architects chose to make extensive use of bronze and brass, as well as various examples of exotic stone and woods. These materials were available to builders at considerably reduced costs during the 1930s because of the economic depression then afflicting the nation. Even so, a number of decorative features, including a 30-foot statue centered on the capitol steps, had to be eliminated.

The construction contract was awarded to the Lundoff-Bicknell Company of Cleveland, Ohio, in June 1932, and construction began soon after. State agencies began moving into the structure in the latter half of 1934. Although the building has had two separate cornerstones, both laid with appropriate ceremonies, there is no record of its ever having been formally dedicated. The second cornerstone was installed in 1933 by newly elected Governor William Langer, who insisted that the original had been damaged by souvenir hunters. That 1933 cornerstone, hewn from rock near St. Anthony, North Dakota, can be found at the east side of the foyer.

The capitol reaches 242 feet – or 19 stories – into the North Dakota sky. The outside dimensions of the tower measure 95 feet by 95 feet. West of the tower are the three stories of the legislative wing. The tower and the legislative wing are joined together by the Memorial Hall, the central feature found in the building and the most beautiful interior setting in North Dakota.

The exterior walls were covered with Bedford white limestone, a material commonly used on both skyscrapers and public buildings; Rosetta black granite from Wisconsin was used around the foundations and on the tower, while Minnesota granite covered the front steps and foyer. A controversy arose in 1932 when the capitol commissioners, intent upon using North Dakota building materials to the greatest extent possible, considered facing the structure with locally manufactured brick. When an investigation determined that state brickmakers could not produce the material in sufficient volume to keep construction on schedule, the commissioners chose limestone to cover the building. This matched the Liberty Memorial Building, the only other structure then standing on the capitol grounds.

There are two revolving bronze doors in the foyer. Above these doors, inside and outside, are bronze figures representing farming and mining. Between the two revolving doors are six bronze columns that have weathered to a black finish. Between the columns and on the bronze canopies atop the glass panels are five raised sculptured bronze figurines representing a blacksmith, a farmer and his family, a woman with three children, a hunter and his family, and a Native American. (Bronze is a metal consisting of copper and tin with traces of other minerals.) The main entrance doors located at ground level are made of bronze and are accessible for all persons. The walls of the ground floor lobby are covered with Yellowstone Travertine, cream-colored marble from Gardiner, Montana. (Yellowstone Travertine marble is found on the north edge of the Yellowstone National Park and is formed by lime and calcium deposits carried in solutions of hot water springs and geysers.) The floor is covered by very dense Tennessee gray marble intermixed with dark cedar Tennessee marble.

On the first floor, the hallway extends 342 feet from the west end of the building to the east side of the Memorial Hall. It is 25 feet wide and 42 feet high, but the effects of the glass windows make it seem much larger. Travertine marble is found throughout the Memorial Hall. This is the first large building in the United States in which Travertine marble was extensively used. The hall is the site of official state functions and hosts the state Christmas tree during the holiday season.

When the Judicial Wing was added in 1981, the corridor was extended another 164 feet east. The corridor plus the length of the Legislative Assembly Hall and Memorial Hall measures 505 feet from the west end to the front door of the Supreme Court office. The corridor went through part of the Secretary of State's office when the new wing was built.

On either side and at the ends of the Memorial Hall are 16 bronze pillars reaching to the ceiling. The pillars are 40 feet tall. Five bronze chandeliers visually portraying a head of wheat hang from the ceiling. They are 12 feet long and 30 inches in diameter. One hundred and nine light bulbs in each fixture light the hallway, making it beautiful by night and by day.

On the north wall, opposite the main entrance, a stairway leads to the ground floor. Black Belgium marble, polished to such a brightness that one gets the impression of dark looking glass, panels the stairwell and accentuates other features in the hall. Bronze railings contribute to the richness of the hall. Again, black marble accentuates the bronze pillars and many other features throughout the hall. All staircases between the first floor and the ground floor are finished with Travertine marble and bronze metal.

Legislative Wing of the Capitol

On the west end of the Memorial Hall is situated the Legislative Assembly Hall. It is 20 feet wide. The walls are covered with dark East Indian rosewood panels offset with lighter curly maple. (Curly maple wood comes from the eastern United States.) Ten canopies of curly maple wood and rosewood cover alcoves found in this area of the Legislative Assembly Hall. The canopies have the Greek Key Meander classical design built into the wood.

The chamber of the House of Representatives feature walls covered with American chestnut wood. The rostrum and furniture are made of American walnut. (Chestnut wood comes from the Appalachia area of the United States, and the black walnut found in this room came from the Missouri Ozarks.) The ceiling could represent the moon and the evening rays radiating outward. Bronze railings and columns encircle the chamber where the 94 representatives sit among 116 desks found on the chamber's floor. The House balcony can accommodate 248 persons sitting behind the bronze railing.

The walls in the Senate chamber are covered with English oak. The rostrum and furniture are made of American oak. The ceiling could represent the rising rays of the sun at sunrise. Bronze railings and columns encircle the chamber where 47 state senators sit among 52 seats on the floor. The Senate balcony can accommodate seating for 184 persons behind the bronze railing. Several small offices are situated at the back of the Senate chamber. These offices, which include a conference room, are covered with American walnut.

There are 17 legislative meeting rooms of various sizes situated throughout the capitol. The Prairie Room is located in the former Supreme Court chambers on the second floor of the tower, and the Coteau and Sheyenne River rooms are located on the second floor of the judicial wing. The remaining rooms are located on the ground floor: the Fort Union, Fort Totten, Peace Garden, Roosevelt, and Medora rooms on the north side of the legislative wing; the Fort Lincoln, Lewis and Clark, Missouri River, and Brynhild Haugland rooms on the south side of the legislative wing; the Sakakawea, Red River, Roughrider, and Harvest rooms in the center of the building; and the Pioneer Room in the judicial wing.

Each committee room features pictures of its namesake North Dakota point of interest, as well as one or more digital signs displaying the committee hearing schedule. Master committee hearing schedules are also available, along with daily House and Senate calendar information, on 12 large digital signs distributed between the legislative wing's ground floor hallway and first floor Information Kiosk.

Administrative Offices and Tower

The architects of the original building added several features to the three main offices located on the east end of the first floor.

The walls of the Governor's reception office are covered with laurel wood, which comes from either East India or the East Indies. The Governor's private office walls are covered with Honduras mahogany. The Lieutenant Governor's private office walls and ceiling are covered with teak wood from Burma. The corridor leading into the Governor's office is covered with prima vera wood. (Prima vera wood may be a species of mahogany from South America.)

The walls of the Secretary of State's office are also covered with prima vera wood. The private entrance to the Secretary of State's office, sometimes referred to as the "Monkey Room," is covered with California walnut. This is very rare and has wavy, highly figured grains known as "wild figure."

The Attorney General's private office walls are covered by English brown oak. (English brown oak is known for its beauty and rich brown color, which comes from the aging process after the tree has been harvested.)

The doors to the elevators on the first floor are finished with sculptured bronze metal. Figurines on those doors represent different eras in North Dakota's pioneer history: American Indians, buffalo hunters, the frontier army, railroads and wagons, pioneer farm families, miners and construction workers, and various kinds of grain grown in the state. All offices located on the first floor have doors and casings made from American walnut.

On the east side of the Memorial Hall is the mezzanine to the second floor. Once the Supreme Court chambers and offices, the floor now houses the Legislative Council. The former Supreme Court chamber, now known as the Prairie Room, has walls covered with rosewood. The walls to the mezzanine and entryway to the Prairie Room are covered with American walnut trimmed with black Belgium marble. The walls in the former Chief Justice's office are covered by Honduras mahogany. This wood comes from Central America and is generally darker in color, finer in texture, and has more pleasing features than other mahoganies.

The upper floors of the capitol contain offices for elected officials, departments, agencies, and their staffs. The top floor of the capitol, now accessible for handicapped persons, is an observation tower allowing visitors to look to the south and west. A southern panoramic view of bluffs of the Missouri River and small buttes can be seen in the distance on clear days.

The legislative assembly approved $3,155,000 in 2005 for a capitol fire suppression system, which included sprinklers, ceiling replacement, and lighting modification. The system was installed on a floor-by-floor basis over a 10-month period. During the project, employees on the affected floors were moved either off-site or into another part of the capitol.

1981 Addition

Facing a need to provide additional office space for state government during the 1960s and 1970s, the legislative assembly formulated a number of plans to solve the problem. Through a combination of political maneuvering and referral elections, several projects to construct state office buildings on the capitol grounds went down to defeat. Finally during the late 1970s, a financing plan was developed based on funds loaned by the Board of University and School Lands, thus avoiding the need for a legislative appropriation.

With the funds finally available, a new building provided office space in the form of an east wing attached to the old capitol. The design, while not completely sympathetic with the architecture of the original structure, placed the bulk of the addition north of and behind the capitol tower. This judicial wing, which houses a number of state agencies, was completed and occupied in 1981. In what has now almost become a North Dakota tradition, outside of the metal and stone utilized in the east-side entry and atrium, very little money was spent on decorative features.

Judicial Wing's Physical Features

The atrium located on the east side of the judicial wing measures 35 feet wide and 64 feet in length, with the ceiling reaching 62 feet. The walls of the foyer are covered with white Indiana limestone. The fig trees located in the foyer were imported from Israel and planted when the building was finished. Mezzanines accentuate each of the upper three floors. Aluminum, terazzo, vinyl, and natural plants add to the beauty of the east entrance. The railings are stainless steel accentuated with bronze.

The Supreme Court chambers, located on the first floor, are covered with Travertine marble behind the justices' chairs with dyed black wool on the remaining walls. The wool is a North Dakota product. The justices' offices are finished with oak woodwork and vinyl. The foyer in front of the Supreme Court reaches to the ceiling. It is also finished with oak and glass. An assortment of plants add a touch of freshness. Terazzo floor tiles and segmented glass panels add to the geometric design of the entrance to the court.

State Office Building

In 1959, the legislative assembly purchased a building on the corner of Highway 83 and Boulevard that had been constructed originally with a local mill levy for Bismarck Junior College (1959 S.L., ch. 369). Currently, the State Office Building houses the State Water Commission, and for approximately six months of each year, staff from the State Tax Department. During the 1991-1993 biennium, the building was totally remodeled and re-faced with an exterior to blend with other capitol complex buildings. The State Office Building contains 28,838 square feet and is the smallest facility housing state agencies on the capitol grounds.

Department of Transportation Building

Prior to 1968 when the State Highway Department first occupied its present home, the agency had been located in various buildings, such as both the original and current capitol buildings, the old Bismarck Junior College building, and rented quarters. The structure became the Department of Transportation Building after the 1989 Legislative Assembly created that agency to assume the functions of the Highway Department, its commissioner, and its chief engineer, as well as those of the Motor Vehicle Department and its registrar. In addition to these, today it houses the Highway Patrol's permit section. The building has 125,000 square feet on five floors and was built with a limestone exterior, which harmonized visually with other capitol grounds structures.

Phase 2 of a three-phase project to remove the asbestos within the central office of the Department of Transportation, formerly known as the "Highway Building" was completed in 2012. Phase 1 (completed in 2010) consisted of abating the fourth and the fifth floor mechanical room, where the original air handlers from 1967 were removed and updated with more efficient and quieter devices. Phase 2 consisted of the abatement and reconstruction of the basement and first floor. In doing so, the department relocated the Motor Vehicle Division to the Kirkwood Mall while the reconstruction took place. Once completed, the first floor was reconfigured to handle all public services, including the Driver's License (formerly on second floor and accessed using the west doors) and Motor Vehicle Divisions, Mapping Services, Administrative Hearings, and the Highway Patrol Permit and Routing section. In addition, the east parking lot belonging to the department was expanded with an additional 66 parking spots to accommodate the influx of citizens using the east entrance. A customer flow management and wait time management system was added to eliminate standing in line and to handle multiple requests, such as driver permitting and exams. The last phase of the abatement project involved abating the final two floors (second and third) within the central office building. The NDDOT completed the project in November 2014.

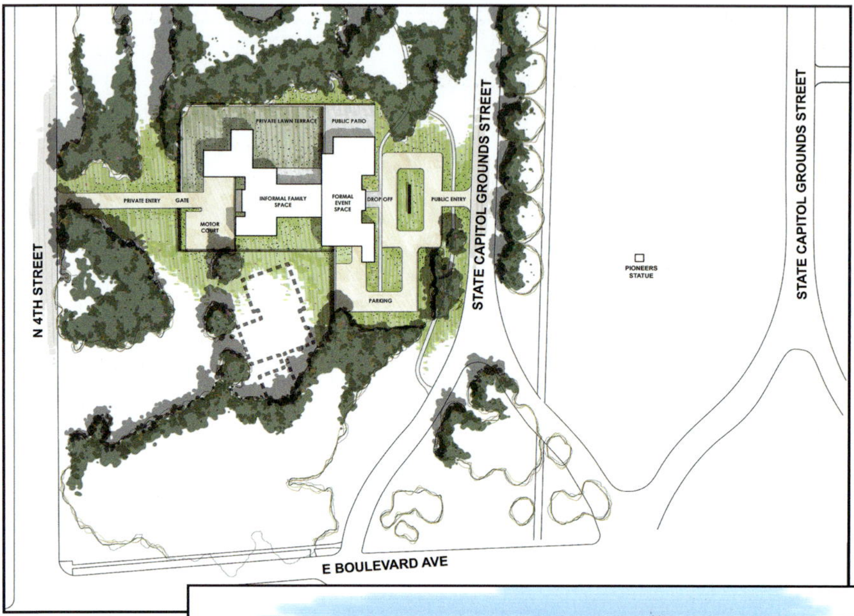

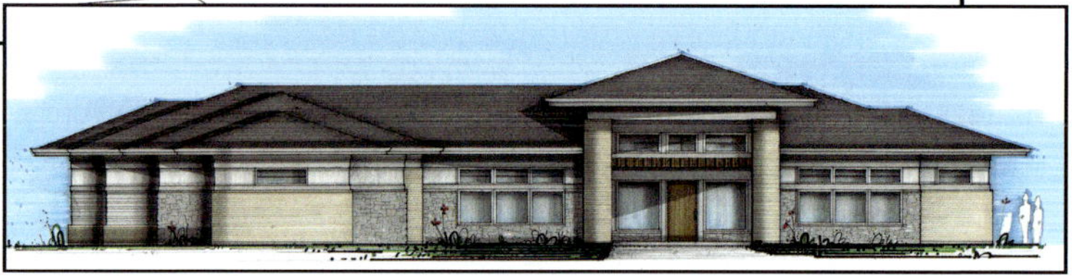

Architectural renderings of new Governor's Residence.

Governor's Residence

Located on the southwest corner of the capitol grounds, the second Governor's Residence was completed in 1960 and replaced an aging Fourth Street mansion of 1884 vintage. A new Governor's Residence, authorized in 2015 by Senate Bill 2304 for $4 million with an additional $1 million in private funding, contains 17,700 square feet. Construction began in 2016. Occupying a site on the southwest corner of the capitol grounds, just north of the 56-year-old former home, the new home will dwarf the current 10,000-square-foot residence built for $250,000 in 1960. Lawmakers said the older residence, which will be demolished, had problems ranging from security to asbestos to a lack of handicapped accessibility and would have cost up to $3 million to repair and upgrade. Occupancy is expected in late 2017.

Liberty Memorial Building

In 1919, the legislative assembly authorized construction of the Liberty Memorial Building to honor the 30,000 North Dakotans who served in the military during World War I. As completed in 1924, it housed the State Historical Society, Adjutant General, Library Commission, and Supreme Court. A proposal to erect a similar building opposite the Liberty Memorial Building on the west side of the capitol mall, to house the Supreme Court, was never funded. Present-day occupants include the State Library and the Tax Department. It is the oldest building on the capitol grounds and was completely renovated in 1982.

The State Library [NDCC 54-24] was established in 1890 and was placed within the Department of Public Instruction in 1989 for administration purposes. The library is administered by the state librarian, who is appointed by the superintendent. The State Library's mission is to provide access to information, which it does through direct service to North Dakota libraries, state agencies, and underserved or unserved citizens. It maintains a collection of more than 155,000 titles, most of which are available for loan; offers technical assistance to public, academic, school, and special libraries; creates continuing educational opportunities for librarians and public library board members; provides library service for persons who are unable to read or use standard printed materials; explores and recommends use of technology to increase library effectiveness; collects both paper and electronic state documents and maintains the State Document Depository Program; provides consultative services in the development and coordination of North Dakota libraries; coordinates the purchase of online resources, including magazine and newspaper databases, that are available statewide; administers state aid to public libraries; and administers the Federal Library Services and Technology Act and state-funded grants. The library's catalog is part of the Online Dakota Information Network (ODIN), an online catalog with participation of more than 70 other libraries in the state.

Capitol Grounds Arboretum Trail

This trail, which winds around various parts of the capitol grounds, was completed in 1985 and allows pedestrians to view and identify about 75 species of trees and shrubs found in North Dakota. It also guides people through the Centennial Grove. Also visible from the trail are many of the statues and memorials located on the capitol grounds.

Capitol Grounds Prairie Trail

Similar to the Arboretum Trail, this trail runs north of the capitol's judicial wing and leads pedestrians into an area filled with grasses and wild flowers typical of North Dakota's native prairie. It was placed on the Natural Areas Registry in 1987.

Centennial Grove

The Centennial Grove is located west of the capitol mall along Fourth Street and north of the Governor's residence. During his North Dakota Centennial visit in 1989, President George Bush dedicated the Centennial Grove. This project was sponsored by the North Dakota Forest Service, the North Dakota Centennial Commission, and the Centennial Decade Trees Committee.

North Dakota Heritage Center

The North Dakota Heritage Center, which began as a 1976 U.S. Bicentennial project for the state, opened its doors in 1981. The original building was designed to be expanded in a 20-year plan. Under the recommendation of Governors Guy, Link, Olson, Sinner, and Schafer, expansion planning began in 2002 with Governor Hoeven's State Historical Society of North Dakota Commission. The Commission was chaired by Lt. Governor Dalrymple. Since 2001, as a result of the Commission Report, $21 million was invested across the state in heritage tourism infrastructure; the last remaining piece was the expansion of the North Dakota Heritage Center. Phase I, the expansion of the State Archives, was completed in 2007. This 25-year plan added 30,000 square feet of collections storage at a cost of $5.7 million, doubling archives collections space.

The second phase of expansion doubled the existing exhibit, visitor services, public and educational programming, collections storage, labs, and office space by adding 97,000 square feet. The 2005 and 2007 Legislative Assemblies allocated planning dollars, and the 2009 Assembly authorized $40 million toward this $52 million project. The remaining $12 million was raised by the State Historical Society of North Dakota Foundation from private sources, corporations, foundations, and other groups.

Collections

The State Historical Society has several different collection responsibilities. Because of trained staff, an environmentally controlled facility, and extensive security, the Heritage Center is the federal repository for the state in all collection areas. The State Archives, by law, is the official repository of state and local government records of enduring value.

The State Archives manages a collection of more than 115,000 books and periodicals; 10,000 maps; 2.5 million photographs; 2,659 manuscript collections; 4,244 archival records series; 1,400 titles of newspapers; 3,000 oral histories; and 132 moving image collections.

Archaeology and historic preservation collections include millions of artifacts representing more than 12,000 years of human activity recovered from across the state. There are also thousands of resource files critical to oil, coal, wind, road, and bridge contractors and developers across the state. Also considered collections, a statewide network of 57 state historic sites is administered from the Heritage Center. Ten of these sites have interpretive centers or museums.

Artifact collections are three-dimensional objects, including items such as natural history specimens, textiles, vehicles, agricultural equipment, art, toys, weapons, and furniture. A collection of more than 60,000 objects range in age from a 10,000-year-old mastodon skeleton to disposable items used yesterday and in scale from tiny glass beads to a locomotive.

Paleontology collections are housed at the Heritage Center through an agreement with the Department of Mineral Resources, North Dakota Geological Survey. The center also houses the Johnsrud Paleontology Laboratory. Representing more than 500 million years of fossil history and geology of North Dakota, specimens in the paleontology lab include a gem, mineral, and rock collection and the state fossil collection containing millions of specimens ranging in scale from microscopic shells of marine animals to huge dinosaur bones.

Public Level

The building areas reference nature's elements of earth, air, fire, and water and correspond to the geography of the state from east to west: Pembina River Plaza, Red, Sheyenne, and Mouse River Halls, James River Café, Missouri River Special Events Center, and Badlands Plaza. Several improvements were made to the Russell Reid Auditorium, and the Museum Store doubled in size. The café features North Dakota-grown and ethnic specialties. All these areas focus on enhancing the visitor's North Dakota experience.

Hub of History

A tourist information center, the Hub of History, directs visitors to all corners of the state to experience the people, landscape, and history where it happened. The expanded Heritage Center is a destination, part of a string of pearls of heritage tourism opportunities across the northern border. The opportunities include North Dakota events, places to visit, and Main Street tourism venues. The hub is a statewide network of partnerships offering the best of the state to those who live near and those visiting from afar.

Exhibit Galleries

The Heritage Center exhibition space increased from 28,000 square feet to more than 47,000 square feet. New galleries, each with a learning lab, include:

- The Adaptation Gallery: Geological Time presents 500 million years of the geologic history of life in North Dakota from the earliest life forms up to the last glaciation, about 10,000 years ago. These exhibits, which include the dinosaurs and many more fossils, set the stage for the fossil fuel stories of North Dakota's oil and coal industries and explain landscape and soil development that will shape the state's agricultural future.

- The Innovation Gallery: Early Peoples covers more than 12,000 years of the earliest human history in what is now North Dakota to the present day. When the Giza pyramids in Egypt or pre-Columbian civilizations of South America flourished, so did American Indian civilizations in North Dakota. The gallery features archaeological artifacts from prehistoric cultures, the international story of the fur trade, oral histories, and stunning collections representing prehistoric, historic, and contemporary tribal life.

- The Inspiration Gallery: Yesterday & Today features the last 150 years of the state's history, with room for the future. It investigates agriculture, industry and energy, newcomers and settlement, conflicts, communities, and cultural expressions through captivating stories that illustrate North Dakota's unique character and its creative thinkers.

- The Governor's Gallery hosts temporary and traveling exhibits, creating regional and world-class blockbuster events. This gallery provides an opportunity to bring the world to North Dakota and share the state with other museums across the country and world.

- The Treehouse provides young children with their very own museum space. This hands-on, fun experience is located on the mezzanine above the Missouri River Event Center.

The Grand Opening of the North Dakota Heritage Center expansion was a centerpiece of the statewide celebration of North Dakota's 125th anniversary of statehood on November 2, 2014.

For more information about the North Dakota Heritage Center expansion project, visit the State Historical Society of North Dakota's website at www.history.nd.gov or the State Historical Society of North Dakota Foundation's website at www.statehistoricalfoundation.com.

✔ More information about the State Historical Society is in the *2015-2017 North Dakota Blue Book.*

References:

North Dakota's State Capitol, by Simons, Kenneth W., 1934

North Dakota State Capitol, Self Guided Walking Tour, State Historical Society of North Dakota, 1991

North Dakota State Capitol, information brochure by Facilities Management, Office of Management and Budget

North Dakota State Capitol, Bidders Specifications Manual, June 10, 1932

Remele, Larry, editor, *The North Dakota State Capitol: Architecture and History,* (Bismarck: State Historical Society of North Dakota, 1989)

Statues, Monuments, and Markers on the Capitol Grounds

Identified As	Title or Description	Artist	Year Dedicated	Sponsor or Donor
Statue	Sakakawea	Leonard Crunelle	1910	ND Federation of Women's Clubs
Marker	Tree planted in memory of President Franklin D. Roosevelt		1945	American War Mothers
Statue	Pioneer Family	Avard Fairbanks	1946	H.F. McLean
Boxcar	French Gratitude Boxcar		1949	French Government
Statue	John Burke	Avard Fairbanks	1963	National Statuary Hall Commission & Legislative Assembly
Statue	American Buffalo	Bennett Brien	1986	Dayton-Hudson, Inc.
Marker	Capitol Grounds Prairie Trail		1987	ND Parks & Recreation Dept.
Marker	Centennial Grove		1989	ND Forest Service, ND Centennial Commission & Centennial Decade Trees Committee
Marker	Flower Bed (Heritage Center Square)		1989	Bismarck/Mandan Junior Service League
Statue	Pioneers of the Future (children holding hands)	Jeff Barber	1989	ND Federation of Women's Clubs
Monument	All Veterans Centennial Memorial	Warren Tvenge (architect)	1989	ND All Veterans Memorial Centenntial Memorial Assn.
Monument	U.S.S. North Dakota Battleship Bowplate	U.S. Navy	1989	State Historical Society of ND
Marker	Petrified Meta-sequoia Tree Stumps and Log		1988, 1991	Central Dakota Gem & Mineral Society
Monument	ND Peace Officers Memorial	Warren Tvenge (architect)	1994	ND Peace Officers Association
Statue	"Cortes" - Arabian Horse	Bennett Brien	1994	ND Heritage Foundation & eight power companies
Marker	Capitol overlook - three plaques showing Capitol complex design, describing native prairie remnant on the Capitol grounds and providing brief history of the Capitol building	Metal Arts Company Mandan foundry	2005	N.D. Dept. of Transportation
Monument	Purple Heart Memorial	DeIasi Enterprises, Jersey City, NJ	2005	Military Order of the Purple Heart and Arnold Maier
Monument	Bronze likeness of the Great Seal in Memorial Hall	Metal Arts Company Mandan foundry	2006	Capitol Grounds Planning Commission

Theodore Roosevelt Rough Rider Award
North Dakota Hall of Fame

On August 29, 1961, Governor William L. Guy announced the establishment of an honorary commission of colonel in the North Dakota Theodore Roosevelt Rough Riders. The first commission was given in a surprise presentation to Lawrence Welk at a Minot Diamond Jubilee Celebration the day before the announcement.

In 1963, the 38th Legislative Assembly authorized the Theodore Roosevelt Rough Rider Award as the highest recognition the state of North Dakota can bestow upon present or former North Dakotans. The award was to go to those "who have been influenced by this state in achieving national recognition in their fields of endeavor thereby reflecting credit upon this state and its citizens."

The initial meeting of the committee was held on August 29, 1963, close to the second anniversary date of the first award. At this first meeting, the committee affirmed three previous awards made to Lawrence Welk, Dorothy Stickney, and Ivan Dmitri. Three new members, Roger Maris, Peggy Lee, and Eric Sevareid, were also selected.

The award has continued to the present day. Recipients of the award are chosen by the Governor, with the concurrence of the Secretary of State and the Director of the State Historical Society of North Dakota.

Forty-three North Dakotans have received the award. Their portraits are on display on the ground floor of the North Dakota State Capitol Building.

Theodore Roosevelt

Theodore Roosevelt was the 26th president of the United States. As a young man, Roosevelt spent several years in the North Dakota Badlands. Of that time, Roosevelt said, "If it had not been for what I learned during the years I spent in North Dakota, I never in the world would have been President of the United States."

Roosevelt vigorously championed the conservation of America's scenic, natural, and historical resources. In recognition of his valuable contributions toward conservation, Theodore Roosevelt National Park was established in 1947, in the North Dakota Badlands that Roosevelt loved.

Portrait artist: Vern Skaug

(Note: Recipients are listed in order of the year the award was presented.)

USV

Lawrence Welk
(1903-1992)

Award Presented:
August 28, 1961, Minot
Governor William Guy

Portrait Artist: Emmett Morgan

North Dakota's most famous "favorite son," Lawrence Welk became one of the greatest entertainers in the world through his weekly television show featuring his distinctive "champagne music."

Welk was one of eight children born on a farm near Strasburg, North Dakota. Welk displayed a musical interest at an early age. After leaving school in his elementary years because of a prolonged illness, he spent more time practicing his talent.

Welk played for local farm dances to pay for a new professional accordion he had purchased. He later added a saxophone player, a drummer, and a piano player, and then Welk had his first band. The band gained recognition for its program on WNAX, Yankton, South Dakota, in 1935. In the years to follow, the band went on to play at hotels and resorts, eventually playing in the top ballrooms in the nation. From 1950-1955, the Lawrence Welk Orchestra appeared on KTLA-TV in Los Angeles, California, and so began the many years of televised performances of Welk and the Champagne Music Makers.

Welk authored several books including *Wunnerful, Wunnerful*; *Ah One, Ah Two*; and *My America, Your America*.

Dorothy Stickney
(1896-1998)

Award Presented:
November 2, 1961, Bismarck
Governor William Guy

Portrait Artist:
Emmett Morgan

A Broadway actress who received stage immortality in the long-running "*Life With Father*," co-starring with her husband, Howard Lindsay, Dorothy Hayes Stickney was one of the great leading ladies of the legitimate theater.

Stickney was born in Dickinson, North Dakota, June 21, 1896. She attended school in St. Paul and Minneapolis, Minnesota, and Auburndale, Massachusetts. Stickney played in stock companies and vaudeville for several years. Her New York performances include *The Way of the World*, *On Borrowed Time*, and *Life with Father*. Stickney received the Barter Award for best performance of the year for her role as Mother in *Life with Father*. The award was given in 1940 by Eleanor Roosevelt.

Stickney is also the author of a number of poems, including *You're Not the Type* and *My Dressing Room*.

Ivan Dmitri
(1900-1968)

Award Presented:
April 13, 1962, Dickinson
Governor William Guy

Portrait Artist: Emmett Morgan

Gaining international fame for his sensitive portrayals in color photography, etchings, and water colors, Ivan Dmitri's work has been exhibited in nearly every major art museum in the western world.

Born Levon West, he moved throughout North Dakota during his youth, as his father was a Congregational preacher. He graduated valedictorian of his high school class at Harvey, North Dakota, taught school for a year, and enlisted in the United States Navy. After WWI, he received a scholarship to the University of Minnesota where, despite his interest in art, he studied business administration at his father's insistence.

His first break as an artist came with the publication of his etching of *The Spirit of St. Louis* upon Charles Lindbergh's arrival in Paris. The etchings of Levon West soon were in great demand.

His interest in photography brought recognition in the new medium and in order to separate his two artistic fields and protect those that had purchased his etchings, West took the name of Ivan Dmitri for his photographic work.

In 1959, Dmitri, in an effort to gain acceptance of photography as an art medium, founded Photography in the Fine Arts.

Roger Maris
(1934-1985)

Selected:
September 4, 1963

Award Presented:
January 4, 1964, Fargo
Governor William Guy

Portrait Artist:
Emmett Morgan

Baseball's Single-Season Home Run King, Roger Maris, hit 61 home runs during the 1961 season, while he was a member of the New York Yankees. This record stood for 37 years until Mark McGwire hit 70 home runs in 1998. Barry Bonds went on to break McGwire's record with 73 home runs in 2001. Maris also played for the Cleveland Indians, Kansas City Athletics, and St. Louis Cardinals.

Raised in Fargo, North Dakota, Maris was a football and basketball star at Shanley High School. After trying out with the Chicago Cubs, he played in the American League until the end of his career when he played for the St. Louis Cardinals. Maris began playing for the Cleveland Indians in 1959 and hit 14 home runs. In 1958 and 1959, he hit 28 and 16 homers respectively, while playing for Kansas City. Maris was traded to the Yankees in 1960, and his legend began. He was voted most valuable player in the American League that year, after hitting 39 home runs with 112 RBIs. The year 1961 saw Maris hit 61 home runs, one more than Babe Ruth hit in a season, and again Maris earned the most valuable player award.

Peggy Lee
(1920-2002)

Selected:
September 4, 1963

Award Presented:
May 23, 1975, Fargo
Governor Art Link and former Governor William Guy

Portrait Artist:
Emmett Morgan

A motion picture actress and singer, a distinctive "rhythm and blues" style, and beautiful voice quickly established Peggy Lee as one of the most brilliant performers in the field of popular music.

Born Norma Delores Egstrom at Jamestown, North Dakota, on May 26, 1920, Peggy Lee was one of eight children. She received much encouragement and recognition for her singing in school and church choirs. In 1938, after graduating from high school, she went to Hollywood, California, but later returned to Fargo and worked for WDAY radio. She moved to Minneapolis, where she met and began touring with the Will Osborne Band and later with Benny Goodman.

Lee wrote music and lyrics, both for herself and the movie industry. She published a book of verse entitled *Softly With Feeling*.

Lee starred in several films with Bing Crosby and Danny Thomas and was nominated for an Academy Award.

Eric Sevareid
(1912-1992)

Selected:
September 4, 1963

Awarded:
April 17, 1964, Minot
Governor William Guy

Portrait Artist:
Emmett Morgan

Nationally known television commentator, news analyst, and author, Eric Sevareid is particularly noted for his perceptive essays on public events and personalities.

Sevareid grew up in Velva, North Dakota, and knew from his youth that he wanted to be a journalist, which accounted for his fascination with the local newspaper. At the age of 18, Sevareid began working as a copy boy. He later became a reporter for *The Minneapolis Journal* while attending the University of Minnesota.

Upon receiving his B.A. degree, Sevareid traveled to London and Paris to continue his studies. He joined the Paris edition of the *New York Herald* and became a radio correspondent for CBS in 1939, covering the war in Europe. In later years, Sevareid was known for his coverage of presidential elections and meetings of the United Nations Assembly in Paris. Sevareid retired as a CBS television news commentator on November 30, 1977.

Sevareid was the author of *Not So Wild a Dream*.

General Harold K. Johnson
(1912-1983)

Award Presented:
April 23, 1965, Fargo
Governor William Guy

Portrait Artist:
Emmett Morgan

A professional soldier who became Chief of Staff of the United States Army in 1965, General Harold Johnson was the youngest man to hold the position since General Douglas MacArthur.

Johnson was born in Bowesmont, North Dakota, in 1912. He graduated from Grafton High School in 1929 and West Point Military Academy in 1933.

Captain Johnson was operations officer for the 57th Infantry in Manila, prior to the Pearl Harbor attack by the Japanese. The 57th was ordered to Bataan where the Japanese were engaged. Johnson was promoted to major and then lieutenant colonel and given command of the battalion. After a surrender to the superior Japanese force, Johnson and the 57th were forced on the Bataan Death March, which claimed 8,150 prisoners.

Johnson saw combat again in Korea, emerging from the conflict as a Full Colonel. In 1956, he was made a Brigadier General. In 1957, Johnson was named Chief of Staff of the U.S. Seventh Army in Germany. General Johnson was chosen Chief of Staff to NATO's Central Army Group in West Germany in 1959. In 1964, General Johnson was named Chief of Staff of the U.S. Army and was awarded his fourth star.

Dr. Anne H. Carlsen
(1915-2002)

Selected:
May 13, 1966

Award Presented:
September 9, 1966, Fargo
Governor William Guy

Portrait Artist: Vern Skaug

Former long-time superintendent of the Crippled Children's School at Jamestown, North Dakota, Dr. Anne Carlsen was born without hands or feet. Nevertheless, her great courage and keen intellect enabled her to earn a Doctor of Philosophy degree and international honors.

Carlsen, born in Gratsburg, Wisconsin, was one of six children. As a child, she received much assistance from her sister, four brothers, and childhood playmates, making it possible for her to participate in their games. She attended and completed elementary school in Gratsburg and high school in St. Paul, Minnesota. She graduated from the University of Minnesota, cum laude in 1936, and set about to realize her dream of self-support, hopefully by teaching.

After some teaching experience, Carlsen accepted a teaching position at the Good Samaritan School in Fargo, North Dakota, a Lutheran school for crippled children. She continued her education, earning a M.A. from Northern University of Colorado in 1946 and a Ph.D. from the University of Minnesota in 1949. The following year she was named superintendent of the Crippled Children's School in Jamestown, which is now named the Anne Carlsen School. Under her guidance, the school, established in 1940, gained national recognition.

Edward K. Thompson
(1907-1996)

Selected:
January 2, 1968

Award Presented:
April 19, 1968, Bismarck
Governor William Guy

Portrait Artist:
Emmett Morgan

A former editor of *Life* magazine, Edward Thompson received his early journalism experience with the *Foster County Independent* in the city of Carrington and later the *Fargo Forum*.

Raised in St. Thomas, North Dakota, Thompson began his journalism career as editor of the *Foster County Independent* in 1927. Two months later, he was the night city editor of the *Fargo Forum*. In another two months, he was a reporter for the *Milwaukee Journal* in Wisconsin. Thompson later became picture editor and assistant news editor at Milwaukee, and in 1937, he joined *Life* magazine.

In 1942, Thompson joined the Army, where he edited a magazine for Air Force intelligence. By 1944, he was in charge of intelligence concerning the German air force.

In 1945, Thompson returned to *Life* magazine and became assistant managing editor. In 1949, he was named managing editor. After his retirement from *Life* in 1968, Thompson served as special assistant to the Secretary of State for Far Eastern Affairs.

Dr. Robert Henry Bahmer
(1904-1990)

Award Presented:
July 28, 1970, Minot
Governor William Guy

Portrait Artist: Vern Skaug

Dr. Robert Bahmer was the fourth Archivist of the United States (1966-1969) in the nation's history. He headed the National Archives and Records Service and directed the offices of the Hoover, Roosevelt, Truman, and Eisenhower Presidential Libraries.

Bahmer was born near Gardena, North Dakota, on September 27, 1904. He attended high school at Omemee and spent a year at the University of North Dakota. He later transferred to Valley City State Teachers College where he received a B.A. degree in 1928.

From 1925 to 1927, Dr. Bahmer was principal at Bentley school in Hettinger County. In 1938, he received his M.A. degree from the University of Colorado and a Ph.D. from the University of Minnesota in 1941.

Bahmer joined the National Archives staff in 1936 and served as a specialist in records management in several governmental agencies, including the Navy Department and the War Department. In 1948, he was appointed Assistant Archivist of the United States, serving until 1966, when he was appointed Archivist of the United States.

Louis L'Amour
(1908-1988)

Selected:
February 15, 1972

Award Presented:
May 26, 1972, Jamestown
Governor William Guy

Portrait Artist: Vern Skaug

An award winning western author and screen writer, Louis L'Amour published more than 400 short stories and more than 100 novels. He wrote 65 TV scripts and sold more than 30 stories to the motion picture industry, including *Hondo*, starring John Wayne.

L'Amour was born in Jamestown, North Dakota, March 22, 1908. At 15, he joined a circus and later worked in mining and lumber camps. He was a prize fighter and traveled throughout the world. During World War II, he was an officer in the Army Tank Corps. He was a self-educated man, whose hobbies included archaeology and the study of wildlife.

L'Amour's books have been translated into 27 languages. He produced the movie *Catlow*, in addition to writing for the film screen. In addition to his prose, he wrote a volume of poetry entitled *Smoke From the Altar*.

Bertin C. Gamble
(1898-1986)

Selected:
September 13, 1972

Award Presented:
October 20, 1972, Grand Forks
Governor William Guy

Portrait Artist: Vern Skaug

With partner Phil Skogmo, Bertin Gamble developed nearly 4,200 merchandising outlets in 38 states and Canada, since the first store was established in 1925, making Gamble-Skogmo one of the largest retailers in the nation.

Born in Chicago, Illinois, in 1898, Gamble claims North Dakota as home, since he was raised and attended school here. He lived with his family in Hunter, North Dakota, and later in nearby Arthur. It was there, at the age of seven, that he met Phil Skogmo, who would be his future partner.

After finishing high school, Gamble went to Minneapolis, Minnesota, where he worked and attended business school. He and Skogmo purchased an auto dealership in Fergus Falls, Minnesota, and prospered.

In 1925, the first Gamble-Skogmo store opened in St. Cloud, Minnesota. The second and third stores opened in Fargo and Grand Forks, North Dakota, respectively. Their business survived many financial crises, including the depression of the 1930s. Gamble was company president at Gamble-Skogmo from 1925-1945 and was board chairman until his retirement in 1977. The company was acquired in 1980 by the California-based Wickes Corporation.

Casper Oimoen
(1906-1995)

Selected:
January 24, 1973

Award Presented:
February 12, 1973, Minot
Governor Art Link

Portrait Artist: Vern Skaug

Captain of the Olympic ski team in 1936, Casper Oimoen won more than 400 medals and trophies during his skiing career. He was inducted into the U.S. Skiing Hall of Fame in 1963.

Born May 6, 1906, in Norway, Casper Oimoen came to Minot, North Dakota, in 1923. He had learned to ski while a boy in Norway and began to compete in ski jumping after coming to North Dakota. He did not compete in the 1928 Olympics because he was not an American citizen, but continued to compete regionally and entered the Olympics as captain of the U.S. team in 1936.

His winning record was unmatched. He won the Northwestern Ski Jumping Championship nine times in nine entries, the Montana State Jumping Championship six times in six entries, the Central United States Championship 10 times, six of them in consecutive years (1925-1931), and the United States National Ski Jumping Championship three times. In 1930, he won the Eastern, Central, and National Championships, plus eight other firsts, a feat which has never been equaled.

Casper Oimoen was also a brick layer, a trade he learned from his uncle when he lived in Minot. During the 1930s, he worked on the construction crew that built the North Dakota State Capitol.

Harold Schafer
(1912-2001)

Selected:
November 18, 1974

Award Presented:
July 4, 1975, Medora
Governor Art Link

Portrait Artist: Vern Skaug

Creator and Chairman of the Board of Gold Seal Company, Harold Schafer was the founder of North Dakota's largest home-owned business. Schafer was the youngest-ever recipient of the Horatio Alger Award, a national award that annually recognizes individuals who have faced and overcome significant personal adversity through hard work, integrity, determination, and have a strong dedication to helping others. He was also responsible for restoration and development of Medora, one of North Dakota's leading tourist attractions.

Schafer was born in Stanton and attended public schools at Stanton, Hazen, Killdeer, Glen Ullin, and Jamestown and graduated from Bismarck High School in 1929. He attended North Dakota State University in Fargo.

Schafer traveled western North Dakota while working for several Bismarck firms before founding the Gold Seal Company on May 1, 1942. At that time, the company was regional, but the products of the Gold Seal Company, among them Glass Wax, Mr. Bubble, and Snowy Bleach, were known worldwide. The Gold Seal Company was also noted for its Medora restoration project and the Medora Musical, which entertains nearly 100,000 visitors each season.

Era Bell Thompson
(1905-1986)

Selected:
April 12, 1976

Award Presented:
August 14, 1976, Bismarck
Governor Art Link

Portrait Artist: Vern Skaug

International editor of *Ebony* magazine, Era Bell Thompson grew up in North Dakota. This noted journalist and author wrote several books, including *American Daughter*, which tells the story of her youth in North Dakota.

Thompson was born in Des Moines, Iowa, and in 1914, moved with her family to the Driscoll area where she attended school. Later she studied at the University of North Dakota, where she established five state women's track records and tied two national intercollegiate women's track records. She graduated from Morningside College in Sioux City, Iowa.

Thompson served as associate editor of *Ebony* for four years, co-managing editor from 1951-1964, and was international editor of Johnson Publishing Company.

Thompson also wrote *Africa, Land of My Father*, and *White on Black*.

Dr. Leon Orris Jacobson
(1911-1992)

Selected:
April 12, 1976

Award Presented:
October 1, 1976, Jamestown
Governor Art Link

Portrait Artist: Vern Skaug

Dr. Leon Jacobson held clinical, teaching, and research positions in the field of medical science with the University of Chicago and served as director of the Franklin McLean Memorial Research Institute. Much of his research dealt with modern cancer chemotherapy.

Jacobson was born in Sims, North Dakota, a small town in Morton County that no longer exists. At age 16, he began college in Fargo, North Dakota, but was forced to drop out for financial reasons. He then taught all eight grades in a two-room schoolhouse. In 1935, he received his bachelor of science degree at North Dakota State University and earned his medical degree from the University of Chicago in 1939.

He was a founder of the Argonne Cancer Research Hospital, now known as the Franklin McLean Memorial Research Institute.

Elizabeth Bodine
(1898-1986)

Selected:
May 2, 1979

Award Presented:
July 27, 1979, Bismarck
Governor Art Link

Portrait Artist: Vern Skaug

Named to the Rough Rider Award Hall of Fame during the International Year of the Child, Mrs. Frank Bodine served as the 1968 North Dakota Mother of the Year.

Education played an important role in Bodine's life. All 18 of the Bodine children received post-high school education. Her 10 sons received college degrees. Six of her daughters attended college, and the other two daughters received business training. For 26 years, including 10 summer sessions, one or more of her family was enrolled at Minot State College.

Bodine was active in church, civic, and community projects for many years. Assisting the Indian people in the Belcourt area, contributing clothing and food to her relatives in Poland during World War II, and sending boxes of clothing to Vietnam are but a few of the many projects to which she contributed.

Cliff Purpur
(1912-2001)

Selected:
September 15, 1980

Award Presented:
May 16, 1981, Grand Forks
Governor Allen Olson

Portrait Artist: Vern Skaug

Cliff "Fido" Purpur was the first North Dakota native to become a National Hockey League player. He achieved this at a time when there were only six NHL teams and an American player playing on any of these teams was an oddity. After his active hockey days were over, Purpur returned to his native state to live and work in Grand Forks. He gained further success as a coach at Grand Forks Central High School and the University of North Dakota.

Purpur was enshrined in the Sports Hall of Fame and also the United States Hockey Hall of Fame. As the first native North Dakotan to play in the National Hockey League, he was as much responsible as anyone for North Dakota's reputation as one of the nation's hockey hotbeds.

Serving as an example to a countless number of young men, Purpur showed the true spirit of North Dakota pioneers. His personal honesty and integrity, plus his determination, enabled him to achieve what few men even dare to dream.

Phyllis Frelich
(1944-2014)

Selected:
January 23, 1981

Award Presented:
April 27, 1981, Bismarck
Governor Allen Olson

Portrait Artist: Vern Skaug

Tony Award winner for the most outstanding performance by an actress for her role in the play *Children of a Lesser God*, Phyllis Frelich is an exceptional woman.

Deaf all her life, Frelich dreamed of becoming an actress. After graduating from the School for the Deaf in her hometown of Devils Lake, North Dakota, she went to Gallaudet College in Washington, D.C., a liberal arts college for the deaf. Few theater courses were offered there, but Frelich devoured the limited number available.

Frelich was one of the founding members of the National Theater of the Deaf (NTD). Through her involvement with the NTD, Frelich met the playwright Mark Medoff. Intrigued by the difficulties of a deaf actress in finding suitable roles, he wrote a play which portrayed the problems of deaf people in a hearing world on one level and the difficulty of all human communication on another level.

Although the play, *Children of a Lesser God*, was written for her and the similarities between the lead character and Frelich are numerous, it is not her life story, but rather illustrates the life of one deaf person in a hearing world.

General David C. Jones
(1921-2013)

Selected:
January 20, 1982

Award Presented:
May 21, 1982, Bismarck
Governor Allen Olson

Portrait Artist: Vern Skaug

Appointed Chairman of the Joint Chiefs of Staff in 1978, General David C. Jones was re-appointed to a second two-year term in 1980. In this capacity, he served as the senior military advisor to the President, the National Security Council, and the Secretary of Defense. He was also responsible for executing the decisions of the National Command Authorities regarding world-wide readiness and employment of combat forces of the United States Army, Navy, Air Force, and Marine Corps. Prior to his appointment, General Jones served four years as Chief of Staff to the United States Air Force.

Jones served as inspector, operator, planner, and Commander in Chief of the United States Air Forces in Europe. He also served as Commander of the Fourth Allied Tactical Air Force and led the way toward establishing the integrated air headquarters in North Atlantic Treaty Organization's Central Region, Allied Air Forces, Central Europe.

Raised in Minot, North Dakota, and a graduate of Minot High School, Jones attended the University of North Dakota and Minot State College until the outbreak of World War II. He entered the Army Air Corps and began aviation training in 1942, receiving his commission and pilot wings in February 1943. He is also a graduate of the National War College in Washington, D.C.

Ronald N. Davies
(1904-1996)

Selected:
May 1987

Award Presented:
June 11, 1987, Bismarck
Governor George Sinner

Portrait Artist: Vern Skaug

Ronald Davies is the federal jurist who ordered the integration of Little Rock, Arkansas, Central High School in September 1957. *The New York Times* called Judge Davies' ruling the "landmark decision on racial integration in our nation."

Davies attended high school in Grand Forks and went on to graduate from the University of North Dakota in 1927. He earned his law degree at Georgetown University and then returned to Grand Forks to practice law. He was a municipal judge from 1931-1940. Davies served in the U.S. Army during World War II, rising from Lieutenant to Lieutenant Colonel before his discharge in 1946.

Davies resumed his practice in Grand Forks after the war, and in 1955, he was appointed U.S. District Judge in Fargo. In Davies' most famous case, while filling a temporary vacancy, he faced down Governor Orval Faubas and the Arkansas National Guard with the simple principle that "integration must begin forthwith."

Davies was named a Senior U.S. District Judge in 1971.

Phil Jackson
(1945-)

Selected:
June 1992

Award Presented:
July 30, 1992, Williston
Governor George Sinner

Portrait Artist:
Vern Skaug

Phil Jackson grew up in Williston, North Dakota, where he was a standout basketball player at Williston High School. While attending the University of North Dakota, he earned consecutive All-American honors for his star performances and was drafted by the New York Knicks in 1967. Jackson was instrumental in leading the Knicks to a National Basketball Association championship in 1973.

Jackson took his brilliant knowledge of the courts to a successful coaching career. He became the head coach of the Chicago Bulls in 1989 and led the Bulls to six national championships in nine years. After nine years as head coach of the Bulls, Jackson resigned and took a one-year sabbatical. In June 1999, he became head coach of the Los Angeles Lakers. He led the team to the 2000 NBA championship title in his first season as head coach and subsequent championships in 2001, 2002, 2009 and 2010. Jackson left the Lakers at the end of the 2004 season and returned as head coach in June 2005.

Self-possessed, focused and confident, Jackson will go down in NBA history not only for his dynamic leadership, but as the only person to both play and coach teams to titles for the NBA and Continental Basketball Association.

Larry Woiwode
(1941-)

Selected:
June 1992

Award Presented:
October 23, 1992, Bismarck
Governor George Sinner

Portrait Artist:
Vern Skaug

Larry Woiwode was born in 1941 in Carrington, near his hometown of Sykeston, North Dakota. In 1950, his family moved to Illinois. This award-winning novelist's writing career began in New York City and by 1966 he was publishing stories and poetry in *The New Yorker*. He has since published two dozen stories in that publication and has also appeared in the *Atlantic, Esquire, Harper's*, and *The Paris Review*.

Woiwode is the author of five novels, *What I'm Going To Do, I Think* (1969), *Beyond the Bedroom Wall* (1975), *Poppa John* (1981), *Born Brothers* (1988), and *Indian Affairs* (1992,) besides books of short stories, poetry, and non-fiction. He has been a Guggenheim Fellow, a John Dos Passos Prize winner, a recipient of the William Faulkner Foundation Award, and the Medal of Merit from the American Academy of Arts and Letters. He has been a finalist for both the Book Critics Circle and the National Book Awards and appears in four volumes of *Best American Short Stories.*

In his success, Woiwode has not forgotten his native state of North Dakota. Many of his books contain references to the state, and two novels are set in North Dakota. Woiwode returned to North Dakota in 1978. He continues his writing on a 160-acre farm near Mott, where he and his wife raised four children.

Angie Dickinson
(1931-)

Selected:
June 1992

Award Presented:
December 2, 1992, Bismarck
Governor George Sinner

Portrait Artist: Vern Skaug

Angie Dickinson was born Angeline Brown in the small farming community of Kulm, North Dakota. She was one of three daughters of Leo and Frederica Brown and grew up around the sights and sounds of her family's weekly newspaper offices in the 1930s. Her family owned and operated the *Kulm Messenger* and later, the *Edgeley Mail.*

Dickinson's family moved to California when she was 10 years old, but her time in North Dakota gave her the grounding she needed to take a shot at stardom. She took her prairie work ethic to the aircraft industry and worked in a parts plant to finance acting lessons. A talent scout spotted her in a beauty contest and so began the career of Dickinson. Her first big break came when Howard Hawks cast her opposite John Wayne in *Rio Bravo.*

Dickinson has appeared on the big screen with such Hollywood notables as Gregory Peck, Richard Burton, Marlon Brando, Roger Moore, Burt Reynolds, Peter Finch, and Ronald Reagan. She has appeared in more than 50 major movies and television productions, most known for her roles in *Police Woman* and *Dressed to Kill.* Among her many accolades, she has a star on Hollywood's Walk of Fame and her work in *Police Woman* earned her a Golden Globe for Best Actress in a Dramatic Series.

Rev. Richard C. Halverson
(1916-1995)

Selected:
December 1993

Award Presented:
March 26, 1994, Bismarck
Governor Ed Schafer

Portrait Artist:
Ann Linton Hodge

Reverend Halverson was born in Pingree, North Dakota. He was the United States Senate Chaplain from February 2, 1981, until his retirement on December 31, 1994.

Before becoming Senate Chaplain, Halverson was a minister at the Fourth Presbyterian Church in Bethesda, Maryland, for 23 years. Since 1956, he was active in the International Prayer Breakfast movement. He was chairman of the Board of World Vision-U.S., from 1966 to 1983. He also wrote several inspirational books.

Halverson was recognized for moving his job beyond that of giving the Senate daily opening prayer to include ministering to those on Capitol Hill. Former President George H. W. Bush wrote that Halverson is "one of God's very special messengers. He is one of the most thoughtful individuals I have ever met...He cared deeply, and his caring was so evident to me and to the members of Congress whose paths crossed his."

Brynhild Haugland
(1905-1998)

Selected:
October 1994

Award Presented:
March 20, 1995, Bismarck
Governor Ed Schafer

Portrait Artist:
Ann Linton Hodge

At her retirement in 1990, Brynhild Haugland was the longest serving incumbent state legislator in the nation, with 52 years in the North Dakota House of Representatives. Former First Lady Eleanor Roosevelt in 1954 wrote in the book *Ladies of Courage*, "Go down the list of laws passed by the North Dakota Legislature in the last 15 years to help meet the farmer's problems and improve his living conditions, and you will find that Brynhild Haugland had a hand in every one of them." Haugland was also instrumental in developing legislation in the 1940s that created a medical care program that other states have modeled. She cast an estimated 22,000 votes during her state service.

Haugland was born in Ward County near Minot, North Dakota, the daughter of Norwegian immigrant parents. She taught in Ward County schools from 1923-1925, before leaving to help run her parents' farm. In 1928, she received a teaching certificate from Minot State Normal School, now Minot State University. In 1988, she was recognized as one of two top award winners in the Public Service category of the Council of Advancement and Support of Education (CASE). Haugland had served on the Board of Directors of the International Peace Garden.

Admiral William A. Owens
(1940-)

Selected:
December 1995

Award Presented:
January 29, 1996, Bismarck
Governor Ed Schafer

Portrait Artist:
Ann Linton Hodge

Admiral William A. Owens was born and raised in Bismarck, North Dakota, and graduated from Bismarck High School in 1958. At the encouragement of his father, who had been in the Navy, he decided to apply to the U.S. Naval Academy in Annapolis. Owens was accepted and graduated in 1962 with a bachelor's degree in mathematics.

In the 1980s, his leadership and management skills brought him to Washington, where he served in several different capacities in the Office of the Chief of Naval Operations. Owens directed the Office of Program Appraisal under the Secretary of the Navy and was the first director of the Navy's Strategic Think Tank.

From November 1990 to July 1992, Owens commanded the U.S. Sixth Fleet, from which the first attacks of Desert Storm were launched, and NATO's Naval Striking and Support Forces Southern Europe. On March 1, 1994, Owens was appointed by President Clinton to serve as Vice Chairman of the Joint Chiefs of Staff. While serving in these demanding military duties, Owens also obtained bachelor's and master's degrees in politics, philosophy, and economics at Oxford University and a MBA from George Washington University.

In addition to numerous medals and awards, Owens has received Defense Distinguished Service and Superior Service Medals, a Legion of Merit with three Gold Stars, a Navy Commendation Medal with one Gold Star, and a Vietnam Service Medal with two Bronze Stars. He has also been awarded high-level foreign awards from France, Sweden, and Indonesia.

Carl Ben Eielson
(1897-1929)

Selected:
July 1997

Award Presented:
August 26, 1997, Hatton
Governor Ed Schafer

Portrait Artist:
Ann Linton Hodge

Pioneer aviator Carl Ben Eielson was born and raised in Hatton, North Dakota. After studying at the University of North Dakota, he enlisted in the Army Air Service in 1917 and completed pilot training.

Following his father's advice in 1921, Eielson enrolled in law school at Georgetown University, abandoning his passion for flying. During his time in Washington, he became friends with an Alaskan representative in Congress, and through him was offered a job at a high school in Fairbanks, Alaska. He quickly realized the value aviation could have for the remote land. He ordered a plane and began flying passengers and supplies throughout the northern territory.

Known as the "Father of Aviation" in Alaska, Eielson piloted the first airmail route in 1924. Eielson was later introduced to Captain George Hubert Wilkins, another outstanding pilot, and the two together earned international acclaim for their non-stop, 2,200 mile flight over the North Pole on April 15, 1928. In September of the same year, Wilkins and Eielson completed a 1,200 mile flight in the Antarctic, where they discovered six new islands.

In 1929, U.S. President Herbert Hoover granted Eielson the Harmon Trophy, an award presented annually to the outstanding aviator of the year. Eielson returned to Alaska and established Alaskan Airways, Inc. In 1929, he was killed while attempting to rescue passengers and cargo from an ice-bound ship in the Bering Strait. Eielson is the first individual to receive the Rough Rider Award posthumously.

Warren Christopher
(1925-2011)

Selected:
December 1997

Award Presented:
June 20, 1998, Scranton
Governor Ed Schafer

Portrait Artist:
Ann Linton Hodge

Warren Christopher was born in Scranton, North Dakota, on October 27, 1925. He graduated magna cum laude from the University of Southern California in 1945 and earned a law degree from Stanford University in 1949.

After law school, Christopher clerked for U.S. Supreme Court Justice William O. Douglas for one year. He joined the O'Melveny & Myers law firm of Los Angeles in 1950. He became a partner in 1958 and has worked with O'Melveny & Myers for 37 years in between several prestigious federal executive branch appointments.

Christopher served as Deputy Secretary of State in the Carter Administration. In that position, he led negotiations for the release of 52 American hostages in Iran, spearheaded the normalization of relations with China, helped to win ratification of the Panama Canal treaties, and headed the first interagency group on human rights. President Carter awarded him the Medal of Freedom on January 16, 1981.

In 1993, Christopher was sworn in by President Bill Clinton as the 63rd Secretary of State. During his four years of service, he logged 780,000 miles representing the United States abroad, more miles than any Secretary of State in a comparable period. At a ceremony honoring his retirement from public service President Clinton said, "The cause of peace and freedom and decency have never had a more tireless or tenacious advocate…." He retired from public service on November 7, 1996.

Bobby Vee
(1943-2016)

Selected:
February 3, 1999

Award Presented:
June 20, 1999, Bismarck
Governor Ed Schafer

Portrait Artist:
Ann Linton Hodge

Bobby Vee's rise to national prominence in the "rock and roll" industry began as the result of tragedy. The 15-year-old Bobby and his band, the "Shadows," were replacements for Buddy Holly, Richie Valens, and the Big Bopper the evening after they were killed in a plane crash on February 3, 1959. Ten days later, Bobby and his band had their first paying gig and later that fall they signed with Liberty Records.

His first regional hit was *Susie Baby*, his first national hit was *Devil or Angel*. Since then Bobby Vee has had 38 songs on *Billboard's* Top 100 chart, six gold singles, 14 top 40 hits, and two gold albums. He produced six gold records: *Devil or Angel*, *Rubber Ball*, *Take Good Care of My Baby*, *Run to Him*, *The Night Has a Thousand Eyes*, and *Come Back When You Grow Up*. He has seven top 10 hits in England and top 10 hits in Australia, Chile, Hong Kong, New Zealand, Israel, and the Philippines. *Billboard* magazine has called Bobby Vee, "One of the top ten most consistent chart makers ever."

Bobby Vee, born Robert Thomas Velline, was born April 30, 1943, in Fargo, North Dakota. In 1963, he married his high school sweetheart, Karen Ann Bergen, and they make their home in St. Cloud, Minnesota. They have four children, Jeff, Tom, Rob, and Jennifer. The boys now form part of his back-up band. Bobby Vee's popularity has remained constant; between Europe and America, Bobby and his band perform about 100 dates a year.

Chester "Chet" Reiten
(1923-2013)

Selected:
February 26, 2002

Award Presented:
October 8, 2002, Minot
Governor John Hoeven

Portrait Artist:
Ann Linton Hodge

Chester "Chet" Reiten was born in Hastings, North Dakota, in 1923 and served in the U.S. Navy during World War II. He graduated from North Dakota State University in Fargo with a degree in agriculture and worked as a county agent until entering the radio and television field in 1951. His company, Reiten Broadcasting Co., eventually owned four television and three radio stations in North Dakota.

In 1978, Chester Reiten and some of his Norwegian friends sat down to discuss a way in which they could celebrate their ancestry. Their discussion led to the birth of Norsk Høstfest, with Reiten as the founding father. Twenty-five years later, Norsk Høstfest has become an international phenomenon, steering the course of a Nordic festival that is both an ethnic celebration and a great source of entertainment. The event draws some 60,000 people from throughout North America and abroad. Over the years, royalty, ambassadors, national war and sports heroes, members of Congress, a former vice president of the United States, and many of North Dakota's governors have attended the festival.

Reiten has a long history of public service to his community and state, as a state senator, mayor of Minot, and community leader. As a result of the success of Norsk Høstfest, His Majesty King Olav V of Norway awarded Reiten the St. Olav Medal, one of the highest honors bestowed by the Norwegian government, outside of Norway.

Thomas J. Clifford
(1921-2009)

Selected:
February 26, 2002

Award Presented:
November 23, 2002, Grand Forks
Governor John Hoeven

Portrait Artist:
Ann Linton Hodge

Thomas J. Clifford, a native of Langdon, North Dakota, is recognized as one of the most effective university presidents in the nation. He became the eighth president of the University of North Dakota (UND) in 1971. Clifford's history with UND spans more than 50 years, as a UND student, faculty member, and administrator. Clifford received his Bachelor of Science in Commerce and Juris Doctorate from the University of North Dakota and a Master of Business Administration from Stanford University. He served in the U.S. Marine Corps during World War II, rising from the rank of Private First Class to Major and earning the Purple Heart, Bronze Star, and Silver Star in the Pacific Campaign.

Under Clifford's leadership, UND evolved into the largest and most comprehensive university in a five-state region: North Dakota, South Dakota, Montana, Wyoming, and Idaho. During his presidency, a four-year medical school, energy and environmental research center, and aviation and aerospace science programs were developed and became world-class, multi-million dollar enterprises. He played a key role in facilitating one of the nation's largest gifts to a public university, resulting in the finest college hockey facility in the world.

Clifford was named to the North Dakota Aviation Hall of Fame in 2002. He was regarded with high esteem for his entrepreneurial spirit, leadership in economic development, and service to his community, state, and nation.

Sister Thomas Welder
(1940-)

Award Presented:
May 1, 2004, Bismarck
Governor John Hoeven

Portrait Artist: Vern Skaug

Sister Thomas Welder, a native of Bismarck, North Dakota, served the University of Mary, formerly Mary College, since 1963 and was named college president in 1978. She attended the College of St. Benedict, graduated from the College of St. Scholastica, Duluth, and earned a master's degree in music from Northwestern University in Evanston, Illinois. She is a member of the Benedictine Sisters of Annunciation Monastery and has led an extraordinary life committed to God and her community.

Under the leadership of Sister Thomas, Mary College expanded to university status in 1986 and added undergraduate and graduate degree programs at locations throughout the state and region, including Fargo, Minot, Grand Forks, New Town, Belcourt, Montana, and Wyoming. During her presidency, enrollment grew from 925 students to nearly 3,000 in 2009. She retired on June 30, 2009, after 40 years of service to the University.

Sister Thomas is recognized as a woman who lives, serves, and leads by example. She has served on numerous boards and has been actively involved in professional organizations and religious affiliations on both a state and national level. Her personal achievements, character, and leadership have been an inspiration to countless individuals, students, entrepreneurs, and business and state leaders.

Envisioning the University of Mary as the nation's premier institution for the preparation of servant leaders, Sister Thomas promotes competence in communication, commitment to values, and service to community. Her strong belief in the ability of an individual to grow into leadership through service is an example for North Dakota and the nation.

Harry J. Pearce
(1942-)

Award Presented:
August 11, 2004, Bismarck
Governor John Hoeven

Portrait Artist: Vern Skaug

Harry J. Pearce is recognized statewide and nationally as an inspirational business leader and philanthropist. A native of Bismarck, North Dakota, he received a bachelor's degree in engineering sciences from the U.S. Air Force Academy and his juris doctor degree from Northwestern University School of Law.

Pearce was a senior partner in the law firm of Pearce & Durick in Bismarck from 1970-1985. He helped rewrite the North Dakota Criminal Code and Rules of Criminal Procedure while serving on several volunteer judicial and legislative committees. He served as a police commissioner, a municipal judge, and a U.S. magistrate. He joined General Motors (GM) in 1985 as Associate General Counsel and two years later was promoted to GM's General Counsel. He was promoted to Executive Vice President in 1992 and was responsible for GM's non-automotive operations, including electronic data systems and Hughes Electronics. In 1996, he was appointed Vice Chairman and served as a Director of the GM Corporation Board of Directors until his retirement from GM in 2001. He was then elected Chairman of the Hughes Electronics Corporation Board of Directors, a subsidiary of GM, and retired in 2003.

With an unbounded commitment to service, Pearce has received numerous state and national awards. He has turned his personal battle with leukemia into a public mission, serving on the boards of six different foundations supporting leukemia and bone marrow research. Pearce is a board member of MDU Resources Group, Inc., and is an active supporter of North Dakota's education system, the Bismarck-Mandan Symphony, the Nature Conservancy, and numerous other state organizations. He has served on the Theodore Roosevelt Medora Foundation Board of Directors and the Bismarck Hospital Board of Trustees and Executive Committee.

Pearce attributes his life of professional achievement and personal compassion to his North Dakota roots and the values he says make this state an extraordinary place to live and work – honesty and integrity, respect and responsibility, diversity and community, and faith in ourselves and our ability to succeed.

William C. Marcil
(1936-)

Award Presented:
May 18, 2006

Portrait Artist: Vern Skaug

William C. Marcil is a visionary state and national leader who has defined his career and business success with a steadfast commitment to respect, integrity, and responsibility. Getting his start as a young retail advertising salesman, Marcil quickly became a prominent leader in the state's newspaper industry as publisher of *The Forum*, and later, as president and chief executive officer of Forum Communications Company, a multi-media company based in Fargo.

A native of Rolette, Marcil graduated from the University of North Dakota in 1958 and then served in the U.S. Army and Reserves. In 1960, he married Jane Black, daughter of Norman D. Black, Jr., who was publisher of *The Forum* at the time. He began his newspaper career at *The Forum* in 1961 in retail advertising, and over the next eight years, worked his way up through the company, eventually becoming its president and publisher in 1969. Marcil placed a strong emphasis on public trust and consistently demonstrated a deep passion for publishing the best possible newspaper for the consumer.

Under Marcil's leadership, Forum Communications Company has retained its identity as an independent, family-owned publishing business, with deep roots in its community, while growing and diversifying into a multi-state, multi-media company. Forum Communications now includes more than 30 daily and community newspapers, as well as broadcasting, interactive media, and commercial printing in North Dakota, South Dakota, Minnesota, and Wisconsin.

Throughout his career, Marcil has had an impact on a national level, as well. He was the first North Dakotan to be elected chair of the American Newspaper Publishers Association, now known as the Newspaper Association of America. He has also been a strong advocate for business growth in general and served as chairman of the U.S. Chamber of Commerce.

Master Sgt. Woodrow W. Keeble

(1917-1982)

Award Presented: July 23, 2008

Portrait Artist: Vern Skaug

Master Sergeant Woodrow "Woody" Wilson Keeble is one of North Dakota's most highly decorated soldiers. A veteran of World War II and the Korean War, Keeble was presented with the Medal of Honor posthumously on March 3, 2008, at the White House. He is the first full-blooded Sioux Indian to receive the nation's highest military honor. He was inducted into the Pentagon Hall of Heroes on March 4, 2008.

Born on the Sisseton-Wahpeton Sioux Reservation in Waubay, South Dakota, he lived much of his life in Wahpeton, North Dakota. He joined the North Dakota National Guard in 1942 and was a member of Company I, 3rd Battalion, 164th Infantry Regiment (Rifle). His unit became the first U.S. Army unit to engage in offensive operations in WWII. They reinforced the 1st Marine Division at Guadalcanal and significantly contributed to decisive victory in the battle. Keeble received his first Bronze Star Medal, his first of four Purple Hearts, and the Combat Infantryman Badge for his actions at Guadalcanal.

Keeble reenlisted with the 164th Infantry Regiment at the beginning of the Korean War and later volunteered for a combat assignment with an active duty Army unit. He served with Company G, 19th Infantry of the 24th Infantry Division in Korea, where his actions would eventually earn him the nation's highest military honor. On October 20, 1951, when all of the officers of his company were killed or wounded, Keeble took charge of the support platoon attempting to complete the company's mission of taking control of a steep, rocky, and heavily fortified hill.

Keeble was treated for over 80 shrapnel wounds one day, but he returned to duty the next to earn the Medal of Honor. Armed with grenades and his rifle, he successfully conducted multiple, single-handed assaults against three well-fortified enemy positions, saving the lives of his fellow soldiers and inspiring his company to achieve its important objective. Keeble's famous comments exemplify his military service. "There were terrible moments that encompassed a lifetime, an endlessness when terror was so strong in me that I could feel idiocy replace reason. Yet I have never left my position, nor have I shirked hazardous duty. Fear did not make a coward out of me."

Doug Burgum
(1956-)

Award Presented:
November 20, 2009, Fargo

Portrait Artist: Vern Skaug

Recognized globally for his visionary business leadership, entrepreneur and philanthropist Doug Burgum credits his success to the values and ethics instilled in his early years by his family and community. Others cite his deep commitment to improving both the personal and business lives of people worldwide as the distinguishing attribute of his leadership.

A native of Arthur, North Dakota, Burgum earned a Bachelor of University Studies degree from North Dakota State University, then went on to achieve a MBA from the Stanford Graduate School of Business. After building national experience as a consultant at McKinsey & Company, he returned to North Dakota in 1983 and joined Great Plains Software – then a very small startup company in the fledgling computer software industry. Driven by a firm belief in the region's people and a powerful dream, he led the company's growth as chairman and CEO to a very successful initial public offering in 1997. He then steered Great Plains through its strategic acquisition by Microsoft Corporation in 2001 for $1.1 billion – at the time the largest acquisition Microsoft had ever made. He remained at Microsoft as senior vice president through 2007, helping the company capture a leading position in the business applications software industry.

As a testimony to his people-centric philosophy, Great Plains was named to *FORTUNE* magazine's list of "100 Best Companies to Work for in America" four times, a distinction also held by Microsoft Corporation during Burgum's tenure there.

In 2006, Burgum reaffirmed his passion for the region by founding Kilbourne Group, a company committed to the redevelopment of downtown Fargo through the restoration of historic buildings and the creation of new buildings that honor the past and inspire the future.

In 2008, Burgum co-founded Arthur Ventures, a regional venture capital fund that seeks to identify and invest in businesses with potential for strong growth. He has also served as a member of the advisory council for the Stanford Graduate School of Business, the board of directors of SuccessFactors, and other companies.

Ronald Offutt

(1942-)

Award Presented: September 15, 2011

Portrait Artist: Vern Skaug

Ron Offutt is one of North Dakota's and the nation's premiere agribusiness leaders and philanthropists. As the nation's largest producer of potatoes and as owner of the largest network of John Deere construction and agricultural equipment dealerships in the U.S., Ron has brought jobs, revenue, and opportunities to North Dakota, especially within the state's agriculture industry.

Ron is the founder and chairman of the R. D. Offutt Company and RDO Equipment Company. With its corporate headquarters in Fargo, North Dakota, the company is comprised of a variety of businesses covering the agriculture, food processing, and retail equipment industries.

His companies and partnerships have resulted in several equipment and truck center locations across the state, the creation of more than 500 North Dakota jobs, an average annual payroll of more than $25 million, and three farm partnerships that grow nearly 12,000 acres of potatoes annually. The company's cornerstone is a 12-state, 190,000-acre farming operation for the production of potatoes.

In addition to his economic contributions, Ron is highly regarded for his philanthropy and civic involvement, serving on multiple boards and dedicating his time to several organizations and charities.

Ron attended Concordia College in Moorhead, Minnesota, where he majored in economics and starred in football and wrestling. After graduating from Concordia in 1964, he became a business partner in his father's farming operation and became the fourth generation to work in his family's potato business. In 1968, he purchased the John Deere store in Casselton, North Dakota, and began laying the foundation for the companies he founded and still owns and operates today.

Louise Erdrich
(1954-)

Award Presented:
April 19, 2013

Portrait Artist: Vern Skaug

Louise Erdrich is an internationally-acclaimed author and prominent literary figure who has numerous professional achievements and philanthropic contributions to her credit. The oldest in a family of seven children, Karen Louise Erdrich was born in Little Falls, Minnesota, in 1954, and grew up in Wahpeton, North Dakota, where her parents worked for the Bureau of Indian Affairs School. She is a member of the Turtle Mountain Band of Chippewa.

Louise graduated from Dartmouth College and received a master of fine arts degree from Johns Hopkins University. She is the author of 14 novels, as well as volumes of poetry, children's books, and a memoir of early motherhood. Her novel *Love Medicine* (1984) won the National Book Critics Circle Award. The *Last Report on the Miracles at Little No Horse* was a finalist for the National Book Award. *The Plague of Doves* (2008) won the Anisfield-Wolf Book Award and was a finalist for the Pulitzer Prize in 2009. In November 2012, Louise won the National Book Award for her novel, *The Round House*.

Louise lives in Minnesota and is the owner of Birchbark Books, a small independent bookstore in St. Paul. In an interview with Bill Moyers, Louise credited her achievements to the support of a widely extended loving family, to her parents, and to "a small, incremental, persistent, insect-like devotion to putting one word next to the next word. It's a very dogged process." In one of her poems, "Advice to Myself," Louise wrote, "Pursue the authentic. Decide first what is authentic, then go after it with all your heart."

Herman Stern

(1887-1980)

Award Presented: March 13, 2014

Portrait Artist: Vern Skaug

Businessman and visionary leader Herman Stern was born in Oberbrechen, Germany, in 1887. He came to America at the age of 16 to work at the Straus Clothing Store in Casselton, a clothing store established by his cousin, Morris Straus. In 1910, Herman became manager of the company's second store located in Valley City, where he remained for the next 70 years. In addition to Casselton and Valley City, the company operated stores in LaMoure, Carrington, Grand Forks, Jamestown, and Devils Lake. Today, after more than 130 years of operation, Straus Clothing has a store in Fargo with a third generation of Stern family members running the business.

In addition to his business contributions, Herman was also very active in community and statewide organizations and initiatives, establishing many programs that were pivotal in North Dakota's progress and remain so today. In 1924, he founded the Greater North Dakota Association, known today as the Greater North Dakota Chamber, and served as the organization's first president.

In 1937, under Herman's vision and direction, the North Dakota Winter Show made its debut in Valley City, and today, is the oldest and longest running agriculture show in the state, drawing visitors and exhibitors from across the country and Canada. He was active with Boy Scouts of America and was instrumental in establishing councils in Fargo, Valley City, Wahpeton, and Grand Forks, and raising money to build Camp Wilderness, a 2,400-acre camp in Minnesota that focuses on character building, citizenship training, and physical and mental fitness.

With family and friends in Germany during the rise of Adolf Hitler and the Nazi Party, Herman became worried about their welfare and embarked on a mission to bring them to America. With assistance from state and federal leaders, he made it possible for between 175 and 200 German Jews to escape the Holocaust and come to America.

Herman was also active in Rotary and the Masonic Order and was instrumental in establishing a program called the Community Chest. That program later became the United Way of Barnes County, another of his visions that is still impacting people today.

Herman passed away in 1980 at the age of 92.

Gerald W. VandeWalle
(1933-)

Award Presented:
January 7, 2015

Portrait Artist: Vern Skaug

Chief Justice Gerald W. VandeWalle has served on the North Dakota Supreme Court for more than 36 years and was recently re-elected to his fourth 10-year term. He has served as the court's Chief Justice for the past 21 years, making him the longest-serving Chief Justice in North Dakota history and the longest-serving of all sitting Chief Justices in the nation.

Throughout his career, Chief Justice VandeWalle has made important contributions to the North Dakota Supreme Court and the state court system. He played an integral role in the unification of the court system, establishing a unified, statewide approach to court proceedings and the administration of justice. He was instrumental in redefining North Dakota's judicial districts and increasing the number of judges to accommodate growth in the state's economy and population. He also promoted the establishment of a mediation program for family law cases and created a trial court administration system to place administrators within the judicial districts to oversee court procedures.

A native of Noonan, North Dakota, Chief Justice VandeWalle attended the University of North Dakota, and in 1955, received a bachelor of science degree in commerce from the School of Business. In 1958, he received a juris doctor degree magna cum laude from the University of North Dakota School of Law.

He was admitted to the State Bar of North Dakota in 1958 and spent the next 20 years working in the Attorney General's Office. In August 1978, VandeWalle was appointed to the North Dakota Supreme Court. That November, he was elected to serve an unexpired term and was re-elected to 10-year terms in 1984, 1994, 2004, and 2014. In 1993, he was elected Chief Justice of the North Dakota Supreme Court and has been re-elected to that post for five consecutive terms.

Chief Justice VandeWalle has served as chair of several prestigious national organizations and has received numerous national awards and recognitions for his outstanding contributions to the justice system and the practice of law.

John D. Odegard

(1941–1998)

Award Presented:
October 15, 2015

Portrait Artist: Vern Skaug

John D. Odegard is the founder and former dean of the John D. Odegard School of Aerospace Sciences at the University of North Dakota (UND) in Grand Forks. In 1968, John pioneered UND's aviation program, which has grown to become one of UND's largest degree-granting colleges, one of the nation's most widely-respected aerospace education programs, and a leader in atmospheric research.

Throughout his 32-year career as an aerospace educator, John's reputation for leadership earned him industry acclaim and numerous recognitions. In 1982, he directed the development of the Federal Aviation Administration's (FAA) four-year degree. He helped initiate a joint effort between UND Aerospace and the FAA to broadcast aviation classes via satellite to college campuses across the country, and in 1986, led the development of the SPECTRUM airline pilot training program, an industry standard for commercial pilot training around the globe.

Under John's leadership, UND Aerospace moved to the forefront of research aimed at modernizing the nation's aging weather radar surveillance system. In 1987, UND Aerospace established the nation's first multi-disciplinary space studies program to provide a comprehensive understanding of the impact of humankind's move into space.

John was honored with the FAA's Excellence in Aviation Award and Distinguished Service Award for his many achievements in aerospace education and aviation safety. He was honored by the National Air Transportation Association with its Excellence in Pilot Training Award and received the prestigious Frank G. Brewer Trophy from the National Aeronautics Association for his distinguished and inspiring leadership in creating new educational opportunities. He was named North Dakota Business Innovator of the Year and was inducted into the North Dakota Entrepreneur Hall of Fame, the North Dakota Aviation Hall of Fame, and the Norsk Hostfest Scandinavian-American Hall of Fame.

John passed away in 1998 at the age of 57.

Eugene Dahl

(1924-2008)

Award Presented:
October 27, 2016

Portrait Artist: Vern Skaug

Eugene Dahl, an entrepreneur and business leader who led the successful growth of several equipment manufacturing businesses in North Dakota, including Bobcat and Steiger, was responsible for creating thousands of manufacturing jobs in the state.

A native of Gwinner, Dahl graduated from Gwinner High School and attended North Dakota State University (NDSU) and Michigan State University before serving in World War II with the 75th Infantry at the Battle of the Bulge as a cryptographer. After the war, he finished his education at the University of North Dakota (UND), earning a degree in math and chemistry.

In 1947, Dahl taught school for one year in Cavalier before returning to his hometown of Gwinner where he became a partner in the Melroe Company. Dahl and his four brothers-in-law built the Melroe Manufacturing Company, now known as Bobcat, before selling it in 1970 to Clark Equipment.

Dahl served in numerous leadership roles in his church and the community, including two terms in the North Dakota House of Representatives.

In 1971, Dahl assumed the role of CEO of Steiger Tractor, and his family moved to Fargo. Under his leadership, the company grew from $2 million to $105 million in sales in six years and became a world leader in the manufacturing of four-wheel drive tractors. While at Steiger, Dahl formed one of the first employee stock ownership plans in the nation. Steiger was sold to JI Case in 1986.

He helped his sons establish Concord, Inc., which became the leading manufacturer in the United States of air seeders. He served as board chairman from 1977 until the company's sale to Case Corporation in 1996. He was also pivotal in the creation of Amity Technology, an industry-leading firm specializing in the manufacturing of agriculture machinery.

Dahl co-founded First Dakota Capital, North Dakota's first venture capital firm, and served as the first chairman of the Center for Innovation at UND. He served on numerous boards and received many honors, including an honorary doctorate from UND, induction into the North Dakota Entrepreneurial Hall of Fame, and the 2008 NDSU Harvest Bowl Agribusiness Award.

North Dakota KIDS COUNT

The KIDS COUNT Data Book annually ranks child health and the well-being of children in the country. Indicators reflect the educational, social, economic, and physical well-being of children. It is produced by the Annie E. Casey Foundation.

Here are some rankings released in 2017 of North Dakota children compared to children in other states:

Ranking	Measure
1	Lowest percentage of children without secure parental employment (families where no parent has full-time, year-round employment)
3	Lowest percentage of children in single-parent families
3	Lowest percentage of low-birthweight babies
5	Lowest percentage of teens not in school and not working (ages 16-19)
25	Lowest teen birth rates

More data is available at www.ndkidscount.org and www.aecf.org.

North Dakota Vital Statistics

	2015	2016
Number of Marriages	4,671	4,514
Number of Divorces	2,149	1,963
Number of Births	11,265	11,364
Number of Deaths	6,051	6,115

Leading Causes of Death by Rank in North Dakota in 2015

1. All Cancers
2. Diseases of the Heart
3. Alzheimer's Disease
4. Chronic Lung Disease
5. Strokes (Cerebrovascular Disease)
6. Diabetes
7. Influenza/Pneumonia
8. Suicide
9. Blood Clots and Embolisms
10. Cirrhosis of the Liver

North Dakota Traffic Fatalities

Year	2012	2013	2014	2015	2016
Fatal Crashes	147	133	121	111	102
Traffic Fatalities	170	148	135	131	113

Military Preparedness in North Dakota

ND National Guard Strength: 4,006 assigned/4,602 authorized (87%)
ND Army National Guard Strength: 3,001 assigned/3,407 authorized (88% strength)
ND Air National Guard Strength: 1,005 assigned/1,195 authorized (84% strength)

Since the 2001 terrorist attacks on America, the North Dakota National Guard has mobilized more than 4,200 soldiers and more than 2,600 airmen in support of the Global War on Terrorism. About 70 percent of all members serving today have joined since that time. With a total force of about 4,100 Guardsmen, the North Dakota National Guard remains ready for stateside response and national defense. For every 10,000 citizens in North Dakota, 65 serve in the North Dakota National Guard, a rate that is more than four times the national average.

✔ More information on the North Dakota National Guard can be found in the *1999-2001 North Dakota Blue Book: The Citizen-Soldiers: An Abbreviated History of the North Dakota National Guard.*

The North Dakota National Guard responds to a wildfire in southern Burleigh County in 2015.

Veterans in North Dakota

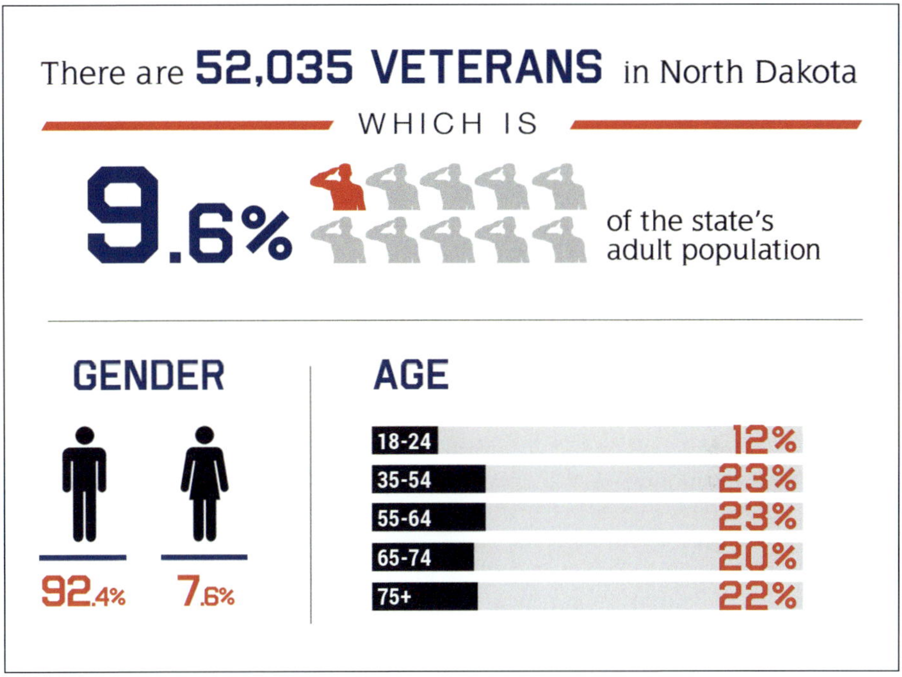

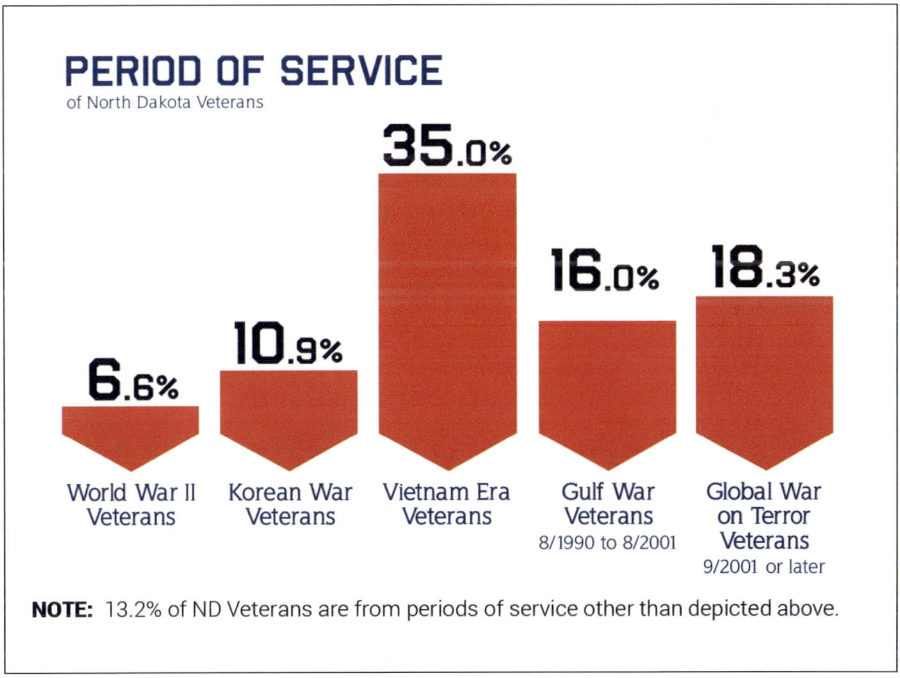

Source: North Dakota Cares

North Dakota Peace Officers Memorial

Police Officers Killed in the Line of Duty

Name	Location of Duty	Date
Fred D. Alderman	Fargo PD	1882
Evan Paulson	Mayville PD	1890
James Rauland	Northern Pacific RR	1899
H. M. Personius	Valley City PD	1906
George E. Moody	Richland County SO	1911
Carl G. Nelson	Carrington PD	1915
Seymour H. Douglas	McKenzie County SO	1917
Evan M. Jones	Richland SO	1917
George Dixon	Wilton PD	1917
Patrick J. Devaney	Minot PD	1918
Kersey E. Gowin	Attorney General's Office	1918
Earnest W. Thompson	Ward County SO	1920
Lee S. Fahler	Minot PD	1921
Julius A. Nielson	Kenmare PD	1921
Christian A. Madison	Stanley PD	1922
Carl Peterson	Westhope PD	1922
Charles R. Sneesby	Devils Lake PD	1924
E. M. "Ned" Morris	New Rockford PD	1926
Nels H. Romer	Mandan PD	1926
Hans C. Jess	Mandan PD	1929
Martin G. Johnson	Ray PD	1930
George Peipkorn	Burleigh County SO	1930
Leo Dagner	Willow City PD	1933
David L. Stewart	Hope PD	1933
Aslak "Oscar" Thorsen	Bottineau County SO	1936
Fred A. Patrickus	Billings County SO	1940
Joesph Runions	Mercer County SO	1941
Arthus M. Sem	Stanley PD	1942
Charles M. Allmaras	Eddy County SO	1942
Jacob M. Hoerner	New Leipzig PD	1942
John Oles	North Dakota Penitentiary	1946
Rudolph F. Howell	Ramsey County SO	1950
William W. Hansen	Velva PD	1950
Henry S. Halvorson	Grand Forks County SO	1952
Edward E. Mumby	New Salem PD	1953
Beryl E. McLane	North Dakota Highway Patrol	1954
John Holcolmb	North Dakota Penitentiary	1954
Ralph L. Burdick	Benson County SO	1954
Lee E. Morrow	Federal Bureau of Investigation	1960
Max L. Taylor	Bowman County SO	1960

Name	Location of Duty	Date
Nathan N. Bear	Bureau of Indian Affairs	1960
Ralph J. Hansen	Ransom County SO	1962
Frank A. Peterson	Rugby PD	1963
Burdette M. Miller	Ray PD	1966
Theodore C. Wanner	Dickinson PD	1966
Robert D. Martin	Grand Forks PD	1966
Raymond A. Wietstock	State Industrial School	1966
Ronald E. Trautman	Jamestown PD	1966
Frank C. Schultz Burlington	Northern RR	1970
P.A. "Tex" Goyne	New Salem PD	1971
Herbert A. Parmeter	Sargent County SO	1974
Kenneth A. Lenerville	Reeder PD	1975
Kenneth B. Muir	United States Marshal	1983
Robert S. Cheshire Jr.	United States Marshal	1983
Timothy L. Wells	Williams County SO	1989
Valence L. Pascal	Benson County SO	1993
Charles V. Pulver	North Dakota Game & Fish	1995
Keith A. Braddock	Watford City PD	1996
Roger C. Sorensen	Youth Correctional Center	1996
Steven R. Kenner	Bismarck PD	2011
Bryan K. Sleeper	Burleigh County SO	2011
Jason Moszer	Fargo PD	2016
Colt Eugene Allery	Rolette County SO	2017

(**Note**: PD means Police Department; SO means Sheriff's Office)

Police Officers Memorial, North Dakota State Capitol Grounds.

Miss North Dakota

1949 Kitty Gates Page, Fargo
1950 Joan Teets, Minot
1951 Marilyn Walker, Minot
1952 Margaret Winnifred Aandahl, Bismarck
1953 Marilyn Joy Wentz, Napoleon
1954 Dolores Ann Paulsen, Bismarck
1955 Mary Ann Gibbs, Crosby
1956 Janet Elizabeth Smith, Steele
1957 Helen Jane Winje, Minot
1958 Helen Estelle Korfhage, Grand Forks
1959 Claudia Jean Gullickson, Grand Forks
1960 Carol Ruth Olson, Fargo
1961 Diane Leda Ulvedal, Grand Forks
1962 Claudia Ellen Revland, Fargo
1963 Jo Ann Syvrud, Mandan
1964 Karen Victoria Kopseng, Bismarck
1965 Onalee Louise Olson, Fargo
1966 Denise Lee Fledderman, Inkster
1967 Wanda Lou Lowry, New Town
1968 Virginia Lee Hanson, Killdeer
1969 Charlene Hope Seifert, Gascoyne
1970 Nancy Jean Tangen, Aneta
1971 Lana Jean Herreid, Williston
1972 Georgia Ann Becker, Napoleon
1973 Linda Joyce Cole, Lisbon
1974 Susan Kaye Myhr, Bottineau
1975 Cathy Marie Woell, Minot
1976 Donna Grotberg , Valley City
1977 Kathryn L. Power, Beulah
1978 Sheila Jean Lindeman, Linton
1979 Daureen Podenski , Edgeley
1980 Karen Moe, Minot
1981 Stacie Anfinson, Hettinger
1982 Jeana Wolf, Rugby
1983 Phyllis Jeanette Hankey, Park River
1984 Callie Lynn Northagen, Grand Forks
1985 Elizabeth Ann Jaeger, Fargo
1986 Barbara Ann Kerzman, Garrison
1987 Susan Campbell, Grand Forks
1988 Tina Curran, Grand Forks
1989 Susan Jacobson, Grand Forks
1990 Lezlie Lund, Tolna
1991 VanNessa Straub, Fargo
1992 Stephanie Jean Fisher, Larimore

Miss North Dakota 2017
Cara Mund

1993 Suzanne Spilde, Casselton
1994 Nicci Elkins, Grand Forks
1995 Kimberly Ann Cooley, Grand Forks
1996 Stephanie Hamilton, Williston
1997 Roxana Saberi, Fargo
1998 Sonja Marie Gedde, Fargo
1999-00 Kay Picconatto, Minot
2001 Carrie Haverstroh, Lisbon
2002 Jillayne Mertens, Wahpeton
2003 Stacey Thomas, Bismarck
2004 Sara Schelkoph, Grand Forks
2005 Ashley Ford, Cavalier
2006 Jacqueline Marie Johnson, Fargo
2007 Annette Olson, Baldwin
2008 Ashley Young, Grand Forks
2009 Tessie Jones, West Fargo
2010 Kate Ralston, Carrington
2011 Beth Dennison, Grand Forks
2012 Arianna Walker, Bismarck
2013 Laura Harmon, Grand Forks
2014 Jacky Arness, Fargo
2015 Delanie Wiedrich, Hazen
2016 Macy Christianson, Minot
2017 Cara Mund, Bismarck

Miss North Dakota Scholarship Organization, PO Box 607, Williston, ND 58802, www.missnorthdakota.org.

Miss Rodeo North Dakota

Miss Rodeo North Dakota 2017
Cassidy Rasmusson

1955	Vonnie Young
1956	Pat Shipley
1957	Kay VanDyke
1958	Jamie Childs
1959	Barbara Kennedy
1960	Ellen Trotter
1961	Sharon Burkhardt
1962	Joan Hecker
1963	Virginia Eck
1964	Bonita Bohnsack
1965	Janice Brettin
1966	Terrilyn Todd
1967	Kathy Sandberg
1968	Celeste Hill
1969	Janet Mutchler
1970	Cathy Moon
1971	Bonnie Kuntz
1972	Patty Backhaus
1973	Pat Carlson
1974	Katie Osborn
1975	Karen Paulson
1976	Vicki Solheim
1977	Judi Fischer
1978	Deb Sterns
1979	Nancy Jo Rustad
1980	Sue Vuylsteke
1981	Lynn Brokaw
1982	Brenda Lee Bonogofsky
	****Miss Rodeo America 1983**
1983	Tammy Schaubert
1984	Shauna Rangen
1985	Tracy Pearce
1986	Janet Voight
1987	Melissa Berger
1988	Jessica Severson
1989	Tammy Peterson
1990	Ellen Thomas
1991	Leah Mecklenberg
1992	Tanya Jo Zahn
1993	Ashlee Ehr
1994	Larri Pfliiger
1995	Nacole Needham
1996	Korrey Tweed
1997	Sonya Dee Froelich
1998	Jamie Erhardt
1999	Shanda Doan
2000	Robyn Nelson
2001	Shannon Rustad
2002	Kami Fladeland (disqualified)
2003	Melanie Marquart
2004	Amanda Schaff
2005	Cara Ness
2006	Ashley Andrews
	****Miss Rodeo America 2007**
2007	Reba Bucholtz (resigned)
2008	Lindy Ellis
2009	Jessinta Hammer
2010	Tiffany Kuntz
2011	Sam Stanke
2012	Sadie Wardner
2013	Krystal Carlascio
2014	Codi Miller
2015	Dani Taylor
2016	Megan Haag
2017	Cassidy Rasmusson

Pictures and list are also available at www.missrodeond.org.

North Dakota's Published Authors

Below are North Dakota authors published in 2015 and 2016:

2015

Peter Brandvold, *Once More Into the Breech*
Peter Brandvold, *Thunder Over the Superstitions*
Ryan C. Christiansen, *Boy Wanted*
Heidi K. Czerwiec, *North Dakota is Everywhere: An Anthology of Contemporary North Dakota Poets*
Kathleen Davison, *Prairie Barns of North Dakota*
Richard Edwards, *Natives of a Dry Place: Stories of Dakota Before the Oil Boom*
Gerald E. Gipp, *American Indian Stories of Success: New Visions of Leadership in Indian Country*
Lois Greiman, *Hearth Stone*
Thomas D. Isern, *The Welk Homestead: A Source Book*
Jill Kandel, *So Many Africas: Six Years in a Zambian Village*
Debra K. Marquart, *Small Buried Things*
Steve C. Martens, *Buildings of North Dakota*
Daniel D. Maurer, *Faraway: A Suburban Boy's Story as a Victim of Sex Trafficking*
Jack McDevitt, *Thunderbird*
James M. McPherson, *The War That Forged a Nation: Why the Civil War Still Matters*
Marcia Mikulak, *Childhood Unmasked: The Agency of Brazil's Street and Working Children*
David W. Mills, *Cold War in a Cold Land: Fighting Communism on the Northern Plains*
Ronda Rousey, *My Fight, Your Fight*
Chris Rylander, *Countdown Zero*
Michelle M. Sauer, *Gender in Medieval Culture*
Amy Scheibe, *A Fireproof Home for the Bride*
Terry L. Shoptaugh, *Red River Floods: Fargo and Moorhead*
Mike Thompson, *Wolf Point*

2016

Sue B. Balcom, *Thoughts and Memories on Country Schools in German-Russian Country*
Kimball M. Banks, *The National Historic Preservation Act: Past, Present, and Future*
Albert I. Berger, *Life and Times of the Atomic Bomb: Nuclear Weapons and the Transformation of Warfare*
John P. Bluemle, *North Dakota's Geologic Legacy: Our Land and How It Formed*
Jeremy T. Bold, *The Walk Across North Dakota*
Peter Brandvold, *The Wild Ones*
William R. Caraher, *The Bakken Goes Boom: Oil and the Changing Geographies of Western North Dakota*

Jessamyn Conrad, *What You Should Know about Politics but Don't: A Nonpartisan Guide to the Issues That Matter*
Lorraine Dopson, *Hard Road Home*
Louise Erdrich, *LaRose*
Louise Erdrich, *Makoons*
Troyd Andrew Geist, *YGGDRASIL: The Norwegian-American Carvings of Gaylord "Guy" Paulson*
Lois Greiman, *Hearth Song*
Clint Hill, *Five Presidents: My Extraordinary Journey with Eisenhower, Kennedy, Johnson, Nixon, and Ford*
Chuck Klostermann, *But What if We're Wrong?: Thinking about the Present as if It Were the Past*
Clinton Romesha, *Red Platoon: A True Story of American Valor*
Chris Rylander, *Clash of the Worlds*
Chris Rylander, *Crisis Zero*
Rolf Sletten, *Roosevelt's Ranches: The Maltese Cross & The Elkhorn*
Renee Splichal Larson, *A Witness: The Haiti Earthquake, A Song, Death, and Resurrection*
Mike Thompson, *The Turbulent Trail*
Larry Watson, *As Good as Gone: A Novel*
Gina Wohlsdorf, *Security: A Novel*
Larry Woiwode, *Land of Sunlit Ice*

North Dakota's Official Poets

The following people have received recognition as official poets in North Dakota. Formal recognition of an individual as poet laureate has been made by resolution of the Legislative Assembly. Such recognition is honorary and carries no duties or stipend.

Larry Woiwode, a native North Dakotan, is the state's fourth poet laureate. He assumed the position in 1995 under Senate Concurrent Resolution 4039. The nominee for state poet laureate requires a joint resolution of the state legislature and confirmation by the governor. According to former Governor George Sinner, Woiwode's work "shows the beauty of the truth prism of life here on the prairie and the broad beauty of the promise of humanity itself."

Woiwode is the author of the poetry collection *Even Tide* (Farrar, Straus, Giroux; New York, 1977) and a chapbook, *Land of Sunlit Ice* (North Dakota State University Press; Fargo, N.D., 2016). His poetry has appeared in several publications, including *The Atlantic, GQ, Harpers, The New Yorker,* and *Transatlantic Review,* and is reprinted in a dozen anthologies. His novels include *Beyond the Bedroom Wall,* which was a finalist for the National Book Award and the Book Critics Circle Award. Six of his books have been selected as "notable books of the year" by the *New York Times Book Review*. His stories appear in four volumes of *Best American Short Stories*. Woiwode has published two memoirs, two collections of essays, the biography of Harold Schafer, and a children's book, among others.

Woiwode is currently a writer in residence at the University of Jamestown where he teaches creative writing, world literature, contemporary American fiction, and Native American literature and religion.

Woiwode has won the William Faulkner Foundation Award and the Medal of Merit from the American Academy of Arts and Letters. He was also a fellow with the John Simon Guggenheim Foundation. Woiwode is also a recipient of the Theodore Roosevelt Rough Rider Award, the highest honor bestowed up a citizen of North Dakota. To read more about Woiwode and his accomplishments, see page 100.

David Solheim, English professor from Dickinson State University, was selected by the North Dakota Centennial Commission as the North Dakota Centennial poet.

Lydia O. Jackson became poet laureate by action of the 1983 Legislative Assembly as Henry R. Martinson died in November 1981. (Senate Concurrent Resolution No. 4055, 1983 S.L., ch. 853) (Lydia Jackson died in April 1984.)

Lydia O. Jackson and **Henry R. Martinson** were given the title of poets laureate by the 1979 Legislative Assembly as Corbin A. Waldron died in April 1978. (Senate Concurrent Resolution No. 4017, 1979 S.L., p. 1871)

Corbin A. Waldron was named North Dakota poet laureate by the 1957 Legislative Assembly. (Senate Concurrent Resolution E, 1957 S.L., p. 843)

James W. Foley, while considered to be North Dakota's first poet laureate, never officially received that designation.

✔ For complete biographies, photos, and poetry by these poets, see the feature of the *2003-2005 North Dakota Blue Book.*

The Pulitzer Prize in North Dakota

Pulitzer Prizes awarded in North Dakota:

- Public Service: *The Bismarck Tribune,* 1938, for the "Self-Help in the Dust Bowl" article series.
- Local Reporting: *The Forum*, 1958, for coverage of the tornado that devastated the Golden Ridge neighborhood in Fargo.
- Public Service: *The Grand Forks Herald*, 1998, for coverage during the blizzard, flood, and fire of 1997.

Pulitzer Prizes won by individuals with ties to North Dakota:

- Drama: Maxwell Anderson, 1933, for his play *Anne of a Thousand Days.* Anderson graduated from Jamestown High School and the University of North Dakota.
- Spot News Reporting: Mel Ruder, 1965, for daily coverage in his Columbia Falls, Montana, newspaper of floodwaters overwhelming the community. Ruder grew up in Bismarck and graduated from the University of North Dakota.
- Editorial Writing: Richard Aregood, 1985, for his work at the *Philadelphia Daily News.* Aregood taught at the University of North Dakota following his career in journalism.
- Breaking News Reporting: William Ketter, 2003, for directing staff as editor and publisher of the *Lawrence Eagle* in Massachusetts in stories of the accidental drowning of four boys in the Merrimack River. Ketter graduated from the University of North Dakota.
- Local Reporting: Rob Kuznia, 2015, for leading a team of three at the *Daily Breeze* in investigating a local school board in Torrance, California. Kuznia graduated from Red River High School in Grand Forks.

Pulitzer Prizes with subject ties to North Dakota:

- Biography: Edmund Morris, 1980, for his book *The Rise of Theodore Roosevelt*, which led Morris to the North Dakota Badlands where Roosevelt heard birds, herded cattle, hunted buffalo, wrote books, and developed his character.
- History: Elizabeth Fenn, 2015, for her book *Encounters at the Heart of the World,* which covers the history of the Mandan people.
- History: T.J. Stiles, 2016, for his book *Custer's Trails*, which included Custer's experience in the country that would become North Dakota.

North Dakota Statistical Information

Highest geographical point: White Butte, Slope County, 3,506 feet
Highest elevation for a city: Rhame, Slope County, 3,194 feet
Mean elevation: 1,900 feet
Lowest elevation: Pembina County, where the Red River enters Canada, 750 feet
Geographic center: McClusky

Square miles in land area 68,976
State ranking in land area 18th
Total acres occupied by farmland and ranches .... 39.2 million

Geographic Description of Location
Border to the north: Saskatchewan and Manitoba, on 49th Parallel
Border to the south: South Dakota, on 45 degrees 55 minutes North
Border to the east: Minnesota, Red River of the North divides the two states
Border to the west: Montana, on 104 degrees 2 minutes West
North Dakota is 310 miles wide at the Canadian border, 360 miles wide at the South Dakota border, and 210 miles from north to south.

The Geographic Center of the North American continent: located precisely six miles west of Balta or 15 miles southwest of Rugby. (National Oceanic & Atmospheric Administration)

The Continental Divide dissects North Dakota, roughly dividing the state from the southeastern part of the state diagonally northwest across the state to the northwest corner of the state. This is a north-south drainage divide. Waters north of this divide drain into the Hudson Bay. Waters south of this divide drain into the Missouri River and the Gulf of Mexico.

Soil: North Dakota has more black humus soil (Chernozem) in the eastern part of the state than any other state in the nation.

North America's tallest structure: 2,063-foot television transmission tower near Blanchard (KVLY television tower).

Tallest buildings in North Dakota:

- The Antelope Valley power plant near Beulah has two buildings that stand 361 feet tall.
- The Coal Creek Station power plant near Underwood has two buildings that measure 290 feet tall.
- The Garrison Dam water intake structure for power generators located on Lake Sakakawea near Riverdale is 249 feet tall.
- The North Dakota State Capitol in Bismarck is 242 feet tall. It is the third tallest capitol building in the country, following Nebraska and Louisiana at 450 feet tall.

Holidays in North Dakota

North Dakota Century Code Section 1-03-01

The Revised Codes of Dakota 1877 list Sunday, January 1, February 22 (Washington's birthday), July 4, December 25, and territorial election days as specific holidays (Civil Code, Part V, Section 2115).

1885 Added May 30, Decoration Day.

1897 Added February 12, Lincoln's birthday, and changed Decoration Day to Memorial Day.

1909 Added Labor Day as the first Monday in September.

1919 Added October 12, Discovery Day.

1921 Added November 11, Armistice Day.

1927 Expanded Discovery Day by adding "to commemorate the discovery of America by Leif Erikson about the year A.D. 1000; and by Christopher Columbus in the year A.D. 1492." Additional language in 1927 provided that legislative meetings held on or decisions made on any of the holidays other than Sunday were legal.

1937 Added Good Friday, which falls two days before Easter.

1945 Added Thanksgiving Day as the last Thursday in November.

1949 Changed Thanksgiving Day to the fourth Thursday in November.

1955 Changed the name of Armistice Day to Veterans Day (leaving it on November 11).

1969 Changed February 22, Washington's birthday, to the third Monday in February; Memorial Day from May 30 to the last Monday in May; Discovery Day from October 12 to the second Monday in October.

1973 Changed Veterans Day to November 11.

1987 Established third Monday of January as Martin Luther King, Jr., Day.

Fishing in North Dakota is popular among residents and visitors.

The Fort Seward Wagon Trail has been an annual family-oriented event since 1969.

North Dakota LEGENDARY

North Dakota Tourism

In 2015, there were 21.9 million trips taken in North Dakota. Travelers are fascinated by the state's legendary things to see and do, and they spent $3.1 billion seeing and doing them. North Dakota is a destination for traditional family vacations and also an important place for business and convention travelers, a popular host for sports tournaments, and a welcoming state to shoppers from other communities, states, and nations. Travelers can easily find hotel accommodations, restaurants, event centers, art galleries, museums, and parks, along with bustling downtowns. North Dakota's travel industry provides the experiences, goods, and services for people spending time and money away from home.

In 2016, North Dakota joined other states in celebrating the 100th anniversary of the National Park Service and in the process welcomed 760,458 visitors to the three units of Theodore Roosevelt National Park (TRNP). Of those, 35,371 chose to stay within the park's borders. TRNP celebrated another milestone in 2017, the 70th anniversary of its naming as a National Memorial Park.

Blockhouse at Fort Abercrombie.

Tourism continues to be a vital component in North Dakota's economic well-being. While energy and agriculture have gone through ups and downs, tourism – the state's third-largest industry – has shown consistent and steady growth. Tourism's contributions to the state's tax base saved each household in the state $1,092.

North Dakota Tourism teamed up with Minot native and actor Josh Duhamel for an advertising campaign that led, in part, to 1 billion social media impressions. In 2016, these efforts resulted in 325 story placements and 25 media trips. Major media included appearances on *The Today Show* (2.89 million viewers) and *Food Network* and articles in *The New York Times*, *USA Today Travel,* and *National Geographic Travel.*

The state is seeing increased interest from overseas markets, with 79 tour operators offering North Dakota product.

Sports continue to be a marketing tool. The University of North Dakota's men's hockey team won an NCAA national championship; North Dakota State University had its run of FCS football championships snapped but continues to be easily marketable as a title contender; Carson Wentz was the No. 2 pick in the NFL draft and started all 16 games as a rookie quarterback with the Philadelphia Eagles; and pitcher Matt Strahm made his major league baseball debut with the Kansas City Royals.

While these are easily promotable, it is the allure of things to see and do that makes North Dakota attractive to travelers. The beautiful sunsets, clear blue skies, welcoming communities, and exciting outdoor activities are unmatched.

The official tourism website (www.NDtourism.com) helps connect hundreds of thousands of people to opportunities, adventures, travel accommodations, and legendary experiences throughout North Dakota.

Canoeing on the Red River.

North Dakota State Historical Sites

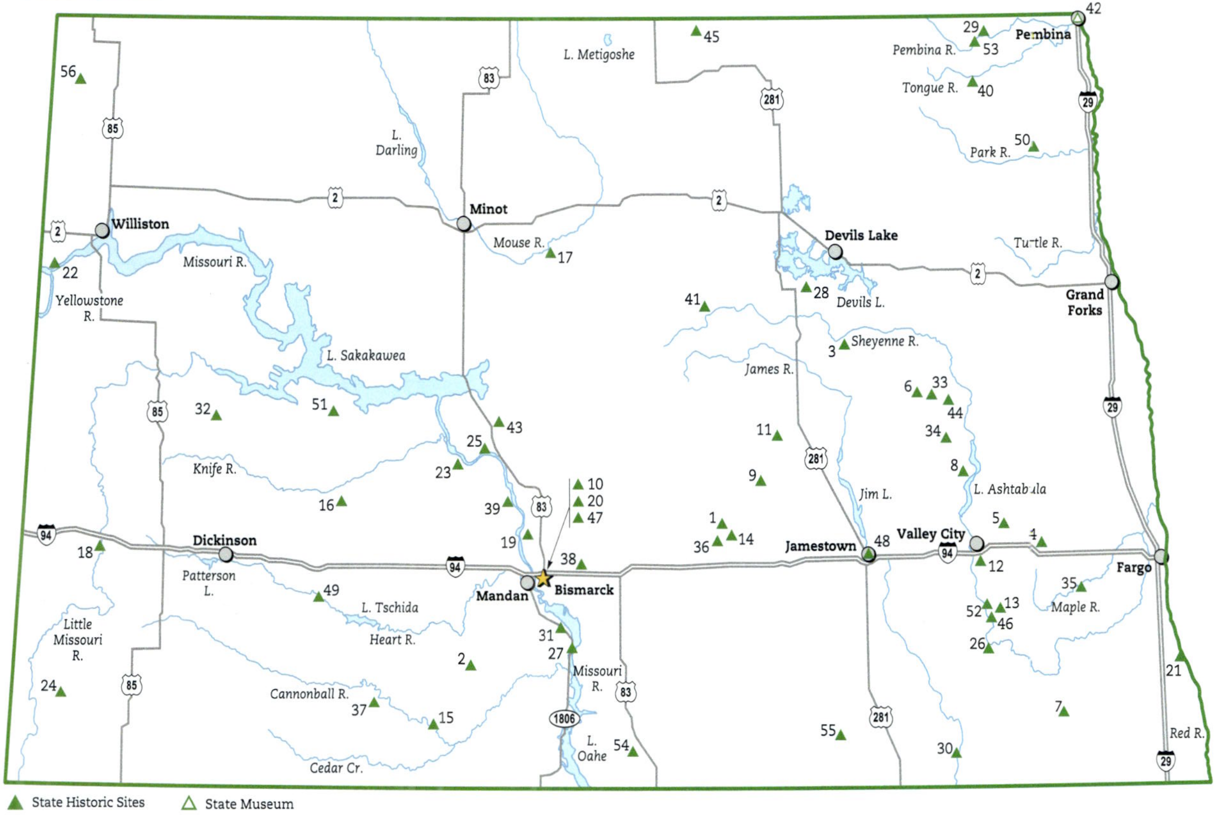

1. Big Mound Battlefield
2. Bismarck-Deadwood Stage Trail
3. Brenner Crossing
4. Buffalo Creek
5. Camp Arnold
6. Camp Atchison
7. Camp Buell
8. Camp Coming
9. Camp Grant
10. Camp Hancock
11. Camp Kimball
12. Camp Sheardown
13. Camp Weiser
14. Camp Whitney
15. Cannonball Stage Station
16. Crowley Flint Quarry
17. David Thompson
18. DeMores
19. Double Ditch Indian Village
20. Former Governors' Mansion
21. Fort Abercrombie
22. Fort Buford & MYCIC
23. Fort Clark Trading Post
24. Fort Dilts
25. Fort Mandan Overlook
26. Fort Ransom
27. Fort Rice
28. Fort Totten
29. Gingras Trading Post
30. Hudson Townsite
31. Huff Indian Village
32. Killdeer Mountain Battlefield
33. Lake Jessie
34. Lake Johnson
35. Maple Creek Crossing
36. McPhail's Butte
37. Medicine Rock
38. Menoken Indian Village
39. Molander Indian Village
40. Oak Lawn
41. Palmer's Spring
42. Pembina State Museum
43. Pulver Mounds
44. Ronald Reagan Minuteman Missile
45. St. Claude
46. Standing Rock
47. Steamboat Warehouse
48. Stutsman County Courthouse
49. Sully's Heart River Corral
50. Sweden
51. Turtle Effigy
52. Walhalla
53. Welk Homestead
54. Whitestone Hill
55. Writing Rock

North Dakota State Parks

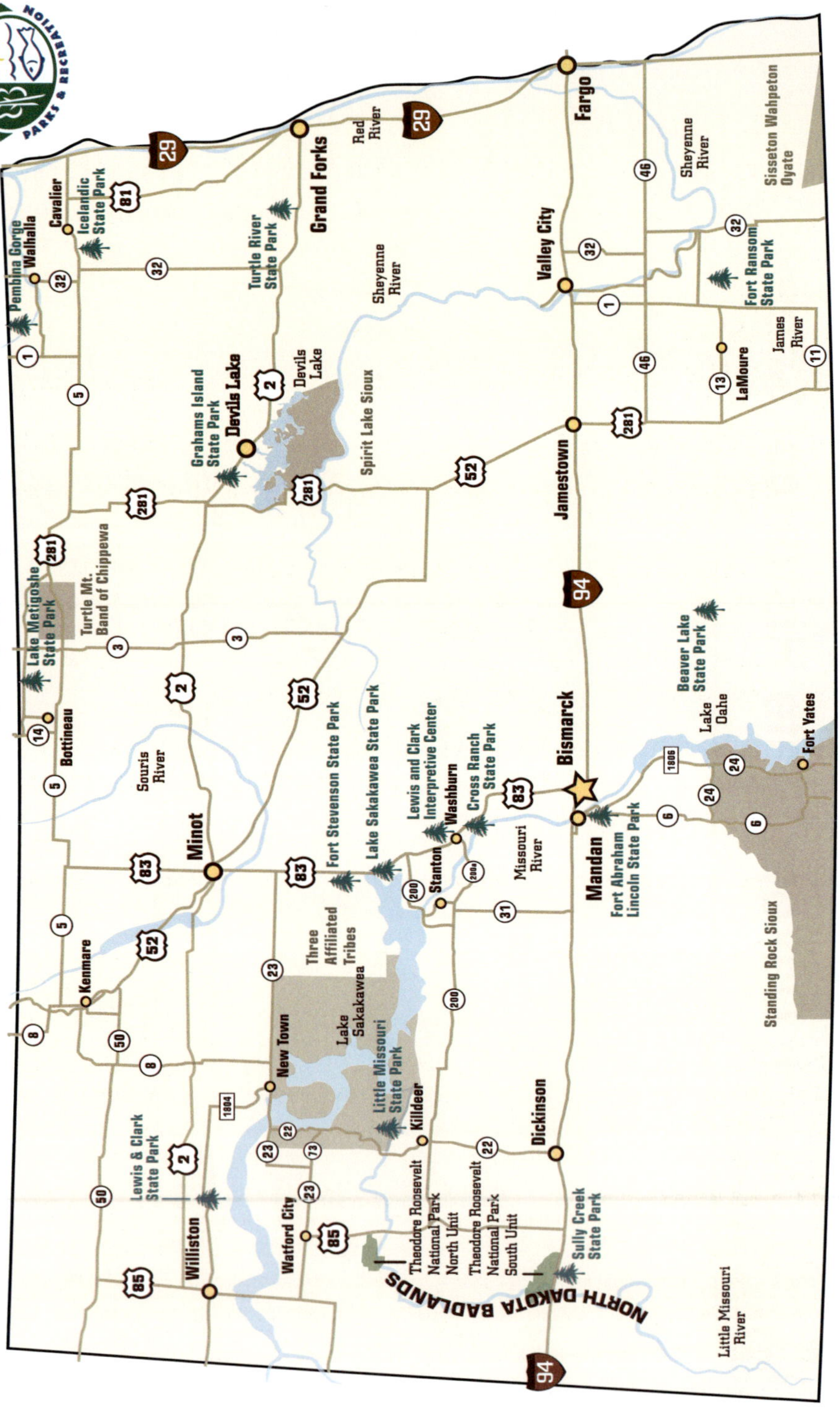

Visitation at North Dakota Sites

	2013	2014	2015	2016
North Dakota State Parks	1,125,231	1,073,146	1,205,598	1,220,918
Theodore Roosevelt National Park	551,668	566,158	580,033	753,880
Fort Union Trading Post National Historic Site	13,518	12,143	13,605	17,502
Knife River Indian Villages National Historic Site	15,111	11,384	11,377	13,328
North Dakota State Fair	320,485	314,446	305,093	293,123
Lewis and Clark Interpretive Center/Fort Mandan	79,003	81,479	52,119	48,532
North Dakota Heritage Center	31,154 (construction)	169,907	305,265	238,313
North Dakota Historic Sites	78,103	73,161	82,409	84,674

North Dakota State Parks that collect visitor data include: Fort Abraham Lincoln State Park, Cross Ranch State Park, Fort Stevenson State Park, Lake Metigoshe State Park, Lake Sakakawea State Park, Lewis and Clark State Park, Little Missouri State Park, Turtle River State Park, Icelandic State Park, Fort Ransom State Park, Sully Creek State Park, and Grahams Island State Park.

The Theodore Roosevelt National Park, Fort Union Trading Post National Historic Site, and Knife River Indian Villages National Historic Sites are all owned and operated by the U.S. government.

✔ More information on state parks is in the *1997-1999 North Dakota Blue Book.*

Theodore Roosevelt National Park.

International Peace Garden

Landscape at the International Peace Garden.

Nestled in the Turtle Mountains, the International Peace Garden (Garden) straddles the North Dakota (United States) – Manitoba (Canada) borders. It is located 30 miles north of the geographical center of North America.

The concept of the Garden was the peaceful coexistence between the United States and Canada, illustrating to the world their commitment to world peace. Inscribed on a simple stone cairn, the only piece at the entrance to the Garden on opening day, July 14, 1932, are the words: "To God in His Glory. We two nations dedicate this Garden and pledge ourselves that as long as man shall live; we will not take up arms against one another."

Nestled amidst lakes and woodlands is the one-of-a-kind garden. More than 150,000 flowers are planted each year, in addition to flowering shrubs and perennials. The most photographed is the working floral clock, and the only displays that remain the same each year are the two floral flag displays.

The Garden's Interpretive Center features a café, retail store, modest library, conference room, and conservatory. The conservatory reveals 40 years of a 6,000-specimen collection of succulents and cacti, many native to Africa. A beautifully landscaped addition has been added to the original conservatory, and the collection is the first of its kind in North Dakota and only the second in Manitoba.

The Sunken Garden is located directly across from the Interpretive Center. The garden's focal point is an octagon-shaped pond with a water feature in the center. The plantings of trees, shrubs, flowers, and walkways surround the pond in repeated octagonal rows.

Visitors may stand with a foot in each country as they see a panoramic view from the Formal Garden area's top terrace. Below is a water feature where garden weddings take place. On each side are gazebos with individual landscaping. At the far end of the Formal Garden is the Peace Chapel. It is the only building in the International Peace Garden straddling the international border. Etched in limestone tablets embossed with marine fossils are inspiring quotes of people of peace. Enclosed in glass is a book of remembrance, listing the names of those who perished on September 11, 2001, in the wreckage of the New York City World Trade Center.

Also along the Formal Garden Border Walk is the Bell Tower; the beautiful tones ring on the hour and half hour. Across from the Bell Tower is the 9/11 Memorial Site with 10 steel girders from the World Trade Center. The Stroll and Contemplative Garden, sponsored by the Rotary International, North American Fire Fighters Union, and Manitoba Infrastructure, surrounds the 9/11 site.

The International Peace Garden is also home to the International Music Camp and Legion Athletic Camp, providing arts appreciation and athletic training to thousands of young people each year.

The more than 2,300-acre International Peace Garden has many buildings to accommodate bus tours, conventions, wedding receptions, reunions, and conferences, as well as private camp sites and hiking and biking trails.

✔ A list of North Dakota Olympians can be found in the *2003-2005 North Dakota Blue Book*.

✔ See *2013-2015 North Dakota Blue Book* for information about the North Dakota Cowboy Hall of Fame.

✔ See *2013-2015 North Dakota Blue Book* for information about the North Dakota Country Woman of the Year.

✔ See *2013-2015 North Dakota Blue Book* for information about the North Dakota Champion Tree Program and answers to common tree questions.

✔ See *2015-2017 North Dakota Blue Book* for information about North Dakota license plates.

✔ North Dakota record fish caught while recreational fishing can be found in the *2015-2017 North Dakota Blue Book*.

✔ See *2015-2017 North Dakota Blue Book* for information on the sister states of North Dakota and Taiwan.

Enriching Lives Through the Arts: The North Dakota Council on the Arts Celebrates 50 Years

The North Dakota Council on the Arts was founded in 1967 as a service and program agency to develop, promote, and support the arts in North Dakota. In 2017, the council celebrated its 50th anniversary and its continued focus on enriching the lives of North Dakotans through the arts.

Two art exhibits celebrated the 50th anniversary and displayed the artwork of 50 North Dakota artists. One exhibit was displayed in the North Dakota Heritage Center & State Museum and the other traveled the state.

The History of the NDCA

On September 29, 1965, President Lyndon B. Johnson signed the National Foundation on the Arts and Humanities Act, which established the National Endowment for the Arts (NEA) and the Humanities Foundation. The legislation also created government support for the arts and the development of state arts councils.

Appointed North Dakotans attended a meeting of the National Council of the Arts and the Arts Councils of America, which provided model legislation for establishing a state arts council. An organizational meeting of a "temporary" North Dakota Council on the Arts and Humanities then approved a survey of the state's arts resources, the submission of a $25,000 application to the NEA to cover a director's salary and the costs of regional workshops, as well as the state's plans for establishing an arts council.

A planning grant was awarded by the NEA and, during the 1967 Legislative Session, House Bill 628 established the North Dakota Council on the Arts and Humanities. The organization officially began operating on July 1, 1967.

The North Dakota Council on the Arts and Humanities received its first state appropriation in 1972. In 1977, the first local arts councils were established, and the first Governor's Awards for the Arts were presented in 1978. In 1979, the name of the organization was officially shortened to the North Dakota Council on the Arts (NDCA).

NDCA's office remained in Fargo until 1994, when all state agencies were moved to Bismarck. At this time, the NDCA Board of Directors was also reduced from 15 members to eight regional members and one at large member.

Supporting the Arts

In its beginning, NDCA funding of arts groups was on a request basis. It then moved to a formal grant program. The largest of the nine grant programs is NDCA's institutional support, which offers operating support to organizations whose primary activity is the presentation, production, or service to the arts.

Additional grant programs provide support for organizations actively involved in the arts and arts in education, as well as folk and traditional arts apprenticeship programs. NDCA also funds Individual Artist Fellowships and has created many important partnerships to help expand the arts in North Dakota.

NDCA's first economic impact study was conducted in 1967 and, in 2007, another survey established the significant impact of the arts on the state, which generates more than $101 million in local activity and supports nearly 2,450 full-time equivalent jobs.

North Dakota Zoos

These four zoos in North Dakota are accredited by the Association of Zoos and Aquariums.

Dakota Zoo, Bismarck

The Dakota Zoo began with the 67-acre Marc and Betty Christianson Farm, located at what was then the northern edge of Bismarck. The Christianson Farm operated for some time as a boarding kennel for domesticated animals such as dogs, cats, and horses. At one point, the land was used to raise mink for profit. The Christiansons began to receive injured or stray animals from friends and neighbors to care for at their farm. As the number of animals increased, curiosity intensified, and the number of visitors that came to view the animals increased. Eventually, in 1958, a petition was filed with the park board to form the land into a self-supporting community zoo.

On June 3, 1961, the Dakota Zoo opened its gates to the public with 75 mammals and 23 birds on approximately 15 acres of developed land. Forty thousand visitors paid a 10-cent admission fee during the first year.

The Dakota Zoo remains self-supporting and operates on money raised through admissions, concession sales, adopt an animal program, memberships, donations, and events.

Red River Zoo, Fargo

The Red River Zoological Society was formed in 1993 with intent to form a zoological facility in Fargo. Through land sold and donated to the Fargo Park District by the Anderson Family, the Red River Zoo was able to obtain a long-term lease of 34 acres. In May 1999, the Red River Zoo was constructed and opened to the public.

The initial site included only seven trees and a few old farm buildings. The land has since been landscaped into different exhibits featuring rolling hills and a series of ponds connected by flowing streams. Hundreds of trees and shrubs were planted to create the illusion of wilderness. The collection plan of the Red River Zoo primarily focuses on species from around the world with climates similar to North Dakota's. Primary areas represented are North America, Northern Asia, and Northern Europe.

The Red River Zoo has experienced steady, continuous growth and has expanded to 22 developed acres featuring a collection of approximately 89 species from around the world.

Roosevelt Park Zoo, Minot

The Roosevelt Park Zoo was established in 1920. The first animal in the zoo was a male bison from Montana. In 1921, a bear den and a zoological building were added. The animal population increased during the 1940s and 1960s, although a flood in 1969 caused every bird and animal to be removed from the grounds. Due to the flood, the zoo was redesigned with a foot bridge, feline house, and new bear den added to the grounds.

The zoo gained its own separate identity from Roosevelt Park in 1970, and the Greater Minot Zoological Society was formed. In 1981, the park board instituted a gate admission at the zoo to help defray costs. New animals, new exhibits, and participation in a Species Survival Program have enhanced the zoo.

Chahinkapa Zoo, Wahpeton

The land for the Chahinkapa Zoo and Chahinkapa Park was first purchased from the federal government in 1903 by the city of Wahpeton. The name of the site, which lies along the banks of the Red River, comes from American Indians who named the site Chahinkapa or "end of the woods."

Thirty years later, the first park board was established. The Chahinkapa Zoo was also established at this time, with modest display of animals on its grounds.

In the 1960s, the zoo was moved to its present 18-acre location at the north end of Chahinkapa Park. The Chanikapa Zoo Association was formed in 1974, and the first zoo director was hired in 1994.

Chapter Three

Federal-State Relationships

Unmanned Aircraft Systems in North Dakota

North Dakota's technology-based businesses are growing and diversifying. Keeping stride with rapid changes in technology and integrating those developments can benefit all North Dakotans. North Dakota is home to a growing cluster of Unmanned Aircraft Systems (UAS) used for research, business, and military interests. North Dakota is a proven leader with the experience, resources, and leadership to help drive the UAS industry's growth. Partnerships among private businesses, universities, and state government, as well as the most open air space in the country and the nation's first unmanned aircraft degree program, strengthen North Dakota's position as a leader in UAS.

UAS are colloquially called drones. Drones have many uses with industries such as real estate, agriculture, and insurance projected to be among the biggest commercial users of UAS technology. Drones help farmers prioritize where to apply fertilizer or monitor crops and livestock. They help energy companies monitor their infrastructure. Cell phone towers could be inspected easily and safely without climbing. Drones could even enable emergency response teams to quickly map the extent of damage after natural disasters and deliver needed medical supplies. Based on the types of initiatives that have already been granted exemptions from the Federal Aviation Administration (FAA), drones used for film, video, and photography will likely lead the way in usage. These projects account for nearly half of all FAA approvals, but experts say higher margins in engineering, surveying, and agriculture could lead these industries to slowly come to the forefront.

North Dakota is one of six FAA UAS test sites conducting research to determine how to best integrate UAS into the national airspace through research, testing, and technology development. The FAA certified the Northern Plains UAS Test Site as the first site ready for operations in April 2014. The site covers more than half of the state, boasting 45,000 square miles of authorized air space – the largest such volume of any single state. In 2016, the North Dakota Department of Commerce announced it was awarded a five-year contract to support National Aeronautics and Space Administration (NASA) unmanned aircraft systems research.

"This NASA contract is more confirmation that our ongoing work to establish North Dakota as a national hub for UAS research, development, and commercialization is gaining more traction every day," said former Governor Jack Dalrymple, who led the state's efforts to make North Dakota a premier destination for America's growing UAS industry, in September 2015. "With onc of only six UAS test sites in the nation, the development of the Grand Sky UAS park, and many other assets, North Dakota is well positioned to lead this growing industry into a role of great importance to the nation."

UAS utilize a diverse group of local partners, including the University of North Dakota, North Dakota State University, North Dakota Department of Commerce,

North Dakota Aeronautics Commission, North Dakota Aviation Council, and the Office of the Adjutant General. The U.S. Air Force, Air National Guard, and border patrol have also supplied needed input as they have all piloted drones from the Grand Forks Air Force Base.

There could be seven million small drones in the sky by 2020, according to U.S. aviation officials, who believe as many as 2.7 million of them will be used for commercial purposes. These same officials predict small unmanned aircraft systems (sUAS) "will be the most dynamic growth sector within aviation" within a few years.

North Dakota is also ready to explore the next big advancement in UAS technology: flying beyond visual line of sight (BVLOS). Aviation officials also predict overall demand for commercial UAS will soar once regulations are cleared for BVLOS. The Northern Plains Test Site staff has been working with officials at Grand Sky, an aviation business park located near the Grand Forks Air Force Base, on concepts and procedures for BVLOS operations. With permission to fly beyond line of sight come new opportunities to expand projects the test site is leading, bring larger unmanned aircraft to the state for eventual commercial operations, and potentially attract new businesses that could develop in North Dakota.

USNS City Of Bismarck

On September 16, 2015, in Bismarck, Secretary of the Navy Ray Mabus announced the naming of a new ship the *USNS City of Bismarck* (T-EFP-9). It is a high-speed transport operated by a 24-member civilian crew. It is capable of carrying 312 personnel in theater-style seating while carrying all of their equipment on a large deck with a roll on/roll off ramp. It displaces 1,515 tons. It is 337 feet in length with a beam of 93 feet 6 inches. It has a catamaran hull and is capable of speeds of up to 42 miles per hour.

The *City of Bismarck* is being built at the Austal USA shipyard in Mobile, Alabama. Its keel laying ceremony was held on January 18, 2017, with former North Dakota State District Court Judge and former Attorney General Robert O. Wefald authenticating the keel. The *City of Bismarck* was christened in May 2017 and will be delivered to the U.S. Navy late in 2017. The second officer of the ship will be Patricia Evenson, a 2010 Bismarck Century High School graduate and a 2014 graduate of the U.S. Merchant Marine Academy.

✔ Information about the *USS North Dakota (B-29)* and *USS North Dakota (SSN-785)* may be found in the *2013-2015* and *2015-2017 North Dakota Blue Books.*

✔ Information regarding laws that honor women veterans can be found in the *2011-2013 North Dakota Blue Book.*

✔ Information regarding Honor Flights can be found in the *2011-2013 North Dakota Blue Book.*

✔ World War II art by Scott Nelson can be found in the *2007-2009* and *2009-2011 North Dakota Blue Books.*

✔ Personal stories of North Dakota soldiers during wartime can be found in the *2009-2011 North Dakota Blue Book.*

North Dakota Military Bases

North Dakota is the home of two U.S. Air Force bases and a Space Warning Squadron. These bases are important assets to the country, the state, and their respective communities.

Minot Air Force Base

Minot Air Force Base (AFB) is located approximately 13 miles north of the city of Minot and covers approximately 5,000 acres. Minot AFB has the distinction of being the only dual-wing Air Force base in the Department of Defense that houses two components of the nuclear triad: nuclear-tipped air-launched cruise missiles and Minuteman III intercontinental ballistic missiles. The base comprises two wings: the 5th Bomb Wing and the 91st Missile Wing. The 5th Bomb Wing flies the B-52H Stratofortress, the Air Force's long-range heavy bomber. The 91st Missile Wing is the home of the Minuteman III intercontinental ballistic missile.

The Minot AFB workforce consists of approximately 5,487 military and 549 civilian personnel, making it one of the largest single employers in North Dakota. The population totals more than 12,129, counting family members and Air Force retirees in the surrounding communities.

Minot AFB was activated February 15, 1957, as an Air Defense Command Base and was host to the 32d Fighter Group. Additional information about the base can be found at www.minot.af.mil.

Grand Forks Air Force Base

Grand Forks Air Force Base (AFB) is located 16 miles west of Grand Forks and covers roughly 5,422 acres. The base is comprised of the 319th Medical Group and the 69th Reconnaissance Group.

The 319th Medical Group is responsible for the medical support and care necessary to maintain the combat readiness of base personnel. The group medically supports a patient population by providing services, including family health, pediatrics, flight medicine, women's health, optometry, dental care, physical therapy, mental health, public health, pharmacy, laboratory, radiology, and TRICARE referrals to the network. The group deploys personnel in support of the wartime mission throughout the world.

The 69th Reconnaissance Group was activated on September 19, 2011, to conduct high altitude reconnaissance and surveillance and provide commanders with real-time intelligence using unmanned aerial vehicles, including the RQ-4 Block 40 Global Hawks UAV.

The base has approximately 2,300 active military and civilian personnel, including family members and retirees in the area.

Grand Forks AFB was activated February 8, 1957. Additional information about the base can be found at www.grandforks.af.mil.

Cavalier Air Force Station

The 10th Space Warning Squadron, Cavalier Air Force Station, keeps watch for sea-launched and intercontinental ballistic missiles launched toward North America. The squadron is a geographically separated unit of the 21st Space Wing at Peterson Air Force Base in Colorado and is located 15 miles south of the Canadian and U.S. border.

This small base currently operates the one surviving component of the U.S. Army's SAFEGUARD anti-ballistic missile system – the Perimeter Acquisition Radar site – built in the early 1970s and deactivated by Congress in February 1976. The site was transferred to the U.S. Air Force in October 1977 and its present name adopted. It became part of the Strategic Air Command on December 1, 1977.

It also supports the space surveillance network by providing space surveillance data, tracking, reporting, and space object identification and also maintains and operates the Perimeter Acquisition Radar Attack Characterization System (PARCS).

The operating unit was designated Detachment 5, 1st Space Wing (Space Command) on May 1, 1983. On August 1, 1986, it was re-designated and activated as the 10th Missile Warning Squadron and assigned to Headquarters 1st Space Wing. In 1992, it became part of the 21st Space Wing, headquartered at Peterson Air Force Base, Colorado.

Additional information about the Cavalier Air Force Station can be found by requesting a search for the station at www.peterson.af.mil.

Medal of Honor Memorial Recognizes State Veterans

A memorial honoring North Dakota's Medal of Honor recipients was dedicated at Roosevelt Park in Minot on July 4, 2007. The park is named after President Theodore Roosevelt, who was a Medal of Honor recipient.

Medal of Honor Memorial.

✔ See the *2007-2009 North Dakota Blue Book* for a listing of North Dakota's Medal of Honor recipients. The latest recipient, Woodrow Wilson Keeble, is recognized in the *2015-2017 North Dakota Blue Book*.

Representation at the Federal Level

North Dakota in Congress

The United States Congress is often known as "the people's branch" of government. It is comprised of 535 members, with 435 in the House of Representatives and 100 in the Senate. Congress serves as both a representative and governing body. Responsibilities of the congressional branch include the development and passage of legislation, constituent service, oversight responsibilities for departments and agencies in the executive branch, and appropriations authority.

To obtain more information about the U.S. Congress, visit www.congress.gov. The website contains information on the federal legislative process, pending legislation, the voting records of members of Congress, and links to congressional news and information. Additional information about the federal government, including links to documents such as the U.S. Constitution, can be found at www.usa.gov/about-the-us.

United States Senators

Under Article I, Section 3, of the U.S. Constitution, "The Senate of the United States shall be composed of two senators from each state...." The Constitution originally provided that senators were to be elected by the legislatures of each state. The 17th Amendment to the Constitution, effective May 31, 1913, amended the Constitution to allow for senators to be elected by popular vote of the people. Senators serve six-year terms and are elected in staggered terms.

Extensive and timely information on the U.S. Senate can be found at www.senate.gov.

United States Representatives

Under Article I, Section 2, of the U.S. Constitution, each state elects one or more representatives to Congress. The number of representatives is based upon each state's population in relation to that of the entire nation as enumerated by the federal decennial census. In 1929, the total number of House members was limited to 435. Had this not occurred, the size of the present House of Representatives using the initial formula would now exceed 8,000 members. Based on the 2010 census, each member of the U.S. House of Representatives represents an average population of 709,760.

Extensive and timely information on the U.S. House can be found at www.house.gov.

Profile of Present Congressional Delegation

U.S. Senator

Heidi Heitkamp

Birthplace
Breckenridge, MN

Party Affiliation
Democratic-NPL

Education
B.A. from University of North Dakota;
J.D. from Lewis and Clark College

Professional Experience
First female senator ever elected from North Dakota; Environmental Protection Agency, lawyer, 1980-1981; Office of the North Dakota State Tax Commissioner, lawyer, 1981-1986; Tax Commissioner of North Dakota, 1986-1992; Attorney General of North Dakota, 1992-2000; candidate for Governor of North Dakota, 2000; Dakota Gasification Company, director; elected to the United States Senate, 2012, took the oath of office on January 3, 2013

Committees
- Committee on Agriculture, Nutrition, and Forestry
  - Subcommittee on Commodities, Trade, and Risk Management (Ranking Member)
  - Subcommittee on Livestock, Marketing, and Agriculture Security
  - Subcommittee on Rural Development and Energy
- Committee on Banking, Housing, and Urban Affairs
  - Subcommittee on Economic Policy (Ranking Member)
  - Subcommittee on Housing, Transportation, and Community Development
  - Subcommittee on National Security and International Trade and Finance
- Committee on Homeland Security and Governmental Affairs
  - Permanent Subcommittee on Investigations
  - Subcommittee on Regulatory Affairs and Federal Management (Ranking Member)
- Committee on Indian Affairs
- Committee on Small Business and Entrepreneurship

U.S. Senator

John Hoeven

Birthplace
Bismarck

Party Affiliation
Republican

Education
B.A. from Dartmouth College; MBA from Northwestern University

Professional Experience
Bank of North Dakota, president and CEO, 1993-2000; Governor of North Dakota, 2000-2010; elected to the United States Senate, 2010 and 2016

Committees

- Committee on Agriculture, Nutrition, and Forestry
  - Nutrition, Specialty Crops, Food, and Agricultural Research
  - Rural Development and Energy
  - Commodities, Risk Management, and Trade
- Committee on Appropriations
  - Agriculture, Rural Development, Food and Drug Administration, and Related Agencies (Chairman)
  - Homeland Security
  - Military Construction, Veterans Affairs, and Related Agencies
  - Interior, Environment, and Related Agencies
  - Energy and Water Development
- Committee on Energy and Natural Resources
  - Energy
  - Public Lands, Forests, and Mining
  - National Parks
- Committee on Homeland Security and Governmental Affairs
  - Federal Spending Oversight and Emergency Management
- Committee on Indian Affairs (Chairman)

Contact Information for North Dakota's Senators

Senator Heidi Heitkamp

Email: senator@heitkamp.senate.gov
Web: http://heitkamp.senate.gov

Washington, D.C., Offices
516 Hart Office Building
Washington, DC 20510-3403
202-224-2043
202-224-7776 (Fax)

Bismarck District Offices
U.S. Federal Building, Room 228
220 East Rosser Avenue
Bismarck, ND 58501
701-258-4648
701-258-1254 (Fax)

Fargo District Offices
U.S. Federal Building, Room 306
657 Second Avenue North
Fargo, ND 58102
701-232-8030
701-232-6449 (Fax)

Grand Forks District Offices
33 South 3rd Street, Suite B
Grand Forks, ND 58201
701-775-9601
701-746-1990 (Fax)

Minot District Offices
U.S. Federal Building, Room 105
100 First Street Southwest
Minot, ND 58701
701-852-0703
701-838-8196 (Fax)

Dickinson District Office
40 First Avenue West, Suite 202
Dickinson, ND 58601
701-225-0974
701-225-3287 (Fax)

Senator John Hoeven

Email: senator@hoeven.senate.gov
Web: http://hoeven.senate.gov

338 Russell Senate Office Building
Washington, DC 20510-3402
202-224-2551
202-224-7999 (Fax)

U.S. Federal Building, Room 312
220 East Rosser Avenue, P.O. Box 2579
Bismarck, ND 58502
701-250-4618
701-250-4484 (Fax)

123 Broadway North, Suite 201
Fargo, ND 58102
701-239-5389
701-239-5112 (Fax)

102 North Fourth Street, Suite 108
Grand Forks, ND 58203
701-746-8972
701-746-5613 (Fax)

U.S. Federal Building, Suite 107
100 First Street Southwest
Minot, ND 58701
701-838-1361
701-838-1381 (Fax)

Western North Dakota
Williston, ND
701-580-4535

Due to the delay in receiving mail at the Washington, D.C., locations, constituents are encouraged to mail all correspondence to the North Dakota addresses.

U.S. Congressman

Kevin Cramer

Birthplace
Rolette; raised in Kindred

Party Affiliation
Republican

Education
Graduate of Kindred High School; B.A. from Concordia College in Moorhead, MN; M.A. in Management from University of Mary in Bismarck

Professional Experience
North Dakota Republican Party, chairman, 1991-1993; North Dakota State Tourism, director, 1993-1997; candidate for United States House of Representatives, 1996; North Dakota State Economic Development and Finance, director, 1997-2000; candidate for United States House of Representatives, 1998; North Dakota Public Service Commissioner, 2003-2012; elected to the United States House of Representatives, 2012, 2014, and 2016

Membership and Committees
- Committee on Energy and Commerce
  - Subcommittee on Communications and Technology
  - Subcommittee on Energy
  - Subcommittee on Environment

Contact Information for Congressman Kevin Cramer

Representative Kevin Cramer

www.cramer.house.gov

Washington, D.C., District Office
1717 Longworth House Office Building
Washington, DC 20515
202-225-2611
202-226-0893 (Fax)

Bismarck District Office
220 East Rosser Avenue
328 Federal Building
Bismarck, ND 58501
701-224-0355
702-224-0431 (Fax)

Fargo District Office
3217 Fiechtner Drive, Suite D
Fargo, ND 58103
701-356-2216
701-356-2217 (Fax)

Grand Forks District Office
4200 James Ray Drive, Office 600
Grand Forks, ND 58202
701-738-4880

Minot District Office
315 Main Street, Suite 203
Minot, ND 58701
701-839-0255

Due to the delay in receiving mail at the Washington, D.C., locations, constituents are encouraged to mail all correspondence to the North Dakota addresses.

Chronology of United States Senators from North Dakota

North Dakota was granted statehood on November 2, 1889. On this date, elections for congress and state-level officials were held. What follows is a chronology of senators elected to the U.S. Congress.

Gilbert A. Pierce (R) (1839-1901) 1889-1891
Elected 1889; defeated for re-election 1891

Lyman R. Casey (R) (1837-1914) 1889-1893
Elected 1889; defeated for re-election 1893

Henry C. Hansbrough (R) (1848-1933) 1891-1909
Elected 1891, 1897, 1903; defeated for re election 1909

William N. Roach (D) (1840-1902) 1893-1899

Porter J. McCumber (R) (1858-1933) 1899-1923
Elected 1899, 1905, 1911, 1916; defeated for re-election 1922

Martin N. Johnson (R) (1850-1909) 1909-1909
Elected 1909; died in office October 21, 1909

Fountain L. Thompson (D) (1854-1942) 1909-1910
Appointed December 7, 1909, to fill vacancy caused by Martin Johnson's death; resigned January 31, 1910

William E. Purcell (D) (1856-1928) 1910-1911
Appointed February 1, 1910, to fill vacancy caused by Fountain Thompson's resignation; defeated for re-election 1911

Asle J. Gronna (R) (1858-1922) 1911-1921
Elected 1911, 1914; defeated for re-election 1920

Edwin F. Ladd (R) (1859-1925) 1921-1925
Elected 1920; died in office June 25, 1925

Lynn J. Frazier (R) (1874-1947) 1923-1941
Elected 1922, 1928, 1934; defeated for re-election 1940

Gerald P. Nye (R) (1892-1971) 1925-1945
Appointed November 14, 1925, to fill vacancy caused by Edwin Ladd's death; elected 1926, 1932, 1938; defeated for re-election 1944

William Langer (R) (1886-1959) 1941-1959
Elected 1940, 1946, 1952, 1958; died in office November 8, 1959

John Moses (D) (1885-1945) 1945-1945
Elected 1944; died in office March 3, 1945

Milton R. Young (R) (1897-1983) 1945-1980
Appointed March 12, 1945, to fill vacancy caused by John Moses' death; elected in special election to fill unexpired term, 1946; elected 1950, 1956, 1962, 1968, 1974; did not seek re-election, 1980

C. Norman Brunsdale (R) (1891-1978) 1959-1960
Appointed November 19, 1959, to fill vacancy caused by William Langer's death; served until August 7, 1960

Quentin N. Burdick (D) (1908-1992)..1960-1992
Elected June 28, 1960, to complete William Langer's unexpired term; re-elected 1964, 1970, 1976, 1982, 1988, died in office September 8, 1992
Mark Andrews (R) (1926-)...1981-1986
Elected 1980; defeated for re-election 1986
Jocelyn Burdick (D) (1922-)... 1992
Appointed September 12, 1992, to fill vacancy caused by her husband's death; sworn in on September 16, 1992; served until December 14, 1992*
Kent Conrad (D) (1948-)..1987-2013
Elected 1986; did not seek re-election, 1992, but following Sen. Burdick's death, won a December 4, 1992, special election to fill Burdick's unexpired term; re-elected 1994, 2000, 2006
Byron L. Dorgan (D) (1942-) 1992-2011
Elected 1992; sworn into office December 15, 1992*, re-elected 1998, 2004; did not seek re-election, 2010
John H. Hoeven (R) (1957-) 2011-present
Elected 2010, 2016
Heidi Heitkamp (R) (1955-)... 2013-present
Elected 2012

* The year 1992 saw a series of unusual events that affected North Dakota's elected federal officeholders. See page 457 of the *2001-2003 North Dakota Blue Book.*

Chronology of United States House Members from North Dakota

The state of North Dakota, based on a 2010 census population of 672,591, has one at-large member of the House of Representatives. North Dakota had one representative from 1889 to 1902, two from 1903 to 1912, three from 1913 to 1932, two from 1933 to 1972, and one since 1973. House members serve for two years.

After every federal decennial (or 10-year) census, the number of House members from each state is determined by population. The U.S. Constitution guarantees every state one representative, no matter how small its population. By law, the total number of House members is set at 435. The number of members given to each state is determined by its proportion of the nation's total population as of the latest decennial census. Congressional districts are those geographical areas within each state represented by a single member of the House of Representatives. For states like North Dakota with only House member, the entire state is considered a congressional district, referred to as a district at large.

The following is a chronology of House members elected to the U.S. Congress.

One Representative, Elected At Large (1889-1902)

Henry C. Hansbrough (R) (1848-1933) 1889-1891
Elected 1889; did not seek re-election 1890
Martin N. Johnson (R) (1850-1909) 1891-1899
Elected 1890, 1892, 1894, 1896; did not seek re-election 1898
Burleigh F. Spalding (R) (1853-1934) 1899-1901
Elected 1898; did not seek re-election 1900
Thomas F. Marshall (R) (1854-1921) 1901-1903
Elected 1900

Two Representatives, Elected At Large (1903-1912)

Thomas F. Marshall (R) (1854-1921) 1903-1909
Elected 1902, 1904, 1906; did not seek re-election 1908
Burleigh F. Spalding (R) (1853-1934) 1903-1905
Elected 1902; defeated for re-election 1904
Asle J. Gronna (R) (1858-1922) 1905-1911
Elected 1904, 1906, 1908; did not seek re-election 1910
Louis B. Hanna (R) (1861-1948) 1909-1913
Elected 1908, 1910; did not seek re-election 1912
Henry T. Helgesen (R) (1857-1917) 1911-1913
Elected 1910

Three Representatives, Elected By District (1913-1932)

District 1
Henry T. Helgesen (R) (1857-1917) 1913-1917
Elected 1912, 1914, 1916; died in office April 10, 1917
John M. Baer (R) (1886-1970) 1917-1921
Elected at July 10, 1917, special election to fill unexpired term of Henry Helgesen elected 1918; defeated for re-election 1920
Olger B. Burtness (R) (1884-1960) 1921-1933
Elected 1920, 1922, 1924, 1926, 1928, 1930; defeated for re-election 1932

District 2
George M. Young (R) (1870-1932) 1913-1924
Elected 1912, 1914, 1916, 1918, 1920, 1922; resigned September 2, 1924
Thomas Hall (R) (1869-1958) 1924-1933
Elected November 4, 1924, to fill unexpired term of George Young; elected 1926, 1928, 1930; defeated for re-election 1932

District 3
Patrick D. Norton (R) (1876-1953) 1913-1919
Elected 1912, 1914, 1916; defeated for re-election 1918

James H. Sinclair (R) (1871-1943)..1919-1933
Elected 1918, 1920, 1922, 1924, 1926, 1928, 1930

Two Representatives, Elected At Large (1933-1962)

James H. Sinclair (R) (1871-1943)..1933-1935
Elected 1932; defeated for re-election 1934
William Lemke (R) (1878-1950)...1933-1941
Elected 1932, 1934, 1936, 1938; did not seek re-election
Usher L. Burdick (R) (1879-1960)..1935-1945
Elected 1934, 1936, 1938, 1940, 1942; did not seek re-election
Charles R. Robertson (R) (1889-1951)...1941-1943
Elected 1940; defeated for re-election 1942
William Lemke (R) (1878-1950)...1943-1950
Elected 1942, 1944, 1946, 1948; died in office May 30, 1950
Charles R. Robertson (R) (1889-1951)...1945-1949
Elected 1944, 1946; defeated for re-election 1948
Usher L. Burdick (R) (1879-1960)..1949-1959
Elected 1948, 1950, 1952, 1954, 1956; did not seek re-election 1958
Fred G. Aandahl (R) (1897-1966)...1951-1953
Elected 1950; did not seek re-election 1952
Otto Krueger (R) (1890-1963)...1953-1959
Elected 1952, 1954, 1956; did not seek re-election 1958
Quentin N. Burdick (D) (1908-1992)...1959-1963
Elected 1958; resigned August 8, 1960
Don L. Short (R) (1903-1982)...1959-1963
Elected 1958, 1960
Hjalmer C. Nygaard (R) (1906-1963)..1961-1963
Elected 1960

Two Representatives, Elected By District (1963-1972)

In 1959, the North Dakota Legislative Assembly created two congressional districts – East and West (Senate Bill No. 73, chapter 181, 1959 Laws of North Dakota).

East District
Hjalmer C. Nygaard (R) (1906-1963)..1963-1963
Elected 1962; died in office July 19, 1963
Mark Andrews (R) (1926-)..1963-1973
Elected October 22, 1963, special election to fill unexpired term of Hjalmer Nygaard; elected 1964, 1966, 1968, 1970

West District
Don L. Short (R) (1903-1982)...1963-1965
Elected 1962; defeated for re-election 1964

Rolland Redlin (D) (1920-2011)..1965-1967
Elected 1964; defeated for re-election 1966
Thomas S. Kleppe (R) (1919-2007) 1967-1971
Elected 1966, 1968; did not seek re-election 1970
Arthur A. Link (D) (1914-2010) 1971-1973
Elected 1970; did not seek re-election 1972

One Representative, Elected At Large (1973)

Mark Andrews (R) (1926-) 1973-1980
Elected 1972, 1974, 1976, 1978; did not seek re-election 1980 (elected to Senate 1980)
Byron L. Dorgan (D) (1942-) 1981-1992
Elected 1980, 1982, 1984, 1986, 1988, 1990, did not seek re-election 1992
Earl Pomeroy (D) (1952-) 1993-2011
Elected 1992*, 1994, 1996, 1998, 2000, 2002, 2004, 2006, 2008; defeated for re-election 2010
Rick Berg (R) (1959-) 2011-2012
Elected in 2010; did not seek re-election 2012
Kevin Cramer (R) (1961-)...2013-present
Elected in 2012, 2014, 2016

* Earl Pomeroy was elected in November 1992 to fill Dorgan's former seat in the House of Representatives and took his oath of office with other representatives on January 3, 1993. The U.S. Constitution specifically prohibits any House member from serving by appointment. As a result, North Dakota's only House seat was officially vacant between December 15, 1992, and January 3, 1993.

United States Judicial System

Justices of the United States Supreme Court

Years of birth, states from which appointed, and periods of service:

Appointed by President Reagan (1981-1989)
Kennedy, Anthony M. (1936-) CA (1988-present)

Appointed by President Bush (1989-1993)
Thomas, Clarence (1948-) GA (1991-present)

Appointed by President Clinton (1993-2001)
Ginsburg, Ruth Bader (1933-) NY (1993-present)
Breyer, Stephen (1938-) MA (1994-present)

Appointed by President George W. Bush (2001-2009)
Roberts, John G. (1955-) DC (2005-present) Chief Justice
Alito, Samuel Anthony (1950-) NJ (2006-present)

Appointed by President Obama (2009-present)
Sotomayor, Sonia (1954-) NY (2009-present)
Kagan, Elena (1960-) MA (2010-present)

Appointed by President Trump (2017-present)
Gorsuch, Neil M. (1967-) CO (2017-present)

Judges of the Eighth Circuit Court of Appeals

Circuit Justice: Samuel A. Alito, Jr.

Active Judges

Chief Judge:	Lavenski R. Smith (Little Rock, AR) appointed July 19, 2002
Chief Judge:	William Jay Riley (Omaha, NE) appointed August 3, 2001
Judge:	Roger L. Wollman (Sioux Falls, SD) appointed July 22, 1985
Judge:	James B. Loken (Minneapolis, MN) appointed October 17, 1990
Judge:	William Jay Riley (Omaha, NE) appointed August 3, 2001
Judge:	Steven M. Colloton (Des Moines, IA) appointed September 30, 2003
Judge:	Raymond W. Gruender (St. Louis, MO) appointed June 5, 2004
Judge:	Duane Benton (Kansas City, MO) appointed July 2, 2004
Judge:	Bobby E. Shepherd (El Dorado, AR) appointed October 10, 2006
Judge:	Jane Kelly (Cedar Rapids, IA) appointed April 24, 2013

Senior Judges

Pasco M. Bowman	(Kansas City, MO) appointed July 19, 1983
C. Arlen Beam	(Lincoln, NE) appointed November 9, 1987
Morris S. Arnold	(Little Rock, AR) appointed May 26, 1992
Michael J. Melloy	(Cedar Rapids, IA) appointed February 14, 2002
Diana E. Murphy	(Minneapolis, MN) appointed October 11, 1994

Judges of the Eighth Circuit Court of Appeals from North Dakota

Charles J. Vogel, (1898-1980) appointed by President Dwight Eisenhower, began 1954, assumed senior status 1968.
Myron H. Bright, (1919-2016) appointed by President Lyndon Johnson, began 1968, assumed senior status 1986.
Frank J. Magill, (1927-2013) appointed by President Ronald Reagan, began 1986, assumed senior status 1998.
John D. Kelly, (1934-1998) appointed by President William Clinton, began 1998, died less than two months after assuming office.
Kermit E. Bye, (1937-) appointed by President William Clinton, began 2000, assumed senior status 2015.

United States District Court for the District of North Dakota Judges

Alfred D. Thomas, (1837-1896) appointed by President Benjamin Harrison, served 1890-1896.
Charles F. Amidon, (1856-1937) appointed by President Grover Cleveland, served 1896-1928.
Andrew Miller, (1870-1960) appointed by President Warren Harding, served 1922-1941.
Charles J. Vogel, (1898-1980) appointed by President Franklin D. Roosevelt, served 1941-1954.
George S. Register, (1901-1972) appointed by President Dwight Eisenhower, served 1955-1971.
Ronald N. Davies, (1904-1996) appointed by President Dwight Eisenhower, served 1955-1971.
Paul Benson, (1918-2004) appointed by President Richard Nixon, served 1971-1985.
Bruce M. Van Sickle, (1917-2007) appointed by President Richard Nixon, served 1971-1985, assumed senior status 1985.
Patrick A. Conmy, (1934-) appointed by President Ronald Reagan, served 1985-2000.
Rodney S. Webb, (1935-2009) appointed by President Ronald Reagan, served 1987-2002.
Daniel L. Hovland, (1954-) appointed by President George W. Bush, served 2002-present.
Ralph R. Erickson, (1959-) appointed by President George W. Bush, served 2003-present.

Chief Judge
U.S. District Court

Ralph Erickson
Fargo

Personal
Born 1959 in Thief River Falls, MN; married to Michele, two children

Education
B.A. Jamestown College, 1980; J.D. University of North Dakota School of Law, 1984

Professional Experience
1984-94, private practice in West Fargo, ND; 1984-91, Assistant City Attorney, West Fargo, ND; 1990-91, Assistant City Attorney, Moorhead, MN; 1993-94, Cass County Magistrate, Cass County, ND; 1994, County Judge, Traill, Steele, Nelson, and Griggs Counties, ND; 1995-2003, District Judge, East Central Judicial District of North Dakota, chambered in Hillsboro and Fargo; 2003-present, U.S. District Court for the District of North Dakota

Judicial
Nominated September 12, 2002, by President George W. Bush; re-nominated January 7, 2003, by President George W. Bush, confirmed by Senate March 12, 2003, sworn in March 14, 2003. On June 7, 2016, Judge Erickson was nominated by President Donald Trump to serve on the U.S. Court of the Appeals for the Eighth Circuit. Senate confirmation hearings have not yet been held.

Judge
U.S. District Court

Daniel L. Hovland
Bismarck

Personal
Born 1954 in Moorhead, MN; married to Kristen, three children

Education
B.A. Concordia College (summa cum laude); J.D. University of North Dakota School of Law

Professional Experience
1979-80, law clerk to Chief Justice Ralph J. Erickstad of the North Dakota Supreme Court; 1980-83, Assistant Attorney General for the State of North Dakota; 1983-2002, private practice in Bismarck, ND; 2002-present, Chief Judge, U.S. District Court for the District of North Dakota

Judicial
Nominated for appointment June 27, 2002, by President George W. Bush, confirmed by Senate on November 14, 2002, sworn in November 26, 2002.

Judge
U.S. Bankruptcy Court
District of North Dakota

Shon Kaelberer Hastings
Fargo

Education
B.B.A. University of North Dakota, 1986; J.D. UND School of Law, 1993

Professional Experience
1993–1995, law clerk to the Honorable Karen K. Klein, United States Magistrate Judge, District of North Dakota; 1995–1997, private practice in Minneapolis, MN; 1998–2011, Assistant United States Attorney, District of North Dakota

Judicial Experience
Appointed U.S. Bankruptcy Judge, District of North Dakota, on September 9, 2011, for a 14-year term.

U.S. Commissioners and Magistrate Judges for the United States District Court for the District of North Dakota

Kenneth M. Knutson served as U.S. Commissioner in Minot from 1958 to 1970; served as part-time Magistrate Judge in Minot from 1970 to 1994.

David Kessler served as U.S. Commissioner in Grand Forks from 1959 to 1970; served as part-time Magistrate Judge in Grand Forks from 1970 to 1990.

Harry J. Pearce served as U.S. Commissioner in Bismarck in 1970; served as part-time Magistrate Judge in Bismarck from 1970 to 1977.

Everett E. Palmer served as part-time Magistrate Judge in Williston from 1970 to 1974.

Odin J. Strandness served as part-time Magistrate Judge in Fargo from 1971 to 1975.

Ted Weisenburger served as part-time Magistrate Judge in Devils Lake from 1972 to 1974.

Robert D. Hartl served as part-time Magistrate Judge in Rolla from 1970 to 1972.

Howard A. Olson served as part-time Magistrate Judge in Minnewaukan from 1970 to 1971.

John E. Rilling served as part-time Magistrate Judge in Fargo from 1970 to 1971.

Charles C. Chinquist served as part-time Magistrate Judge in Rolla from 1973 to 1975.

William A. Hill served as part-time Magistrate Judge in Fargo from 1975 to 1984.

Lewis C. Jorgenson served as part-time Magistrate Judge in Minnewaukan from 1975 to 1979.

Arne F. Boyum served as part-time Magistrate Judge in Rolla from 1976 to 1980 and 1981 to 1984.

Alan K. Grindberg served as part-time Magistrate Judge in Bismarck from 1977 to 1978.

Ronald M. Dosch served as part-time Magistrate Judge in Devils Lake from 1979 to 1985.

Dwight C. H. Kautzmann served as part-time Magistrate Judge in Bismarck from 1978 to 1994; served as part-time Magistrate Judge in Bismarck and Minot from 1994-1996; served as full-time Magistrate Judge in Bismarck 1996 to 2004.

Karen K. Klein served as part-time Magistrate Judge in Fargo in 1985; served as full-time Magistrate Judge in Fargo from 1985 to 2014; designated Chief Magistrate Judge in 2004.

Alice R. Senechal served as part-time Magistrate Judge in Grand Forks from 1990 to 2014; serves as full-time Magistrate Judge in Fargo from 2015 to present.

Charles S. Miller, Jr., serves as full-time Magistrate Judge in Bismarck from 2004 to present.

Magistrate Judge
U.S. District Court

Charles S. Miller, Jr.
Mandan

Personal
Born in 1951, Fargo

Education
B.A. University of North Dakota, 1973; J.D. University of North Dakota, 1976

Professional Experience
1976-1977, private practice West Fargo, ND; 1977-1982, staff attorney Basin Electric Power Cooperative; 1982-1987, Assistant U.S. Attorney for District of North Dakota; 1987-2004, private practice Bismarck, ND; 2004 to present, Magistrate Judge U.S. District Court North Dakota

Judicial
Appointed in 2004 and 2012 for eight-year term as federal Magistrate Judge, chambered in Bismarck.

Magistrate Judge
U.S. District Court

Alice R. Senechal
Grand Forks

Personal
Born in 1955, Rugby

Education
B.S. North Dakota State University, 1977; J.D. University of Minnesota, 1984 (cum laude)

Professional Experience
1984-86, law clerk to Hon. Bruce M. Van Sickle, United States District Court, District of North Dakota; 1986 to present, private practice (part-time), Grand Forks, ND

Judicial
Appointed United States Magistrate Judge (part-time) November 15, 1990; appointed United States Magistrate Judge (full-time) February 2015, chambered in Fargo.

Chapter Four

Judicial Branch

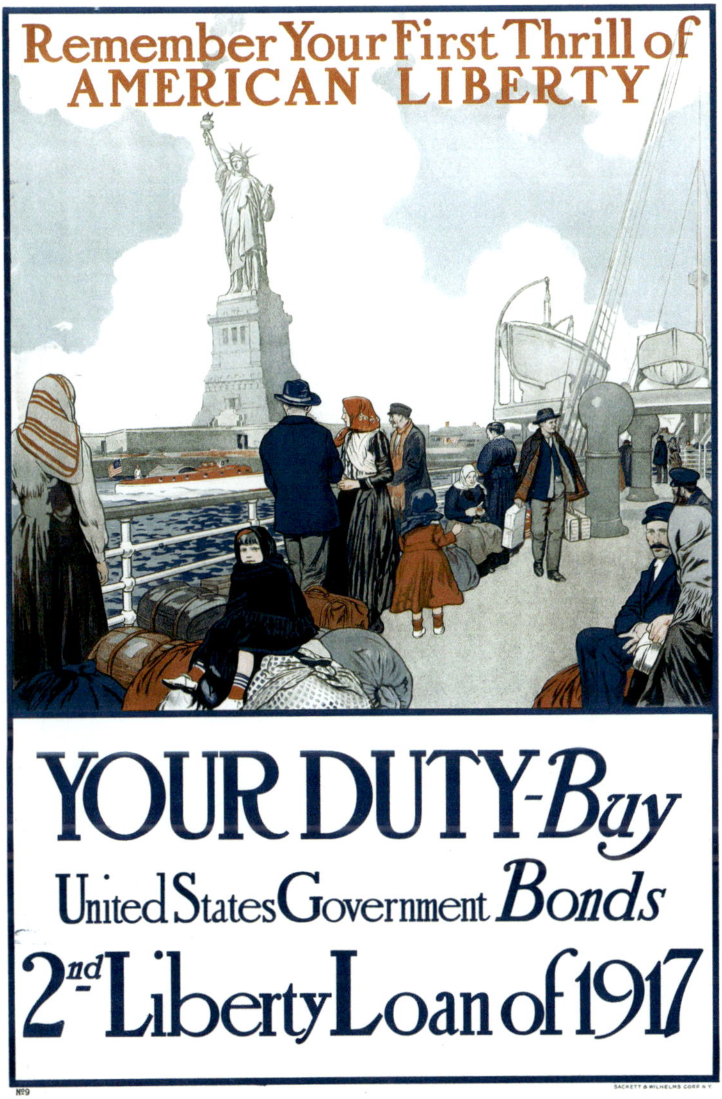

Judiciary

Supreme Court
The Supreme Court is the appellate court of final authority in North Dakota. It consists of five justices.

Court of Appeals
The Court of Appeals is an intermittent court established to assist the Supreme Court with its caseload. Judges of this court are detailed from the ranks of retired justices or sitting district court judges.

District Court
This court is the trial court with original and general jurisdiction over all state cases. There are 51 court judgeships assigned to eight judicial districts.

Municipal Courts
This court hears violations of municipal ordinances. Appeals are heard de novo in district court. There are approximately 65 municipal judges serving 118 municipal courts.

Profile of the North Dakota Judicial System

Structure of the Court System

The original constitution of the state of North Dakota created a judicial system consisting of the Supreme Court, district courts, county courts, and such municipal courts as provided by the law. This judicial structure remained intact until 1959 when the Legislative Assembly abolished the justice of peace courts in the state.

The adoption of a new judicial article to the state constitution in 1976 significantly modified the constitutional structure of the judicial system. The new judicial article vested the judicial powers of the state in a unified judicial system consisting of a Supreme Court, district courts, and such other courts as provided by law. Thus, under the new judicial article, only the Supreme Court and the district courts retained their status as constitutional courts. All other courts in the state are statutory courts.

In 1981, the Legislative Assembly further altered the structure of the judicial system by enacting legislation that replaced the multi-level county court structure with a uniform system of county courts throughout the state. This new county court structure became effective on January 1, 1983.

With the county court system in place, the judicial system of the state consisted of the Supreme Court, district courts, county courts, and municipal courts.

This changed again as the county courts were abolished by 1991 House Bill 1517, effective January 1, 1995. The bill, with a final completion date of January 1, 2001, also transferred the jurisdictional workload to an expanded number of district judges. The 1991 total of 26 county judges and 27 district court judges had been reduced to 42 district court judges by January 1, 2001, as provided by statute. The number of judges increased to 44 in 2010, to 47 in 2013, and to 51 in 2015.

Administrative Authority

The 1976 constitutional judicial article clarified the administrative responsibilities of the Supreme Court by designating the chief justice as the administrative head of the judicial system and by granting the chief justice the authority to assign judges for temporary duty in any non-federal or tribal court in the state. It also acknowledged the Supreme Court's rulemaking authority in such areas as court procedure and attorney supervision.

Selection and Removal of Judges

All judges in North Dakota are elected in nonpartisan elections. Justices of the Supreme Court are elected for 10-year terms, district court judges for six-year terms, and municipal court judges for four-year terms.

Vacancies in the Supreme Court and the district courts can be filled either by a special election called by the governor or by gubernatorial appointment. However, before a vacancy can be filled by gubernatorial appointment, the Judicial Nominating Committee must first submit a list of nominees to the governor from which the governor makes an appointment. Whether the vacancy is filled by a special election or by appointment, the appointed judge serves for a minimum of two years and then until the next general election, at which time the office is filled by election for the remainder of the term.

If a vacancy occurs in a municipal court, it is filled by the executive officer of the municipality with the consent of the governing body of the municipality.

Under the North Dakota Constitution, only Supreme Court justices and district court judges can be removed from office by impeachment. All judges are subject to removal, censure, suspension, retirement, or other disciplinary action for misconduct by the Supreme Court upon the recommendation of the Judicial Conduct Commission. Other methods for the retirement, removal, and discipline of judges can be established by the Legislative Assembly.

Chief Justice

Gerald W. VandeWalle

Personal
Born and raised in Noonan, North Dakota.

Education
Awarded a Juris Doctor (JD) Magna Cum Laude from UND School of Law in 1958. Editor of *North Dakota Law Review* in senior year.

Professional Experience
Served as an assistant attorney general from 1958 to 1975. Appointed first assistant attorney general in 1975. As an assistant attorney general, held portfolios for elementary, secondary, and higher education, oil and gas, and the state retirement system. Served as the North Dakota delegate to the Interstate Oil Compact Commission. Appointed to the Supreme Court in August 1978 and elected to serve the unexpired term in November 1978. Elected for a full 10-year term in 1984 and re-elected in 1994, 2004, and 2014. Elected Chief Justice in January 1993 by vote of the district court judges and Supreme Court justices. Re-elected as Chief Justice January 1995, 2000, 2005, 2010, and 2015.

Memberships and Committees
Chaired North Dakota Judicial Conference, 1985 to 1987; President of the Conference of Chief Justices, 2000 to 2001; appointed by Chief Justice Rehnquist to the Federal/State Jurisdiction Committee of the Judicial Conference of the United States; Chairperson of the Section on Legal Education and Admissions to the Bar of the American Bar Association (ABA), 2000 to 2001; recipient of the University of North Dakota Sioux Award, 1992; recipient of the North Dakota State Bar Association Distinguished Service Award, June 1998; inducted into the Warren E. Burger Society, October 2002; recipient of the National Center for State Courts Paul C. Reardon Award, 2003; American Inns of Court Professionalism Award for the Eighth Circuit, 2008; recipient of the ABA Section of Legal Education and Admissions to the Bar 2009 Robert J. Kutak Award; 42nd recipient of the North Dakota Theodore Roosevelt Rough Rider Award, 2015; recipient of National Center for State Courts Harry L. Carrico Award, 2015; recipient of National Lambda Chi Alpha Fraternity Order of Achievement, 2015; recipient of University of North Dakota Honorary Degree of Doctor of Letters, 2015; recipient of University of Mary Degree of Doctor of Leadership, 2015.

Justice

Daniel J. Crothers

Personal
Born January 1957 and raised in Fargo, American Samoa, and Albuquerque, New Mexico; married to Holly Crothers; two children.

Education
Graduated from University of North Dakota, 1979. Major studies in Political Science and Journalism, Early American History Minor, and earned a Juris Doctorate from the University of North Dakota School of Law, 1982.

Professional Experience
Law Clerk, New Mexico Court of Appeals, Santa Fe, New Mexico, 1982 to 1983; Assistant State's Attorney, Walsh County, ND, 1983 to 1984; private practice, 1983 to 1986 in Santa Fe, Grafton, and Fargo, 1987 to 2005; member and partner with the Nilles Law Firm, Fargo; appointed June 2005 to the North Dakota Supreme Court and elected to unexpired four-year term November 2008 and 10-year term in 2012.

Memberships and Committees
President of the State Bar Association of North Dakota from 2001 to 2002 and has served as a member and chair of several Bar Association and Court committees relating to lawyer and judicial ethics and professional conduct. Currently serves on North Dakota's Committee on Judiciary Standards; Chair of the Court Services Administration Committee and member of the American Bar Association Center for Professional Responsibility Policy Implementation Committee; past-chair of the ABA Standing Committee on Client Protection and Policy Implementation Committee.

Justice

Lisa K. Fair McEvers

Personal
Born in Grafton and raised in Minto, North Dakota; married to James P. McEvers; one child and three step-children.

Education
Graduated Cum Laude from the University of North Dakota in 1993 with a BBA in Information Management. Awarded a Juris Doctorate, with distinction, from the University of North Dakota School of Law in 1997.

Professional Experience
Worked for the Northeast Judicial District in court administration prior to attending law school. After law school, law clerk to the North Dakota Supreme Court, 1997-1998 term; private legal practice, 1998-2001; Cass County Assistant State's Attorney, 2001 to 2005; appointed North Dakota Commissioner of Labor by Governor John Hoeven in 2005; appointed District Judge by Governor John Hoeven in 2010 and elected to the post in 2012; appointed by Governor Jack Dalrymple to the North Dakota Supreme Court to fill the vacancy created by the retirement of Justice Mary Muehlen Maring in 2011, and in November 2016, elected to complete that term set for re-election in 2018.

Memberships and Committees
Served on the Judicial Branch Education Committee, 1992 to 1994; the Judiciary Standards Committee, 2004 to 2009; the State Bar Association's Commission for Continuing Education, 2006 to 2010, Chair, 2009-2010; the Pattern Jury Instruction Commission, 2012 to 2013; the Domestic Violence Benchbook Subcommittee, 2009 to 2011; the Rough Rider Industries Prison Advisory Board, 2005 to 2013; and the Cass County Resource Committee on Elder Abuse, 2013. Currently, chairs the Juvenile Drug Court Advisory Committee, 2014 to present; the Juvenile Policy Board, 2013 to present; the Personnel Policy Board, 2013 to present; the Commission on the Alternatives to Incarceration, 2011 to present; the North Dakota Judges Association, 2013 to present, President, 2014 to 2015; and the United Tribes Criminal Justice Advisory Board, 2014 to present; the Court Technology Committee's File and Serve User Group Subcommittee, 2015 to present; and the North Dakota Attorney General's Human Trafficking Commission, 2015 to present.

Justice

Jerod E. Tufte

Personal
Born in Minot, North Dakota, in 1975; married to Mylynn Tufte; three children.

Education
Attended West Fargo Public Schools; BS Computer Engineering from Case Western Reserve University, Cleveland, Ohio; and JD from Arizona State University, Tempe, Arizona.

Professional Experience
Worked as computer engineer for Motorola prior to law school. Private practice in Phoenix, Arizona, and Steele, North Dakota. Appointed Kidder County State's Attorney in 2005 and elected in 2006 and 2010. Judge Advocate, North Dakota Army National Guard from 2008-2016, including overseas service in Kosovo. Legal counsel to Governor Jack Dalrymple from 2011-2014. Appointed District Court Judge in 2014 and elected to Supreme Court in 2016.

Membership and Committees
Member of Court Technology Committee and Joint Committee on Attorney Standards. Chair, Judicial Conference Standing Committee on Legislation. Past member of Judicial Ethics Advisory Committee.

Justice

Jon J. Jensen

Personal
Born in 1965 in Grand Forks and raised in Grand Forks, Helena, Montana, and East Grand Forks, Minnesota; married to Linda Bata.

Education
Graduated with a BS in Accounting from Minnesota State University Mankato, Mankato, Minnesota, 1987. Earned a Juris Doctorate from the University of North Dakota School of Law, 1990.

Professional Experience
Law Clerk, North Dakota Supreme Court, Bismarck, 1990 to 1991; private practice, Grand Forks, 1991 to 2013; Northwest Airlines, Egan, Minnesota, 2000-2001; District Judge, Northeast Central Judicial District, Grand Forks, 2013-2017, appointed by Governor Jack Dalrymple in 2013 and elected to a six-year term in 2016; appointed to the North Dakota Supreme Court by Governor Doug Burgum in August 2017.

Memberships and Committees
Caseflow Management Committee, 2016-2017. President, Grand Forks County Bar Association, 1999. Past Chair, North Dakota CPA Taxation Committee. Chair (North Dakota), ABA Real Property Taxation Section, 1996-1999. Member: American Bar Association; North Dakota State Bar Association Taxation Section; Minnesota State Bar Association; Ninth Judicial District (Minnesota) Bar Association. Member: North Dakota Society of Public Accountants – Taxation Section; Grand Forks County Society of Public Accountants.

North Dakota Supreme Court

The North Dakota Supreme Court has five justices. Each justice is elected for a 10-year term in a nonpartisan election. The terms of the justices are staggered so only one judgeship is scheduled for election every two years. Each justice must be a licensed attorney and a citizen of the United States and North Dakota.

One member of the Supreme Court is elected as Chief Justice by the justices of the Supreme Court and the district court judges. The term is for five years or until the justice's elected term on the court expires. The Chief Justice's duties include presiding over Supreme Court conferences, representing the judiciary at official state functions, and serving as the administrative head of the judicial system.

Functions and Powers

The North Dakota Supreme Court is the highest court for the state. It has two major types of responsibilities: adjudicative and administrative.

In its adjudicative capacity, the Supreme Court is primarily an appellate court with jurisdiction to hear appeals from decisions of the district courts. All appeals from these courts must be accepted for review. In addition, the court also has original jurisdiction in matters, such as certain habeas corpus cases and decisions of the secretary of state in the petition process, and can issue such original and remedial writs as are necessary to exercise this authority.

The state constitution requires a quorum, composed of a majority of the justices, is necessary before the court can conduct its judicial business. It also stipulates the court cannot declare a legislative enactment unconstitutional unless four of the justices so decide. When the court decides an appeal, it is required to issue a written opinion stating the rationale for its decision. Any justice disagreeing with the majority decision may issue a dissenting opinion that explains the reasons for the disagreement with the majority.

In its administrative capacity, the Supreme Court has major responsibilities for ensuring the efficient and effective operation of all courts in the state, except federal and tribal courts; maintaining high standards of judicial conduct; supervising the legal profession; and promulgating procedural rules that allow for the orderly and efficient transaction of judicial business. Within each area of administrative responsibility, the court has general rulemaking authority.

The court carries out its administrative responsibilities with the assistance of various committees and boards. It exercises authority to admit and license attorneys through the State Board of Law Examiners. Supervision of legal ethics is exercised through the Disciplinary Board of the Supreme Court and supervision of judicial conduct is exercised through the Judicial Conduct Commission. Continuing review and study of specific subject areas within its administrative jurisdiction are provided through five advisory committees: the Joint Procedure Committee, the Joint Committee on Attorney Standards, the Judiciary Standards Committee, the Court Services Administration Committee, and the Judicial Planning Committee. Other committees, such as the Continuing Judicial Education Commission, Personnel Policy Board, and the North Dakota Legal Counsel for Indigents Commission, also provide valuable assistance to the Supreme Court in important administrative areas.

Administrative personnel of the Supreme Court also play a vital role in helping the court fulfill its administrative functions. The clerk of the Supreme Court supervises the calendaring and assignment of cases, oversees the distribution and publication of opinions and administrative rules and orders, and decides certain procedural motions filed with the court. The state law librarian supervises the operation of the state law library.

North Dakota Court of Appeals

The Court of Appeals was established in 1987 to assist the Supreme Court in managing its workload.

Since it was established, the Court of Appeals has written opinions disposing of 90 cases.

Cases assigned to the Court of Appeals under Administrative Rule 27 may include family law issues, appeals from administrative agency decisions, appeals from trial court orders on motions for summary judgment, appeals involving cases originating under the Uniform Juvenile Court Act, and appeals from misdemeanor convictions.

Authorization for the Court of Appeals must be granted by the Legislature every four years.

Supreme Court Communication Information

Supreme Court
600 East Boulevard Avenue
Judicial Wing, 1st Floor
Bismarck, ND 58505-0530
Telephone: 701-328-2221
Fax: 701-328-4480
Website: www.ndcourts.gov

Penny Miller
Clerk of the Supreme Court
Telephone: 701-328-2221
Fax: 701-328-4480
Email: pmiller@ndcourts.gov
TTY: 800-366-6888

Sally A. Holewa
State Court Administrator
Telephone: 701-328-4216
Fax: 701-328-2092
Email: sholewa@ndcourts.gov

Ted Smith
Law Librarian
Telephone: 701-328-4594
Fax: 701-328-3609
Email: tsmith@ndcourts.gov
TTD: 701-328-2885

Office of State Court Administrator

Article VI, Section 3, of the North Dakota Constitution authorizes the chief justice of the Supreme Court to appoint a court administrator for the unified judicial system. Pursuant to this constitutional authority, the Supreme Court has outlined the powers, duties, qualifications, and term of the state court administrator in Administrative Rule 1. The duties delegated to the state court administrator include assisting the Supreme Court in the preparation and administration of the judicial budget, providing for judicial education services, coordinating technical assistance to all levels of courts, planning for statewide judicial needs, and administering a personnel system.

Judicial Education

The office of state court administrator, under the guidance of the Judicial Branch Education Commission and through the director of education and communication, develops and implements education programs for all judicial and non-judicial personnel. To supplement the education programs presently being offered, an audio and video library has been established and is housed in the Supreme Court Law Library. To complement this library, the University of North Dakota Law School provides additional materials upon request.

Research and Planning

Staff services are provided to the Judicial Planning Committee and other advisory committees of the Supreme Court by staff in the office of state court administrator. The duties of these staff personnel include research, bill drafting, rule drafting, arrangement of committee meetings, and any other tasks assigned by various committees. Specific activities and projects of the Supreme Court standing committees are provided in a latter section of this chapter.

Personnel Management

To ensure uniformity in personnel administration across districts, personnel policies and a pay and classification plan for district court employees were developed under the direction of the state court administrator. This program is administered by the director of human resources. The Personnel Policy Board provides oversight and guidance.

Fiscal Responsibilities

One of the primary functions of the office of state court administrator is to obtain adequate financial resources for judicial operations and to manage these resources.

In viewing the judicial budget, it should be noted the state funds the Supreme Court, the Judicial Conduct Commission, approximately half of the expenses of the Disciplinary Board, and district court expenses, including 14 of the clerk of district court offices. The remaining clerk offices are funded by the state through a service contract. Municipal courts are funded by the municipalities they serve.

Information Technology

The state court administrator's office is responsible for providing information technology services to the judicial branch. These services are provided through the judicial branch Information Technology Department.

Through the Unified Court Information System and the Data Warehouse, the Information Technology Department provides access to district court case information to more than 2,000 court and non-judicial personnel.

North Dakota Administrative Units
Judicial Districts 2017

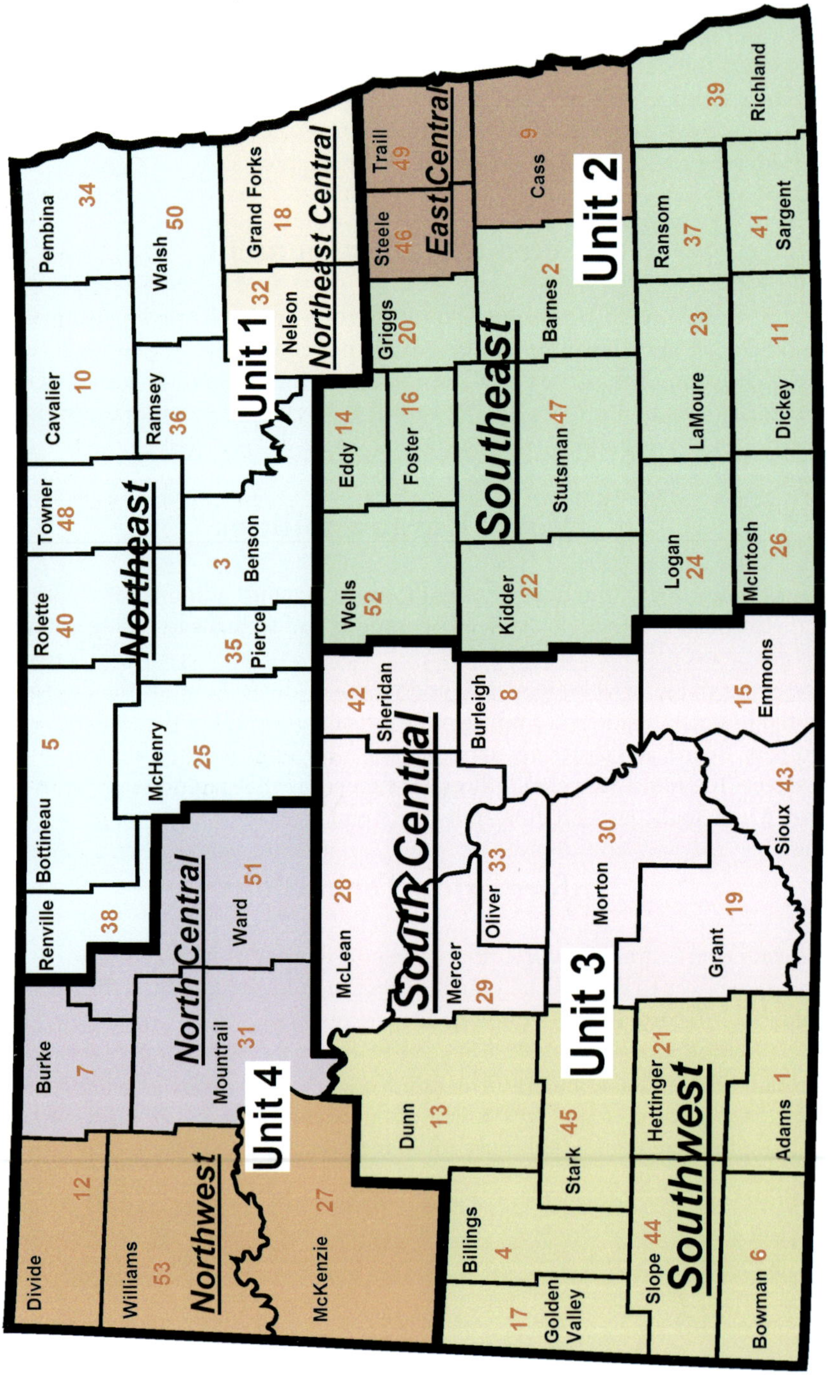

District Courts

There are district court services in each of the state's 53 counties. The district courts are funded by the state of North Dakota. The district courts have original and general jurisdiction in all cases except as otherwise provided by law. They have the authority to issue original and remedial writs. They have exclusive jurisdiction in criminal cases and have general jurisdiction for civil cases.

The district courts also serve as the juvenile courts in the state and have exclusive and original jurisdiction over any minor who is alleged to be unruly, delinquent, or deprived. This jurisdiction includes cases in which a female minor is seeking judicial authorization to obtain an abortion without parental consent. The responsibility for supervising and counseling juveniles who have been brought into court lies with the judicial branch of government in North Dakota.

The district courts are also the appellate courts of first instance for appeals from the decisions of many administrative agencies. Acting in this appellate capacity, district courts do not conduct a retrial of the case. Their decisions are based on a review of the record of the administrative proceeding conducted by the administrative agency.

Under the authority granted to the Supreme Court in Article VI, Section 3 of the Constitution of North Dakota, the court has organized the district courts into eight judicial districts operating within four administrative units. In each district, there is a presiding judge who oversees the courts' judicial services in the district's geographical area. The duties of the presiding judge, as established by the Supreme Court, include convening regular meetings of the judges within the judicial district to discuss issues of common concern, assigning cases among the judges of the district, and assigning judges within the judicial district in cases of demand for change of judge. The administrative unit structure consolidates the managerial and administrative functions of the courts within the districts under one trial court administrator for every two districts. The trial court administrator serves as a liaison with governmental and other agencies and is responsible for personnel, fiscal, facilities, contracts, and records management for the unit.

There are 51 district judges in the state. Nine judges in four chamber city locations serve the South Central Judicial District. Six judges in the Northwest Judicial District serve in two chamber city locations. Five judges serve the North Central Judicial district in one chamber city location. Nine judges serve the East Central Judicial District in two chamber city locations. Five judges serve the Northeast Central Judicial District in one chamber city location. Six judges serve the Northeast Judicial District in five chamber city locations. Seven judges serve the Southeast Judicial District in five chamber city locations. Four judges serve the Southwest Judicial District in one chamber city location. All district court judges are required by the state constitution to be licensed North Dakota attorneys, citizens of the United States, and residents of North Dakota.

The office of district court judge is an elected position which is filled every six years in a nonpartisan election held in the district in which the judge will serve. If a vacancy in the office of district judge occurs, the Supreme Court must determine whether the vacancy should be filled or whether the vacant office should be abolished or transferred. If the vacancy is to be filled, the governor may either fill the vacancy by appointing a candidate from a list of nominees submitted by the Judicial Nominating Committee or by calling a special election to fill the vacancy. If the vacancy is filled by the nomination process, the appointed judge serves for a minimum of two years and then until the next general election, at which time the office is filled by election for the remainder of the term.

Northeast Judicial District – Administrative Unit 1

Presiding Judge Laurie A. Fontaine

Court Administrator Scott Johnson
Asst. Court Administrator Kelly Hutton
Pembina County Courthouse
301 Dakota Street West, #3
Cavalier, ND 58220-4100
Telephone: 701-265-8783

LAURIE A. FONTAINE, Cavalier, Presiding

Born in 1956 in Grand Forks and raised in Cavalier. BS, Mayville State University, 1978. JD, UND School of Law, 1983. Private practice in Pembina County, 1983 to 1998. Pembina County State's Attorney, 1987 to 1998. Elected District Judge in 1998; re-elected 2004, 2010, and 2016. Elected Presiding Judge in 2013.

ANTHONY SWAIN BENSON, Bottineau

Born in 1970. BUS, NDSU, 1994. JD, UND School of Law, 2000. Private practice in Bottineau, 2000 to 2015. Assistant Bottineau County State's Attorney, 2000 to 2015. Appointed District Judge in 2015.

DONOVAN FOUGHTY, Devils Lake

Born in 1955 in Devils Lake. BA, UND. JD, UND School of Law, 1983. Admitted to the North Dakota Bar in 1983. County Judge, 1987 to 1994. Elected District Judge in 1994; re-elected 1996, 2002, 2008, and 2014. Presiding Judge, 2007 to 2012.

M. RICHARD GEIGER, Grafton

Born in 1951 in Grand Forks. BA, NDSU, 1973. JD, UND School of Law, 1979. Member of North Dakota Law Review, 1978 to 1979. Admitted to North Dakota Bar in 1979. Private practice in Grafton, 1979 to 1987. County Judge Walsh, Pembina, and Cavalier Counties, 1987 to 1994. Past President of Northeast District Bar Association, 1990 to 1992. Board of Governors, State Bar Association, 1990 to 1992. Member, ABA. Elected District Judge in 1994; re-elected 2000, 2006, and 2012. Presiding Judge, 2001 to 2007. Resigned effective October 31, 2017.

MICHAEL P. HURLY, Rugby

Born in 1976. BS, NDSU, 2000. JD, UND School of Law, 2005. Clerk for Montana 16th Judicial District. Private practice in Devils Lake, 2007 to 2017. Appointed District Judge in 2017.

LONNIE OLSON, Devils Lake

Born in 1962. Graduate, Devils Lake Central High School, 1980. BA, UND, 1984. JD, UND School of Law, 1987. Private practice, 1987 to 1989. Special Assistant State's Attorney for the Lake Region Child Support Enforcement Unit, 1990. Elected Ramsey County States Attorney, 1990. Elected District Judge in 2016.

Northeast Central Judicial District – Administrative Unit 1

Presiding Judge Vacant

Court Administrator Scott Johnson
Asst. Court Administrator Kelly Hutton
Grand Forks County Courthouse
124 South 4th Street
Grand Forks, ND 58201
Telephone: 701-787-2730

DONALD HAGER, Grand Forks

Born in 1955. BSBA, Mayville State University, 1983. JD, UND School of Law, 1986. Served in the U.S. Navy, 1974 to 1980. Private practice in Larimore, 1986 to 2014. Appointed District Judge in 2014.

JASON McCARTHY, Grand Forks

Born in 1971. BA, Minnesota State University Moorhead, 1995. JD, with distinction, UND School of Law, 1999. Served in the Grand Forks County State's Attorney's Office for 13 years. Appointed District Judge in 2016.

LOLITA G. ROMANICK, Grand Forks

Born in 1956. BS, UND, 1979. JD, University of Idaho School of Law, 1983. BA, UND, 1995. Private practice in Grand Forks and Minot, 1984 to 2014. Appointed District Judge in 2014.

JOHN A. THELEN, Grand Forks

Born in 1952. BS, 1978. JD, UND School of Law, 1981. Private practice, 1981 to 2009. Judicial Referee and Magistrate, 2009 to 2015. Appointed District Judge in 2015.

East Central Judicial District – Administrative Unit 2

Presiding Judge Frank L. Racek

Court Administrator Rodney Olson
Asst. Court Administrator Chris Iverson
Cass County Courthouse
PO Box 2806
Fargo, ND 58108-2806
Telephone: 701-451-6940

FRANK L. RACEK, Fargo, Presiding

Born in 1957. BA, Cum Laude, St. John's University, Collegeville, MN, 1979. JD, with distinction, UND School of Law, 1982. Private practice in Fargo, 1982 to 1988. Appointed Judge of County Court, 1988. Elected District Judge in 1994; re-elected 1996, 2002, 2008, and 2014. Elected Presiding Judge in 2010. CPA certificate.

NORMAN G. ANDERSON, Fargo

Born in 1950 in Fargo. U.S. Marine Corps, 1969 to 1971. BA, UND, 1975. MA, University of Minnesota, 1977. JD, UND School of Law, 1982. Law Clerk, North Dakota Supreme Court, 1982 to 1983. Assistant U.S. Attorney, 1983 to 2007. Contract Hearing Officer for the state of North Dakota, 2007 to 2013. Appointed District Judge in 2013; elected in 2016.

SUSAN L. BAILEY, Fargo

Born in 1963. BS, UND, 1986. MA, UND, 1988. JD, UND School of Law, 1997. Served as Administrative Law Judge, 2006 to 2014. Municipal Judge of West Fargo and Horace, 2004 to 2014. Municipal Judge of Tower City, Kindred, and Davenport, 2009 to 2014. Assistant Cass County State's Attorney, 2001 to 2006. Elected District Judge in 2014.

DOUGLAS R. HERMAN, Fargo

Born in 1949. BA, Baylor University, 1971. JD, University of Michigan Law School, 1975. General counsel, Great Plains Software, 1997 to 2004. Private practice, 1977 to 1997. Appointed District Judge in 2004; elected in 2006; re-elected 2010 and 2016.

JOHN C. IRBY, Fargo

Born in 1956 in Warroad, MN. Graduate, Falls Senior High School, International Falls, MN. BA, Moorhead State University. JD, University of Wyoming. Legal intern for Legal Services for Southeastern Wyoming, Inc., 1980. Private practice in Casselton, 1982 to 2002. Casselton City Prosecutor and Assistant City Attorney, 1982 to 2002. Appointed District Judge in 2002; elected in 2004; re-elected 2006 and 2012.

STEVEN L. MARQUART, Fargo

Born in 1954. Graduate, Moorhead High School. BA, Moorhead State University. JD, UND School of Law. Private practice in Fargo, 1979 to 2004. Law Clerk to U.S. District Court Judge Paul Benson. Elected District Judge in 2004; re-elected 2010 and 2016.

STEVEN E. McCULLOUGH, Fargo

Born in 1962. Graduate, West Fargo High School. BA, Moorhead State University. JD, UND School of Law. Private practice in Fargo, 1987 to 2004. Elected District Judge in 2004; re-elected 2010 and 2016.

THOMAS R. OLSON, Fargo

Born in 1952. BA, Augsburg College, 1976. Studied at Luther Theological Seminary, 1975 to 1976. JD, William Mitchell College of Law, 1981. Served in Clay County, MN, Attorney's Office, 1983 to 1985. Private practice in Fargo, 1985 to 2014. Appointed District Judge in 2014; elected in 2016.

WADE L. WEBB, Fargo

Born in 1970 in Grafton. Graduate, Oak Grove Lutheran High School, Fargo, 1988. BA, Concordia College, Moorhead, MN, 1992. JD, UND School of Law, 1995. Law Clerk, Minnesota District Court, 1995 to 1996. Assistant Cass County State's Attorney, leading the Personal Crimes Team, 1996 to 2003. Appointed District Judge in 2003; elected in 2006; re-elected 2008 and 2014.

Southeast Judicial District – Administrative Unit 2

Presiding Judge Daniel D. Narum

Court Administrator Rodney Olson
Asst. Court Administrator Chris Iverson
LaMoure County Courthouse
PO Box 128
LaMoure, ND 58458
Telephone: 701-883-6057

DANIEL D. NARUM, Ellendale, Presiding

Born in 1969. BS, NDSU, 1996. JD, UND School of Law, 1999. Private practice, 1999 to 2006. LaMoure County State's Attorney, 2001 to 2006. U.S. Navy, 1987 to 1990. Appointed District Judge in 2006; elected in 2008. Elected Presiding Judge in 2016; re-elected 2008, 2010, and 2016.

MARK T. BLUMER, Valley City

Born in 1955. Graduate, North Sargent High School, Gwinner. U.S. Navy, 1976 to 1980. BA, University of Colorado. JD, UND School of Law. Private practice, 1989 to 2016. Dickey County State's Attorney. Elected District Judge in 2016.

CHERIE L. CLARK, Jamestown

Born in 1969. BS, University of South Dakota (USD), 2000. JD, USD School of Law, 2000. Assistant County Attorney, Otter Tail County, Minnesota, 2002 to 2006. Assistant Cass County State's Attorney, 2006 to 2017. Appointed District Judge in 2017.

BRADLEY A. CRUFF, Wahpeton

Born in 1964 in Valley City and raised in rural Rogers. Graduate, Barnes County North, 1982. Graduate, Valley City State College, 1986. JD, UND School of Law, 1994. Served as Barnes County State's Attorney, City Attorney for Valley City, Municipal Judge for Valley City, and Barnes County Commissioner. Private practice in Valley City. Elected District Judge in 2012.

JAMES D. HOVEY, New Rockford

Born in 1964. BA, UND, 1987. MA, University of Arizona, 1991. JD, with distinction, UND School of Law, 1996. Private practice in Grand Forks, 1996 to 2010. City Attorney for Larimore, 2001 to 2010. Instructor, UND Center for Legal Studies, 2002. Taught Basic Russian as a graduate student and completed 260 hours of language instruction at Moscow State University, Moscow, Russia. Appointed District Judge in 2010; elected in 2014; re-elected 2016.

TROY J. LeFEVRE, Jamestown

Born in 1974 in Jamestown. Graduate, Jamestown High School, 1992. BA, UND, 1996. JD, UND School of Law, 2002. Private practice, 2002 to 2004. Law Clerk, Southeast Judicial District, 2004 to 2006. Stutsman County Chief Assistant State's Attorney, 2006 to 2016. Elected District Judge in 2016.

JAY A. SCHMITZ, Valley City

Born in 1962 in Pierre, SD, and raised on a cattle ranch near Verona. Graduate, Oakes High School, 1980. BA, Moorhead State University, 1985. JD, Southwestern University School of Law, Los Angeles, CA, 1989. Private practice in Los Angeles, 1989 to 1995. Private practice in Oakes, 2000 to 2002. Stutsman County Chief Assistant State's Attorney, Jamestown, 2003 to 2010. Member of Southeast Judicial District Caseload Management Committee. Elected District Judge in 2010; re-elected 2016.

South Central Judicial District – Administrative Unit 3

Presiding Judge Gail Hagerty
Court Administrator Donna Wunderlich
Burleigh County Courthouse
PO Box 1013
Bismarck, ND 58502-1013
Telephone: 701-222-6682

GAIL HAGERTY, Bismarck, Presiding
Born in 1953 in Bismarck. BA, UND, 1975. JD, UND School of Law, 1978. MJS, University of Nevada, Reno, 1994. Served as Burleigh County State's Attorney, 1982 to 1986. Also served as Assistant Burleigh County State's Attorney and Assistant Attorney General. Burleigh County Judge, 1987 to 1994. Elected District Court Judge in 1994; re-elected 1996, 2002, 2008, and 2014. Elected Presiding Judge in 2004. President, State Bar Association of North Dakota, 2012 to 2013. Chair, North Dakota Judicial Conference, 1995 to 1997. Commissioner, National Conference of Commissioners on Uniform State Laws.

SONNA M. ANDERSON, Bismarck
Born in 1958 in Bismarck. Graduate, Century High School, Bismarck, 1976. Undergraduate education in Trondheim, Norway, 1978. BA, UND, 1981. JD, University of Denver College of Law, 1985. Admitted to North Dakota State Bar, 1985. Clerked for Mountain States Legal Foundation during law school. Clerked for Judge Patrick Conmy, 1985 to 1987. Private practice in Bismarck, 1987 to 2004. Appointed District Judge in 2003; elected in 2006; re-elected 2010 and 2016.

CYNTHIA M. FELAND, Bismarck
Born in 1965. BA, UND, 1987. JD, UND School of Law, 1990. Grant County State's Attorney, 1992 to 1998, while also in private practice in Mandan. Assistant Burleigh County State's Attorney, 1999 to 2010. Elected District Judge in 2010; re-elected 2016.

JOHN W. GRINSTEINER, Mandan
Born in 1972 in Bismarck. Graduate, UND and Bismarck State College. JD, UND School of Law, 1998. Private practice in Bismarck, 1998 to 2003. Judicial Referee and Magistrate for South Central Judicial District, 2003 to 2015. Appointed District Judge in 2015.

BRUCE B. HASKELL, Bismarck
Born in 1957 in Breckenridge, MN. BA, UND, 1980. JD, UND School of Law, 1983. Law Clerk, U.S. Department of Justice, Bureau of Prisons, 1981. Law Clerk, South Central Judicial District, 1982. Assistant Attorney General, Securities Commissioner's Office, 1983 to 1984. Assistant Morton County State's Attorney, 1984 to 1987. Assistant Burleigh County State's Attorney, 1987 to 1994. Elected District Judge in 1994; re-elected 2000, 2006, and 2012.

JAMES S. HILL, Mandan
Born in 1949 in Grand Forks. JD, UND School of Law, 1974. Served five years as Assistant U.S. Attorney in Bismarck. Private practice in Bismarck, 1981 to 2014. Served as representative of the State Bar Association to the American Bar Association House of Delegates and served on the ABA Board of Governors. Chair, ABA Commission on IOLTA. Appointed District Judge in 2014; elected 2016.

DAVID E. REICH, Bismarck
Born in 1956 in Jamestown. BA, UND, 1979. JD, UND School of Law, 1982. Law Clerk, North Dakota Supreme Court, 1982 to 1983. Private practice in Bismarck, 1983 to 2006. Appointed District Judge in 2006; elected in 2008; re-elected 2014.

BRUCE A. ROMANICK, Bismarck
Born in 1960 in Washburn. BS, UND, 1982. JD, UND School of Law, 1986. Private practice in Washburn and Bismarck, 1986 to 1988. Judge Advocate, U.S. Army, Fort Carson, CO, and Kingdom of Saudi Arabia, 1989 to 1992. Private practice in Moorhead, MN, 1992 to 1994. Assistant Burleigh County State's Attorney, 1995 to 2000. Elected District Judge in 2000; re-elected 2006 and 2012.

THOMAS J. SCHNEIDER, Mandan
Born in 1950 in Dickinson. BA, UND, 1972. JD, UND School of Law, 1981. Private practice, 1981 to 1985. Mandan Municipal Judge, 1982 to 1986. Judicial Referee, South Central Judicial District, 1982 to 1986. County Judge, Morton, Grant, and Sioux Counties, 1986 to 1994. Elected District Judge in 1994; re-elected 1996, 2002, 2008, and 2014.

Southwest Judicial District – Administrative Unit 3

Presiding Judge William A. Herauf
Court Administrator Donna Wunderlich
Stark County Courthouse
51 3rd Street East, Suite 202
Dickinson, ND 58601
Telephone: 701-227-3150

WILLIAM A. HERAUF, Dickinson, Presiding
Born in 1957 in Dickinson. Graduate, Dickinson High School, 1975. BA, UND, 1979. JD, UND School of Law, 1982. Private practice in Dickinson, 1982 to 2006. Appointed District Judge in 2006; elected in 2008; re-elected 2010 and 2016. Elected Presiding Judge in 2010.

RHONDA R. EHLIS, Dickinson
Born in 1968 in Bowman. Graduated, Scranton High School, 1986. BA, UND, 1990. JD, UND School of Law, 1993. Staff attorney and outreach attorney, Legal Assistance of North Dakota, Devils Lake, 1993 to 1995. Staff attorney, Regional Child Enforcement Unit, Bismarck, 1995 to 2001. Private practice in Dickinson, 2001 to 2006. Assistant Stark County State's Attorney, 2006 to 2015. Appointed District Judge in 2015.

JAMES D. GION, Dickinson

Born in 1953. Graduated, Regent High School, 1971. BA, UND, 1976. JD, UND School of Law, 1982. Private practice in Hettinger County, 1982 to 2015. Hettinger County State's Attorney, 1991 to 2015. Also served as State's Attorney of Bowman and Slope Counties. Appointed District Judge in 2015.

DANN E. GREENWOOD, Dickinson

Born in 1952 in Dickinson. Earned rank of Eagle Scout in the Boy Scouts of America, 1968. Graduate, Dickinson High School, 1970. Attended Dickinson State College, 1970 to 1972. Graduate, UND, 1974. JD, UND School of Law, 1977. Private practice in Dickinson, 1977 to 2012. President, North Dakota Trial Lawyers Association, 1987. President, State Bar Association of North Dakota, 1998 to 1999. Elected District Judge in 2012.

North Central Judicial District – Administrative Unit 4

Presiding Judge Gary H. Lee

Court Administrator Carolyn Probst
Ward County Courthouse
PO Box 5005
Minot, ND 58702-5005
Telephone: 701-857-6625

GARY H. LEE, Minot, Presiding Judge

Born in 1955. BA, UND. JD, UND School of Law. Private practice in Minot, 1982 to 2004. Assistant Attorney General, 1980 to 1982. Elected District Judge in 2004; re-elected 2010 and 2016. Elected Presiding Judge in 2014.

TODD L. CRESAP, Minot

Born in 1961 in Valley City. BS, Minot State College, 1983. JD, UND School of Law, 1986. Admitted to practice in North Dakota, 1986. Private practice in Minot, 1986 to 2009. Appointed District Judge in 2009; elected in 2012; re-elected 2016.

RICHARD L. HAGAR, Minot

Born in 1957, Clark AFB, Pampanga, Philippines. Graduate, Santa Paula Union High School, Santa Paula, CA, 1975. Appointed to U.S. Air Force Academy by President Gerald Ford. BS, U.S. Air Force Academy, Colorado Springs, CO, 1979. JD, UND School of Law, 1988. Private practice in Minot, 1988 to 2006. Elected District Judge in 2006; re-elected 2012.

STACY J. LOUSER, Minot

Born 1973 in Minot. BS, UND, 1996. MS, Minot State University, 2001. JD, UND School of Law, 2007. Private practice in Minot, 2007 to 2014. Appointed District Judge in 2014; elected in 2016.

DOUGLAS L. MATTSON, Minot

Born in 1955 in Minot. Served in ND House of Representatives, 1978 to 1982. JD, UND School of Law, 1985. Worked for Federal Energy Regulatory Commission and Senator Mark Andrews in Washington, D.C., 1985 to 1986. Private practice in Minot, 1987 to 1990. Ward County States' Attorney, 1990 to 2002. Elected District Judge in 2002; re-elected 2008 and 2014.

Northwest Judicial District – Administrative Unit 4

Presiding Judge Robin A. Schmidt

Court Administrator Carolyn Probst
McKenzie County Courthouse
201 5th Street Northwest
Watford City, ND 58854
Telephone: 701-842-8237

ROBIN A. SCHMIDT, Watford City, Presiding Judge

Born in 1976. Graduate, Sawyer High School. BS, UND, 1999. JD, UND School of Law, 2004. Judicial Clerk, North Dakota Supreme Court, 2004 to 2005. Private practice in Fargo, 2005 to 2010, and in Watford City, 2010 to 2013. Appointed District Judge in 2013; elected in 2016. Elected Presiding Judge in 2017.

DANIEL S. EL-DWEEK, Watford City

Born in 1981. BS, UND, 2003. JD, UND School of Law, 2006. Managing Attorney, Dakota Plains Legal Services, 2006 to 2010. Staff Attorney, Regional Native Public Defense Corporation, 2010 to 2013. Supervising Attorney, Williston Public Defender's Office, 2013 to 2015. Appointed District Judge in 2015.

PAUL W. JACOBSON, Williston

Born in 1948 in Valley City. Graduate, Fargo North High School, 1966. BA, NDSU, 1970. JD, University of Minnesota Law School, 1973. Served in U.S. Army Judge Advocate General's Corps, 1974 to 1979. Private practice in Williston, 1979 to 1993. Assistant Disciplinary Counsel, 1993 to 1999. Disciplinary Counsel, 1999 to 2013. Appointed District Judge in 2013; elected in 2016.

BENJAMEN J. JOHNSON, Williston

Born in 1982 in Williston and raised in Froid, MN. BS, University of Mary, Bismarck, 2004. JD, UND School of Law, 2008. Private practice in Tioga, 2008 to 2016. Public Defender, Three Affiliated Tribes, 2008 to 2010 and 2012 to 2016. Assistant Burke County State's Attorney, 2008 to 2010. Prosecutor, Three Affiliated Tribes, 2010 to 2012. Burke County State's Attorney, 2010 to 2011. Appointed District Judge in 2017.

JOSHUA B. RUSTAD, Williston

Born in 1972. Graduate, Williston High School, 1991. Graduate, UND, 1995. JD, UND School of Law, 1999. Private practice in Williston, 1999 to 2006. Supervising attorney, North Dakota Legal Counsel for Indigents Commission, Williston office, 2006 to 2010. Elected District Judge in 2010; re-elected 2016.

KIRSTEN M. SJUE, Williston

Born in 1981. Graduate, Williston High School, 1999. BA, UND, 2003. JD, with distinction, UND School of Law, 2006. Law Clerk, Chief Justice Gerald W. VandeWalle, 2006 to 2007. Law Clerk, U.S. District Judge Ralph Erickson, 2007 to 2009. Private practice in Williston, 2013 to 2015. Appointed District Judge in 2015.

For a listing of former district court judges, see www.ndcourts.gov/history/district/contents.htm.

Municipal Courts

There are approximately 363 incorporated cities in North Dakota. Currently, there are 65 municipal judges serving 118 municipal courts.

Each municipality under 5,000 in population has the option of deciding whether or not to have a municipal court. Municipalities may contract with the state to provide municipal ordinance violation court services so that district judges may hear municipal ordinance violations.

Municipal judges have jurisdiction over all violations of municipal ordinances, except certain violations involving juveniles. Violations of state law are not within the jurisdiction of the municipal courts.

A municipal judge is elected for a four-year term. The judge must be a qualified elector of the city, except in cities with a population below 5,000. In cities with a population of 5,000 or more, the municipal judge is required to be a licensed attorney, unless an attorney is unavailable or not interested in serving. At present, there are approximately 19 legally-trained and 46 lay municipal judges in the state. Vacancies that occur between elections are filled by the executive officer of the municipality with the consent of the governing body of the municipality.

State law requires each new municipal judge attend two educational seminars and all others attend one course conducted by the Supreme Court in each calendar year. If a municipal judge fails to meet this requirement without an excused absence from the Continuing Judicial Education Commission, the judge's name is referred to the Judicial Conduct Commission for disciplinary action.

North Dakota Judicial System Committees, Councils, Commissions, and Boards

Advisory Committees

In the North Dakota judicial system, a system of committees has been established to develop new ideas and evaluate proposals for improving public services. These advisory committees include citizen members, legislators, lawyers, district court judges, municipal court judges, and members of the Supreme Court. Committee minutes can be found on the court's website located at www.ndcourts.gov/Court/Index.htm.

Administrative Council

The Administrative Council is established by Administrative Rule 22. Duties of the Council are to develop uniform administrative policies and procedures for the trial courts and juvenile courts and make recommendations for their implementation; to review the biennial budget proposals submitted by the trial court administrators for the respective administrative units; to review and approve for submission to the Supreme Court a proposed trial court component of the unified judicial system budget for each biennium; to monitor trial court budget expenditures; and to perform other duties as directed by the Chief Justice.

Judicial Planning Committee

The Judicial Planning Committee is established by Supreme Court rule. The Committee studies the judicial system and makes recommendations concerning long-range and strategic planning and future improvements for the system.

Joint Procedure Committee

The Joint Procedure Committee is the standing committee of the Supreme Court responsible for proposing adoption, amendment, or repeal of rules of civil procedure, criminal procedure, appellate procedure, evidence, and specialized court procedure. The Committee membership of 10 judges and 10 attorneys is appointed by the Supreme Court, except for one liaison member appointed by the State Bar Association.

Informal Complaint Panel

The Informal Complaint Panel is established by Supreme Court rule. It provides an informal forum to address complaints or concerns about judges or other employees of the state judicial system. It is confidential, non-confrontational, and educational. It is intended to constructively influence conduct and resolve issues before they rise to the level of a formal grievance or disciplinary proceeding.

Joint Committee on Attorney Standards

The Joint Committee on Attorney Standards, established by Supreme Court rule, is comprised of members appointed by the Chief Justice and the Board of Governors of the State Bar Association. The Committee is responsible for the study and review of all rules and proposals concerning attorney supervision, including admission to the bar, attorney discipline, rules of professional conduct, and law student practice.

Judiciary Standards Committee

The Judiciary Standards Committee, established by Supreme Court rule, studies and reviews all rules relating to the supervision of the judiciary, including judicial discipline, judicial ethics, and the judicial nominating process.

Court Services Administration Committee

The Court Services Administration Committee, established by Supreme Court rule, is responsible for the study and review of all rules and orders relating to the administrative supervision of the judicial system.

Committee on Tribal and State Court Affairs

The Committee on Tribal and State Court Affairs was established following adoption of Administrative Rule 37 by the Supreme Court. The Committee is comprised of tribal and state court judges, tribal and state court support services representatives, and public members. It provides a vehicle for expanding awareness about the operation of tribal and state court systems, identifying and discussing issues regarding court practices, procedures, and administration, which are of common concern to members of the two court systems, and for cultivating mutual respect for, and cooperation between, tribal and state courts.

Gender Fairness Implementation Committee

The Gender Fairness Implementation Committee was established by Supreme Court Administrative Order 7 to oversee implementation of the recommendations of the Supreme Court's Commission on Gender Fairness in the Courts. It is further charged with monitoring the progress of the judicial branch in eliminating gender bias in the courts.

Minority Justice Implementation Committee

The Minority Justice Implementation Committee was established by Supreme Court Administrative Order 21 to oversee the implementation of the recommendations of the North Dakota Commission to Study Racial and Ethnic Bias in the Courts.

Personnel Policy Board

The Personnel Policy Board was established by Supreme Court Administrative Rule 33. The Board is comprised of a Supreme Court justice, district court judges, Supreme Court department heads, and employees of the supreme and district courts. The Board is tasked with the responsibility of reviewing and implementing the personnel system and developing a salary administration plan for the judiciary.

Court Technology Committee

The Court Technology Committee is established by Administrative Order and is responsible for the planning and implementation of information technology for the Judicial Branch. The Committee's coordinated efforts are responsible for consistent and efficient management of information technology resources.

Jury Standards Committee

The Jury Standards Committee, established by Supreme Court rule, studies and oversees the operation of North Dakota's jury system. The Committee is responsible for reviewing the Uniform Jury Selection Act, studying and making recommendations concerning juror use and management, and reviewing the operation, management, and administration of the state's jury system.

North Dakota Judicial Conference

The North Dakota Judicial Conference is established by statute for the purpose of soliciting, receiving, and evaluating suggestions relating to the improvement of the administration of justice; considering and making recommendations to the Supreme Court for changes in rules, procedures, or any matter pertaining to the judicial system; coordinating continuing judicial education efforts for judges and support staff; and establishing methods for reviewing proposed legislation, which may affect the operation of the judicial branch.

Committee on Legislation

The Committee on Legislation, a standing committee of the Judicial Conference, drafts, reviews, and tracks proposed legislation that may affect the North Dakota judicial system. During legislative sessions, the Committee provides weekly reports to the members of the conference on legislation that could affect judicial services.

Advisory Commission on Electronic Media in the Courtroom

The Advisory Commission on Electronic Media in the Courtroom is established by Supreme Court rule and governs electronic and photographic media coverage of court proceedings. The Commission generally monitors the experience with electronic media in the North Dakota Supreme Court, district courts, and municipal courts.

Pattern Jury Instruction Commission

The Pattern Jury Instruction Commission, established by Supreme Court rule, is composed of six lawyer-members appointed by the State Bar Association of North Dakota Board of Governors and six judge-members appointed by the chair of the Judicial Conference after consultation with the Executive Committee. In addition to revising and developing instructions corresponding to current law, the Commission is engaged in an extensive review of all pre-1986 civil and criminal instructions. A primary goal is rewriting the instructions using plain English, that is, language that is understandable by jurors without a legal background.

Judicial Branch Education Commission

The Judicial Branch Education Commission was established by Supreme Court rule in 1993. The responsibilities of the Commission are to establish policies that affect the implementation of the mandatory education provision of the rule, develop judicial education programs for judges and court support personnel, develop and recommend a biennial budget for judicial education activities to the North Dakota Supreme Court, and develop a library of resource materials for judges and court support personnel.

Juvenile Policy Board

The Juvenile Policy Board is established by Supreme Court rule to define the mission of juvenile court services consistent with N.D.C.C. 27-20-01, to provide the administrative mechanism and authority to ensure the implementation of the policies, and to ensure the full involvement of the judges and personnel of the North Dakota judicial system in the development of juvenile court policies and procedures.

Court Improvement Project Committee

The Court Improvement Project Committee became a committee of the Administrative Council with the approval of Policy 520 on December 15, 2006. The committee oversees three grants related to court improvement in the area of child abuse and neglect. Four permanent subcommittees were created: Lay Guardian Ad Litem, Indian Child Welfare, Education and Training, and Data Collection and Analysis.

Parenting Investigator Review Board

The Parenting Investigator Review Board is established by Supreme Court rule. It addresses complaints about parenting investigators. It has nine members: three judges and one lawyer appointed by the Chief Justice, two lawyers appointed by the State Bar Association, and three parenting investigators appointed by the Chief Justice and the president of the State Bar Association acting together.

Caseflow Management Committee

Established by Policy 510, the Caseflow Management Committee is developed under the auspices of the Administrative Council to provide recommendations to the Council on case management activities governing all trial courts statewide. The purpose of the Committee is to establish and monitor caseflow management practices in each judicial district of the state.

State Board of Law Examiners

The State Board of Law Examiners was created by the 1905 Legislative Assembly to assist the Supreme Court in its constitutional responsibility to regulate the admission to practice. The Board's three members must all be licensed members of the North Dakota Bar.

Disciplinary Board

The Disciplinary Board was created in 1965 to provide for investigating, evaluating, and acting upon complaints alleging unethical conduct by attorneys licensed in North Dakota. The Rules of Professional Conduct are the primary guide for lawyer conduct, and the North Dakota Rules for Lawyer Discipline provide the procedural framework for the handling and disposition of complaints.

Judicial Conduct Commission

The Judicial Conduct Commission was established in 1975 to receive, evaluate, and investigate complaints against any judge in the state and, when necessary, conduct hearings concerning the discipline, removal, or retirement of any judge. The Commission consists of four non-lawyers, two judges, and one lawyer. The non-lawyers are appointed by the governor, the judges are appointed by the North Dakota Judges Association, and the lawyer member is appointed by the State Bar Association.

Chronology of Justices of the North Dakota Supreme Court

Under the provisions of the 1889 Constitution, the Supreme Court consisted of three judges elected for terms of six years. So that terms might be staggered, the first three judges elected drew lots so that there would initially be one term of three years, one of five years, and one of seven years.

Guy C.H. Corliss (R)(1858-1937) 1889-1898
Elected 1889, received the three-year term; elected 1892; resigned April 15, 1898

Joseph M. Bartholomew (R)(1843-1901) 1889-1901
Elected 1889, received the five-year term; elected 1894; did not seek re-election 1900

Alfred M. Wallin (R)(1836-1923)..1889-1903
Elected 1889, drew the seven-year term; elected 1896; did not seek re-election 1902

Newton C. Young (R)(1862-1923)..1898-1906
Appointed August 19, 1898, to replace Corliss; elected 1898, 1904; resigned August 15, 1906

David E. Morgan (R)(1849-1912)..1901-1911
Elected 1900, 1906

John M. Cochrane (R)(1859-1904)..1903-1904
Elected 1902; died in office July 20, 1904

Edward Engerud (R)(1869-1921)..1904-1907
Appointed August 9, 1904, to replace Cochrane; elected 1904; resigned January 1907

John Knauf (R)(1868-1952)..1906-1906
Appointed August 15, 1906, to replace Young; defeated in November 1906 general election

Charles J. Fisk (D)(1862-1932)..1907-1910
Elected 1906 to fill unexpired term of Young

Burleigh F. Spalding (R)(1853-1934)..1907-1910
Appointed January 30, 1907, to replace Engerud; elected 1908

A constitutional amendment, adopted November 3, 1908, increased the number of judges from three to five. The two new judges were appointed by Governor John Burke.

John Carmody (1854-1920)..1909-1910
Appointed January 15, 1909; defeated in June 1910 primary election

Sidney E. Ellsworth (1862-1945)..1909-1910
Appointed January 15, 1909; defeated in June 1910 primary election

The 1909 Legislature enacted a law providing that Supreme Court Judges should henceforth be elected on a no party ballot. This measure became effective with the 1910 elections.

David E. Morgan (1849-1912)..1911-1911
Incumbent; resigned October 31, 1911

Burleigh F. Spalding (1853-1934)..1911-1914
Incumbent; defeated in June 1914 primary election

Charles J. Fisk (1862-1932)..1911-1916
Incumbent; defeated in June 1916 primary election

Edward T. Burke (1870-1935)..1911-1916
Elected 1910; defeated in June 1916 primary election

Evan B. Goss (1872-1930)..1911-1916
Elected 1910; defeated in June 1916 primary election

Andrew A. Bruce (1866-1934)... 1911-1918
Appointed October 31, 1911, to replace Morgan; elected 1912; did not seek re-election 1918; resigned December 1, 1918

Adolph M. Christianson (1887-1954).. 1915-1934
Elected 1914, 1920, 1926, 1932

Luther E. Birdzell (1880-1973)... 1917-1933
Elected 1916, 1922, 1928; resigned November 1, 1933

Richard H. Grace (1868-1929) 1917-1922
Elected 1916; did not seek re-election 1922

James E. Robinson (1844-1933).. 1917-1922
Elected 1916; defeated in June 1922 primary election

Harrison A. Bronson (1873-1947) 1919-1924
Elected 1918; did not seek re-election 1924

Sveinbjorn Johnson (1883-1946)... 1923-1926
Elected 1922; resigned November 29, 1926

William L. Nuessle (1878-1959).. 1923-1934
Elected 1922, 1928

John Burke (1859-1937)... 1925-1934
Elected 1924, 1930

Alexander G. Burr (1871-1951) 1926-1934
Appointed November 29, 1926, to replace Johnson; elected 1928

George H. Moellring (1878-1935)... 1933-1934
Appointed November 1, 1933, to replace Birdzell; defeated in November 1934 general election

A constitutional amendment approved June 25, 1930, increased the term of office to 10 years. So that terms might be staggered, this provision did not take effect until the 1934 elections, when three judges were elected. Of the three, a 10-year term went to the judge receiving the highest vote, an eight-year term to the judge receiving the second highest, and a six-year term to the judge receiving the third highest vote.

John Burke (1859-1937)... 1935-1937
Incumbent; elected 1936; died in office May 14, 1937

Adolph M. Christianson (1887-1954).. 1935-1954
Incumbent; elected 1938, 1948; died in office February 11, 1954

James Morris (1893-1980) 1935-1964
Elected 1934 to a 10-year term; elected 1944, 1954; did not seek re-election 1964

Alexander G. Burr (1871-1951) 1935-1949
Elected 1934 to an eight-year term; elected 1942; resigned September 2, 1949

William L. Nuessle (1878-1959).. 1935-1950
Elected 1934 to a six-year term; elected 1940; resigned December 31, 1950

P. O. Sathre (1878-1968) 1937-1938
Appointed December 7, 1937, to replace John Burke; defeated November 1938 general election

Thomas J. Burke (1896-1966) 1939-1966
Elected 1938 to fill unexpired term of John Burke; elected 1946, 1956; died in office March 20, 1966

Gudmunder Grimson (1878-1965) 1949-1958
Appointed September 15, 1949, to replace Burr; elected 1950; resigned November 20, 1958, effective December 31, 1958

P. O. Sathre (1878-1968) 1951-1962
Elected 1950 to fill unexpired term of Alexander Burr; elected 1952; did not seek re-election 1962

Nels G. Johnson (1896-1958) 1954-1958
Appointed February 26, 1954, to replace Christianson; elected 1954 to fill unexpired term; elected 1958; died in office December 2, 1958

Obert C. Teigen (1908-1978) 1959-1974
Appointed December 23, 1958, effective January 13, 1959, to replace Grimson; elected 1960, 1970; resigned May 1, 1974, effective July 1, 1974

Alvin C. Strutz (1903-1973) 1959-1973
Appointed February 6, 1959, effective April 1, 1959, to replace Johnson; elected 1960 to fill unexpired term; elected 1968; died in office June 16, 1973

Ralph J. Erickstad (1922-2001) 1963-1992
Elected 1962, 1972, 1982; did not seek re-election 1992

Harvey B. Knudson (1903-1978) 1965-1974
Elected 1964 to 10-year term; did not seek re-election

William S. Murray (1916-1998) 1966
Appointed April 1, 1966, to replace Thomas Burke; defeated in 1966 general election

William L. Paulson (1913-2000) 1967-1983
Elected 1966, 1976; resigned effective September 5, 1983

Robert L. Vogel (1918-2005) 1973-1978
Appointed June 27, 1973, to replace Strutz; elected 1974 to 10-year term; resigned effective August 11, 1978

J. Philip Johnson (1938-) 1974
Appointed June 20, 1974, effective July 1, 1974, to replace Teigen; defeated in September 1974 primary election

Paul M. Sand (1914-1984) 1973-1984
Elected 1974 to fill unexpired term of Vogel; re-elected 1978; died in office December 8, 1984

Vernon R. Pederson (1919-2017) 1975-1984
Elected 1974 to fill unexpired term of Teigen; re-elected 1980; resigned November 8, 1984, effective January 7, 1985

Gerald Wayne VandeWalle (1933-)..1978-present
Appointed July 8, 1978, effective August 13, 1978, to replace Vogel; elected to unexpired term 1978, re-elected to 10-year term in 1984, 1994, 2004, 2014

Herman F. Gierke (1943-2016)...1983-1991
Appointed effective September 30, 1983, to replace Paulson; elected to fill unexpired term 1984; re-elected 1986; resigned November 20, 1991, effective immediately

Beryl J. Levine (1935-)...1985-1996
Appointed January 17, 1985, to replace Sand; elected to unexpired term 1986; re-elected to 10-year term in 1988; resigned effective March 1, 1996

Herbert L. Meschke (1928-2017)...1985-1998
Appointed January 17, 1985, to replace Pederson; elected to unexpired term 1986; re-elected to a 10-year term in 1990; resigned effective September 30, 1998

J. Philip Johnson (1938-)..1992
Appointed February 11, 1992; defeated for election 1992

Dale V. Sandstrom (1950-)..1992-2016
Elected 1992 to fill unexpired term of Gierke; assumed office December 31, 1992; re-elected to a 10-year term in 1996 and 2006; did not seek re-election 2016

William A. Neumann (1944-)...1993-2005
Elected to a 10-year term in 1992 and 2002; resigned effective March 14, 2005

Mary Muehlen Maring (1951-)...1996-2013
Appointed March 1, 1996, to replace Levine; elected to fill unexpired term in 1996; re-elected to a 10-year term in 1998 and 2008; resigned effective December 31, 2013

Carol Ronning Kapsner (1947-)...1998-2017
Appointed November 1, 1998, to replace Meschke; elected to a 10-year term in 2000 and 2010; retired effective July 31, 2017

Daniel J. Crothers (1957-)..2005-present
Appointed June 10, 2005, to replace Neumann; elected to unexpired term in 2008; re-elected to a 10-year term in 2012

Lisa K. Fair McEvers (1962-)...2014-present
Appointed November 18, 2013, to replace Maring; elected to unexpired term 2016

Jerod E. Tufte (1976-)...2017-present
Elected to 10-year term in 2016

Jon J. Jensen (1965-)...2017-present
Appointed July 12, 2017, to replace Kapsner

Chapter Five

Executive Branch

Executive Branch

This chapter begins with a listing of North Dakota's 13 elected executives. Each official is pictured along with biographical information and a short summary of duties.

The 13 elected officials are the:

- Governor
- Lieutenant Governor
- Secretary of State
- State Auditor
- Attorney General
- State Treasurer
- Commissioner of Insurance
- Agriculture Commissioner
- Public Service Commissioners (3)
- Tax Commissioner
- Superintendent of Public Instruction

✔ The *2001-2003 North Dakota Blue Book* contains a comprehensive overview of the duties and responsibilities of each of the 13 officials.

✔ See the *2011–2013 North Dakota Blue Book* for information regarding the 2010 Governor Transition Ceremony.

Elected State Officials

Governor
Doug Burgum

Personal
Born August 1, 1956; married to Kathryn Helgaas Burgum; two sons, Joe and Tom, and a daughter, Jesse

Party Affiliation
Republican

Education
Graduate of North Dakota State University in 1978 and Stanford University Graduate School of Business in 1980 with an M.B.A.

Professional Experience
Consultant at McKinsey & Co. in Chicago from 1980 to 1983; returned to North Dakota to join Great Plains Software in 1983 and grew it from a small startup company to an award-winning global software company; former chairman and CEO of Great Plains Software through its initial public offering in 1997 and acquisition by Microsoft Corp. in 2001; senior vice president of Microsoft through 2007; founder of Kilbourne Group, a real estate development firm committed to creating smart, healthy cities through vibrant downtowns; co-founder of Arthur Ventures, a venture capital firm that invests in ambitious, mission-driven software companies; awarded the Theodore Roosevelt Rough Rider Award in 2009; elected Governor on November 8, 2016; sworn in as Governor on January 3, 2017.

Summary of Duties
The Governor is the chief executive officer of the state and has general supervision over executive branch state agencies. He serves as commander-in-chief of the state's military forces except when they are called into service of the United States. In addition, the Governor has the authority to convene special sessions of the Legislative Assembly; veto legislation and line items on appropriations bills; recommend legislative measures; and grant reprieves, commutations, and pardons for all offenses except treason and impeachment.

The Governor chairs the Industrial Commission, Emergency Commission, Board of University and School Lands, State Board of Equalization, State Water Commission, and North Dakota Indian Affairs Commission.

Lieutenant Governor

Brent Sanford

Personal
Born December 23, 1971; married to Sandi; three children, Sydney, Nicolas, and Erin

Party Affiliation
Republican

Education
Earned a degree in accounting from the University of North Dakota in 1994 and is a certified public accountant

Professional Experience
Worked at Eide Bailly in Fargo for eight years; served as chief financial officer for Transwest Trucks, a multi-location truck dealership, financing, and manufacturing operation headquartered in Brighton, Colo.; became owner and president of S & S Motors in Watford City; served as mayor of Watford City from 2010 to 2016 and as a city councilman for four years prior; served as a board member with the McKenzie County Job Development Authority; sworn in as Lieutenant Governor of North Dakota on January 3, 2017.

Summary of Duties
The Lieutenant Governor acts as chief executive in case of the Governor's death, resignation, or on other occasions when the Governor is unable to fulfill his responsibilities; serves as President of the Senate and, in the event of a tie, may cast the decisive vote; leads the North Dakota Trade Office; chairs the State Investment Board, Capitol Grounds Planning Commission, Higher Education Challenge Fund Commission, Early Childhood Education Council, and Northern Plains Unmanned Aircraft Systems Authority; and assumes other board chairmanships and functions as prescribed by the Governor.

Secretary of State
Alvin (Al) A. Jaeger

Personal
Born December 10, 1943, in Beulah, N.D.; wife, Kathy (deceased November 24, 2016); three children, Todd, Stacy, and Heidi

Party Affiliation
Republican

Education
Beulah High School; Bismarck State College, A.A.; Dickinson State University, B.S.; University of North Dakota and Montana State University, post-graduate work

Professional Experience
Military: 1966-1972, North Dakota Army National Guard; Career: 1966-1969, Killdeer High School, 1969-1971, Kenmare High School, teacher of business education; 1971-1973, Mobil Oil Corporation, marketing analyst; 1973-1992, real estate broker; 1992, elected Secretary of State, re-elected 1996, 2000, 2004, 2006, 2010, and 2014.

Jaeger is a member of the National Association of Secretaries of State and has served several times on the Executive Committee. He has been chair of the awards committee since 1994.

Summary of Duties
The Secretary of State commissions notaries public, registers lobbyists, issues contractor licenses, registers charitable organizations, regulates boxing and mixed fighting styles, maintains a central database for the recording of various security documents (e.g., uniform commercial code, crop, and livestock liens), registers and administers laws pertaining to more than 40 different business entity categories, and is the state's chief election officer.

In addition, the Secretary of State attests the official acts of the Governor and maintains a related registry, is the custodian of the Great Seal, and receives and files the original signed copies of legislative bills and resolutions.

The Secretary of State is a member of the Emergency Commission, Board of University and School Lands, State Historical Board, State Canvassing Board, Theodore Roosevelt Rough Rider Awards Committee, and State Information Technology Advisory Committee.

State Auditor

Joshua C. Gallion

Personal

Born 1979 in Spokane, Wash.; married to Rebecca (Becky); two daughters, Brooklyn and Sasha

Party Affiliation

Republican

Education

Central Valley High School, Spokane, Wash.; Bismarck State College, Associate of Arts; Dickinson State University, bachelor's degrees, accounting and business administration; University of North Dakota, Master of Business Administration

Professional Experience

United States Air Force, Minot Air Force Base, 1998-2002; office manager, R.W. Gallion Floors, Spokane, Wash., 2002; office manager, Fougner Engineered Sales, Bismarck, 2002-2008; transportation management officer and finance, Department of Transportation, Bismarck, 2008-2010; accounting manager, Public Service Commission, Bismarck, 2010-2016; elected as State Auditor, 2016.

Summary of Duties

The State Auditor is the chief accountability officer for the state of North Dakota that provides accountability to both internal and external stakeholders.

The internal stakeholders, primarily the citizen's representation in the legislature and government managers in the executive and judicial branches, rely on independent, professional audits conducted in accordance with performance audit standards issued by the Comptroller General of the United States to verify compliance and improve operations. The State Auditor performs three distinct types of performance audits. The first are audits conducted as determined necessary by the State Auditor, Legislative Audit and Fiscal Review Committee, or as specified by state law. The second are referred to as operational audits and are performed on most state agencies on a biennial basis. The third type is conducted by the office's Higher Education Audit Division.

The State Auditor also conducts independent, professional audits of the state's financial statements, the university system's financial statements, various state agencies, and political subdivisions. The State Auditor also audits federal funds in accordance with the Single Audit Act and federal oil and gas royalties under agreement with the federal Office of Natural Resource Revenues. These reports are often referred to as external financial reporting, providing accountability to external stakeholders outside of state government, primarily citizens, creditors, investors, and grantors.

Attorney General
Wayne Stenehjem

Personal
Born February 5, 1953, in Mohall, N.D.; married to Beth Bakke Stenehjem; one son, Andrew

Party Affiliation
Republican

Education
Graduate of Bismarck High School; A.A. from Bismarck Junior College; B.A. from University of North Dakota; J.D. from UND School of Law

Professional Experience
Formerly a partner in the Grand Forks law firm of Kuchera, Stenehjem, Walberg & Sharp. Licensed to practice law in North Dakota and North Dakota U.S. district courts since 1977. Member of the North Dakota House of Representatives from 1976 to 1980. State Senator from 1980 to 2000. Chairman of the Senate Judiciary Committee, 1995 to 2000. President Pro Tem of the Senate, 1999. Member of the Legislative Council, 1997 to 2000. Elected Attorney General 2000, re-elected 2004 (two-year term), 2006 (four-year term), 2010, and 2014.

Summary of Duties
The Attorney General represents the state in all legal matters, civil and criminal, where the state is named as a party or the state may have an interest in the outcome of the litigation; provides legal services and opinions to state legislators, state officials, constitutional officers, state agencies, boards, and commissions; enforces open meetings and open records laws and consumer fraud laws. The attorney general's office issues licenses for retail alcohol beverage establishments, Class A and Class B gambling organizations, polygraph (lie detector) examiners, amusement games and devices, and concealed weapons permits; maintains the state's criminal history records and offender registration systems; performs fire safety inspections of public buildings; conducts arson investigations and criminal investigations; and is responsible for the North Dakota Lottery and the state Crime Laboratory.

The Attorney General is a member of numerous boards and commissions, including the Board of University and School Lands, Industrial Commission (which oversees all state-owned industries), ND Public Employees Retirement System Board, and Judicial Council and Pardon Advisory Board.

State Treasurer

Kelly L. Schmidt

Personal
Born in 1962 in Elmhurst, Ill.; married to Charles (Chuck); four sons, five grandsons

Party Affiliation
Republican

Education
Graduate of Moorhead High School, Moorhead, Minn.; attended the University of Minnesota-Moorhead and North Dakota State University, majoring in behavioral sciences

Professional Experience
Investment/insurance firm brokerage manager; self-employed/contractual services working for advocacy issues such as the Bush Clear Skies Initiative; North Dakota House of Representatives Appropriations Committee in the 2003 Legislative and special sessions. Founding member and immediate past chair of the State Financial Officers Foundation (SFOF). She was awarded the SFOF Servant Leadership Award in October 2016. She served as president of the National Association of State Treasurers (NAST) in 2011 and also chaired its foundation. The Council of State Governments has also named her a "Toll Fellow" for her achievement and service to state government. In 2015, Schmidt was awarded the Desjardins Financial Education Award by the Credit Union National Association for her leadership on behalf of financial literacy. She is a founding member of the North Dakota Jump$tart Coalition and a past member of the board of directors for the National Jump$tart Coalition and the American Savings Education Council. Elected State Treasurer in 2004; re-elected 2008, 2012, and 2016.

Summary of Duties

1. Cash Management: The management of the state "checkbook." The forecasting and cash management expertise offered by the Office of State Treasurer (OST) is necessary to ensure the availability of sufficient funds to cover state obligations while optimizing investment earnings.
2. Accounting: The State Treasurer is responsible for paying all warrants or checks drawn against the state. Bank balances are reconciled daily to the state accounting system (PeopleSoft) and the Bank of North Dakota. All state funds received by agencies are deposited through the OST for investment in the general fund.
3. Investments: The Treasurer serves as custodian for all state funds. The OST is responsible for the investment of the state's general and special funds, as well as several trust funds, including the Veterans Postwar Trust Fund. State funds are invested as CDs with the Bank of North Dakota. Trust fund money is invested in banks and credit unions throughout the state of North Dakota.
4. Tax Collections and Distributions: The OST disburses more than 30 tax distributions to political subdivisions. Its web-based system TDOC (Tax Distribution Outstanding Check) pulls data from a variety of sources, which streamlines distributions and ensures greater accuracy, transparency, and efficiency. The office also provides analysis, data, and education of various tax distributions and state laws to legislators, employees of state agencies, officials and employees of local political subdivisions, and the general public.
5. Financial Literacy: Treasurer Schmidt worked collaboratively to pass legislation to promote financial literacy as a responsibility of the State Treasurer and a priority of the office. NDCC 54-11-01 outlines the duty: "May work to promote access to financial education tools that can help all North Dakotans make wiser choices in all areas of personal financial management."
6. Boards and Commissions: The Treasurer serves on the State Investment Board, Board of University and School Lands, Teacher's Fund for Retirement Board, State Board of Equalization, State Historical Board, and State Canvassing Board.

Insurance Commissioner

Jon Godfread

Personal
Born in Bismarck in 1982; married to Amanda; two children

Party Affiliation
Republican

Education
B.A., Business Administration, University of Northern Iowa, cum laude, 2005; summer session, McGeorge School of Law, University of the Pacific, 2008, including study abroad in Austria under U.S. Supreme Court Justice Anthony Kennedy; member, North Dakota Law Review, UND; J.D./M.B.A., UND School of Law, 2011

Professional Experience
Professional basketball player, Ehingen Steeples, Ehingen, Germany, October 2005-March 2006; branch manager/personal banker, Alerus Financial, Grand Forks, July 2005-August 2007; legislative intern, House Finance and Taxation Committee and House Transportation Committee, 2009 North Dakota Legislative Session; legislative aide, North Dakota Office of the State Tax Commissioner, December 2010-August 2011; vice president of governmental affairs, Greater North Dakota Chamber, August 2011-December 2016; elected Insurance Commissioner, November 8, 2016.

Summary of Duties
The Commissioner regulates insurance companies doing business in the state, which includes licensing, registering and/or approving, and examining for business conduct and financial stability. Oversight of more than 52,000 insurance agents involves the administration of continuing education and pre-licensing requirements. The Insurance Department also interprets and applies laws dealing with the insurance industry and aids policyholders in receiving fair treatment during disputes.

The Commissioner is responsible for the State Health Insurance Counseling and Prescription Connection programs, State Fire and Tornado Fund, State Bonding Fund, Petroleum Tank Release Compensation Fund, and the Boiler Inspection Program and also receives and investigates inquiries and insurance fraud referrals.

Agriculture Commissioner

Doug Goehring

Personal
Born in 1965; raised on a family farm near Menoken, Burleigh County, N.D.; married to Annette; six children and seven grandchildren

Party Affiliation
Republican

Education
Graduate of Century High School, Bismarck; graduate of Bismarck State College

Professional Experience
Third generation family farmer from Burleigh County, 1990-present; president of Nodak Mutual Insurance, 2002-2008; licensed medical laboratory technician; appointed Agriculture Commissioner in 2009; elected to four-year terms in 2010 and 2014.

Summary of Duties
The Agriculture Commissioner oversees and coordinates the activities of the Department of Agriculture and represents the agricultural community in the formulation of public policy.

The Department of Agriculture is organized into six divisions:

1. Administrative Services includes fiscal management, human resources and procurement functions, and the North Dakota Mediation Service.
2. Plant Industries includes noxious weeds, plant protection, apiary, and waterbank programs.
3. Livestock Services includes livestock licensing, dairy/poultry, state meat and poultry inspection, livestock pollution prevention, feed inspection and registration, beef age and source verification, and wildlife services.
4. Marketing & Information offers promotional and market enhancement programs for North Dakota agricultural commodities and value-added agricultural products, both domestically and internationally, and provides public information and information technology services.
5. Animal Health/State Veterinarian protects the health of domestic animals and nontraditional livestock of the state and administers all rules and orders of the State Board of Animal Health.
6. Pesticide & Fertilizer regulates pesticides, fertilizers, and anhydrous ammonia to protect human health and the environment.

The Agriculture Commissioner is a member of numerous boards and commissions, including the Industrial Commission (which oversees the North Dakota Mill, the Bank of North Dakota, the Department of Mineral Resources, and the Oil and Gas Division), the Board of Tax Equalization, the State Water Commission, and the State Board of Agricultural Research and Education.

Public Service Commissioner

Randy Christmann

Personal

Outside of government service, Randy owns a 111-year-old, third generation cattle ranch west of Hazen, N.D. He is married to Bethanie.

Party Affiliation

Republican

Education

Before graduating from Hazen High School in 1978, Christmann enlisted in the North Dakota Army National Guard. He enrolled at North Dakota State University and graduated in 1982 with a bachelor's degree in business administration.

Professional Experience

Christmann has a background in agriculture, telecommunications, and 18 years in the North Dakota Senate representing energy country. He was elected to the North Dakota Senate in 1994 and initially focused mostly on energy, taxation, and natural resources issues. Governor Ed Schafer appointed Christmann to serve as one of the two legislative appointees on the Lignite Research Council. He continued to serve in that position under Governor John Hoeven and Governor Jack Dalrymple. Senate Republicans chose Christmann to serve as Assistant Majority Leader in 2002. He was re-elected to that post every two years through 2012. He also served on the Senate Appropriations Committee. From 1999 through 2012, the members of West River Telecommunications (WRT) Cooperative elected Christmann to serve on its board of directors. During part of this time, he also served as the president of the North Dakota Association of Telecommunications Cooperatives. He was elected to the Public Service Commission in 2012.

Summary of Duties

Originally established as the Railroad Commission, the name was changed to the Public Service Commission in 1940. The Commission maintains jurisdiction over railroads; telecommunications companies; pipeline utilities engaged in the transportation of gas and oil; electric utilities engaged in the generation and distribution of natural, synthetic, or artificial gas; all heating utilities engaged in the distribution of heat; warehouse companies engaged in the marketing, storage, or handling of grain; and all other public utilities engaged in business in the state or any of its political subdivisions.

The Abandoned Mine Lands Division administers a federal program to remove hazards and environmental problems associated with abandoned mines, investigates abandoned mine land sites, designs reclamation projects, submits applications for federal funds, and manages construction projects under public contracts.

Public Service Commissioner

Julie Fedorchak

Personal

Third generation North Dakotan; born in 1968 in Williston, N.D.; husband Mike Fedorchak of Minot; three children, Elizabeth, Nathan, and Samuel

Party Affiliation

Republican

Education

Century High School, Bismarck, 1986; University of North Dakota, bachelor's degree in journalism, 1990

Professional Experience

Julie Fedorchak was appointed to the Public Service Commission in December 2012 by Governor Jack Dalrymple and elected by North Dakota voters in 2016. She holds the pipeline, railroad, electric transmission, and consumer affairs portfolios. She has focused on improving reclamation standards, minimizing environmental and cultural resource impacts, and improving safety. She launched her professional career with the University of North Dakota Alumni Association and Foundation where she was director of communications and editor of alumni publications. Julie lived in Washington, D.C., and worked at the University of Maryland College Park from 1993-1995. She returned to North Dakota in 1995 to be communications director for Governor Ed Schafer, serving as a senior advisor and principal speech writer, spokesperson, and media liaison until he retired from office in 2000. For the next decade, Julie managed Liffrig Communications, a small firm that provided marketing, communications, media, and government relations services. She also published a bi-weekly column in the *Bismarck Tribune* and collaborated with her mother on two books. Upon U.S. Senator John Hoeven's election in 2010, Julie helped lead his state offices as state director.

Summary of Duties

See description of Summary of Duties on previous page.

Public Service Commissioner

Brian Kroshus

Personal

Born in 1963 in Fargo, N.D.; two daughters, Megan and Alyssa, and son-in-law, Michael

Party Affiliation

Republican

Education

Graduate of North Dakota State University, B.S.

Professional Experience

Kroshus was appointed to the Public Service Commission in March 2017 by Governor Doug Burgum. He has a background in business, agriculture, and energy. Prior to his appointment to the Public Service Commission, Kroshus spent 30 years in business management in the publishing industry, including 10 years (1987-1997) at Forum Communications, Fargo, and 20 years (1997-2017) with Lee Enterprises, Bismarck. During his time with Lee Enterprises, Brian spent 10 years as publisher of *The Bismarck Tribune*, 17 years as publisher of *Farm and Ranch Guide*, and 13 years as group publisher of Lee Agri-Media.

Kroshus has served as a board member and trustee for numerous organizations, including United Way, Bismarck-Mandan Chamber, Bismarck-Mandan Development Foundation, Sanford Health Foundation, Lewis and Clark Fort Mandan Foundation, and Bismarck State College Foundation. He served as president of the Bismarck State College Foundation in 2012-2013 and co-chaired the United Way Missouri Slope Area Wide Annual Gift Giving Campaign in 2009.

Summary of Duties

See description of Summary of Duties on page 215.

Tax Commissioner

Ryan Rauschenberger

Personal
Born in 1982 in Kenmare, N.D.; resides in Bismarck

Party Affiliation
Republican

Education
Graduate of University of North Dakota with a bachelor's degree in accounting and a master's degree in business administration

Professional Experience
Auditor for PricewaterhouseCoopers; manager of energy development for the North Dakota Department of Commerce; deputy tax commissioner, July 2009-December 2013; appointed Tax Commissioner by Governor Jack Dalrymple to fill a vacancy, effective January 2014; elected Tax Commissioner in November 2014.

Summary of Duties
The Tax Commissioner is responsible for the fair and effective administration of the tax laws of North Dakota. As the primary revenue-producing agency for the state of North Dakota, the department collects more than 95 percent of all general fund dollars. The Office of State Tax Commissioner collects revenue from 36 tax types, such as sales and use taxes; individual and corporate income; oil and gas taxes; motor fuels; excise taxes, including motor vehicle, alcohol, and tobacco product taxes; estate; and other miscellaneous taxes. The department also issues sales and use tax permits.

The Tax Commissioner provides assistance in establishing uniformity of procedures for the administration of property taxes. The Property Tax Division makes annual tentative valuations of centrally assessed properties (railroads, utility companies, wind farms, pipelines, airlines, and telecommunications companies) for the Tax Commissioner to submit to the State Board of Equalization, which makes the final assessments.

The Tax Commissioner researches and prepares opinions answering tax-related questions; drafts proposals for changes in the tax laws; assists the Office of Management and Budget with preparing the revenue forecast; estimates the fiscal impact of all tax-related legislation; conducts all litigation for the department and the State Board of Equalization; and helps draft rules and regulations for the administration of the various state taxes.

Superintendent of Public Instruction

Kirsten Baesler

Personal

Born 1969 in Flasher, N.D.; three adult sons, Lee and twins, Mitchel and Chancellor

Education

Master's degree in education and library information technology, Valley City State University; bachelor's degree in elementary education, magna cum laude, Minot State University; associate of arts degree, Bismarck State College; associate of science degree, Bismarck State College

Professional Experience

Baesler worked for 23 years in the Bismarck school district as an assistant principal, a library media specialist, a technology integration specialist, and as an aide to children with intellectual disabilities. In 2004, she was elected to the Mandan School Board, serving for nine years, including seven years as president of the board. She is a former chairwoman of the board of trustees of Morton County's public library. Baesler was elected as North Dakota's superintendent of public instruction in November 2012 and was re-elected in 2016. Baesler serves on 15 boards, including the Education Standards and Practices Board; the Educational Technology Council; the Teachers' Fund for Retirement Board; and the Board of University and School Lands, which manages state land holdings and oversees a $3 billion trust fund that benefits North Dakota's public schools. She is a member of the board of directors for the National Dropout Prevention Center at Clemson University and a member of the Joe Foss Institute's Civics Education Initiative advisory board. She has completed the Harvard Graduate School Educational Leadership Program.

Summary of Duties

The Superintendent of Public Instruction is an advocate for more than 110,000 North Dakota students in grades kindergarten through 12. The superintendent oversees compliance with state and federal laws and regulations that affect education. The job's duties include oversight of elementary and secondary education, school accreditation, review of proposed school construction projects, and the development of course content standards and assessments of student progress. The superintendent adopts rules for the credentialing of teachers and administrators. She administers state and federal programs, including state aid to schools, assistance for students who need extra help in reading and mathematics, instruction for students who are not fluent in English, and school breakfast and lunch programs. She is in charge of implementing a uniform system for accounting, budgeting, and reporting school district data and responsible for publishing yearly reports on school finance and teacher compensation. The superintendent selects the North Dakota Teacher of the Year. In addition to the Department of Public Instruction, the superintendent has charge of the State Library, the North Dakota School for the Deaf/Resource Center for the Deaf and Hard of Hearing in Devils Lake, and North Dakota Vision Services/School for the Blind in Grand Forks.

Executive Officials Contact Information

The Constitution establishes all elective offices. This distribution of power has traditionally been seen as severely limiting the power of the Governor. However, the Governor's powers have increased over the more recent history of the state with greater control of the budgeting process and more direct appointments of the heads of the state's largest executive agencies. At the same time, North Dakota has a larger number of elected officials than most states outside of southern states.

Three elected officials – the Governor, Agriculture Commissioner, and Attorney General – exercise joint power through the Industrial Commission. This product of the industrial program of the Nonpartisan League was established to manage state-owned industries. The use of commissions and boards headed by elected officials has been common in North Dakota state government, although the Industrial Commission is a unique expression of that phenomenon.

The following is contact information and term requirements for the executive official's offices:

Governor

600 East Boulevard Avenue, 1st Floor
Bismarck, ND 58505-0001
Phone: 701-328-2200
Fax: 701-328-2205
Web: www.governor.nd.gov
[Constitution, Article V, Section 1; NDCC 54-07]

Term: four years. Qualifications: citizen of the United States, qualified elector of the state, at least 30 years old, resident of the state for five years immediately prior to the election.

Lieutenant Governor

600 East Boulevard Avenue, 1st Floor
Bismarck, ND 58505-0001
Phone: 701-328-2200
Fax: 701-328-2205
Web: www.governor.nd.gov
[Constitution, Article V, Section 2; NDCC 54-08]

Term: four years. Qualifications: same as Governor, elected on joint ballot with Governor since 1975.

Agriculture Commissioner

600 East Boulevard Avenue, Dept. 602
Bismarck, ND 58505-0200
Phone: 701-328-4754
Toll Free: 800-242-7535
North Dakota Mediation Services: 701-328-4158
Fax: 701-328-4567
Web: www.agdepartment.com
Email: ndda@nd.gov
[Constitution, Article V, Section 2; NDCC 4-01]

Term: four years. Qualifications: qualified elector of the state, at least 25 years old. Originally the Commissioner of Agriculture and Labor, the office was divided in 1965, and the term of office was lengthened from two years to four.

Attorney General

600 East Boulevard Avenue, Dept. 125
Bismarck, ND 58505-0040
Phone: 701-328-2210
Fax: 701-328-2226
Web: www.attorneygeneral.nd.gov
Email: ndag@nd.gov
TTY: 800-366-6888
Consumer Protection Division: 800-472-2600
Gaming Division: 701-328-4848
Bureau of Criminal Investigation (BCI): 800-472-2185
[Constitution, Article V, Section 2; NDCC 54-12]

Term: four years, except in 2004 when the term was two years. Qualifications: qualified elector of the state, at least 25 years old, licensed attorney. The Attorney General was elected to a two-year term until passage of a constitutional amendment in 1964 established a four-year term of office.

State Auditor

600 East Boulevard Avenue, Dept. 117
Bismarck, ND 58505-0060
Phone: 701-328-2241
Fax: 701-328-1406
Web: www.nd.gov/auditor
Email: ndsao@nd.gov
[Constitution, Article V, Section 2; NDCC 54-10]

Term: four years. Qualifications: qualified elector of the state, at least 25 years old.

Insurance Commissioner

600 East Boulevard Avenue
Bismarck, ND 58505-0320
Phone: 701-328-2440
Toll Free: 800-247-0560 - Consumer Hotline
Fax: 701-328-4880
Web: www.nd.gov/ndins
[Constitution, Article V, Section 2; NDCC 26.1-01]

Term: four years. Qualifications: qualified elector of the state, at least 25 years old.

Superintendent of Public Instruction

600 East Boulevard Avenue, Dept. 201
Floors 9, 10 and 11
Bismarck, ND 58505-0440
Phone: 701-328-2260
Fax: 701-328-2461
Web: www.dpi.state.nd.us
Email: dpi@nd.gov
[Constitution, Article V, Section 4; NDCC 15.1-02-01]

Term: four years. Qualifications: qualified elector of the state, at least 25 years old, resident of North Dakota for five years preceding the election to office.

Public Service Commission

600 East Boulevard Avenue, Dept. 408
Bismarck, ND 58505-0480
Phone: 701-328-2400
Fax: 701-328-2410
TTY: 800-366-6888
Web: www.psc.state.nd.us
Email: ndpsc@nd.gov
[Constitution, Article V, Section 2; NDCC 49-01]

Term: three commissioners serving six-year terms with one commissioner's term expiring every two years. Qualifications: qualified elector of the state, at least 25 years old.

Secretary of State

600 East Boulevard Avenue, Dept. 108
Bismarck, ND 58505-0500
Phone: 701-328-2900
Toll Free: 800-352-0867
Fax: 701-328-2992
TTY: 701-328-4083
Web: www.nd.gov/sos
Email: sos@nd.gov
[Constitution, Article V, Section 2; NDCC 54-09]

Term: four years. Qualifications: qualified elector of the state, at least 25 years old. The Secretary of State was elected to a two-year term prior to passage of a constitutional amendment in 1964 establishing a four-year term of office.

Tax Commissioner

600 East Boulevard Avenue, Dept. 127
Bismarck, ND 58505-0599
Phone: 701-328-7088
Toll Free: 877-328-7088
Fax: 701-328-3700
Relay ND: 800-366-6888
Web: www.nd.gov/tax
Email: taxinfo@nd.gov
[Constitution, Article V, Section 2; NDCC 57-01]

Term: four years. Qualifications: qualified elector of the state, at least 25 years old. The Tax Commissioner was first elected in 1940.

State Treasurer

600 East Boulevard Avenue, 3rd Floor, Dept. 120
Bismarck, ND 58505-0600
Phone: 701-328-2643
Fax: 701-328-3002
Web: www.nd.gov/treasuer
Email: treasurer@nd.gov
[Constitution, Article V, Section 2; NDCC 54-11]

Term: four years. Qualifications: qualified elector of the state, at least 25 years old. The State Treasurer was elected to a two-year term prior to passage of a constitutional amendment in 1964 establishing a four-year term of office.

Executive Branch

Chronology of Elective State Officers Since Statehood

Elected officials take office on January 1 except the Governor and Lieutenant Governor who take office on December 15. (Legislators take office on December 1.)

Governor

The office was created by the 1889 state constitution and originally provided for a two-year term. By constitutional amendment, adopted June 30, 1964, the term was increased to four years (Article V, Section 1).

John Miller (R) (1843-1908) 1889-1890
Elected 1889, did not seek re-election 1890
Andrew H. Burke (R) (1850-1918) 1891-1892
Elected 1890; defeated for re-election 1892
Eli C. D. Shortridge (Pop) (1830-1908) 1893-1894
Elected 1892; did not seek re-election 1894
Roger Allin (R) (1848-1936) 1895-1896
Elected 1894; did not seek re-election 1896
Frank A. Briggs (R) (1858-1898) 1897-1898
Elected 1896; died in office August 9, 1898
Joseph M. Devine (R) (1861-1938) 1898
Lieutenant Governor; completed Frank Briggs' term
Frederick B. Fancher (R) (1852-1944) 1899-1900
Elected 1898; defeated for renomination 1900
Frank White (R) (1856-1940) 1901-1904
Elected 1900, 1902; did not seek re-election 1904
Elmore Y. Sarles (R) (1859-1929) 1905-1906
Elected 1904; defeated for re-election 1906
John Burke (D) (1859-1937) 1907-1912
Elected 1906, 1908, 1910; did not seek re-election 1912
Louis B. Hanna (R) (1861-1948) 1913-1916
Elected 1912, 1914; did not seek re-election 1916
Lynn J. Frazier (R) (1874-1947) 1917-1921
Elected 1916, 1918, 1920; recalled October 28, 1921
Ragnvold A. Nestos (R) (1877-1942) 1921-1924
Elected 1921, 1922; defeated for re-election 1924
Arthur G. Sorlie (R) (1874-1928) 1925-1928
Elected 1924, 1926; died in office August 28, 1928
Walter J. Maddock (R) (1880-1951) 1928
Lieutenant Governor; completed Arthur G. Sorlie's term
George F. Shafer (R) (1888-1948) 1929-1932
Elected 1928, 1930; did not seek re-election 1932
William Langer (R) (1886-1959) 1933-1934
Elected 1932; removed from office July 17, 1934

Ole H. Olson (R) (1872-1954) 1934
Lieutenant Governor; completed William Langer's term

Thomas H. Moodie (D) (1878-1948) 1935
Elected 1934; removed from office February 16, 1935

Walter Welford (R) (1868-1952) 1935-1936
Lieutenant Governor; completed Thomas H. Moodie's term; defeated for election 1936

William Langer (R) (1886-1959) 1937-1938
Elected 1936; did not seek re-election 1938

John Moses (D) (1885-1945) 1939-1944
Elected 1938, 1940, 1942; did not seek re-election 1944

Fred G. Aandahl (R) (1897-1966) 1945-1950
Elected 1944, 1946, 1948; did not seek re-election 1950

C. Norman Brunsdale (R) (1891-1978) 1951-1956
Elected 1950, 1952, 1954; did not seek re-election 1956

John E. Davis (R) (1913-1990) 1957-1960
Elected 1956, 1958; did not seek re-election 1960

William L. Guy (D) (1919-2013) 1961-1972
Elected 1960, 1962, 1964, 1968; did not seek re-election 1972

Arthur A. Link (D) (1914-2010) 1973-1980
Elected 1972, 1976; defeated for re-election 1980

Allen I. Olson (R) (1938-) 1981-1984
Elected 1980; defeated for re-election 1984

George A. Sinner (D) (1928-) 1985-1992
Elected 1984, 1988; did not seek re-election 1992

In the General Election November 4, 1986, voters approved a constitutional amendment changing the date of office for Governor and Lieutenant Governor from January 1 to December 15. (1987 Session Laws, Chapter 776). That provision is now found in Article V, Section 5, of the North Dakota Constitution.

Edward T. Schafer (R) (1946-) 1992-2000
Elected 1992, 1996; did not seek re-election 2000

John H. Hoeven (R) (1957-) 2000-2010
Elected 2000, 2004, 2008; resigned December 7, 2010, following election to U.S. Senate

John (Jack) Dalrymple (R) (1948-) 2010-2016
Appointed in 2010 to fill unexpired term of John Hoeven; elected 2012; did not seek re-election 2016

Doug Burgum (R) (1956-) 2016-present
Elected 2016

Lieutenant Governor

In 1974, voters approved a constitutional amendment requiring the Governor and the Lieutenant Governor be of the same party (joint ballot) (Article V, Section 4).

Alfred Dickey (R) (1846-1901)..1889-1890
Elected 1889; did not seek renomination 1890
Roger Allin (R) (1848-1936)..1891-1892
Elected 1890; defeated for renomination at 1892 Republican convention
Elmer D. Wallace (D-I) (1844-1928)...1893-1894
Elected 1892; did not seek re-election 1894
John H. Worst (R) (1850-1945) 1895-1896
Elected 1894; defeated for renomination at 1896 Republican convention
Joseph M. Devine (R) (1861-1938)..1897-1900
Elected 1896, 1898; did not seek re-election 1900
David Bartlett (R) (1854-1913) 1901-1906
Elected 1900, 1902, 1904; did not seek re-election 1906
Robert S. Lewis (R) (1856-1956)..1907-1910
Elected 1906, 1908; did not seek re-election 1910
Usher L. Burdick (R) (1879-1960)..1911-1912
Elected 1910; did not seek re-election 1912
Anton T. Kraabel (R) (1862-1934)..1913-1914
Elected 1912; defeated in June 1914 Republican primary
John H. Fraine (R) (1861-1943)..1915-1916
Elected 1914; did not seek re-election 1916
Anton T. Kraabel (R) (1862-1934)..1917-1918
Elected 1916; defeated in June 1918 Republican primary
Howard R. Wood (R) (1887-1958)..1919-1922
Elected 1918, 1920; did not seek re-election 1922
Frank H. Hyland (R) (1880-1934)..1923-1924
Elected 1922; did not seek re-election 1924
Walter J. Maddock (R) (1880-1951) 1925-1928
Elected 1924, 1926; did not seek re-election 1928
John W. Carr (R) (1874-1932)..1929-1932
Elected 1928, 1930; died in office June 14, 1932
Ole H. Olson (R) (1872-1954) 1932-1934
Elected 1932; defeated in June 1934 Republican primary
Walter Welford (R) (1868-1952)...1935-1936
Elected 1934; did not seek re-election 1936
Thorstein H. H. Thoresen (R) (1885-1956)...1937-1938
Elected 1936; did not seek re-election 1938
Jack A. Patterson (R) (1890-1971) 1939-1940
Elected 1938; did not seek re-election 1940
Oscar W. Hagen (R) (1884-1945)..1941-1942
Elected 1940; did not seek re-election 1942
Henry Holt (D) (1888-1944)...1943-1944
Elected 1942; died in office March 2, 1944
Clarence P. Dahl (R) (1892-1976)...1944-1950
Elected 1944, 1946, 1948; did not seek re-election 1950
Ray Schnell (R) (1893-1970) 1951-1952
Elected 1950; defeated in June 1952 Republican primary

Clarence P. Dahl (R) (1892-1976)... 1953-1956
Elected 1952, 1954; did not seek re-election 1956

Francis Clyde Duffy (R) (1890-1977).. 1957-1958
Elected 1956; did not seek re-election 1958

Clarence P. Dahl (R) (1892-1976)... 1959-1960
Elected 1958; did not seek re-election 1960

Orville W. Hagen (R) (1915-2007)... 1961-1962
Elected 1960; did not seek re-election 1962

Frank A. Wenstrom (R) (1903-1997).. 1963-1964
Elected 1962; defeated in November 1964 general election

Charles Tighe (D) (1927-2004).. 1965-1968
Elected 1964; defeated in November 1968 general election

Richard F. Larsen (R) (1936-).. 1969-1972
Elected 1968; did not seek re-election 1972

Wayne G. Sanstead (D) (1935-).. 1973-1980
Elected 1972, 1976; defeated for re-election 1980

Ernest Sands (R) (1922-2012)... 1981-1984
Elected 1980; defeated for re-election 1984

Ruth Meiers (D) (1925-1987).. 1985-1987
Elected 1984; died in office March 19, 1987

Lloyd B. Omdahl (D) (1931-).. 1987-1992
Appointed April 22, 1987, eff. May 15, to complete Ruth Meiers' term; elected 1988; did not seek re-election 1992

Rosemarie Myrdal (R) (1929-)... 1992-2000
Elected 1992, 1996; did not seek re-election 2000

John (Jack) Dalrymple (R) (1948-).. 2000-2010
Elected 2000, 2004, 2008; became governor December 7, 2010

Drew H. Wrigley (R) (1965-)... 2010-2016
Appointed in 2010 to fill the unexpired term of Jack Dalrymple; elected 2012; did not seek re-election 2016

Brent Sanford (R) (1971-)... 2016-present
Elected 2016

Secretary of State

Originally a two-year term, the office became a four-year term with adoption of a constitutional amendment in June 1964 (Article V, Section 12). Voters approved a change to the Constitution at the Primary Election on June 13, 2000, that puts one-half of the elected officials on the ballot each election year. To begin that process, the Secretary of State, the Commissioner of Agriculture, the Attorney General, and the Tax Commissioner were elected for two-year terms in 2004. Those offices then returned to four-year terms (2001 Laws of North Dakota, Chapter 591).

John Flittie (R) (1856-1913)... 1889-1892
Elected 1889, 1890; did not seek re-election 1892

Christian M. Dahl (R) (1865-1923).. 1893-1896
Elected 1892, 1894; did not seek re-election 1896
Fred Falley (R) (1859-1907).. 1897-1900
Elected 1896, 1898; did not seek re-election 1900
Edward F. Porter (R) (1858-1915) 1901-1906
Elected 1900, 1902, 1904; did not seek re-election 1906
Alfred Blaisdell (R) (1875-1946) 1907-1910
Elected 1906, 1908; did not seek re-election 1910
Patrick D. Norton (R) (1876-1953) 1911-1912
Elected 1910; did not seek re-election 1912
Thomas Hall (R) (1869-1958).. 1913-1924
Elected 1912, 1914, 1916, 1918, 1920, 1922; did not seek re-election 1924
Robert Byrne (R) (1886-1967)... 1925-1934
Elected 1924, 1926, 1928, 1930, 1932; defeated in June 1934 Republican primary
James D. Gronna (R) (1884-1963).. 1935-1940
Elected 1934, 1936, 1938; did not seek re-election 1940
Herman Thorson (R) (1880-1960) 1941-1942
Elected 1940; defeated in November 1942 general election
Thomas Hall (R) (1869-1958).. 1943-1954
Elected 1942, 1944, 1946, 1948, 1950, 1952; did not seek re-election 1954
Ben Meier (R) (1918-1995) 1955-1988
Elected 1954, 1956, 1958, 1960, 1962, 1964, 1968, 1972, 1976, 1980, 1984; did not seek re-election 1988
Jim Kusler (D) (1947-)... 1989-1992
Elected 1988; defeated for re-election 1992
Alvin A. Jaeger (R) (1943-) 1993-present
Elected 1992, 1996, 2000, 2004, 2006, 2010, 2014

State Auditor

Originally a two-year term, the office became a four-year term with adoption of a constitutional amendment in June 1964 (Article V, Section 12).

John P. Bray (R) (1859-1917)...1889-1891
Elected 1889, 1890; resigned September 1892
Archie Currie (R) (1860-1943) 1892-1892
Appointed September 1892 to complete John P. Bray's term
Arthur W. Porter (D-I) (1857-1952) 1893-1894
Elected 1892; defeated in November 1894 general election
Frank A. Briggs (R) (1858-1898) 1895-1896
Elected 1894; did not seek re-election 1896
Nathan B. Hannum (R) (1851-1920)...1897-1898
Elected 1896; did not seek re-election 1898
Albert N. Carlblom (R) (1865-1920) 1899-1902

Elected 1898, 1900; did not seek re-election 1902

Herbert L. Holmes (R) (1853-1922)..1903-1908

Elected 1902, 1904, 1906; did not seek re-election 1908

David K. Brightbill (R) (1865-1949)..1909-1912

Elected 1908, 1910; did not seek re-election 1912

Carl O. Jorgenson (R) (1881-1951)..1913-1916

Elected 1912, 1914; defeated in June 1916 Republican primary

Carl R. Kositzky (R) (1876-1940)..1917-1920

Elected 1916, 1918; defeated in June 1920 Republican primary

David C. Poindexter (R) (1891-1927)...1921-1924

Elected 1920, 1922; defeated in June 1924 Republican primary

John Steen (R) (1874-1959)...1925-1934

Elected 1924, 1926, 1928, 1930, 1932; did not seek re-election 1934

Berta E. Baker (R) (1875-1964)...1935-1956

Elected 1934, 1936, 1938, 1940, 1942, 1944, 1946, 1948, 1950, 1952, 1954; did not seek re-election 1956

Curtis G. Olson (R) (1908-2004)..1957-1972

Elected 1956, 1958, 1960, 1962, 1964, 1968; did not seek re-election 1972

Robert W. Peterson (R) (1929-2013)..1973-1996

Elected 1972, 1976, 1980, 1984, 1988, 1992, did not seek re-election 1996

Robert R. Peterson (R) (1951-)...1997-2016

Elected 1996, 2000, 2004, 2008, 2012; did not seek re-election 2016

Joshua C. Gallion (R) (1979-).. 2017-present

Elected 2016

State Treasurer

Originally a two-year term, the office became a four-year term with adoption of a constitutional amendment in June 1964 (Article V, Section 12). Article V, Section 12, prohibits any person from serving more than two consecutive terms as State Treasurer; that prohibition was removed in 1996 by a vote of the people (S.L. 1995, ch. 646, HCR 3009).

Lewis E. Booker (R) (1846-1918)... 1889-1892

Elected 1889, 1890; defeated in November 1892 general election

Knud J. Nomland (D-I) (1852-1922).. 1893-1894

Elected 1892; defeated in November 1894 general election

George E. Nichols (R) (1856-1935)... 1895-1898

Elected 1894, 1896; ineligible for re-election 1898

Dennis W. Driscoll (R) (1849-1905).. 1899-1900

Elected 1898; defeated for renomination in 1900 Republican convention

Donald H. McMillan (R) (1849-unknown).. 1901-1904

Elected 1900, 1902; ineligible for re-election 1904

Albert Peterson (R) (1862-1944) 1905-1908

Elected 1904, 1906; ineligible for re-election 1908

George L. Bickford (R) (1874-1937) 1909-1910

Elected 1908; defeated in June 1910 Republican primary

Gunder Olson (R) (1852-1948) 1911-1914

Elected 1910, 1912; ineligible for re-election 1914

John Steen (R) (1874-1959) 1915-1918

Elected 1914, 1916; ineligible for re-election 1918

Obert A. Olson (R) (1882-1938) 1919-1920

Elected 1918; did not seek re-election 1920

John Steen (R) (1874-1959) 1921-1924

Elected 1920, 1922; ineligible for re-election 1924

Chessmur A. Fisher (R) (1868-1948) 1925-1928

Elected 1924, 1926; ineligible for re-election 1928

Berta E. Baker (R) (1875-1964) 1929-1932

Elected 1928, 1930; ineligible for re-election 1932

Alfred S. Dale (R) (1896-1974) 1933-1934

Elected 1932; defeated in June 1934 Republican primary

John Gray (R) (1877-1952) 1935-1938

Elected 1934, 1936; ineligible for re-election 1938

John R. Omland (R) (1893-1970) 1939-1940

Elected 1938; defeated in June 1940 Republican primary

Carl Anderson (R) (1897-1945) 1941-1944

Elected 1940, 1942; ineligible for re-election 1944

Otto G. Krueger (R) (1890-1963) 1945

Elected 1944; resigned September 7, 1945

Hjalmer W. Swenson (R) (1885-1958) 1945-1948

Appointed October 3, 1945, to fill Otto G. Krueger's term; elected 1946; defeated in June 1948 Republican primary

Albert Jacobson (R) (1899-1958) 1949-1952

Elected 1948, 1950; ineligible for re-election 1952

Ray Thompson (R) (1911-1957) 1953-1954

Elected 1952; defeated in June 1954 Republican primary

Albert Jacobson (R) (1899-1958) 1955-1958

Elected 1954, 1956; died in office October 27, 1958

Mike J. Baumgartner (R) (1895-1969) 1958

Appointed November 1, 1958, to fill Albert Jacobson's term

John R. Erickson (R) (1905-1980) 1959-1962

Elected 1958, 1960; ineligible for re-election 1962

Phil Hoghaug (R) (1906-1971) 1963-1964

Elected 1962; defeated in November 1964 general election

Walter Christensen (D) (1910-1979) 1965-1968

Elected 1964; defeated in November 1968 general election

Bernice Asbridge (R) (1919-2004) 1969-1972

Elected 1968; defeated in November 1972 general election

Walter Christensen (D) (1910-1979) 1973-1979

Elected 1972, 1976; died in office August 3, 1979

Robert E. Hanson (D) (1947-2015) 1979-1980

Appointed September 28, 1979, to fill Walter Christensen's term; defeated for election 1980

John S. Lesmeister (R) (1955-2006)... 1981-1984

Elected 1980; defeated for re-election 1984

Robert E. Hanson (D) (1947-2015)... 1985-1992

Elected 1984, 1988; ineligible for re-election 1992

Kathi Gilmore (D) (1944-) 1993-2004

Elected 1992, 1996, 2000, did not seek re-election in 2004

Kelly L. Schmidt (R) (1962-) 2005-present

Elected 2004, 2008, 2012, 2016

Attorney General

Originally a two-year term, the office became a four-year term with adoption of a constitutional amendment in June 1964 (Article V, Section 12). Voters approved a change to the Constitution at the Primary Election on June 13, 2000, that puts one-half of the elected officials on the ballot each election year. To begin that process, the Secretary of State, the Commissioner of Agriculture, the Attorney General, and the Tax Commissioner were elected for two-year terms in 2004. Those offices then returned to four-year terms (2001 Laws of North Dakota, Chapter 591).

George F. Goodwin (R) (1849-1918)...1889-1890

Elected 1889; defeated for renomination in 1890 Republican convention

Clarence A. M. Spencer (R) (1850-1933) 1891-1892

Elected 1890; did not seek re-election 1892

William H. Standish (D-I) (1843-1923)..1893-1894

Elected 1892; defeated in November 1894 general election

John F. Cowan (R) (1858-1917)...1895-1900

Elected 1894, 1896, 1898; did not seek re-election 1900

Oliver D. Comstock (R) (1865-1945) 1901-1902

Elected 1900; defeated for renomination in 1902 Republican convention

Carl N. Frich (R) (1867-1927)...1903-1906

Elected 1902, 1904; did not seek re-election 1906

Thomas F. McCue (R) (1866-1938) 1907-1908

Elected 1906; defeated in June 1908 Republican primary

Andrew Miller (R) (1870-1960)..1909-1914

Elected 1908, 1910, 1912; did not seek re-election 1914

Henry J. Linde (R) (1879-1917) 1915-1916

Elected 1914; defeated in June 1916 Republican primary

William Langer (R) (1886-1959)..1917-1920

Elected 1916, 1918; did not seek re-election 1920

William Lemke (R) (1878-1950)... 1921

Elected 1920; recalled October 28, 1921

Sveinbjorn Johnson (R) (1883-1946) 1921-1922

Elected October 28, 1921; did not seek re-election 1922

George F. Shafer (R) (1888-1948)...1923-1928

Elected 1922, 1924, 1926; did not seek re-election 1928
James Morris (R) (1893-1980) 1929-1932
Elected 1928, 1930; defeated in June 1932 Republican primary
Arthur J. Gronna (R) (1897-1965) 1933
Elected 1932; resigned November 1, 1933
P. O. Sathre (R) (1878-1968) 1933-1937
Appointed November 1, 1933, to fill Arthur J. Gronna's term; elected 1934, 1936; resigned December 6, 1937
Alvin C. Strutz (R) (1903-1973) 1937-1944
Appointed December 7, 1937, to fill P. O. Sathre's term; elected 1938, 1940, 1942; did not seek re-election 1944
Nels G. Johnson (R) (1896-1958) 1945-1948
Elected 1944, 1946; defeated in June 1948 Republican primary; resigned September 1, 1948
P.O. Sathre (R-NPL) (1878-1968) 1948
Appointed September 1, 1948, to fill Nels G. Johnson's term
Wallace E. Warner (R) (1916-1994) 1949-1950
Elected 1948; did not seek re-election 1950
Elmo T. Christianson (R) (1920-1996) 1951-1954
Elected 1950, 1952; resigned May 5, 1954
Paul Benson (R) (1918-2004) 1954
Appointed May 15, 1954, to fill Elmo T. Christianson's term
Leslie R. Burgum (R) (1890-1984) 1955-1962
Elected 1954, 1956, 1958, 1960; did not seek re-election 1962
Helgi Johanneson (R) (1906-1994) 1963-1972
Elected 1962, 1964, 1968; did not seek re-election 1972
Allen I. Olson (R) (1938-) 1973-1980
Elected 1972, 1976; did not seek re-election 1980
Robert Wefald (R) (1942-) 1981-1984
Elected 1980; defeated for re-election 1984
Nicholas Spaeth (D) (1950-2014) 1985-1992
Elected 1984, 1988; did not seek re-election 1992
Mary Kathryn "Heidi" Heitkamp (D) (1955-) 1993-2000
Elected 1992, 1996; did not seek re-election 2000
Wayne Stenehjem (R) (1953-) 2001-present
Elected 2000, 2004, 2006, 2010, 2014

Commissioner of Insurance

Originally a two-year term, the office became a four-year term with adoption of a constitutional amendment in June 1964 (Article V, Section 12).

A. L. Carey (R) (1846-1906) 1889-1892
Elected 1889, 1890; did not seek re-election 1892
James Cudhie (D-I) (1858-1941) 1893-1894
Elected 1892; defeated in November 1894 general election
Frederick B. Fancher (R) (1852-1944) 1895-1898

Elected 1894, 1896; did not seek re-election 1898

George W. Harrison (R) (1867-1931).. 1899-1900

Elected 1898; defeated for renomination at 1900 Republican convention

Ferdinand Leutz (R) (1854-1934).. 1901-1904

Elected 1900, 1902; defeated for renomination at 1904 Republican convention

Ernest C. Cooper (R) (1856-1917) 1905-1910

Elected 1904, 1906, 1908; did not seek re-election 1910

Walter C. Taylor (R) (1870-1929).. 1911-1916

Elected 1910, 1912, 1914; defeated in June 1916 Republican primary

Sveinung A. Olsness (R) (1866-1954).. 1917-1934

Elected 1916, 1918, 1920, 1922, 1924, 1926, 1928, 1930, 1932; defeated in June 1934 Republican primary

Harold Hopton (R) (1894-1984) 1935-1936

Elected 1934; defeated in June 1936 Republican primary

Oscar E. Erickson (R) (1884-1945) 1937-1945

Elected 1936, 1938, 1940, 1942, 1944; died in office August 15, 1945

Otto G. Krueger (R) (1890-1963)..1945-1950

Appointed September 7, 1945, to fill Oscar E. Erickson's term; elected 1946, 1948; did not seek re-election 1950

Alfred J. Jensen (R) (1893-1973)... 1951-1962

Elected 1950, 1952, 1954, 1956, 1958, 1960; did not seek re-election 1962

Frank Albers (R) (1909-1974)... 1963-1964

Elected 1962; defeated in June 1964 Republican primary

Kelly O. Nygaard (D) (1906-1979) 1965-1968

Elected 1964; defeated in November 1968 general election

Joris O. Wigen (R) (1917-1987) 1969-1976

Elected 1968, 1972; defeated for re-election 1976

Byron Knutson (D) (1929-) 1977-1980

Elected 1976; defeated for re-election 1980

Jorris O. Wigen (R) (1917-1987)... 1981-1984

Elected 1980; did not seek re-election 1984

Earl Pomeroy (D) (1952-)... 1985-1992

Elected 1984, 1988; did not seek re-election 1992

Glenn Pomeroy (D) (1956-)... 1993-2000

Elected 1992, 1996; did not seek re-election 2000

Jim Poolman (R) (1970-) 2001-2007

Elected in 2000, 2004; resigned August 31, 2007

Adam Hamm (R) (1971-) 2007-2016

Appointed October 9, 2007, to fill Jim Poolman's term; elected 2008, 2012; did not seek re-election 2016

Jon Godfread (R) (1982-) 2017-present

Elected in 2016

Commissioner of Agriculture and Labor

Originally a two-year term, the office became a four-year term with adoption of a constitutional amendment in June 1964 (Article V, Section 12). This combination office existed until 1967.

Henry T. Helgesen (R) (1857-1917) 1889-1892
Elected 1889, 1890; did not seek re-election 1892
George E. Adams (D-I) (1859-1946)
Elected 1892; but failed to qualify for office
Nelson Williams (D-I) (1856-1941) 1893-1894
Appointed January 3, 1893, to fill George E. Adams' term; did not seek re-election 1894
Andrew H. Laughlin (R) (1848-1914) 1895-1896
Elected 1894; defeated for renomination at 1896 Republican convention
Henry U. Thomas (R) (1853-1926) 1897-1900
Elected 1896, 1898; did not seek re-election 1900
Rollin J. Turner (R) (1850-1918) 1901-1904
Elected 1900, 1902; did not seek re-election 1904
William C. Gilbreath (R) (1851-1921) 1905-1914
Elected 1904, 1906, 1908, 1910, 1912; did not seek re-election 1914
Robert F. Flint (R) (1872-1941) 1915-1916
Elected 1914; defeated in June 1916 Republican primary
John N. Hagan (R) (1873-1952) 1917-1921
Elected 1916, 1918, 1920; recalled October 28, 1921
Joseph A. Kitchen (R) (1878-1942) 1921-1932
Elected October 28, 1921, 1922, 1924, 1926, 1928, 1930; defeated in June 1932 Republican primary
John Husby (R) (1884-1965) 1933-1934
Elected 1932; defeated in June 1934 Republican primary
Theodore Martell (R) (1894-1967) 1935-1936
Elected 1934; defeated in June 1936 Republican primary
John N. Hagan (R) (1873-1952) 1937-1938
Elected 1936; did not seek re-election 1938
Matt Dahl (R) (1884-1976) 1939-1964
Elected 1938, 1940, 1942, 1944, 1946, 1948, 1950, 1952, 1954, 1956, 1958, 1960, 1962; did not seek re-election 1964
Arne Dahl (R) (1907-1974) 1965-1966
Elected 1964

Commissioner of Agriculture

A constitutional amendment adopted June 28, 1960, authorized the Legislative Assembly, if it so chose, to separate agriculture and labor into two distinct offices. The 1965 Legislative Assembly enacted the necessary legislation, and in January 1967, the former Commissioner of Agriculture and Labor became the new Commissioner of Agriculture. Voters approved a change to the Constitution at the Primary Election on

June 13, 2000, which put one-half of the elected officials on the ballot each election year. To begin that process, the Secretary of State, the Commissioner of Agriculture, the Attorney General, and the Tax Commissioner were elected for two-year terms in 2004. Those offices then returned to four-year terms (2001 Laws of North Dakota, Chapter 591).

Arne Dahl (R) (1907-1974) 1967-1974
Elected 1968, 1972; died in office February 2, 1974
Myron Just (D) (1941-) 1974-1980
Appointed February 14, 1974, to fill Arne Dahl's term;
elected 1976; did not seek re-election 1980
H. Kent Jones (R) (1926-1995) 1981-1988
Elected 1980, 1984; 1988 on ballot as independent, defeated for re-election
Sarah Vogel (D) (1946-) 1989-1996
Elected 1988, 1992; did not seek re-election 1996
Roger Johnson (D) (1953-) 1997-2009
Elected 1996, 2000, 2004, 2006; resigned April 4, 2009
Doug Goehring (R) (1965-).......... 2009-present
Appointed April 6, 2009; elected 2010, 2014

Commissioner of Labor

Following passage of the June 28, 1960, constitutional amendment, the 1965 Legislative Assembly created the office of Commissioner of Labor, to be elected on a no-party ballot for a four-year term, beginning with the general election in 1966 (1965 S.L., ch. 236) (North Dakota Century Code Sections 34-05-01.2 and 16.1-11-08). Beginning January 1, 1999, the Governor appoints the Labor Commissioner (1995 S.L., ch. 334, amendment to NDCC 34-05-01.2).

Orville W. Hagen (1915-2007) 1967-1986
Elected 1966, 1970, 1974, 1978, 1982; defeated for re-election 1986
Byron Knutson (1929-) 1987-1990
Elected 1986; defeated for re-election 1990
Craig Hagen (1965-).......... 1991-1998
Elected 1990, 1994; resigned August 13, 1998

Superintendent of Public Instruction

Originally a two-year term, the office became a four-year term with adoption of a constitutional amendment in June 1964 (Article V, Section 12).

William Mitchell (R) (1830-1890) 1889-1890
Elected 1889; died in office March 10, 1890
William J. Clapp (R) (1857-1934) 1890
Appointed April 10, 1890, to fill William Mitchell's term;
defeated for nomination at 1890 Republican convention
John Ogden (R) (1824-1910).......... 1891-1892
Elected 1890; did not seek re-election 1892

Laura J. Eisenhuth (D-I) (1858-1937).. 1893-1894
Elected 1892; defeated in November 1894 general election
Emma F. Bates (R) (1854-1920).. 1895-1896
Elected 1894; defeated for renomination in 1896 Republican convention
John G. Halland (R) (1863-1938)... 1897-1900
Elected 1896, 1898; did not seek re-election 1900
Joseph M. Devine (R) (1861-1938).. 1901-1902
Elected 1900; did not seek re-election 1902
Walter L. Stockwell (R) (1868-1950)... 1903-1910
Elected 1902, 1904, 1906, 1908; did not seek re-election 1910
Edwin J. Taylor (R) (1869-1956).. 1911-1914
Elected 1910, 1912

An act of the 1913 Legislative Assembly provided for the election of the Superintendent of Public Instruction on a no-party ballot, effective in 1914 (1913 S.L., ch. 153) (North Dakota Century Code Section 16.1-11-08).

Edwin J. Taylor (1869-1956).. 1915-1916
Elected 1914; did not seek re-election 1916
Neil C. MacDonald (1876-1923).. 1917-1918
Elected 1916; defeated in November 1918 general election
Minnie J. Nielson (1874-1958)... 1919-1926
Elected 1918, 1920, 1922, 1924; did not seek re-election 1926
Bertha R. Palmer (1880-1959)...1927-1932
Elected 1926, 1928, 1930; defeated in June 1932 Republican primary
Arthur E. Thompson (1891-1969) 1933-1946
Elected 1932, 1934, 1936, 1938, 1940, 1942, 1944; resigned August 31, 1946
Garfield B. Nordrum (1906-1995) 1946-1951
Appointed August 31, 1946, to fill Arthur E. Thompson's term;
elected 1946, 1948, 1950; resigned January 4, 1951
Marvell F. Peterson (1908-1996) 1951-1976
Appointed January 4, 1951, to fill Garfield B. Nordrum's term; elected 1952, 1954, 1956, 1958, 1960, 1962, 1964, 1968, 1972; did not seek re-election 1976
Howard J. Snortland (1912-2006)..1977-1980
Elected 1976; defeated for re-election 1980
Joseph Crawford (1944-)...1981-1984
Elected 1980; did not seek re-election 1984
Wayne G. Sanstead (1935-)..1985-2012
Elected 1984, 1988, 1992, 1996, 2000, 2004, 2008
Kirsten Baesler (1969-) 2013-present
Elected 2012, 2016

Tax Commissioner

The 1919 Legislature replaced the three-member Tax Commission, created in 1911, with a single Tax Commissioner, appointed by the Governor for a six-year term with the advice and consent of the Senate. The first commissioner was to be appointed on or before the last Monday in February 1919 (S.L. 1919, Ch. 213).

George E. Wallace (1873-1952) 1919-1921
  Appointed March 3, 1919, eff. July 28, 1919; removed December 31, 1921, by Governor Nestos

C. C. Converse (1878-1961) 1922-1925
  Appointed January 3, 1922, by Governor Nestos; removed March 27, 1925, by Governor Sorlie

Thorstein H. Thoresen (1885-1956) 1925-1929
  Appointed March 28, 1925, by Governor Sorlie; removed July 1, 1929, by Governor Shafer

Iver A. Acker (1886-1969) 1929-1932
  Appointed June 24, 1929, eff. July 1, 1929, by Governor Shafer; removed December 31, 1932, by Governor Langer

F. A. Vogel (1888-1951) 1933
  Appointed January 3, 1933, by Governor Langer; resigned March 15, 1933

J. J. Weeks (1871-1936) 1933-1935
  Appointed March 15, 1933, by Governor Langer; removed from office, following extensive litigation, March 24, 1935

Lyman Baker (1886-1972)
  Appointed August 9, 1934, by Governor Olson; didn't take office due to Week's litigation

Ingram J. Moe (1872-1942)
  Appointed January 17, 1935, by Governor Moodie; didn't take office due to Week's litigation

Lee Nichols (1883-1966) 1935-1937
  Appointed March 25, 1935, by Governor Welford; removed from office, January 12, 1937, by Governor Langer

John Kenneth Murray (1882-1960) 1937
  Appointed January 13, 1937, by Governor Langer; resigned April 10, 1937

Owen T. Owen (1890-1989) 1937-1938
  Appointed April 10, 1937, eff. April 12, 1937, by Governor Langer; resigned, December 15, 1938

Claude P. Stone (1891-1946) 1938-1939
  Appointed December 27, 1938, by Governor Langer; removed from office January 3, 1939, by Governor Moses

William T. DePuy (1903-1982) 1939
  Appointed January 3, 1939, by Governor Moses; resigned, March 31, 1939

Lee Nichols (1883-1966) 1939
  Served as Acting Tax Commissioner, April 1 to May 17, 1939

John Gray (1877-1952) 1939-1940
Appointed May 17, 1939, effective May 18, by Governor Moses

By constitutional amendment adopted June 28, 1938, the Tax Commissioner became an elected office with a term of four years. The measure also provided for the election of the Tax Commissioner on a no-party ballot and that the first commissioner would not be elected until the 1940 general election (Article V, Section 12). In 1987, the Tax Commissioner was removed from no-party ballot (1987, S.L., ch. 253) (NDCC 16.1-11-08).

Voters approved a change to the Constitution at the Primary Election on June 13, 2000, which puts one-half of the elected officials on the ballot each election year. To begin that process, the Secretary of State, the Commissioner of Agriculture, the Attorney General, and the Tax Commissioner were elected for two-year terms in 2004. Those offices then returned to four-year terms (2001 Laws of North Dakota, Chapter 591).

John Gray (1877-1952) 1941-1952
Elected 1940, 1944, 1948; died in office July 17, 1952

Burtis B. Conyne (1890-1974) 1952
Appointed July 22, 1952, to fill John Gray's term; defeated in 1952 general election

J. Arthur Engen (1897-1963) 1953-1963
Elected 1952, 1956, 1960; died in office March 21, 1963

Lloyd B. Omdahl (1931-) 1963-1966
Appointed April 15, 1963, to fill J. Arthur Engen's term; elected 1964; resigned May 1, 1966

Edwin O. Sjaastad (1903-1969) 1966-1969
Appointed May 1, 1966, to fill Lloyd B. Omdahl's term; elected 1968; died in office March 20, 1969

Byron L. Dorgan (D) (1942-) 1969-1980
Appointed March 31, 1969, to fill Edwin O. Sjaastad's term; elected 1972, 1976; did not seek re-election 1980

Kent Conrad (D) (1948-) 1981-1986
Elected 1980, 1984; resigned December 2, 1986

Mary Kathryn "Heidi" Heitkamp (D) (1955-) 1986-1992
Appointed December 2, 1986, to fill Kent Conrad's term; elected 1988; did not seek re-election 1992

Robert Hanson (D) (1947-2015) 1993-1996
Elected 1992; defeated 1996

Rick Clayburgh (R) (1960-) 1997-2005
Elected 1996, 2000, 2004; resigned May 31, 2005

Cory Fong (R) (1972-) 2005-2013
Appointed June 1, 2005, to fill Rick Clayburgh's term; elected 2006, 2010; resigned December 31, 2013

Ryan Rauschenberger (R) (1982-) 2014-present
Appointed January 2014 to fill Cory Fong's term; elected 2014

Public Service Commissioners

The Board of Railroad Commissioners, as originally created by the 1889 Constitution, consisted of three commissioners, each elected for a two-year term (Article V, Section 12).

David Barlett (R) (1854-1913)....................1889-1890
Elected 1889; defeated for renomination at 1890 Republican convention
George S. Montgomery (R) (1856-1936)....................1889-1890
Elected 1889; defeated for renomination at 1890 Republican convention
T. S. Underhill (R) (1834-1928)....................1889-1890
Elected 1889; did not seek re-election 1890
George W. Harmon (R) (1842-1902)....................1891-1892
Elected 1890; did not seek re-election 1892
Andrew Slotten (R) (1840-1902)....................1891-1892
Elected 1890; defeated for renomination at 1892 Republican convention
George H. Walsh (R) (1845-1913)....................1891-1892
Elected 1890; defeated for renomination at 1892 Republican convention
Peter Cameron (D-I) (1847-1916)....................1893-1894
Elected 1892; defeated in November 1894 general election
Nels P. Rasmussen (D-I) (1849-1909)....................1893-1894
Elected 1892; did not seek re-election 1894
Benjamin B. Stevens (D-I) (birth and death date unknown)....................1893-1894
Elected 1892; defeated in November 1894 general election
John W. Currie (R) (1847-1937)....................1895-1896
Elected 1894; defeated for renomination at 1896 Republican convention
George H. Keys (R) (1845-1935)....................1895-1898
Elected 1894, 1896; did not seek re-election 1898
John J. Wamberg (R) (1854-1915)....................1895-1896
Elected 1894; defeated for renomination at 1896 Republican convention
John R. Gibson (R) (1860-1940)....................1897-1898
Elected 1896; defeated for renomination at 1898 Republican convention
Luther L. Walton (R) (1844-1922)....................1897-1900
Elected 1896, 1898; did not seek re-election 1900
Henry Erickson (R) (1866-1924)....................1899-1900
Elected 1898; did not seek re-election 1900
John Simmons (R) (1858-1925)....................1899-1900
Elected 1898; defeated for renomination at 1900 Republican convention
Curtis J. Lord (R) (1862-1936)....................1901-1904
Elected 1900, 1902; did not seek re-election 1904
James F. Shea (R) (1856-1932)....................1901-1904
Elected 1900, 1902; did not seek re-election 1904
Joseph J. Youngblood (R) (1864-1938)....................1901-1902
Elected 1900; did not seek re-election 1902
Andreas Schatz (R) (1858-1928)....................1903-1904
Elected 1902; did not seek re-election 1904

John Christianson (R) (1862-1954) 1905-1906
Elected 1904; did not seek re-election 1906
Christian S. Deisem (R) (1848-1919) 1905-1908
Elected 1904, 1906; did not seek re-election 1908
Erick A. Stafne (R) (1848-1925) 1905-1908
Elected 1904, 1906; defeated in June 1908 Republican primary
Simon Westby (R) (1876-1963) 1907-1908
Elected 1906; defeated in June 1908 Republican primary
Olaf P. N. Anderson (R) (1872-1939) 1909-1916
Elected 1908, 1910, 1912, 1914; defeated in June 1916 Republican primary
William H. Mann (R) (1857-1935) 1909-1916
Elected 1908, 1910, 1912, 1914; defeated in June 1916 Republican primary
William H. Stutsman (R) (1866-1950) 1909-1916
Elected 1908, 1910, 1912, 1914; defeated in June 1916 Republican primary
Sam J. Aandahl (R) (1869-1922) 1917-1920
Elected 1916, 1918; did not seek re-election 1920
Charles W. Bleick (R) (1881-1964) 1917-1918
Elected 1916; did not seek re-election 1918
Myron P. Johnson (R) (1873-1937) 1917-1918
Elected 1916; defeated in June 1918 Republican primary
Charles F. Dupuis (R) (1865-1940) 1919-1920
Elected 1918; defeated in June 1920 Republican primary
Frank Milhollan (R) (1885-1944) 1919-1926
Elected 1918, 1920, 1922, 1924, 1926
William H. Stutsman (R) (1866-1950) 1921-1922
Elected 1920; did not seek re-election 1922
Clark W. McDonnell (R) (1870-1952) 1921-1926
Elected 1920, 1922, 1924
Fay A. Harding (R) (1875-1943) 1923-1926
Elected 1922, 1924

By constitutional amendment, approved June 30, 1926, terms of Commissioners of Railroads were increased to six years. This took effect with the November 1926 general election. So that the terms might be staggered, the three commissioners elected that year were elected for terms of six, four, and two years (Article V, Section 12).

Frank Milhollan (R) (1885-1944) 1927-1928
Elected 1926 for six-year term; resigned April 1, 1928
Clark W. McDonnell (R) (1870-1952) 1927-1936
Elected 1926 for four-year term; elected 1930; defeated in June 1936 Republican primary
Fay A. Harding (R) (1875-1943) 1927-1934
Elected 1926 for two-year term; elected 1928; defeated in June 1934 Republican primary

Ben C. Larkin (R) (1873-1949) 1928-1944
Appointed April 1, 1928, to fill Frank Milhollan's term; elected 1932, 1938
Elmer W. Cart (R) (1891-1980) 1935-1940
Elected 1934; defeated in June 1940 Republican primary
Simon S. McDonald (R) (1869-1956).. 1937-1942
Elected 1936

A constitutional amendment, adopted June 25, 1940, created the Public Service Commission and transferred to it the powers and duties of the Board of Railroad Commissioners. It also provided that two commissioners would be elected at the 1940 general election, one for a six-year term and one for a four-year term.

Ben C. Larkin (R) (1873-1949) 1941-1949
Elected 1940 for six-year term; elected 1946; died in office November 22, 1949
Clark W. McDonnell (R) (1870-1952) 1941-1950
Elected 1940 for four-year term; elected 1944; won the June 1950 Republican primary but resigned his place on the ballot September 30, 1950
Simon S. McDonald (R) (1869-1956) 1943-1948
Incumbent in 1940; elected 1942; defeated in June 1948 Republican primary
Elmer W. Cart (R) (1891-1980) 1949-1954
Elected 1948; defeated in June 1954 Republican primary
Ernest D. Nelson (R) (1897-1961) 1949-1961
Appointed December 3, 1949, to fill Ben C. Larkin's term; elected 1952, 1958; died in office September 10, 1961
Everett H. Brant (R) (1885-1954).. 1951-1954
Elected 1950; died in office November 3, 1954
Martin Vaaler (R) (1927-2014) 1954-1962
Appointed November 15, 1954, to fill Everett H. Brant's term; elected 1956; did not seek re-election 1962
Anson J. Anderson (R) (1905-1996) 1955-1960
Elected 1954; did not seek re-election 1960
Richard J. Thompson (R) (1913-1973)... 1961-1966
Elected 1960; did not seek re-election 1966
E. Bruce Hagen (D) (1930-) 1961-2000
Appointed September 19, 1961, to fill Ernest D. Nelson's term; elected 1964, 1970, 1976, 1982, 1988, 1994; did not seek re-election in 2000
Ben J. Wolf (R) (1907-1986)... 1963-1980
Elected 1962, 1968, 1974; did not seek re-election 1980
Richard Elkin (R) (1932-) 1967-1983
Elected 1966, 1972, 1978; resigned May 1, 1983
Leo M. Reinbold (R) (1933-2010)... 1981-2003
Elected 1980, 1986, 1992, 1998; resigned July 31, 2003
Dale Sandstrom (R) (1950-) 1983-1992
Appointed May 5, 1983, to complete Richard Elkin's term; elected 1984, 1990; resigned December 31, 1992

Susan Wefald (R) (1947-) 1993-2008
Appointed effective January 1, 1993, to complete Sandstrom's term; elected 1996, 2002; did not seek re-election 2008

Tony Clark (R) (1971-) 2001-2012
Elected 2000, 2006; resigned June 2012 to become Commissioner at Federal Energy Regulatory Commission

Bonny Fetch (I) (1943-) 2012
Appointed July 1, 2012, to December 31, 2012, to complete Tony Clark's term; did not seek election in 2012

Kevin Cramer (R) (1961-) 2003-2012
Appointed August 1, 2003, to complete Leo Reinbold's term; elected 2004, 2010; resigned December 31, 2012

Brian Kalk (R) (1966-) 2009-2017
Elected 2008, 2014, resigned 2017

Julie Fedorchak (R) (1968-) 2012-present
Appointed December 2012 to complete Kevin Cramer's term; elected 2014 to complete term ending in 2016; elected 2016

Randy Christmann (R) (1960-) 2013-present
Elected 2012

Brian Kroshus (R) (1963-) 2017-present
Appointed March 2017 to fill Brian Kalk's term

State Officials Appointed by the Governor to Head State Agencies

This segment of the *Blue Book* is based on the agencies that currently have gubernatorial appointed heads. (The Tourism Division of the North Dakota Department of Commerce is included because of the 2001 changes made as noted on that entry.)

Adjutants General
NDCC 37-03-01

Alan S. Dohrmann	Major General	December 13, 2015 –present
David A. Sprynczynatyk	Major General	August 26, 2006 –December 13, 2015
Michael J. Haugen	Major General	December 19, 2000– August 25, 2006
Keith D. Bjerke	Major General	1993–2000
Alexander P. Macdonald	Major General	1984–1993
C. Emerson Murry	Major General	1975–1984
LaClair A. Melhouse	Major General	1962–1975
Heber L. Edwards	Major General	1937–1962
Frayne Baker	Brigadier General	1935–1937

Earle R. Sarles	Brigadier General	1933–1935
G. A. Fraser	Brigadier General	1917–1933
Thomas Tharalson	Major General	1915–1917
Ira A. Berg	Major General	1913–1915
William C. Treumann	Major General	1911–1913
Amasa Peake	Major General	1909–1911
Thomas H. Poole	Major General	1907–1909
Heber M. Creel	Brigadier General	1905–1907
Eliot S. Miller	Brigadier General	1895–1905
W. H. Topping	Brigadier General	1893–1895
William A. Bentley	Brigadier General	1891–1893
William Devoy	Brigadier General	1890

Department of Corrections and Rehabilitation
NDCC 54-23.3-03

Leann K. Bertsch	Director	July 1, 2005–present
Elaine Little	Director	1989–July 1, 2005

Department of Corrections and Rehabilitation was created in 1989 (1989 S.L., ch. 156). Prior to 1989 correctional institutions fell under the jurisdiction of the Director of Institutions. See entries for Director of Institutions for additional history.

Director of Institutions

See Department of Corrections and Rehabilitation, was NDCC 54-21-06 until repealed in 1991.

Director of Institutions

Richard L. Rayl	Director	1987–December 14, 1988
Clarence A. Bina	Director	November 25, 1985–May 31, 1986
Erwin Giegle	Acting Director	July 1, 1985–September 30, 1985
Alton L. Lick	Director	1979-1985
Edward J. Klecker	Director	July 16, 1973–1979
Isak Hystad	Acting Director	April 5, 1973–July 15, 1973
Walter R. Fiedler	Director	July 1, 1969–1973

Board of Administration

Isak Hystad	Chairman	December 1, 1964–June 30, 1969
Howard I. Henry	Chairman	October 3, 1963–September 30, 1964
H. H. Joos	Chairman	August 1, 1957–September 10, 1963
R. H. Sherman	Chairman	December 8, 1947–July 31, 1957
Mark I. Forkner	Chairman	June 15, 1939–December 1, 1947
J. D. Harris	Chairman	March 20, 1939–June 15, 1939
Jennie Ulsrud	Chairman	July 1, 1937–March 20, 1939
J. D. Harris	Chairman	August 1, 1935–June 30, 1937
Nelson Sauvain	Chairman	December 22, 1930–August 1, 1935
J. E. Davis	Chairman	July 9, 1929–December 28, 1930

R. B. Murphy	Chairman	December 1, 1922–July 9, 1929
Robert T. Muir	Chairman	May 1, 1922–November 30, 1922
George A. Totten	Chairman	July 7, 1919–April 30, 1922

Board of Control of State Institutions

James A. Brown	Chairman	December 1, 1917–June 30, 1919
R. S. Lewis	Chairman	March 1, 1913–December 1, 1917
John Carmody	Chairman	June 15, 1911–March 1, 1913

In 1991, the Legislative Assembly transferred the Director of Institutions responsibilities to other agencies, including the Department of Corrections and Rehabilitation (1991 S.L., ch. 592).

In 1969, the Legislative Assembly established a Director of Institutions and abolished the Board of Administration (1969 S.L., ch. 440).

In 1919, the Legislative Assembly combined the Board of Control, Board of Education, and Board of Regents into the Board of Administration (1919 S.L., ch. 71).

In 1911, the Legislative Assembly created the Board of Control of State Institutions (1911 S.L., ch. 62).

Department of Transportation
NDCC 24-02-01.3

Thomas Sorel	Director	August 7, 2017–present
Ron Henke	Interim Director	June 1, 2017–August 6, 2017
Grant Levi	Director	May 22, 2013–May 31, 2017
Francis Ziegler	Director	October 5, 2006–May 21, 2013
Grant Levi	Interim Director	August 28, 2006–October 4, 2006
David A. Sprynczynatyk	Director	January 1, 2001–August 25, 2006
Tom D. Freier	Director	March 2, 2000–December 31, 2000
Marshall W. Moore	Director	January 4, 1993–February 29, 2000
Richard J. Backes	Director	January 16, 1989–December 14, 1992

On January 1, 1990, the North Dakota Highway Department became the Department of Transportation – "Commissioner" became "Director" (1989 S.L., ch. 72).

Walter R. Hjelle	Commissioner	January 14, 1985–December 31, 1988
Duane R. Liffrig	Commissioner	January 1, 1982–January 7, 1985
Walter R. Hjelle	Commissioner	January 3, 1961–January 31, 1981

The North Dakota State Highway Department was created in 1953 (1953 S.L., ch. 177).

One-Man Highway Commission

A. W. Wentz	Commissioner	April 1, 1957–January 3, 1961
S. W. Thompson	Commissioner	May 1, 1951–April 1, 1957
M. P. Wynkoop	Commissioner	January 2, 1951–May 1, 1951
N. O. Jones	Commissioner	April 2, 1945–December 31, 1950
J. S. Lamb	Commissioner	January 18, 1939–April 2, 1945
P. H. McGurren	Commissioner	January 19, 1937–January 18, 1939
W. J. Flannigan	Commissioner	April 21, 1935–January 18, 1937
Ole H. Olsen	Commissioner	January 17, 1935–April 21, 1935
T. G. Plomasen	Commissioner	September 13, 1934–January 17, 1935
Bert M. Salisbury	Commissioner	July 21, 1934–September 13, 1934
F. A. Vogel	Commissioner	March 15, 1933–July 22, 1934

In 1933, the office of Highway Commissioner was established, abolishing the commission. The commissioner was appointed by the Governor (1933 S.L., ch. 125).

Chief Highway Commissioner and Two-Man Highway Commission Members

Chief Highway Commissioner
A. D. McKinnon
July 30, 1931– March 14, 1933

Members
C. D. King
February 1, 1933–March 14, 1933

J. A. Dinnie
July 30, 1931–January 30, 1933

H. R. Lapman
July 30, 1931–March 14, 1933

In 1931, the Legislative Assembly established the commission, three members appointed by the Governor, one of whom was appointed Chief Highway Commissioner (1931 S.L., ch. 153).

Three-Man Highway Commission With Executive Secretary

Governor	Executive Secretary	Two Appointed Members
George Schafer January 1, 1929– July 20, 1931	H. C. Frahm April 1, 1929– July 29, 1931	I. J. Moe March 15, 1927– July 29, 1931
	Joe J. Ermatinger March 15, 1927– April 1, 1929	J. A. Dinnie February 15, 1929– July 29, 1931
	Ray S. Ashley March 15, 1927 to February 14, 1929	
Walter Maddock August 30, 1928– December 31, 1928	Joe J. Ermatinger March 15, 1927– April 1, 1929	I. J. Moe March 15, 1927– July 29, 1931

	Ray S. Ashley March 15, 1927– February 14, 1929	
A. G. Sorlie March 15, 1927– August 29, 1928	Joe J. Ermatinger March 15, 1927– April 1, 1929	I. H. Moe March 15, 1927– July 29, 1931
		Ray S. Ashley March 15, 1927– February 14, 1929

In 1927, the membership of the Highway Commission changed to include the Governor and two members appointed by the Governor (1927 S.L., ch. 158).

In 1927, the Department of State Highways was created (1927 S.L., ch. 159).

Five-Man Highway Commission

Governor	State Engineer	Commissioner of Agriculture and Labor	Two Members Appointed by Governor
A. G. Sorlie January 9, 1925– March 14, 1927	H. C. Frahm September 14, 1925– March 14, 1927	Joseph H. Kitcher November 23, 1921– March 14, 1927	I. J. Moe April 15, 1925– March 14, 1927
	W. G. Black April 2, 1923– September 13, 1925		Herman Hardt April 15, 1925– March 14, 1927
			Ormanzo A. Brown April 15, 1923– April 14, 1925
			Joseph Poupore April 2, 1923– April 14, 1925
R. A. Nestos November 23, 1921– January 8, 1925	W. G. Black April 2, 1923– September 13, 1925	Joseph H. Kitcher November 23, 1921– April 15, 1923	Ormanzo A. Brown March 14, 1927– April 14, 1925
	W. H. Robinson October 26, 1918– April 1, 1923		Joseph Poupore April 2, 1923– April 14, 1925
			Herman Hardt May 13, 1921– April 14, 1923

			Benton Baker November 23, 1921– April 1, 1923
Lynn J. Frazier April 20, 1917– November 22, 1921	W. H. Robinson October 26, 1918– April 1, 1923	John N. Hagan April 20, 1917– November 22, 1921	Herman Hardt May 13, 1921– April 14, 1923
	Jay W. Bliss April 20, 1917– October 25, 1918		J. J. Marquart April 4, 1919– May 12, 1921
			Two Members Appointed by Governor
			Frayne Baker July 15, 1919– November 22, 1921
			Theodore Andrew April 20, 1917– April 3, 1919 Ed White April 20, 1917– November 18, 1918

In 1917, the membership of the commission was changed to include the Governor, State Engineer, Commissioner of Agriculture and Labor, and two members appointed by the Governor (1917 S.L., ch. 131).

Three-Man State Highway Commission
January 14, 1914

Governor	**State Engineer**	**One Member Appointed by Governor**
Louis B. Hanna	Jay W. Bliss	C. A. Grow

In 1913, the State Highway Commission was created to consist of the Governor, the State Engineer, and one other member appointed by the Governor (1913 S.L., ch. 179).

Game and Fish Department
NDCC 20.1-02-01

Terry Steinwand	Director	January 1, 2006–present
Dean Hildebrand	Director	1996–December 31, 2005
K. L. Cool	Director	1993–1996
Lloyd A. Jones	Director	1989–1993
Dale Henegar	Commissioner	1981–1989

Larry Kruckenberg	Commissioner	1979–1981
Russell Stuart	Commissioner	1961–1979
Dr. I. G. Bue	Commissioner	1957–1961
H. R. Morgan	Commissioner	1948–1957
Wm. J. Lowe	Commissioner	1938–1948
O. W. Hulterstrom	Commissioner	1936–1938
A. I. Swenson	Commissioner	1934–1936
Thoralf Swenson	Commissioner	1932–1934
Burnie Maurek	Commissioner	1930–1932

Commissioner changed to director. References removed to commissioner and made instead to Game and Fish Department and its director (1991 S.L., ch. 231).

Information Technology Department
NDCC 54-59-03

Shawn Riley	Chief Information Officer	April 17, 2017–present
Daniel Sipes	Interim Chief Information Officer	December 15, 2016–April 16, 2017
Mike Ressler	Chief Information Officer	October 10, 2013–December 31, 2016
Mike Ressler	Interim Chief Information Officer	May 20, 2013–October 9, 2013
Lisa Feldner	Chief Information Officer	May 8, 2006–May 19, 2013
Mike Ressler	Acting Chief Information Officer	January 1, 2006–May 7, 2006
Curtis L. Wolfe	Chief Information Officer	October, 1999–December 31, 2005

Job Service North Dakota
NDCC 52-02-01

Michelle Kommer	Interim Executive Director	September 2017–present
Cheri Giesen	Executive Director	July 2014–August 2017
Darren Brostrom	Interim Director	October 2013–June 2014
Maren Daley	Executive Director	2000–2013
Jennifer Gladden	Executive Director	1996–2000
Gerald Balzer	Executive Director	1993–1996
Michael Deisz	Executive Director	1985–1992
Shirley Peterson	Executive Director	1981–1984
Therman Kaldahl	Executive Director	1977–1981
Martin Gronvold	Executive Director	1965–1976

In 1979, Job Service North Dakota was created (1979 S.L., ch. 522). The Employment Security Bureau was created in 1965 (1965 S.L., ch. 333).

North Dakota Department of Commerce
NDCC 54-60-03

Jay Schuler	Commissioner	February 27, 2017–present
Al Anderson	Commissioner	May 2, 2011–December 31, 2016
Paul Govig	Acting Commissioner	January 1, 2011–May 2, 2011
Shane Goettle	Commissioner	December 1, 2005–December 31, 2010
Lee Peterson	Commissioner	July 1, 2001–November 30, 2005

Lee Peterson	Director	December 2000–June 30, 2001
Kevin Cramer	Director	June 1, 1997–December 2000
Ron Rauschenberger	Interim Director	May 22, 1997–May 30, 1997
Charles (Chuck) W. Stroup	Director	January 1, 1993–May 15, 1997
Mitchell Bohn	Director	January 6, 1992–January 1, 1993
Bill Davis	Director	September 1, 1991–January 5, 1992
Carol Jean Larsen	Acting Director	May 1, 1991–August 31, 1991
Joe Cascalenda*	Director	May 1, 1991–December 1991
Fred A. Haeffner	Director	August 1990–May 1, 1991
William S. Patrie	Director	September 1986–June 30, 1990
Robert Whitney	Director	May 1985–September 1986
Sylvan Melroe	Director	April 9, 1984–May 24, 1985
Edwin Becker	Director	November 1980–February 29, 1984
Bruce L. Bartch	Director	April 10, 1969–November 1980
Fred P. Brandt	Acting Director	March 1969
Robert H. Huey	Director	1961–February 1969
Lawrence A. Schneider	Director	1957–September 1961

In 2001, the North Dakota Department of Commerce was created, placing the agency under a commissioner of commerce (2001 S.L., ch. 488).

In 1991, Growing North Dakota legislation abolished the Economic Development Commission by establishing in its place the Department of Economic Development and Finance (1991 S.L., ch. 95). The Governor was given authority to appoint the department's director. The Governor appointed Fred Haeffner to the position.

In 1987, the Legislative Assembly moved the appointment of the agency director to the Economic Development Commission (1987 S.L., ch. 622).

In July 1987, the Economic Development Commission named William Patrie its director. Governor George Sinner had, prior to the 1987 change, appointed William Patrie as director of the Economic Development Commission.

In 1981, the name reverted to Economic Development Commission (1981 S.L., ch. 528).

In 1969, the Business and Industrial Development Department replaced the Economic Development Commission (1969 S.L., ch. 446).

In 1957, the Legislative Assembly created the Economic Development Commission (1957 S.L., ch. 343).

*Governor Sinner hired Joe Cascalenda, Minnesota consultant, to find Fred Haeffner's replacement, as well as to design the organizational structure for the newly created Department of Economic Development and Finance.

North Dakota Department of Human Services
NDCC 50-06-01.3

Christopher D. Jones	Executive Director	February 27, 2017–present
Maggie Anderson	Interim Executive Director	December 1, 2016–February 26, 2017
Maggie Anderson	Executive Director	April 29, 2013–December 1, 2016
Carol K. Olson	Executive Director	July 1997–April 28, 2013
Henry C. "Bud" Wessman	Executive Director	February 1993–June 1997
John A. Graham	Executive Director	February 1984–December 1992
Dale E. Moug	Executive Director	January 1982–December 1983
Thorfin N. Tangedahl	Executive Director	December 1972–December 1981
Leslie O. Ovre	Executive Director	October 1962–June 1972
Carlyle D. Onsrud	Executive Director	July 1944–October 1962
E. A. Wilson	Executive Director	May 1935–June 1944

The North Dakota Department of Human Services was created in 1981 (1981 S.L., ch. 486).

In 1971, the Public Welfare Board became the Social Service Board of North Dakota (1971 S.L., ch. 465).

The State Board of Public Welfare was established in 1935 (1935 S.L., ch. 221).

North Dakota Department of Labor and Human Rights
NDCC 34-05-01.2

Michelle Kommer	Commissioner	December 19, 2016–present
Troy T. Seibel	Commissioner	October 1, 2014–November 23, 2016
Bonnie Storbakken	Commissioner	May 16, 2013–September 30, 2014
Tony J. Weiler	Commissioner	September 7, 2010–May 15, 2013
Lisa Fair McEvers	Commissioner	July 25, 2005–August 31, 2010
Leann K. Bertsch	Commissioner	September 1, 2004–June 30, 2005
Mark Bachmeier	Commissioner	January 1, 2001–August 18, 2004
Tony Clark	Commissioner	September 16, 1999–December 14, 2000
Mark Bachmeier	Interim Commissioner	August 14, 1998–September 15, 1999

During the 2013 Legislative Session, the name of the Labor Department was changed to the Department of Labor and Human Rights (HB 1369).

In 1995, the Legislative Assembly made the position appointive by the Governor, beginning January 1, 1999 (1995 S.L., ch. 334). The last elected Commissioner of Labor, Craig Hagen, resigned the position effective August 13, 1998.

North Dakota Indian Affairs Commission
NDCC 54-36-02

Scott J. Davis	Standing Rock Sioux Tribe	Executive Director	April 2009–present
Cheryl M. Kulas	Oglala Lakota Nation	Executive Director	April 2001–April 2009
Cynthia A. Mala	Spirit Lake Nation	Executive Director	January 1998–March 2001
Deborah A. Painte	Three Affiliated Tribes	Executive Director	January 1991–January 1998
Juanita Helphrey	Three Affiliated Tribes	Executive Director	March 1975–December 1990
Earl Azure	Turtle Mountain Band of Chippewa	Executive Director	August 1971–February 1975
Rev. Austin Engel		Executive Director	January 1965–August 1971
Hans Walker, Jr.	Three Affiliated Tribes	Executive Director	February 1962–January 1965
Edward A. Milligan		Executive Director	October 1960–January 1962
John B. Hart		Executive Director	August 1949–September 1960

Office of Administrative Hearings
NDCC 54-57-01

Timothy J. Dawson	Director	January 1, 2016–present
Wade C. Mann	Director	January 1, 2014–December 31, 2015
Allen C. Hoberg	Director	July 1, 1991–December 31, 2014

Office of Management and Budget
NDCC 54-44-03

Pam Sharp	Director	June 2003–present
Pam Sharp	Acting Director	January 2003–June 2003
Rod Backman	Director	December 15, 1992–January 2003
Charles Mertens	Director	January 3, 1992–December 15, 1992
Richard Rayl	Director	January 1, 1985–December 1992
Lee M. Stenehjem	Director	August 1, 1983–December 31, 1984
Robert B. Melland	Director	January 1, 1983–May 1983
Darrell R. Ohlhauser	Acting Director	January 1982–December 31, 1982
Dale Moug	Director	January 1, 1981–December 31, 1981
Dean L. Conrad	Director	December 1, 1976–December 31, 1980
Dale Moug	Acting Director	September 9, 1976–November 30, 1976
Lloyd Omdahl	Director	1975–1976
Ralph Dewing	Director	January 1961–1975

In 1981, the Office of Management and Budget was created (S.L. Chapter 534).
In 1959, the Department of Accounts and Purchases was created (S.L. Chapter 372).

Parks and Recreation Department
NDCC 55-08-01.2

Melissa Baker	Director	2017–present
Jesse Hanson	Interim Director	2016–2017
Mark Zimmerman	Director	2011–2016
Douglass A. Prchal	Director	1994–2010
Douglas K. Eiken	Director	1981–1994
Robert Horne	Director	1978–1981
Gary Leppart	Director	1975–1977
Einar Johnson	Director	1973–1975
David L. O'Brien	Director	1968–1972
James R. Kittle	Director	1964–1967

In 1993, the agency name reverted back to Parks and Recreation Department as tourism became its own department (1993 S.L., ch. 80).

In 1991, the Legislative Assembly created the Parks and Tourism Department with the director of the Parks and Outdoor Recreation Division and the director of the Tourism Division being appointed by the Governor (1991 S.L., ch. 640).

In 1977, the Parks and Recreation Department was created, combining the Park Service and State Outdoor Recreation Agency (1977 S.L., ch. 503).

In 1965, the North Dakota Park Service was created (1965 S.L., ch. 379).

State Department of Health
NDCC 23-01-05

Mylynn Tufte	State Health Officer	February 17, 2017–present
Avry Smith	Co-Acting State Health Officer	December 15, 2016–February 16, 2017
David Glatt	Co-Acting State Health Officer	December 15, 2016–February 16, 2017
Terry L. Dwelle, M.D.	State Health Officer	October 23, 2001–December 15, 2016
Robert A. Barnett	Interim State Health Officer*	December 15, 2000–October 23, 2001
Murray G. Sagsveen	State Health Officer	February 1, 1998–December 14, 2000
Robert A. Barnett	Interim State Health Officer*	September 8, 1997–January 31, 1998
Jon R. Rice, M.D.	State Health Officer	February 22, 1993–August 31, 1997
Robert A. Barnett	Interim Director*	December 15, 1992–February 21, 1993
Robert M. Wentz, M.D.	State Health Officer	January 11, 1985–December 14, 1992
Gene A. Christianson	Acting Administrator*	December 1, 1984–January 10, 1985

M. A. K. Lommen, M.D.	State Health Officer	January 1, 1982–November 30, 1984
Gene A. Christianson	Acting Administrator*	January 6, 1981–December 31, 1981
Joan G. Babbott, M.D.	State Health Officer	July 1, 1980–January 5, 1981
Gene A. Christianson	Acting Administrator*	October 4, 1979–July 1, 1980
Thomas Campbell	Executive Officer*	October 1, 1979–October 4, 1979
Jonathan B. Weisbuch, M.D.	State Health Officer	June 1, 1976–September 30, 1979
Willis Van Heuvelen	Executive Officer*	January 1, 1975–May 31, 1976
James R. Amos, M.D.	State Health Officer	September 1, 1961–December 31, 1974
Willis Van Heuvelen	Executive Officer*	June 1, 1957–August 31, 1961
Jerome H. Svore	Director of Public Health*	July 1, 1953–May 31, 1957
Russell O. Saxvik, M.D.	State Health Officer	July 1, 1947–June 30, 1953
William M. Smith, M.D.	Acting State Health Officer	1946–June 30, 1947
George F. Campana, M.D.	State Health Officer	1944–1946
Frank J. Hill, M.D.	Acting State Health Officer	1942–1944
Maysil M. Williams, M.D.	State Health Officer	1933–1942
Arthur A. Whittemore, M.D.	State Health Officer	1923–1933
Harley E. French, M.D.	Secretary–Superintendent of Health	1921–1923
Charles J. McGurren, M.D.	Secretary–Superintendent of Health	1913–1921
James Grassick, M.D.	Secretary–Superintendent of Health	1907–1913
Herbert H. Healy, M.D.	Secretary–Superintendent of Health	1901–1907
Amos Flaten, M.D.	Superintendent, State Board of Health	1897–1901
John Montgomery, M.D.	Superintendent, State Board of Health	1895–1997
Francis H. DeVaux, M.D.	Superintendent, State Board of Health	1893–1995
Harry D. Quarry, M.D.	Superintendent, State Board of Health	1891–1993
J. G. Millspaugh, M.D.	Superintendent, State Board of Health	1890–1991

*State Health Officer position vacant

In 1995, the name reverted back to the State Department of Health (1995 S.L., ch. 243).

The 1987 Legislative Assembly changed the agency's name to State Department of Health and Consolidated Laboratories (1987 S.L., ch. 263).

In 1923, the State Department of Health was created with a state health officer as its head (1923 S.L., ch. 227).

The State Board of Health was created in 1890.

State Department of Financial Institutions
NDCC 6-01-08

Bob Entringer	Commissioner	2011–2017
Timothy J. Karsky	Commissioner	2001–2010
Gary D. Preszler	Commissioner	1986–2001
Jane M. Lundberg	Commissioner	1985–1986
Marilyn Foss	Commissioner	1983–1985
L. M. Stenehjem, Jr.	Commissioner	1981–1983
LeRoy Gilbertson	Commissioner	1977–1981
G. W. Ellwein	Commissioner	1969–1977
H. L. Thorndal	State Examiner	1966–1969
Eugene Rich	State Examiner	1961–1966
G. H. Russ, Jr.	State Examiner	1956–1961
John A. Graham	State Examiner	1939–1956
Adam A. Lefor	State Examiner	1933–1939
Gilbert Semingson	State Examiner	1921–1933
O. E. Loftus	State Examiner	1919–1921
J. R. Waters	State Examiner	1917–1919
G. J. Johnson	State Examiner	1915–1917
S. G. Severtson	State Examiner	1913–1915
Oliver Knudson	State Examiner	1907–1913
D. K. Brightbill	State Examiner	1905–1907
Evan S. Tyler	State Examiner	1903–1905
R. E. Wallace	State Examiner	1901–1903
H. A. Langlie	State Examiner	1895–1901
Kemper Peabody	State Examiner	1893–1895
R. E. Wallace	State Examiner	1891–1893
Wm. G. Hayden	Public Examiner	1889–1891

In 2001, the State Department of Financial Institutions was created (2001 S.L., ch. 88).

In 1969, the Legislative Assembly created the Department of Banking and Financial Institutions with the commissioner known as the State Examiner (1969 S.L., ch. 96).

The Department of Banking came into existence in 1911 (1911 S.L., ch. 55).

In 1905, the State Banking Board was created (1905 S.L., ch. 165).

In 1893, the position of State Examiner was created (1893 S.L., ch. 95). Prior to that time, the office of Public Examiner had been established in 1887 and given duties to audit/examine the county records in the new state of North Dakota in 1890 (1890 S.L., ch. 116).

State Highway Patrol
NDCC 39-03-02

Michael Gerhart	Superintendent	2014–present
James Prochniak	Superintendent	2009–2014
Mark Nelson	Superintendent	2007–2009
Bryan R. Klipfel	Superintendent	2003–2007
James M. Hughes	Superintendent	1993–2003
Brian C. Berg	Superintendent	1985–1992
Norman D. Evans	Superintendent	1981–1985
James D. Martin	Superintendent	1978–1981
Ralph M. Wood	Superintendent	1961–1978
Clark J. Monroe	Superintendent	1953–1961
E. M. Klein	Superintendent	1943–1953
John Jeffery	Superintendent	1941–1943
Archie O'Connor	Superintendent	1939
Frank Putman	Superintendent	1939–1941
H. G. Lund	Superintendent	1937–1938
Frank Putman	Superintendent	1935–1937

In 1951, the Governor was granted authority to appoint the superintendent (1951 S.L., ch. 237). Prior to that time, the highway commissioner, with the Governor's consent, made the appointment (1935 S.L., ch. 148).

State Securities Department
NDCC 10-04-03

Karen Tyler	Commissioner	September 1, 2001–present
Syver Vinje	Commissioner	January 1, 1998–August 31, 2001
Harold P. Kocher	Acting Commissioner	November 17, 1997–December 31, 1997
Calvin Hoovestol	Commissioner	February 15, 1993–November 16, 1997
Harold P. Kocher	Acting Commissioner	January 1, 1993–February 14, 1993
Glenn A. Pomeroy	Commissioner	March 1, 1988–December 31, 1992
Harold P. Kocher	Acting Commissioner	December 29, 1987–February 28, 1988
Peter A. Quist	Commissioner	May 6, 1983–January 31, 1988
Dale Sandstrom	Commissioner	May 1, 1981–May 5, 1983
Arly Richau	Commissioner	May 7, 1977–April 30, 1981
Peter A. Quist	Acting Commissioner	December 27, 1976–May 6, 1977
Robert Holte	Commissioner	January 1, 1976–December 24, 1976
Donald R. Holloway	Commissioner	March 12, 1968–December 31, 1975
Wallace E. Warner	Commissioner	July 1, 1965–March 11, 1968
Charles L. Hughes	Commissioner	July 1, 1959–June 30, 1965

In 1961, the Legislative Assembly gave the Governor the authority to appoint the commissioner (1961 S.L., ch. 116).

In 1951, the Securities Commission was abolished and agency functions placed under the state examiner in the Department of Banking (1951 S.L., ch. 106).

The Securities Commission was created in 1923 (1923 S.L., ch. 182).

Division of Tourism
NDCC 54-60-02

Sara Otte Coleman	Director	2003–present
Allan Stenehjem	Director	2001–2002
Bob Martinson	Director	1997–2000
Kevin Cramer	Director	1993–1997
James Fuglie	Director	1985–1992
Michael Foster	Director	1981–1985
Wally Reber	Director	1977–1981
Joe Satrom	Director	1968–1977
James Hawley	Director	1962–1967

In 2001, the North Dakota Tourism Department again became a division, this time within the North Dakota Department of Commerce (2001 S.L., ch. 488). The statutory language provided that until August 1, 2005, the Governor appointed the director of the Tourism Division. After that date, the appointment was made by the commissioner of the North Dakota Department of Commerce.

In 1993, the Legislative Assembly created the North Dakota Tourism Department with its director appointed by the Governor (1993 S.L., ch. 80).

In 1991, Tourism was merged with Parks to become the Department of Parks and Tourism with the director of tourism portion of the agency being appointed by the Governor (1991 S.L., ch. 640).

In 1981, the Tourism Division was placed under the Economic Development Commission (1981 S.L., ch. 528).

The Travel Division was created as part of the North Dakota State Highway Department in 1953 but did not have its own budget/funding until 1961 (1953 S.L., ch. 177), (1961 S.L., ch. 205).

Executive Commissions and Boards

Emergency Commission
Phone: 701-328-2900 (Secretary of State)
[NDCC 54-16]

The 1915 Legislative Assembly established the Emergency Commission. Since that time, its function has been to respond to natural disasters or unforeseen events and funding circumstances when the legislature is not in session and which were not anticipated during the legislative session. Some examples include considering and approving requests from state agencies to transfer spending authority between appropriated line items, accepting and authorizing disbursement of federal funds, accepting and authorizing disbursement of funds received from other sources, authorizing spending authority from a contingency fund appropriated to the

Commission, and granting borrowing authority from the Bank of North Dakota in response to a disaster declaration by the Governor.

The original members were the Governor, Secretary of State, and State Auditor. In 1919, the State Auditor was replaced by the Commissioner of Agriculture and Labor. The 1949 Legislature added the respective chairmen of the House and Senate Appropriations Committees if the amount being considered was more than $10,000. In 1967, the title of the Commissioner of Agriculture and Labor was changed to the Commissioner of Agriculture, who was subsequently replaced on the Commission in 1995 by the Chairman of the Legislative Council (now known as Legislative Management). During the same session, the respective chairman of the appropriations committees became full members of the Commission regardless of the amount of the request being considered. In 2005, the Chairman of the Legislative Council was replaced by the respective majority leaders in the House and the Senate.

The Commission now consists of six members, two from the executive branch and four from the legislative branch. Since its creation, the Secretary of State has served as the Commission's secretary.

Equalization, State Board of

Phone: 701-328-7088, option 6
[NDCC 57-13-01]

The State Board of Equalization consists of the Governor, State Treasurer, State Auditor, Commissioner of Agriculture, and State Tax Commissioner. The Governor acts as chair and the Tax Commissioner as secretary.

The Board equalizes the valuation and assessment of property throughout the state and has the power to equalize assessments between assessment districts of the same county and between the different counties of the state.

Industrial Commission

600 East Boulevard Avenue
Bismarck, ND 58505-0310
Phone: 701-328-3722
Fax: 701-328-2820
Web: www.nd.gov/ndic
Email: ndicinfo@nd.gov
[NDCC 54-17]

The Industrial Commission consists of the Governor as chairman, the Attorney General, and the Agriculture Commissioner. In addition to an Executive Director and Secretary, the Commission employs other staff as the public interest dictates. As the management authority for all utilities, industries, enterprises, and business projects owned, administered, and operated by the state, the Commission has under its jurisdiction the Bank of North Dakota, North Dakota Mill and Elevator

Association, North Dakota Housing Finance Agency, North Dakota Public Finance Authority, North Dakota Student Loan Trust, North Dakota Building Authority, North Dakota Transmission Authority, and North Dakota Pipeline Authority. In addition to the business entities, the Commission also has regulatory responsibilities through the Department of Mineral Resources, which consists of the North Dakota Oil and Gas Division and North Dakota Geological Survey. The Commission also provides research grants through the Lignite Research, Development, and Marketing Program; Oil and Gas Research Program; and Renewable Energy Program. In 2013, the Industrial Commission was given oversight of the Outdoor Heritage Fund and the industrial water sales of the Western Area Water Supply Authority.

The Bank of North Dakota (BND) was established to promote agriculture, commerce, and industry in the state. It is the only legal depository for all state funds. As of December 31, 2016, the bank's assets were $7.29 billion, including loans of approximately $4.7 billion. The bank's capital was $863 million. The bank's profits in 2016 exceeded $136 million; in 2015, the profits were $130 million. BND serves as a central clearinghouse for many North Dakota financial institutions and partners with financial institutions to provide loan programs for businesses and agriculture, residential loans, and special loan programs established by the Legislature or the Industrial Commission. Supporting agriculture and economic development are in the mission statement of the bank. The Industrial Commission has directed that the bank serve as the Farm Finance Agency to facilitate first-time farmer loans. For more advanced agriculture producers, BND provides loans for financing real estate, equipment, and livestock. Businesses in North Dakota are supported through a variety of economic development programs, such as PACE (Partnership in Assisting Community Expansion), Flex Pace, Beginning Entrepreneur Programs, and Export Enhancement Programs. Through its Mortgage Programs, the Bank of North Dakota provides a secondary market for mortgage loans and assists rural financial institutions in originating loans if they do not have a mortgage department. The Bank helps keep college affordable by providing low-cost student loans through the DEAL (Dakota Education Alternative Loan) and introduced a student loan consolidation and refinancing program, the DEAL One loan, in 2014. It administers the College Planning Center, a resource for North Dakota families to assist with planning for college from cradle to career. College Save, North Dakota's 529 plan, and North Dakota Dollars for Scholars are also managed by BND. BND's profits are used to support the state's economic development, community infrastructure, and disaster assistance programs. For the 2015-2017 biennium, the Legislature appropriated more than $257 million of BND profits for these types of programs. BND can also be called upon by the Legislature to provide General Fund appropriations. Since the Bank's inception, $685 million has been appropriated to the General Fund. The Industrial Commission appoints the Bank President. Phone: 701-328-5600; Fax: 701-328-5632; 800-472-2166; TYY: 800-366-6888; Web: www.bnd.nd.gov; Mailing Address: 1200 Memorial Highway, Bismarck, ND 58506-5509.

The Mill and Elevator Association is located in Grand Forks. The Mill and Elevator Association was established for the purpose of encouraging and promoting agriculture, commerce, and industry by engaging in the business of manufacturing and marketing farm products. The North Dakota Mill is the largest single site wheat flour mill in the United States and the ninth largest wheat-durum-rye milling company in the United States, with sales of more than $288 million in FY2017. The Mill is primarily a spring-wheat mill, shipping 90 percent spring wheat products and 10 percent durum products. The Mill and Elevator Association currently has the capacity to produce 4.95 million pounds of finished product per day and a terminal elevator with total available storage of more than four million bushels of grain. The Mill and Elevator Association processes up to 100,000 bushels of top quality North Dakota spring and durum wheat per day, adding value to more than 30 million bushels per year. Seventy-five percent of all products are shipped in bulk trucks or railcars, with 25 percent shipped in bags or totes. A portion of the Mill's profits are appropriated each biennium to the state's General Fund. The Industrial Commission appoints a President and General Manager to oversee operations. Phone: 701-795- 7000; Web: www.ndmill.com; Mailing Address: PO Box 13078, Grand Forks, ND 58208-3078.

The Commission, acting as the North Dakota Student Loan Trust, acquires and holds in trust United States government or North Dakota guaranteed student loans. The creation of the North Dakota Student Loan Trust enabled the state of North Dakota to obtain low cost funds (through the sale of tax-exempt and taxable bonds) and use those funds for purchasing student loans originated by the Bank of North Dakota. The Trust provides funding for the North Dakota Guarantee Agency, and the Legislature has appropriated funds from the Trust for certain North Dakota University System programs and other education-related programs. The Commission's Executive Director serves as the authorized officer for the trust. Financial audits of the Trust are available on the Industrial Commission website at www.nd.gov/ndic/ic-public.htm. Phone: 701-328-3722.

The North Dakota Housing Finance Agency's (NDHFA) mission is to make safe, decent, and affordable housing for every North Dakotan. The agency assists low- and moderate- income residents in financing their homes by issuing bonds and generating funds to purchase mortgage loans originated by local lenders. Since its creation in 1982, the agency has purchased more than 41,000 loans valued at more than $3.2 billion. The agency administers the state's Housing Incentive Fund, the federal Low Income Housing Tax Credit Program, and other development programs that provide incentives for the production or rehabilitation of affordable rental housing. These programs have created or rehabilitated more than 17,000 units statewide. NDHFA also administers rental subsidies and provides regulatory oversight for privately-owned rental units for low-income households. The Commission appoints the Executive Director. Phone: 701-328-8080; 800-292-8621; Fax: 701-328-8090; TTY: 800-366-6888; Web: www.ndhfa.org; Mailing Address: PO Box 1535, Bismarck, ND 58502.

The North Dakota Public Finance Authority (NDPFA), formerly the Municipal Bond Bank, was established to make loans to political subdivisions by issuing bonds and using the proceeds to purchase municipal securities issued by the borrowing political subdivisions. In addition to its general financing programs for political subdivisions, the NDPFA issues industrial revenue bonds for projects that qualify under the IRS definition of small issue manufacturing. The NDPFA also acts as the financial administrator of the state's Revolving Loan Fund established by the state in conformity with the federal Clean Water and Safe Drinking Water Acts. The NDPFA operates and is managed under the control of the Commission. The Executive Director is appointed by the Commission. Phone: 701-328-7100; Web: www.nd.gov/pfa; Mailing Address: 1200 Memorial Highway, Bismarck, ND 58504.

In its role as the North Dakota Building Authority, the Commission, as authorized under North Dakota Century Code Chapter 54-17.2, provides financing through the issuance of bonds for acquiring, constructing, altering, repairing, and maintaining certain projects as directed by the Legislative Assembly. The Commission has appointed two authorized officers to administer this program – the Commission's Executive Director and the Director of the Office of Management and Budget. Phone: 701-328-3722; Web: www.nd.gov/ndic/ba-info.htm; Mailing Address: See Industrial Commission office address.

The Commission administers the Lignite Research, Development, and Marketing Program established in 1987 as a partnership between the private and public sectors. By executive order, a Lignite Research Council, consisting of 30 members, advises the Commission on the administration of this program. The Commission approves or disapproves research, development, and marketing projects and activities; accepts and distributes funds; and enters into contracts for the various projects. Phone: 701-328-3722; Web: www.nd.gov/ndic/lrc-infopage.htm. Mailing Address: See Industrial Commission office address.

The Industrial Commission has jurisdiction over the investigation and publication of geological information and the regulation of coal exploration, geophysical exploration, geothermal energy, paleontology resources, subsurface minerals, and the production of oil and gas in North Dakota through the Department of Mineral Resources Geological Survey and Oil and Gas Division. The Industrial Commission appoints the Director of the Department of Mineral Resources, who serves as Director of the Oil and Gas Division and appoints the State Geologist and Assistant Director of the Oil and Gas Division.

The Geological Survey of North Dakota serves as the primary source of geological information in the state, conducts research relative to the state's mineral resources, and conducts programs to promote better public understanding of the state's natural resources, along with a variety of regulatory duties. The Geological Survey was originally established under the trustees of the University of North Dakota by the Legislative Assembly in 1895 with the "professor of geology" at the university as ex-officio State Geologist. Early work of the Survey included studies of water supplies and lignite resources. In 1953, the Industrial Commission was given jurisdiction and authority over Survey enforcement of North Dakota oil and gas conservation laws. The relationship of the State Geologist and the Industrial Commission was tied closer by a series of legislative acts until 1989, when the Legislative Assembly placed the Geological Survey under the North Dakota Industrial Commission and the Survey offices were moved from the University of North Dakota in Grand Forks to Bismarck. The Survey is headed by the State Geologist, who is appointed by the Director of the Department of Mineral Resources. Phone: 701-328-8000; Fax: 701-328-8010; Web: www.dmr.nd.gov/ndgs/; Mailing Address: State Capitol, 600 East Boulevard Avenue, Bismarck, ND 58505; Physical Address: 1016 East Calgary, Bismarck, ND 58501.

The Oil and Gas Division, headed by the Director, was formed in 1981 to provide the technical expertise needed for enforcement of Industrial Commission jurisdiction over statutes, rules, regulations, and orders pertaining to geophysical exploration, drilling, production of oil and gas, restoration of drilling and production sites, and proper disposal of oil field brine and other oil field wastes in North Dakota. The Division facilitates the electronic storage of and provides access to oil and gas production, reservoir, well, and geophysical exploration data for use by industry, royalty owners, and other governmental agencies and citizens. In 2009, regulation of carbon dioxide storage was added to the Oil and Gas Division responsibilities. In 2013, regulation of underground gathering pipeline infrastructure was added to the Oil and Gas Division's responsibilities. In 2015, this authority was broadened to include bonding requirements on underground gathering pipelines. Phone: 701-328-8020; Fax: 701-328-8022; Web: www.dmr.nd.gov/oilgas; Mailing Address: State Capitol, 600 East Boulevard Avenue, Bismarck, ND 58505; Physical Address: 1016 East Calgary, Bismarck, ND 58501.

In 2003, the Legislature established the Oil and Gas Research Fund to promote the growth of the oil and gas industry through research and education. The Industrial Commission is assisted in the administration of the Oil and Gas Research Program by a nine-member Oil and Gas Research Council. The Commission approves or disapproves research and education projects and enters into contracts for the various projects that promote the program's mission. The Director of the Oil and Gas Research Program is appointed by the Industrial Commission. Phone: 701-328-3722; Web: www.nd.gov/ndic/ogrp-infopage.htm; Mailing Address: See Industrial Commission office address.

The Outdoor Heritage Fund was established in 2013 to provide access to private and public lands for sportsmen, including projects that create fish and wildlife habitat; improve, maintain, and restore water quality, soil conditions, plant diversity, animal systems, and other practices of stewardship to enhance farming and ranching; develop, enhance, conserve, and restore wildlife and fish habitat on private and public lands; and conserve natural areas for recreation through the establishment and development of parks and other recreation areas. The Industrial Commission is assisted by a 16-member Advisory Board (12 voting members). Through June 30, 2016, the Commission has awarded funding for 95 projects totaling $28,497,374. Deadlines are established by the Commission for submission of grant applications. After receiving recommendations from the Advisory Board, the Commission acts on their recommendations and, if funding is awarded, contracts are entered into with the applicant. Web: www.nd.gov/ndic/outdoor-infopage.htm; Phone: 701-328-3722; Fax: 701-328-2820; Mailing Address: See Industrial Commission office address.

The North Dakota Transmission Authority was established on August 1, 2005, to serve as a catalyst for developing transmission in North Dakota, offer an alternative source of financing, partner with investors and transmission providers, foster the development of transmission corridors, and serve as a transmission developer as a builder of last resort. The Director of the Transmission Authority is appointed by the Industrial Commission. The annual reports of the Transmission Authority are available on the Industrial Commission website at www.nd.gov/ndic/ic-public.htm Phone: 701-328-3722; Fax: 701-328-2820; Address: See Industrial Commission office address.

The North Dakota Pipeline Authority was established on April 10, 2007, to diversify and expand the North Dakota economy by facilitating development of pipeline facilities to support the production, transportation, and utilization of North Dakota energy-related commodities. Similar to the Transmission Authority, the Pipeline Authority may offer an alternative source of financing, partner with investors and pipeline providers, and serve as a pipeline developer as a builder of last resort. The Director of the Pipeline Authority is appointed by the Industrial Commission. Web:www.dmr.nd.gov/pipeline/; Phone: 701-328-3722; Fax: 701-328-2820; Mailing Address: See Industrial Commission office address.

In 2007, the Legislature established the Renewable Energy Development Fund and the Renewable Energy Program to promote the growth of renewable energy industries through research, development, marketing, and education. The Industrial Commission is assisted in the administration of the Renewable Energy Program by a six-member Renewable Energy Council and staff from the Department of Commerce. The Commission approves or disapproves projects and enters into contracts for the various projects that promote the program's mission. Phone: 701-328-3722; Web: www.nd.gov/ndic/renew-infopage.htm; Mailing Address: See Industrial Commission office address.

In 2013, the Legislature directed that the Industrial Commission receive monthly reports on revenues and expenditures and establish rates for industrial water sales made by the Western Area Water Supply Authority (Authority). The Authority's Board of Directors oversees the operations of the Authority for their domestic and industrial water sales, but additional reporting on industrial water sales must be provided to the Industrial Commission. The Commission's Executive Director works with the Authority's Executive Director in preparing the information for the Commission's review. Phone: 701- 328-3722; Mailing Address: See Industrial Commission office address.

Department of Trust Lands (University and School Lands, Board of)

Phone: 701-328-2800
Fax: 701-328-3650
Web: www.land.nd.gov
Email: landinfo@nd.gov

[Constitution, Article IX, and Section 21 of Article X; NDCC Chapters 15-01 through 15-08.1, 15-68, 15.1-36, 47-30.1, and 57-62 and NDCC § 57-51.1-07.5 and § 61-33-07]

The Governor, Secretary of State, State Treasurer, Attorney General, and Superintendent of Public Instruction make up the Board of University and School Lands. The Governor serves as chair and the Secretary of State as vice chair. The Commissioner, who is appointed by the Board, serves as the Department Director and as the Board's Secretary.

The primary responsibility of the Department of Trust Lands is to manage the permanent educational trust funds and assets under the control of the Board of University and School Lands in a manner that preserves the purchasing power of the funds and provides stable distributions to fund beneficiaries. Revenues are generated through prudent management of trust assets, consisting of more than 706,000 surface acres, 1.8 million mineral acres, and $3.8 billion in permanent trust financial assets. The surface acres are leased to ranchers and farmers across the state. The mineral acres are offered for oil, gas, coal, gravel, and scoria leasing. Trust Fund revenues are invested in a diversified portfolio that includes farm loans, U.S. Treasury notes and bonds, real estate, corporate stocks and bonds, and other financial assets. According to Article IX of the Constitution, biennial distributions from the permanent trust funds must be 10 percent of the five-year average value of the trust financial assets. Distributions are made to schools (public grades K-12), various higher education institutions, and other public institutions at specific intervals throughout the biennium.

Besides management of the permanent trust assets, the Department has three additional major functions that include:

1. Operation of the State Unclaimed Property Division, which serves as the repository for financial accounts, cash assets, and securities that have been not been claimed by the rightful owners or their heirs and successors. Acting as a custodian, the Department manages financial assets (no real estate) received from businesses referred to as "holders" and works to reunite owners with those assets. Assets that go unclaimed are invested and support the Common Schools Trust Fund.

2. Management of the Energy Infrastructure and Impact Office, which is a statutory division within the Department responsible for administering the coal impact loan fund and an oil impact grant program to support political

subdivisions' efforts to manage the direct impacts of energy development. The Office develops a plan for assistance through grants to counties, cities, school districts, and other political subdivisions in oil and gas development areas. The Land Board determines the amount of individual grants; however, the total amount available to grant is set by legislative appropriation. Recent biennial grant authority follows:

- $6 million – 2007-2009 Biennium
- $8 million – 2009-2011 Biennium
- $135 million – 2011-2013 Biennium
- $240 million – 2013-2015 Biennium
- $139.3 million – 2015-2017 Biennium

3. Oversight and management of four important state trust funds:

   a) The Strategic Investment and Improvements Fund (SIIF) holds the assets and revenues earned from 800,000 sovereign mineral acres, including those formerly owned by the Bank of North Dakota and State Treasurer and minerals located under navigable rivers and lakes. The SIIF also receives a portion of the oil and gas production and extraction taxes collected by the state. This fund may be expended by the Legislature for one-time expenditures relating to improving state infrastructure or for initiatives to improve the efficiency and effectiveness of state government.
   b) The Coal Development Trust Fund is a permanent fund administered by the Board to provide loans to coal-impacted counties, cities, and school districts as provided in section 57-62-03 and for loans to school districts pursuant to chapter 15.1-36.
   c) The Capitol Building Fund was created under Article IX of the North Dakota Constitution for the construction and maintenance of public buildings at the capitol. This fund is not permanent; the balance of the fund is subject to legislative appropriation each biennium.
   d) The Indian Cultural Education Trust was created in 2003 for the purpose of generating income to benefit the Mandan, Hidatsa & Arikara Nation Cultural Education Foundation.

Agencies Headed by Gubernatorial Appointees

Consolidation of governmental responsibilities in a number of areas has increased the scope of activity under agencies headed by direct gubernatorial appointees. Since at least 1942, there have been calls for a greater consolidation of state government, with fewer agencies and more direct control by the Governor. While general efforts to consolidate all of state government have failed, individual efforts to establish multi-functional departments have been more successful.

Administrative Hearings, Office of

2911 North 14th Street – Suite 303
Bismarck, ND 58503
Phone: 701-328-3200
Fax: 701-328-3254
Email: oah@nd.gov
[NDCC 54-57-01]

Established in 1991, the office is administered by a Director who is appointed by the Governor for a term of six years and whose appointment is confirmed by the Senate. The Director must be a licensed attorney in good standing.

The Director or appointed administrative law judges preside at administrative hearings as requested by agencies. With specified exceptions, all administrative hearings must be conducted by this office. The office is to assure all proceedings are conducted in a fair and impartial manner.

There is a State Advisory Council for Administrative Hearings, which is a committee of the State Bar Association appointed by its president. The committee is to meet with the Director at least semi-annually and advise on rules and policy matters.

Adjutant General and North Dakota National Guard

Fraine Barracks
P.O. Box 5511
Bismarck, ND 58506-5511
Phone: 701-333-2000
Fax: 701-333-2017
Website: www.ndguard.com
[NDCC 37-03-01]

Appointed by the Governor, the Adjutant General must have been a federally recognized commissioned officer of the National Guard for a period of at least three years immediately preceding the appointment, be in the rank of lieutenant colonel or higher, and must have completed the educational requirements for appointment as a federally recognized general officer. The Adjutant General serves as Commander of the State Army and Air National Guard. The Governor is Commander-in-Chief of this military establishment, except portions called to service in a Title 10 Federal Status in support of the United States.

The North Dakota National Guard is organized into three major commands: the Joint Force Headquarters, Army Command, and Air Command. Located in Bismarck at Fraine Barracks, the North Dakota National Guard's Joint Force Headquarters is comprised of the Adjutant General's Office; the Deputy Adjutant General's Office, which includes the Director of Intelligence (J-2), Director of Training and Military Operations (J-3/7), Director of Strategic Plans and Outreach

(J-5/9), and Chief Information Office (J-6); and United States Property and Fiscal Office. The Adjutant General's Office also includes the special staff offices of the Chaplain, State Surgeon, Staff Judge Advocate, Public Affairs Office, Environmental Services, and Facilities Engineering. The Adjutant General's Personal Staff includes the Inspector General, Government Affairs Officer, and Senior Enlisted Leader. The Joint Headquarters provides command, control, and supervision of the two military service components. It receives, manages, and provides support to civil authorities by activating units and providing resources during domestic operations and state emergencies as directed by the Governor.

The North Dakota Army National Guard provides personnel (soldiers) to the Army Command, which provides a full range of military support to fulfill federal, state, and community missions. The Army Command is headquartered at the Raymond J. Bohn Armory in Bismarck and consists of five major subordinate commands: the 141st Maneuver Enhancement Brigade (Fargo); the 68th Troop Command (Bismarck); the Recruiting & Retention Command (Bismarck); the 164th Regiment (Regional Training Institute); and Camp Grafton Training Center, both located at Devils Lake.

The North Dakota Air National Guard provides personnel (airmen) to the Air Command and the 119th Wing, nicknamed "The Happy Hooligans." The 119th Wing, headquartered at Hector Field in Fargo, provides personnel and military assets in support of federal, state, and community missions and is divided into four groups: Operations Group; Mission Support Group; Medical Group; and the Intelligence, Surveillance, and Reconnaissance Group. Primary missions include gathering and utilizing intelligence to perform target system analysis and target development, missile field security at Minot Air Force Base, medical, logistics, security forces, engineering, communications, personnel, and services support.

In addition to commanding the North Dakota National Guard, the Adjutant General serves as the Director of the North Dakota Department of Emergency Services (NDDES) and is the Chairman of the Department of Emergency Services Advisory Committee. NDDES provides 24/7 emergency communications through the Divisions of State Radio and Homeland Security in collaboration with more than 50 lead and support agencies, private enterprise, and voluntary organizations to assist local jurisdictions in disaster and emergency response and planning activities. NDDES supports response and recovery coordination with emergency managers in each county and tribal nation within the state of North Dakota, as well as the cities of Bismarck and Fargo. The department administers several federal disaster recovery programs and the Homeland Security Grant Programs.

Additionally, NDDES administers the Hazardous Chemicals Preparedness and Response Program and works in collaboration with the North Dakota State and Local Intelligence Center (NDSLIC) to manage homeland security information, such as threats to critical infrastructure, so appropriate actions can be implemented to protect citizens. NDDES also manages the Emergency Management Assistance

Compact (EMAC) that serves as a national clearinghouse through which member states may request and provide mutual aid assistance.

Commerce Department

Department of Commerce
1600 E. Century Ave., Suite 2
Bismarck, ND 58503
Phone: 701-328-5300
Fax: 701-328-5320
Web: www.NDcommerce.com
Email: commerce@nd.gov

Division of Community Services
Phone: 701-328-5300
Fax: 701-328-2308
Web: www.NDcommunityservices.com
Email: commerce@nd.gov

Division of Tourism
Phone: 701-328-2525
Toll Free: 800-HELLO-ND
Fax: 701-328-4878
Web: www.NDtourism.com
Email: tourism@nd.gov

Division of Workforce Development
Phone: 701-328-5345
Fax: 701-328-5320
Web: www.NDworkforce.com
Email: commerce@nd.gov

Division of Economic Development and Finance
Phone: 701-328-5300
Fax: 701-328-5320
Web: www.NDbusiness.com
Email: commerce@nd.gov

The North Dakota Department of Commerce is the lead agency charged by the Governor and Legislature to attract, retain, and expand wealth in North Dakota. The Department of Commerce serves businesses and communities statewide through four divisions: Community Services, Economic Development and Finance, Tourism, and Workforce Development. The agency has hundreds of partners – local, state, federal, public, tribal, private, and nonprofit – and is the primary facilitator for all entities involved in the economic and community development process.

The North Dakota Department of Commerce was created in 2001, absorbing four previous state entities. The Department is headed by a Commissioner, appointed by the Governor with the advice and counsel of the North Dakota Economic Development Foundation. The Department of Commerce must consist of a Division of Community Services; a Division of Economic Development and Finance; a Division of Tourism; a Division of Workforce Development; and any other divisions the Commissioner determines necessary. It must also encompass the Office of Renewable Energy and Energy Efficiency, the Office of International Business and Trade, the North Dakota Women's Business Development Office, and the Rural Development Office. The Commissioner appoints the directors of the Divisions of Community Services, Economic Development and Finance, Tourism, and Workforce Development.

The North Dakota Economic Development Foundation, also created in 2001, is composed of a minimum of 15 and a maximum of 30 members appointed by the Governor for two-year terms. Appointment of the foundation members must ensure a cross section of business, tourism, and economic development representation and must ensure that at least one member represents rural concerns. The foundation members elect an executive committee with a minimum of five and a maximum of seven foundation members. The executive committee members elect a chairman, vice chairman, and secretary. The foundation is to seek funding for administrative expenses from private sector sources and seek and distribute private sector funds for use in commerce-related activities. The purpose of the foundation is to provide the Governor advice and counsel in selecting the Commissioner; serve in an advisory role to the Commissioner; administer a strategic plan for economic development in the state and set accountability standards, measurements, and benchmarks to evaluate the effectiveness of the department in implementing the strategic plan; and monitor economic development activities and initiatives of the department.

The Department of Commerce manages programs that lead to growth and innovation within the state's economy. These include the Research North Dakota and Innovate North Dakota programs. The Research North Dakota program was established in 2013 to build upon earlier efforts in the Centers of Excellence and Centers of Research Excellence programs and is governed by the Centers of Excellence Commission with staff services provided by the department. The program supports research, development, and commercialization of North Dakota projects and ideas by partnering private sector businesses with North Dakota's research universities.

The Innovate North Dakota program is a statewide economic development initiative designed to help entrepreneurs turn business ideas into viable new business ventures. It is coordinated by the Department of Commerce in partnership with the UND Center for Innovation, NDSU Research and Technology Park, IDEA Center in Bismarck, and the Severson Entrepreneurship Academy at Minot State University. Through expert guidance from business coaches and extensive leadership courses, Innovate ND provides the entrepreneurial community of North Dakota the resources needed to help turn an innovative idea into a profitable business.

The Division of Economic Development and Finance [NDCC 54-34.3] assumes the functions of the department of the same name, which was created in 1991 to assume the functions, powers, and duties of the Economic Development Commission. The Economic Development Commission was created in 1957 and consisted of the Governor as chair and nine members, one from each of the eight planning districts and one at-large member representing minorities. A predecessor agency, the North Dakota Research Foundation, existed from 1943-1957.

The mission of the division includes attracting and creating new wealth-generating enterprises in the state; promoting economic diversification and innovation within targeted industries and economic sectors; promoting increased productivity and value-added products and processes; maintaining and revitalizing economically depressed rural areas; supporting partnerships with sources of financial and intellectual capital; and identifying state statutes, rules, and policies which impede economic development. The Division of Economic Development and Finance is broken down into three major areas: Business Development, Research, and Finance and works closely with the Bank of North Dakota. Finance programs within the division include the North Dakota Development Fund (NDDF) and the Agricultural Products Utilization Commission (APUC).

The North Dakota Development Fund, Inc., [NDCC 10-30.5] is a state-wide nonprofit development corporation that has authority to take equity positions in, provide loans to, or use other innovative financing mechanisms to provide capital for new and expanding businesses in North Dakota or for relocating businesses in North Dakota. The Governor appoints the eight members who comprise the Board of Directors to serve three-year terms. The Board must include at least one member enrolled in a North Dakota tribe and one member from a rural area.

The Agricultural Products Utilization Commission [NDCC 4-14.1-03] creates wealth and jobs through the development of new and expanded uses of North Dakota's agricultural products. This is accomplished through the administration of a grant program. The Governor appoints five of the nine commission members, three of whom must be actively engaged in farming and two actively engaged in business. The Commissioner of Agriculture also appoints one member who must be actively engaged in farming. All appointees serve two-year terms. Other members are the Commissioner of Agriculture, the Commissioner of Commerce, and the President of North Dakota State University or their designees.

The Division of Workforce Development [NDCC 54-60-09] was established in the 2001 legislation that created the Department of Commerce. The division is responsible for monitoring local, regional, and national workforce initiatives and leading the development and implementation of the state's talent and workforce intelligence coordination strategies. Its goals are to ensure North Dakota employers have access to a skilled talent pool to meet their workforce needs, encourage young people to remain in state for career opportunity, and to support volunteerism in the state.

Programs administered by the division include the AmeriCorps state formula program, Operation Intern, Workforce Enhancement Grant Program, Relocation Program, Youth Office, Rural Healthcare Workforce Grant Program, and Tribal College Grants. The division administers Early Childhood Education Provider grants in cooperation with the Department of Public Instruction. The division also provides administrative support to the North Dakota State Commission on National and Community Service.

The Division of Tourism [NDCC 54-34.4-01] began as the Tourist Promotion Bureau in the State Highway Department in 1965. The bureau was transferred to the

Economic Development Commission in 1981, merged with the Department of Parks and Recreation in 1991, and established as a separate agency in 1993. The Tourism Division became part of the North Dakota Department of Commerce in 2001.

The division fosters and promotes tourism to, and within, the state; promotes the full development of the state's tourism resources; and serves as a planning and coordinating agency for tourism-related programs of the state and the state's political subdivisions. The Legislative Assembly established a state tourism policy in 1993, which was updated during the 2011 Legislative Session.

The mission of the Tourism Division is to bring new wealth to North Dakotans by increasing the number of out-of-state visitors who choose the state as a travel destination and to enhance North Dakota's image.

Program areas within the Tourism Division include: General Leisure Tourism Marketing, Group Travel Marketing, Outdoor Promotion, International Marketing, Public and Media Relations, and Tourism Development.

The division continues to strengthen its partnerships with the hospitality industry and local tourism organizations, as well as numerous state and federal agencies in the following areas:

- Cooperative marketing programs
- Brochure distribution programs
- Trade show and sales mission participation
- Familiarization tour opportunities
- Access to the division's comprehensive photo library and research
- Hospitality training
- Merchandise sales
- Marketing and infrastructure grants
- Packages and education vacation marketing
- Complimentary website and publication listings

The division has also used research to create compelling advertising to attract regional visitors and adventure tourists from across the United States interested in activities like mountain biking, golfing, fishing, and birding. The research drives the creative strategy and the types of media purchased. In addition, it measures the return on investment the state receives for all advertising investment. The $3.17 million 2016 advertising campaign generated 354,000 new trips to North Dakota and $328.3 million in visitor spending. That means for every $1 invested, North Dakota businesses and government entities received $104 back. Additional research showed, in 2015, North Dakota hosted 22 million visitors, and they spent $3.1 billion. Tourism makes up 4 percent of gross domestic product and impacts all 53 counties. Tax revenue of $327 million was generated through visitor activity.

The Division of Community Services [NDCC 54-44.5] provides technical assistance to local governments, state agencies, and the executive branch in the areas of community and rural planning and development, policy research and development, and grant program implementation.

The division provides the people of North Dakota with effective, efficient, and customer-oriented administration of federal and state programs for Community Development, Energy Efficiency and Renewable Energy, and Self Sufficiency. These programs help create a quality of life that makes North Dakota a good place in which to live, work, and do business. The Division of Community Services consists of four different program areas: Community Development, Office of Renewable Energy and Energy Efficiency, Self Sufficiency, and Technical Assistance.

The Division of Community Services' primary partners for administering grant programs are the Community Action Agencies and the Regional Planning Councils. They are directly involved in the implementation of the Community Services Block Grant, Community Development Block Grant, HOME, Emergency Shelter Grants, and Weatherization programs. Other partners assisting in implementing programs include such entities as the North Dakota Building Officials Association, Interstate Compact on Industrialized Buildings, North Dakota Manufactured Housing Association, North Dakota Association of Builders, Institute for Building Technology and Safety, and each city with a Renaissance Zone. The division also administers grants to homeless shelters, domestic violence shelters, and child care facilities.

The Department of Commerce also works with other strategic partners, such as the North Dakota Trade Office, Impact Dakota, Center for Technology and Business, Small Business Development Center (SBDC), and North Dakota Rural Development Council.

The purpose of the Office of International Business and Trade (North Dakota Trade Office) is to increase exports of North Dakota products to international markets. The office's goal of increasing exporting strengthens and diversifies the economy with new money; creates new, interesting career opportunities; and prepares businesses to become more globally competitive with higher growth.

The office assists North Dakota businesses expand exports to international markets by:

- Advocating for exporters;
- Offering export educational opportunities to North Dakota businesses;
- Researching and raising awareness of export opportunities, issues, and challenges impacting North Dakota businesses;
- Assisting North Dakota businesses in identifying, developing, and cultivating international markets for products; and
- Organizing and carrying out trade missions that seek to facilitate contact and communication between North Dakota businesses and international markets.

Impact Dakota is organized as a nonprofit organization [501(c)(3)] and is an affiliate of the Manufacturing Extension Partnership – the nation's largest assistance network dedicated to developing domestic manufacturing. It has a Board of Directors representing progressive North Dakota businesses and the state of North Dakota (through the North Dakota Department of Commerce). As an MEP affiliate, Impact Dakota is able to introduce world class best practices complemented by objective assessment, technical assistance, and training services locally to manufacturers, other new wealth creating companies, and related industries in order to strengthen their economic vitality and that of the region and nation. Services provided by Impact Dakota include: leadership and people development; strategic and business planning; process improvement; and accelerating growth and innovation.

The Center for Technology and Business (CTB) delivers the services of the Women's Business Development Office and the Rural Development Office. These programs are involved with computer education, rural outreach, rural housing, childcare, and the North Dakota Young Professionals Network.

The Small Business Development Center (SBDC) provides high-quality business assistance in the form of counseling, training, and research to existing and prospective small businesses.

Corrections and Rehabilitation, Department of

3100 Railroad Avenue
PO Box 1898
Bismarck, ND 58502-1898
Phone: 701-328-6390
Fax: 701-328-6651
Web: www.nd.gov/docr/
Email: docr@nd.gov

Created in 1989, the Department of Corrections and Rehabilitation (DOCR) is responsible for the direction and general administrative supervision, guidance, and planning of adult and juvenile correctional facilities and programs within the state. The Director is appointed by the Governor. The Director's qualifications include a minimum of a bachelor's degree from an accredited college or university and at least five years' experience in a management position in correctional or related work.

The Board of Control was established in 1911 to manage the state's charitable, reformatory, and penal institutions; it was succeeded by the Board of Administration in 1919. In turn, the Director of Institutions replaced that Board in 1969. The office of the Director of Institutions was abolished in 1989. The Department of Corrections and Rehabilitation was created in 1989 and consists of the Adult Services Division and Juvenile Services Division.

The Division of Adult Services manages almost 9,100 adult offenders. It has organized itself in a manner that effectively transitions offenders through the adult corrections system while enhancing public safety. Adult correctional assets are organized as follows:

Transitional Planning implements strategies that best utilize DOCR resources when managing offender movement throughout the DOCR. This unit provides administrative support for the Parole Board and Pardon Advisory Board, the development of the Department's correctional sentencing report, the management of male classification and movement, the coordination for the transportation of offenders throughout the system, victim services, and discharge coordination, as well as the coordination for the Department's adult offender case planning committee and legal records.

The maximum security facility for male inmates, known as the North Dakota State Penitentiary (NDSP), provides housing for 800 maximum and medium custody inmates. The male orientation unit, an administrative segregation and disciplinary detention unit, and medical infirmary are also located at NDSP.

The medium security facility for male inmates, known as the James River Correctional Center (JRCC), provides housing for 440 inmates in Jamestown. The Special Assistance Unit (SAU) located within JRCC is a 24-bed housing unit for inmates with serious mental illness or other special needs.

More than 540 male and female inmates are housed across the state in transitional and prison facilities that are managed by the Division of Adult Services. Transitional Facilities consists of a 196-bed minimum security facility known as the Missouri River Correctional Center. This facility includes a 36-bed transitional housing unit allowing inmates to live in an apartment-type setting which facilitates efficient and effective reintegration. Transitional Facilities also includes residential treatment programs located at the Tompkins Rehabilitation and Corrections Center on the State Hospital campus in Jamestown; a transition assessment program located at the Bismarck Transition Center in Bismarck; and residential re-entry programs located at Lake Region Reentry Center in Devils Lake, as well as Centre, Inc. facilities, located in Mandan, Grand Forks, and Fargo.

The 2003 Legislative Assembly passed House Bill No. 1271, which directed the North Dakota Department of Corrections to contract with county entities for the housing of female inmates sentenced to the DOCR. The Southwest Multi-County Correctional Center was awarded the contract and has been housing female inmates at their facility in New England (Dakota Women's Correctional Rehabilitation Center) since November 2003. DWCRC is a 126-bed women's prison, consisting of a 70-bed minimum unit, a 40-bed medium unit, a five-bed special management unit, and a 16-bed orientation unit. Following a period of orientation and assessment at the prison, female inmates are classified and designated to the appropriate housing units. Roughly 75 percent of female inmates are serving sentences for non-violent offenses, allowing for large numbers of female inmates to serve their sentences in minimum security housing at DWCRC or residential treatment programs and halfway houses. In addition to DWCRC, classified female inmates are housed at the Tompkins Rehabilitation and Corrections Center in Jamestown and at halfway houses in Devils Lake, Bismarck, Mandan, and Fargo.

The Behavioral Health Department delivers individual and group programming using the evidence of what works to reduce recidivism and improve psychosocial outcomes. People in prison participate in comprehensive behavioral health intervention to determine their specific needs. They may be referred for Thinking for a Change, substance abuse treatment, conflict resolution or domestic violence programming, and sexual offender treatment, as well as individual counseling and psychiatric services. The behavioral health staff also provides referrals for people leaving prison to access necessary community-based resources.

The Industry Training Program is commonly referred to as Rough Rider Industries and operates within all three institutional facilities. The program helps provide vocational learning and employment skills training to incarcerated individuals enrolled in the training program. It also helps reduce resident idleness by giving individuals an opportunity to participate in productive work activities. These activities help lessen both security and behavioral situations while instilling transferrable job skills necessary in helping make a successful transition back into the community.

The Education Department provides appropriate educational, vocational, employment skills, post-secondary, and training opportunities for inmates to assist them in re-entering into the community successfully. Education has a number of programs that have been established to assist inmates with personal and career development at all three institutions. Inmates go through an assessment to determine their education and literacy levels and needs. Several of the programs provided are Adult Basic Education, General Education Development (GED), Computer Literacy Programs, Read Right, AutoCAD, Construction Technology, Welding Technology, Career Readiness, and a Post-Secondary Program.

Parole and Probation delivers supervision and services for nearly 7,300 people that are placed on parole or probation supervision in the community. Parole and Probation utilizes a validated risk assessment tool to identify risk and formulate supervision plans to serve as the roadmap for an offender's success. Specialized programs include a parole specialist, re-entry, drug court, sex offender specialist, domestic violence specialist, and mental health specialist. Parole and Probation manages about 5,500 male offenders and more than 1,800 female offenders.

The Division of Juvenile Services (DJS) [NDCC 27-21] is responsible for the custody of delinquent and unruly children placed in its care, custody, and control by the District Courts. The Division includes the operation of the North Dakota Youth Correctional Center and Community Services, which operates through eight regionalized offices.

Community Services (in cooperation with the Department of Human Services, North Dakota Association of Counties, and Department of Public Instruction) provides a continuum of placement options and an array of services for committed youth. Among the programs are Intensive In-Home (family therapy services); Day Treatment (providing assessment, counseling, cognitive intervention programming, behavior management, and academic remediation); Restorative Justice programming (providing accountability conferences, victim empathy seminars, and restorative councils); and Attendant Care (statewide detention support services designed to reduce the number of juveniles held in adult jails).

The North Dakota Youth Correctional Center (NDYCC) opened southwest of Mandan in 1903 with a land grant of 40,000 acres. The Center assumes responsibility for the detention, rehabilitation, and education of juveniles legally committed to the Division by the courts. Individual and group interventions are focused on reducing risk for future crime, along with helping offenders learn skills to manage criminogenic need areas, including substance use, violence, and sexual offending. A variety of academic and vocational programs are provided. The Youth Correctional Center has a fully accredited high school and middle school called Marmot Schools.

The Division of Juvenile Services utilizes an integrated approach across its system. During the intake phase, youth undergo assessment at NDYCC while Community Services staff assesses the home and family. A treatment plan is developed based on the assessment findings. Placement is fluid, and youth move across the system based on their changing needs for level of structure and individualized treatment requirements.

Financial Institutions, Department of

2000 Schafer St., Suite G
Bismarck, ND 58501-1204
Phone: 701-328-9933
Fax: 701-328-0290
Web: www.nd.gov/dfi
Email: dfi@nd.gov
[NDCC 6-01]

Established in 1969, the Department is headed by the Commissioner. The State Examiner was established in 1893. The Department of Financial Institutions was established in 1969, and the title of the agency's head changed from State Examiner to Commissioner.

The Commissioner is appointed by the Governor and confirmed by the Senate for a four-year term. The Commissioner must be a skilled accountant and may not be an incumbent of any other public office. The Commissioner may not own, hold, or control any stocks, capital, or bonds or hold the office of trustee, assignee, officer, agent, or employee of any financial institution under his jurisdiction or of any corporation engaged in the business of guarantying or ensuring the fidelity or faithful performance of duties or the solvency of public officers or of public depositories.

The Department executes all laws relating to state banks; trust companies; building and loan associations; mutual investment corporations; mutual savings corporations; banking institutions; other financial corporations, exclusive of the Bank of North Dakota; and all credit unions, organized or doing business under the laws of this state. The Commissioner chairs the State Banking Board and the State Credit Union Board.

Additionally, the Department issues licenses to money brokers, mortgage loan originators, collection agencies, consumer finance, debt settlement providers, deferred presentment service providers, and money transmitter businesses. The Department is responsible to the depositors and creditors of the financial institutions by determining the soundness of the financial institutions and monitoring compliance with applicable rules and regulations.

The State Banking Board consists of the Commissioner and six members appointed by the Governor to terms of five years. Four members must be in an executive capacity in management of a state bank for five years; one member in an executive capacity in management of a state bank or national bank for five years; and one member is from the public. The Board may adopt rules for the government of financial corporations to the extent the rules do not conflict with any law of this state or of the United States. The Board makes and enforces orders necessary or proper to protect the public and the depositors or creditors of state financial corporations and institutions.

The State Credit Union Board has the same powers with respect to credit unions as the State Banking Board has to other financial institutions. The State Credit Union Board consists of the Commissioner and four members appointed by the Governor for terms of five years. Two members must have at least three year's experience as an officer, director, or committee member of a North Dakota state-chartered credit union; one member must have at least three year's experience as an officer, director, or committee member.

Game and Fish Department

100 North Bismarck Expressway
Bismarck, ND 58501-5095
Phone: 701-328-6300
Fax: 701-328-6352
Report All Poachers (RAP): 800-472-2121
Web: www.gf.nd.gov
Email: ndgf@nd.gov
[NDCC 20.1-02]

Game and fish laws were first established in Dakota Territory in 1861, but it was not until 1893, when the Superintendent of Irrigation and Forestry was designated as Game Commissioner, that a Game and Fish Department was formed. In 1909, the Game and Fish Board of Control was established. The Board continued to function as the agency controlling fish and game until 1929, when legislation was passed providing for a single commissioner charged with administering a Game and Fish Department.

The Game and Fish Director is appointed by the Governor. The Director names a deputy director, chief game warden, district game wardens, biologists, technicians, and other staff to enforce game laws, establish hunting and fishing seasons, and perform other duties.

The Department consists of five divisions:

- Administrative Services, which performs accounting and basic operations, data processing, licensing, and planning.
- Enforcement, which enforces game and fish laws and rules necessary for proper management of fish and game resources.
- Fisheries, which is responsible for the programs of fish production, sport fish research, and lake and stream management and access.
- Conservation and Communications, which is divided into the program areas of hunter education, fish and wildlife information and education, and boating education. It also includes environmental project review and the Department's nongame wildlife program.
- Wildlife, which is divided into the program areas of wildlife management area maintenance and development, private land habitat and access improvement, and game management.

Health, Department of

600 East Boulevard Avenue
Bismarck, ND 58505-0200
Phone: 701-328-2372
Fax: 701-328-4727
Web: www.ndhealth.gov
Email: health@nd.gov
[NDCC 23-01]

The Territorial Board of Health was created in 1885. At the time of statehood in 1889, the State Board of Health was established. In 1923, the Legislative Assembly authorized the State Department of Health. Among administrative changes made in 1933 was the transfer of public health laboratories previously connected with the University of North Dakota to the State Health Department. In 1947, the State Health Department was reorganized to provide for hospital registration and licensure.

In 1987, the State Department of Health and the State Laboratories Department were consolidated to form the State Department of Health and Consolidated Laboratories. The name was shortened to its present form in 1995, and the Department was designated the primary environmental agency for the state.

The North Dakota Department of Health is dedicated to the goal of ensuring North Dakota is a healthy place to live and each person has an equal opportunity to enjoy good health. It is committed to the promotion of healthy lifestyles, protection and enhancement of health and the environment, and provision of quality health care services for the people of North Dakota.

It advances its mission by networking, facilitating local efforts, collaborating with partners and stakeholders, and providing expertise in developing creative public health solutions.

The administrative head of the Department is the State Health Officer appointed by the Governor. If the Governor does not appoint as State Health Officer a physician licensed in this state, the Governor shall appoint at least three licensed physicians recommended by the state medical association to serve as an advisory committee to the state health officer. The State Health Officer carries out the rules and recommendations of the State Health Council; oversees operations of the agency; and serves as the primary spokesperson and authority on health issues, voicing public health policies on behalf of the Governor.

The State Health Council consists of 11 members appointed by the Governor for three-year terms. These members include four persons from the health care field, five persons representing consumer interests, one person from the energy industry, and one from the manufacturing and processing industry.

The State Health Council establishes standards and rules for the maintenance of public health, including sanitation and disease control; develops, establishes, and enforces basic standards for hospitals and related medical institutions; holds hearings related to licensing of medical facilities; and advises the State Health Officer to do all things required in the proper performance of the various responsibilities placed upon the State Department of Health.

The Department consists of the following sections: Administrative Support, Community Health, Environmental Health, Emergency Preparedness and Response, Health Resources, and Medical Services.

The Administrative Support Section provides services to support the Department's activities and programs. Within Administrative Support are the Division of Accounting, Office of Public Information, Information Technology Coordinator, Division of Vital Records, Office of Human Resources, and Office of Education Technology.

The goal of the Community Health Section is to improve the health of North Dakota citizens by working actively to promote healthy behaviors and prevent disease and injury. Many of the services are provided through local public health units. The section includes the divisions of Cancer Prevention and Control, Children's Special Health Services, Chronic Disease, Family Health, Injury Prevention and Control, and Nutrition and Physical Activity.

The Environmental Health Section safeguards the quality of North Dakota's air, land, and water resources. The section deals with issues that affect the comfort, health, safety, and well-being of North Dakota citizens and their environment. Primary functions and responsibilities of the section include coordinating communication with the U.S. Environmental Protection Agency regarding state programs and related environmental issues; monitoring and enforcing compliance with state and federal environmental laws; carrying out environmental analyses; and providing public education, contaminant remediation, and emergency response. The section consists of the following divisions: Air Quality, Laboratory Services, Municipal Facilities, Waste Management, and Water Quality.

The Emergency Preparedness and Response Section is responsible for improving and maintaining public health response to disasters and large-scale emergencies. The overall goal is to promote a state of emergency readiness and response. Future activities will improve public health infrastructure for the detection and mitigation of chemical threats, naturally occurring phenomena such as tornadoes and floods, and other disasters and emergencies. The section includes the following divisions: Emergency Medical Systems, Public Health Preparedness, and Hospital Preparedness.

The Health Resources Section consists of four divisions: Health Facilities, Food and Lodging, Life Safety and Construction, and Medical Marijuana. These divisions work to promote quality care and services for the people of North Dakota.

The goal of the Medical Services Section is to promote health and prevent illness and disease. The section includes the following: Office of the State Forensic Examiner and Division of Disease Control.

Highway Patrol

600 East Boulevard Avenue, Department 504
Bismarck, ND 58505-0240
Phone: 701-328-2455
After Hours: 800-472-2121
Fax: 701-328-1717
Email: ndhpinfo@nd.gov
Web: www.nd.gov/ndhp

During the first years of the organization, the State Highway Commissioner appointed the Superintendent of the Highway Patrol. In 1951, the Legislative Assembly gave the responsibility of appointing the Superintendent to the Governor. All officers are appointed by the Superintendent.

The Patrol is divided into two main components: Field Operations and Administration. The Field Operations component includes three divisions: east, west, and motor carrier. The administration component includes the finance section and two divisions, support services and administrative services.

The Patrol enforces criminal and traffic laws, including those governing commercial motor vehicles on roadways open to the public. Other primary responsibilities include investigating vehicle crashes, promoting safe driving practices, assisting other law enforcement agencies, inspecting school buses, and administering a federal commercial vehicle safety inspection program. In addition, the Patrol has jurisdiction on state-owned and leased property, such as the Capitol grounds. The Patrol is responsible for providing security and protection for the Governor, the Governor's family, the Legislative Assembly while in session, and the Supreme Court. The Patrol also has an aircraft equipped with infrared equipment to assist in search and rescue operations.

The Law Enforcement Training Academy provides basic and advanced training to members of the public safety community. Certification and curriculum offered by the Law Enforcement Training Academy, located in Bismarck, must meet criteria established by the Peace Officer Standards and Training Board.

Human Services, Department of

600 East Boulevard, 3rd Floor-Judicial Wing
Bismarck, ND 58505-0250
Phone: 701-328-2310
Fax: 701-328-1545
Toll Free: 800-472-2622
Web: www.nd.gov/dhs

Established in 1981, the Department of Human Services consolidated programs formerly operated under multiple agencies. The Department's Executive Director is appointed by and serves at the pleasure of the Governor. The Department serves as the official agency for administration of federal social and rehabilitation programs in the areas of medical services, economic assistance, community services, and vocational rehabilitation. The role of the Department is to provide services that help vulnerable individuals maintain or enhance their quality of life, which may be threatened by lack of financial resources, emotional crises, disabling conditions, or an inability to protect themselves. This role is carried out directly and through partnerships with county social service offices and contracts with an array of public and private providers.

The Department is organized into these divisions: Aging Services, Child Support, Children and Family Services, Developmental Disabilities, Economic Assistance, Medical Services (Medicaid, Medicaid Expansion, State Children's Health Insurance Program, and the Home and Community-based Services Administration Unit that includes autism services), Behavioral Health Services, Vocational Rehabilitation, and Administrative Support Services. These divisions are responsible for receiving, distributing, and monitoring the use of state and federal funds; providing direction and technical assistance for implementing programs, setting standards and policy for service delivery, and providing training. For some programs, division staff members are involved directly in service delivery, including determining eligibility for services, paying provider claims, distributing benefits, and conducting assessments.

The Department's Field Services area is comprised of eight regional human service centers located in Bismarck, Devils Lake, Dickinson, Fargo, Grand Forks,

Jamestown, Minot, and Williston; the North Dakota State Hospital in Jamestown; and the Life Skills and Transition Center (LSTC) in Grafton.

- The North Dakota State Hospital, established in 1884 and continuously accredited by the Joint Commission since 1956, provides acute, sub-acute, and specialized rehabilitation hospital services for individuals with severe and persistent mental illnesses and substance use disorders. The hospital also provides specialized residential addiction services for adults under the custody of the Department of Corrections and Rehabilitation and specialized residential services for individuals committed as sexually dangerous.
- The LSTC became a part of the Department in 1989. The LSTC is a state-operated comprehensive support agency for people with intellectual and developmental disabilities. It is accredited by The Council and certified as an Intermediate Care Facility. It provides specialized services including residential, vocational, and outreach services to meet the unique needs of individuals with intellectual and developmental disabilities residing on campus, in supported living arrangements in Grafton, and in communities across the state. Outreach services that support individuals in their homes and communities include clinical and direct support consultation and services and behavioral analyst assessment and intervention services.
- Human service centers provide a comprehensive set of community-based services, including a continuum of behavioral health care services for individuals with severe mental illnesses and substance use disorders, either directly or through contracts. Other community services include vocational rehabilitation, developmental disability services, and vulnerable adult protective services. In addition, staff members provide direction and oversight of services offered through county social service offices and other providers, such as child care licensing and child welfare services.

Indian Affairs Commission, North Dakota

Phone: 701-328-2428
Fax: 701-328-1537
Email: ndiac@nd.gov
[NDCC 54-36]

The North Dakota Indian Affairs Commission consists of the Governor as Chairman; three members appointed by the Governor from the state at large, two of whom must be of Indian descent, must be enrolled members of a tribe, and must be current voting residents of the state of North Dakota; and the chairperson or the chairperson's designee of the Standing Rock Sioux Tribe; Spirit Lake Tribe; Three Affiliated Tribes of the Fort Berthold Reservation; Turtle Mountain Band of Chippewa Indians; and Sisseton-Wahpeton Oyate of the Lake Traverse Reservation. The Commission meets quarterly or as otherwise agreed. Members of the Commission or the chairperson's designee are entitled to receive mileage and expenses for attending each meeting as are allowed other state officers. The Governor appoints the Executive Director of the Commission after consultation with the members of the Commission. The Executive Director serves at the pleasure of the Governor.

The Indian Affairs Commission has the power to assist and to mobilize the support of state and federal agencies in assisting Indian individuals and groups in North Dakota, especially the five tribal councils, as they seek to develop their own goals, project plans for achieving those goals, and implement those plans. The Commission's duties are to:

- Investigate any phase of Indian affairs and to assemble and make available the facts needed by tribal, state, and federal agencies to work effectively together.
- Assist tribal, state, and federal agencies in developing programs whereby Indian citizens may achieve more adequate standards of living.
- Assist tribal groups in developing increasingly effective institutions of self-government.
- Work for greater understanding and improved relationships between Indians and non-Indians.
- Seek increased participation by Indian citizens in local and state affairs.
- Confer with and coordinate officials and agencies of other governmental units and congressional committees with regard to Indian needs and goals.
- Encourage and propose agreements and accords between federal, state, and local agencies and the several tribal governments, and, pursuant to NDCC 54-40.2, to assist in monitoring and negotiating agreements and accords when asked by an affected tribe.

Information Technology Department

4201 Normandy Street
Bismarck, ND 58503-1324
Telephone: 701-328-3190
Fax: 701-328-3000
TYY: 701-328-2001

The North Dakota Information Technology Department (ITD) supports the IT needs of state government, K-12, and higher education. Because of the diverse needs of state entities, ITD provides varied amounts of support to its customers. While some entities have their own IT departments that partner with ITD for necessary services, others utilize ITD for all of their IT needs. In all situations, it is ITD's vision to be a leader and trusted business partner for strategic IT services within government and education.

ITD provides a wide range of services, broken into four categories: infrastructure, professional services, information management, and communication. Some of these services include: help desk management, software development, hosting, network infrastructure, records management, email, and video conferencing.

In addition to ITD's core service offerings, the organization houses or has representatives in a number of statewide alliances. Statewide alliances are programs made up of stakeholders from various government entities working toward a common goal. For example, the Educational Technology Council (ND ETC) is a state board responsible for developing technology systems and coordinating their use to enhance and support the educational opportunities for elementary and secondary education. The board is made up of representatives from ITD, the Department of Public Instruction, University System, and State Board of Career & Technical Education, among other stakeholders. Other statewide alliances include the Statewide Longitudinal Data System (SLDS), Graphic Information System Hub (GIS), and Health Information Technology (HIT).

To learn more about ITD, statewide alliances, and the progress of information technology within North Dakota State Government, visit www.nd.gov/itd.

Job Service North Dakota

1000 East Divide Avenue
PO Box 5507
Bismarck, ND 58506-5507
Phone: 701-328-2836
Fax: 701-328-4000
TTY: 800-366-6888
Web: www.jobsnd.com
Webmaster Email: JSNDweb@nd.gov
[NDCC 52-02]

Job Service North Dakota, the state's workforce agency and administrator of the unemployment insurance program, delivers state and federally-funded workforce services, as well as programs funded through a competitive bidding process. The Governor appoints the Job Service North Dakota Executive Director.

Job Service North Dakota serves a customer base that is vast and includes employers, employees, job seekers, and unemployment insurance claimants. The agency's mission is to provide customer-focused services to meet the current and emerging workforce needs of the state.

Job Service North Dakota:

- Helps businesses find workers and job seekers find jobs.
- Accepts and processes unemployment insurance claims.
- Gathers and publishes in-depth labor market information and analysis to provide employers and job seekers detailed employment, wage, job growth, and other valuable workforce data.
- Helps businesses develop a cost containment strategy for unemployment insurance.
- Provides 24-hour access to workforce and unemployment information via jobsnd.com.

- Assists businesses to address short-term and long-term workforce needs and skill development.
- Processes unemployment insurance benefits and subsequently applies statute to assign unemployment insurance tax rates.
- Collects and administers unemployment insurance taxes.
- Gives priority of service to veterans.
- Provides online access to local, state, and national job openings.
- Provides a variety of workshops to help job seekers learn and develop job search and job retention skills.
- Partners with businesses and local communities to host job fairs.

Through various federal and state partnerships, Job Service North Dakota has administered and continues to be involved with many workforce programs.

The unemployment insurance program provides temporary financial benefits to unemployed workers who lose their jobs through no fault of their own. Benefits paid to claimants come from monies held in the North Dakota unemployment insurance trust fund, which is funded through unemployment insurance taxes paid by employers. A key component in the administration of the unemployment insurance program is maintaining a sound trust fund balance.

The federal Workforce Innovation and Opportunity Act (WIOA) was signed into law in 2014 to increase participant employment, retention, earnings, and skill levels with the ultimate goal of improving the quality of the workforce, reducing welfare dependency, and enhancing productivity and competitiveness. Funding through the WIOA allows Job Service North Dakota to provide specialized services to targeted groups (adults, dislocated workers, and youth). Services focus on job seeking, skills identification, and work readiness. Wagner-Peyser Act programs provide a public labor exchange service to help businesses find workers and workers find jobs.

Workforce 20/20 is a state-funded job training program designed to help North Dakota industry and business retain and upgrade workers' skills to meet demands brought about by the introduction of new technologies and work methods.

The North Dakota New Jobs Training Program is a state-funded program that provides incentives to businesses that are creating, expanding, or locating employment opportunities within the state.

Trade Adjustment Assistance (TAA) and Alternative Trade Adjustment Assistance (ATAA) help workers who have lost their jobs as a result of increased imports or jobs outsourced to other countries. Certified individuals who are found eligible for the programs may be entitled to benefits such as reemployment assistance, training, income support, and more.

Job Service North Dakota delivers services to Temporary Assistance to Needy Families (TANF) recipients through the Job Opportunities and Basic Skills (JOBS) program in two locations in North Dakota. This program is designed to get TANF recipients back to work and help them become self-sufficient quickly and for the long term.

The Parental Responsibility Initiative for the Development of Employment (PRIDE) program is a nationally-recognized and an award-winning program administered by Job Service North Dakota. PRIDE addresses the unemployment and underemployment of noncustodial parents through one-on-one case management employment services. The PRIDE program helps individuals obtain employment, resulting in more frequent and more substantial child support payments.

The Jobs for Veterans State Grant provides services to veterans in North Dakota. Services from the grant include assistance from staff who are veterans and understand the many changes that veterans experience from military to civilian life. Staff provides one-on-one assistance to help veterans work through employment barriers. In addition to providing individual services, routine outreach services are conducted throughout the state.

The Work Opportunity Tax Credit (WOTC) is a federal income tax credit incentive provided to private sector employers. An employer may be eligible for WOTC when they hire from certain target groups of job seekers who face employment barriers. The WOTC tax credit is a one-time tax credit for each new hire – and there is no limit to the number of new hires who can qualify an employer for a tax credit. The requirements for this program are set by the Internal Revenue Service and the U.S. Department of Labor, Employment, and Training Administration.

Labor and Human Rights, Department of

600 East Boulevard Avenue, Department 406
State Capitol, 1st Floor Judicial Wing
Bismarck, ND 58505-0340
Phone: 701-328-2660
Toll Free within ND: 800-582-8032
TTY (Relay ND): 800-366-6888 or -6889
Fax: 701-328-2031
Web: www.nd.gov/labor or www.nd.gov/humanrights
Email: labor@nd.gov or humanrights@nd.gov
[NDCC Chapters 34-01–34-14, 14-02.4, 14-02.5 and NDAC Chapter 46-02-07]

In 1889, the North Dakota Constitution created the Department of Agriculture and Labor. In 1960, North Dakota citizens approved a constitutional amendment authorizing the legislature to establish a Department of Labor separate from the Department of Agriculture, which the legislature did in 1965.

The Department is administered by the Commissioner of Labor. The Commissioner was originally elected statewide to a four-year term. In 1995, the

Legislature changed the office to gubernatorial appointee effective January 1, 1999. Today, the Commissioner of Labor is appointed by and serves at the pleasure of the Governor.

The original primary responsibilities of the Commissioner of Labor were to promote the welfare of wages earners and industries, to promote friendly relations between employers and employees, and to prescribe and enforce standards relating to wages and working conditions of employment in the state. These responsibilities continue today. In addition, legislative action in 1983, 1999, and 2001 added responsibilities to the Department relating to the enforcement of anti-discrimination laws in North Dakota.

Today, the Department has two primary divisions: the Wage and Hour Division and the Human Rights Division. The Wage and Hour Division carries out the traditional responsibilities of the Department relating to wage and working conditions of employment. The division administers and enforces state labor laws and regulations, such as those relating to child labor, minimum wage, overtime compensation, breaks, paid time off, and deductions from pay. The division also investigates and enforces claims for unpaid wages and educates the public about the rights and responsibilities of employers and employees.

The Human Rights Division is responsible to receive and investigate complaints alleging discriminatory practices in the areas of employment, housing, public services, public accommodations, and credit transactions. In addition, the division educates the public about rights and responsibilities under the state's human rights laws and studies the nature and extent of discrimination in the state.

In addition to its two main divisions, the Department licenses employment agencies, makes determinations regarding the independent contractor status of workers, and issues sub-minimum wage licenses.

Management and Budget, Office of

600 East Boulevard Avenue, Department 110
Bismarck, ND 58505-0400
Phone: 701-328-2680
Fax: 701-328-3230
Web: www.nd.gov/omb
Email: omb@nd.gov

The 1941 Legislative Assembly appointed a governmental survey commission to study the field of governmental reorganization and make recommendations.

Among the recommendations was a single agency to handle the state's fiscal affairs. That study was reviewed by directive of the 1957 Legislative Assembly. The 1959 Legislative Assembly established the Department of Accounts and Purchases to become operative in 1961. In 1981, the agency became the Office of Management and Budget.

The Director is appointed by and serves at the will of the Governor. As agency head, the Director is vested with control and supervision of the fiscal administration of the executive branch of state government. There are five divisions within the Office of Management and Budget. The directors of three of the divisions are appointed by and serve at the pleasure of the Director of the Office of Management and Budget. The remaining two division directors are classified employees.

The Fiscal Management Division is responsible for budget preparation and the monitoring of spending after legislative appropriations are made, preparing revenue forecasts, processing state financial transactions, including agency payrolls, preparing the statewide Comprehensive Annual Financial Report (CAFR), and maintaining the integrity, integration, and configuration of statewide financial systems in full compliance with policies, procedures, laws, and rules. The fiscal management director and budget analysts prepare the Governor's executive recommendation for submission to the Legislative Assembly. As the sole financial plan for providing state services, the executive budget recommendation is presented to the Legislative Assembly prior to the convening of each session. Part of the budget process involves fiscal management staff appearing at hearings for each agency budget request, on-site visits, and comparative analyses. Once the executive budget recommendation has been submitted, the office works closely with the Legislative Assembly and its committees by explaining the budget or by providing information on other fiscal concerns. During both the Legislative Session and the Legislative Management's interim study period, the Office of Management and Budget assists legislators and other key policy makers in resolving budget-related issues. Phone: 701-328-2680; email: omb@nd.gov.

The Human Resource Management Services Division provides services related to establishing and maintaining a unified system of human resource management for the classified service. The division and the State Personnel Board were created by executive order in 1974 and by the Legislative Assembly in 1975. The 2003 Legislative Assembly changed the name of the Central Personnel Division to the North Dakota Human Resource Management Services Division. The division establishes and maintains the statewide classification and compensation plans, as well as general policies and rules, which are binding on the agencies with employees in the classified service. In 1995, the administration of the merit system function was decentralized to those agencies required to have a merit system of personnel administration. The Human Resource Management Services Division maintains the merit system auditing function and provides consultative services to agencies on a multitude of human resource issues including, but not limited to, recruitment, screening, and selection of applicants; performance management; classification; salary administration; discipline; grievances; investigations; appeals; and federal and state employment requirements. In addition, the division develops, coordinates, and conducts training programs; plans, coordinates, and leads activities for the statewide human resource information system; provides mediation services; and administers a cooperative education and internship program. Phone: 701-328-3290; TTY: 800-366-6888; email: hrms@nd.gov.

The Central Services Division provides five areas of service to the state of North Dakota and state government agencies: central duplicating, central supply, state procurement, surplus property, and vendor registry. Central duplicating provides print related services and issues state identification cards. Central supply orders and houses office supplies. State procurement provides comprehensive purchasing services, maintains the state's bidders list and online solicitation database, and provides procurement training to state government agencies. Surplus property acquires and distributes state and federal surplus property to qualified recipients. Vendor registry manages the state payee database, provides 1099 reporting services, and manages the purchasing module software. Phone: 701-328-1726; email: csd@nd.gov.

The Facility Management Division was created July 1, 1991, with the elimination of the Director of Institutions office. The division manages the physical plant operations, provides capitol tours, operates the central mail bureau, and coordinates event scheduling for all of the buildings located on the 132-acre capitol complex. The division is also responsible for providing space management services for the state agencies located on the capitol complex through its state planner. Phone: 701-328-2471; email: facmgt@nd.gov.

The Risk Management Division was established in 1995 in response to a North Dakota Supreme Court decision that eliminated the state's sovereign immunity for tort claims. The division's objectives are to implement proactive loss control practices to address the state's exposures to loss and to appropriately administer claims and lawsuits. The 2001 Legislative Assembly established the Risk Management Workers Compensation Program and assigned the division the duty of administering the single workers' compensation account that consolidated 143 state agency accounts and authorized a $100,000 deductible per claim and a cross agency return-to-work program. Phone: 701-328-7584; email: rminfo@nd.gov.

Parks and Recreation Department

1600 East Century Avenue
Bismarck, ND 58503
Phone: 701-328-5357
Toll Free: 800-807-4732 (for reservations at state parks)
Fax: 701-328-5363
Web: www.parkrec.nd.gov (for online reservations)
Email: parkrec@nd.gov
[NDCC 55-08]

Before 1965, all state parks were under the jurisdiction of the State Historical Society of North Dakota. In 1965, the North Dakota Park Service and the State Outdoor Recreation Agency were established as separate entities. In 1977, the State Outdoor Recreation Agency was joined with the Park Service. The Department's Director is appointed by the Governor.

The North Dakota Parks and Recreation Department consists of four divisions:

Administrative Services, State Parks Division, Planning and Natural Resources Division, and Recreation Division.

The Administrative Division provides fiscal management, human resources management, information technology, and public information.

The State Parks Division manages 13 state parks and five recreation areas. State parks include Beaver Lake, Cross Ranch, Fort Abraham Lincoln, Fort Ransom, Fort Stevenson, Grahams Island, Icelandic, Lake Metigoshe, Lake Sakakawea, Lewis and Clark, Little Missouri, Sully Creek, and Turtle River. The recreation areas are Butte Saint Paul, Crow Flies High, Indian Hills, Little Metigoshe, and Pelican Point. The Parks Division also oversees the Campground Host program, Campsite Reservation program, and the Friends of Recreation and Parks.

The Planning and Natural Resources Division includes park planning, development, capital construction, and major repairs in support of all Department lands, facilities, and infrastructure. The Division also manages programs associated with North Dakota's Natural Areas and Nature Preserve Act.

The Nature Preserves and Natural Areas Program, mandated in 1975, required the Department to establish a system of natural areas and nature preserves for public use and to promote the protection of natural areas throughout the state. Nature preserves include the Gunlogson Nature Preserve (Icelandic State Park), Head of the Mountain Nature Preserve in Sargent County, Sentinel Butte in Golden Valley County, H.R. Morgan State Nature Preserve in Ransom County, and Cross Ranch Nature Preserve in Oliver County. Natural Areas include the Stumpf Fossil Site in Morton County, Missouri River Natural Area in Morton County, and Smokey Lake in Pierce County.

The Recreation Division manages the federal outdoor recreation grant programs, off-highway vehicle and snowmobile programs, recreation trails, statewide outdoor recreation planning, the Pembina Gorge State Recreation Area, and the Lewis and Clark Interpretive Center and Fort Mandan.

Securities Department

600 East Boulevard Avenue
State Capitol, 5th Floor
Bismarck, ND 58505-0510
Phone: 701-328-2910
ND Toll Free: 800-297-5124
Fax: 701-328-2946
Web: www.nd.gov/securities
Email: ndsecurities@nd.gov
[NDCC 10-04-10]

The Securities Commissioner is appointed by the Governor and confirmed by the Senate for a four-year term.

In protecting the investing public, the Commissioner regulates all securities offered and sold in this state. Salesmen and companies dealing in securities, sales agents, issuers, broker-dealers, and investment advisor firms are required to comply with the statutory registration process. When necessary, the Commissioner investigates violations of the Securities Act and may bring injunctive administrative or civil criminal action against persons who violate the state's securities law or refer those violators for criminal prosecution. The Commissioner also administers the franchise investment law and those statutes regulating pre-need funeral services.

Transportation, Department of

608 East Boulevard Avenue
Bismarck, ND 58505-0700
Phone: 701-328-2500
Toll Free: 855-637-6237
Fax: 701-328-1427
Web: www.dot.nd.gov
Email: dot@nd.gov
[NDCC 28-32-02.1]

The North Dakota State Highway Department was created in March 1917 and became the North Dakota Department of Transportation (NDDOT) in 1990. At that time, the State Highway Department and Motor Vehicle Department were consolidated. The first Highway Commission, consisting of the Governor as the chair, the State Engineer, and one member appointed by the Governor, was established in 1913. In 1917, the Commission was expanded to five members and given authority to designate a state highway system and take advantage of federal aid. In 1933, the Commission was abolished and the first independent Highway Commissioner was named.

Mission – Safely move people and goods.

Vision – North Dakota's Transportation Leader Promoting:
Safe Ways, Superior Service, and Economic Growth.

Strategic Focus Areas and Goals

Safety – Provide a safe and secure transportation system and workplace.
Team – Recruit, develop, and retain a high performing workforce that results in everyone working together to achieve our mission and vision.
Service – Be proactive and adaptive to provide superior external and internal services, products, and programs.
Innovation – Promote a culture of innovation to enhance external and internal services, products, and programs.
Assets – Preserve and enhance assets managed by NDDOT.

Overview

As of December 2015, NDDOT maintained 8,614 roadway miles, including interstate and national highways. North Dakota has more miles of road per capita than any state in the nation.

NDDOT oversees the development of surface transportation (highways, bridges, transit, pedestrian and bikeway paths, and safe routes to school) in the state.

Organization

NDDOT is led by a Director appointed by the Governor. The Department also has three Deputy Directors: Business Support, Engineering, and Driver and Vehicle Services. The Director appoints one of the Deputy Directors to serve as Deputy Director for the Department and to perform the Director's duties in his absence. The NDDOT Director's responsibility is to oversee the activities of the Department and provide an integrated state highway system, built on sound engineering, with full regard for the interest and wellbeing of the entire state. The Highway Distribution Fund is to be spent in the following order: (1) maintenance of the state highway system; (2) cost of construction and reconstruction in an amount necessary to ensure that federal aid match is available to the state; and (3) other construction, improvement, or maintenance purposes. The Governor has designated the Director to act on his behalf in administering the National Highway Safety Act of 1966.

Services

The NDDOT provides service to the traveling public in three areas, which includes Driver and Vehicle Services, Engineering, and Business Support.

The Deputy Director for Driver and Vehicle Services is responsible for three divisions:

- The Drivers License Division tests drivers, grants licenses, and maintains drivers' records.
- The Safety Division is responsible for analyzing and compiling data for the annual crash report book and creating and implementing traffic safety programs.
- The Motor Vehicle Division is responsible for registering and titling vehicles, collecting fees and excise taxes, and maintaining motor vehicle records.

The Deputy Director for Engineering is responsible for completing the planning, project development, construction, and maintenance as needed to meet the public needs on the state's roadways. Engineering also consists of the following offices, divisions, and districts:

- District Offices are located in eight cities throughout North Dakota, including

Fargo, Valley City, Devils Lake, Grand Forks, Bismarck, Dickinson, Williston, and Minot. Each district also has a number of local maintenance sections and shops located throughout the state. The districts are responsible for highway construction, engineering, administration, roadway and bridge maintenance, roadside maintenance, rest area/visitor center maintenance, materials testing, equipment and vehicle maintenance, traffic engineering, and highway sign maintenance.

- The Office of Operations encompasses the following divisions: Construction Services Division is responsible for administering highway construction bid openings, contracts, bonds, records, and contractor payments. The Maintenance Division is responsible for coordinating district maintenance efforts, employee safety, health and emergency responses, the Roadway Weather Information System (RWIS), the Intelligent Transportation Systems (ITS), and providing load restriction and road condition reports. The Civil Rights Division is responsible for EEO/affirmative action, labor and contract compliance, disadvantaged business enterprise, workplace investigations, and mediation.
- The Office of Project Development encompasses the following divisions: The Bridge Division is responsible for the overall planning, design, and upkeep of state bridges. The Design Division is responsible for designing improvements for rural highways and some urban highways, performs right-of-way activities, and deals with billboards. The Environmental and Transportation Services Division includes cultural resource compliance, environmental documentation, consultant agreement services, technical services, and right of way. The Materials and Research Division tests and researches soil and materials on highway projects.
- The Office of Transportation Programs encompasses the following divisions: the Local Government Division is responsible for general administration of all county, urban, and transit federal aid programs and projects. The Planning and Asset Management Division is responsible for administering rail programs, data collection, data management, analysis, and mapping activities. The Programming Division is responsible for coordinating the development of the Statewide Transportation Improvement Program, managing federal funds, implementing the Department's scoping process, and completing traffic operations activities.

The Deputy Director for Business Support is responsible for overseeing the tasks and duties of seven divisions, as well as managing the Aviation Services and Business Planner functions of the Department:

- The Audit Services Division is responsible for performing and overseeing Internal Audit functions, such as an annual DOT Inventory Review, and annual review of physical inventory of NDDOT fixed assets and inventoried materials as required by NDDOT policy and North Dakota Century Code. They are also responsible for Motor Carrier Program Audits and federally required audits of International Fuel Tax Agreement (IFTA) and International Registration Program (IRP) registered North Dakota-based motor carriers.

- The Communication Division is responsible for media relations, public information, public relations, and public involvement, as well as all internal NDDOT communications. The Communication Division also includes video, photography, graphic art, and website design services.
- The Financial Management Division is responsible for the Department's accounting and reporting functions, budgeting, payroll, procurements, revenue forecasting, central supply, cash management, and the disposal of highway equipment and materials.
- The Human Resources Division provides staffing for the Department through the following: recruitment and selection, employment records, performance reviews, training, discipline, staffing plans, employment law compliance, workplace investigations, personnel policies, and payroll. The Division also coordinates Department position classifications and implements salary plans.
- The Information Technology Division is responsible for all automated devices hardware and software and other technology support, information processing, records management, internet and intranet development and maintenance, printing and mail operations, telecommunications/radio, and Transportation Building physical security and maintenance.
- The Legal Division is responsible for providing legal services to NDDOT in all areas, with emphasis on pre-litigation, risk management, driver's license administrative matters, contract development/negotiation/drafting/administration assistance, administration of non-construction contracts, legislation, and administrative rulemaking.
- The State Fleet Services Division is responsible for state fleet vehicles, liability and property damage insurance, alcohol and controlled substance testing for state employees and commercial drivers, statewide refueling program, and risk management.

Water Commission, State

State Office Building
900 East Boulevard Avenue, Department 770
Bismarck, ND 58505-0850
Phone: 701-328-2750
Fax: 701-328-3696
TTY: 800-366-6888
Web: www.swc.nd.gov
Email: swc@nd.gov
[NDCC 61-02-02]

The Office of State Engineer and the Board of Water Commissioners were created in 1905 to administer an irrigation program passed that same year. In 1937, the State Water Conservation Commission came into being. Through 1983 legislation, the agency became known as the State Water Commission.

The State Water Commission consists of the Governor as Chairman, the Commissioner of Agriculture as an ex-officio member, and seven members who are appointed by the Governor to serve terms of six years each. The Commission appoints a Secretary (the State Engineer) as its executive officer, who employs a staff as needed to carry out the work of the State Water Commission. Agency staff are organized into six divisions: Administration Services, Atmospheric Resources, Planning and Education, Regulatory, Water Appropriations, and Water Development.

Divisions and Responsibilities within the State Water Commission

The Administrative Services Division provides agency operational support, including accounting, human resources, records management, and legal support coordination for all agency projects and programs.

The Atmospheric Resources Division is responsible for the administration of cloud seeding activities in the state, conducts atmospheric research, and performs weather-related data collection and analysis.

The Planning and Education Division develops and maintains the State Water Management Plan and the agency's Strategic Plan and manages the agency's information and education programs, including public outreach and water education.

The Regulatory Division is responsible for floodplain and sovereign lands management; the Silver Jackets program; dam safety; and the processing of dam, dike, and drainage permits.

The Water Appropriations Division is responsible for the processing of water permit applications, water rights evaluations, hydrologic data collection, water supply investigations, and economic development support activities.

The Water Development Division is responsible for project engineering, construction, and maintenance; Municipal, Rural, and Industrial water supply programs; State Water Supply Program administration; flood response and recovery; cost-share program administration; Southwest Pipeline and Northwest Area Water Supply projects management; and Devils Lake outlets construction and operations.

Workforce Safety and Insurance

1600 East Century Avenue, Suite One
Bismarck, ND 58504-5685
Phone: 701-328-3800
Toll Free: 800-243-3331 (Safety and Fraud Hotline)
Fax: 701-328-3820
TDD: 701-328-3786
Email: ndwsi@nd.gov
[NDCC 65-02]

In 1919, the 16th Legislative Assembly created the Workmen's Compensation

Bureau. Its purpose was to provide "sure and certain relief regardless of questions of fault to the exclusion of every other remedy, proceeding or compensation." The intent of the law was to provide relief to workers injured while on the job. This relief would be in the form of compensation for lost earnings and payment of medical bills incurred. It was anticipated that the law would help employers by eliminating the risk of damaging lawsuits by injured employees.

Today, Workforce Safety & Insurance (WSI) remains an exclusive, employer financed, no-fault insurance state fund covering workplace injuries, illnesses, and death. WSI is the sole provider and administrator of the workers' compensation system in North Dakota. North Dakota is one of four "exclusive" state funds in the country (the other three are Ohio, Washington, and Wyoming). This means that all employers, except those authorized to self-insure, must purchase workers' compensation insurance from the state fund, rather than from private insurance companies. In the other 46 states and the District of Columbia, employers have options to buy workers' compensation insurance from private insurance companies, competitive state funds, or to self-insure. In November 2008, voters in North Dakota returned control of WSI back to the Governor, who now appoints the agency's Executive Director, while leaving the Board as quasi-advisory.

The 11-member Board of Directors is appointed by the Governor with members serving four-year terms. Six members represent employers that maintain active accounts with WSI, three members represent employees, one member is a member of the North Dakota Medical Association, and one is appointed as an at-large member.

As administrator of workers' compensation laws, WSI collects premiums from employers and adjusts rates of premium for each classification to assure the solvency of the organization. WSI also provides workers' compensation for injured employees, cooperates in making arrangements for rehabilitation of persons injured in employment, provides safety grants and incentives to employers, and classifies types of employment with respect to degree of hazard.

Workforce Safety & Insurance is administered by the Director and consists of Employers Services, Injury Services, and Administrative Services functions.

Injury Services

The Claims Department processes new injured worker claims that are filed. Injured workers, employers, and medical providers can file claims either by mail, over the telephone, or online. The claims technicians work closely with the claim adjusters to provide clerical support and assistance in the collection of required documentation needed in the processing of claims. Benefit levels for injured workers are tied to the state's average annual wage as reported by Job Service North Dakota. The maximum disability benefit an injured worker may receive is 125 percent of the state's average weekly wage. Return-to-Work Services assists injured workers and employers to coordinate stay-at-work or a return-to-work plan quickly and safely. Medical Services administers the managed care and medical bill audit programs and the medical and hospital fee schedules. The department administers the medical dispute resolution process for disputes arising out of managed care recommendations. WSI uses the Official Disability Guidelines-Treatment in Workers' Comp (ODG) as developed by Work Loss Data Institute, an independent database company focusing on workplace health and productivity. ODG is a nationally recognized, evidence-based treatment and disability guideline to evaluate the necessity and/or effectiveness of medical care. The department also provides technical support to the claims and rehabilitation department in the processing of medical bills and in computer and claim form functions. Provider Relations works to ensure good communication is taking place between WSI and medical providers. A pharmacy benefit management system has allowed WSI to continue to provide for the medication needs of injured workers, while addressing the issue of continued rising costs in the pharmaceutical area. Injury Services also oversees the Customer Service Call Center, which receives and answers more than 700 calls per day.

Employer Services

Policyholder Services manages employer insurance accounts, develops annual rate and classification structures (in consultation with WSI's actuarial consultant), rates employer loss experience, determines coverage status, and manages extraterritorial agreements with other states. The department's field representatives audit employer accounts and investigate uninsured employers. The Safety and Loss Prevention Department assists employers with safety and loss prevention program design, implementation, and training; conducts workplace safety inspections; and investigates industrial accidents. The department works with employers to establish their own safety programs and provides opportunities through matching grants to purchase safety intervention to eliminate hazards in the workplace. WSI offers safety grant and discount programs aimed at further reducing the frequency of workplace injuries. These programs can reduce a qualifying employer's premium by up to 25 percent. In addition, associations and employee organizations may qualify for grants to help promote safety through training and education.

Other Administrative Services

- Communications: The department's primary efforts are designed to maintain close relationships with the news media and the public they serve, as well as contact with the legislature and other governmental leaders. It also works to enhance the agency's internal communications.

- Facility Management: Operates Century Center, WSI's home since May 2003. The building was formally dedicated in September 2003. Century Center is also the home for North Dakota's Department of Commerce, Parks and Recreation Department, Council on the Arts, Risk Management, and Human Service's Child Support Enforcement and Provider Audit Divisions.

- Finance: Monitors, records, and reports on all WSI financial activity to ensure WSI resources are used effectively and efficiently and WSI fund solvency is maintained.

- Human Resources: Administers the personnel functions of WSI and maintains the performance management system of WSI.

- Information Services: Provides support and services for all computers, software, and telephones for the WSI staff at the Century Center building and remote facilities and offices.

- Internal Audit: Plans, directs, and completes internal audits and compliance reviews to ensure WSI departments and major programs are properly functioning and operating in accordance with applicable laws, rules, and Board outcomes.

- Legal: Provides support services to legal counsel and assistance to the staff of injury services, employer services, and other administrative departments.

- Special Investigations Unit: Provides WSI's Claims, Employer Services, and Medical Services departments with investigation resources for claims adjudication, employer and medical provider non-compliance, and fraud.

- Quality Assurance: Ensures the continual improvement of WSI operations by statistically tracking performance and identifying areas that need improvement and new initiatives that would serve to improve the overall efficiency and cost effectiveness of WSI.

- Office Services: Provides support services to all of WSI through mail processing, document imaging, claims registration, fax and photocopying services, forms processing, medical and non-medical bill entry, records retention, and off-site storage.

- Decision Review Office: Established by the North Dakota Legislature in 1995 in response to two needs: providing injured workers with a no-cost, speedy claims dispute resolution alternative to litigation and reducing the amount of attorney fees paid by the agency.

Administrative Departments Under Boards, Commissions, Committees, and Councils

Traditionally the most common form of executive agency, many agencies operate under the authority of a board or commission. The boards or commissions are most frequently appointed by the Governor and often have ex-officio members. The board or commission is then responsible for appointing a chief executive officer. Although traditionally seen as a check or limitation upon the power of the Governor, the

Governor has the authority to replace the membership of most boards under his appointing authority upon assuming office. However, in some cases, boards have multiple appointing authorities or ex-officio membership, which provides a degree of independence from any single official.

Aeronautics Commission

Phone: 701-328-9650
Fax: 701-328-9656
Web: https://aero.nd.gov
[NDCC 2-05]

The commission shall have general supervision over aeronautics within this state and shall:

1. Encourage the establishment of airports and air navigation facilities;
2. Cooperate with and assist the federal government, the municipalities of this state, and other persons in the development and coordination of all aeronautical activities;
3. Represent the state in aeronautical matters before state and federal agencies;
4. Participate as party plaintiff or defendant or as intervenor on behalf of the state or any municipality in any controversy which involves the interest of the state in aeronautics;
5. Establish or promote with the public sector or private sector, or both, and provide financing, in whole or in part, of aeronautical educational programs and support of the educational programs of aeronautical museums in the state; and
6. Establish or promote with the public sector or private sector, or both, and provide financing, in whole or in part, of programs informing the public of commercial and general aviation services available in the state.

Animal Health, State Board of

Phone: 701-328-2654
Fax: 701-328-4567
Email: doa-bah@nd.gov
Web: www.nd.gov/ndda
[NDCC 36-01-01; 36-01-08]

The State Board of Animal Health consists of nine members appointed by the Governor for seven-year terms. Two members are licensed, practicing veterinarians and seven are livestock operators, each representing a different segment of the livestock industry: dairy cattle, commercial beef cattle, swine, sheep, bison, non-traditional livestock, and registered purebred beef cattle. Recommendations for appointments are made by the professional and industry associations represented.

The Commissioner of Agriculture, with the consent of the board, appoints the State Veterinarian and Deputy State Veterinarian who graduated from a recognized college or university in veterinary medicine and surgery. As the State Veterinarian, the executive officer is not a member of the board. A veterinarian on staff at North Dakota State University is chosen to act as consulting veterinarian to the board.

The board protects the health of animals in the state and determines and employs the most efficient and practical means for the prevention, suppression, control, and eradication of dangerous, contagious, and infectious diseases among the domestic animals and non-traditional livestock of this state. In the interest of public and animal health, the board may restrict the importation, sale, and distribution of infected domestic and non-traditional livestock. The board is also empowered to impose quarantine and to kill animals infected with contagious diseases. The board also registers feedlots and inspects livestock in transit for ownership identification and health verification.

Arts, Council on the

Phone: 701-328-7590
Fax: 701-328-7595
Email: comserv@nd.gov
Web: www.nd.gov/arts
[NDCC 54-54-02]

The nine-member Board of Directors of the North Dakota Council on the Arts is appointed by the Governor and broadly represents all fields of the performing and fine arts. Members appointed for five-year terms are North Dakotans known for their competence and experience in the arts. The Governor names a chair from the board membership. The Council appoints an Executive Director to administer the agency and oversee the agency's full-time staff.

The North Dakota Council on the Arts works with other state agencies to assist with five important priorities of North Dakota government: 1) economic development, 2) education, 3) health and wellness, 4) sense of place and quality of life, and 5) culture and heritage.

Canvassing Board, State

Phone: 701-328-2900 (Secretary of State)
[NDCC 16.1-15-33]

After each statewide election, the State Canvassing Board meets to canvass the election results received from each county and to officially certify the statewide and district totals for candidates and measures.

Its members are the Clerk of the Supreme Court, Secretary of State, State Treasurer, and the chairman, or chairman's designee, of the two political parties which had the highest vote cast for governor in the last general election at which the office of the Governor was on the ballot.

Capitol Grounds Planning Commission

Phone: 701-328-2471
(Office of Management and Budget, Facility Management Division)
[N.D.C.C. Chapter 48-10]

In addition to the Lieutenant Governor, who serves as the chairman, the Capitol Grounds Planning Commission has eight members. Selected biennially for a two-year term, the Governor appoints two citizens, one licensed architect, and one representative from the State Historical Society. The President of the Senate appoints two Senators, and the Speaker of the House appoints two Representatives.

Among its duties, the Commission may confer with the state Council on the Arts regarding the artistic value of monuments, memorials, or works of art to be constructed on the capitol grounds; work with consultants to select sites for buildings, facilities, monuments, memorials, or works of art to be constructed on the capitol grounds; develop and modify long-term plans for the development of the capitol grounds; and approve or disapprove the basic style and exterior construction of any building, facility, monument, memorial, or work of art constructed on the capitol grounds.

The Commission meets whenever major interior changes, including new construction, remodeling, or renovation of any kind, are proposed or considered for the buildings or facilities on the capitol grounds. It must also be consulted before the purchase or installation of furniture or fixtures in the public areas of the capitol and other buildings on the capitol grounds.

Career and Technical Education, State Board for

Phone: 701-328-3180
Fax: 701-328-1255
Email: cte@nd.gov
Web: www.nd.gov/cte
[NDCC 15-20.1-02]

The State Board for Career and Technical Education consists of the six members of the State Board of Public School Education, the Superintendent of Public Instruction, the executive director of Job Service North Dakota, and the chancellor of the University System or the chancellor's designee. The board appoints a director and executive officer of the Department of Career and Technical Education.

The six members, one from each of the six districts described in the governing statute, are appointed by the Governor for six-year terms and come from a list of nominees. The list of nominees for each vacant position is submitted by a committee comprised of the president of the North Dakota United, the president of the North Dakota Council of Educational Leaders, and the president of the North Dakota School Boards Association.

The Board's authority includes administering state legislation passed in conformity with acts of Congress relating to career and technical education; administering funds provided by the state and federal government for career and technical education; formulating plans for the promotion of career and technical education in subjects taught in the public schools; providing for the preparation and prescribing the qualification and certification of teachers and directors; making studies relating to career and technical education; and promoting and aiding in the establishment of schools, departments, or classes.

Career and Technical Education, Department of

Phone: 701-328-3180
Fax: 701-328-1255
Email: cte@nd.gov
Web: www.nd.gov/cte
[NDCC 15-20.1-02]

The Department of Career and Technical Education (CTE) is governed by the State Board for Career and Technical Education and carries out the policies of the Board. The Department works with other education agencies and business and industry in planning, conducting, and evaluating career and technical education programs. Business and industry involvement is present in all CTE programs through local advisory committees. Beyond ensuring high school students have career and technical education opportunities, the Department develops career and technical education programs in cooperation with the State Board of Higher Education and the state's post-secondary institutions. To assist adults in upgrading skills or in retraining for employment, the Department offers such programs as farm business management and short-term adult classes. The Department administers all federal and state legislation affecting career and technical education, including congressional and Legislative Assembly appropriations.

Credit Review Board

Phone: 701-328-4158
[NDCC 6-09.10-02]

The Credit Review Board consists of six members. The Governor, Attorney General, and Commissioner of Agriculture each appoint two members to the Board. The Governor and Attorney General each appoints one member with experience as a director or officer of a financial institution and one member actively engaged in farming in the state. The Commissioner of Agriculture appoints two members who are actively engaged in farming in the state. No member of the Board may hold state office or serve in state office or state government in any capacity at any time of appointment or during service on the Board. The Credit Review Board members serve terms of two years. The Board establishes policy for the North Dakota Mediation Service and recommends policies and procedures to the Industrial Commission regarding farm loan programs to the Bank of North Dakota.

Education Commission of the States

[NDCC 15-64]

The Education Commission of the States (ECS) – created by states for states in 1965 to improve student success across the nation – is an unbiased organization that does not advocate for specific education policies. ECS tracks state policy trends, provides research-based advice, and creates opportunities for state leaders to learn from one another. It brings together governors, state legislators, K-12 leaders, higher education officials, and other education leaders to work on education issues along the full spectrum – from pre-K to postsecondary and beyond. Elected officials, members of the media, and the public can access ECS resources on the web (www.ecs.org) or through its information hotline (303-299-3675). The North Dakota delegation of commissioners includes the Governor, two legislators, and four gubernatorial appointees.

Fair Association, State

Phone: 701-857-7620
Email: ndsf@minot.com
Web: www.ndstatefair.com
[NDCC 4-02.1]

The North Dakota State Fair Association consists of three members from each county in the state chosen for one-year terms. One member from each county is selected by the county fair board, the second by the board of county commissioners, and the third by the county agent. The Board of Directors, which manages the affairs of the Association, consists of nine members elected to three-year terms from the Association membership. The Association conducts an annual state fair at Minot to exhibit agricultural, horticultural, industrial, mechanical, mining, stock breeding, and other products and resources of North Dakota. The Association also cooperates in year-round promotion of 4-H, FFA, and agricultural and industrial enhancements in order to make the state fair a North Dakota showcase.

Firefighters' Association

1502 Grumman Lane
P.O. Box 6127
Bismarck, ND 58506-6127
Phone: 701-222-2799
Fax: 701-222-2899
Email: renee@ndfa.net
Web: www.ndfa.net
[NDCC 18-03]

The North Dakota Firefighters' Association is made up of dues-paying fire departments in the state. It is governed by a 10-member executive board and has been given the responsibility of conducting fire service training throughout the state by the North Dakota Legislature. The Association hosts an annual fire school and offers regional fire schools, specialized training, and other firefighting training following national standard recommendations. Firefighting training is held to promote the safety and welfare of the Association members through uniform and established training following national standards. Firefighting training conveys information to members on safety, health, and equipment issues based on the duties that firefighters are expected to perform on the fire ground. New skills are required for the ever-changing demands placed on fire departments.

Forest Service

307 1st Street East
Bottineau, ND 58318-1100
Phone: 701-228-5422
Fax: 701-228-5448
Email: forest@nd.gov
Web: www.ndsu.edu/ndfs
[NDCC 4.1-21]

The NDSU North Dakota Forest Service is organized under the North Dakota Board of Higher Education. The agency is administered by a State Forester who reports to the president of North Dakota State University at Fargo and supports the land grant mission in public service. The mission of the North Dakota Forest Service is to "care for, protect, and improve forest resources to enhance the quality of life for present and future generations."

A wide variety of customers depend on the North Dakota Forest Service for technical, financial, and educational forestry assistance. The State Forester administers forestry programs serving communities, rural landowners, soil conservation districts, rural fire districts, schools, and citizens of North Dakota. All the programs utilize a voluntary, educational, and incentives-based approach to address forestry and related natural resource needs and customer requests.

The agency also operates a nursery at Towner that produces one-million conifer (evergreen) seedlings in more than 30 different species and stock types annually for distribution to landowners. The trees are used for farmstead, living snow fence, field windbreaks, wildlife, forestry, and other conservation plantings. The agency also owns and manages approximately 13,290 acres of state forestlands.

Garrison Diversion Conservancy District

Phone: 701-652-3194
Toll free: 800-532-0074
Fax: 701-652-3195
Email: gdcd@gdcd.org
Web: www.garrisondiversion.org
[NDCC 61-24]

The Garrison Diversion Conservancy District was created by the North

Dakota State Legislature in 1955 to contract with the federal government for the development and operation of the Garrison Diversion Unit. The Board of Directors held its first meeting on July 18, 1955, in Harvey, N.D., with representatives from 22 counties.

Over the years, federal legislation has evolved Garrison Diversion Conservancy District's focus from strictly irrigation to a more multi-purpose effort. In 1965, legislation enacted called for the construction of the Garrison Diversion Unit Principal Supply Works. It also reduced the number of acres for irrigation development in North Dakota, originally authorized in the 1944 Flood Control Act, from 1.2 million to 250,000 acres. A focus on municipal and industrial water, fish and wildlife development, and recreation was also added.

The Garrison Diversion Unit Reformulation Act of 1986 further reduced authorized acres for irrigation development to 130,940 acres. In addition, the act authorized a $200 million grant program to facilitate municipal, rural, and industrial water service.

The Dakota Water Resources Act of 2000 authorized a $200 million increase in municipal, rural, and industrial project funding, $200 million to meet the Indian water needs, and $200 million to provide reliable, high-quality water to areas in eastern North Dakota. In addition, $31.5 million was authorized for recreation and wildlife facilities and programs in North Dakota.

The Dakota Water Resources Act further reduced the number of acres authorized for irrigation development to 75,480 acres. In 2011, Garrison Diversion completed the 3,500-acre McClusky Canal Mile Marker 7.5 Irrigation Project. Additional projects have since been added, bringing the total to nearly 5,000 irrigated acres.

The Garrison Diversion Conservancy District headquarters are located in Carrington, with additional operations and maintenance offices in McClusky, New Rockford, and Oakes. The district consists of 28 counties. Each member county elects a citizen to a four-year term on a no-party ballot at the general election to serve on the Garrison Diversion Conservancy District Board of Directors. The Board of Directors elects a chairman, vice chairman, and second vice chairman. An Executive Committee is elected from the board. Any county may petition to join the district upon application of its board of county commissioners.

Garrison Diversion's mission is "to provide a reliable, high quality, and affordable water supply to benefit the people of North Dakota." Garrison Diversion Conservancy District is responsible for the development and operation of the Garrison Diversion Unit. The district has the power of eminent domain and may levy, to cover expenses, a tax not to exceed one mill on each dollar of taxable valuation within the district. The district also acts as fiscal agent on behalf of the federal government in connection with any Garrison Diversion Unit business.

Higher Education, State Board of

All public colleges and universities
Phone: 701-328-2960
Fax: 701-328-2961
Email: ndus.office@ndus.edu
Web: www.ndus.edu/
[Constitution, Article VIII, Section 6; NDCC 15-10-02]

The State Board of Higher Education consists of eight members. Seven members must be qualified electors and state residents for at least five years preceding appointment; one must be a full-time resident student in good academic standing at an institution under the jurisdiction of the Board. All members except the student are appointed by the Governor for four-year terms and confirmed by the Senate. Members are limited to serving two terms. The student member, appointed by the Governor upon recommendation of the North Dakota Student Association, serves a one-year term. The student member cannot serve more than two consecutive terms. The seven appointments outside of the student member are made from a list of names selected by action of at least four of the following five people: the president of the North Dakota United, the Chief Justice of the North Dakota Supreme Court, the Superintendent of Public Instruction, the President Pro Tempore of the Senate, and the Speaker of the House of Representatives. In addition, the Council of College Faculties selects one nonvoting advisor for a one-year term, and the North Dakota University System Staff Senate selects one nonvoting staff advisor for a one-year term.

The Constitution provides that the Board employ an individual as the Commissioner of Higher Education. The Commissioner serves as Chancellor of the North Dakota University System and as the chief executive officer of the Board and University System. Under Board policy, the president of each institution of higher education governed by the Board is responsible to the Chancellor and through the Chancellor to the Board.

All public colleges and universities in North Dakota are under the Board's jurisdiction. The Board seeks appropriations through the executive and legislative budget review process.

In coordinating and planning development of North Dakota's state higher education, the Board approves all new programs of instruction, research, and public service, including the establishment of a college, school, division, department, or other unit. Plans for all capital improvements also are subject to the Board's approval.

Historical Society of North Dakota, State

Phone: 701-328-2666
Fax: 701-328-3710
Email: histsoc@nd.gov
Web: www.history.nd.gov
[NDCC 55-01]

A State Historical Commission and authorization for a State Historical Society were established in 1895. In 1905, the Legislative Assembly provided an appropriation and facilities in the Capitol and named the Society trustee for the state. The Society remained a quasi-public institution until 1965, when legislative action created the State Historical Board as the governing body of the agency. In 1967, the private membership organization was severed from official connection with the state agency. In 1987, the Legislative Assembly authorized the State Historical Society of North Dakota to create a new membership adjunct without voice in governance of the agency.

The Society is under the supervision of the 12-member State Historical Board. Seven members of the board are appointed by the Governor for three-year terms. The remaining members are ex-officio: Commissioner of Commerce, Director of the Department of Transportation, Secretary of State, Director of Parks and Recreation Department, and State Treasurer. From among the appointed members, the Board elects a president, vice president, and secretary. The Board appoints the Director of the State Historical Society of North Dakota to administer the agency and carry out policies and directives. The agency is organized into five divisions:

The Administration Division is headed by the Assistant Director and is responsible for overall agency support, budgeting and fiscal matters, store operations, and security.

The Archaeology and Historic Preservation Division protects and manages cultural resources by identifying and recording sites related to North Dakota's prehistory; surveying, identifying, and recording structures and sites eligible for listing on the North Dakota Historic Sites Registry; and nominating structures and sites for listing on the National Register of Historic Places. The Director of the State Historical Society of North Dakota serves as the State Historic Preservation Officer. The Director of the Archeology and Historic Preservation Division is also the Deputy Historic Preservation Officer. The Division also preserves and manages 57 state-owned historic sites ranging in size from nearly 200 acres (Fort Clark State Historic Site) to markers occupying less than one-tenth acre.

The Museum Division collects and manages artifact collections representative of North Dakota history and culture, designs and mounts interpretive exhibits at the North Dakota Heritage Center and 10 branch museums, and oversees a traveling exhibit program. The North Dakota Heritage Center is fully accredited by the American Association of Museums.

The Communications and Education Division produces public and educational programs and events for adults and children at the North Dakota Heritage Center and other locations; provides liaison services to North Dakota's 140 county and local historical societies; produces publications including a quarterly journal, *North Dakota History*, and a quarterly newsletter, *Plains Talk;* and coordinates visitor services for the Heritage Center. The division oversees the agency's IT operations.

The State Archives Division collects, manages, and references documentary resources relating to state history and culture. The Division is the official state archives, preserving North Dakota government records of enduring value. Its extensive collections also include the state's official newspapers, books, photographs, maps, manuscript collections, and audiovisual materials. The Director of the Division is also the North Dakota State Archivist.

State Historical Society of North Dakota activities are headquartered in the North Dakota Heritage Center on the Capitol grounds.

Indian Scholarships, State Board for North Dakota

Phone: 701-328-2964
Fax: 701-328-2979
Web: www.ndus.edu/students/paying-for-college/grants-scholarships/#NDIS
[NDCC 15-63-01]

The Board is comprised of the Executive Director of the North Dakota Indian Affairs Commission as secretary, the Chancellor or Chancellor's designee of the North Dakota University System as chair, and an American Indian appointed by the Governor.

The Board awards scholarships each year for North Dakota residents who are members of federally recognized Indian tribes. The scholarships may be used to attend any North Dakota institution of higher learning or state career and technical education program. The scholarship funding is appropriated through the biennial budget request of the North Dakota University System.

Investment Board, State

Phone: 701-328-9885
Toll Free: 800-952-2970
Fax: 701-328-9897
Email: rio@nd.gov
Web: www.nd.gov/rio
[NDCC 21-10-01]

The State Investment Board consists of the Governor (or designee), State Treasurer, Commissioner of University and School Lands, Director of Workforce Safety & Insurance (or designee), Commissioner of Insurance, three members of the Teachers' Fund for Retirement board, and three members of the Public

Employees Retirement System board. The Board appoints an investment director. The State Investment Board serves as the administrative board to the Retirement and Investment Office, an agency of the state of North Dakota.

The Board administers the investment programs for the following funds in accordance with their stated investment goals and objectives: Statutory – State Bonding Fund, State Fire and Tornado Fund, Insurance Regulatory Trust Fund, Petroleum Tank Release Compensation Fund, Public Employees Retirement System Fund, Risk Management Fund, Risk Management Workers Compensation Fund, Teachers' Fund for Retirement, Workforce Safety & Insurance, Budget Stabilization Fund, Cultural Endowment Fund, and the Legacy Fund. Contractual – City of Bismarck Employees Retirement Fund, City of Bismarck Police Retirement Fund, City of Bismarck Deferred Sick Leave Fund, City of Fargo Fargo Dome Permanent Fund, North Dakota Association of Counties Fund, North Dakota Job Service Retirement Fund, Public Employees Retirement System Group Health Insurance Fund, Public Employees Retirement System Retiree Health Insurance Fund, City of Grand Forks Pension Fund, City of Grand Forks Park District Pension Fund, and State Board of Medicine.

Judicial Nominating Committee

Phone: 701-255-1404
[NDCC 27-25]

Six members of the Judicial Nominating Committee are appointed for three-year terms as follows: two by the Governor, two by the Chief Justice, and two by the president of the State Bar Association. In each case, one appointee is to be a judge or attorney and the other is to be a citizen who is not a judge, former judge, or attorney. The Committee of six sits to consider nominees for Supreme Court vacancies. For district court vacancies, each appointing authority appoints an additional temporary member from the judicial district with a vacancy to serve on the committee until the vacancy is filled. The Executive Director of the State Bar Association serves as nonvoting Secretary for the Judicial Nominating Committee. The Governor appoints the chairman.

The committee recruits, screens, nominates, and submits to the Governor a list of two to seven nominees for each vacancy in a district court or the Supreme Court. The Governor then may fill the vacancy by appointment from the list, call a special election to fill the vacancy, or return the list of nominees to the committee with directions to reconvene. Any gubernatorial appointment made from the list of nominees submitted by the Committee continues for at least two years and until the next general election immediately following those two years, at which time the office will be filled by election for the remainder of the term.

Milk Marketing Board

410 E. Thayer Avenue
Bismarck, ND 58501
Phone: 701-328-9588
[NDCC 4.1-26]

The Milk Marketing Board consists of five members appointed by the Governor for five-year terms. The Governor appoints one Grade A dairy farmer selling to a processor, one processor, one retailer, and two consumers not engaged in the milk business. The Board meets at the call of the chairman.

The Board promotes the North Dakota dairy industry through the following means. The Board establishes a minimum Grade A dairy farmer hundredweight price and wholesale and retail prices as a result of public hearings. The Board licenses all Grade A dairy farmers, processors, distributors, and retailers in the marketing area. The Board regulates disruptive trade practices.

Natural Resources Trust, Inc.

[Garrison Diversion Unit Reformulation Act of 1986] and
[Dakota Water Resources Act of 2000]
Phone: 701-223-8501
Fax: 701-233-6937
Email: mary@naturalresourcestrust.com
Web: www.ndnrt.com

The Trust is dedicated to the preservation, enhancement, restoration, and management of wetlands and associated wildlife habitat, grasslands, and riparian areas in the state of North Dakota. The director of the Game and Fish Department is an ex-officio member. Three members are appointed by the Governor for terms of two years. Three additional members represent the North Dakota Chapter of The Wildlife Society, National Audubon Society, and National Wildlife Federation.

Parole Board, State

Phone: 701-328-6664
Web: www.nd.gov/docr/parole/board.html
[NDCC 12-59-01]

The State Parole Board consists of six members appointed by the Governor for three-year terms: one member must be experienced in law enforcement; one must be a licensed attorney; and four must be qualified by special experience, education, or training. The Board is the sole authority for all parole-related decisions in North Dakota. Department of Corrections and Rehabilitation-Division of Adult Services staff are designated to serve as clerk for the Board and provide all administrative support including docketing, information gathering, and execution of the Board's orders.

Personnel Board, State

Web: www.nd.gov/hrms/employees/board.html
[NDCC 54-44.3.03]

The State Personnel Board is composed of the Director of the North Dakota Human Resource Management Services Division of the Office of Management and Budget, who serves as chair; two members appointed by the Governor, one who must have a professional human resource background; and two members elected by state employees in classified positions. The Board meets at least once a year, and except for the chair, terms are for six years.

The primary responsibilities of the Board are to review classification and pay grade appeals, promulgate rules, and approve positions not to be included in the classified service.

Protection and Advocacy, Committee on

Phone: 701-328-2950
Toll Free: 800-472-2670
Fax: 701-328-3934
Relay ND: 711TTY
Email: panda@nd.gov
Web: www.ndpanda.org
[NDCC 25-01.3-02]

The Committee on Protection and Advocacy consists of seven members, two of whom are appointed by the Governor and two by the Legislative Management. The Arc of North Dakota, a North Dakota nonprofit advocacy group for people with disabilities, and the Mental Health Association in North Dakota, Inc., each appoint one member. Members appointed by the Governor and the Legislative Management serve two-year terms.

The Committee appoints a director who serves at the will of the Committee. The Committee oversees the North Dakota Protection and Advocacy Project, which provides advocacy and legal services to persons with all types of disabilities so they may realize the rights and services to which they are entitled.

Public Employees Retirement System Board

400 East Broadway, Suite 505
PO Box 1657
Bismarck, ND 58502
Phone: 701-328-3900
Toll Free: 800-803-7377
Fax: 701-328-3920
Email: ndpers-info@nd.gov
Web: https://ndpers.nd.gov/
[NDCC 54-52]

The North Dakota Public Employees Retirement System (NDPERS) is governed by a nine-member Board of Trustees. One member, the chairman, is appointed by the Governor; one member is appointed from the Attorney General's staff; one member is the North Dakota State Health Officer's appointee; three members are elected by the active membership of the NDPERS system; one member is elected by the retired public employees; and two legislators are appointed by the chairman of Legislative Management. The Board appoints an executive director.

NDPERS manages six defined benefit retirement plans and two defined contribution retirement plans. In addition to the retirement programs, the system administers the group health plan, dental plan, vision plan, long-term care plan, employee assistance plan, and life insurance program for public employees. The Board is also responsible for the administration of the state Flex Comp program.

NDPERS investments are under the supervision of the State Investment Board, pursuant to investment policies and asset allocations approved by the Board of Trustees.

Public School Education, State Board of

Phone: 701-328-2283
[NDCC 15.1-01]

The State Board of Public School Education consists of the Superintendent of Public Instruction and a qualified elector from each of six districts in the governing law. The Superintendent is the board's director and executive secretary. The six members are appointed by the Governor and come from a list of nominees submitted by a committee made up of the presidents of North Dakota United, North Dakota Council of Educational Leaders, and the North Dakota School Boards Association.

Retirement and Investment Office

Phone: 701-328-9885
Toll Free: 800-952-2970
Fax: 701-328-9897
Email: rio@nd.gov
Web: www.nd.gov/rio
[NDCC 54-52.5]

The North Dakota Retirement and Investment Office (RIO) was established in 1989 to coordinate the activities of the State Investment Board (SIB) and the Teachers' Fund for Retirement (TFFR). The administrative board for the agency is the State Investment Board, which consists of the Governor (or designee), State Treasurer, Commissioner of University and School Lands, Director of Workforce Safety and Insurance (or designee), Commissioner of Insurance, three members of the Teachers' Fund for Retirement board, and three members of the Public Employees Retirement System board. The Board appoints an executive director.

Seed Department, State

Phone: 701-231-5400
Fax: 701-231-5401
Email: ndseed@ndseed.ndsu.edu
Web: www.ndseed.com
[NDCC 4.1-52]

The State Seed Commission is the governing board for the North Dakota State Seed Department. The nine-member group is comprised of members from various industries the Department serves and represents a broad cross-section of agricultural commodities grown in this state and region. Established in 1931 by the state legislature, the Department is the state-designated authority for seed certification and seed regulatory and laboratory testing services to North Dakota producers and the agriculture industry. A self-funded agency of government, it derives its revenues from fees for services provided and receives no general fund revenues from the state of North Dakota.

Headquartered at North Dakota State University in Fargo, it maintains close working relationships with a variety of affiliates in North Dakota and surrounding states, including the North Dakota Crop Improvement Association, North Dakota Certified Seed Potato Growers Association, North Dakota State University Foundation Seedstocks Project, and numerous other public associations and private businesses.

Soil Conservation Committee, State

Phone: 701-328-9718
Fax: 701-328-9721
Email: scott.hochhalter@ndsu.edu
Web: www.ag.ndsu.nodak.edu/ndsscc
[NDCC 4-22-03]

Of the seven members on the State Soil Conservation Committee, two are appointed by the Governor and five are elected by supervisory board members of their soil conservation districts. Committee members serve three-year terms. Representatives from the following agencies serve in an advisory capacity to the committee: State Association of Soil Conservation Districts, North Dakota Extension Service, Natural Resources Conservation Service, Commissioner of Agriculture, and Game and Fish Department.

The Committee encourages conservation of soil and soil resources. It may offer assistance to supervisors of soil conservation districts in the carrying out of their programs; facilitate exchange of advice and experience between districts; coordinate the programs of several conservation districts; secure the cooperation and assistance of state, federal, regional, and other agencies with conservation districts; and review programs and agreements affecting soil conservation districts. All surface mining operators file an annual detailed report of their activities with the Committee which, in turn, transmits the information to the district.

Teachers' Fund for Retirement

Phone: 701-328-9885
Toll Free: 800-952-2970
Fax: 701-328-9897
Email: rio@nd.gov
Web: www.nd.gov/rio
[NDCC 15-39.1]

The Teachers' Fund for Retirement (TFFR) is a trust fund established to provide retirement income for all public schools and state educators. The Teachers' Fund for Retirement, formerly the Teachers' Insurance and Retirement Fund, dates back to 1913. In 1971, a new law created the Teachers' Fund for Retirement.

Responsibility for the administration of the fund is assigned to a seven-member board of trustees. This board consists of the State Treasurer, the Superintendent of Public Instruction, and five members appointed by the Governor: one full-time school administrator; two full-time classroom teachers; and two retired members of the fund.

The State Investment Board is responsible for the investment of the assets of TFFR. The TFFR program and State Investment program are administered by the Retirement and Investment Office.

Theodore Roosevelt Rough Rider Award

[NDCC 54-02-07]

The Theodore Roosevelt Rough Rider Award is the highest recognition given by the state of North Dakota. It is awarded to present or former North Dakotans who have been influenced by the state in achieving national recognition in their fields of endeavor, thereby reflecting credit and honor upon the state and its citizens. Presented in the name of the Legislative Assembly and the citizens of this state, the award is not for momentary success, but for genuine achievements of lasting significance. The Governor bestows the award upon the concurrence of the Secretary of State and the Director of the State Historical Society.

Upper Great Plains Transportation Institute

Phone: 701-231-7767
Fax: 701-231-1945
Email: info@ugpti.org
Web: www.ugpti.org

The Upper Great Plains Transportation Institute conducts applied and advanced research in highway, transit, rail, air, and waterway transportation that addresses the critical issues of the state, region, and nation. It educates the transportation workforce of tomorrow through multidisciplinary curricula that focus on transportation economics, management, infrastructure planning, mobility, and supply chain logistics.

The Institute also improves the skills and knowledge of the existing workforce through training, technical assistance, and the transfer of research results to practitioners. The Institute is a research and outreach education center at North Dakota State University, which is guided in part by an advisory council composed of representatives of various organizations, industries, and agencies affecting or affected by transportation.

Veterans Affairs, Administrative Committee on

Phone: 701-239-7165
Fax: 701-239-7166
Toll Free: 866-634-8387
[NDCC 37-18.1]

Fifteen members with equal representation from the American Legion, Veterans of Foreign Wars, Disabled American Veterans, AMVETS, and the Vietnam Veterans of America are appointed by the Governor for three-year terms to the Committee. Appointments are made from lists of nominees submitted to the Governor by the respective organizations. From the 15, the Governor names a chair and a secretary on an annual basis. Ex-officio committee members include the Adjutant General, Center Director of Veterans Administration, and the Executive Director of Job Service North Dakota. The chairman and secretary, acting jointly, shall appoint: a seven-member governing board for administration of the Veterans Home, from within or outside the Committee, subject to ratification of a majority vote of the Committee; and a subcommittee to be responsible for supervision and government of the Department of Veterans Affairs. Each nominating organization listed in section 37-18.1-01 must have at least one voting member nominated by the organization serving on the subcommittee.

The governing board has the power to establish qualifications for the selection of an administrator (for the Veterans Home) who serves at the pleasure of the governing board. The Committee appoints the commissioner of the Department of Veterans' Affairs who serves at the pleasure of the Committee. The commissioner serves as the executive secretary for the subcommittee.

Veterans Affairs, Department of

Phone: 701-239-7165
Fax: 701-239-7166
Toll Free: 866-634-8387
[NDCC 37-18]

The Department's mission is to ensure that every veteran in the state of North Dakota who has served in the military receives every benefit to which he or she may be entitled from the U.S. Department of Veterans Affairs (VA), allied agencies, and the state of North Dakota. The Department has the responsibility of training and assisting the work of the Tribal Service Officers and County Veterans Service Officers (who service 53 counties), appointed by their respective County Board of Commissioners.

The Department of Veterans Affairs is governed by a subcommittee appointed by the chairman and secretary of the Administrative Committee on Veterans Affairs. The Administrative Committee appoints the Commissioner of Veterans Affairs and sets the salary. The Commissioner serves at the pleasure of the board. The Commissioner also acts as Executive Secretary of the Subcommittee on Veterans Affairs.

Veterans Home

Phone: 701-683-6500
Fax: 701-683-6550
[Constitution, Article IX, Section 13; NDCC 37-15]

In operation since 1893, the North Dakota Veterans Home is located on a 90-acre tract of land adjacent to the Sheyenne River in Lisbon, N.D. The chairman and secretary of the Administrative Committee on Veterans Affairs appoint a Governing Board consisting of seven members to oversee administration of the Home. Day-to-day management is the responsibility of the Administrator, who is hired by the Governing Board.

The Home provides care and service to veterans and their spouses. Services at the Home include activities, housekeeping, dietary, medical care, therapy services, and social services. The North Dakota Veterans Home has an in-house pharmacy that provides services for eligible veterans. The Basic Care Unit has 98 beds and requires that potential residents have total independence with personal care needs, such as bathing, dressing, eating, ambulating (walking), toileting, and transferring. The Skilled Care Unit has 52 beds and requires that a potential resident meet the North Dakota criteria for nursing home placement.

North Dakota Boards and Commissions

A number of boards and commissions exist in North Dakota to regulate or license occupations and professions. Others provide agencies with advice and expertise, plans, and recommendations relating to a broad range of issues. Others coordinate activities and planning among entities in a common area. Some are established under state law, while others are required by federal laws or rules. Most members of state boards and commissions generally serve without compensation.

North Dakota's boards and commissions are coordinated by the Governor's Office. For more information on boards and commissions, and for a listing of current members, call 701-328-2219 or visit the website at www.governor.nd.gov/boards.

A number of boards and commissions are listed in the profiles in this chapter. The name and a contact phone number of others not mentioned elsewhere in this chapter are listed below.

Abstracters' Board of Examiners	701-271-8500
Accountancy, State Board of	701-755-7100
Addiction Counseling Examiners, Board of	701-255-1439
Aging, Committee on	701-328-4601
Agricultural Products Utilization Commission	701-328-5350
Air Pollution Control Advisory Council	701-328-5188
Alternatives to Incarceration, Commission on	701-857-4638
Architecture and Landscape Architecture, State Board of	701-223-3540
Athletic Trainers, North Dakota Board of	701-417-6171
Atmospheric Resource Board, North Dakota	701-328-2788
Audiology and Speech-Language Pathology, Board of Examiners on	701-775-7165
Autism Spectrum Disorder Task Force	701-328-8924
Bank of North Dakota, Advisory Board of Directors to the	701-328-5600
Banking Board, State	701-328-9933
Barber Examiners, Board of	701-837-0826
Beef Commission, North Dakota	701-328-5120
Cares, North Dakota	701-333-2026
Chiropractic Examiners, State Board of	701-213-0476
Clinical Laboratory Practice, North Dakota Board of	701-530-0199
Cosmetology, State Board of	701-224-9800
Counselor Examiners, Board of	701-667-5969
Credit Union Board, State	701-328-9933
Criminal Justice Information Sharing Board	701-328-1110
Crop Insurance Development Board	701-328-2231
Crop Protection Product Harmonization and Registration Board	701-328-1505
Dairy Promotion Commission, North Dakota	701-782-4154
Dental Examiners, State Board of	701-258-8600
Development Fund, Incorporated, Board of Directors for North Dakota	701-328-5334
Developmental Disabilities, State Council on	701-328-4847
Devils Lake Outlet Management Advisory Committee	701-328-4940
Dietetic Practice, Board of	701-838-0218
Drug Use Review Board	701-328-4023
Drugs and Alcohol, Governors Prevention Advisory Council on	701-328-8920

Dry Bean Council, North Dakota	218-334-6351
Early Childhood Education Council, North Dakota	701-328-2200
Economic Development Foundation, North Dakota	701-328-5300
Education Factfinding Commission	701-456-6302
Education Standards and Practices Board	701-328-9646
Educational Technology Council, North Dakota	701-231-6032
Electrical Board, State	701-328-9522
Employment of People with Disabilities, Committee on	701-328-8926
Energy Policy Commission (EmPower North Dakota Commission)	701-328-5300
Engineers and Land Surveyors, State Board of Registration for Professional	701-258-0786
Funeral Service, State Board of	701-776-6222
Game and Fish Advisory Board, State	701-328-6300
Gaming Commission, State	701-328-4848
Governor's Task Force for Military Issues in North Dakota	701-333-2234
Grape and Wine Advisory Committee	701-328-4763
Health Council	701-328-2372
Health Information Technology Advisory Committee	701-328-1991
Hearing Aid Specialists, Board of	701-237-9977
Higher Education Grant Review Committee	701-328-2937
Historical Board, State	701-328-2666
Historical Records Advisory Board, State	701-328-2090
Homelessness, Interagency Council on	701-328-8072
Humanities Council, North Dakota State	701-255-3360
Integrative Health Care, State Board of	701-255-1881
Interagency Coordinating Council	701-328-8936
Intergovernmental Relations, Advisory Commission on	701-258-8988
International Peace Garden, Inc., Board of Directors of the	888-432-6733
Interstate Adult Offender Supervision, North Dakota State Council for	701-328-6616
Interstate Juvenile Supervision, North Dakota Council for	701-328-6362
Interstate Oil and Gas Compact Commission (IOGCC)	701-328-3722
Judicial Conduct Commission	701-328-3925
Juvenile Justice Advisory Group	701-328-7300
Legal Counsel for Indigents, Commission on	701-845-8632
Library Coordinating Council, North Dakota	701-328-2492
Lignite Research Council	701-328-3722
Marriage and Family Therapist Licensure Board, North Dakota	701-400-2696
Massage, North Dakota Board of	701-872-4895
Medical Facility Infrastructure Loan Task Force	701-224-9732
Medical Imaging and Radiation Therapy Board of Examiners, North Dakota	701-328-2219
Medicine, State Board of	701-328-6500
Mental Health and Substance Abuse Planning Council, North Dakota	701-328-8920
Midwest Interstate Passenger Rail Compact Commission	630-810-0210
Midwestern Higher Education Commission	612-626-8288
Military Interstate Children's Compact Commission	701-333-2268
National and Community Service, State Commission on	701-328-5345
Nursing Home Administrators, State Board of Examiners for	701-222-4867
Nursing, State Board of	701-328-9777

Occupational Therapy Practice, Board of	701-250-0847
Oil and Gas Research Council	701-328-3722
Oilseed Council, North Dakota	701-328-5107
Olmstead Commission	701-328-2538
Optometry, North Dakota State Board of	701-690-7937
Pardon Advisory Board	701-328-6192
Petroleum Tank Release Compensation Advisory Board	701-328-9600
Pharmacy, State Board of	701-328-9535
Physical Therapy, North Dakota Board of	701-352-3093
Plumbing, State Board of	701-328-9977
Podiatric Medicine, North Dakota Board of	701-390-7190
Prison Industry Advisory Committee	701-328-6163
Private Investigative and Security Board	701-222-3063
Property Tax Reform, Task Force on	701-328-2200
Psychologist Examiners, State Board of	701-590-1754
Racing Commission, North Dakota	701-328-4633
Real Estate Appraiser Qualifications and Ethics Board, North Dakota	701-222-1051
Real Estate Commission, State	701-328-9749
Reflexology, North Dakota Board of	701-331-2435
Rehabilitation Council, State	701-328-8926
Renewable Energy Council	701-328-5300
Respiratory Care, State Board of	701-222-1564
Rural Development Council	701-223-0707
Small Business Air Pollution Compliance Advisory Board	701-328-5150
Social Work Examiners, North Dakota Board of	701-222-0255
Soil Classifiers, State Board of Registration for Professional	701-952-9049
State Employees Compensation Commission	701-328-2680
State Information Technology Advisory Committee	701-328-3193
Statewide Independent Living Council	701-328-8950
Statewide Longitudinal Data System Committee	701-328-4134
Status of Women, Commission on	602-318-4239
STOP Violence Against Women Advisory Committee	701-328-2455
Supervision of Adult Offenders, Advisory Council to the	701-328-6616
Teachers' Fund for Retirement, Board of Trustees of the	701-328-9885
Tobacco Prevention and Control Advisory Committee	701-328-5130
Unemployment Insurance Advisory Council	701-328-2843
Uniform State Laws, Commission on	701-328-2916
Veterinary Medical Examiners, State Board of	701-328-9540
Water Pollution Control Board, State	701-667-2492
Water Well Contractors, State Board of	701-328-3440
Wheat Commission, North Dakota State	701-328-5111
Workforce Development Council, North Dakota	701-328-3105
Youth Development Council, North Dakota	701-328-3105

✔ See the *1997-1999 North Dakota Blue Book* for a more detailed description of the duties of the Boards, Commissions, Committees, and Councils.

✔ See the *2011-2013 North Dakota Blue Book* for the Guide to North Dakota Statutes on Licensing, Certification, Registration, and Permits.

Chapter Six

Legislative Branch

Legislative Branch

General Background

The Legislative Assembly of the State of North Dakota is the bicameral legislative body established and governed by the Constitution of North Dakota as the Legislative Branch of North Dakota State Government. As the policy making branch for the state, the Legislative Assembly enacts laws and appropriates money for state government operations; conducts oversight on state and local government spending and authority; places proposed Constitutional amendments before North Dakota voters; voices opinions on behalf of North Dakota to federal agencies, other states, and interstate organizations; and provides constituent services to assist North Dakotans in their interactions with government entities.

Redistricting

Every 10 years the Legislative Assembly redistricts itself based upon the decennial census. The most recent legislative district boundaries are in effect following a November 2011 special session for redistricting.

Elections

The Legislative Assembly currently comprises 47 senators and 94 representatives, with one senator and two representatives serving each legislatively apportioned district. Voters in the state elect one-half of each chamber biennially to four-year terms: elections for even-numbered district seats took place in 2016, and odd-numbered district seats will be on the 2018 ballot.

Legislator Qualifications

Article IV, Section 5, of the Constitution of North Dakota specifies that "Each person elected to the legislative assembly must be, on the day of the election, a qualified elector in the district from which the member was chosen and must have been a resident of the state for one year immediately prior to that election" and, following voter approval of Measure No. 1 on the 2016 general election ballot, "An individual may not serve in the legislative assembly unless the individual lives in the district from which selected."

Legislative Sessions

A legislator formally begins service to constituents on December 1 following election. The regular biennial session of the Legislative Assembly commences the first Tuesday after the third day in January, or as prescribed by law, but no later than the 11th day of January. The state constitution limits the session to 80 natural, but not necessarily consecutive, days per biennium and specifies that neither chamber may recess or adjourn for more than three days without the consent of the other chamber. Legislators also meet for a three-day organizational session, for committee meetings throughout the biennium, and if necessary, for special sessions called by the Governor or for impeachment proceedings.

Presiding Officers

The President of the Senate and the Speaker of the House are the presiding officers of their respective bodies. They conduct legislative floor sessions, issue rulings on procedures, and sign all bills and resolutions passed by the Legislative Assembly. North Dakota's Lieutenant Governor serves as the President of the Senate and may cast a vote if there is a tie vote among senators voting on a procedural or substantive matter. The Senate elects one of its members to be a fully voting President Pro Tempore in times of absence of the President of the Senate. The House of Representatives chooses its Speaker from its membership, and the Speaker votes on all questions before the House.

Chamber Leadership

Majority and minority leaders, assistant majority and minority leaders, caucus chairmen, and committee chairmen and vice chairmen serve as party leadership within the Legislative Assembly. The majority and minority leaders are senior party members who promote their respective party policies and platforms and who influence legislative workflow through decisions about committee membership and leadership, bill assignment and consideration, and legislative procedures. The assistant leaders of each caucus work to unify their members for votes on important issues, and the assistant majority leader assists the presiding officer in coordinating floor sessions and states most procedural motions. The caucus chairmen develop party cohesion through formal and informal caucuses where members discuss positions and strategy and participate in politically oriented social events. Committee chairmen direct committee workflow and appoint conference committees, and their vice chairmen support them in organizing committee activities.

Committees

Committees meet throughout session to receive testimony, to deliberate, and to recommend legislative action. During the regular session of the Legislative Assembly, standing committees make policy and appropriation recommendations to their respective houses, select committees consider special matters such as confirmation of executive nominees, and procedural committees address the Legislative Assembly's working mechanics in terms of committee appointments and room arrangements, journal revisions and corrections, delayed bills, employment, inaugural planning, and rules. Conference committees, comprising like committees from the Senate and the House, meet toward the end of legislative sessions to resolve chamber discrepancies on, and to produce final versions of, bills and resolutions. When the Legislative Assembly is not in session, interim committees of the Legislative Management conduct studies as directed by the Legislative Assembly and develop legislation.

Members of the 65th Legislative Assembly – 2017
Convened January 3, 2017; Adjourned April 27, 2017

Senate

Lieutenant Governor Brent Sanford, President
Gary A. Lee (R), President Pro Tempore
Rich Wardner (R), Majority Leader
Joan Heckaman (D), Minority Leader
Shanda Morgan, Secretary

District	Name	County	Post Office
8	Howard C. Anderson, Jr.	Pt. Burleigh, Pt. McLean	Turtle Lake
36	Kelly M. Armstrong	Pt. Dunn, Pt. Hettinger, Pt. Morton Pt. Stark	Dickinson
1	Brad Bekkedahl	Pt. Williams	Williston
39	Bill L. Bowman	Adams, Billings, Bowman Pt. Dunn, Golden Valley, Pt. McKenzie, Slope	Bowman
5	Randall A. Burckhard	Pt. Ward	Minot
19	Tom Campbell	Pt. Grand Forks, Pt. Walsh	Grafton
27	Jonathan Casper	Pt. Cass	Fargo
16	David A. Clemens	Pt. Cass	West Fargo
34	Dwight Cook	Pt. Morton	Mandan
41	Kyle Davison	Pt. Cass	Fargo
32	Dick Dever	Pt. Burleigh	Bismarck
26	*Jim Dotzenrod	Pt. Dickey, Pt. Ransom Pt. Richland, Sargent	Wyndmere
28	Robert Erbele	Pt. Burleigh, Pt. Dickey Emmons, Pt. LaMoure, Logan, McIntosh	Lehr
12	*John Grabinger	Pt. Stutsman	Jamestown
23	*Joan Heckaman	Pt. Benson, Eddy, Griggs Nelson, Steele	New Rockford
38	David Hogue	Pt. Ward	Minot
17	Ray Holmberg	Pt. Grand Forks	Grand Forks
4	Jordan Kannianen	Pt. Dunn, Pt. McKenzie Pt. McLean, Pt. Mercer, Pt. Mountrail, Pt. Ward	Stanley
47	Ralph Kilzer	Pt. Burleigh	Bismarck
14	Jerry Klein	Pt. Benson, Kidder, Pierce Sheridan, Wells	Fessenden
40	Karen K. Krebsbach	Pt. Ward	Minot
42	Curt Kreun	Pt. Grand Forks	Grand Forks
43	Lonnie J. Laffen	Pt. Grand Forks	Grand Forks
3	Oley Larsen	Pt. Ward	Minot
30	Diane Larson	Pt. Burleigh	Bismarck
22	Gary A. Lee	Pt. Cass	Casselton
13	Judy Lee	Pt. Cass	West Fargo
25	Larry Luick	Pt. Cass, Pt. Richland	Fairmount
9	*Richard Marcellais	Rolette	Belcourt

11	*Tim Mathern	Pt. Cass	Fargo
18	Scott Meyer	Pt. Grand Forks	Grand Forks
10	Janne Myrdal	Cavalier, Pembina, Pt. Walsh	
21	*Carolyn C. Nelson	Pt. Cass	Fargo
35	*Erin Oban	Pt. Burleigh	Bismarck
15	Dave Oehlke	Ramsey, Towner	Devils Lake
20	Arne Osland	Pt. Cass, Pt. Grand Forks, Traill	Mayville
44	*Merrill Piepkorn	Pt. Cass	Fargo
7	Nicole Poolman	Pt. Burleigh	Bismarck
24	*Larry J. Robinson	Barnes, Pt. Cass, Pt. Ransom	Valley City
46	Jim P. Roers	Pt. Cass	Fargo
2	David S. Rust	Burke, Divide, Pt. Mountrail Pt. Williams	Tioga
31	Donald Schaible	Grant, Pt. Hettinger, Pt. Morton, Sioux	Mott
45	Ronald Sorvaag	Pt. Cass	Fargo
33	Jessica Unruh	Pt. Mercer, Pt. Morton, Oliver	Beulah
6	Shawn Vedaa	Bottineau, McHenry, Renville	Velva
29	Terry M. Wanzek	Foster, Pt. LaMoure, Pt. Stutsman	Jamestown
37	Rich Wardner	Pt. Stark	Dickinson

House

Larry Bellew (R), Speaker
Al Carlson (R), Majority Leader
Corey Mock (D), Minority Leader
Buell J. Reich, Chief Clerk

District	Name	County	Post Office
2	Bert Anderson	Burke, Divide, Pt. Mountrail Pt. Williams	Crosby
6	Dick Anderson	Bottineau, McHenry, Renville	Willow City
41	*Pamela Anderson	Pt. Cass	Fargo
27	Thomas Beadle	Pt. Cass	Fargo
43	Rich S. Becker	Pt. Grand Forks	Grand Forks
7	Rick C. Becker	Pt. Burleigh	Bismarck
38	Larry Bellew	Pt. Ward	Minot
42	Jake G. Blum	Pt. Grand Forks	Grand Forks
9	*Tracy Boe	Rolette	Mylo
27	Randy Boehning	Pt. Cass	Fargo
30	Glenn Bosch	Pt. Burleigh	Bismarck
44	*Joshua A. Boschee	Pt. Cass	Fargo
5	Roger Brabandt	Pt. Ward	Minot
28	Mike Brandenburg	Pt. Burleigh, Pt. Dickey, Emmons Pt. LaMoure, Logan, McIntosh	Edgeley
41	Al Carlson	Pt. Cass	Fargo
10	Chuck Damschen	Cavalier, Pembina, Pt. Walsh	Hampden
43	*Lois Delmore	Pt. Grand Forks	Grand Forks
8	Jeff Delzer	Pt. Burleigh, Pt. McLean	Underwood
23	Bill Devlin	Pt. Benson, Eddy, Griggs, Nelson, Steele	Finley

11	*Gretchen Dobervich	Pt. Cass	Fargo
7	Jason Dockter	Pt. Burleigh	Bismarck
26	Sebastian Ertelt	Pt. Dickey, Pt. Ransom Pt. Richland, Sargent	Lisbon
12	Jim Grueneich	Pt. Stutsman	Jamestown
11	*Ron Guggisberg	Pt. Cass	Fargo
44	*Karla Rose Hanson	Pt. Cass	Fargo
1	Patrick Hatlestad	Pt. Williams	Williston
29	Craig Headland	Foster, Pt. LaMoure, Pt. Stutsman	Montpelier
32	Pat D. Heinert	Pt. Burleigh	Bismarck
21	*Kathy Hogan	Pt. Cass	Fargo
20	*Richard G. Holman	Pt. Cass, Pt. Grand Forks, Traill	Mayville
22	Michael Howe	Pt. Cass	West Fargo
6	Craig A. Johnson	Bottineau, McHenry, Renville	Maxbass
15	Dennis Johnson	Ramsey, Towner	Devils Lake
45	Mary Johnson	Pt. Cass	Fargo
24	Daniel Johnston	Barnes, Pt. Cass, Pt. Ransom	Kathryn
4	Terry B. Jones	Pt. Dunn, Pt. McKenzie, Pt. McLean Pt. Mercer, Pt. Mountrail, Pt. Ward	New Town
45	Tom Kading	Pt. Cass	Fargo
35	Karen Karls	Pt. Burleigh	Bismarck
46	Jim Kasper	Pt. Cass	Fargo
47	George J. Keiser	Pt. Burleigh	Bismarck
39	Keith Kempenich	Adams, Billings, Bowman, Pt. Dunn Golden Valley, Pt. McKenzie, Slope	Bowman
24	Dwight Kiefert	Barnes, Pt. Cass, Pt. Ransom	Valley City
47	Lawrence R. Klemin	Pt. Burleigh	Bismarck
16	Ben Koppelman	Pt. Cass	West Fargo
13	Kim Koppelman	Pt. Cass	West Fargo
33	Gary Kreidt	Pt. Mercer, Pt. Morton, Oliver	New Salem
8	Vernon Laning	Pt. Burleigh, Pt. McLean	Bismarck
37	Mike Lefor	Pt. Stark	Dickinson
2	Donald W. Longmuir	Burke, Divide, Pt. Mountrail Pt. Williams	Stanley
5	Scott Louser	Pt. Ward	Minot
28	Jeffery J. Magrum	Pt. Burleigh, Pt. Dickey, Emmons Pt. LaMoure, Logan, McIntosh	Hazelton
3	Andrew G. Maragos	Pt. Ward	Minot
16	Andrew Marschall	Pt. Cass	Fargo
35	Bob Martinson	Pt. Burleigh	Bismarck
20	Aaron McWilliams	Pt. Cass, Pt. Grand Forks, Traill	Hillsboro
32	Lisa Meier	Pt. Burleigh	Bismarck
25	*Alisa Mitskog	Pt. Cass, Pt. Richland	Wahpeton
18	*Corey Mock	Pt. Grand Forks	Grand Forks
10	David Monson	Cavalier, Pembina, Pt. Walsh	Osnabrock
30	Mike Nathe	Pt. Burleigh	Bismarck
14	Jon O. Nelson	Pt. Benson, Kidder, Pierce Sheridan, Wells	Rugby
9	*Marvin E. Nelson	Rolette	Rolla
42	Emily O'Brien	Pt. Grand Forks	Grand Forks

4	Bill Oliver	Pt. Dunn, Pt. McKenzie, Pt. McLean Pt. Mercer, Pt. Mountrail, Pt. Ward	New Town
13	Christopher D. Olson	Pt. Cass	West Fargo
17	Mark S. Owens	Pt. Grand Forks	Grand Forks
19	Gary Paur	Pt. Grand Forks, Pt. Walsh	Gilby
29	Chet Pollert	Foster, Pt. LaMoure, Pt. Stutsman	Carrington
34	Todd Porter	Pt. Morton	Mandan
22	Brandy Pyle	Pt. Cass	Casselton
46	Shannon M. Roers Jones	Pt. Cass	Fargo
31	Karen M. Rohr	Grant, Pt. Hettinger, Pt. Morton, Sioux	Mandan
38	Dan Ruby	Pt. Ward	Minot
40	Matthew Ruby	Pt. Ward	Minot
17	Mark Sanford	Pt. Grand Forks	Grand Forks
12	Bernie Satrom	Pt. Stutsman	Jamestown
36	Mike Schatz	Pt. Dunn, Pt. Hettinger, Pt. Morton Pt. Stark	New England
31	Jim Schmidt	Grant, Pt. Hettinger, Pt. Morton, Sioux	Huff
21	*Mary Schneider	Pt. Cass	Fargo
40	Randy A. Schobinger	Pt. Ward	Minot
25	Cynthia Schreiber-Beck	Pt. Cass, Pt. Richland	Wahpeton
33	Jay Seibel	Pt. Mercer, Pt. Morton, Oliver	Beulah
36	Luke Simons	Pt. Dunn, Pt. Hettinger, Pt. Morton Pt. Stark	Dickinson
26	Kathy Skroch	Pt. Dickey, Pt. Ransom, Pt. Richland Sargent	Lidgerwood
37	Vicky Steiner	Pt. Stark	Dickinson
3	Roscoe Streyle	Pt. Ward	Minot
1	Gary R. Sukut	Pt. Williams	Williston
34	Nathan Toman	Pt. Morton	Mandan
19	Wayne A. Trottier	Pt. Grand Forks, Pt. Walsh	Northwood
18	Steve Vetter	Pt. Grand Forks	Grand Forks
23	Don Vigesaa	Pt. Benson, Eddy, Griggs, Nelson Steele	Cooperstown
14	Robin Weisz	Pt. Benson, Kidder, Pierce, Sheridan Wells	Hurdsfield
15	Greg Westlind	Ramsey, Towner	Cando
39	Denton Zubke	Adams, Billings, Bowman, Pt. Dunn Golden Valley, Pt. McKenzie, Slope	Watford City

(*) Democrats - All other Republicans

On the following pages, contact information and short biographies for all senators and representatives are listed by legislative district. Maps of North Dakota cities that include multiple legislative districts are included at the end of this section.

DISTRICT #1

Brad Bekkedahl

418 12th Avenue West, Williston, ND 58801-4730; bbekkedahl@nd.gov; (R) Pt. Williams • Dentist • BA, University of Jamestown; BS, U of M; DDS, U of M School of Dentistry • US Army Reserves, 1996-2002; ND National Guard, 2002-present, Rank: Col. • Williston Park Board, 1988-1996; Williston City Finance Commissioner, since 1996; USA Hockey Director Emeritus • Senate since 2015
FINANCE AND TAXATION; GOVERNMENT AND VETERANS AFFAIRS

Patrick Hatlestad

P.O. Box 1342, Williston, ND 58802-1342; phatlestad@nd.gov; (R) Pt. Williams • Retired, Part-time Teacher • BA, Western Washington University; MEd. EA, UND • Past President, TriCounty ED Board; Past President, Williston Chamber of Commerce; President, Williston Rotary; Board, USND; Board, Williams County Social Service; Board, Northwest Human Services; TrainND, Instructor; Past President, ND Elks Association; PER Williston Elks; Renaissance Zone Committee; RC&D Board; Marketplace 4 Kids; Shrine; API • Married (Durelle); 2 Children • House since 2007
FINANCE AND TAXATION; POLITICAL SUBDIVISIONS

Gary R. Sukut

1603 Fourth Avenue East, Williston, ND 58801-4324; gsukut@nd.gov; (R) Pt. Williams • Retired Office Equipment Business Owner/Operator • BA & MA, UND • Williston Western Star Award; Past President, Williston Chamber of Commerce; Williston Jobs & Industries, Communities for a Modern US 2; Past Board, Prairie Rose State Games; Williston City Commissioner; Board, Williston Star Fund; Board, Williston Economic Development Foundation; Past President, Williston Rotary; Former Republican Caucus Chair; Past Chairman, Workers Compensation Review Committee • Married (Leora); 3 Children • House since 2007
INDUSTRY, BUSINESS AND LABOR; TRANSPORTATION

DISTRICT #2

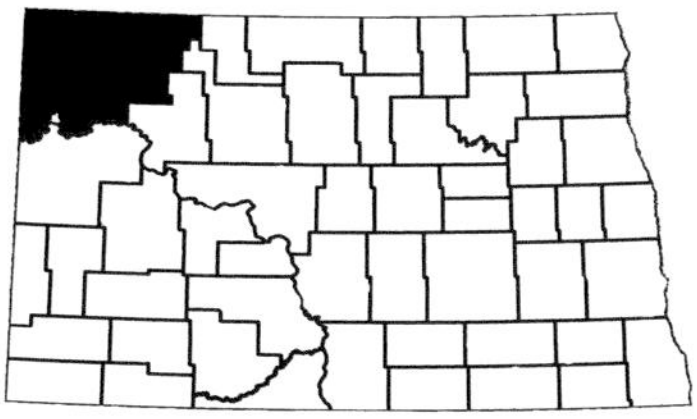

David S. Rust

P.O. Box 1198, Tioga, ND 58852-1198; drust@nd.gov; (R) Burke, Divide, Pt. Mountrail, Pt. Williams • Retired Superintendent, Tioga Public School • BS, VCSU; MA, Bowling Green State University; EDS, NDSU • Past President, ND Association of Oil & Gas Producing Counties; Past President, ND Council of Educational Leaders; President, Tioga Community Medical Center; Board, Tioga EDC; ND Superintendent of the Year, 1996; First Baptist Church of Tioga • Married (Claudia); 4 Children; 9 Grandchildren • House 2009-2014; Senate since 2015
EDUCATION; TRANSPORTATION

Bert Anderson

P.O. Box 604, Crosby, ND 58730-06040; bertanderson@nd.gov; (R) Burke, Divide, Pt. Mountrail, Pt. Williams • Business Owner • Lake Region College; Northwest Bible College • Mayor of Crosby; Crosby City Council; Board, St. Luke's Hospital; Crosby Assembly of God • Married (Diane); 2 Children; 4 Grandchildren • House since 2015
HUMAN SERVICES; TRANSPORTATION

Donald W. Longmuir

P.O. Box 519, Stanley, ND 58784-0519; dlongmuir@nd.gov; (R) Burke, Divide, Pt. Mountrail, Pt. Williams • Small Business Owner • BS, Business Economics, NDSU • Stanley Public School Board, 21 years; Past President, ND Land Title Assoc.; Past President, ND Planning Assoc.; Lions International Melvin Jones Fellow; ND Emergency Managers Assoc. Achievement Award; Stanley Lions Club; Stanley Boy Scouts Troop Committee; Stanley Boy Scout Trust Committee; Stanley Area Community Foundation; Trinity Health Foundation; Stanley American Lutheran Church • Married (Connie); 2 Children; 7 Grandchildren • House since 2017
EDUCATION; POLITICAL SUBDIVISIONS

DISTRICT #3

Oley Larsen

11051 20th Avenue SE, Minot, ND 58701-2658; olarsen@nd.gov; (R) Pt. Ward • Self Employed, Insurance • Diesel Technology, WSC; BA, Vocational Education, VCSU; MS, Educational Leadership, NDSU • Young Educator of the Year, NDACTE; Teacher of the Year; VFW; EAA Skills-USA • Married (Elizabeth); 2 Children • Senate since 2011
AGRICULTURE; HUMAN SERVICES

Andrew G. Maragos

1535 16th Street SE, Minot, ND 58701-6091; agmaragos@nd.gov; (R) Pt. Ward • Businessman • BS, UND • Vietnam Veteran • American Legion; Veterans of Foreign Wars; Flemming Fellow, 1995 • Married (Sherry) • House 1993-2006; Senate since 2011
JUDICIARY; POLITICAL SUBDIVISIONS

Roscoe Streyle

3408 21st Street SE, Minot, ND 58701-7568; rstreyle@nd.gov; (R) Pt. Ward • Banker; Small Business Owner • AS, Banking and Finance, NDSCS • MCSA Certificate, BUCEC; Rotary • Married (Kristi); 3 Children • House since 2011
APPROPRIATIONS; APPROPRIATIONS - EDUCATION AND ENVIRONMENT DIVISION

DISTRICT #4

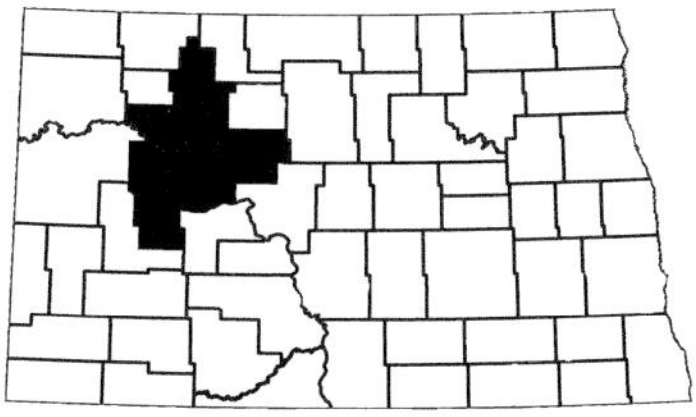

Jordan Kannianen

8011 51st Street NW, Stanley, ND 58784-9562; jkannianen@nd.gov; (R)
Pt. Dunn, Pt. McKenzie, Pt. McLean, Pt. Mercer, Pt. Mountrail, Pt. Ward
• Electrical Contractor • BS, MS, Management, MSU • Director, Sikes Township Board, President, Belden Finnish Cemetery Assoc.; Bishop's Counselor, The Church of Jesus Christ of Latter-day Saints • Married (Elizabeth); 8 Children • Senate since 2017
EDUCATION; POLITICAL SUBDIVISIONS

Terry B. Jones

P.O. Box 1964, New Town, ND 58763-1964; tbjones@nd.gov; (R)
Pt. Dunn, Pt. McKenzie, Pt. McLean, Pt. Mercer, Pt. Mountrail, Pt. Ward
• Farmer, Rancher, Contractor • AS, Business • Married (Kelly); 6 Children
• House since 2017
JUDICIARY; TRANSPORTATION

Bill Oliver

P.O. Box 1264, New Town, ND 58763-1264; boliver@nd.gov; (R)
Pt. Dunn, Pt. McKenzie, Pt. McLean, Pt. Mercer, Pt. Mountrail, Pt. Ward
• Line Patroller/Damage Prevention • BS, Business, University of Maryland
• USAF; New Town City Council • House since 2017
AGRICULTURE; EDUCATION

DISTRICT #5

Randall A. Burckhard

1837 15th Street SW, Minot, ND 58701-6158; raburckhard@nd.gov; (R) Pt. Ward • Retired, SRT Communications Executive • Past President, Minot CVB and MSU Alumni Association; Past Chair, Minot Area Chamber of Commerce; Minot Area Development Corporation; Souris Valley United Way; Task Force 21 Executive Committee; AF Global Strike Command Civic Leaders' Program; MSU Board of Regents; MSU Alumni Golden Award; Rotary Club; Past Member, Minot City Council; Catholic • Married (Pat); 3 Children; 8 Grandchildren • Senate since 2011
INDUSTRY, BUSINESS AND LABOR; POLITICAL SUBDIVISIONS

Roger Brabandt

1317 Third Street SW, Minot, ND 58701-5802; rbrabandt@nd.gov; (R) Pt. Ward • Retired • BS, MSU • Lions Club; Moose Club • Married (Juell); 1 Child • House since 2011
APPROPRIATIONS; APPROPRIATIONS - GOVERNMENT OPERATIONS DIVISION

Scott Louser

1718 Birch Place SW, Minot, ND 58701-7097; sclouser@nd.gov; (R) Pt. Ward • Realtor/Owner; NextHome Legendary Properties • BS & MS, MSU • VP, National Association of Realtors, 2012 • Married (Alexa); 3 Children • House since 2011
GOVERNMENT AND VETERANS AFFAIRS; INDUSTRY, BUSINESS AND LABOR

DISTRICT #6

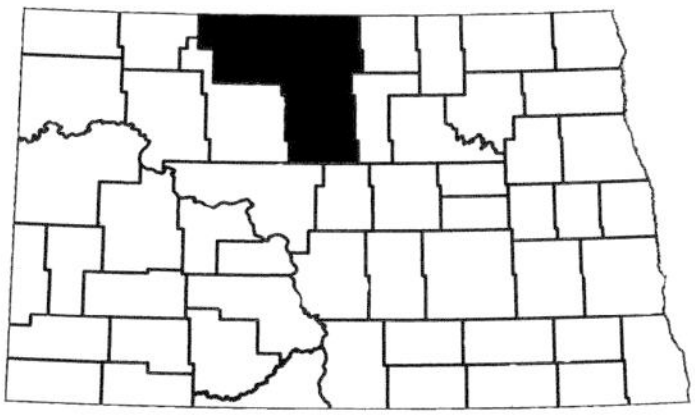

Shawn Vedaa

P.O. Box 550, Velva, ND 58790-0550; svedaa@nd.gov; (R) Bottineau, McHenry, Renville • Grocery Store Owner • Attended MSU • ND Army National Guard • Stanley City Council • Married (Geneil); 5 Children • Senate since 2017
EDUCATION; GOVERNMENT AND VETERANS AFFAIRS

Dick Anderson

1187 77th Street NE, Willow City, ND 58384-9109; dickanderson@nd.gov; (R) Bottineau, McHenry, Renville • Farmer • BA, UND • District Advisor, ND Game and Fish Dept.; Board, Rugby Airport Authority; Board, Rugby Farmers Elevator; Board, North Central Experiment Station; Board, Heart of America Medical Center; Board, All Seasons Water Users; Normal Town Board; Harvest Bowl Award; NDSU McHenry County Extension; McHenry County Conservation Award, 2013 • Married (Susan); 2 Children • House since 2011
ENERGY AND NATURAL RESOURCES; HUMAN SERVICES

Craig A. Johnson

8080 17th Avenue NW, Maxbass, ND 58760-9769; craigjohnson@nd.gov; (R) Bottineau, McHenry, Renville • Farmer and Rancher • BS, Agricultural Engineering, NDSU • Clerk/Treasurer, Chatfield Township; Bottineau County Farmers Union; Trinity Lutheran Church • Married (Julia); 2 Children • House since 2017
GOVERNMENT AND VETERANS AFFAIRS; INDUSTRY, BUSINESS AND LABOR

DISTRICT #7

Nicole Poolman

3609 Bogey Drive, Bismarck, ND 58503-9195; npoolman@nd.gov; (R) Pt. Burleigh • English Teacher, Century High School • BS, Ed, English and Secondary Education, UND • Commission of the States; ND Interagency Coordinating Council; Board, Anne Carlson Center • Married (Jim); 3 Children • Senate since 2013
GOVERNMENT AND VETERANS AFFAIRS; INDUSTRY, BUSINESS AND LABOR

Rick C. Becker

6140 Ponderosa Avenue, Bismarck, ND 58503-9156; rcbecker@nd.gov; (R) Pt. Burleigh • Plastic Surgeon • BS, UND; MD, UND School of Medicine • UND General Surgery Residency; Wayne State University Plastic Surgery Residency; University of Arkansas for Medical Sciences Microvascular and Breast Fellowship • 4 Children • House since 2013
INDUSTRY, BUSINESS AND LABOR; TRANSPORTATION

Jason Dockter

4443 Turnbow Lane, Bismarck, ND 58503-5814; jddockter@nd.gov; (R) Pt. Burleigh • Small Business Owner • BSC; UND • ND Army National Guard • Lions; Faith Lutheran Church • 2 Children • House since 2013
FINANCE AND TAXATION; GOVERNMENT AND VETERANS AFFAIRS

DISTRICT #8

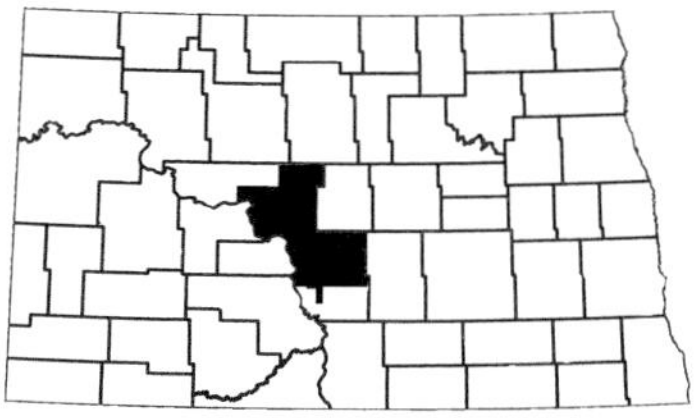

HOWARD C. ANDERSON, JR.

2107 Seventh Street NW, Turtle Lake, ND 58575-9667; hcanderson@nd.gov; (R) Pt. Burleigh, Pt. McLean • Retired Executive Director, ND State Board of Pharmacy; HC Anderson Consulting • Pharmacy, NDSU • Honorary President, NABP; Lions; Rotary; Masons; Eagle Scout; State Health Council; ND Pharmacist Association; Lifetime NRA; DU; Methodist Church • Married (Joan); 4 Sons; 9 Grandchildren • Senate since 2013
HUMAN SERVICES; POLITICAL SUBDIVISIONS

JEFF DELZER

2919 Fifth Street NW, Underwood, ND 58576-9603; jdelzer@nd.gov; (R) Pt. Burleigh, Pt. McLean • Farmer • Attended Dawson Community College • Single • House 1991-1992, since 1995
APPROPRIATIONS

VERNON LANING

4121 78th Avenue NE, Bismarck, ND 58503-6396; vrlaning@nd.gov; (R) Pt. Burleigh, Pt. McLean • Retired • BS, Mechanical Engineering, NDSU • US Army Active Duty 1971-1974 • Mayor of Stanton; City Councilman; Park Board; Chairman, Mercer County Planning and Zoning Commission • Married (Rose); 4 Children • House since 2013
GOVERNMENT AND VETERANS AFFAIRS; INDUSTRY, BUSINESS AND LABOR

DISTRICT #9

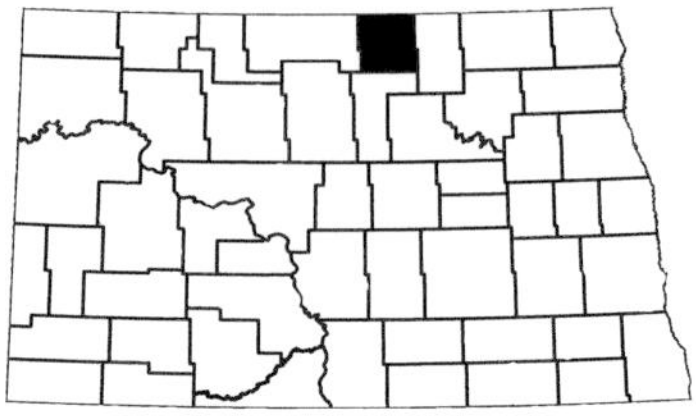

RICHARD MARCELLAIS

301 Laite Loop NE, Belcourt, ND 58316-3877; rmarcellais@nd.gov; (D) Rolette • AAS, Business Administration; Structural Drafting Degree • US Army, Vietnam Veteran • Chairman, Turtle Mountain Band of Chippewa, 2008-2010; Vice Commander, American Legion Central Region; American Legion Post #262; Veteran of Foreign Wars Post 4516; NARFE Charter #2168; ND Native American Hall of Honor • Married (Betty); 2 Children • Senate since 2007

GOVERNMENT AND VETERANS AFFAIRS; INDUSTRY, BUSINESS AND LABOR

TRACY BOE

5125 89th Street, Mylo, ND 58353-9438; tboe@nd.gov; (D) Rolette • Farmer • President, Northern Plains Electric Cooperative; ND Farm Bureau; ND Farmers Union; ND Grain Growers; Our Saviors Lutheran Church • Married (Sandy) • House since 2003

APPROPRIATIONS; APPROPRIATIONS - EDUCATION AND ENVIRONMENT DIVISION

MARVIN E. NELSON

P.O. Box 577, Rolla, ND 58367-0577; menelson@nd.gov; (D) Rolette • Agricultural Consultant • AS, Agriculture, NDSU; BBIF, BS, Entomology, NDSU • ND Farm Bureau; ND Farmers Union; ND Agricultural Consultant's Association; AHEC; ND Stockmen's Association; Church of the Lutheran Brethren in America; Ebenezer Lutheran Brethren Church • Married (Susan); 2 Children • House since 2011

JUDICIARY; TRANSPORTATION

DISTRICT #10

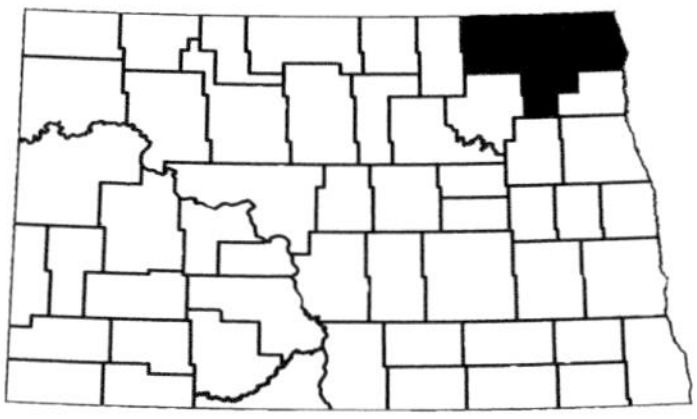

Janne Myrdal

jmyrdal@nd.gov; (R) Cavalier, Pembina, Pt. Walsh • Homemaker, Farmer • Valley Edinburg School Board; Board, CWA; NDGOP Rules Committee; Board, Pembina Gorge Foundation • Married (Mark) • Senate since 2017
AGRICULTURE; JUDICIARY

Chuck Damschen

9461 80th Street NE, Hampden, ND 58338-9351; cdamschen@nd.gov; (R) Cavalier, Pembina, Pt. Walsh • Clerk and Assessor, Storlie Township • Hampden High School • Board, Cavalier County Water Resource; Member, Pembina County JDA; Ex-officio Director, LAND; Zoar Lutheran Church • Married (Alice); 3 Children • House since 2005
ENERGY AND NATURAL RESOURCES; HUMAN SERVICES

David Monson

P.O. Box 8, Osnabrock, ND 58269-0008; dmonson@nd.gov; (R) Cavalier, Pembina, Pt. Walsh • Farmer; Retired School Administrator; Retired Insurance Agent/Owner • AA, UND-Williston; BS, UND; MEd, UND • Speaker of the House - 2008-2010; Asst. Majority Leader - 1998-2008; Boards: Pres., Family Mutual Ins. Co.; Pres., Dovre Lutheran Church; North American Industrial Hemp Council; ND Atmospheric Resource Board; NE ND Heritage Assoc.; Past Boards: Prairie Public Broadcasting; Pres., North Central Council of School TV; Pres., Upper Valley Special Education Unit; Pres., Osnabrock School District; Memberships: Past Grand Chancellor, Knights of Pythias - Life Member; Eagles; ND Pulse Growers; Farm Bureau; Northern Canola Growers; NRA - Life Member; National Wildlife Federation - Life Member; Legislator of the Year: ND Township Officers - 2011; ND Career and Technical Education - 2007 • Married (Mary); 3 Sons, 5 Grandchildren • House since 1993
APPROPRIATIONS; APPROPRIATIONS - EDUCATION AND ENVIRONMENT DIVISION

DISTRICT #11

Tim Mathern

429 16th Avenue South, Fargo, ND 58103-4329; tmathern@nd.gov; (D) Pt. Cass • Director of Public Policy, Prairie St. John's • BA, NDSU; MSW, University of Nebraska; MPA, Harvard University • Board, UND School of Medicine and Health Sciences; CSG Health and Human Services; Prairie Roots Food Cooperative; YMCA Child Care Committee; Commission on National and Community Service; Advocacy Award, National Association of Psychiatric Health Systems; Mental Health Service Award, Psychiatric Society; MADD Legislator of the Year; Golden Apple Award, Council of Educational Leaders; Affordable Housing Award; EMS Vision Award; Roman Catholic • Married; 4 Children; 5 Grandchildren • Senate since 1987
APPROPRIATIONS

Gretchen Dobervich

1625 23rd Street South, Fargo, ND 58103-3722; gdobervich@nd.gov; (D) Pt. Cass • Policy Project Manager, American Indian Public Health Resource Center, NDSU • BSW, MSU; Attending NDSU • Chair, ND Rural Health Association; American Legion Auxiliary; ND Public Health Association; ND Farmers Union; Awesome Foundation Cass Clay; Pierce Congregational Church • Married (Eric) • House since 2016
INDUSTRY, BUSINESS AND LABOR; TRANSPORTATION

Ron Guggisberg

1621 17th Street South, Fargo, ND 58103-4027; rguggisberg@nd.gov; (D) Pt. Cass • Fire Department Captain • House since 2011
EDUCATION; POLITICAL SUBDIVISIONS

DISTRICT #12

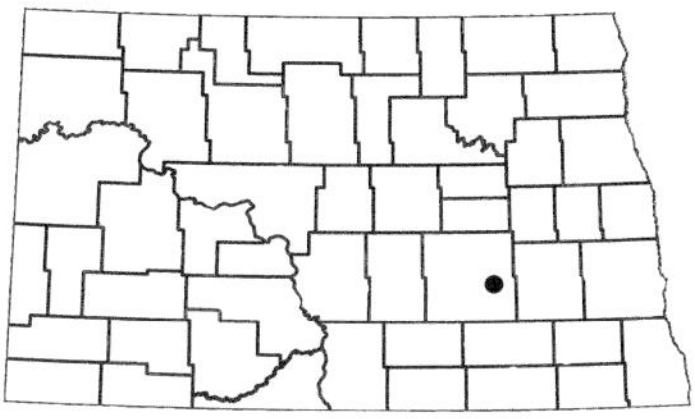

JOHN GRABINGER

1008 Eighth Avenue NE, Jamestown, ND 58401-3507; jgrabinger@nd.gov; (D) Pt. Stutsman • Owner, Grabinger Marine • Jamestown High School • Lifetime/Honorary Member, Jamestown Volunteer Fire Department; Jamestown City Council; Former President, St. John's Academy School Board; St. James Basilica Church • Married (Debra); 1 Child • Senate since 2013

APPROPRIATIONS

JIM GRUENEICH

3051 83 1/2 Avenue SE, Jamestown, ND 58401-9600; jgrueneich@nd.gov; (R) Pt. Stutsman • Business Owner • Alexandria Tech College • US Air Force • Elks; Shriners; Jamestown Clowns • Married (Naomi); 3 Children • House since 2017

FINANCE AND TAXATION; TRANSPORTATION

BERNIE SATROM

P.O. Box 950, Jamestown, ND 58402-0950; blsatrom@nd.gov; (R) Pt. Stutsman • President, Maranatha • BS, Business Finance, Montana State University • Salvation Army Advisory Board; Gideons Jail Ministry; Elder, Temple Baptist Church • Married (Dianne); 4 Children • House since 2017

AGRICULTURE; JUDICIARY

DISTRICT #13

Judy Lee

1822 Brentwood Court, West Fargo, ND 58078-4204; jlee@nd.gov; (R) Pt. Cass • Retired Real Estate Broker • BS, Medical Technology, UND • Board, 2015, UND Masters in Public Health; Board, Vocational Training Center; President Pro Tempore, 2007; Board, CHAND; First Lutheran Church • Widow; 2 Children; 3 Grandchildren • Senate since 1995
HUMAN SERVICES; POLITICAL SUBDIVISIONS

Kim Koppelman

513 First Avenue NW, West Fargo, ND 58078-1101; kkoppelman@nd.gov; (R) Pt. Cass • President/CEO, Koppelman & Associates, LLC • NDSCS • BILLD Fellow; Toll Fellow; Past National Chairman, Council of State Governments (CSG); Chairman, CSG Suggested State Legislation Committee; Past: City Councilman; Executive Committee, NCSL and CSG; Committee Chair, MLC, CSG Public Safety & Justice Task Force; Co-Chairman, Interstate Compact on Transmission Line Siting; Founder/Chairman, National Interbranch Summit of the States; Founder/Chairman, Interbranch Working Group; R Street Board; ALEC; Chairman, VCLA Board; Church Elder/Chairman; Legislative Awards: NDSAA, SBAND; Stueben Eagle Leadership Award; CSG Champion Award; NDFA Champion Award • Married (Torey); 3 Children • House since 1994
JUDICIARY; POLITICAL SUBDIVISIONS

Christopher D. Olson

138 West Beaton Drive, West Fargo, ND 58078-2657; cdolson@nd.gov; (R) Pt. Cass • President, Treasure Island Coins, Inc. • Army Infantry, Active Duty (Former) • Immanuel Lutheran Church-Missouri Synod • Married (Lisa); 5 Children • House since 2015
FINANCE AND TAXATION; GOVERNMENT AND VETERANS AFFAIRS

DISTRICT #14

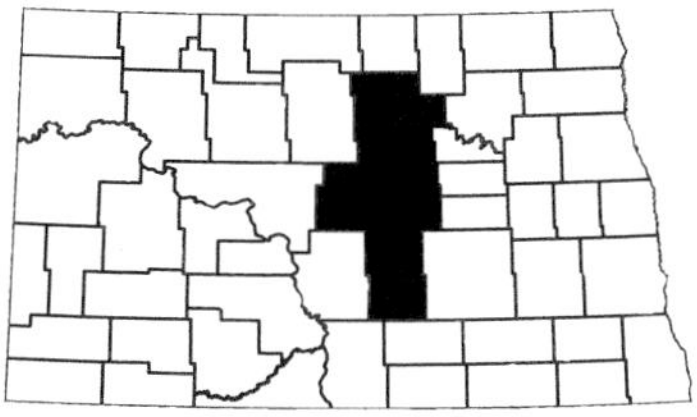

Jerry Klein

P.O. Box 265, Fessenden, ND 58438-0265; jklein@nd.gov; (R) Pt. Benson, Kidder, Pierce, Sheridan, Wells • Retired Grocery Store Owner, 35 years • BSC; U of Mary • Assistant Majority Leader since 2013; President Pro Tempore, 2009-2011; Past Board, Carrington Health Center; Member, Harvey Knights of Columbus; President, Fessenden Economic Development; Past Chair, ND Grocers Association; Past President, Civic & Commerce Association; ND Grocer of the Year, 2005; Fessenden Fire Department; Past Jaycees; Past Kiwanis; St. Augustine Catholic Church • Married (Bev); 4 Children; 8 Grandchildren • Senate since 1997
AGRICULTURE; INDUSTRY, BUSINESS AND LABOR

Jon O. Nelson

420 Sixth Avenue SE, Rugby, ND 58368-2320; jonelson@nd.gov; (R) Pt. Benson, Kidder, Pierce, Sheridan, Wells • Farmer • Attended MSU & Dakota College at Bottineau • Executive Committee, ND Rural Water Association; ND Farm Bureau; State Public Finance & Education Committee; Board, All Seasons Water Users; Wolford Wildlife Club; Wolford School Board, 12 years; Moving the Marble Award, American Cancer Society; Past Board, Heart of America Hospital; Wolford Lutheran Church Council • Married (Shirley "Sid"); 3 Children • House since 1997
APPROPRIATIONS; APPROPRIATIONS - HUMAN RESOURCES DIVISION

Robin Weisz

2639 First Street SE, Hurdsfield, ND 58451-9029; rweisz@nd.gov; (R) Pt. Benson, Kidder, Pierce, Sheridan, Wells • Farmer, Businessman • Attended UND • Chairman, Lynn Township; BILLD Fellowship, 1999; Legislator of the Year, NDEMSA, 1999, 2011; Legislator of the Year, NDTOA, 2003, 2009; Legislator of the Year, MHA, 2006; Henry Toll Fellow, 2006; Farm Bureau • Married (Lori); 2 Children • House since 1997
HUMAN SERVICES; TRANSPORTATION

DISTRICT #15

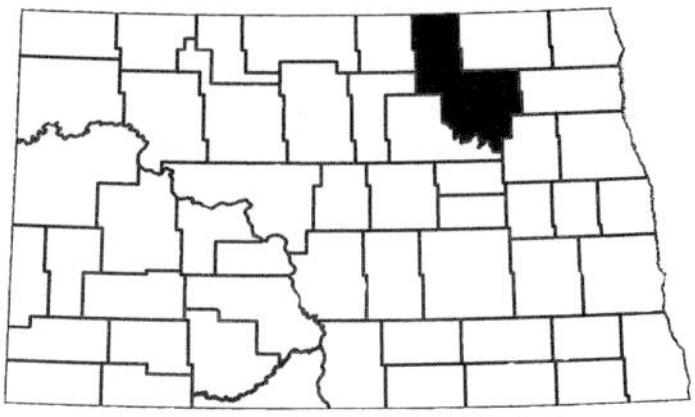

DAVE OEHLKE

125 Woodlea Drive, Devils Lake, ND 58301-8545; doehlke@nd.gov; (R) Ramsey, Towner • Insurance Agent, CIC • BA, Concordia College • Master Graduate of Rapport Leadership Int'l; Lake Region Search & Rescue Team; Elks; Rotary • Married (Vicki); 2 Children • Senate since 2007
APPROPRIATIONS

DENNIS JOHNSON

7871 45th Street NE, Devils Lake, ND 58301-9089; djohnson@nd.gov; (R) Ramsey, Towner • Farmer • Vietnam Veteran; US Navy Seabees • MHEC, Commissioner; Farm Bureau; Farmers Union; ND Stockmen's Association; ND Grain Growers; American Legion; VFW • Married (Donna); 3 Children; 2 Grandchildren • House since 1993
AGRICULTURE; EDUCATION

GREG WESTLIND

205 13th Street, Cando, ND 58324-6613; gwestlind@nd.gov; (R) Ramsey, Towner • Retired Farmer/Businessman • AA, Agriculture Science; BA, Arts, Brooks Institute of Photography, Santa Barbara, CA • National Guard • 9 Years, Cando School Board; 11 Years, Towner County Medical Center, Board of Directors • Married (Janet); 2 Children • House since 2016
HUMAN SERVICES; TRANSPORTATION

DISTRICT #16

David A. Clemens

1682 Oakwood Drive, West Fargo, ND 58078-4315; dclemens@nd.gov; (R) Pt. Cass • Owner, Clemens Transport • BS, Industrial Engineering, NDSU • US Army, Vietnam Veteran • Chairman, Republican Party District 16; VFW; American Legion; NRA • Married (Jody); 4 Children • Senate since 2017

HUMAN SERVICES; TRANSPORTATION

Ben Koppelman

205 36 1/2 Avenue Place East, West Fargo, ND 58078-7931; bkoppelman@nd.gov; (R) Pt. Cass • Building Contractor • Attended NDSU • West Fargo School Board, 2008-2012; School Board President, 2011-2012 • Married (Julie); 2 Children • House since 2013

FINANCE AND TAXATION; GOVERNMENT AND VETERANS AFFAIRS

Andrew Marschall

4469 Santiago Boulevard South, Fargo, ND 58103-1069; amarschall@nd.gov; (R) Pt. Cass • Small Business Owner, Three Lyons Pub • BS, Occupational Education; Major in Business and Automotive Tech • Air National Guard, 2.5 Years; Air Force; 24.5 Total Military Service • DAV; VFW; American Legion; NRA • 1 Child • House since 2017

EDUCATION; ENERGY AND NATURAL RESOURCES

DISTRICT #17

Ray Holmberg
621 High Plains Court, Grand Forks, ND 58201-7717; rholmberg@nd.gov; (R) Pt. Grand Forks • Retired School Counselor • WICHE Commissioner; Member, MHEC Legislative Advisory Committee; Member, GF Chamber • Single; 2 Children; 4 Grandchildren • Senate since 1977
APPROPRIATIONS

Mark S. Owens
5865 Fountain Vista Drive, Grand Forks, ND 58201-2820; mowens@nd.gov; (R) Pt. Grand Forks • Associate Vice President, Transportation Services, Iteris Inc. • BS, Troy State; MS, Central Michigan University • USAF Retired • Lifetime Member, Disabled American Veterans and NRA; Member, Intelligent Transportation Society (ITS) of America; Past President, Rocky Mountain Chapter of ITS America; Vice Chairman, First Liberty Federal Credit Union; Past President, Current Member, Grand Forks Optimist Club; Cornerstone Baptist Church • 1 Child • House 2005-2008, since 2011
EDUCATION; TRANSPORTATION

Mark Sanford
675 Vineyard Drive, Grand Forks, ND 58201-2904; masanford@nd.gov; (R) Pt. Grand Forks • Retired School Administrator • BS, Math and History, MSU; MEd. EA, UND; Ed.D. School Leadership, UND • Married (Gloria); 2 Children • House since 2011
APPROPRIATIONS; APPROPRIATIONS - EDUCATION AND ENVIRONMENT DIVISION

DISTRICT #18

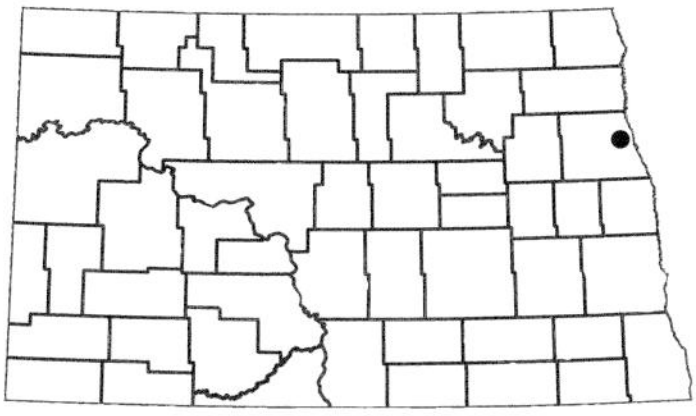

Scott Meyer

1624 Seventh Avenue North, Grand Forks, ND 58203-3010; scottmeyer@nd.gov; (R) Pt. Grand Forks • Home Mortgage Consultant, Cornerstone Mortgage • BS, Psychology, UND • Single • Senate since 2017

FINANCE AND TAXATION; GOVERNMENT AND VETERANS AFFAIRS

Corey Mock

P.O. Box 12542, Grand Forks, ND 58208-2542; crmock@nd.gov; (D) Pt. Grand Forks • Executive Director, Greater Grand Forks Young Professionals; Owner, Dr. Eliot's Twice Sold Tales • BA, History (Magna Cum Laude), UND • Board of Trustees, Grand Forks Public Library; Board, Evolve Grand Forks; Board, Kennedy Memorial Foundation; Grand Forks/East Grand Forks Chamber of Commerce; Sons of Norway; Rotary International; ND Farmers Union; American Legion Boys State Staff; BILLD Fellowship; State Legislative Leadership Foundation, Emerging Leaders Program Fellowship; Global Bridges Alumni • House since 2009

EDUCATION; ENERGY AND NATURAL RESOURCES

Steve Vetter

804 South 17th Street, Grand Forks, ND 58201-4241; smvetter@nd.gov; (R) Pt. Grand Forks • Real Estate Appraiser • Attending U of Mary • House since 2017

GOVERNMENT AND VETERANS AFFAIRS; JUDICIARY

DISTRICT #19

Tom Campbell

15135 County Road 11, Grafton, ND 58237-8802; tomcampbell@nd.gov; (R) Pt. Grand Forks, Pt. Walsh • Farming/Businessman; Co-Founder, Campbell Farms • BS, Economics, NDSU • Chairman, Choice Financial Banks Holding Co; Board/Partner, Campbell Property Group; Board, NDSU Alumni Association; Board, Unity Medical Center; Past Chairman, Florida Potato Growers Association; Past Director, National Potato Board; Board, Mission for Homeless; Board, Teen Challenge; National Outstanding Farmer Award • Married (Lori); 2 Children • Senate since 2013

INDUSTRY, BUSINESS AND LABOR; TRANSPORTATION

Gary Paur

2710 28th Street NE, Gilby, ND 58235-9706; gpaur@nd.gov; (R) Pt. Grand Forks, Pt. Walsh • Farmer • UND • Past President, Northarvest Bean Growers Association; Knights of Columbus; Past Chairman, District 19 Republicans; Farm Bureau; St. Timothy's Catholic Church • Married (Ruth); 3 Children • House since 2011

JUDICIARY; TRANSPORTATION

Wayne A. Trottier

115 North Lincoln Street, Northwood, ND 58267-4010; wtrottier@nd.gov; (R) Pt. Grand Forks, Pt. Walsh • Auctioneer • US Army • Past Board, North Dakota State Fair; Past Commissioner, City Council; Past Legion Commander • Married (Gladys); 1 Child; 2 Grandchildren • House since 2011

AGRICULTURE; FINANCE AND TAXATION

DISTRICT #20

Arne Osland

15333 13th Street NE, Mayville, ND 58257-9225; aosland@nd.gov; (R) Pt. Cass, Pt. Grand Forks, Traill • Retired Farmer/Businessman • BS, Mayville State • Traill County Commissioner; ND Society of CPA; American Institute of CPAs; Goose River Masons; Kem Shriner; ND Farm Bureau; ND Stockmen's Assoc. • Married (Pat); 4 Children • Senate since 2017

AGRICULTURE; JUDICIARY

Richard G. Holman

622 153rd Avenue NE, Mayville, ND 58257-9000; rholman@nd.gov; (D) Pt. Cass, Pt. Grand Forks, Traill • Retired Math Teacher, Farmer, College Professor • BS, Mayville State; MS, Bemidji State; EdD, UND • Board, AHEC; Red River HS Foundation; Board, Center for Rural Health RN to BSN Nursing Program; MSU Distinguished Alumni and Professor Emeritus; Hillsboro Kiwanis; Goose River Masonic Lodge; Gran Lutheran Church • Married (Marilyn); 3 Children • House since 2009

APPROPRIATIONS; APPROPRIATIONS - HUMAN RESOURCES DIVISION

Aaron Mcwilliams

P.O. Box 1, Hillsboro, ND 58045-0001; amcwilliams@nd.gov; (R) Pt. Cass, Pt. Grand Forks, Traill • Business Owner • BA, Psychology, Communications, Theology • Fargo, "The 100" • Married (Sara); 1 Child • House since 2017

AGRICULTURE; HUMAN SERVICES

DISTRICT #21

CAROLYN C. NELSON

210 11th Street North, Apt. #205, Fargo, ND 58102-4687; cnelson@nd.gov; (D) Pt. Cass • Senior Lecturer, Emeritus of Mathematics, NDSU • BS & MS, NDSU • President, National Federation of Music Clubs; Board, International Music Camp; Board, Consensus Council, Inc.; Past President, Fargo Board of Education; Past President, ND PTA; American Guild of English Handbell Ringers; LWV; AAUW; First United Methodist Church • Married (Gil); 3 Children; 9 Grandchildren • House 1987 and 1993; Senate since 1995
JUDICIARY; TRANSPORTATION

KATHY HOGAN

710 South University Drive, Fargo, ND 58103-2632; khogan@nd.gov; (D) Pt. Cass • Retired • BS, Jamestown College; MS, NDSU • Board, Villa Nazareth; ND Assistive; Presentation Associates; St. Anthony of Padua • Married (Dennis); 2 Children • House since 2009
AGRICULTURE; FINANCE AND TAXATION

MARY SCHNEIDER

1011 Eighth Street South, Fargo, ND 58103-2725; mschneider@nd.gov; (D) Pt. Cass • Attorney • NUI Galway; Emory University School of Law; UND School of Law; BS, Sociology, NDSU • Bush Foundation Fellow, 2004-2005; MN State Assembly Delegate; President, County Bar Association; National ABA Delegate; YWCA Lifetime Achievement Award; Champion of Justice Award; Human Rights Award; Soroptimists International • Married (Mark); 2 Children • House since 2015
GOVERNMENT AND VETERANS AFFAIRS; HUMAN SERVICES

DISTRICT #22

Gary A. Lee
P.O. Box 3, Casselton, ND 58012-0003; galee@nd.gov; (R) Pt. Cass • Small Business Partner • BA, NDSU • Vietnam Veteran • Casselton City Council; Central Cass School Board; Past Director, Cass Rural Water Users; EFC Church • Married (Joan); 2 Children; 5 Grandchildren • Senate since 2001
APPROPRIATIONS

Michael Howe
1011 Westport Parkway, West Fargo, ND 58078-8291; mchowe@nd.gov; (R) Pt. Cass • Farmer/Business Owner • BS, NDSU • ND Grain Growers; ND Corn Growers; ND Farm Bureau • Single • House since 2017
AGRICULTURE; FINANCE AND TAXATION

Brandy Pyle
P.O. Box 337, Casselton, ND 58012-0337; bpyle@nd.gov; (R) Pt. Cass • Self Employed • Finance, Carlson School of Management, University of Minnesota • Former MN Army National Guard • Cass County Park Board; RLND Class VII; Casselton Business Association; Westminster Presbyterian Church • Married (Nicholas); 4 Children • House since 2017
EDUCATION; POLITICAL SUBDIVISIONS

DISTRICT #23

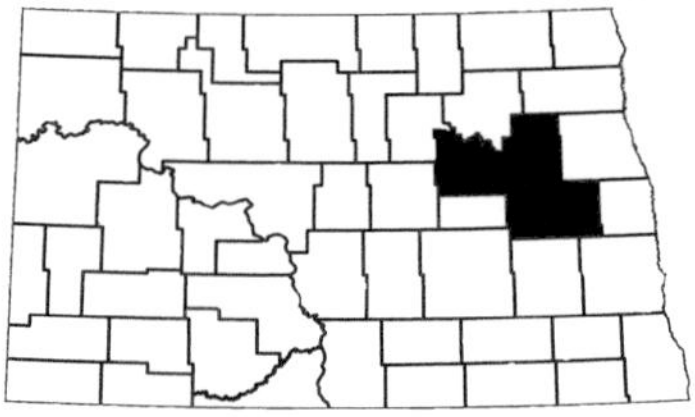

Joan Heckaman

322 Second Avenue North, New Rockford, ND 58356-1712; jheckaman@nd.gov; (D) Pt. Benson, Eddy, Griggs, Nelson, Steele • Retired Teacher • BS, Ed, VCSU; MS, Special Education, MSU • Board/Secretary, Central ND Steam Threshers; Governor's Autism Task Force; Legislative Procedures and Arrangements; Eastern Star; New Rockford Golf Club; New Rockford Book Club; Eagles Auxiliary; First Lutheran Church • Married (Dewey); 4 Children; 10 Grandchildren • Senate since 2007
HUMAN SERVICES

Bill Devlin

P.O. Box 505, Finley, ND 58230-0505; bdevlin@nd.gov; (R) Pt. Benson, Eddy, Griggs, Nelson, Steele • Former Newspaper Publisher • Attended Mayville State College • Director, Nodak Mutual Insurance Company; Past President, ND Newspaper Association; Distinguished Service Award; ND Long Term Care Association; Legislative Service Award; ARC of ND; Sunshine Award, ND Newspaper Association; BILLD Fellow, CSG Midwest; ND Farm Bureau • Married (Margie); 2 Children; 5 Grandchildren • House 1997-2005, since 2011
ENERGY AND NATURAL RESOURCES; HUMAN SERVICES

Don Vigesaa

P.O. Box 763, Cooperstown, ND 58425-0763; dwvigesaa@nd.gov; (R) Pt. Benson, Eddy, Griggs, Nelson, Steele • Auto Dealer • BS, Business Economics, NDSU • Farm Bureau; Elder, Zion Lutheran Church • Married (Cheryl); 3 Children • House since 2003
APPROPRIATIONS; APPROPRIATIONS - GOVERNMENT OPERATIONS DIVISION

DISTRICT #24

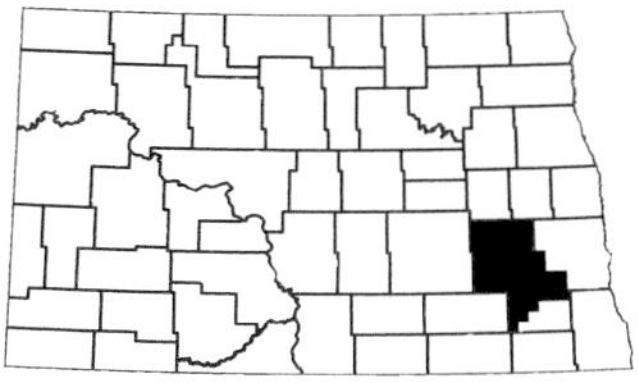

Larry J. Robinson

3584 Sheyenne Circle, Valley City, ND 58072-9545; lrobinson@nd.gov; (D) Barnes, Pt. Cass, Pt. Ransom • Executive Director, University Advancement, VCSU • BS, VCSU; MS, NDSU • Past President, Valley City Area Chamber of Commerce; Barnes County Wildlife Federation; Valley City Area Chamber of Commerce; Governor's Alcohol & Drug Prevention Advisory Task Force; Board, MHA; Drug Court Advisory Committee; Legislative Council, 1991-2014; Member, VCSU-V-500; Century Club Scholarship; Organizations: Elks; Eagles; Knights of Columbus; Kiwanis; St. Catherine's Catholic Church • Married (Mary Lee); 2 Children; 3 Grandchildren • Senate since 1989
APPROPRIATIONS

Daniel Johnston

5807 Valley Road, Kathryn, ND 58049-9308; dljohnston@nd.gov; (R) Barnes, Pt. Cass, Pt. Ransom • Self Employed • BA, Interdisciplinary Studies, Accounting/Religion • Army, Active 1996-2008 • VFW; DAV; American Legion • Married (Wendi) • House since 2017
GOVERNMENT AND VETERANS AFFAIRS; JUDICIARY

Dwight Kiefert

3721 115th Avenue SE, Valley City, ND 58072-9312; dhkiefert@nd.gov; (R) Barnes, Pt. Cass, Pt. Ransom • Farmer, Contractor • Valley City High School • Married (Robbin); 3 Children • House since 2013
AGRICULTURE; HUMAN SERVICES

DISTRICT #25

Larry Luick

17945 101st Street SE, Fairmount, ND 58030-9522; lluick@nd.gov; (R) Pt. Cass, Pt. Richland • Farmer, Excavation Contractor • AAS, Diesel Mechanic, NDSCS • Past President, Fairmount Public School Board; Past Director, Organic Crop Improvement Association (OCIA); Past Member, OCIA Internal Review Committee; Past Director, South East Education Cooperative; Vice-chair, Agriculture Interim Committee, 2014; Water Topics Interim Committee, 2014; ND Representative, US Ag Summit, 2012-2015; International Legislative Forum, Steering Committee Director; Red River Basin Commission • Married (Yolanda); 5 Children
• Senate since 2011
AGRICULTURE; JUDICIARY

Alisa Mitskog

1504 Oakwood Avenue, Wahpeton, ND 58075-3553; amitskog@nd.gov; (D) Pt. Cass, Pt. Richland • Chiropractor • NDSCS; UND; Logan College of Chiropractic • Breckenridge/Wahpeton Community Foundation; Past President, Wahpeton City Council • Married (Allen); 3 Children
• House since 2015
ENERGY AND NATURAL RESOURCES; FINANCE AND TAXATION

Cynthia Schreiber-Beck

1251 Pegasus Road, Wahpeton, ND 58075-4868; cschreiberbeck@nd.gov; (R) Pt. Cass, Pt. Richland • Business Owner • BS, Speech Language Pathology • ND Aeronautics Commission; Board, Fargo Air Museum; Executive Director, ND Agricultural Aviation Association • 1 Child
• House since 2015
AGRICULTURE; EDUCATION

DISTRICT #26

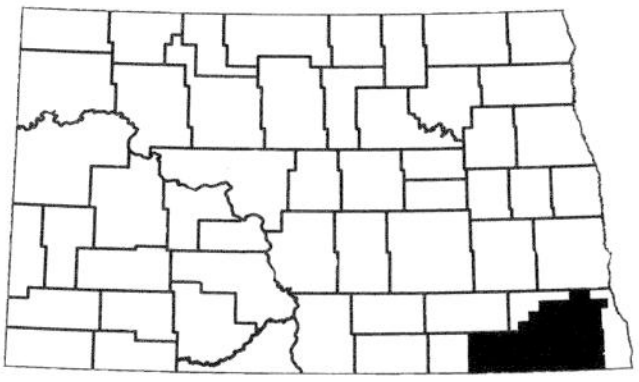

Jim Dotzenrod

P.O. Box 69, Wyndmere, ND 58081-0069; jdotzenrod@nd.gov; (D) Pt. Dickey, Pt. Ransom, Pt. Richland, Sargent • Farmer • BS, Engineering, NDSU • Air Force; ND Air National Guard • American Legion; Wyndmere Lutheran Church • 2 Children • Senate 1978-1994, since 2009
FINANCE AND TAXATION; POLITICAL SUBDIVISIONS

Sebastian Ertelt

906 Ash Street, Lisbon, ND 58054-4316; sertelt@nd.gov; (R) Pt. Dickey, Pt. Ransom, Pt. Richland, Sargent • Manufacturing Engineer • MBA, Management, U of Mary; BS, Mechanical Engineering, NDSU • Eagles Post #2968 • Single • House since 2017
FINANCE AND TAXATION; POLITICAL SUBDIVISIONS

Kathy Skroch

10105 155th Avenue SE, Lidgerwood, ND 58053-9761; kskroch@nd.gov; (R) Pt. Dickey, Pt. Ransom, Pt. Richland, Sargent • Farmer/Rancher; Restorative Nurse/CNA; School Bus Route/Activity Driver; Co-Manager/ Owner, Vinnie's Mud Bog, LLC • CNA Certification, Moorhead Technical College • Lidgerwood Public School Board; Board, Lidgerwood Ambulance; ND Long Term Care Assoc. Certificate of Recognition; Nominated, CNA of the Year 2016; American Legion Auxiliary • Married (Michael); 7 Children • House since 2017
AGRICULTURE; HUMAN SERVICES

DISTRICT #27

Jonathan Casper

P.O. Box 6457, Fargo, ND 58109-6457; jcasper@nd.gov; (R) Pt. Cass • Attorney • BA, Saint John's University; JD, Creighton University School of Law • FMWF Chamber of Commerce • Single • Senate since 2015
INDUSTRY, BUSINESS AND LABOR; TRANSPORTATION

Thomas Beadle

4266 Russet Avenue South, Fargo, ND 58104-8429; tbeadle@nd.gov; (R) Pt. Cass • Commercial Broker, KW Commercial Real Estate • BA, Business Economics, Concordia College • State Debate Coach of the Year, NDHSAA, 2009 • Married (Shana) • House since 2011
INDUSTRY, BUSINESS AND LABOR; POLITICAL SUBDIVISIONS

Randy Boehning

5599 36th Avenue South, Fargo, ND 58104-5249; rboehning@nd.gov; (R) Pt. Cass • Self Employed, General Construction • AAS, Business Administration, NDSCS • Past Advisory Board, Department of Corrections Rough Rider Industries; Past Squad Leader and President, Hankinson Ambulance • Single • House since 2003
APPROPRIATIONS; APPROPRIATIONS - GOVERNMENT OPERATIONS DIVISION

DISTRICT #28

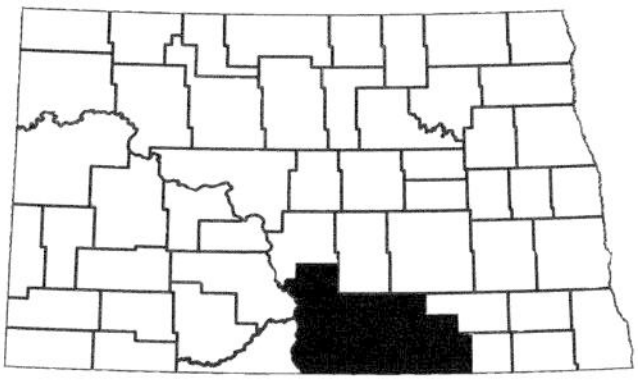

Robert Erbele

6512 51st Avenue SE, Lehr, ND 58460-9149; rerbele@nd.gov; (R) Pt. Burleigh, Pt. Dickey, Emmons, Pt. LaMoure, Logan, McIntosh • Rancher • University Studies, Ag Econ, Animal Science and Music, NDSU • ND Stockmen's Association; President, Prairie Bible Camp (Lehr); WICHE Veterinary Advisory Council; UND Medical Advisory Board; Lay Leader, United Methodist Church • Married (Susan); 4 Children • Senate since 2001

APPROPRIATIONS

Mike Brandenburg

8044 County Road 34, Edgeley, ND 58433-9761; mbrandenburg@nd.gov; (R) Pt. Burleigh, Pt. Dickey, Emmons, Pt. LaMoure, Logan, McIntosh • Farmer • Edgeley High School • North Dakota National Guard • Trump Ag Advisory Group; Nora Township Supervisor; Board, ND Chemical Harmonization; Board, Dakota Prairie Ag; Board, LaMoure County Farm Bureau; Farmers Union; Zions Club; Zion Lutheran Church Council • Married (Lovice); 6 Children; 14 Grandchildren • House 1997-2001, since 2005

APPROPRIATIONS; APPROPRIATIONS - GOVERNMENT OPERATIONS DIVISION

Jeffrey J. Magrum

P.O. Box 467, Hazelton, ND 58544-0467; jmagrum@nd.gov; (R) Pt. Burleigh, Pt. Dickey, Emmons, Pt. LaMoure, Logan, McIntosh • Self Employed, Businessman, Rancher • Environmental Systems, NDSSS; Licensed Master Plumber • Mayor, City of Hazelton; Emmons County Commissioner; Beaver Valley Horse Club; ND Water Well Association; Voices for Lake Oahe • Married (Donna); 2 Children • House since 2017

AGRICULTURE; JUDICIARY

DISTRICT #29

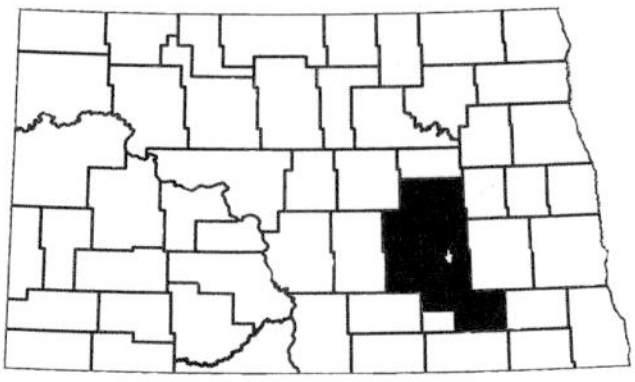

Terry M. Wanzek

900 Seventh Avenue SW, Jamestown, ND 58401-4542; tmwanzek@nd.gov; (R) Foster, Pt. LaMoure, Pt. Stutsman • Farmer; Rancher; Businessman • Cum Laude BA, Jamestown College; Texas A&M TEPAP Graduate • Board, Global Farmers Network; Community Leadership Award, GNDC; Kernel Award, NDGGA; Past President, Board, ND Grain Growers; Board, Nodak Mutual Insurance; Knights of Columbus; Farm Bureau; NAWG; Basilica of St. James Catholic Church • Married (Janice); 3 Children; 3 Grandchildren • House 1993-1994; Senate 1995-2002, since 2007
APPROPRIATIONS

Craig Headland

4950 92nd Avenue SE, Montpelier, ND 58472-9630; cheadland@nd.gov; (R) Foster, Pt. LaMoure, Pt. Stutsman • Farmer • Attended MSU Moorhead and NDSU • Elks Club; Montpelier Lutheran Church • Married (Dawn); 1 Child • House since 2003
AGRICULTURE; FINANCE AND TAXATION

Chet Pollert

151 Crossroads Estates Drive, Carrington, ND 58421-8919; cpollert@nd.gov; (R) Foster, Pt. LaMoure, Pt. Stutsman • Owner/Operator, G & R Grain and Feed, New Rockford, ND • Trinity Lutheran Church • Married (Jo) • House since 1999
APPROPRIATIONS; APPROPRIATIONS - HUMAN RESOURCES DIVISION

DISTRICT #30

Diane Larson

2525 Larson Road, Bismarck, ND 58504-8926; dklarson@nd.gov; (R) Pt. Burleigh • Retired, Youth Worker, Bismarck Police Department • AA, BSC; BS, Ed, UND • National Conference of State Legislatures: Co-chair, Law, Criminal Justice and Public Safety Committee, Ex-officio member; ND State Council for Interstate Juvenile Supervision; Interstate Commission on Juveniles; Supreme Court's Judiciary Standards Committee; Governor's Juvenile Justice Advisory Group; State Historical Board • Married (Greg); 2 Children; 4 Grandchildren • House 2013-2016; Senate since 2017

JUDICIARY; POLITICAL SUBDIVISIONS

Glenn Bosch

3613 Mayflower Circle, Bismarck, ND 58504-6487; gdbosch@nd.gov; (R) Pt. Burleigh • Executive VP, AVI Systems • AAS, Electronic Technology, BSC • Corpus Christi Catholic Church • Married (Julie); 2 Children • House since 2017

ENERGY AND NATURAL RESOURCES; INDUSTRY, BUSINESS AND LABOR

Mike Nathe

1899 Bonn Boulevard, Bismarck, ND 58504-7019; mrnathe@nd.gov; (R) Pt. Burleigh • Owner, Bismarck Funeral Home • BS, Mortuary Science, U of M • Kiwanis; NRA; NFIB; CANA; BILLD • Married (Karen); 3 Children • House since 2009

APPROPRIATIONS; APPROPRIATIONS - GOVERNMENT OPERATIONS DIVISION

DISTRICT #31

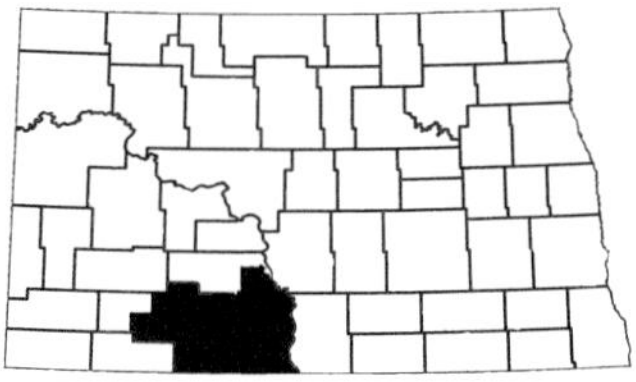

Donald Schaible

9115 Highway 21, Mott, ND 58646-9200; dgschaible@nd.gov; (R) Grant, Pt. Hettinger, Pt. Morton, Sioux • Farmer • AS, Agriculture, NDSU • Past President, Mott/Regent School Board; EMT-1, Mott Ambulance Service; FFI, Mott Volunteer Fire Brigade; Trustee, Zoar Congregational Church • Married (Carmen); 4 Children • Senate since 2011
EDUCATION; ENERGY AND NATURAL RESOURCES

Karen M. Rohr

1704 Fourth Street NE, Mandan, ND 58554-3814; kmrohr@nd.gov; (R) Grant, Pt. Hettinger, Pt. Morton, Sioux • Bioethics and Faculty Formation Director • PhD, Nursing Research; MSN, Nursing Administration & Board Certified Nurse Practitioner • 3 Children • House since 2011
GOVERNMENT AND VETERANS AFFAIRS; HUMAN SERVICES

Jim Schmidt

5165 Highway 1806, Huff, ND 58554-8721; jeschmidt@nd.gov; (R) Grant, Pt. Hettinger, Pt. Morton, Sioux • Retired, USDA; Farmer; Small Business Owner • BS, Utah State University • Morton County Water Resource Board; Board, Missouri West Water Systems; Board, Morton County Soils Committee; Member, Jacobson Memorial Hospital Foundation • 2 Children • House since 2011
APPROPRIATIONS; APPROPRIATIONS - EDUCATION AND ENVIRONMENT DIVISION

DISTRICT #32

Dick Dever

1416 Eastwood Street, Bismarck, ND 58504-6226; ddever@nd.gov; (R) Pt. Burleigh • Self Employed; DEVCO; Manufacturers Representative • UND • US Army • PERS Board Member; Chair, Committee on Protection and Advocacy; Chair, Legislative Veterans Caucus; Farwest Rotary Club; BILLD Fellow; 2004 ND Small Business Champion of the Year, NFIB; Life Member, VFW & AmVets; Bis-Man Chamber; Legislator of the Year, MHA, 2007; Elder, Shepherd of the Valley Lutheran Church • Married (Pam); 3 Children; 12 Grandchildren • Senate since 2001
APPROPRIATIONS

Pat D. Heinert

1501 Eastwood Street, Bismarck, ND 58504-6230; pdheinert@nd.gov; (R) Pt. Burleigh • Sheriff, Burleigh County • St. Mary's Central High School; BA, Management, U of Mary; MA, Management, U of Mary • Knights of Columbus; Elks • Married (Lynn); 2 Children • House since 2017
EDUCATION; ENERGY AND NATURAL RESOURCES

Lisa Meier

1713 South Third Street, Bismarck, ND 58504-7114; lmeier@nd.gov; (R) Pt. Burleigh • Sales and Interior Designer • AS, BSC • District Commissioner, Boy Scouts; Board, Pride Industries; American Council of Young Political Leaders Delegate to South Korea, 2001; Delegate, Asian Summit in Tokyo, Japan, 2006; Participant, Government of Canada's Rising State Leader Program, 2007 • Married (Dennis); 1 Son; 3 Stepsons; 6 Grandchildren • House since 2001
APPROPRIATIONS; APPROPRIATIONS - HUMAN RESOURCES DIVISION

DISTRICT #33

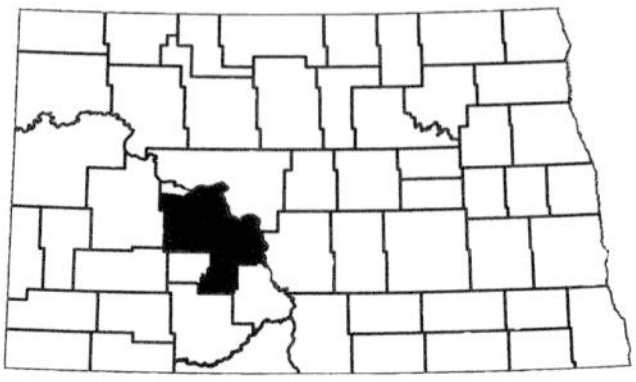

Jessica Unruh

2108 Seventh Street NE, Beulah, ND 58523-7101; jkunruh@nd.gov; (R) Pt. Mercer, Pt. Morton, Oliver • Environmental Specialist, Coteau Properties Co. Freedom Mine • BS, Natural Resources Management, Economics, NDSU • Supervisor, Mercer County Soil Conservation District; Member, Energy Council since 2013; Commission on Legal Council for Indigents; State Council for Interstate Adult Offender Supervision • Married (KC); 2 Children • Senate since 2013
ENERGY AND NATURAL RESOURCES; FINANCE AND TAXATION

Gary Kreidt

3892 County Road 86, New Salem, ND 58563-9406; gkreidt@nd.gov; (R) Pt. Mercer, Pt. Morton, Oliver • Nursing Home Administrator; Farmer • Past President, West River Transportation; Past President, New Salem School Board; Past President, NDLTCA; Past Secretary/Treasurer, New Salem Development Corporation; Past Region VI Vice President, American Healthcare Association; American Healthcare Association Presidential Citation; National Leadership, Republican Party; Elks; Peace Church New Salem • Married (Judy); 5 Children; 10 Grandchildren; 5 Great-grandchildren • House since 2003
APPROPRIATIONS; APPROPRIATIONS - HUMAN RESOURCES DIVISION

Jay Seibel

5801 Lakeshore Estates, Beulah, ND 58523-9124; jayseibel@nd.gov; (R) Pt. Mercer, Pt. Morton, Oliver • Retired Funeral Home Director • Jamestown College; BS, Mortuary Science, U of Central Oklahoma • ND National Guard; Past President, NDFDA; Past Board, NFDA; Past Member, ND State Board of Funeral Service; Asst. Scoutmaster, Boy Scouts; Youth Football and Wrestling Coach; Lions Club; American Legion; Prince of Peace Lutheran Church • Married (Karen); 2 Children • House since 2015
ENERGY AND NATURAL RESOURCES; HUMAN SERVICES

DISTRICT #34

Dwight Cook

1408 17th Street SE, Mandan, ND 58554-4895; dcook@nd.gov; (R) Pt. Morton • Owner, Cook Industrial Sales • Chair, Morton County Housing Authority; Streamlined Sales Tax Governing Board; Kiwanis; American Legion; Lutheran • Married (Shirley); 3 Children; 8 Grandchildren • Senate since 1997
ENERGY AND NATURAL RESOURCES; FINANCE AND TAXATION

Todd Porter

4604 Borden Harbor Drive SE, Mandan, ND 58554-7961; tkporter@nd.gov; (R) Pt. Morton • Part Owner/Paramedic, Metro-Area Ambulance Service • Century College (Paramedic Program) • Chair, Bismarck/Burleigh County 911 Center; Elks; Pheasants Forever; Rocky Mountain Elk Foundation; Bismarck/Mandan Chamber of Commerce; Bismarck/Mandan Development Association; Greater North Dakota Chamber • Married (Shirley); 2 Children • House since 1999
ENERGY AND NATURAL RESOURCES; HUMAN SERVICES

Nathan Toman

203 Fourth Avenue NW, Mandan, ND 58554-3135; nptoman@nd.gov; (R) Pt. Morton • Information Systems, Ducks Unlimited Inc. • AA, BSC • Married (Jessica); 5 Children • House since 2013
FINANCE AND TAXATION; POLITICAL SUBDIVISIONS

DISTRICT #35

ERIN OBAN

1319 Apache Street, Bismarck, ND 58501-2632; eoban@nd.gov; (D) Pt. Burleigh • Consultant • BS, Mathematics Education, U of Mary • NDSU Foundation; 2015 BILLD Fellow; Governing Institute Women in Government, 2014-2015; '40 under 40', Bismarck Tribune, 2014; NDFU Alumni Council; Board, Designer Genes; Good Shepherd Lutheran Church • Married (Chad); 1 Son • Senate since 2015
EDUCATION; ENERGY AND NATURAL RESOURCES

KAREN KARLS

2112 Senate Drive, Bismarck, ND 58501-1978; kkarls@nd.gov; (R) Pt. Burleigh • Self Employed • BS, Medical Technology, MSU • Board Secretary, Bis-Man Rifle & Pistol Association; NRA; Chair, District 35 Republicans, 20 years; ND Council on Educational Opportunity for Military Children; Cathedral of the Holy Spirit • Married (Ken); 4 Children • House since 2007
GOVERNMENT AND VETERANS AFFAIRS; JUDICIARY

BOB MARTINSON

2749 Pacific Avenue, Bismarck, ND 58501-2513; bmartinson@nd.gov; (R) Pt. Burleigh • Independent Landman • BSC; BS, U of Mary • Retired NDARNG, Lt. Col. • Majority Leader, 1993-1995; ND Tourism Director, 1997-2000; American Legion; AMVETS; Elks; Moose; Eagles • Married (Jodi) • House 1973-1997, since 2000
APPROPRIATIONS; APPROPRIATIONS - EDUCATION AND ENVIRONMENT DIVISION

DISTRICT #36

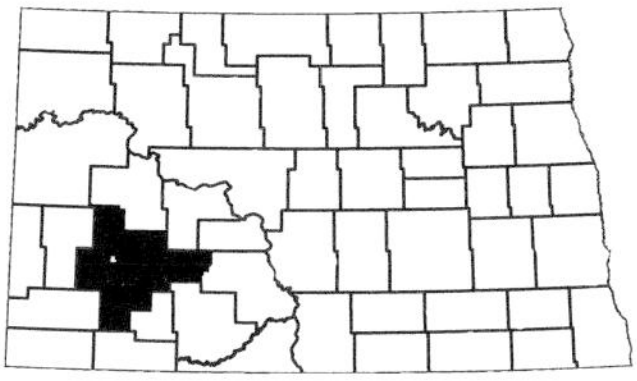

KELLY M. ARMSTRONG

513 Elks Drive, Dickinson, ND 58601-2947; karmstrong@nd.gov; (R) Pt. Dunn, Pt. Hettinger, Pt. Morton, Pt. Stark • Partner, Reichert Armstrong Law Firm • Psychology, UND; JD, UND School of Law • Vice President, Armstrong Corporation; Chairman, ND Republican Party; President, Dickinson Baseball Club 2006-2012; Volunteer Fireman 2004-2012 • Married (Kjersti); 2 Children • Senate since 2013
JUDICIARY; ENERGY AND NATURAL RESOURCES

MIKE SCHATZ

400 Ninth Street East, New England, ND 58647-7528; mischatz@nd.gov; (R) Pt. Dunn, Pt. Hettinger, Pt. Morton, Pt. Stark • Businessman • MSU • Former Vice President, Education Standards & Practices Board; Former President, New England Park Board; Lifetime Member, ND Coaches Association; NRA; Rotary; ND Stockmen's Association; Elks • Married (Patti); 4 Children • House 1989-1990, since 2009
APPROPRIATIONS; APPROPRIATIONS - EDUCATION AND ENVIRONMENT DIVISION

LUKE SIMONS

11509 27th Street SW, Dickinson, ND 58601-8238; lsimons@nd.gov; (R) Pt. Dunn, Pt. Hettinger, Pt. Morton, Pt. Stark • Rancher • Married (Aliesha); 5 Children • House since 2017
JUDICIARY; POLITICAL SUBDIVISIONS

DISTRICT #37

RICH WARDNER

1042 12th Avenue West, Dickinson, ND 58601-3654; rwardner@nd.gov; (R) Pt. Stark • Retired Educator; Former Executive Director of the Dickinson Area Chamber of Commerce • BS, DSU; MS, Northern State University • Past President Pro Tempore of the Senate; Chairman, Sunrise Youth Bureau; Chair, Midwest Legislative Conference; Member, Legislative Management; Elks; Rotary • Married (Kayleen); 2 Children • House 1991-1998; Senate since 1999

MIKE LEFOR

P.O. Box 1347, Dickinson, ND 58602-1347; mlefor@nd.gov; (R) Pt. Stark • President/CEO, DCI Credit Services, Inc.; President, Blackridge Enterprises, LLC • DSU • President, Dickinson Park Board; Chairman, St. Joseph Hospital Board; Board, CHI Home Health; Board, St. Joseph Foundation, 1997-2008; Elks • Married (Sherryl); 3 Children • House since 2015

ENERGY AND NATURAL RESOURCES; INDUSTRY, BUSINESS AND LABOR

VICKY STEINER

859 Senior Avenue, Dickinson, ND 58601-3755; vsteiner@nd.gov; (R) Pt. Stark • Owner, Big Sky Condos • BS, MSU Moorhead, MN • Vision West ND; TR Presidential Library and Museum Foundation; DSU Community Committee; Rotary; ND Right to Life; St. Patrick's Church Building Committee • Married (Calvin); 4 Children; 5 Grandchildren • House since 2011

FINANCE AND TAXATION; GOVERNMENT AND VETERANS AFFAIRS

DISTRICT #38

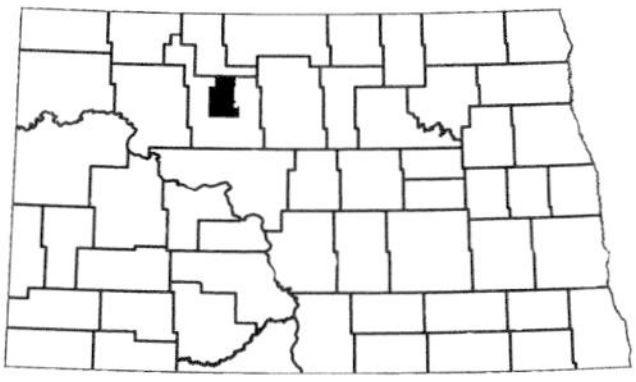

David Hogue

6811 27th Avenue NW, Minot, ND 58703-8849; dhogue@nd.gov; (R) Pt. Ward • Attorney • BA, Cornell College; U.S. Army War College; JD, UND • Veteran • Married (Paula); 2 Children • Senate since 2009
APPROPRIATIONS

Larry Bellew

812 Bel Air Place, Minot, ND 58703-1751; lbellew@nd.gov; (R) Pt. Ward • Retired Golf Course Superintendent; Part-time School Bus Driver • AA, Horticulture • US Air Force • Sertoma; Board, Minot Commission on Aging; Board, MUAW • Married (Carol); 4 Children • House since 2001

Dan Ruby

4620 46th Avenue NW, Minot, ND 58703-8710; druby@nd.gov; (R) Pt. Ward • Circle Sanitation Inc. and Noonan Landfill LLC • Married (Lori); 10 Children; 14 Grandchildren • House since 2001
TRANSPORTATION; INDUSTRY, BUSINESS AND LABOR

DISTRICT #39

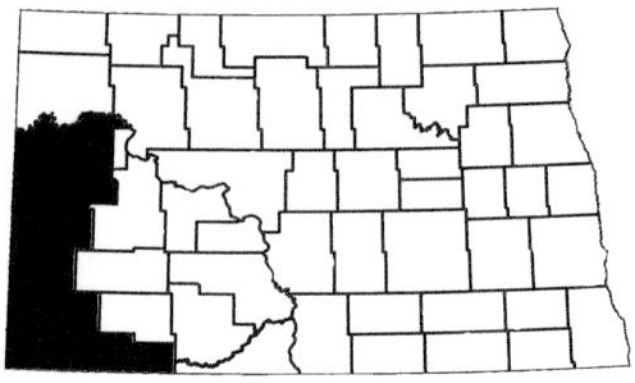

Bill L. Bowman

408 First Street SW, Bowman, ND 58623-4272; bbowman@nd.gov; (R) Adams, Billings, Bowman, Pt. Dunn, Golden Valley, Pt. McKenzie, Slope • Auctioneer • BS, Education, DSU • US Army • Bowman County Commissioner; Past President Pro Tempore • 3 Children • Senate since 1991

APPROPRIATIONS

Keith Kempenich

(R) Adams, Billings, Bowman, Pt. Dunn, Golden Valley, Pt. McKenzie, Slope • Rancher; Crop Adjuster; Owner, Box K Trucking • Black Hills State • Farm Bureau; Farmers Union; AOPA • Married (Melinda); 3 Children • House since 1993

APPROPRIATIONS; APPROPRIATIONS - GOVERNMENT OPERATIONS DIVISION

Denton Zubke

P.O. Box 927, Watford City, ND 58854-0927; dzubke@nd.gov; (R) Adams, Billings, Bowman, Pt. Dunn, Golden Valley, Pt. McKenzie, Slope • Retired CEO, Financial Institution • Chairman, McKenzie County Water RD; Director, Past Chairman, Western Area Water Supply Project; McKenzie County Job Development Authority; Watford City Chamber of Commerce; Midwest Federal Corporate Credit Union • Married (Margaret); 5 Children; 3 Grandchildren • House since 2015

EDUCATION; POLITICAL SUBDIVISIONS

DISTRICT #40

Karen K. Krebsbach

P.O. Box 1767, Minot, ND 58702-1767; kkrebsbach@nd.gov; (R)
Pt. Ward • President, Krebsbach Realty Co., Inc. • BS, MSU • Board of Regents, MISU; MISU Foundation; Board, Trinity Health; TR Medora Foundation; Minot Area Development Corporation; Norsk Hostfest Association; Minot Community Ambulance; Past Chair, Minot Area Chamber of Commerce; Greater North Dakota Chamber; Minot Job Service Employer's Committee; Souris Valley United Way; SBA Advisory Committee; President Pro Tempore, 2001; First Lutheran Church • Widow; 2 Children; 4 Grandchildren • Senate since 1989
APPROPRIATIONS

Matthew Ruby

315 Fourth Street NW, Minot, ND 58703-3129; mruby@nd.gov; (R)
Pt. Ward • Owner, 5R Construction • 7 years, SGT, 815th Engineer, Edgeley • Apathy Original Motorcycle Club; Loyal Order of the Moose • Married (Dana); 2 Children • House since 2017
EDUCATION; ENERGY AND NATURAL RESOURCES

Randy A. Schobinger

3500 30th Street NW, Minot, ND 58703-0312; rschobinger@nd.gov; (R) Pt. Ward • Insurance Agent • Economics, MSU • Single • Senate 1995-2006; House since 2017
FINANCE AND TAXATION; TRANSPORTATION

DISTRICT #41

Kyle Davison

4918 Meadow Creek Drive South, Fargo, ND 58104-7116; kdavison@nd.gov; (R) Pt. Cass • Executive Director, South East Education Cooperative • BS, Business Administration, VCSU • Married (Laura); 3 Children • Senate since 2015
EDUCATION; GOVERNMENT AND VETERANS AFFAIRS

Pamela Anderson

3001 40th Avenue South, Unit H, Fargo, ND 58104-4406; pkanderson@nd.gov; (D) Pt. Cass • Retired; Sr. Vice President, Regional Trust Manager, Wells Fargo • BA, MA, Economics, UND • Board, Union State Bank; Board, NDPERS; Past Board, Bethany Retirement Living; MeritCare; FM Symphony; Sanford Health System; YWCA; FM Community Theatre • Widow; 3 Children; 4 Grandchildren • House since 2015
GOVERNMENT AND VETERANS AFFAIRS; HUMAN SERVICES

Al Carlson

2548 Rose Creek Parkway South, Fargo, ND 58104-6699; acarlson@nd.gov; (R) Pt. Cass • Contractor; Partner, Up North Recreation • NDSCS; Secondary Education, NDSU • Past President, F-M Homebuilders Association; Past President, North Dakota Association of Builders; State Chairman, State Legislative Leaders Foundation; St. Anthony's Catholic Church • Married (Sharon); 3 Children; 12 Grandchildren • House since 1993

DISTRICT #42

Curt Kreun

3111 Longbow Court, Grand Forks, ND 58203-2193; ckreun@nd.gov; (R) Pt. Grand Forks • Retired • BS • City Council; School Board; Prairie Harvest Human Services Foundation; Automobile Dealers Assoc. of ND; Greater Grand Forks Senior Men's Club; Grand Forks Housing Authority; Grand Forks Chamber of Commerce • Married (Linda); 2 Children • House 2011-2014; Senate since 2017

ENERGY AND NATURAL RESOURCES; HUMAN SERVICES

Jake G. Blum

2310 Second Avenue North, Grand Forks, ND 58203-8314; jblum@nd.gov; (R) Pt. Grand Forks • Attending UND • Sigma Alpha Epsilon; State Director for Students, Marco Rubio, Donald Trump • House since 2017

AGRICULTURE; JUDICIARY

Emily O'Brien

2002 University Avenue, Apt. #2, Grand Forks, ND 58203-3346; eobrien@nd.gov; (R) Pt. Grand Forks • Entrepreneur Coach, Center for Innovation • Masters Student; BA, Entrepreneurship, UND • Single • House since 2017

INDUSTRY, BUSINESS AND LABOR; TRANSPORTATION

DISTRICT #43

Lonnie J. Laffen

3549 15th Avenue South, Grand Forks, ND 58201-3706; llaffen@nd.gov; (R) Pt. Grand Forks • President/CEO, JLG Architects • BArch, NDSU • Vice Chairman, Altru Health System; NDSU Architecture Advisory Board; Board, Grand Forks Special Assessment Commission; American Institute of Architects; ND 20/20 & and Beyond; Past Chairman, Grand Forks Chamber of Commerce; Past President, AIA North Dakota; Streamlined Sales Tax Governing Board • Married (Pam); 3 Children • Senate since 2011

FINANCE AND TAXATION; TRANSPORTATION

Rich S. Becker

3633 Lynwood Circle, Grand Forks, ND 58201-3934; rsbecker@nd.gov; (R) Pt. Grand Forks • Management/Marketing Consultant • BS, BA, UND • Theodore Roosevelt Medora Foundation; Dakota Certified Development Corp; Past Board, UND Alumni Association; UND Energy & Environmental Research Center; Prairie Public Broadcasting; GF/EGF Chamber of Commerce; Grand Forks Regional Airport Authority; Board, GF Youth for Christ; Hope Covenant Church • Married (Joanne); 3 Children; 4 Grandchildren • House since 2015

EDUCATION; POLITICAL SUBDIVISIONS

Lois Delmore

714 South 22nd Street, Grand Forks, ND 58201-4138; ldelmore@nd.gov; (D) Pt. Grand Forks • Retired School Teacher • UND • Board, Crime Victims Services; 2001 Flemming Fellow; Lottery Commission; Higher Education Round Table; Steering Committee, International Legislators Forum; UND School of Medicine & Health Sciences Advisory Council; ND Professional Health Program; Director, BIO ND; Director, WIG ND; Board, ND EPSCoR • Married (Michael); 1 Child • House since 1995

APPROPRIATIONS; APPROPRIATIONS - GOVERNMENT OPERATIONS DIVISION

DISTRICT #44

MERRILL PIEPKORN

1321 Third Street North, Fargo, ND 58102-2728; mpiepkorn@nd.gov; (D) Pt. Cass • President, Prairie Airwaves Inc.; Producer, Dakota Air: The Radio Show, Film, Television and Radio Projects; Radio Stars Band • BA, Concordia College • Horace Mann Area Neighborhood Assoc.; Messiah Lutheran Church's "Hour of Worship" Telecast • Married (Connie) • Senate since 2017
AGRICULTURE; HUMAN SERVICES

JOSHUA A. BOSCHEE

517 First Street North, Fargo, ND 58102-4540; jboschee@nd.gov; (D) Pt. Cass • Sales Manager, Realtor, Hatch Realty • BA, Political Science, NDSU; MEd., Educational Leadership, NDSU • Partnered • House since 2013
AGRICULTURE; INDUSTRY, BUSINESS AND LABOR

KARLA ROSE HANSON

1114 Fifth Street North, Fargo, ND 58102-3713; krhanson@nd.gov; (D) Pt. Cass • Small Business Owner • BA, NDSU • 2013 Woman of the Year, ND Women's Network • Married (Shawn); 2 Children • House since 2017
JUDICIARY; POLITICAL SUBDIVISIONS

DISTRICT #45

Ronald Sorvaag

3402 Birdie Street North, Fargo, ND 58102-1201; rsorvaag@nd.gov; (R) Pt. Cass • Small Business Owner • BA, Sociology, Concordia College • Past Commissioner, Fargo Park District; Past Director, Prosper Farmers Elevator; Member, Fargo/Moorhead/West Fargo Chamber of Commerce • Married (Carla); 2 Children • Senate since 2011
APPROPRIATIONS

Mary Johnson

3407 Birdie Street, Fargo, ND 58102-1203; marycjohnson@nd.gov; (R) Pt. Cass • Controller, Valley Bus, LLC • BS, Accounting, MSUM; JD, UND School of Law • Fargo Park Board • Married (David); 2 Children • House since 2015
EDUCATION; POLITICAL SUBDIVISIONS

Tom Kading

7205 County Road 31, Fargo, ND 58102-6117; tkading@nd.gov; (R) Pt. Cass • Attorney; Entrepreneur • BS, Civil Engineering Degree, NDSU; JD, UND; MS, Business Administration, UND • Salem Evangelical Free Church • Married (Ashley) • House since 2015
APPROPRIATIONS; APPROPRIATIONS - HUMAN RESOURCES DIVISION

DISTRICT #46

Jim P. Roers

200 45th Street South, Fargo, ND 58103-0907; jroers@nd.gov; (R) Pt. Cass • Owner, Roers Companies • BS, Agriculture, NDSU • 2016 Service Award, NDSU Foundation; NDSU Alumni Assoc.; The Chamber; NDSU Foundation; Valley Prosperity Partnership • Married (Sandra); 5 Children • Senate 2012, since 2017
ENERGY AND NATURAL RESOURCES; INDUSTRY, BUSINESS AND LABOR

Jim Kasper

1128 Westrac Drive, Fargo, ND 58103-2342; jkasper@nd.gov; (R) Pt. Cass • President, Asset Management Group, Inc. • Business Economics, NDSU • US Army Reserve • Business Champion Legislator, Greater North Dakota Chamber, 2011; Friend of Farm Bureau, 2011 & 2009; Distinguished Friend of ND Pharmacy Award, 2010; Keynote Speaker, ACLI, Boston, 2008; Keynote Speaker, Mealey's Conference, NY City Harvard Club, 2007; Keynote Speaker, Life Settlements Conference, Orlando, 2007; Outstanding Legislator, NDAIFA, 2007; Testified, US Senate Banking Committee, Privacy Matters, 2002; Chair, District 46; Former Chair, Fargo Area Republican Party; ND and F-M Life Underwriter of the Year; 44-Year Member, MDRT; Bethel Evangelical Free Church • Married (Sandy); 2 Sons • House since 2001
GOVERNMENT AND VETERANS AFFAIRS; INDUSTRY, BUSINESS AND LABOR

Shannon M. Roers Jones

5948 Silverleaf Drive South, Fargo, ND 58104-7127; sroersjones@nd.gov; (R) Pt. Cass • Attorney • JD, UND; MBA, Univ. of St. Thomas; BA, Business, St. Benedict College • Married (Ross); 3 Children • House since 2017
ENERGY AND NATURAL RESOURCES; JUDICIARY

DISTRICT #47

RALPH KILZER

1982 Mesquite Loop, Bismarck, ND 58503-0198; rkilzer@nd.gov; (R) Pt. Burleigh • BA, St. John's University; MD, Marquette University School of Medicine; MPH, Medical College of Wisconsin • US Army • UND School of Medicine Clinical Professor of Surgery; Past President, 6th District Medical Association; AMA; AAOS; Founder, Bone & Joint Center; St. Mary's High School DSA; McCarthy Award, University of Mary; Physician Community and Professional Services Award; Schafer Excellence in Healthcare Award; Friend of Nursing Award; Legislative Service Award, ND Bar Association; Elks; Knights of Columbus; Knight of the Holy Sepulcher • Married (Marcia); 6 Children • House 1997-1998; Senate since 1999
APPROPRIATIONS

GEORGE J. KEISER

422 Toronto Drive, Bismarck, ND 58503-0276; gkeiser@nd.gov; (R) Pt. Burleigh • Owner, Quality Printing Service • PhD, University of Utah • US Army • Past Bismarck City Commissioner • Married (Kathy); 4 Children • House since 1993
ENERGY AND NATURAL RESOURCES; INDUSTRY, BUSINESS AND LABOR

LAWRENCE R. KLEMIN

3929 Valley Drive, Bismarck, ND 58503-1729; lklemin@nd.gov; (R) Pt. Burleigh • Lawyer, Schweigert, Klemin & McBride, PC • BA, English, UND; JD, UND • US Army, Vietnam Veteran, 101st Airborne Division (Air Assault) • Who's Who in American Law; American Legion; Elks; Eagles; Optimist Club; National Uniform Law Commission; Church of Corpus Christi • Married (Rita); 2 Children • House since 1999
JUDICIARY; POLITICAL SUBDIVISIONS

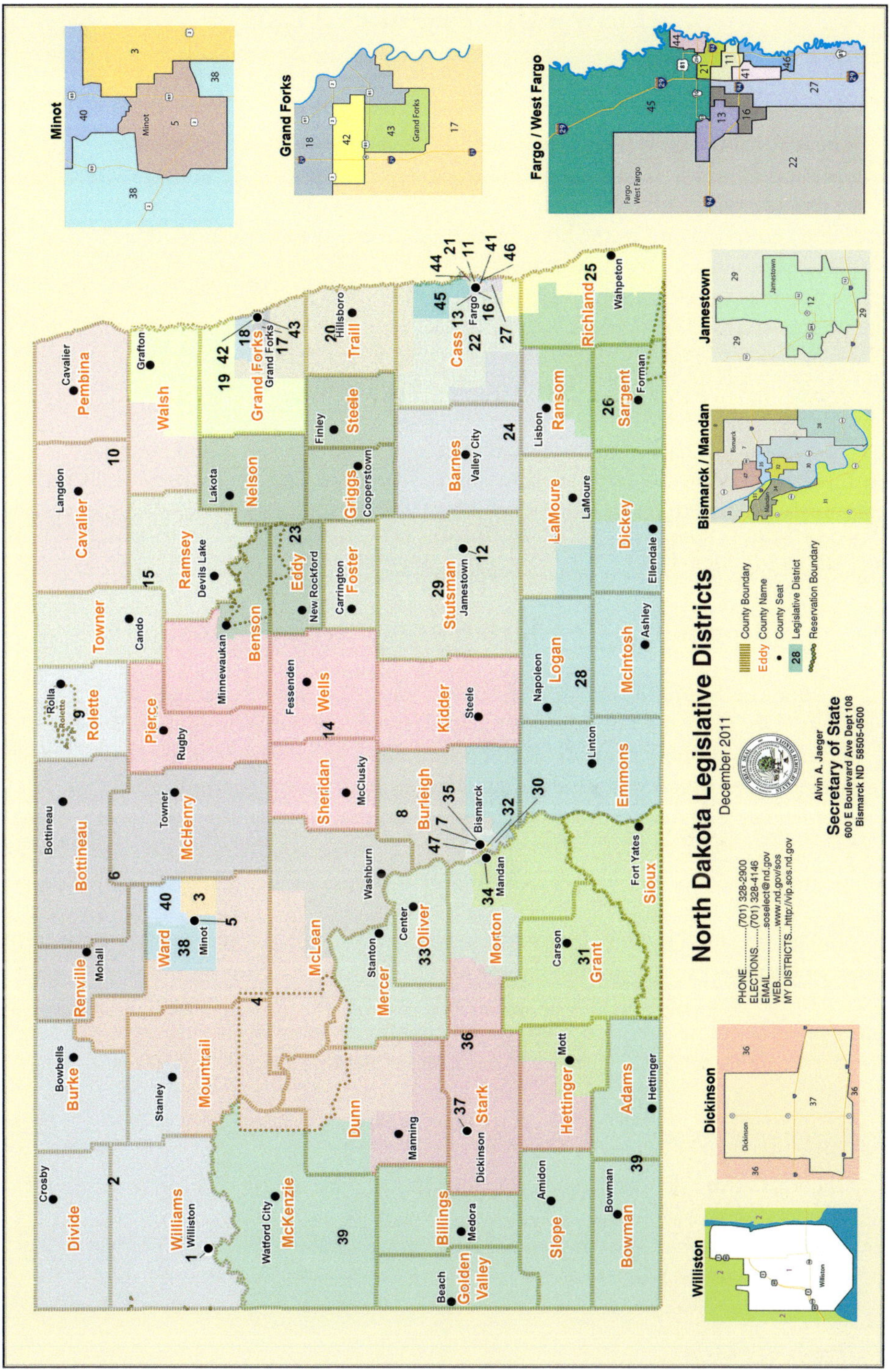
North Dakota Legislative Districts
December 2011
County Boundary
Eddy County Name
County Seat
28 Legislative District
Reservation Boundary
Alvin A. Jaeger
Secretary of State
600 E Boulevard Ave Dept 108
Bismarck ND 58505-0500
PHONE..........(701) 328-2900
ELECTIONS.......(701) 328-4146
EMAIL..........soselect@nd.gov
WEB..........www.nd.gov/sos
MY DISTRICTS....http://vip.sos.nd.gov
Minot
Grand Forks
Fargo / West Fargo
Jamestown
Bismarck / Mandan
Dickinson
Williston
Divide
Burke
Renville
Bottineau
Rolette
Towner
Cavalier
Pembina
Williams
Mountrail
Ward
McHenry
Pierce
Benson
Ramsey
Walsh
Nelson
Grand Forks
McKenzie
Dunn
McLean
Sheridan
Wells
Eddy
Foster
Griggs
Steele
Traill
Golden Valley
Billings
Stark
Mercer
Oliver
Burleigh
Kidder
Stutsman
Barnes
Cass
Slope
Hettinger
Morton
Grant
Emmons
Logan
LaMoure
Ransom
Richland
Bowman
Adams
Sioux
McIntosh
Dickey
Sargent

How a Bill Becomes a Law

Introduction and Standing Committee Referral

Legislative Assembly members, standing committees, and the Legislative Management sponsor bills that conform to statutory requirements and legislative rules. The presiding officer of a bill's chamber of origin refers each bill to an appropriate standing committee unless the body by motion assigns it to a select or other standing committee or to the Committee of the Whole in the case of the House of Representatives. A journal entry records the bill's official introduction, title, and committee referral.

Committee Hearing

The committee chair designates and posts a hearing date, time, and place for each bill assigned. The committee convenes as scheduled, and the chairman calls the committee to order and announces the bill under consideration. The committee receives testimony and other information from interested parties such as the bill's author, concerned citizens, and state agency representative.

Committee Consideration and Recommendation

A standing committee makes its final decision in an executive session, and committee staff members prepare a report for chamber submission conveying the committee's recommendation. A standing committee either reports a bill favorably, unfavorably, or without recommendation. Where applicable, a committee may recommend amendment of referral of a bill in addition to one of the foregoing options.

Amendment

The Senate and House first consider a bill's recommended amendments on the sixth order of business prior to placing the bill on the daily calendar for second reading and final passage. The House considers all amendments on the calendar simultaneously unless a representative requests that an amendment be voted upon separately, whereas the Senate deliberates and votes upon each recommended amendment in turn.

Engrossment

The legislative rules deem a bill amended in its house of origin properly engrossed upon amendment adoption, but an amended bill must also undergo a formal engrossment process of inserting all adopted amendments into place to produce a new official version of the bill.

Second Reading and Final Passage

Second reading and final passage occurs on the 11th order of business in a bill's chamber of origin and on the 14th order of business in the opposite chamber. Prior to voting on final passage, the Senate may amend a bill from the floor or rerefer it to a committee for further action, and the House may rerefer a bill to a standing committee or to the Committee of the Whole, amend a bill's title, or by unanimous consent otherwise amend a bill. To obtain final passage, every bill requires a favorable majority vote, and amendment or repeal of any law initiated or referred within the past seven years requires a two-thirds vote of the members-elect. Each chamber must record and print in its journal any vote on a bill's final passage.

Secondary House Procedure

A bill successfully passed by its house of origin goes through the same series of steps in the opposite house as in its house of origin. If the opposite house amends a bill, the house of origin must concur or refuse to concur with the proposed amendments. If the opposite house passes a bill without change, or if the house of origin agrees to the opposite house's amendments, the originating chamber may enroll the bill.

Conference Committee

If the house of origin does not concur in the opposite house's amendments, each chamber may organize a committee to meet in conference with a like committee from the other chamber to further discuss the bill. Conference committees may agree to recede from the opposite house's amendments, accede to the opposite house's amendments, recede and propose new amendments, accede and propose further amendments, or state an inability or unwillingness to agree. In the latter case, chambers may reappoint conference committee members or appoint entirely new conference committees.

Enrollment

The enrollment process involves final bill proofreading and editing, code section clean-up, line number removal, replacement of the words "A Bill for ..." with the words "An Act ...," -and printing of an official bill version for signatures.

Presiding Officer's Signature

The constitution requires that the presiding officer of each house sign all bills the Legislative Assembly passes and each chamber to enter the fact of such signing in the journal. As a formal procedure, the Chief Clerk of the House and the Secretary of the Senate also sign these bills before messaging them to the Governor for consideration.

Governor's Signature or Veto

The Legislative Assembly must present to the Governor for consideration every bill they pass. If the Governor approves a bill by signing it, the bill becomes law on its effective date. If the Governor vetoes a bill or any parts of a bill, the items approved become law and the portions disapproved are void unless subsequently enacted through a veto override by the Legislative Assembly. If during session the Governor neither signs nor vetoes a bill within three business days, the bill becomes law on its effective date without the Governor's signature. If the Legislative Assembly adjourns within three days after the Governor receives a bill, the bill becomes law automatically unless the Governor files it in the office of the Secretary of State within 15 business days after adjournment of the Legislative Assembly, along with a veto message detailing the Governor's objections to the bill.

Veto Consideration

If the Governor vetoes part or all of a bill during session, the Governor must return it to its house of origin, along with a veto message that details the Governor's objections to the bill. If the originating house chooses to reconsider the bill or the applicable bill items and two-thirds of its members-elect agree to override the Governor's veto, the bill or bill items, together with the Governor's objections thereto, proceed to the opposite house for reconsideration. If two-thirds of the members-elect of the opposite house also override the Governor's veto, the bill becomes law.

Effective Date

Following filing with the Secretary of State, the effective dates of bills are as follows: July 1 for all taxation and appropriations bills, August 1 for all other bills that do not specify other effective dates, and the effective date specified for bills containing approved emergency or delayed effective clauses.

North Dakota's Revenue Forecasting Process

Office of Management and Budget (1)

The Executive Budget Office (Office of Management and Budget) has primary authority for revenue forecasting in North Dakota. Historically, during each biennium, the Office of Management and Budget issues three revenue forecasts:

Preliminary	July	Issued in the year prior to the start of the legislative session
Executive Budget	December	Presented, along with the executive budget recommendations, to the Budget Section and organizational session of the Legislative Assembly
Revised	February	Updated and presented to the Appropriations Committees

Tax Department (2)

The Tax Department is responsible for the basic methodology for forecasting the following general fund tax types: sales, motor vehicle excise, individual income, corporation income, financial institution, oil extraction, oil and gas production, cigarette and tobacco, coal conversion, and wholesale liquor taxes.

Moody's Analytics (3)

The Office of Management and Budget contracts with Moody's Analytics to provide economic projections for the state of North Dakota. Moody's Analytics provides tax-based forecasts for each of the major taxable sectors. Reports prepared by Moody's Analytics include analyses and forecasts of sweet crude oil prices and production. As needed, Moody's Analytics also provides analyses and forecasts of North Dakota's major crops and livestock, including farm income and cash receipts for livestock and products.

Revenue Advisory Committee (4)

The Revenue Advisory Committee, created by the Office of Management and Budget, is a committee generally consisting of private sector members, at least two legislators, and other public officials. The Revenue Advisory Committee meets before the issuance of each forecast to review the economic projections and resulting tax-based forecasts.

Legislative Assembly (5)

The Legislative Assembly receives and reviews the revenue forecast from the Office of Management and Budget during its organizational session in December and an updated forecast in February during the regular session. The Appropriations Committees may adopt the forecast as presented or change the forecast prior to adopting it as the "official" legislative revenue forecast.

Forecasting Process

2	Updates the historical tax base statistics and provides the results to Moody's Analytics.
3	Processes the historical data through forecasting models, adjusting forecast equations or "drivers" as needed.
1 2 3	Participate in conference calls to discuss views on the economies of the United States and North Dakota.
3	Creates North Dakota's tax-based forecasts for each of the next two fiscal years.
4 5	Review the tax-based forecasts and recommend modifications.
2	Applies the appropriate tax rates and statutory distributions through the use of in-house tax revenue models to produce the tax revenue forecast, which is supplied to the Office of Management and Budget.

North Dakota's Budgeting Process

North Dakota's Legislative Assembly meets for up to 80 legislative days beginning in January and usually concluding in April of each odd-numbered year. By the close of each regular legislative session, the Legislative Assembly approves North Dakota's biennial budget, which takes effect on July 1 of that year and ends on June 30 of the following odd-numbered year.

North Dakota's budgeting process begins in March of the year prior to the legislative session with state agencies and institutions preparing and submitting their biennial budget requests to the Office of Management and Budget. The Office of Management and Budget holds executive budget hearings, attended by the legislative budget analyst and auditor's staff, that allow agencies an opportunity to explain and justify their budget requests for inclusion in the Governor's budget recommendations to the Legislative Assembly.

The Governor develops the executive budget recommendation using revenue forecast information based on data provided by the Tax Department, input from the Advisory Council on Revenue Forecasting, and an analysis by the economic forecasting firm under contract with the state. The Legislative Assembly also uses this revenue information, as well as updated revenue information provided in February during the legislative session, as it develops the legislative budget.

The Legislative Assembly receives the Governor's executive budget recommendation during its organizational session in December preceding the legislative session, and the Legislative Management's Budget Section meets afterward to receive more detailed information about the recommendation. Prior to the legislative session, the Legislative Council fiscal staff prepares a comprehensive analysis of the executive budget, presents this analysis to the Appropriations Committee of each house, and makes it available to all members of the Legislative Assembly for the members' use in developing the legislative budget.

The Office of Management and Budget introduces bills to provide for the revenue and appropriations levels recommended in the Governor's budget. Individual legislators may also introduce bills affecting state revenues or appropriations for an agency, and the Legislative Assembly may consider bills for deficiency appropriations relating to the current biennium. As it develops the legislative budget, the Legislative Assembly considers the Governor's recommendations and information received through public hearings held in each chamber on each appropriations and revenue bill.

The rules of the Legislative Assembly require that the Senate and the House of Representatives refer each bill having an appropriation of $5,000 or more and each bill with a fiscal note indicating a fiscal impact of $50,000 or more to their respective Appropriations Committee. The Senate Appropriations Committee (14 members in 2017) forms ad hoc subcommittees to consider specific issues or funding levels for select agencies. The House Appropriations Committee (21 members in 2017) organizes itself into three formal divisions: Education and Environment, Human Resources, and Government Operations. These subdivisions hold budget hearings on assigned agencies, develop budget recommendations, and report their recommendations to the full Appropriations Committee.

The Legislative Council fiscal staff serves the Appropriations Committees and all members of the Legislative Assembly by conducting research, analyzing budgets, preparing amendments, and monitoring the status of revenues, appropriations, and fund balances included in the legislative budget. The fiscal staff also publishes the "budget status" report throughout the legislative session, which provides the updated status of general fund revenues, appropriations, and ending general fund balance for the next biennium's budget.

The Legislative Assembly approves approximately 75 appropriations bills each session, providing for the operations of state government for the subsequent biennium. Once passed by both chambers of the Legislative Assembly, each bill moves from its originating chamber to the Governor for signature, and when signed, the bill becomes law. Unless otherwise indicated, appropriations bills or tax measure bills become effective on July 1 following the legislative session, and other bills become effective on August 1.

If defined unforeseen circumstances arise following an appropriation, North Dakota Century Code Chapter 54-16 grants authority to the state's Emergency Commission to approve agency requests for line item transfers, for acceptance of additional federal or other funds, and for use of state contingencies appropriations. Transfer or additional spending of federal or other funds exceeding $50,000 requires Budget Section approval.

Documents in the Budget Process

Planning, preparing, and managing a state budget is a continuous process throughout which the Office of Management and Budget (OMB) and the Legislative Council produce a variety of budget documents that provide information about state revenues and appropriations. Following is a chart of North Dakota's budget publications produced each biennium.

	Date	Publication	Author	Description
Even-numbered years	March or April	*Guidelines for Preparation of Biennium Agency Operating and Capital Budget Requests*	Governor and OMB	Agency guidelines for the preparation of the next biennium's budget
Even-numbered years	By July 15	Budget Requests	State Agencies	Agency/institution budget requests, narratives of functions and programs, and appropriations for the last two biennia
Even-numbered years	December	*Budget Message of the Governor and Executive Budget Summary*	Governor and OMB	Governor's budget recommendations and message delivered to the Legislative Assembly
Odd-numbered years	By January	*Executive Budget Detail*	OMB	Agency budget requests and details about the Governor's budget recommendations
Odd-numbered years		*Supplement to the Report of the Legislative Council, Budget Section: Analysis of . . . Executive Budget*	Legislative Council	Narrative and schedules analyzing the executive budget recommendations
Odd-numbered years	Crossover	*Analysis of Legislative Changes to the Governor's Budget*	Legislative Council	List and explanation of legislative changes made through crossover to agency budgets for the upcoming biennium
Odd-numbered years	End of the legislative session	*Analysis of Legislative Changes to the Governor's Budget*	Legislative Council	List and explanation of legislative changes made to agency budgets for the upcoming biennium
Odd-numbered years	After legislative session adjournment	*State Budget Actions . . . Biennium*	Legislative Council	Comparison of total legislative appropriations, executive budget recommendations, and the previous biennium's agency/institution appropriations; analyses of special funds and FTE positions; pie graphs and schedules on general fund revenues and appropriations
Odd-numbered years		*Legislative Appropriations for the . . . Biennium*	Governor's Office and OMB	Summary of and Governor's policies relating to the budget passed by the Legislative Assembly; agency/institution total appropriations

	Date	Publication	Author	Description
Odd-numbered years	Following a legislative session	*Report on Appropriations and Estimated Revenues for the Biennium . . .*	Legislative Council	Final budget status report showing Legislative Assembly changes and final agency/institution appropriations from the general fund and special funds; comparison of agency/institution appropriations changes listed by bill number
	Between legislative sessions	*Biennium Report on Compliance with Legislative Intent*	Legislative Council	Report on agency/institution compliance with legislative intent included in appropriations measures; information on the status of selected special funds
		Audit Reports	State Auditor	Report on agencies' use of appropriated funds
	End of the biennium	*Biennium Budget and Actual Detail (Budgetary Basis)*	OMB	Individual agency/institution revenues and expenditures; information on each agency's/institution's total approved, adjusted, spent, and unspent or uncollected appropriations for the biennium
	End of the fiscal year	*Comprehensive Annual Financial Report for the Fiscal Year Ended June 30, . . .*	OMB	Financial statements on the state's revenues, expenditures, and funding sources; section defining all special funds

Legislative Documents and Resources

Legislative documents and resources related to a particular Legislative Assembly, including most of the materials listed in this section, are available by clicking on the applicable link online at www.legis.nd.gov/assembly.

	Resource	Description
General	*Constitution of North Dakota*	Supreme legal document of the state of North Dakota
	North Dakota Century Code	North Dakota's codification of general and permanent law, first published between 1959 and 1960 and named to commemorate the 100th anniversary of the establishment of Dakota Territory in 1861
	Legislative events calendar	List of legislative session dates, interim committee meeting dates, and other dates important to the legislative process
	News page	Key information about the legislative branch, such as announcements about upcoming meetings and updates on legislator activities

	Resource	Description
Session	Bill action pages	Date and chamber information, descriptions, and journal links for legislative measures
	Bill version pages	Official amendments, fiscal notes, and versions for legislative measures
	Senate and House Legislative Manual	Procedural guidelines for floor sessions of the Senate and House of Representatives and a legislative directory
	Legislative deadlines	List of important session dates such as bill filing, introduction, rereferral, and reporting deadlines and crossover
	Legislative calendars	Legislative floor session agendas
	Committee hearing schedules	Meeting information organized by date and time, committee, room, bill number, and legislator
	Journals of the Senate and House of Representatives	Records mandated by the state constitution of the actions of the Legislative Assembly
	Standing and conference committee minutes	Summaries of committee deliberation on bills and resolutions and attached testimony showing support for, opposition to, and additional information about each bill
	Major topics index	List of proposed legislation by category, with links to bill status and bill version pages as well as a short descriptive heading for each bill or resolution
	North Dakota *Session Laws*	Compilation of a given biennium's enacted laws, adopted resolutions, gubernatorial vetoes, and ballot measures
Interim	*Legislative Management Final Report* and interim committee memoranda, notices, agendas, minutes, and bill drafts	Information about interim study research, deliberation, and recommendations
	North Dakota Administrative Code	Administrative rules through which state boards, departments, and commissions classified as administrative agencies implement their statutory responsibilities

Legislative Technology

The Legislative Bill Tracking system, introduced by the Legislative Assembly prior to the 2013 legislative session, allows users to track measures based upon bill or resolution number, committee assignment, Senate and House calendars, standing or conference committee schedules, or bill status and to search the bill tracking database by bill number, introduction date, sponsor, committee, emergency clause, major topic index keyword, or North Dakota Century Code title or chapter.

In-room audio systems, installed over the past two interims following Legislative Procedure and Arrangements Committee approval, increase the quality of projected and recorded sounds within the House and Senate chambers and committee rooms.

North Dakota Legislative Daily, the mobile app introduced by the Legislative Assembly for the 2017 legislative session, features access to standing, conference, interim, and administrative rulemaking committee hearing schedules; bill status and bill documents; floor session schedules; and a meeting rooms map. The app can additionally link with the Legislative Bill Tracking System for viewing one's own personalized schedule.

Citizen Involvement

Research

During sessions of the Legislative Assembly, members of the public may obtain legislative documents, including bills and resolutions; committee hearing schedules; and daily calendars, journals, and bill status reports through the bill and journal room or through the Legislative Document Subscription Service. Additional information about the Legislative Assembly, pending legislation, and other related topics is available when the Legislative Assembly is in session through *North Dakota Legislative Daily* or at the first floor information kiosk and on the legislative branch website (www.legis.nd.gov).

Visit

High school and junior high school classes may arrange for student tours by contacting the legislative tour coordinator, and members of the general public are welcome to tour the Capitol complex throughout the year. Information on legislative meeting times is available via standing committee hearing and meeting, conference committee meeting, and legislative session schedules published in hard copy, on electronic signs located throughout the Capitol, or online on the legislative branch website.

Participate

North Dakota has one of the most open legislatures in the nation. Constituents may contact legislators during a legislative session through the legislative branch website or by leaving a message at the legislative telephone message center and may contact legislators throughout the biennium by telephone, mail, or email. North Dakota citizens have the right to testify during scheduled committee hearings on any bill or resolution before the Legislative Assembly, may request that legislators introduce bills or resolutions on their behalf for consideration by the Legislative Assembly, and may refer or initiate measures to be voted upon by the state's electorate in a primary or general election.

Serve

The Legislative Assembly encourages students to participate in the page for the day program and offers a number of legal internships, as well as a fiscal internship and a library internship, to students enrolled in North Dakota institutions of higher education. Qualified individuals may also participate in the chaplain for the day or the doctor of the day programs, apply for Legislative Council or session employment opportunities, or run for legislative office.

Legislative Management

The Legislative Assembly created the Legislative Research Committee in 1945 and renamed it the Legislative Council in 1969 and the Legislative Management in 2009. By statute, Legislative Management membership includes the majority and minority leaders of both houses, the Speaker of the House, six senators, and six representatives appointed based on the proportionate representation of each party in the Senate and the House. At least two senators and two representatives must represent the minority party.

Following each regular legislative session, the Legislative Management prioritizes interim studies and assigns each legislator to serve on one or more interim committees in the period between legislative sessions. Several interim committees, including the Administrative Rules, Budget Section, Employee Benefits Programs, Energy Development and Transmission, Information Technology, Legislative Audit and Fiscal Review, Water Topics Overview, and Workers' Compensation Review committees function under statutory authority. Interim committees allow citizen legislators to keep up with rapidly changing developments in complex fields such as the Budget Section, which receives the Governor's executive budget just prior to each legislative session, and the Administrative Rules Committee, which monitors executive branch rules. The Legislative Management names and assigns other interim committees, and if the need arises, the Chairman of the Legislative Management may assign additional studies to interim committees.

Between sessions, interim committees hold hearings, take testimony, and review information provided by the Legislative Council, state agencies, and interested parties as they consider alternative approaches to issues raised by studies. The Legislative Council staff handles the vast majority of work associated with interim studies, although the Legislative Management occasionally contracts with universities, consulting firms, or outside professionals on specialized studies and projects.

In November of each even-numbered year, the Legislative Management meets to consider the results of all interim committee work and may accept, reject, or amend committee reports. The Legislative Management then presents its recommendations, together with bills and resolutions necessary for implementation, to the Legislative Assembly.

The Legislative Management interim studies over the past 72 years have influenced nearly every facet of state government. The Legislative Management is, in a sense, the Legislative Assembly working between sessions.

Legislative Council

Providing continuity between legislative sessions, the Legislative Management, through its attorneys, accountants, and other personnel known as the Legislative Council, provides a wide range of services to legislators, other state agencies, and the public, including:

- Staffing interim study committees.
- Drafting bills and resolutions.
- Providing fiscal and budget analyses.
- Supervising the publication of the *Laws of North Dakota* (Session Laws), the *North Dakota Century Code*, and the *North Dakota Administrative Code*.
- Providing legal advice on legislative matters to legislators and legislative committees.
- Considering problems of statewide significance that arise during the interim.
- Handling financial administration for the legislative branch.
- Developing and managing information technology services for the Legislative Assembly.
- Reviewing information technology in all three branches of state government.
- Representing the Legislative Assembly in interstate organizations, such as the National Conference of State Legislatures, Midwestern Legislative Conference, Council of State Governments, and the National Conference of Commissioners on Uniform State Laws.
- Encouraging coordination between the Legislative Assembly and other branches of state government.
- Responding to informational needs of legislators and their constituents.
- Handling miscellaneous interim business for the Legislative Assembly.
- Maintaining a library of contemporary and historical legislative reference sources.
- Preparing and submitting to the Secretary of State the estimated fiscal impact of an initiated measure, then tracking and reporting on actual fiscal impact if voters approve the initiated measure.
- Providing technical expertise to budget and appropriation committees.
- Reviewing audit reports for the Legislative Audit and Fiscal Review Committee (LAFRC).
- Assisting LAFRC in conducting studies designed to improve the state's fiscal practices.

Legislative Compensation

The 1889 Constitution of North Dakota entitled legislators to compensation of $5 per day during a legislative session and 10 cents per mile for travel to and from the Capitol. As the cost of serving in the Legislative Assembly rose, expense reimbursements gradually increased.

In 1969, the Legislative Assembly established a five-member committee of gubernatorial appointees called the Legislative Compensation Commission to determine appropriate rates of expense allowance and compensation for legislators. The Legislative Assembly repealed this commission in 1979 but recreated it in 1983 following voter approval of a constitutional amendment that repealed the 1889 constitutional provision of $5 per day, authorized the Legislative Assembly to set compensation levels, provided that legislators' expenses could not exceed those of other state employees, and prohibited the practice of unvouchered expense reimbursements (Article XI, Section 26 of the Constitution of North Dakota).

In 2011, the Legislative Assembly repealed the Legislative Compensation Commission once again and amended North Dakota Century Code (NDCC) Section 54-03-20 to require that the Legislative Management make recommendations and submit any necessary legislation to adjust legislative compensation amounts prior to each regular legislative session. Since 2011, legislator compensation has increased by the same percentage as state employees.

Legislative Compensation and Reimbursement 1969-2016

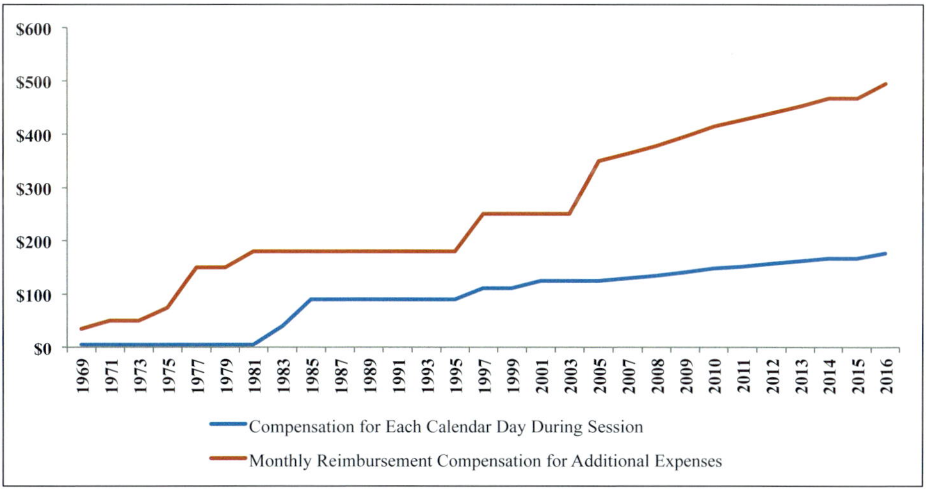

Salary and Other Reimbursement Legislators Receive under Current Law (as of October 2016)

Compensation During Term of Office (NDCC § 54-03-20)

- Compensation paid monthly to legislators during term of office — $495 per month

- Additional compensation for majority leaders, minority leaders, and chairman of the Legislative Management — $355 per month

Compensation for Regular, Special, or Organizational Sessions

- Salary (NDCC § 54-03-20) — $177 per calendar day

- Additional compensation (NDCC § 54-03-10)
  - Speaker of the House, majority leaders, and minority leaders — $15 per calendar day
  - Substantive standing committee chairmen, assistant majority leaders, and assistant minority leaders — $10 per calendar day

Expense Reimbursement for Regular, Special, or Organizational Sessions

- Reimbursement for lodging expenses (NDCC § 54-03-20)
  90 percent of the rate established by the U.S. General Services Administration for lodging reimbursement in the state plus tax per calendar day up to 30 times 70 percent of the state daily lodging reimbursement rate for legislators who reside outside of Bismarck and Mandan (currently $81.90 plus tax per calendar day up to $1,682 per month for legislators who reside outside of Bismarck or Mandan)

- Mileage
  Mileage reimbursement rate per mile for legislators who reside outside of Bismarck for one round trip each calendar week going to and from the meeting of the Legislative Assembly (current mileage reimbursement rate is 53.5 cents per mile)

Compensation for Interim Meetings (NDCC § 54-35-10)

- Compensation for attendance at meetings of the Legislative Management and its committees — $177 per day

- Additional compensation for the chairman of the Legislative Management and committee chairmen — $5 per day

Expense Reimbursement for Interim Meetings

- Meals (NDCC § 44-08-04)
  Up to $35 per day in state; an amount equal to the federal per diem meals rate for out-of-state travel

- Lodging (NDCC § 44-08-04)
  Actual expenses per day not to exceed 90 percent of the rate established by the U.S. General Services Administration for lodging reimbursement in the state (current lodging reimbursement rate is $81.90 per night), plus any applicable state or local taxes in state; actual expenses for out-of-state travel

- Mileage (NDCC § 54-06-09)
  Mileage reimbursement rate per mile by motor vehicle (current mileage reimbursement rate is 53.5 cents); 18 cents per mile by motor vehicle 300 miles beyond the state border; 80 cents per mile by private airplane (1.5 times the state mileage reimbursement rate per mile by motor vehicle)

Reconvened Sessions of the North Dakota Legislative Assembly

In 1976, voters approved a constitutional amendment allowing the Legislative Assembly to meet for 80 natural days during a two-year period (Article IV, Section 7, of the Constitution of North Dakota). The Legislative Assembly used this provision in 1981 to call itself back into session for redistricting purposes, and on June 16, 2015, the 64th Legislative Assembly reconvened to consider the final report of the Special Committee on the Resolution of Senate Bill No. 2022.

Special Sessions of the North Dakota Legislative Assembly

Under Article V, Section 7, of the Constitution of North Dakota, the Governor may call a special session of the Legislative Assembly on "extraordinary occasions." In 2016, Governor Jack Dalrymple called a special session "to make needed adjustments to the state budget due to lower than forecasted tax revenue totals." Previous Legislative Assembly special sessions took place in 1892, 1918, 1919, 1944, 1965, 1984, 1986, 1991, 1994, 2001, 2003, and 2011.

✔ See the 2011-2013 and 2013-2015 editions of the *North Dakota Blue Book* for details on special sessions.

Chairmen and Vice Chairmen of the North Dakota Legislative Management

Interim	Chairman	Vice Chairman
1945-46 (Legislative Research Committee)	Representative E. J. Langley (R-ROC) Rock Lake	Representative Palmer Levin (R-NPL) Park River
1947-48		Senator E. H. (Everett Hall) Brant (R-ROC) Linton
1949-50	Senator Carroll E. Day (R-ROC) Grand Forks	Representative Walter Bubel (R-NPL) Center
1951-52	Representative Roy A. Holand (R-ROC) LaMoure	
1953-54	Representative Ralph Beede (R-NPL) Elgin	Senator Orris G. Nordhaugen (R-NPL) Leeds
1955-56	Representative Ralph Beede (R) Elgin	Senator Iver Solberg (R-NPL) Ray
1957-58		Senator Ralph Dewing (D-NPL) Columbus
1959-60	Senator Donald Holand (R) Lisbon	Representative George R. Bernston (D-NPL) Edinburg
1961-62 1963-64 1965-66	Senator George Longmire (R) Grand Forks	Representative Oscar Solberg (D-NPL) Mylo
1967-68	Representative George Unruh (R) Grand Forks	
1969-70 (Legislative Council)	Representative Bryce Streibel (R) Fessenden	Senator Herbert L. Meschke (D-NPL) Minot
1971-72		Senator Robert M. Nasset (R) Regent
1973-74		Senator L. D. (Lee) Christensen (D-NPL) Kenmare
1975-76	Senator Robert Melland (R) Jamestown	Representative Richard J. Backes (D-NPL) Glenburn

Interim	Chairman	Vice Chairman
1977-78	Representative Roy Hausauer (R) Wahpeton	Senator James Smykowski (R) Cayuga
1979-80		Senator Chuck Goodman (R) Grand Forks
1981-82		Senator Jack Olin (R) Dickinson
1983-84 1985-86		Senator David E. Nething (R) Jamestown
1987-88 1989-90	Representative Charles F. Mertens (D-NPL) Devils Lake	Senator Corliss Mushik (D-NPL) Mandan
1991-92 1993-94	Senator Corliss Mushik (D-NPL) Mandan	Representative Bill Oban (D-NPL) Bismarck
1995-96 1997-98 1999-2000	Senator Gary J. Nelson (R) Casselton	Representative John Dorso (R) Fargo
2001-02	Representative Wesley R. Belter (R) Leonard	Senator Bob Stenehjem (R) Bismarck
2003-04 2005-06	Senator Bob Stenehjem (R) Bismarck	Representative Rick Berg (R) Fargo
2007-08 2009-10 (Legislative Management)	Representative Al Carlson (R) Fargo	Senator Bob Stenehjem (R) Bismarck
2011-12	Representative Al Carlson (R) Fargo	Senator Bob Stenehjem (R) Bismarck Senator Rich Wardner (R) Dickinson
2013-14 2015-16 2017-18	Senator Ray Holmberg (R) Grand Forks	Representative Al Carlson (R) Fargo

North Dakota Legislators Who Served in the Army or Naval Service (Including the Marine Corps) During World War I

Aker, Maurice Sanford
Anderson, Andy John
Andre, Jacob Raymond
Baldwin, Murray Alpheus
Balerud, Bert Arthur
Beede, Ralph Gordon
Belzer, LeRoy William
Bjerkan, Ingval
Bjorgo, Lawrence Knute
Blaisdell, Josiah Crosby, Jr.
Blanchard, Horace James
Blank, Philip William
Boyd, Robert James
Brickner, Clair Francis
Burgum, Leslie Ranard
Burke, Thomas Joseph
Carlson, Arthur Berton "Buck"
Carlson, Harry Ernest
Conway, William Daniel
Correll, Lafayette Eugene
Currie, Jack McPherson
Dahlen, Peder Ingelbert
Downey, Romanus James
Fitch, Kenneth Alfred
Flannigan, William John "Pat"
Flatt, Jonathan Lloyd "Mike"
Fleenor, Walter W.
Fraine, John Henry
Fredrickson, Fred Joseph
Freeman, Charles Vernon
Gray, Robert Thomas
Hageman, Walter Read
Hanley, James Martin
Harrington, Philo George
Harris, Charles Frank
Henderson, Floyd Enoch
Indergaard, Elling Melvin
Johnson, Arthur C.
Johnson, Ole Martin
Johnson, Ole Sylvester
Keidel, Carl George
Kelly, Milton G.
Kitchen, Joseph Ambrose
Larson, Roy
Locken, Gustav Ingram
Loftesnes, Melvin Louis
Lynch, Mathew Hoyt
Lynn, Harry C.
Magill, John
McGillic, James Theodore
McIlraith, Edward John
Morris, Harry James
Mostad, Alfred
Mudgett, Charles Frederick
Nelson, Arthur Burton
Nelson, Arthur Zachary
O'Brien, Harry Francis
Olson, Raymond E.
Page, Franklin
Panko, Dan
Peterson, Frederick Jacob
Preszler, Adam John
Ritter, Christ Peter
Rue, Milton L.
Ruemmele, Frank Joseph
Rulon, Arthur Jackson
Rygg, Arthur
Sagehorn, Eldor George
Sauer, Philip Jacob
Schantz, William Marzelius
Schlosser, Walter Howard
Semling, Harold Victor
Severson, Hans G.
Simonson, Edward Elias
Skartvedt, Selmer Kalob
Smith, Leland Jennings
Starck, Nathaniel Carl "Tony"
Starke, Charles Henry
Swanson, Harley Roy
Symington, Earl Duncan
Tester, Walter Robert
Thompson, Harry Lawrence
Thompson, Sivert W.
Tollefson, Carl Gerhard
Vinje, Martin Edwin
Wadeson, Harry William
Wahlund, Oscar
Welk, Joseph
Whelan, Thomas Edward
White, Frank
Witteman, Orville Phillip
Wright, Dana Monroe

Women in Leadership
North Dakota Legislative Assembly: 1889-2017

Leadership Position	Senate	Years	Party	House	Years	Party
President	Lieutenant Governor Ruth Meyers Lieutenant Governor Rosemarie Myrdal	1985-1987 1992-2000	D-NPL R			
Speaker of the House				Representative Minnie Craig Representative Patricia "Tish" Kelly Representative Janet Wentz	1933-1934 1983-1984 2003-2004	R-NPL D-NPL R
President Pro Tempore	Senator Bonnie Heinrich Senator Corliss Mushik Senator Karen K. Krebsbach Senator Judy Lee	1991-1992 1993-1994 2001-2002 2007-2008	D-NPL D-NPL R R			
Interim President Pro Tempore	Senator Shirley Lee	1983-1984	R			
Majority Leader[1]	*None*			*None*		
Minority Leader[1]	Senator Joan Heckaman	2017-	D-NPL	*None*		
Assistant Majority Leader[2]	*None*			Representative Corliss Mushik	1983-1984	D-NPL
Assistant Minority Leader[2]	Senator Carolyn C. Nelson Senator Joan Heckaman	2007-2010 2013-2016	D-NPL D-NPL	Representative Corliss Mushik Representative Pam Gulleson Representative Kathy Hogan	1979-1982 1997-2002 2017-	D-NPL D-NPL D-NPL
Democratic Caucus Leader[2]	Senator Carolyn C. Nelson	2001-2006, 2017-	D-NPL	Representative Bonnie Heinrich	1979-1980	D-NPL
Republican Caucus Leader[2]	Senator Donna Nalewaja Senator Karen K. Krebsbach	1989-1990 1991-1992	R R	Representative Cathy Rydell Representative Clara Sue Price	1989-1990 1993-1994	R R

[1]Senate records 1941-present, House records 1925-present   [2] Records 1979-present

The 65th Legislative Assembly

Regular Session: Tuesday, January 3 – Thursday, April 27, 2017 (77 Legislative Days)

Bills and Resolutions

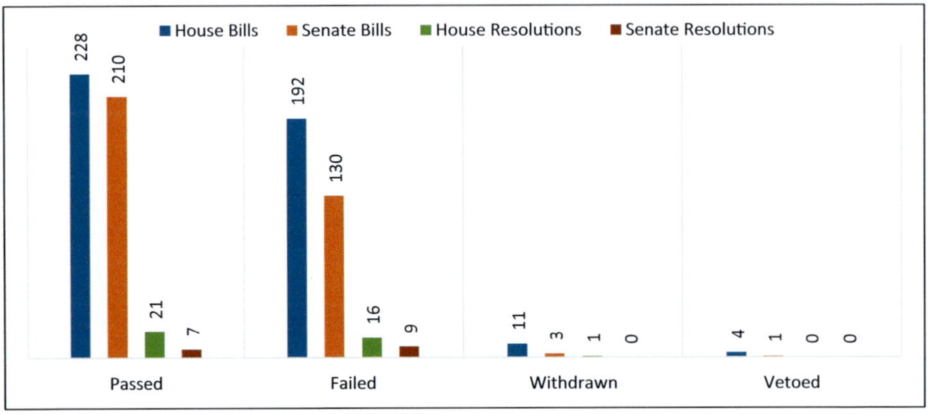

Composition

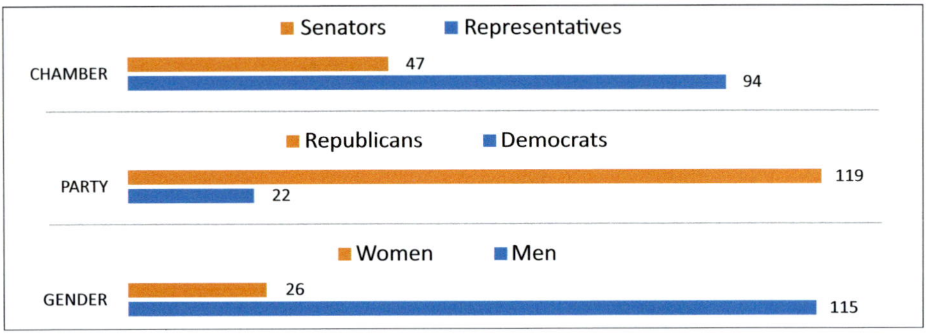

Leadership

Position	Senate	House
President President Pro Tempore Interim President Pro Tempore	Lieutenant Governor Brent Sanford Senator Gary A. Lee Senator Dave Oehlke	
Speaker		Representative Larry Bellew
Majority Leader	Senator Rich Wardner	Representative Al Carlson
Assistant Majority Leader	Senator Jerry Klein	Representative Don Vigesaa
Minority Leader	Senator Joan Heckaman	Representative Corey Mock
Assistant Minority Leader	Senator John Grabinger	Representative Kathy Hogan
Republican Caucus Leader	Senator David Hogue	Representative Mike Lefor
Democratic Caucus Leader	Senator Carolyn C. Nelson	Representative Joshua A. Boschee

Budget Overview

General Fund

The Legislative Assembly projected general fund revenues for the 2017-19 biennium of $4.36 billion – $1.29 billion, or 22.8%, less than the 2015-17 biennium revenues as included in the 2017 legislative revenue forecast. The Legislative Assembly anticipated state agency general fund turnback of $57 million at the end of the 2015-17 biennium. Major areas of tax and fee revenue change as compared to the revised revenue forecast for the 2015-17 biennium included an estimated increase of $21.3 million, or 19.6%, in insurance premium tax collections; an estimated increase of $4.1 million, or 15.7%, in mineral leasing fees; and an estimated decrease of $57.8 million, or 36.1%, in corporate income taxes. Oil tax revenue allocations to the general fund were $400 million, an increase of $100 million from the 2015-17 biennium.

The Legislative Assembly provided general fund appropriations of $4.31 billion – $1.38 billion, or 24.2%, less than the 2015-17 adjusted legislative appropriations. Major general fund appropriation increases included $57.6 million for the Department of Human Services and $9.8 million for the Department of Corrections and Rehabilitation. Major general fund appropriation decreases related to the Department of Transportation ($613.4 million), Department of Public Instruction ($266.1 million), State Treasurer ($241.3 million), Higher Education ($212.1 million), Department of Commerce ($21.2 million), Parks and Recreation Department ($16.5 million), Industrial Commission ($7.3 million), Attorney General ($7.0 million), and Office of Management and Budget ($6.1 million).

Special Funds

The Legislative Assembly provided special funds appropriations of $9.24 billion – $924.1 million, or 11.1%, more than the 2015-17 adjusted legislative appropriations. Major special funds appropriations increases included $1,993.3 million for Higher Education, $309.4 million for the Department of Human Services, $272.9 million for the Department of Public Instruction, $90.2 million for the Department of Trust Lands, $72.9 million for the Information Technology Department, $13.6 million for the State Department of Health, and $12.3 million for the Attorney General.

Tax Relief

The Legislative Assembly provided for property tax relief as follows:

1. $160.7 million to the Department of Human Services for a state-paid economic assistance and social services pilot program during the 2017-19 biennium.
2. $23.3 million to the Department of Human Services to continue state funding for certain county costs of child welfare and service payments for elderly and disabled services.

3. $22.9 million to the Tax Department, including $14.8 million for the homestead tax credit program and $8.1 million for the disabled veterans' property tax credit program.

Summary of Selected Appropriations

Higher Education: $625.8 million – $212.1 million, or 25.3%, decrease
(a decrease of $68.8 million in ongoing funding and a decrease of $143.4 million in one-time funding)

- $15.2 million added for student residency positions at the University of North Dakota School of Medicine and Health Sciences.
- $2 million added for the higher education challenge fund to provide matching grants of $1 for every $2 of private donations for academic enhancements to North Dakota University System institutions.
- $59.5 million removed from campus base funding formula distributions.

Elementary and Secondary Education: $2,015.9 million – $12.5 million increase

- In 2013, the Legislative Assembly approved a change in the K-12 state school aid funding formula. The formula change provides the state will determine an adequate base level of support necessary to educate students, and this base level of support will be provided through a combination of local tax sources, local revenue, and state integrated formula payments. The Legislative Assembly appropriated $1.935 billion of integrated formula payments for the 2017-19 biennium.
- $6 million of one-time funding for rapid enrollment grants.
- $5.5 million for PowerSchool.

Human Services: $1,339.2 million –$57.6 million, or 4.5%, increase

- $224.9 million for cost, caseload, utilization, rate, and other changes in programs authorized by the 2017 Legislative Assembly.
- $160.7 million for a county social services financing pilot program.
- $40.8 million federal one-time funding for a health information technology and care coordination system.
- $40.4 million for Medicare Part D "clawback" payments.
- $7.5 million to implement, in conjunction with the Department of Corrections and Rehabilitation, a community behavioral health program.
- $3 million federal one-time funding for a child care licensing system.
- $5 million decrease for a department-wide reduction of 33 FTE positions.

Capital Construction: $1.32 billion

- $714.5 million for transportation-related projects.
- $305.4 million for water projects.
- $261.2 million for major capital projects.
- $23.1 million for extraordinary repairs.
- $12.5 million for bond payments.
- $2.7 million for other projects.

State Employees

- The 2017-19 biennium FTE level of 15,847.38 is an overall decrease of 620.18 FTE positions compared to the adjusted 2015-17 biennium total, including a decrease of 313.27 FTE positions in higher education and a decrease of 306.91 FTE positions in all other state agencies.
- $42.8 million for a health insurance premium increase.

Corrections: $214.3 million – $9.8 million, or 4.8%, increase

- Added 9 new FTE positions.
- $27.2 million for contract housing and programming.
- $10.8 million for female inmate contract housing.
- $7 million for a community behavioral health program in cooperation with the Department of Human Services.

Information Technology: $144.1 million for state agency information technology projects, including:

- $43.5 million, including $40.8 million in federal funds, for a North Dakota Health Information Network expansion project.
- $28.7 million for the statewide interoperable radio network.
- $11.2 million in federal funds to Job Service North Dakota for an unemployment insurance modernization project.
- $9.5 million for information technology equipment costs.
- $8.9 million to Workforce Safety and Insurance, including $8.1 million for Phase 3 of the claims and policy system project, $538,500 for an extranet enhancement project, and $275,000 for an Oracle Reports enhancement project.
- $3.6 million to the Department of Trust Lands for an information technology system replacement.
- $3 million to the Department of Human Services for a child care licensing system.

Economic Development

- $10.9 million for North Dakota Tourism.
- $3.2 million for the Agricultural Products Utilization Commission.
- $3 million one-time funding for enhanced use lease grants.
- $2.3 million for entrepreneurship grants and vouchers, also known as Innovate North Dakota.
- $2 million for the North Dakota Trade Office.
- $2 million for workforce training in the Department of Career and Technical Education.
- $950,000 for Operation Intern, a program providing matching funds to help expand the number of internships, work experience, and apprenticeship positions with North Dakota employers.
- $600,000 one-time funding for providing grants of up to $200,000 each to assist in base retention efforts in three communities with Air Force bases – Minot Air Force Base, Grand Forks Air Force Base, and Fargo Air National Guard Base.
- $500,000 to the Department of Commerce for a grant to be awarded to the Energy and Environmental Research Center at the University of North Dakota, which must be utilized for economic development and diversification of the North Dakota economy and which may be provided only to the extent the Energy and Environmental Research Center provide $1 of matching funds from private or other public sources for each $1 provided by the department.
- $500,000 one-time funding to the Department of Commerce for providing workforce grants to tribally controlled community colleges in North Dakota.
- $1.6 million decrease for elimination of the Job Service North Dakota Workforce 20/20 program.

Child Care

- $22.6 million to the Department of Human Services for child care assistance programs.
- $6.7 million to the Department of Human Services for workforce development and training, including $4 million for grants to child care providers for workforce development pursuant to North Dakota Century Code Section 50-11.1-14.1 and $2.7 million, including $2.6 million in federal funds, for contracts to provide technical assistance.
- $1.5 million to the Department of Public Instruction for a grant pool that may be used for preschool continuing education grants, as well as other non-child care programs, including leveraging the senior year, leadership program, continuing education grants, curriculum alignment grants, and teacher and principal evaluation system grants.
- $1.5 million to the Department of Commerce for early childhood education grants.

Infrastructure

- $713.6 million, including $523.8 million from federal funds, for road projects.
- $652.5 million for water projects.
- $46.7 million for airport grants.

Transportation

- The Legislative Assembly anticipated $615.1 million in regular federal highway construction funds for the 2017-19 biennium with $141.9 million in state and local matching funds.
- The Legislative Assembly anticipated $21.7 million in funding for federal emergency relief projects for the 2017-19 biennium, including $2.3 million in state and local matching funds.

Summary of Selected Legislation

House Bill No. 1015, the appropriation bill for the Office of Management and Budget, increases from $10 million to $50 million the maximum loan authority of the Bank of North Dakota to the State Treasurer and to the Office of Management and Budget if the balance of the general fund is insufficient to meet legislative appropriations and directs the Office of Management and Budget to report any loan from the Bank of North Dakota obtained under this law to the Budget Section of the Legislative Management.

The bill requires each county auditor to submit a report to the Tax Commissioner that provides each taxing district's property valuation, property tax levy, and any other information the Tax Commissioner requests. The bill repeals the requirement the county auditor certify the tax list prepared by each taxing district or municipality in the county. The bill requires the Tax Commissioner, using the information submitted by the county auditors, to prepare and to provide to the Legislative Management by April 1 of each year a statewide report of property tax increase, which must include the annual increase in property taxes levied by each taxing district. The bill provides property subject to a tax increment financing development agreement before August 1, 2017, is not subject to the specific county and school district notice, approval, and negotiation requirements relating to the granting of property tax incentives.

The bill also allows an individual who has completed a full year of teaching at a nonpublic school to receive loan forgiveness under the student loan forgiveness program for teaching in an area of critical need, authorizes a state agency to charge a fee for providing a paper copy of an agency publication, suspends the Tribal and State Relations Committee, provides the North Dakota Board of Physical Therapy may not disclose a record of a criminal history background check performed as part of physical therapist or physical therapist assistant licensure to the Physical Therapy Compact Commission or similar entity, removes a restriction that disallows a qualified alcoholic beverage licensee who receives a special event permit from the local governing body from holding the special event on the licensee's fixed or permanent licensed premises, provides an appropriation of $1,634,854 to North Dakota State University to pay costs associated with the collapse of Minard Hall and an appropriation of $875,000 to Dickinson State University to pay for institutional operations, amends House Bill No. 1228 to allow real estate investment trusts to own interests in real property within the state, and defines a "real estate investment trust."

House Bill No. 1025 requires the Director of the Game and Fish Department to issue special allocation turkey, deer, elk, and moose hunting licenses to nonprofit organizations for raffles, auctions, or special hunts for individuals served by the organizations.

House Bill No. 1040 directs the Department of Human Services to adopt rules for an evidence-based alcohol and drug education program for individuals who have violated the law relating to underage consumption of alcohol and requires an individual under the age of 21 who unlawfully enters a licensed premises that sells alcoholic beverages to complete the evidence-based alcohol and drug education program as part of the individual's sentence for committing the offense.

House Bill No. 1041 provides an individual is guilty of a Class B misdemeanor for ingestion of marijuana and of a Class A misdemeanor for the ingestion of any other controlled substance; reduces the offense level for use of a controlled substance analog; updates the mandatory terms of imprisonment for the manufacture, delivery, or possession with intent to manufacture or deliver a controlled substance; and provides the increased penalties for a person manufacturing or possessing a controlled substance near a school property apply if the individual commits the offense within 300 feet of the school property and during a school-sponsored activity or during the hours of 6 a.m. to 10 p.m. if school is in session. The bill removes the Class C felony designation for automobile, aircraft, or other motor-propelled vehicle theft.

The bill requires a sentencing court to sentence an individual who has pled guilty to, or has been found guilty of, a Class C felony offense or Class A misdemeanor offense to a term of probation at the time of initial sentencing, except for a sexual offense subject to registration or for an offense involving domestic violence against a child; involving a firearm or dangerous weapon, explosive, or incendiary device; or for which the law requires a mandatory term of incarceration. The bill requires the sentence for an assault, reckless endangerment, terrorizing, or menacing offense against an actor's family or household member must include an order to complete a domestic violence offender evaluation and treatment program as determined by the court. The bill authorizes the court to provide as an intermediate condition of probation one period of incarceration during a period of probation not to exceed 30 consecutive days in lieu of a probation revocation petition and to terminate any probation for a driving under the influence offense when a defendant completes an applicable drug treatment program.

The bill authorizes the Department of Corrections and Rehabilitation to place an individual in a drug and alcohol treatment program. The bill directs the Department of Corrections and Rehabilitation to allow faith-based organizations to provide services to individuals in need of addiction treatment services and includes intermittent imprisonment in a facility with an available faith-based program deemed appropriate for the treatment of an individual offender into a term of imprisonment. The bill provides an individual sentenced to a correctional facility under North Dakota Century Code Chapter 12-44.1 is eligible to earn sentence reductions for good conduct and for time spent in custody before sentencing, but prohibits the Department of Corrections and Rehabilitation from allowing an offender sentence reduction credit for time spent on probation under the supervision of the department.

The bill also prohibits the Department of Human Services from denying supplemental nutrition assistance program (SNAP) and temporary assistance for needy families (TANF) program assistance based on the conviction of a felony offense that has as an element the possession, use, or distribution of a controlled substance.

House Bill No. 1045 disqualifies investments made after June 30, 2017, from the current angel fund investment tax credit and creates a new angel fund investor credit applicable for investments made beginning July 1, 2017. The bill provides a credit against individual income tax liability for investments made by a certified angel fund in the amount of 35 percent of the amount invested in an in-state qualified business and 25 percent of the amount invested in an out-of-state qualified business. The bill requires the investor to claim the credit in the taxable year of the investment in the qualified business and limits claims to no more than $45,000 in credits in any single taxable year and $500,000 in credits over any combination of taxable years. The bill imposes reporting requirements on angel funds, including disclosure of the total amount invested in each qualified business, and attaches penalties for failing to file the required reports.

House Bill No. 1098 allows an individual who has a minor in early childhood education to be eligible to teach kindergarten or prekindergarten if licensed by the Educational Standards and Practices Board.

House Bill No. 1150 provides a hunting license lottery applicant may purchase only one bonus point for the year if the applicant enters the lottery with the intent to forfeit any license received. The bill requires allocation of bonus point fees to the private land open to sportsmen program.

House Bill No. 1151 requires any person having control over a receptacle or facility associated with oil and gas or water production, injection, processing, or well servicing to report any leak or spill to the Industrial Commission unless it amounts to less than a total of 10 barrels over a 15-day period, remains on the site or facility, and is on a well site where the well was spud after September 1, 2000, or on a facility other than a well site, which was constructed after September 1, 2000. The bill requires the commission to place any written notice it issues in regard to a fire, leak, spill, blowout, or leak and spill cleanup violation in the file associated with the well or facility where it occurred and to make the files available to surface owners for review.

House Bill No. 1152 modifies allocations of oil extraction and gross production tax revenues designated for deposit in the general fund. The bill provides after deposit of the first $200 million in the general fund, the amount deposited in the tax relief fund decreases from the next $300 million to the next $200 million. Following the deposit of revenue in the tax relief fund, the bill designates the next $75 million for deposit in the budget stabilization fund, so long as the amount deposited does not bring the balance of the budget stabilization fund to more than 9.5 percent of the current biennial general fund budget. The bill requires the next deposit to be to the general fund, in the amount of $200 million during the 2017-19 biennium and $100 million for periods after July 31, 2019. The bill requires the next $100 million to be deposited 80 percent into the strategic investment and improvements fund and 20 percent into the lignite research fund until the latter reaches $3 million, after which $100 million must be deposited into the strategic investment and improvements fund. The bill reduces the last distribution into the state disaster relief fund from $22 million to $20 million and provides it must not bring the unobligated fund balance to more than $20 million in lieu of the previous $25 million cap.

House Bill No. 1159 requires each plate assigned to a vehicle to be mounted in a visible manner that clearly displays its distinctive assigned number and state of issue and authorizes the number plates assigned to a motorcycle or to a trailer to be displayed vertically.

House Bill No. 1169 allows an individual who is not otherwise prohibited from possessing a Class 2 firearm and dangerous weapon license and who has been a resident of the state for at least one year to carry a concealed firearm if the individual possesses a North Dakota driver's license or identification card issued by the Department of Transportation. The bill allows an individual to show proof of a valid driver's license or nondriver identification card on a mobile device upon demand of proof of residency by a law enforcement officer and requires an individual who is carrying a concealed firearm to inform a law enforcement officer who initiates a traffic stop or other in-person contact of the individual's possession of a concealed weapon.

House Bill No. 1178 directs the Information Technology Department to begin implementing the Statewide Interoperable Radio Network (SIRN), according to the findings of the Statewide Interoperability Executive Committee, and provides legislative intent regarding the use of the network. The bill excludes financing of SIRN and its equipment and services from the list of Information Technology Department powers, but authorizes the department to obtain a loan up to $15 million from the Bank of North Dakota for the network. The bill establishes a statewide interoperable radio network fund in the State Treasury for the state share of expenses of SIRN, requires political subdivisions to increase the fee on assessed communications services and put the increased collections into the statewide interoperable radio network fund, increases the prepaid wireless emergency 911 fee, and creates exceptions for agreements and financing related to SIRN to allow long-term financing and financing of larger software or equipment purchases. The bill adds the Executive Director of the Indian Affairs Commission, a member of the House of Representatives, and a member of the Senate to the Statewide Interoperability Executive Committee.

House Bill No. 1183 creates a Class A misdemeanor for a person exposing one's private body parts by unsolicited electronic means or by any electronic means to a minor. The bill enhances the offense from a Class A misdemeanor to a Class C felony for a subsequent offense if the victim is a minor. The bill defines "electronic means" and expands the definition of "sexual conduct" to include "actual or simulated nude or partially denuded human figure" and "physical contact with a person's clothed or unclothed" private body parts.

House Bill No. 1206 expands the definition of the term "relative," as used with respect to adoption and child relinquishment, to include a first cousin. The bill creates an alternate reporting requirement for interfamily adoptions by replacing the preplacement adoption assessment with a criminal history assessment and three written character statements.

House Bill No. 1222 creates a civil restraining order process for victims of sexual assault. The bill prohibits the sexual assault assailant from harassing, stalking, or threatening the individual requesting the order; appearing at the victim's residence, school, or place of employment; or contacting the victim. A violation of a sexual assault restraining order is a Class A misdemeanor and for a second or subsequent offense is a Class C felony.

House Bill No. 1269 classifies the intentional ingestion, inhalation, or injection of marijuana as a Class B misdemeanor; reduces the offense level for an individual guilty of use of a controlled substance analog; reduces the mandatory terms of imprisonment for manufacturing, delivering, or possessing with the intent to manufacture or deliver a controlled substance; and provides the increased penalties for a person manufacturing or possessing a controlled substance near a school property apply if the individual commits the offense within 300 feet of the school property and during a school-sponsored activity or during the hours of 6 a.m. to 10 p.m. if school is in session. The bill makes it a Class A misdemeanor for a person to possess five or fewer capsules, pills, or tablets of a schedule II, III, IV, or V controlled substance or controlled substance analog and removes the Class C felony designation for prescription drug theft of five or fewer capsules, pills, or tablets. The bill increases from one-half ounce to one ounce the minimum amount of marijuana a city council or city commission may prohibit an individual from possessing.

The bill provides immunity from the criminal prosecution of certain offenses to an individual who in good faith seeks medical assistance for another individual in need of emergency medical assistance due to a drug overdose. To receive immunity, the individual must have remained on the scene until assistance arrived and must have cooperated with the medical treatment of the reported drug-overdosed individual, and the overdosed individual must have been in a condition a layperson would reasonably believe to be a drug overdose requiring immediate medical assistance.

The bill also provides an offender convicted of a Class C felony aggravated assault or an attempt to commit the offense who has received a sentence of imprisonment or a sentence of imprisonment upon revocation of probation before August 1, 2015, is eligible to have the offender's sentence considered by the parole board.

House Bill No. 1275 allows a student at a public or private school to voluntarily participate in studentinitiated prayer at activities held on school premises.

House Bill No. 1279 authorizes an individual to store a firearm or dangerous weapon in a building owned or managed by the state or a political subdivision if the individual resides in the building, the storage is inside the residential unit, and the state, governing board, or designee approves the storage of the firearm or dangerous weapon.

House Bill No. 1293 creates a noncriminal offense for an individual who, knowing that individual is not licensed or privileged to do so, enters or remains in a place where notice against trespass is posted in a manner reasonably likely to come to the attention of intruders and provides a fine of $250 for each violation of the noncriminal offense.

House Bill No. 1311 increases the penalty for littering on a highway from $100 to $500.

House Bill No. 1321 authorizes the Department of Transportation to permit a farmer's farm vehicle or a motor carrier hired by a farmer to exceed specified weight limitations by 10 percent for the movement of agricultural products from the field of harvest to the point of initial storage or to the first point of sale and transfer of possession during harvest or from the point of initial storage to the first point of sale and transfer of possession during the current year's harvest.

House Bill No. 1334 prohibits an individual assessed as a high-risk sexual offender from residing within 500 feet of a public or nonpublic preschool or elementary, middle, or high school. The bill defines the term "reside" as "to live permanently or be situated for a considerable time in a home or a particular place."

House Bill No. 1341 provides a person who willfully manufactures, delivers, or possesses with intent to manufacture or deliver a controlled substance is subject to increased penalties if the person commits a second offense and was at least 21 years of age and delivered a controlled substance to a person under the age of 18 at the time of the second offense. The bill provides a person who willfully possesses a controlled substance or a controlled substance analog is guilty of a Class A misdemeanor for a first offense and a Class C felony for a second offense and provides the increased penalties for a person manufacturing or possessing a controlled substance near a school property apply if the individual commits the offense during a school-sponsored activity or during the hours of 6 a.m. to 10 p.m. if school is in session or if the defendant was at least 21 years of age at the time of the offense and the offense involved delivery of a controlled substance to a minor.

House Bill No. 1352 removes the time requirement a motor vehicle must have remained on private property without consent of the person in control of the property for the motor vehicle to be considered abandoned. The bill defines a "commercial towing service" and allows a commercial towing service to remove and to take into custody an abandoned motor vehicle located on private property if requested by an owner, lessee, tenant, or occupant of that property. The bill requires a commercial towing service provide notice to the owner of, and provides a process for an owner to reclaim, an abandoned motor vehicle that has been taken into custody. The bill provides a disposal process for an abandoned motor vehicle that has been taken into custody and has not been reclaimed by the owner, a secured party, or a lienholder and exempts a commercial towing service that lawfully disposes of an abandoned motor vehicle from the requirement that receipts from the sale or the disposal of an abandoned motor vehicle be deposited in the common schools trust fund. The bill allows a unit of government to reimburse itself for the costs of towing, storing, and disposing of an abandoned motor vehicle.

House Bill No. 1354 requires the Tax Commissioner to disclose the amount of a tax deduction or credit claimed or earned by a taxpayer upon receiving a written request for this information from the Chairman of the Legislative Management or the chairman of a standing committee of the Legislative Assembly. The bill provides the Tax Commissioner shall notify taxpayers of potential disclosures and subjects disclosures to certain restrictions.

House Bill No. 1374 provides requirements for State Water Commission composition and operation, including the intent for a commissioner to represent each of the seven major drainage basins, and establishes criteria for water projects the commission funds. The bill prohibits the commission from providing a cost-share for operation and maintenance costs of water conveyance projects, requires the commission to review progress reports for water projects, and allows the commission to terminate funding for projects not making sufficient progress. The bill requires the State Engineer to develop an economic analysis process for water conveyance projects and flood-related projects expected to cost more than $750,000 and a life cycle analysis for municipal water supply projects.

House Bill No. 1378 requires the Public Service Commission to adopt rules relating to the implementation of lightmitigating technology systems on wind energy conversion facilities. The bill requires all wind energy conversion facilities sited after June 5, 2016, to be equipped with a light-mitigating technology system by December 31, 2019, and those sited before June 5, 2016, to be equipped with a light-mitigating technology system by December 31, 2021.

House Bill No. 1389 allows a parent to direct a school district to not administer any required state test or assessment to the parent's child and creates exceptions for which a parent may not issue such a directive. The bill requires school districts to submit reports to the Superintendent of Public Instruction regarding parental directives.

House Bill No. 1390 amends permitting requirements for installation of subsurface water management systems comprising 80 acres of land area or more and requires water resource board members to attend courses on water management.

House Bill No. 1395 includes in the definition of "dangerous weapon" a device that uses a projectile and voltage or a device that uses a projectile and may be used to apply multiple applications of voltage during a single incident. The bill revises the definition of "law enforcement officer" to include a retired public servant, who was authorized by law or a government agency for at least 10 years to enforce the law and to conduct or engage in investigations or prosecutions for violations of the law; maintains the same level of firearms proficiency as is required by the Peace Officer Standards and Training Board for law enforcement officers, maintains the standards for qualifications in firearms training for law enforcement officers as determined by the former agency of the individual, or maintains the standards used by a certified firearms instructor qualified to conduct firearms qualification tests for active duty officers in the state where the individual resides; has a photo identification card issued by a local law enforcement agency that identifies the individual as having been employed by a government agency or branch as a law enforcement officer and indicates the individual has passed the firearms proficiency test within 12 months from the date of issue; and has not been found by a qualified medical professional to be unqualified for reasons relating to mental health.

House Bill No. 1409 requires the results of water quality tests that a mineral developer must conduct before commencing production operations on a surface owner's property to be reported to the State Department of Health, analyzed by a state-certified laboratory, and recorded in a database maintained by the department. The bill provides a mineral developer's failure to conduct a water quality test before commencing production operations is prima facie evidence of injury to a surface owner's water supply in any claim for relief and the refusal of a surface owner to allow the mineral developer to conduct a water quality test serves to bar a surface owner's claim for relief.

Senate Bill No. 2013, the appropriation bill for the Commissioner of University and School Lands, changes 2017-19 biennium gross production tax revenue allocations by excluding the first two percentage points of mining employment in the hub city allocation formula and by using allocations to counties in the most recently completed even-numbered fiscal year as the basis for determining political subdivision allocations and for establishing benchmarks to determine supplemental allocations to school districts. The bill creates an energy impact fund and provides to it a $2 million total allocation per fiscal year, drawn proportionally on the basis of monthly oil and gas gross production tax revenue collections from each county that received more than $5 million in the most recently completed even-numbered fiscal year.

Senate Bill No. 2037 prohibits an individual from receiving loan forgiveness under the technology occupations student loan program or the teacher shortage loan forgiveness program if the individual is receiving loan forgiveness under another program. The bill revises eligibility for the technology occupations student loan program to require a graduate to have a salary or equivalent hourly wage under $60,000 per year and for the teacher shortage loan forgiveness program to require a teacher to have an existing student loan and to have signed a contract to teach at grade levels, in content areas, or in geographical locations identified by the Superintendent of Public Instruction as having a teacher shortage or critical need. The bill provides criteria for how much an eligible teacher may receive in loan forgiveness each year based upon multiple factors and limits the number of teachers the State Board of Higher Education may approve for loan forgiveness in each school district to no more than two per year.

Senate Bill No. 2042, as part of an update of references to mental health professionals, creates a multi-tier framework of mental health professionals, updates provisions to utilize this new framework, and updates definitions. The bill corrects the provision of Senate Bill No. 2033 that addresses licensure of social workers licensed in another jurisdiction and revises provisions relating to mandatory reporting for abuse and neglect of children and of vulnerable adults.

Senate Bill No. 2047 establishes a negotiation process for water resource boards to follow before taking ownership of rights of way using quick take eminent domain. The bill provides for automatic termination of a right of way acquired through quick take eminent domain when a water resource district no longer needs the right of way for the original purpose.

Senate Bill Nos. 2091 and 2185 amend the minimum requirements for high school graduation, the North Dakota career and technical education scholarship, and the North Dakota academic scholarship.

Senate Bill No. 2134 defines the ordinary high water mark of the Missouri riverbed to establish state sovereign land mineral ownership and provides a method for the Department of Mineral Resources and the Industrial Commission to review the ordinary high water mark for segments of the riverbed. The bill includes an appropriation to the Commissioner of University and School Lands for repayment of mineral lease, bonus, rent, and royalty collections from the state to other mineral owners.

Senate Bill No. 2206 creates a two-year pilot program for the state payment of county-funded economic assistance and social service costs and repeals, for taxable years beginning after 2016, the 12 percent state-paid property tax credit. The bill suspends a county's ability to levy up to 20 mills for human service purposes for taxable years 2017 and 2018, requires property tax statements to reflect savings realized by suspending county social service mill levy authority, and creates a credit to provide comparable savings to centrally assessed companies that make payments in lieu of taxes.

The bill establishes baseline funding amounts, provides for service area human services funds and the social services finance fund, and revises the duties of county social service boards and the Department of Human Services. The bill removes information specific to taxable years 2015 and 2016 from the requirements for county officers to furnish a departmental budget to the county commissioners and provides the county social service board budget for 2020 may not exceed the 2016 budget as a starting point.

Senate Bill No. 2231 directs the Insurance Department to publish data on its website regarding the health insurance network status of each air ambulance service provider authorized to operate in the state. The bill requires if a hospital refers a patient to, or initiates contact on behalf of a patient with, an air ambulance provider for air transportation, the hospital must inform that patient of the provider's health insurance network status in order to facilitate an informed patient decision regarding the service.

The bill prohibits an insurer from issuing a health benefit plan unless the plan provides the out-of-network air ambulance provider service's reimbursement rate is equal to the average of the insurer's in-network rates for air ambulance providers in the state and, for purposes of settling a claim made by the insured under the plan, the payment is deemed to be the same as an in-network payment and is considered a full and final payment by the insured for out-of-network air ambulance services billed to the insured. The bill provides an air ambulance provider may not sell a subscription agreement or contract relating to services or the billing of services provided by an air ambulance provider and removes the criminal penalty for violation of the preferred provider organization law.

The bill also provides if a court finds the law relating to out-of-network payments is invalid, a law would become effective that health insurance preferred provider arrangements must require the health care provider to seek prior approval before accessing air ambulance services and provide a written disclosure regarding out-of-network air ambulance providers and require the insurer to develop a program and to establish an air ambulance provider mediation process for payment of out-of-network air ambulance provider bills.

Senate Bill No. 2249 requires the board of a school district to prohibit a student from participating in extracurricular activities if the student has pled guilty to or been convicted of certain criminal offenses; has an order prohibiting contact, a disorderly conduct restraining order, or a protection order issued against them; or if the principal obtains information that the student has an applicable offense or order. The bill allows the juvenile court system to notify the principal of a school if records open to inspection regarding a student of the school exist in the court system.

Senate Bill No. 2277 provides a monthly child support obligation expires upon the incarceration of the obligor if the sentence is 180 days or more. The bill provides a monthly obligation may be established for an obligor incarcerated for a period of 180 days or more if the obligation is based on actual income of the obligor and the obligee can establish the obligor's income exceeds the minimum amount owed.

Senate Bill No. 2283 prohibits a person from claiming certain state or local tax incentives until the person satisfies all state and local tax obligations and tax liens of record for taxes owed to the state or to a political subdivision. The bill requires a person to attach a county property tax clearance record to any return or filing on which the person claims a state tax incentive and to attach a state tax clearance record when claiming a local tax incentive. The bill authorizes the Tax Commissioner to disallow a state tax exemption or credit claimed under any law authorizing the Tax Commissioner to audit and assess the additional tax due.

Senate Bill No. 2288 changes property tax levy increase notice and public hearing provisions and assessment dates. The bill requires the governing body of a taxing district to provide the county auditor with a preliminary budget statement and the date, time, and location of the taxing district's public hearing on its property tax levy. The bill requires the county treasurer to provide a written notice to the owner of each parcel of taxable property containing the date, time, and location of the budget hearings for all applicable taxing districts; the true and full value of the property owner's property; the amount levied against the parcel by each taxing district in the preceding year; the estimated tax, in dollars, which will be levied in the current year; the difference between the prior and current year levy in dollars; information pertaining to estimated property tax savings; and notification that citizens may provide oral or written comments regarding each taxing district's property tax levy. The bill requires municipalities to provide notice of a preliminary budget on or before August 10 of each year and municipalities levying less than $100,000 to include additional information in the notice, such as a statement of the total proposed expenditures for each fund in the preliminary budget. The bill provides an annexation is effective for the purpose of general taxation on and after the first day of the next January.

Senate Bill No. 2298 requires an out-of-state seller that does not have a physical presence in this state, but has gross sales exceeding $100,000 from taxable items delivered in this state or has sold taxable items for delivery in this state in 200 or more transactions to collect and remit sales and use tax in the event the Supreme Court overturns *Quill v. North Dakota*, 504 U.S. 298 (1992), or confirms a state may constitutionally impose sales or use tax on an outofstate seller under conditions similar to those specified.

Senate Bill No. 2300 provides it is a Class B felony for a person to commit an aggravated assault on a peace officer or a correctional institution employee who is acting in an official capacity.

Senate Bill No. 2303 provides an individual who is required to register as a sexual offender must inform the law enforcement agency having local jurisdiction of the individual's place of residence, residential address, school, and place of employment.

Senate Bill No. 2313 requires the Agriculture Commissioner to create a wind energy restoration and reclamation oversight program to provide assistance, support, and outreach to wind property owners and authorizes the Agriculture Commissioner to contract for ombudsmen to serve as a resource for technical assistance on wind property issues. The bill removes the sunset date on the requirement each retail provider submit to the Public Service Commission a report on the provider's previous calendar year energy sales and a summary of the provider's progress in meeting the state's renewable energy and recycled energy objectives. The bill expands the exclusion and avoidance areas for wind turbines to areas less than one and one-tenth times the height of a turbine from the property line of a nonparticipating landowner and areas less than three times the height of a turbine from an inhabited rural residence of a nonparticipating landowner when considering a site for a wind energy conversion area. The bill allows the commission to grant a variance to reduce the setback requirements upon written authorization by the agent or representative of the permittee, the nonparticipating landowner, and any other affected parties. The bill defines "nonparticipating landowner" and "height of the turbine."

Senate Bill No. 2327 establishes a Department of Environmental Quality by transferring duties and responsibilities of the Environmental Health Section of the State Department of Health to the new department, contingent upon the Section Chief certifying all necessary federal approvals for the new department have been received and all agreements requiring amendment have been amended to ensure the state continues to meet primacy requirements. The bill changes various statutory references from the State Department of Health to the Department of Environmental Quality. The bill authorizes the Department of Environmental Quality to request the Bureau of Criminal Investigation conduct a criminal history background check for a final applicant or an employee; an individual under investigation by the department; or an applicant for registration, certification, or licensure by the department. The bill requires the newly created department to visit, upon request of the Board of University and School Lands, leased land under the board's control that may contain oil, gas, coal, or other natural resources and to make a report to the board of the visit. The bill provides limited x-ray operators are no longer exempt from regulation by the North Dakota Medical Imaging and Radiation Therapy Board.

Senate Bill No. 2333 provides any land disturbed by oil and gas activity that is within the jurisdiction of the Industrial Commission must be reclaimed as close as practicable to its condition before the disturbance. The bill allows the commission to waive reclamation requirements for site and access roads after a well's plugging or a treating plant's or saltwater handling facility's decommissioning if the commission receives consent from the surface owner or appropriate government land manager and records documentation of the waiver.

Senate Bill No. 2344 provides for the use and sale of medical marijuana, restricts the Commissioner of Commerce from certifying a compassion center as a primary sector business, excludes an individual growing medical marijuana from the definition of a "farmer" for purposes of qualifying for the farm residence property tax exemption, and excludes any structure or improvement used in processing medical marijuana from qualifying for a farm-related property tax exemption.

Chapter Seven

Tribal-State Relationships

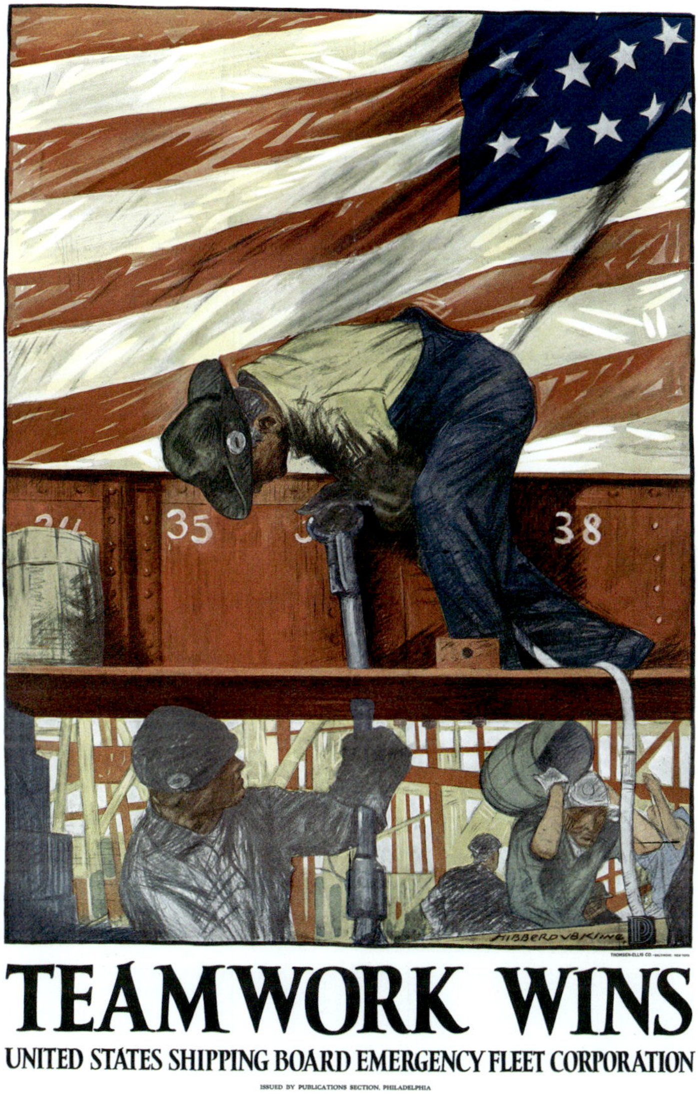

Native American Hall of Honor

The North Dakota Native American Hall of Honor is an annual program that recognizes traditional and contemporary achievements of Native Americans who have gone above and beyond representing their tribes and cultures. Scott Davis, executive director of the North Dakota Indian Affairs Commission, and a committee of representatives from North Dakota were instrumental in moving the North Dakota Native American Hall of Honor from a dream to a reality in partnership with the State Historical Society of North Dakota and the State Historical Society of North Dakota Foundation.

The Native American Hall of Honor provides a place where the public can honor and commemorate significant achievements of Native Americans in North Dakota. The program recognizes the achievements of the chosen inductees in four categories: Leadership, Veterans, Culture and Arts, and Athletics. Information, selected personal objects, and a video about each chosen honoree are placed on exhibit for one year in the Native American Hall of Honor at the North Dakota Heritage Center and State Museum.

Nominations for the award can be made of people who are living or in memory of those who have passed away. Up to two people per category are considered for acceptance into the Hall of Honor each year. The selection of inductees is done by a committee with membership representation from all the tribal nations in North Dakota. A description of the nominee's accomplishments, a biography, photos, other documentation, and two letters of reference are also used to determine those chosen for induction into the Native American Hall of Honor.

The criteria for each category include:

Leadership

Individuals, groups, elected leaders, community leaders, grassroots leaders, elders, spiritual leaders, teachers, and educational leaders can be nominated for this award. Nominees considered have made innovative contributions to their field, community, or state and have distinguished themselves as models in leadership. Also considered in the selection process are awards received and volunteer service.

Military – Veteran

An individual or group can be nominated who was honorably discharged, served during war time or peace time, and demonstrated a positive impact in and around their community or state. Also considered during the selection process are awards and medals received by the nominee and volunteer service.

Culture/Arts

Those eligible for this award include dancers, drum groups, singers, writers, artists in all forms of media art, poets, and designers who have had an impact on the preservation of the culture and art of their specific tribe and state. Also considered in the selection process are other awards received and volunteer service.

Sports/Teams

An individual or group can be nominated who has shown sportsmanship, dedication, and character and made contributions to team, charity, and athletic achievements. Nominees are considered that have provided leadership and support, displayed qualities of an active role model, have distinguished themselves as models in personal and professional conduct, and have performed volunteer services to the local community and state. Also considered during the selection process are other awards received.

Grand Opening and First Inductee Ceremony Held in 2016

The Grand Opening and first inductee ceremony of the North Dakota Native American Hall of Honor was held on September 8, 2016. The event was attended by the inductees, along with their families, as well as many other individuals who filled the Russell Reid Auditorium at the North Dakota Heritage Center and State Museum as well as overflow areas. Approximately 350 people attended the event and also enjoyed a traditional meal with bison stew provided free of charge by United Tribes Technical College.

Scott Davis served as emcee for the inaugural event. During the induction ceremony, videos created by Makoché Studios were premiered, which showcased the accomplishments of each honoree. Each inductee then shared comments, followed by an honor song and celebration of the new exhibit.

The 2017 Native American Hall of Honor induction ceremony took place on September 7, 2017, at the North Dakota Heritage Center and State Museum. This event occurred prior to the United Tribes Technical College International Powwow held September 8-10.

To nominate an individual or group for the Native American Hall of Honor, visit the North Dakota Indian Affairs Commission's North Dakota Native American Hall of Honor website at http://indianaffairs.nd.gov/hall-of-honor. For additional information, call 701-328-2428.

2016 Honorees

Seven individuals were selected for the Hall of Honor in 2016. Below is a list of inductees and a summary of their accomplishments.

Leadership

Harriett Skye
Standing Rock Sioux Tribe

Harriett Skye, Ph.D., (b. 1931) has dedicated her life to the advancement of Native endeavors. She has been an educator, activist, journalist, mentor, poet, student, and filmmaker, often at the same time.

From 1972 to 1982, as the director of the Office of Public Relations at United Tribes Technical College (UTTC), Skye hosted the local KFYR television program *Indian Country Today*. The program placed prominent Native Americans before the public to talk about issues from a tribal point of view.

At age 55, "too young to retire, and too old to train," she picked up the phone and called a community college. She received her doctorate in ethnic studies from the University of California-Berkley in 2003. She returned to North Dakota and retired in 2011 as Vice President Emeritus of Intertribal Programs at UTTC.

Other significant accomplishments include directing the documentary *The Right to Be*, which was screened at the Sundance Film Festival in 1994, serving as editor of the *Standing Rock Star* and *United Tribes News*, and serving on a North Dakota advisory board to the U.S. Commission on Civil Rights.

In addition to her accomplishments, Skye was honored in the Native American Hall of Honor for showing leadership at a time when it was difficult for Native communities to have a voice.

Marcellus Red Tomahawk
Standing Rock Sioux Tribe

Marcellus Red Tomahawk, *Tacanipiluta* (1849-1931), was born in Montana Territory as a member of the Hunkpapa-Tanktonai tribe. He was 24 when he moved to the Standing Rock Sioux Reservation. He served as an Indian Police Duty Sergeant and First Lieutenant for 18 years. In 1890, under order of James McLaughlin, he participated in the arrest of Sitting Bull.

In 1911, Red Tomahawk became the first Tribal Chairman of the Standing Rock Sioux Tribe. He served on the Tribal Council repeatedly over many years, always striving to improve the welfare of his tribe. He was recognized as a peace negotiator, working to educate and create awareness about Native culture among the public. Representing the tribe, he frequently met with dignitaries, including President Theodore Roosevelt.

For more than 90 years, his profile was recognized across the state as the symbol on North Dakota highway signs. The North Dakota Highway Patrol also adopted his profile as its emblem and continues to use it.

A friend of all people, Red Tomahawk is recognized as one of North Dakota's great historical leaders.

Military – Veteran

U.S. Army Corporal Nathan Goodiron Mandan, Hidatsa, and Arikara Nations and Standing Rock Sioux Tribe

Corporal Nathan J. Goodiron (1981-2006) served with the 1st Battalion, 188th Air Defense Artillery, North Dakota National Guard. He died November 23, 2006, when his unit came in contact with enemy forces using small-arms fire and rocket-propelled grenades in Qarabagh, Afghanistan.

He was a fourth generation of Goodiron military veterans, beginning with his great-grandfather, who served as a code talker with the U.S. Army during World War I. Goodiron carried warrior names since infancy; his maternal great-grandmother named him "Young Eagle" and "Distant Thunder."

A high achiever in academics and sports, he played basketball for the Mandaree Warriors, continuing his education at Minot State University and Fort Berthold Community College. Enfolded by the Hidatsa way, he participated in ceremonies, powwows, giveaways, and honorings.

A family member wrote that Corporal Goodiron "represents the ancient way of the Hidatsa people and their willingness to give all [so] that our people remain safe, true to our traditions, and free in this land that is now the United States of America."

He was honored in the Native American Hall of Honor for his military endeavors and for the honor, humility, and compassion he showed toward his community.

Richard Marcellais
Turtle Mountain Band of Chippewa

Senator Richard Marcellais (b. 1947) served in the U.S. Army from 1968 to 1971. From 1971 to 1994, he was a computer specialist with the U.S. Veterans Administration, Bureau of Indian Affairs, and Indian Health Services. Marcellais serves in the North Dakota Senate (2006-present) and was Tribal Chairman for the Turtle Mountain Band of Chippewa (2008-2010).

A colleague describes him as "a man of integrity, respect, common sense, and someone who represents his state, his district, and his people with pride and distinction." Another praises his "colorful dress and humor. He understands that occasional independence from convention and laughter can be soothing to his spirit and the spirit of others."

Marcellais was honored in the Native American Hall of Honor for his ongoing work with Native American veterans throughout various communities in North Dakota.

Culture/Arts

Anthony McDonald
Spirit Lake Nation

A member of the Spirit Lake Nation, Anthony McDonald (b. 1937) was the first Native American to be ordained a deacon of the Roman Catholic Church in North Dakota.

Ordained in 1983, McDonald has dedicated his life to serving people with prayer and support. He held healing services combining Native culture with Catholic faith to bring about better understanding of both worlds. Abstaining from alcohol himself, he remains a role model for those seeking support and help with addiction through counseling and treatment programs.

A fluent Dakota speaker, McDonald taught Dakota culture and language class to elementary school students. He established an Indian club for children to learn dancing and singing to promote positive self-worth and pride in their ancestry. He also served on local school boards, mentored young cowboys in the rodeo club, and, along with his family, coordinated community events to honor veterans.

In addition to his endeavors in the field of arts and culture, McDonald has shown great leadership in sharing his culture with dignity, humility, and compassion.

Sports/Teams

Robert Eaglestaff
Standing Rock Sioux Tribe

Robert "Bob" Eaglestaff (1953-1996) excelled at both academics and basketball. A member of the National Honor Society at Standing Rock High School, he set several basketball scoring records, including the most points in one game (69) and the individual scoring record (1,792 points), which is still unbroken. He chose college over playing professional basketball. Recruited to Brigham Young University, he later transferred to the University of North Dakota (UND). During his time as starting forward, the team won the conference title for three consecutive years. He was inducted into the UND Hall of Fame in 2004.

After graduating with a bachelor's degree from UND in 1976, Eaglestaff attended the University of South Dakota, earning a master's degree in education administration in 1980.

From 1983 until 1996, Eaglestaff worked as an educator in Washington, leading the American Indian Heritage School in Seattle from a place of little hope to a proud community of high-achieving students.

Eaglestaff was honored in the North Dakota Native American Hall of Honor, not only for his endeavors in sports, but for setting an example for all young athletes in Native communities.

Arnold Charging, Sr.
Mandan, Hidatsa, and Arikara Nation

Arnold Charging, Sr. (1933-2011) was a stellar athlete, excelling in both football and basketball, who played during the golden years of the Elbowoods Warriors in North Dakota.

Charging competed in football, basketball, and track, but football was his favorite. He played fullback when the Warriors won the 1950 Conference Championship. He was also on the Warriors team that won its way to third place in the 1951 State Class B Basketball Tournament.

During his senior year of high school, Charging was named to the All-State Basketball Team. That year he was also nominated to the National High School All-American All-Star Football Team and invited by the Winnipeg Blue Bombers football team to tryouts. Offered athletic scholarships from several universities, he enrolled at Dickinson State College on a scholarship in 1952. He left college to assist his family and others in the massive relocation caused by the completion of the Garrison Dam.

2017 Honorees

The following six inductees were inducted into the Hall of Honor in 2017.

Leadership

David Gipp, Standing Rock Sioux Tribe
Leigh Jeanotte, Turtle Mountain Band of Chippewa

Culture/Arts

Daniel Jerome, Turtle Mountain Band of Chippewa
Mary Louise Defender Wilson, Standing Rock Sioux Tribe

Sports/Teams

1973 Fort Yates Warriors Basketball Team, Standing Rock Sioux Tribe
Pete Fredericks, Mandan, Hidatsa, and Arikara Nation

First Nations Day

First Nations Day, held in October each year, recognizes North Dakota's indigenous peoples and their unique role in shaping the history and culture of the state, as well as the history and culture of the nation. It also recognizes the role American Indian people continue to play in shaping the future of the state and nation by making important and distinctive contributions to culture and society, as well as the critical role American Indian people, tribal governments, colleges, and businesses play in strengthening their communities and growing North Dakota's economy.

The 2016 First Nations Day celebration, "Preserving Our Culture," was held on October 7 in the North Dakota Heritage Center and State Museum auditorium. The event included a flag presentation from the United Tribes Technical College Honor Guard and the Wise Spirit Singers. In addition, opening remarks were made by Scott Davis, executive director of the North Dakota Indian Affairs Commission, and a keynote address was presented by Dakota Goodhouse, a writer, editor, and artist, as well as instructor at United Tribes Technical College. The First Nations Day celebration also included the governor's and the city of Bismarck's Proclamation on First Nations Day. A traditional meal was provided by United Tribes Technical College.

Indian Youth Leadership Academy

The North Dakota Indian Youth Leadership Academy (NDIYLA), held each year in June, creates and fosters an environment for Native youth to learn and develop leadership skills, which will open doors for them in their local communities, the state of North Dakota, and throughout the United States. The academy is a peer-to-peer mentorship program that utilizes current college students and/or former youth leadership academy attendees to help participants learn about pursuing a career or expanding on their educational aspirations. These participants are challenged by motivational speakers and mentors, visit college campuses, learn about military opportunities, and have multiple opportunities to talk about the challenges they face.

Native American Youth Leadership Summit

The North Dakota Native American Youth Leadership Summit, held during the United Tribes Technical College Tribal Leaders Summit in September, offers youth leaders from throughout the state the opportunity to talk about issues they see in their communities. The event includes group discussions and an opportunity to present the issues to tribal leaders. More than 75 youth leaders from each of the North Dakota tribal nations were in attendance at the 2016 Leadership Summit, as well as a group of youth leaders living off-reservation.

North Dakota Tribal Nations

Here are summaries of each of the tribal nations located in North Dakota, their governance structure, and contact information.

Spirit Lake Nation

816 3rd Avenue North
Fort Totten, ND 58335
701-766-1219
www.spiritlakenation.com

Demographics

• Tribal enrollment	7,256 (Spirit Lake Enrollment Office 2014)
• Population (All Races)	4,323 (American Community Survey 2015)
• Population (Indian)	3,648 (American Community Survey 2015)

Government

The reservation was created by the "Treaty with the Sioux – Sisseton and Wahpeton Bands" in February 1867. The treaty provided for the establishment of Lake Traverse Reservation in eastern South Dakota, and another reservation south of Devils Lake in North Dakota for the Cut-Head bands of Yanktonai Sioux who did not go to Lake Traverse.

The Spirit Lake Tribe operates under a constitution approved on February 3, 1944. Originally known as the Devils Lake Sioux Tribe, the name was changed to Spirit Lake Tribe in May 1995 by a general referendum vote of its members.

The Tribal Council is made up of six members, including a chairman and secretary, elected at large by the tribal membership residing on the reservation.

Spirit Lake Casino and Resort.

One district representative is elected from each of the four districts of Fort Totten, Mission (St. Michael), Woodlake, and Crow Hill. Council members serve four-year terms, and elections are held once every two years in May.

The reservation is located in east-central North Dakota. There are 7,256 enrolled members of the Spirit Lake Tribe. The topography of the reservation is generally consistent with the Northern Plains region, with flat terrain, rolling hills, and some wooded areas. The major surface water feature of the reservation is Devils Lake, which comprises 90,000 acres of area stretched over 200 miles. There are also numerous small lakes on the reservation, including Twin Lakes, Spring Lake, Free Peoples Lake, Elbow Lake, and Skin and Bone Lake.

The Spirit Lake Tribe Indian Reservation covers approximately 405 square miles. It is located primarily in Benson County, but its southern boundary is in Eddy County, eastern boundary is in Nelson County, and northern boundary is in Ramsey County. Its total acres are as follows: total tribally owned, allocated trust land – 26,283 acres; trust – 34,026 acres; U.S. government and state – 375 acres; and fee land – 184,451 acres. Total acres within the exterior boundaries equal 245,141 acres.

The major river surface water body is the Sheyenne River, which forms the southern boundary of the reservation. The portion of the Sheyenne within the reservation is approximately 50 miles long. Ultimately the Sheyenne River discharges into the Red River, which flows north between North Dakota and Minnesota into Manitoba, Canada. Numerous small streams and springs within the reservation also contribute flows to the Sheyenne River. In addition, the rivers and streams of the reservation have substantial areas of associated wetlands and prairie potholes.

Turtle Mountain Band of Chippewa Indians

PO Box 900
Highway 5 West
Belcourt, ND 58316
701-477-2600
tmbci.org

Demographics

- Tribal enrollment — 32,036 (Turtle Mountain Enrollment Office 2015)
- Population (All Races) — 9,271 (American Community Survey 2015)
- Population (Indian) — 8,839 (American Community Survey 2015)

Government

The Turtle Mountain Reservation lies entirely in Rolette County in the extreme north-central portion of North Dakota, about seven miles from the Canadian border and near the exact geographic center of the North American continent. The reservation is almost equally divided between tribally owned and individually allotted lands. The terrain ranges in elevation from 200 to 2,300 feet above sea level and is dotted with lakes, rolling hills, and a relative abundance of trees. The unincorporated town of Belcourt is the only community on the Turtle Mountain Reservation. Near the reservation are the towns of Rolla, Rolette, Dunseith, and St. John.

The reservation was established by the Executive Orders of December 21, 1882, and March 29, 1884, on an area of 72,000 acres of land. The 72,000 acres proved to be inadequate for the population of the reservation. Consequently, the U.S. government, as specified in an 1892 Treaty Agreement, provided public domain land in western North Dakota and eastern Montana consisting of approximately 69,860 acres. The land was available to Turtle Mountain Chippewa who were willing to relocate and homestead in that area. The treaty agreement assured services would be provided to the relocated membership as if they resided on reservation land.

The Turtle Mountain Tribe's governing body, the Tribal Council, consists of a chairman and eight members elected to two-year terms. The chairman is elected at large by the general membership; the vice-chairman is elected by the eight council members at the first meeting of each newly elected council. The tribal government is organized according to a 1959 constitution and bylaws. In 1976, the tribe adopted a Tribal Code, covering criminal and civil law.

An elected board of directors consisting of a chairperson and six representatives now governs the Trenton Indian Service Area (TISA). Election of directors is held every four years, and terms are staggered. TISA has been divided into three districts (Williston, Trenton, and Montana), with two representatives from each district.

The Chippewa proudly referred to themselves as Anishinabe, meaning "The Original People." The Turtle Mountain Band of Chippewa is primarily a member of the Pembina Band of Chippewa. Ancestry may include intermarriage with other Chippewa bands, Cree, and other nations who make up the membership of the Turtle Mountain Band.

The name Chippewa, a mispronunciation of Ojibwa, Ojibway, Ojibwe, Saulteaux, and Anishinabe, are all nations that refer to the same group of people. The term "Chippewa" is used after European contact.

The Ojibway are members of the Algonquin language group, which are located from Newfoundland to the Rocky Mountains and from Hudson Bay to North Carolina. Other tribes in this language group are the Cree, Ottawa, Sauk, Fox, Menominee, Potawatomi, Miami, Shawnee, Delaware, Cheyenne, Blackfeet, and Arapaho. Scholars have established this classification by language, but this does not mean the tribes were closely related or that they were allies.

Mandan, Hidatsa, and Arikara Nation

(Three Affiliated Tribes)
404 Frontage Road
New Town, ND 58763
701-627-4781
www.mhanation.com

Demographics

• Tribal enrollment	14,322 (Three Affiliated Enrollment Office 2015)
• Population (All Races)	7,611 (American Community Survey 2015)
• Population (Indian)	5,081 (American Community Survey 2015)

Government

The reservation was established under the Fort Laramie Treaty of 1851 and modified over the years, resulting in the final establishment of the reservation by the Executive Order of April 12, 1870. Congressional acts and executive orders gradually reduced the reservation to its present size from the initial 12.5 million acres. In 1972, a federal court ruling determined that land lost to homesteaders through the 1910 Homestead Act had, in fact, always been part of the reservation.

The constitution for the Three Affiliated Tribes was adopted on May 15, 1936. The Tribal Council is made up of seven members, including a chairman elected at-large by the tribal membership and one representative from each of the reservations six districts of Four Bears, Mandaree, Little Shell (New Town), Lucky Mound (Parshall), Twin Buttes, and White Shield. Council members serve four-year terms. Elections are held once every two years in November.

The Fort Berthold Reservation spans approximately one million acres of both flat prairie land and rolling terrain in west-central North Dakota, southeast of Minot and northwest of Bismarck. The reservation is intersected by the Missouri River. About 11 percent of the total surface area is covered by Lake Sakakawea, the reservoir formed behind the Garrison Dam. While there are Indian families living throughout the reservation, the majority live in the local communities of Mandaree, White Shield, Twin Buttes, Four Bears (location of the tribal headquarters), and the incorporated towns of Parshall and New Town (location of the Bureau of Indian Affairs headquarters).

The U.S. Government, as defined by the U.S. Constitution, has governmental relationships with international, tribal, and state entities. The tribal nations have a government-to-government relationship with the United States. The tribes signed treaties in the 1800s with the United States, which are the legal documents that established boundaries and recognized their rights as a sovereign government. The tribal government maintains jurisdiction within the boundaries of the reservation including all rights-of-way, waterways, water courses, and streams running through any part of the reservation and to such other lands as may hereafter be added to the reservation under the laws of the United States.

The tribal government operates under a constitution consistent with the Indian Reorganization Act of 1934 and a Business Council approved by the tribal membership of the Three Affiliated Tribes. The Business Council consists of a chairman, vice-chairman, secretary, treasurer, and three additional council members who are elected by the tribal members. The chairman is the administrative head of the tribe. The chairman and officers serve a four-year term and are elected at large with the three members elected from their districts.

At the time of initial contact with Euro-American culture (around 1790), the three tribes lived along the Missouri River, hunting buffalo and growing squash, corn, and beans. Contact brought some predictable consequences, notably a devastating smallpox epidemic in 1837. To escape the disease, a group of Hidatsa moved up the Missouri River in 1845 and established the village of Like-A-Fishhook. Eventually they were joined by the other two tribal bands, and by 1862, formal unification of the tribes had begun.

Though the Treaty of Fort Laramie granted the three tribes more than 12 million acres, executive orders and allotments eventually reduced the reservation's size to less than one million acres, its approximate size today. During 1954, the tribes lost another 152,300 acres, along with innumerable natural resources, due to the U.S. Army Corps of Engineers' filling of the Garrison Reservoir (which is now Lake Sakakawea). The flooding destroyed long-established Indian population centers, and families who had supported themselves by ranching and farming along the fertile Missouri bottomlands watched the land become dry, windy uplands. Though the tribes received $12 million in compensation for their flooded land, an independent evaluator placed the loss at more than $20 million.

Today, the reservation continues to support limited farming and ranching, but the tribes have been more successful in establishing or attracting businesses in electronics manufacturing, construction, and gaming. Traditional culture has also seen an increase, with Native American church ceremonies, sweat lodges, and the use of native languages all making a comeback. The tribes continue to maintain discreet tribal identities through the preservation of language, customs, and residence.

Prairie Knights Casino and Resort.

Standing Rock Sioux Tribe
PO Box D
Fort Yates, ND 58538
701-854-8500
www.standingrock.org

Demographics

• Tribal enrollment	15,782 (Standing Rock Enrollment Office 2015)
• Population (All Races, ND & SD)	8,542 (American Community Survey 2015)
• Population (Indian, ND & SD)	6,360 (American Community Survey 2015)

Government

The Standing Rock Reservation was established by the 1851 Fort Laramie Treaty and was a part of the Great Sioux Nation. The center of the reservation was the Black Hills, the "paha sapa," sacred to all Lakota. The size of the reservation has been reduced through various ways. The 1868 Fort Laramie Treaty broke the Great Sioux Nation and divided the land for some of the tribes, but took the Black Hills. The series of allotment acts that began in 1868 and ended in 1915 divided the land even further, assigning to individuals and families timber allotments to provide for fuel and home sites. Finally, nearly one million acres of western reservation lands were opened for white settlement.

The Standing Rock Reservation is situated in southwest North Dakota on the North Dakota-South Dakota border. The reservation encompasses all of Sioux County in North Dakota, and all of Corson County and small portions of Dewey and Ziebach Counties in South Dakota. The size of the reservation is more than 2.3 million acres. As of 2015, approximately 925,000 acres of this land is Indian-owned trust land. The remainder of the land is more than 1.4 million acres of fee land, primarily non-Indian owned lands, school and township lands, and approximately 50,000 acres that was a result of the creation of the Oahe Reservoir.

The Tribal Council, as the Standing Rock Sioux Tribe's supreme governing body, is constitutionally empowered to enter into negotiations with the federal, state, and local governments on the tribe's behalf; employ attorneys and protect tribal land and political rights; appoint tribal officials, boards, and organizations; evict non-enrolled people whose presence may be detrimental to the tribe; administer the tribal budget; regulate property; and pass laws and establish courts for the administration of justice. Although the Standing Rock Sioux Tribe has considerable authority, federal law mandates the Secretary of the Interior approve or disapprove certain council actions.

The people of each of the eight districts on the Standing Rock Reservation comprise a local district council which elects officers to consult, make recommendations to and advise the Tribal Council, Bureau of Indian Affairs agency superintendent, and Secretary of the Interior on all matters of local or tribal interest. Tribal Council members are obligated to attend local district council meetings and report tribal business to the local people, ensuring input on a local level.

North Dakota Tribal Colleges

The 1970s brought the establishment of five two-year tribal colleges. Created to retain students on the reservations and prepare them for the job market, they provide both academic and vocational training.

The schools and the year they were established are United Tribes Technical College, Bismarck, 1969; Turtle Mountain Community College, Belcourt, 1972; Nueta Hidatsa Sahnish College, New Town, 1973; Sitting Bull College, Fort Yates, 1973; and Cankdeska Cikana (Little Hoop) Community College, Fort Totten, 1974.

Tribal College Fall 2016 Enrollment

Cankdeska Cikana Community College	179
Sitting Bull College	291
Nueta Hidatsa Sahnish College	273
Turtle Mountain Community College	476
United Tribes Technical College	428

Cankdeska Cikana Community College

214 1st Avenue
Fort Totten, ND 58335
701-766-4415
www.littlehoop.edu

Mission

To provide higher education opportunities at the community college level, including vocational and technical training. As a tribal college, we emphasize the teaching and learning of Dakota culture and language toward the perpetuation of the Spirit Lake Dakota Nation. The goal is student independence and self-sufficiency through academic achievement.

Vision

Through the education and training of its residents, we are maintaining a strong and viable Dakota community that enjoys physical, mental, emotional, and spiritual wellness and growth.

Turtle Mountain Community College

PO Box 340
BIA Highway #7 North
Belcourt, ND 58316
701-477-7862
www.tm.edu

Mission

Turtle Mountain Community College is committed to functioning as an autonomous Indian-controlled college on the Turtle Mountain Chippewa Reservation focusing on general studies, undergraduate education, career and technical education, scholarly research, and continuous improvement of student learning. By creating an academic environment in which the cultural and social heritage of the Turtle Mountain Band of Chippewa is brought to bear throughout the curriculum, the college establishes an administration, faculty, and student body exerting leadership in the community and providing service to it.

Institutional Philosophy

Turtle Mountain Community College is a tribal community college with obligations of direct community service to the Turtle Mountain Chippewa Tribe. Under this unifying principle, the college seeks to maintain, seek out, and provide comprehensive higher education services in fields needed for true Indian self-determination.

Nueta Hidatsa Sahnish College

PO Box 490
220 8th Avenue North
New Town, ND 58763
701-627-4738
https://nhsc.edu

Mission

The Nueta Hidatsa Sahnish College will provide quality cultural, academic, and vocational education and services for the Mandan, Hidatsa, and Arikara Nation.

Values

Nueta Hidatsa Sahnish College's values are illustrated through the earth lodge, which is the common home to the Nueta, Hidatsa, and Sahnish people. Unity, being the key value, is located in the center (fire pit), which the rest of the values built around. Spirituality, people, culture, and future are the four domains represented by the four main posts. The outer 12 posts represent values within each of the four domains.

Sitting Bull College

1341 92nd Street
Fort Yates, ND 58538
701-854-8000
www.sittingbull.edu

Mission

Sitting Bull College is an academic and technical institution committed to improving the levels of education and training, economic, and social development of the people it serves while promoting responsible behavior consistent with the Lakota/Dakota culture and language.

Vision

Catching the spirit to fulfill a dream through culture, academics, technical training, and responsible behavior for now and the future.

United Tribes Technical College

3315 University Drive
Bismarck, ND 58504
701-255-3285
www.uttc.edu

UNITED TRIBES TECHNICAL COLLEGE

Mission

United Tribes Technical College is dedicated to providing American Indians with postsecondary and technical education in a culturally diverse environment that will provide self-determination and economic development for all tribal nations.

Vision

United Tribes Technical College (UTTC) is a premiere college, a leader in tribal education, arts, cultural preservation, technology, research, and the humanities. UTTC foresees a campus community with state-of-the-art facilities. UTTC aspires to be self-sustaining in line with its mission for tribal self-sufficiency and self-determination. Most importantly, UTTC envisions skilled, knowledgeable, culturally-grounded, healthy graduates who will achieve their educational goals; empower their communities; and preserve the environment, tribal land, water, and natural resources.

Economic Development Through Alliances

North Dakota Indian Business Alliance

"Creating Independence in the Spirit of Entrepreneurship in Indian Country"

The North Dakota Indian Business Alliance (NDIBA), founded in 2012, supports Native-owned businesses by helping Native entrepreneurs' dreams become a reality and progress together toward prosperity, jobs, and asset-building.

There are many challenges to economic and business development in Native American communities throughout the region. According to the 2011 Growing Economies in Indian Country (GEIC) report, these challenges fall into eight broad categories. They include (1) insufficient access to capital; (2) capacity constraints of small business resource providers; (3) insufficient workforce development and business education training; (4) tribal governance constraints; (5) regulatory constraints on land held in trust; (6) underdeveloped physical infrastructure; (7) insufficient research and data; and (8) a lack of regional collaboration.

While such challenges may seem insurmountable, the state of North Dakota has maintained a long-standing commitment to working with tribal nations to address workforce and economic development issues both on and off reservations located across the state. The results have been "hit and miss," due in large part to a lack of continuity and consistency in the efforts. For example, past efforts have been hampered by frequent turnover among elected tribal leaders, as well as ever-changing approaches employed by the various consultants hired by the state to coordinate such efforts.

In an effort to find a more effective and lasting approach to promoting economic development within Native American communities, leaders from the North Dakota Governor's Office, Indian Affairs Commission, and Commerce Department sought and received legislative funding in 2011 to explore the merits of establishing an Indian Business Alliance, much like surrounding states had done in prior years. After conducting exploratory meetings, as well as an economic summit with tribal leaders, Native American business owners, and state agencies in 2012, the NDIBA was officially incorporated with the North Dakota Secretary of State on April 10, 2013, as a nonprofit organization.

Although NDIBA is one of the newest Indian Business Alliances in this region, it is quickly gaining traction thanks to the support it has received from the other IBAs, especially those in South Dakota and Montana. NDIBA has also benefitted from the efforts of the Northwest Area Foundation to encourage more collaborative planning and program development among the region's Indian Business Alliances.

The timing for the creation of a strong IBA in North Dakota has never been better. The economy is strong and growing. All stakeholders are anxious to find ways for Native Americans to share in the prosperity. Elected leaders within the state and tribal nations are ready to join with private businesses, tribal colleges, government agencies, charitable foundations, and others to promote the creation of more jobs and businesses in Indian country.

NDIBA
NORTH DAKOTA
INDIAN BUSINESS ALLIANCE

Business Development in Indian Country

A Strategic Approach to Sustainability

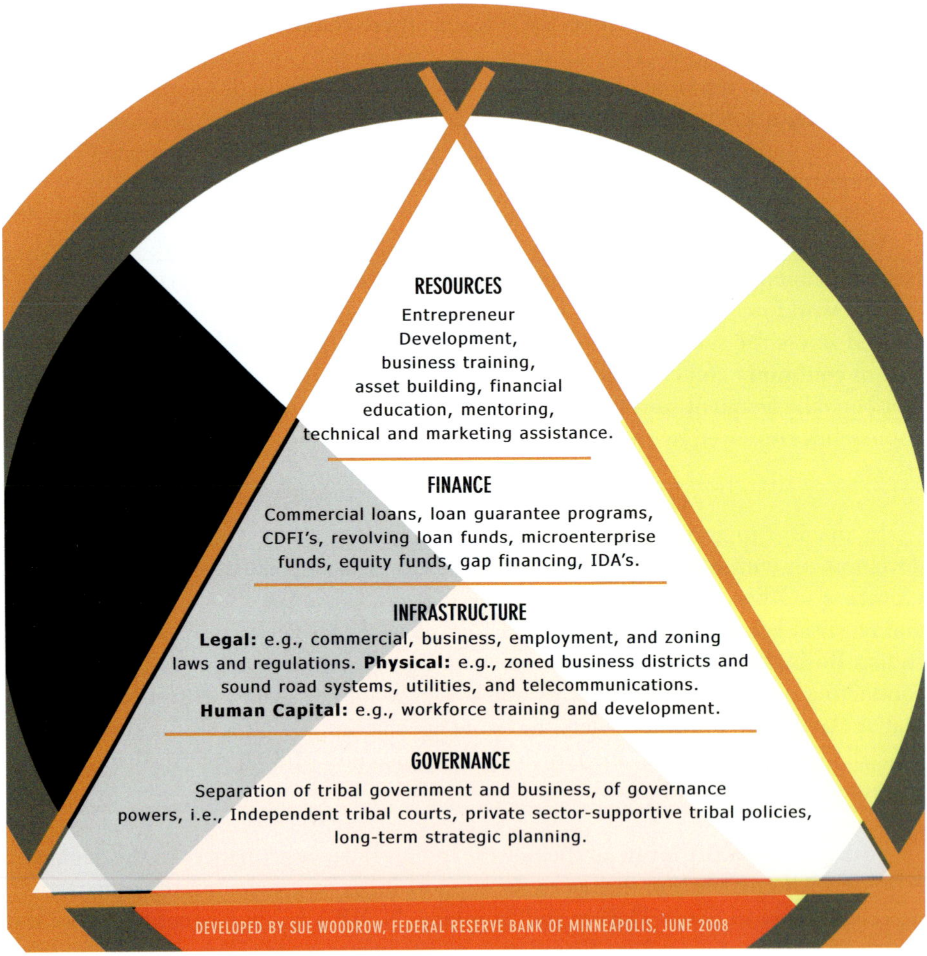

Officers

Mike Mabin, President
Stacey LaCompte, Executive Director
Scott Davis, Secretary/Treasurer
Bonnie Malo, Advisor/Board Member
Brek Maxon, Advisor/Board Member
Erik Cutler, MMGT, Advisor/Board Member
Al Nygard, Advisor/Board Member
Patrice Kunesh, Advisor Member
Terry Lee, Advisor Member

Contact Information

1003 Gateway Avenue
Bismarck, ND 58503
701-250-0728
www.ndiba.com

Regional Indian Business Alliances

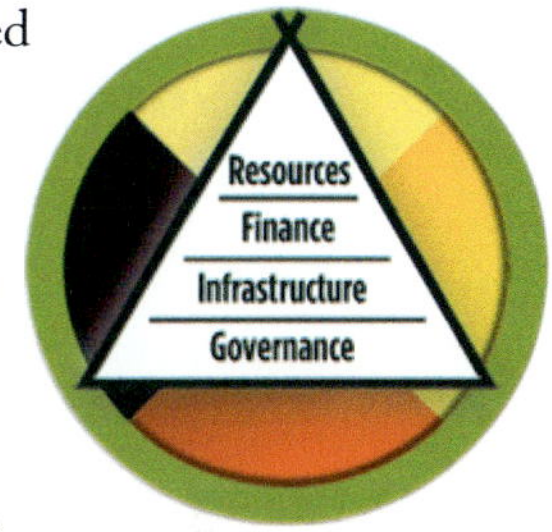

The Regional Indian Business Alliance (RIBA), comprised of the North Dakota Indian Business Alliance (NDIBA), Minnesota Indian Business Alliance (MNIBA), Montana Indian Business Alliance (MIBA), South Dakota Indian Business Alliance (SDIBA), and Wisconsin Indian Business Alliance (WIBA), shares the same vision of community and economic development work for native businesses and entrepreneurs on and off reservations. The Center for Indian Country Development, Federal Reserve Bank of Minneapolis, serves as founding member and co-leader of the Indian Business Alliances. A majority of the RIBAs receive funding from the Northwest Area Foundation.

These statewide coalitions of tribes, financial institutions, nonprofit organizations, corporations, colleges and universities, and government agencies work to maximize and develop resources that encourage and support Native small business owners and entrepreneurs. Although each alliance has created a unique communication, networking, and initiative platform, all have pledged to continue working on the four building blocks of a model for sustainable development in Indian Country: governance, infrastructure, finance, and resources.

- Resources include the awareness and effective use of information and programs that deepen the understanding of the barriers to and opportunities for economic development in Indian country and further the economic development efforts of tribes, native consumers, and native business owners. Activities include entrepreneur development, business training, asset building, financial education, mentoring, and technical and marketing assistance.

- Finance involves the attainment of national parity with respect to access to commercial and consumer capital and financial services. Activities include commercial loans, loan guarantee programs, Community Development Financial Institution's resolving loan funds, microenterprise funds, equity funds, gap financing, and individual development accounts.
- Infrastructure includes the promotion of sound economic infrastructure, including land use and property right's policies and legal systems, and human capital development initiatives that are culturally appropriate and supportive of local goals. Activities include legal (e.g., commercial, business, employment, and zoning laws and regulations), physical (e.g., zoned business districts and sound road systems, utilities, and telecommunications), and human capital (e.g., workforce training and development).
- Governance involves the design and implementation of governance structures (including tribal constitutions, courts, and ethics systems, as well as cross-jurisdictional arrangements) which promote attainment of local goals for investment, employment, and entrepreneurship. Activities include separation of tribal government and business and of governance powers, i.e., independent tribal courts, private sector-supportive tribal policies, and long-term strategic planning.

North Dakota Native Tourism Alliance

"Enhancing Tribal Tourism while Preserving Our Tribal Traditions and Sharing Our Own Stories"

The North Dakota Native Tourism Alliance (NDNTA) was founded in May 2016, and its board was officially formed June 10, 2016. NDNTA received nonprofit status in September 2016. The purpose of the NDNTA is to protect, promote, preserve, and educate the world about the culture, history, and environment of our sovereign nations. The NDNTA promotes and educates through sustainable tourism while developing economic opportunities for its people and nations. NDNTA works in conjunction with the North Dakota Indian Business Alliance on different projects.

The NDNTA's vision is to enhance and promote tribal tourism as a means of economic development, education, and sustainable growth for all North Dakota Tribal Nations, while maintaining respect for sovereignty, tribal traditions, and lands.

The NDNTA views its role as a planning and facilitating tourism organization responsible for:

- Creating an overarching destination strategy for North Dakota Indian country to build capacity and develop tourism products.
- Building partnerships with state agencies, educational institutions, and other organizations that prioritize tourism as an economic development strategy.
- Educating tribal communities and visitors through the promotion of historic sites and cultural traditions.

The NDNTA is a coalition representing the tourism interest of the reservations of North Dakota: Spirit Lake Nation, Standing Rock Sioux Tribe, Three Affiliated Tribes, Sisseton Wahpeton Oyate, Turtle Mountain Band of Chippewa Indians, and Trenton Indian Service Area.

Board Members

Turtle Mountain Band of Chippewa Indians
Leslie Thomas – NDNTA President – Vice-Chair, Turtle Mountain Heritage Center
Lyle Poitra – NDNTA Board Member at Large – Grant Writer/Development Officer, Turtle Mountain Community College

Mandan, Hidatsa, Arikara Nation
Darian Morsette – NDNTA Vice-President – Director, MHA Tourism
Jason Morsette – NDNTA Board Member at Large – Special Projects, MHA Tourism

Spirit Lake Nation
Natasha Gourd – NDNTA Secretary/ Treasurer
Doug Sevigny – NDNTA Board Member at Large – Director, Spirit Lake Nations Tourism

Standing Rock Sioux Tribe
Jennifer Martel – NDNTA Board Member at Large – Tourism Coordinator, Sitting Bull Visitor Center
Cynthia Antelope – NDNTA Board Member at Large – Tribal Planner, Standing Rock Sioux Tribe

Sisseton Wahpeton Oyate
Tamera St. John – NDNTA Board Member at Large – Archivist, Tribal Historic Preservation, Sisseton Wahpeton Oyate
Elias Mendoza – NDNTA Board Member at Large – Executive Assistant to the Tribal Chairman, Sisseton Wahpeton Oyate

Trenton Indian Service Area
In the process of appointing a representative.

NativeWays

The purpose of NativeWays, a nonprofit corporation, is to preserve, celebrate, and advance Native American culture through guided tours, educational activities, cultural performances and demonstrations, and other travel and tourism-related experiences.

NativeWays provides tourists with an authentic exposure to the intriguing world of American Indians, Alaska Natives, and Native Hawaiians through language, art, food, history, and nature. The organization's experiential and educational efforts are conducted in collaboration with sovereign tribal nations, respecting each tribe's unique history, values, and traditions. Beyond providing positive travel experiences for tourists, NativeWays provides jobs and economic benefit to tribes and their members.

The founders and initial board of directors included enrolled members of North Dakota's tribal nations: Scott Davis (Standing Rock), Mike Mabin (Turtle Mountain), Brek Maxon (Three Affiliated Tribes), Robert Shepherd (Sisseton Wahpeton), and Stacey LaCompte (Standing Rock).

In 2017, NativeWays researched the possibility of initially offering a handful of day tours provided by Native American tour guides in the Bismarck-Mandan area, including the North Dakota Heritage Center and State Museum (Early People's Gallery), On a Slant and Knife River Villages, Lewis & Clark Interpretive Center, and United Tribe's International Powwow. Additionally, NativeWays explored the feasibility of offering guided, multi-day charter tours.

NativeWays works in collaboration with the North Dakota Native Tourism Alliance, North Dakota Tourism Office, North Dakota Indian Affairs, North Dakota Heritage Center and State Museum, Fort Lincoln Foundation, Five Nations Art, United Tribes College, and other partners to refine this plan and identify other possible tours and attractions to offer in the future.

NativeWays is also planning to offer travel agency services as an independent contractor of OPOS Tours & Travel, the first solely-owned Indian travel agency in the United States.

Urban Programs for Native Americans

Native American Development Center – Bismarck

The mission of the Native American Development Center (NADC) is to strengthen and advance Native American individuals and families by providing supportive services and resources designed to preserve culture and promote economic security.

Headquartered in Bismarck since August 2014, the NADC is a 501(c)(3) Native-led nonprofit corporation. The NADC was founded to provide social-economic and cultural education, resources, and support services to Native Americans living in the Bismarck metro area, which has the largest diverse tribal Native American population in an urban city within North Dakota. The NADC works toward helping people and families obtain social, emotional, spiritual, and economic security. The organization integrates tribally diverse values including kinship to best meet the cultural needs of Native Americans.

Incorporated on September 10, 2012, the NADC is led by founding Executive Director Lorraine Davis and also has a board of directors and advisory board.

The core focus areas of the NADC are financial capability, housing and homeownership, employment and career development, and parent and youth. Mentoring and cultural are integrated into each program, event, and activity.

Services provided by the NADC include:

- Affordable housing development strategies with national housing leaders, state, rural, and tribal agencies/organizations.
- A guide to homeownership partner resources and loan programs.
- Financial literacy workshops and counseling services.
- Home buyer education workshops and homeownership counseling services.
- Direct supportive services through a mentor and volunteer network for inmates, parolees, youth, and any individual seeking positive personal transformative and transitional change.
- Referrals to emergency transitional support service providers for housing shelter for individuals and families, food pantries, first months' rent and deposit, and bus passes.
- Referrals to churches and traditional spiritual leaders.
- Referrals to a supportive professional network of psychologists, behavior health providers, attorneys, and medical doctors and other career talented individuals.
- An annual Sweetheart Pow-wow in February.
- Currently designing community events and ongoing activities with community partners and community leadership volunteers.
- Educator on cultural sensitivity.

Other NADC activities include:

- Talking Circles (support groups) with child watch.
- Storytelling.

The role of the NADC was identified as a need by its partners to be the grassroots entity to create a volunteer and mentor network program comprised of Native American talents specific to the needs of the Native American people.

Contact Information
205 North 24th Street
Bismarck, ND 58501
701-595-5181
ndnativecenter.org

Sacred Pipe Resource Center – Mandan

The Sacred Pipe Resource Center (SPRC) is a North Dakota- and Native-based nonprofit organization founded in 2007 by long-term American Indian residents committed to maintaining a home away from home for the off-reservation Indian population and building positive relationships within the diverse Bismarck-Mandan community. The founders realized the need for an organization to assist Native people and families who are living away from their homelands, while respecting the sovereign nature of their individual tribal citizenship.

The mission of SPRC is to address and support the social/cultural, emotional, mental, spiritual, and physical needs of Native people of all tribes living in the Bismarck-Mandan area in order to foster strong, self-sufficient individuals and families and to provide liaison services between American Indian and non-Native people in order to foster a cohesive community.

The SPRC takes its name from the meaning behind the pipe as a tool for sharing spirit, truth, reconciliation, and peace. Although the Native peoples and the settlers who came to this area have had a history of conflict, today this history also includes survival, reconciliation, peace, and shared love of land. The SPRC uses the symbol of the sacred pipe to demonstrate the mission of serving the American Indian population by creating partnerships and positive collaborations based on the shared experience of living in this region.

The SPRC is a 501(c)(3) organization, which seeks to enhance existing services by providing critical data, outreach, and cultural brokering needs, rather than replicating or competing for existing services. Through the use of quantitative and qualitative data, SPRC addresses service gaps which may be met by partnering with organizations already providing similar services and by seeking funding to fulfill gaps in services.

The SPRC was founded on the concept of making data-based decisions. The executive director received a Bush Foundation fellowship and used that to design and execute the first-ever Bismarck-Mandan American Indian Community Survey, a survey specifically for the views and perspectives of American Indians living in the Bismarck-Mandan community. The survey was conducted in 2014 and again in 2016. The information from the survey informs a variety of programs and services of the organization. The data also supports community-based research conducted by SPRC and informs partnerships with other community organizations.

The SPRC seeks to build positive relationships and understanding through education as well as data. SPRC began operation by hosting a North Dakota Humanities Council-sponsored speaker series entitled "A Tribe Called Urban." The series featured American Indian scholars discussing the history and development of "urban Indians," as well as the issues unique to the population. SPRC has also sponsored community-wide events to foster healing, such as a series of Cultural Competency workshops to help facilitate positive relationships and, in May 2016, SPRC sponsored the "Armed Forces Day: Honoring All Heroes" event – a parade of Native and non-Native servicemen across the Bismarck-Mandan Memorial Bridge.

SPRC's central focus is coordinating community engagement teams (CETs), groups of Native and non-Native community members committed to working on issues important to American Indian people in the Bismarck-Mandan community, such as American Indian youth issues, cultural events, and health issues/disparities. This includes after-school youth/family activities, American Indian Health Fairs, a program to assist Native homeless, the development of a community health center, and economic/cooperative development efforts. To accomplish these goals, SPRC seeks strong and fair partnerships with other community organizations and individuals.

SPRC collects insightful data about the local American Indian population to create better opportunities for Native Americans living in the area. This data can be utilized to develop programs, make connections, identify needed services, access grants, and create partnerships in the Bismarck-Mandan community.

SPRC Radio Program & Community Interview provides weekly updates on SPRC events, interesting interviews with local Natives, and informative discussion of Native community issues and events.

The Cultural Competency Workshop Series is geared toward professionals in the Bismarck-Mandan area who work with – and care about – Native Americans in the community. Each workshop focuses on a specific issue, providing cultural context and background as well as concrete strategies that can be applied by professionals who work with Native populations.

The SPRC Speaker Series are community conversations about issues important to American Indians. The series features presentations by Native experts in a variety of fields from around the country.

Contact Information
400 West Main
Mandan, ND 58554
701-663-3886
www.sacredpipe.net

American Indian Student Services – University of North Dakota, Grand Forks

The motto of the American Indian Student Services (AISS) office at the University of North Dakota (UND) is to help build strong American Indian communities across the state and nation – one successful student at a time. This program works with all aspects of the university to maintain a climate that is responsive to the needs of American Indians and serves as general institutional contact for American Indian students. AISS provides culturally appropriate student support services designed to enhance the academic and personal success of American Indian students attending UND. Services include recruitment, transitional support, a highly successful retention program, tutoring, study skills, ongoing encouragement, and advisement (academic, financial aid, personal, social, and cultural).

AISS is staffed with culturally knowledgeable, sensitive, and genuinely caring individuals who are passionate about assisting American Indian students to realize success every step of the way from admission to graduation. AISS has assisted and empowered students for more than 40 years by providing support and guidance for thousands of highly successful American Indian alumni now serving their tribal communities as professionals.

AISS is housed in the American Indian Center, a state-of-the-art facility that provides many services to the university community. AISS utilizes a unique team approach to assist students in realizing success and persisting through graduation. Staff provides expertise in the areas of admissions, financial aid, housing, and academic, personal, and cultural advisement. AISS administers walk-in tutoring Sunday through Thursday evenings and provides a computer lab. In addition, AISS is responsible for administering the American Indian Center, coordinating recruitment, establishing communication channels, assisting with institutional planning, advising faculty and staff as to the needs of American Indian students, and serving as an advocate for students. The program also acts as a liaison with reservation communities to bring the university and the students' home communities closer together. American Indian Student Services and the American Indian Center facility are open and welcoming to all UND students.

American Indian Studies Department

UND features an American Indian Studies Department, offering a bachelor's degree program and opportunities to pursue a valuable and diverse minor in American Indian Studies. The department also advises the Indian Studies Association, a student group that plans and implements the annual Time Out American Indian Education Week held on campus each spring and hosts the American Indian Film Festival held annually during November (National American Indian Heritage Month).

The Department of American Indian Studies offers either a major leading to the bachelor's degree or a minor in association with another discipline. Courses include classes on tribal histories, contemporary issues, health and Native cultures, oral traditions, philosophy and religions, resource development, Lakota language, indigenous identities, sustainable communities, and other subjects. Students must also complete coursework required by the university and the College of Arts & Sciences. Many American Indian studies courses meet university requirements in essential studies for social sciences, humanities, and world cultures. The department offers small classes to assist students in refining writing and discussion skills.

American Indian Leaders of Distinction

This permanent gallery exhibition recognizes the exceptional contributions of American Indian alumni to the University of North Dakota, the state, and the communities they serve. The alumni in this gallery received degrees from the university in education, business, counseling, art, psychology, and nursing at undergraduate and graduate levels. They are recognized as leaders of their communities for their advocacy in improving health and wellbeing, preserving and promoting American Indian culture, and supporting education and diversity. They are committed to improving the lives of others. The gallery, located in the Anna Mae Hughes Gallery Hughes Fine Arts Building, Room 103, is free and open to the public.

Contact Information

315 Princeton, Stop 8274
Grand Forks, ND 58202
701-777-4291
http://und.edu/student-life/american-indian-student-services/

FM Native American Center – Fargo

The FM Native American Center, located in Fargo, serves Cass and Clay counties.

Contact Information

109 9th St South
Fargo, ND 58103
701-478-1255

Dancers at the Earthlodge Village on Lake Sakakawea in New Town.

The inside of an earthlodge at Knife River Indian Villages National Historic Site.

Chapter Eight

Elections

Vote of the People

Since the adoption of the North Dakota Constitution on October 1, 1889, four types of questions have been submitted to the electorate for approval or rejection:

1. Amendments to the constitution as proposed by the Legislative Assembly or as proposed by the people through a petition procedure.
2. Statutory proposals initiated by the people through a petition procedure.
3. Acts of the Legislative Assembly referred to the electorate by a petition procedure.
4. A proposed new constitution, with four alternate propositions to certain sections, submitted by a Constitutional Convention (April 28, 1972).

Amending the Constitution

The original North Dakota Constitution provided for submission of amendments to the people after approval of two consecutive sessions of the Legislative Assembly. A majority vote of the legislators was required. In 1918, the constitution was amended to require a majority vote in only one legislative session before submission of the amendment to the people.

On the crest of the "Progressive Party" reform movement, North Dakota changed its constitution in 1914 to provide for an amendment through a procedure of petition by the people. Petitions proposing amendments were to be filed with the Secretary of State at least six months before the election. Those petitions carried the signatures of at least 25 percent of the legal voters in at least one-half of the counties of the state. If the people approved the amendment, it was then referred to the Legislative Assembly for consideration. If the Legislative Assembly adopted the amendment, it became a part of the North Dakota Constitution. If the Legislative Assembly did not approve, the measure returned to the ballot for another test at the polls. If approved again by the people, it became a part of the constitution.

This cumbersome procedure met its fate at the polls in 1918 when the people approved a new initiative procedure calling for petitions with 20,000 signatures to be filed 120 days before the election. Approval by a majority of the voters made the measure a part of the constitution. The Legislative Assembly was no longer involved in the initiative process.

On four occasions, the Legislative Assembly has submitted proposed amendments to the people for an increase in the required number of signatures to initiate constitutional amendments:

- On March 15, 1932, the people voted 104,953 to 51,459 against increasing the number of signatures from 20,000 to 40,000.

- On June 30, 1942, a proposed increase from 20,000 to 30,000 signatures was defeated by a vote of 69,904 to 52,275.

- On November 4, 1958, the people defeated by a vote of 127,290 to 47,814 a proposal to change from 20,000 signatures to the number of signatures equal to 10 percent of the vote cast for governor at the last general election.

- On November 7, 1978, the people approved by a vote of 102,182 to 75,413 a proposal that required a petition to carry signatures equal to four percent of the population based on the last federal census.

1971-72 Constitutional Convention

On April 28, 1972, when the people voted on a proposed new constitution, they approved by a vote of 76,585 to 71,062 the alternate proposition to increase the number of signatures required for initiating constitutional amendments. The increase would have changed from 20,000 required signatures to a number of signatures equal to four percent of the state's population, or around 25,000 signatures. The increase did not occur because none of the four alternate propositions on the ballot took effect if the proposed constitution was defeated, and it was.

Initiating and Referring Laws

Even though "initiative" and "referendum" are different types of political action(s), they have been treated as companion procedures since their original adoption in 1914.

The 1914 amendment to the constitution called for petitions proposing new laws to be signed by at least 10 percent of the legal voters in a majority of counties, then submitted to the Secretary of State at least 30 days before the Legislative Assembly convened. When the Legislative Assembly met, the Secretary of State would then present the measure for its consideration. The Legislative Assembly had the option of adopting the measure, submitting it to the people for a vote, rejecting it, or offering a counter proposal. If the Legislative Assembly failed to act or rejected the proposal, the measure went on the ballot at the next election. If the Legislative Assembly offered a counter proposal, both the counter proposal and the original measure appeared together on the ballot; the measure receiving the highest number of votes won.

The power of "referendum" was included in the 1914 constitutional amendment. Acts, or parts of the acts of the Legislative Assembly, would be referred when a petition was signed by 10 percent of voters from a majority of counties. Petitions were filed within 90 days of adjournment of a Legislative Assembly. A referendum could also be held if a majority of legislators decided to submit legislation to a vote of the people. Measures pertaining to preservation of the public peace, health, or safety that passed both houses by a two-thirds majority could not be referred.

Mired down in cumbersome and unworkable machinery, reformers proposed an amendment on November 5, 1918, which greatly simplified both the initiative and referendum processes. This amendment eliminated the Legislative Assembly from the process and simply required petitions signed by 10,000 qualified electors to be filed no later than 90 days before an election. The referendum was changed to require 7,000 signatures to place the measure on the next election ballot or 30,000 signatures to force a special election.

	For	**Against**
October 1, 1889 Article XV established requirements for future amendments to the North Dakota Constitution	27,441	8,107
November 3, 1914 Signatures of 10 percent of legal voters in majority of counties to initiate or refer measures	48,783	19,964
November 5, 1918 10,000 signatures to initiate 7,000 signatures to refer	47,447	32,598

The Legislative Assembly has on numerous occasions asked the voters to make the provisions of the initiative and referendum more stringent.

	For	Against
March 15, 1932		
30,000 signatures to initiate	50,967	105,581
25,000 signatures to refer		
June 24, 1936		
20,000 signatures to initiate or refer	41,500	127,511
June 25, 1940		
15,000 signatures to initiate or refer	61,573	64,636
June 30, 1942		
20,000 signatures to initiate	53,925	70,927
30,000 signatures to refer		
40,000 signatures to force special election – referring emergency measures		
November 4, 1958		
10 percent of votes cast for governor to initiate	47,814	127,290
Seven percent of votes cast for governor to refer		
November 8, 1966		
Three percent of population to initiate	69,116	84,131
Two percent of the population to refer		

In addition to the increases proposed by the Legislative Assembly, the Constitutional Convention of 1971–1972 submitted to the people the question of increasing the required signatures for the initiative and the referral to the number of signatures equal to two percent of the population, or around 12,500 signatures. This proposal was approved by a vote of 76,585 to 71,062, but did not become effective because the proposed constitution itself was defeated.

On November 7, 1978, the people approved by a vote of 102,182 to 75,413 a proposal to amend the constitution to initiate or refer laws by petition. The petitions required signatures equal to two percent of the population based on the last federal decennial census to refer and initiate statutory changes and four percent to initiate constitutional change(s).

Special Elections

The first special election involving referred measures occurred on June 26, 1919, after the Non-Partisan League (NPL) successfully passed legislation creating the Industrial Commission, Bank of North Dakota, and State Mill and Elevator. Voters approved the NPL programs.

The second special election, called because of recall petitions filed against the NPL Governor, Attorney General, and Commissioner of Agriculture and Labor, meant the defeat of nine different measures – some designed to hobble the NPL program. The program was sustained, but the three primary NPL architects were turned out of office as a result of the recall election of October 28, 1921. This was the first recall of state officials in the United States.

In 1933, the Legislative Assembly adopted a sales tax to bolster the state's waning finances through the tough Depression era. However, the proposal was referred, and another special election was required on September 22 of that year. The measure was defeated 41,241 to 113,807. There were actually seven measures for voter consideration at this special election.

In 1935, the Legislative Assembly passed another sales tax measure, and it was referred. At a July 15 special election, the measure was adopted by a vote of 75,166 to 65,890.

At a July 11, 1939, special election, voters considered four measures, one of which would have established a two percent income tax on businesses and professions. The measure was defeated 36,117 to 168,976.

The 1963 Legislative Assembly's tax program was referred and submitted to a vote of the people on July 17. The program, presented as several measures, was defeated by margins of five to one.

In 1965, the Legislative Assembly passed another tax program. It was referred, and on September 21 was defeated by a vote of 37,886 to 99,269.

In 1971, a special election brought before voters the referred measure that appropriated funds for the operation of the Department of Accounts and Purchases. Voters upheld the appropriation on a 61,342 to 39,076 vote.

On April 28, 1972, voters considered a proposed new constitution and four alternate propositions submitted by the 1971–1972 Constitutional Convention. The new constitution was defeated and as a result made null the votes on the four alternate propositions.

In 1973, the legislative apportionment plan was referred, and a constitutional amendment requiring single-member Senate and House districts initiated. Both measures considered in a special election on December 4 were defeated. The apportionment plan lost by a vote of 44,363 to 50,729, and the initiated constitutional amendment lost by a vote of 43,178 to 53,831.

In 1987, the people voted on two measures. The first dealt with the effective date of measures dealing with appropriations. The second provided for increases in state income tax with mandatory withholding. Both measures were approved on March 18, 1987.

On December 5, 1989, the people considered eight measures. The first, a proposed constitutional amendment, dealt with the reorganization of state government. The other measures referred 1989 legislation, including increases in motor fuel tax, state sales tax and state income tax, use of seatbelts, use of electronic video gaming devices, a retirement plan for legislators, and health care education in the schools. All measures were defeated by the voters.

In 1990, the people voted on a measure that would have provided for a one percent increase in state sales and use tax, motor vehicle excise tax, and aircraft excise tax to support elementary, secondary, adult, and vocational education. The measure was defeated by a vote of 52,610 to 74,207.

On November 3, 1992, the people voted on a measure that would establish water development objectives and impose a one-half of one percent sales and use tax. The measure was defeated by a vote of 110,045 to 181,960.

Summary of Initiative and Referendum Activity in North Dakota

Since statehood in 1889 through the end of the 2016 election cycle, approximately 510 measures have been placed on the ballot for consideration by North Dakota's voters. These have included constitutional measures resulting from legislative action, initiated constitutional measures, initiated statutory measures, and referred measures.

While the greatest single majority (242 of 510) of measures voted upon have been those resulting from legislative action or the Constitutional Convention, more than half (268, or 52 percent of 510) of all measures voted upon represent initiated or referred measures that required petitions to be circulated and signatures gathered. Of those, 142 have been initiated statutory measures, and 50 have been initiated constitutional measures. Actions of the Legislative Assembly have been referred to the voters of North Dakota 76 times. The 510 measures that have been considered by North Dakota voters include the four alternate propositions from the 1972 special election to approve a new constitution.

It is also important to note that the power to initiate and refer laws was not adopted in North Dakota until 1914. Since 1914, 489 measures have been placed on the ballot for consideration by North Dakota's voters. This demonstrates that 55 percent (268 of 489) of all ballot measures voted upon since the adoption of the initiative and referendum process in 1914 represent ballot measures that have required petitions to be circulated and signatures gathered. These statistics strengthen the percentage of measures that have gained ballot access in North Dakota through the initiative and referendum process versus through legislative action.

These statistics support the fact that North Dakota's initiative and referendum laws generally have not created overwhelming hurdles or obstacles to the initiative process. Rather, the statistics demonstrate the citizens of North Dakota have taken advantage of the initiative and referendum process more than the state's Legislative Assembly has taken advantage of its authority to propose constitutional change through the ballot box.

✔ A complete chronology of all measures before the voters since statehood is found in the *2009–2011 North Dakota Blue Book*. In subsequent elections, updates from each election will be published to ensure a complete ongoing listing.

North Dakota Measures Before the Voters 2016 to Present

	For	Against	Action
505. Primary 2016 (June 14) **Referendum** Relating to corporate farming.	32,045	99,976	Rejected
506. General 2016 (November 8) **Const. Amend. (Legis.)** Relating to legislator residency requirements.	282,231	45,542	Accepted
507. General 2016 (November 8) **Const. Amend. (Legis.)** Relating to oil extraction tax distribution.	209,651	116,418	Accepted
508. General 2016 (November 8) **Const. Amend. (Initiative)** Relating to crime victim rights.	207,248	126,884	Accepted
509. General 2016 (November 8) **Statutory (Initiative)** Relating to tobacco tax increase.	130,508	209,832	Rejected
510. General 2016 (November 8) **Statutory (Initiative)** Relating to medical marijuana.	216,042	122,615	Accepted

2016 General Election Report of Vote Totals

United States President
Donald Trump, Republican 216,794
Hillary Clinton, Democratic-NPL 93,758
Gary Johnson, Libertarian 21,434
Jill Stein, Green 3,780
Darrell Castle, Constitution 1,833
Roque "Rocky" De La Fuente 364

United States Senator
John Hoeven, Republican 268,788
Eliot Glassheim, Democratic-NPL 58,116
Robert N. Marquette, Libertarian 10,556
James Germalic, Independent 4,675

Representative in Congress
Kevin Cramer, Republican 233,980
Chase Iron Eyes, Democratic-NPL 80,377
Jack Seaman, Libertarian 23,528

Governor and Lt. Governor
Doug Burgum & Brent Sanford, Republican 259,863
Marvin E. Nelson & Joan Heckaman, Democratic-NPL 65,855
Marty Riske & Joshua Voytek, Libertarian 13,230

State Auditor
Josh Gallion, Republican 236,751
Roland Riemers, Libertarian 70,818

State Treasurer
Kelly L. Schmidt, Republican 204,733
Tim Mathern, Democratic-NPL 95,191
Eric Olson, Libertarian 24,829

Insurance Commissioner
Jon Godfread, Republican 206,067
Ruth Buffalo, Democratic-NPL 85,696
Nick Bata, Libertarian 27,642

Public Service Commissioner
Julie Fedorchak, Republican 218,961
Marlo Hunte-Beaubrun, Democratic-NPL 72,028
Thomas Skadeland, Libertarian 26,913

Superintendent of Public Instruction
Kirsten Baesler, No Party 220,079
Joe Chiang, No Party 73,350

Justice of the Supreme Court
Jerod Elton Tufte, No Party 166,229
Robert V. Bolinske Sr., No Party 105,825

Justice of the Supreme Court
Unexpired Two-Year Term
Lisa Fair McEvers, No Party **261,255**

(Candidates indicated in bold letters were elected.)

2018 North Dakota Election Calendar

Offices to be Filled in 2018

Federal-Congressional Offices (Party)
United States Senator .... Six-year Term
Representative in Congress .... Two-year Term

Statewide Offices (Party)
Secretary of State .... Four-year Term
Attorney General .... Four-year Term
Agricultural Commissioner .... Four-year Term
Public Service Commissioner .... Six-year Term
Tax Commissioner .... Four-year Term

Statewide Offices (No Party)
Justice of the Supreme Court .... Ten-year Term

Judicial District Offices (No Party)
Judges of the District Courts .... Six-year Term

State Legislative Seats (Party)
North Dakota Senate .... Four-year Term
(odd-numbered districts)
North Dakota House of Representatives .... Four-year Term
(odd-numbered districts)

County Offices (No Party)
Commissioners .... Four-year Term
Auditor .... Four-year Term
State's Attorney .... Four-year Term
Recorder .... Four-year Term
Treasurer .... Four-year Term
Sheriff .... Four-year Term
Director, Southwest Water Authority .... Four-year Term
Supervisor, Soil Conservation District .... Six-year Term
Director, Garrison Diversion Conservancy District .... Four-year Term
Official County Newspaper .... Four-year Term

Election Dates
Townships .... March 20, 2018
School Districts .... Between April 1 and June 30, 2018
Cities .... June 12, 2018
Statewide Primary .... June 12, 2018
Statewide General .... November 6, 2018

Note: Cities with home rule charters may have different election dates.

Voters in Burleigh County in 2016.

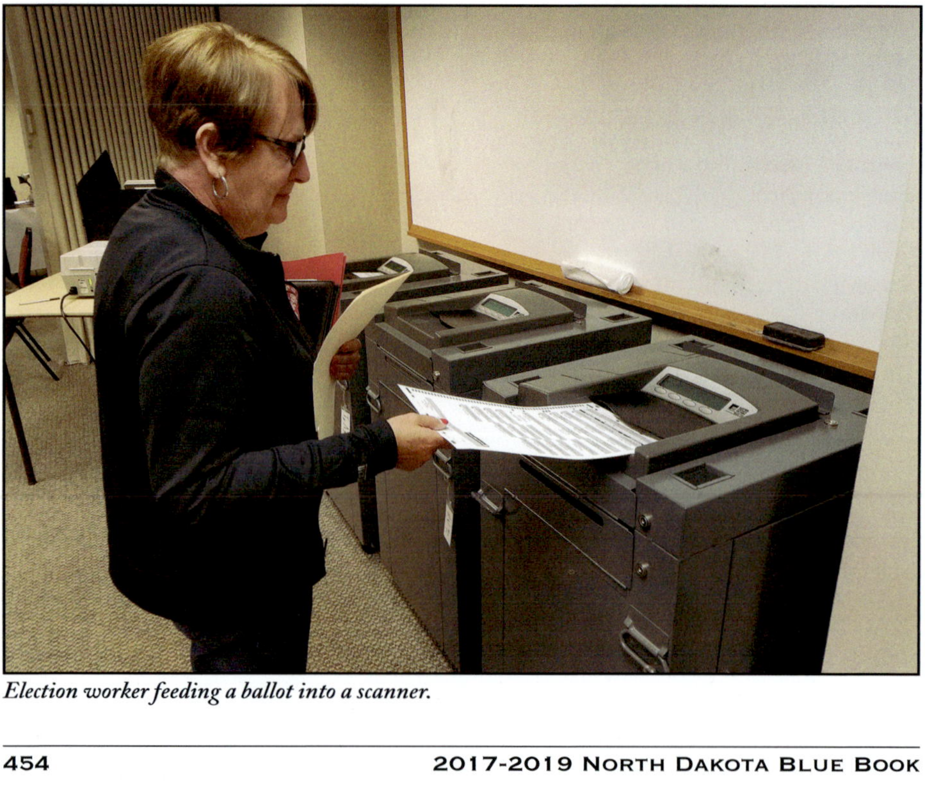

Election worker feeding a ballot into a scanner.

Chapter Nine

Education

North Dakota Education

✔ To review additional history of education in our state, refer to previously published Blue Books.

- The *1995 North Dakota Blue Book* gives a short history of public education in the state and includes material about the early private colleges in North Dakota.

- The *1997-1999 North Dakota Blue Book* features more detailed information about the history of education and Native American education in North Dakota.

- The *1999-2001 North Dakota Blue Book* has a map showing the locations of the institutions of higher education. It also lists North Dakota Rhodes Scholars and United States Senate Youth Winners.

- The *2001-2003 North Dakota Blue Book* contains a detailed list of supplemental programs provided to school districts by federal and state agencies. It also contains a description and history of "Home Education" in North Dakota. This edition also profiles a number of programs administered by the Department of Public Instruction, including the Division of Independent Study, Schools for the Blind and the Deaf, and alternative education.

- The *2003-2005 North Dakota Blue Book* contains a listing of teacher compensation for every school district in North Dakota covering the school year 2001-2002. It also contains a description of several private and public residential school facilities for special needs students and at-risk children.

- The *2005-2007 North Dakota Blue Book* contains summaries of educational trends, open enrollment, reorganization trends, joint powers, and the Education Fact Finding Commission.

- The *2007-2009 North Dakota Blue Book* contains a description regarding the education funding that was established in 2007 and the number of schools and students served with the Department of Career and Technical Education. It also includes a description of the North Dakota School for the Deaf and North Dakota Vision Services/School for the Blind.

- The *2009-2011 North Dakota Blue Book* highlights the programs at state colleges and universities that have a global impact.

- The *2011-2013 North Dakota Blue Book* provides a list of North Dakota Teachers of the Year from 1978-2011. It also provides a chronology of the chief executive officers of North Dakota's colleges and universities.

- The *2013-2015 North Dakota Blue Book* lists Area Career and Technology Education Centers in North Dakota.

Teacher of the Year Program

It is the mission of the state and national Teacher of the Year programs to recognize and honor the contributions of the American classroom teacher. The program is the oldest and most prestigious honors program to focus public attention on excellence in teaching. Begun in 1952, the state and national Teacher of the Year programs are sponsored by the North Dakota Department of Public Instruction in conjunction with the Council of Chief State School Officers and the Voya Foundation.

Nominations for North Dakota Teacher of the Year must come from a teacher, school administrator, school district trustee, local education association, student, or parent. Candidates nominated must:

- Be an exceptionally dedicated, knowledgeable, and skilled teacher in any state-approved or accredited school, pre-kindergarten through grade 12, who is planning to continue in an active teaching status;
- Inspire students of all backgrounds and abilities to learn;
- Have the respect and admiration of students, parents, and colleagues;
- Play an active and useful role in the community as well as in the school; and
- Be poised, articulate, and possess the energy to withstand a taxing schedule and have a background of self-advancement through advanced degree work; and participation in seminars and workshops.

North Dakota State Teacher of the Year
2012 to Present

2012 Brenda Werner
Bismarck High School
Bismarck

2013 Andrea Noonan
Cheney Middle School
West Fargo

2014 Aaron Knodel
West Fargo High School
West Fargo

2015 Dean Aamodt
Wahpeton Public
Wahpeton

2016 Amy Neal
Lewis & Clark Elementary School
Minot

2017 Nanci Jo Dauwen
Sheyenne High School
West Fargo

✔ See the *2011-2013 North Dakota Blue Book* for the North Dakota State Teacher of the Year list from 1978 to 2011.

North Dakota School Data

	School Year 2015-2016
Number of Public School Districts	
High School Districts	149
Elementary Districts	22
One-Room Rural Districts	5
Non-Operating Districts	2
Number of Non-Public Schools	
Approved Non-Public Schools	43
K-12 Enrollment	7,293
Licensed Staff	758
Accreditation Status of Schools	
Approved Public High School Units	167
Approved Public Middle School Units in High School LEAs	28
Approved Public Middle School Units in Graded Elementary LEAs	1
Approved Public Elementary School Units in High School LEAs	253
Approved Public Elementary School Units in Graded Elementary LEAs	24
Approved Public Elementary School Units in Rural LEAs	5
Non-Approved Public Elementary School Units in Rural LEAs	1
Approved Non-Public High School Units	15
Approved Non-Public Middle School Units	4
Approved Non-Public Elementary School Units	46
Non-Approved Non-Public Elementary School Units	1
Approved BIE/Grant High School Units	1
Approved BIE Elementary School Units	5
Approved State Institution High School Units	2
Approved State Institution Middle School Units	1
Approved State Institution Elementary School Units	2
Schools Using AdvancEd for Education Review Process	
Elementary Schools	292
Middle/Junior High Schools	34
High Schools	176

Enrollment by Type of System – Fall 2016

Kindergarten	8,834
One-Room Rural	46
Elementary	67,640
Secondary	30,343
Total K-12 Public Enrollment	106,863

Cost of Education and Average Cost Per Pupil – 2016

	Cost of Education	Cost Per Pupil
Preschool Special Education	$14,977,996	$13,252
Kindergarten	$85,341,576	$9,518
Elementary 1-6	$600,482,092	$11,619
Elementary 7-8	$184,158,263	$11,775
Elementary 1-8	$784,640,355	$11,656
Elementary K-8	$869,981,931	$11,404
Secondary 9-12	$406,221,826	$13,240

Cost of education figures include per pupil cost expenditures from the school district, special education units, and vocational education centers.

Type of School Plants in Session – Fall 2016

Elementary Schools	172
Middle Level/Junior High Schools	24
Senior High Schools	36
Elementary/Secondary Combination	131
One-Teacher Schools	10

K-12 School Enrollment Growth in North Dakota 2012-2016

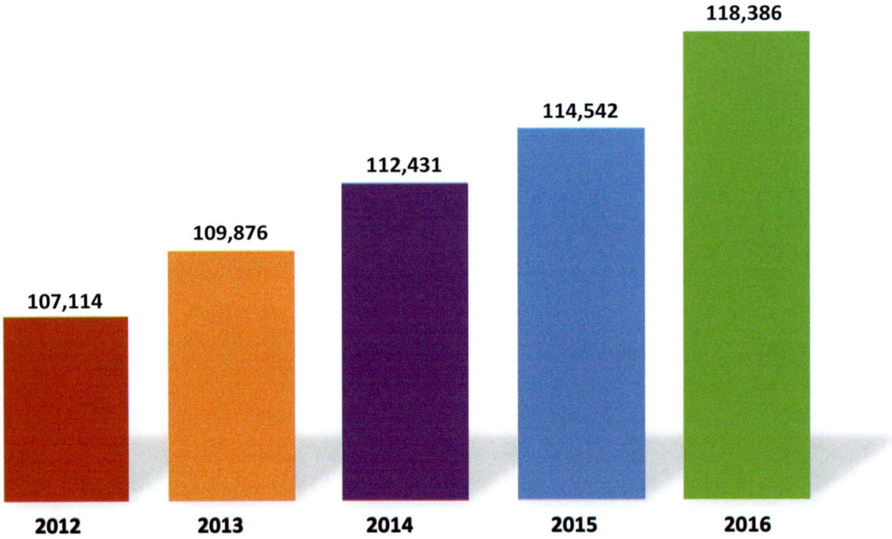

Source: North Dakota Department of Public Instruction

Teacher Growth in North Dakota 2012-2016

(Full-time Equivalent Positions)

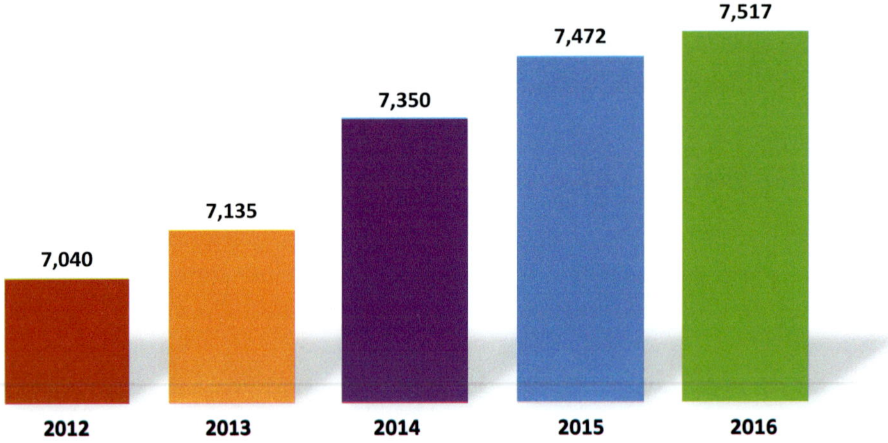

Source: North Dakota Department of Public Instruction

New Schools in North Dakota

2014
Independence Elementary, West Fargo
Liberty Elementary School, Bismarck
Lincoln Elementary School, Lincoln
Red Trail Elementary, Mandan

2015
Discovery Elementary School, Grand Forks
South Prairie High School, south of Minot
Ed Clapp Elementary, Fargo
Legacy High School, Bismarck

2016
John Hoeven Elementary School, Minot
Nedrose High School, Minot
Wahpeton Elementary School
Watford City High School
Williston High School

Source: Public School Districts

New Math and English Standards

The Department of Public Instruction's major initiatives for the 2015-2017 biennium included an update for North Dakota's classroom content standards for mathematics and English and a plan to bring the new Every Student Succeeds Act federal education law into North Dakota's schools.

Two groups of more than 30 North Dakota math and English teachers took on the work of rewriting the standards, which had not been reviewed since 2011. The standards are benchmarks of what a student should know, and be able to do, at different grade levels. For example, a kindergarten student is expected to be able to count to 100 by ones and by 10s and write numbers, in sequence, from one through 20. Seventh graders are expected to be able to solve geometry problems during scale drawing of geometric figures.

Two drafts of the writing committees' work were posted for public comment. In addition, a separate review committee with community leaders and representation from business, industry, labor, and the general public reviewed the proposed new standards and suggested revisions. The standards were approved by Superintendent of Public Instruction Kirsten Baesler in April 2017 and put into use in North Dakota schools in fall 2017.

Every Student Succeeds Act

The new Every Student Succeeds Act (ESSA) was approved by Congress and signed by the president in December 2015. The legislation, which was supported by North Dakota's congressional delegation, Senators John Hoeven and Heidi Heitkamp and Representative Kevin Cramer, restored a great deal of authority to the state and communities about how best to educate North Dakota's students.

State Superintendent Kirsten Baesler subsequently assembled a planning group of more than 50 people, including teachers, parents, school administrators, school board members, business people, legislators, and representatives of gifted students and students with disabilities.

The group drafted a state ESSA blueprint with the goal of ensuring all North Dakota high school students graduate "Choice Ready," "with the knowledge, skills, and disposition to be successful in whatever they choose to do, whether they pursue a post-secondary degree, enroll in a technical college, enter the workforce, or join the military."

Nine implementation committees, each consisting of educators and representatives of stakeholder groups, then took up the job of working through the details of how the Every Student Succeeds Act would improve North Dakota education, emphasize a culture of continuous educational improvement, and make school operations more accountable and transparent to parents and taxpayers.

Superintendent's Student Cabinet

To hear student opinions about how North Dakota's K-12 education system was working, and to solicit suggestions on how to improve it, State Superintendent Kirsten Baesler organized a Superintendent's Student Cabinet after she took office. The Cabinet was made up of students from across North Dakota, representing rural and urban school districts. Student members ranged in age from fourth graders to college freshmen. They were appointed to serve for about 18 months. Baesler's first 20-member Cabinet was appointed in April 2015. The second Cabinet was appointed in November 2016. Several education policy suggestions from Cabinet members were introduced in the Legislature and eventually became law, such as a proposal to make advanced high school coursework more widely available in North Dakota schools.

Career and Technical Education

In the early 1900s, advocates of "practical education" argued for a different curriculum in education that would provide students with a background to better prepare students for jobs. Many people felt the current system did not meet the needs of students or industry.

In 1914, Senator Hoke Smith of Georgia chaired a national commission on providing federal aid for vocational education. In December 1915, he introduced a bill "to provide for the promotion of vocational education." In 1916, Representative Dudley Hughes, also of Georgia, introduced similar legislation in the House.

In 1917, the Smith-Hughes Act was passed, which provided $1.7 million for vocational programs and created a federal board for vocational education. The state of North Dakota developed its first state plan in 1919. The State Board of Administration served as the administering body, and Chauncey E. Cavett of Lisbon was the state director and executive officer for vocational training. This act provided for programs in agriculture, home economics, trade, and industry.

The North Dakota Vocational Association was formed in 1928 and continues today as the North Dakota Association for Career and Technical Education, providing educators with a voice for what is happening in career and technical education. A complete history of that organization, entitled *60th Anniversary NDVA*, was written in 1987 by Marjore Lovering. The George-Dean Act was passed in 1936, expanding the dollars for vocational education and adding distributive education as a program area.

North Dakota operated under the State Board of Administration until 1937. At that time, the State Board of Higher Education was designated as the State Board for Vocational Education. In 1955, the Legislative Assembly created a new State Board for Vocational Education. This board consisted of the Governor, Attorney General, Superintendent of Public Instruction, and one representative each from the North Dakota Education Association and the North Dakota School Officers Association. The Superintendent of Public Instruction served as state director and executive secretary. This board also served as the State Board of Public School Education.

In the mid-1960s, a Committee of 100, chaired by State Representative Art Link, was formed to study ways to improve vocational education in North Dakota. Many recommendations came out of this committee, including one creating a new seven-member board that consisted of six members appointed by the Governor, to represent six judicial districts of the state, and the Superintendent of Public Instruction. A full-time state director and executive officer were to be hired by this board. This was passed by the 1967 Legislative Assembly. During the 1997 legislative session, the board was expanded to include the Chancellor of Higher Education and the director of Job Service North Dakota, making it a nine-member board. This is the current structure.

Prior to 1967, state staff officers were located at the teacher education colleges. Between 1967 and 1969, all staff were brought into Bismarck as one unit under the direction of LeRoy Swenson, state director. The office was located in the lower level of the State Office Building at 900 East Boulevard Avenue.

Over the next 15 years, the staff was expanded under Carrol Burchinal and Reuben Guenthner to include new service areas and special federal and state initiative projects to meet the growing demand for vocational education in the state. In 1981, the State Office was moved to its present location on the 15th floor of the State Capitol.

In 1984, a new federal law, the Carl D. Perkins Vocational Act, was enacted. It was named after Representative Carl Perkins of Kentucky for his continued work (more than 20 years) to improve vocational education in the United States. In 1990, the vocational act was reauthorized as the Carl D. Perkins Vocational and Applied Technology Education Act of 1990. In 1998, and again in 2006, the Perkins Act was reauthorized, providing greater flexibility in how funds are spent with increased accountability. These acts drastically changed how funding was distributed to local education agencies and what the funds could be used for at those levels.

In 1993, the Legislative Assembly changed the agency's name to the State Board for Vocational and Technical Education. In 2003, the agency name was changed to the Department of Career and Technical Education and the state board's name was changed to the State Board for Career and Technical Education. The 2003 Legislature also required every school to offer a minimum of two credits in career and technical education by 2006.

Beginning in 2007, an initiative supported by Governor Hoeven and endorsed by the Legislative Assembly sought to increase access to Career and Technical Education (CTE) programming across the state. It initially focused on the western third of the state, establishing three new virtual Area Career and Technology Centers, and has since established two additional virtual Area Centers across the state. From an original five Area Centers established in the 1970s, there are now 10 Area Career and Technology Centers statewide. Additional funding has been provided to encourage schools to cooperate and share CTE courses and resources, through interactive video (ITV) and online, which increases the number of CTE courses available to schools.

The Legislative Assembly also earmarked funding for an elementary entrepreneurship grant program for schools, which brought CTE into the elementary grades for the first time, with funding to encourage entrepreneurship education at that level.

In 2013, Senate Concurrent Resolution 4015 recognized CTE as the state Science, Technology, Engineering, and Mathematics (STEM) agency to recommend and assist in the coordination of statewide STEM activities. The agency supports the

STEM Network and several statewide STEM activities, including grants to schools which involve private industry participation.

There have been 12 directors of the State Board for Career and Technical Education in North Dakota:

1919-1922	Chauncey Cavett
1922-1942	Edward Erickson
1942-1947	Dr. A.F. Arnason
1947-1955	E.F. Riley
1955-1956	M.F. Peterson
1956-1957	Edward Erickson
1957-1960	M.F. Peterson
1960-1970	LeRoy Swenson
1970-1992	Carrol Burchinal
1992-1995	Reuben Guenthner
1995-2000	Mel Olson
2000-present	Wayne Kutzer

Area Career and Technology Centers Member Schools 2017-2018

Cass County Area CTC (Virtual)
Central Cass, Fargo, Northern Cass, West Fargo

Grand Forks Area CTC (Virtual)
Central Valley, Grand Forks, Hatton, Hillsboro, Larimore, May-Port CG, Northwood, Thompson

James Valley Area CTC (Jamestown)
Jamestown, Montpelier, Pingree-Buchanan

Lake Area CTC (Devils Lake)
Devils Lake Central, Maddock, Minnewaukan, Munich, School for the Deaf, Starkweather

Missouri River Area CTC (Virtual)
Ashley, Beulah, Bismarck, Center-Stanton, Elgin-New Leipzig, Flasher, Garrison, Goodrich, Hazen, HMB (Hazelton, Moffit, Braddock), Kidder County, Linton, Mandan, McClusky, Napoleon, New Salem, Selfridge, Solen-Cannonball, Standing Rock, Strasburg, Turtle Lake-Mercer, Underwood, Washburn, White Shield, Wilton, Wing, Wishek, Zeeland

North Valley Area CTC (Grafton)
Drayton, Grafton, Inkster (Midway), Park River, St. Thomas, Valley-Edinburg

Roughrider Area CTC (Virtual)
Beach, Belfield, Dickinson, Glen Ullin, Hebron, Hettinger, Killdeer, Mott-Regent, New England, Richardton-Taylor, Scranton, South Heart

Sheyenne Valley Area CTC (Valley City)
Barnes County North at Wimbledon, Maple Valley-Tower City, Valley City

Southeast Region CTC (Wahpeton and Oakes)
Campbell-Tintah, Ellendale, Fairmount, Hankinson, Lidgerwood, Lisbon, Oakes, Richland-Colfax, Sargent Central, Wahpeton, Wyndmere

Western Star Area CTC (Virtual)
Alexander, Trenton, Watford City, Williston

21st Century Community Learning Centers

The 21st Century Community Learning Centers Program establishes and/or expands community learning centers that provide students with academic enrichment opportunities along with activities designed to complement the students' regular academic program.

1. **Great Northwest Education Cooperative (GNWED)**
   Director – David Richter
   www.gnwec.k12.nd.us/

2. **Mid-Dakota Education Cooperative (MDEC)**
   Director – Luke Schaefer
   www.ndmdec.org/

3. **Missouri River Education Cooperative (MREC)**
   Director – Lyle Krueger
   www.mrecnd.org/

4. **North Central Education Cooperative (NCEC)**
   Director – Cynthia Jelleberg
   www.ncecnorthdakota.org/

5. **Northeast Education Services Cooperative (NESC)**
   Director – Jennifer Carlson
   www.nesc.k12.nd.us/

6. **Red River Valley Education Cooperative (RRVEC)**
   Director – Janet O'Hara
   https://sites.google.com/a/rrvecnd.org/rrvec/home

7. **Roughrider Education Services Program (RESP)**
   Director – Riley Mattson
   www.resp-k12-education.org/

8. **South East Education Cooperative (SEEC)**
   Director – Kyle Davison
   www.ndseec.com/

Higher Education in North Dakota

During the last quarter of the 19th century, when North Dakota was on the frontier of white settlement, a number of colleges were established. One of the first was the University of North Dakota, which was founded in 1883. Many other colleges were created by religious denominations. These include the Presbyterians (Jamestown College, 1883), the Congregationalists (Fargo College, 1887), the Methodists (Red River Valley University, Wahpeton, 1891), the Norwegian Lutherans (Grand Forks College, 1891), and the Baptists (Tower University, Tower City, 1886, and Dakota College, Lisbon, 1891). In 1961, Assumption College, operated by the Catholic Church, opened in Richardton.

Some survived only a short time. Tower University closed in 1889, while Dakota College operated for two years in a converted hotel building, which burned down in February 1895. The Methodists moved their institution from Wahpeton to Grand Forks in 1905; it affiliated itself with the University of North Dakota as Wesley College. The old building at Wahpeton was immediately occupied by the newly created State School of Science. Assumption College closed in 1971 after just 10 years.

A change in synodical boundaries forced closure of Grand Forks College in 1910; the faculty moved west to Velva where Northwestern College struggled on for two more years. Fargo College had a sizable campus and three brick buildings, but massive debt put it out of business in 1922. Even Jamestown College was closed from 1893 to 1909 for similar reasons, but good organization and strong local support enabled it to reopen and continue.

Several schools were established primarily to provide "normal" or teacher's training. This reflected the hard realities of financial survival, since the 1887 territorial legislature had provided for limited public support of teacher's training in private schools. Milnor Normal School, Rolla University, and Bruflat Academy (also known as Portland Normal School and Business College) came into existence in the last years of territorial government. The first array of public institutions was specified in the 1889 Constitution of North Dakota. Included in this group were Mayville Normal School, the agricultural college at Fargo, the university at Grand Forks, Valley City Normal School, a scientific school at Wahpeton, and a school of forestry at Bottineau.

During the 22nd Legislative Assembly, Senator Lynn Sperry sponsored Senate Bill 209 authorizing the establishment of junior colleges. The bill was approved and signed into law on March 11, 1931. This enabling legislation was the vehicle for the establishment of three two-year colleges: Bismarck Junior College (1939), Devils Lake Junior College (1941), and University of North Dakota – Williston (1957). Two new institutions, Trinity Bible College (1948) and the University of Mary (1955), also came into being. In the 1970s, five two-year tribal colleges were established to provide academic and vocational training for the state's native peoples under their own governance.

Governance of North Dakota's Public Institutions of Higher Education

Prior to 1911, all public colleges – and the university – were governed by independent boards of trustees whose members were appointed by the Governor. In that year, the State Board of Normal School Trustees was created specifically to administer the affairs of the normal schools (or teacher colleges). This board consisted of three gubernatorial appointees serving staggered four-year terms and the Superintendent of Public Instruction, who served as ex-officio president.

In 1915, the State Board of Regents was created and given authority over all public colleges, including the normal schools, and the university. This board consisted of five members appointed by the Governor for six-year terms.

The 1919 Legislative Assembly abolished the Board of Regents and placed the administration of the public colleges and the university under a new agency, the Board of Administration. This board consisted of three gubernatorial appointees as well as the Superintendent of Public Instruction and Commissioner of Agriculture and Labor, serving as ex-officio members. Since the Board was charged with "the general supervision and administration of all state penal, charitable and educational institutions of the state, and the general supervision of the public and common schools," the situation was not altogether a satisfactory one.

The controversy surrounding the charges of political interference in the administration of the North Dakota Agriculture College and the firing of its president and seven high-ranking faculty members in 1937 precipitated a movement to create an independent board to govern the state's institutions of higher learning. A constitutional amendment was initiated to create a board of higher education, which was approved by voters in June 1938. The new board consisted of seven members, each appointed by the Governor for seven-year terms, under a carefully outlined procedure intended to remove the board members as far as possible from political influence. The new law also required the board to appoint a Commissioner of Higher Education to serve as its chief executive officer. The board's first meeting took place in Bismarck on July 6, 1939.

Commissioners of the Board of Higher Education who have served since inception:

Robert Murphy	1940 to December 1942
Albert Arnason	December 1942 to September 1957
Arthur Mead	October 1957 to November 1963
Kenneth Raschke	July 1964 to September 1978
Kent Alm	September 1978 to September 1981
John Richardson	September 1981 to May 1990

In February 1990, the board created a one-university system headed by a chancellor who serves as the system's chief executive officer. Presidents of each institution report directly to the chancellor.

Chancellors who have served since 1990:

John Richardson	May 1990 to September 1990
Thomas Clifford	October 1990 to July 1991
Douglas Treadway	July 1991 to February 1994
Larry Isaak	(co-chancellor), February 1994 to July 1994
Gene Kemper	(co-chancellor), February 1994 to July 1994
Larry Isaak	July 1994 to November 2003
Michael Hillman (interim)	November 2003 to June 2004
Robert L. Potts	July 2004 to August 2006
Eddie Dunn	August 2006 to June 30, 2007
William Goetz	July 1, 2007 to June 30, 2012
Hamid A. Shirvani	July 1, 2012 to June 20, 2013
Larry C. Skogen (interim)	June 20, 2013 to June 30, 2015
Mark R. Hagerott	July 1, 2015 to present

The State Board of Higher Education (SBHE) currently consists of seven citizen members, one student member, one non-voting staff adviser, and one non-voting faculty adviser. The Governor appoints the voting citizen members to four-year terms. In 1996, voters approved a constitutional amendment reducing terms from seven to four years. These appointments require the consent of the majority of the state Senate. The Governor also appoints the voting student member to a one-year term on the board from a list of names submitted by the North Dakota Student Association. The Council of College Faculties annually selects the faculty representative to serve on the board, and the NDUS Staff Senate selects the staff representative.

The SBHE is the policy-setting and advocacy body for the North Dakota University System (NDUS). Decisions on issues with system-wide implications are made by the board and chancellor in consultation with the cabinet (composed of the university presidents, executive dean, and vice-chancellors). The CEOs of the institutions retain their authority in managing campus affairs.

The chancellor's office supports the SBHE in developing public policy for the NDUS' governance and in advocating on its behalf.

SBHE Membership	**Appointment Date**	**Term Ends**
Don Morton, Chair	July 1, 2012	June 30, 2021
Greg Stemen, Vice Chair	July 1, 2015	June 30, 2019
Kathleen Neset	June 20, 2012	June 30, 2021
Nick Hacker	July 1, 2015	June 30, 2019
Kevin Melicher	May 20, 2014	June 30, 2018
Mike Ness	February 26, 2015	June 30, 2018
Casey Ryan	July 1, 2017	June 30, 2021
Jacob Dailey, Student	July 1, 2017	June 30, 2018
Andy Wakefield, Staff Advisor	July 1, 2016	June 30, 2018
Birgit Pruess, Faculty Advisor	July 1, 2017	June 30, 2018

Dr. Mark R. Hagerott, Chancellor

Dr. Mark R. Hagerott is chancellor for the North Dakota University System. He was appointed to the position following a unanimous vote by the State Board of Higher Education on April 30, 2015. Most recently Hagerott served as the senior civilian and deputy director of the Center for Cyber Security Studies at the Naval Academy in Annapolis, Maryland, and panel co-lead of the Defense Science Board in Washington, D.C.

Prior to his most recent position, Hagerott held numerous academic leadership roles to include the dean of humanities and social sciences, special assistant to the provost, chair of the admissions board, chairmanship of senior faculty senate committees pertaining to assessment and accreditation, and as a planning and strategy director in one of the largest U.S. Army educational organizations. Prior to his transition to an academic career path, he held numerous leadership positions in the U.S. Navy, both aboard ships and in administrative positions in the Department of Defense, most recently serving in the Pentagon during the second Bush administration. He hails from a fourth generation North Dakota family, the great-grandson of homesteaders of the Dakota Territory, and 25 years ago began to buy crop and pasture land northwest of Mandan, nearby the family homestead. During his military and educational career, he spent much of his leave time helping his father and uncles on the farm.

A certified naval nuclear engineer in power generation and distribution, who also served as chief engineer for a major environmental project involving the defueling of two atomic reactors, Hagerott changed from engineering to a career in higher education in 2005. Hagerott has conducted research and writing about the evolution of technology, education, and changes in career and the workplace. He is personally committed to sharing his knowledge and experience and working with the students and other stakeholders of North Dakota to help each of the member colleges and universities achieve greater success in this time of rapid social and technological change.

Hagerott holds a B.S. from the U.S. Naval Academy, a M.A. in political science and economics from Oxford University where he attended as a Rhodes Scholar, and a Ph.D. in history from University of Maryland, and he also served as a White House Fellow in the first Bush administration.

Contact information:

Website: www.ndus.edu
Email: mark.hagerott@ndus.edu
Phone: 701-328-2974
Fax: 701-328-2961

North Dakota Colleges and Universities

Four-Year Institutions (Public)	Four-Year Institutions (Private)	Two-Year Colleges (Public)	Tribal Colleges (Two-Year)*
Dickinson State University	Trinity Bible College & Graduate School	Bismarck State College	Cankdeska Cikana Community College
Mayville State University	University of Jamestown	Dakota College at Bottineau	Nueta Hidatsa Sahnish College
Minot State University	University of Mary	Lake Region State College	Sitting Bull College
North Dakota State University		North Dakota State College of Science	Turtle Mountain Community College
University of North Dakota		Williston State College	United Tribes Technical College
Valley City State University			

*See Chapter 7 for complete information.

✔ A summary of the names changes of North Dakota colleges and universities can be found in the *2015-2017 North Dakota Blue Book.*

North Dakota University System

The North Dakota University System (NDUS) is a unified system of higher education governed by the State Board of Higher Education. Organized in 1990, the system includes two research universities, four regional universities, and five community colleges.

Led by the chancellor, the NDUS staff supports the State Board of Higher Education's mission to enhance the quality of life for all those served by the NDUS as well as the economic and social vitality of North Dakota.

NDUS Fall 2016 Enrollment

Four-Year

Dickinson State University	1,386
Mayville State University	1,130
Minot State University	3,412
North Dakota State University	14,432
Valley City State University	1,452
University of North Dakota	14,648

Two-Year

Bismarck State College	3,976
Dakota College at Bottineau	811
Lake Region State College	1,947
North Dakota State School of Science	3,003
Williston State College	1,039

NDUS Four-Year Institutions

Dickinson State University

291 Campus Drive
Dickinson, ND 58601-4896
701-483-2507
800-279-HAWK
www.dickinsonstate.edu

President: Dr. Thomas Mitzel
Nickname: Blue Hawks

Mission, Role, and Scope Statement

Dickinson State University is a regional four-year institution within NDUS, whose primary role is to contribute to intellectual, social, economic, and cultural development, especially in southwestern North Dakota. The university's mission is to provide high-quality, accessible programs; to promote excellence in teaching and learning; to support scholarly and creative activities; and to provide service relevant to the economy, health, and quality of life for the citizens of the state.

History

The "College on the Hill" began as Dickinson State Normal School when it was established by a constitutional amendment in 1916. Classes began in 1918 with a two-year program designed to train elementary and secondary school teachers. One hundred four students attended the first classes at Dickinson High School because the new normal school had no buildings. The sessions were free of charge, although students paid their own room and board. Subsequent classes were held at the historic Elks Building until May Hall was completed in 1924. In 1931, four-year degrees were offered for the first time under the school's new name, Dickinson State Teachers College. In 1963, the name was changed to Dickinson State College, and university status was granted in 1987.

Mayville State University

330 Third Street Northeast
Mayville, ND 58257
701-788-4687
800-437-4104
www.mayvillestate.edu

President: Dr. Gary Hagen
Nickname: Comets

Mission

The mission of Mayville State University is to educate and guide students, as individuals, so that they may realize their full career potential and enhance their lives. We do this in an environment that reflects our tradition of personal service, commitment to innovative technology-enriched education, and dynamic learning relationships with community, employers, and society.

History

Mayville Normal School, located in the heart of the Red River Valley in east-central North Dakota, was established in 1889, and classes began in 1890. Funds for a building, Old Main, were provided in 1891, and classes were held there beginning in 1893. The school became Mayville State Teachers College in 1925, Mayville State College in 1963, State University of North Dakota – Mayville on April 1, 1987, and finally, Mayville State University on April 27, 1987. Today, the university is a regional four-year institution within NDUS.

Minot State University

500 University Avenue West
Minot, ND 58707
701-858-3000
800-777-0750
www.minotstateu.edu

President: Dr. Steven Shirley
Nickname: Beavers

Mission, Core Values, and Core Purpose

Minot State University is dedicated to student success, engaged and lifelong learning, advancement of knowledge, effective student service, and development of students of character. The university values critical and creative thinking, vitality of communities and cultures, stewardship of place, and the multicultural and global environment. It honors and supports the dignity and rights of diverse individuals, freedom of expression, academic freedom, ethical and moral behavior, integrity, fairness, and honesty. The university is dedicated to the success of all students: their growth and development as educated citizens, their confidence, and their lifelong devotion to the common good and the welfare of others. The university is committed to teaching and learning with excellence, integrity, and engagement; serving students and others respectfully and responsibly; following high ethical and moral principles; and supporting the values of community and place where all community members are valued and respected for their work, contributions, and freedom of expression. The core purpose of Minot State University is to help people appreciate life and learning and contribute meaningfully to the lives of others.

History

Minot State University is a regional public institution located in Minot (the "Magic City") in the northwest region of the state. It began as Minot Normal School when it was created by popular vote in November 1910 when the state constitution was amended. The first classes met in September 1913 in the city armory. The school's first building, Old Main, came into use in April 1914.

North Dakota State University

NDSU NORTH DAKOTA STATE UNIVERSITY

1340 Administration Avenue
PO Box 6050
Fargo, ND 58108-6050
701-231-8011
800-488-NDSU (6378)
www.ndsu.edu

President: Dr. Dean Bresciani
Nickname: Bison

Mission

With energy and momentum, North Dakota State University addresses the needs and aspirations of people in a changing world by building on our land-grant foundation.

Vision

We envision a vibrant university that will be globally identified as a contemporary metropolitan land-grant institution.

History

The 1889 state constitution located North Dakota Agricultural College at Fargo, an action ratified by the 1890 Legislature, which established it as North Dakota Agricultural College. The first classes met in January 1891. The first building, College Hall (now called Old Main), was completed in 1892. In 1960, the institution's name was changed to North Dakota State University. Today, it is a student-focused, land-grant, research university located in the northwest part of Fargo. The university also has a major presence in Fargo's downtown area.

University of North Dakota

3501 University Avenue, Stop 8357
Grand Forks, ND 58202
701-777-3000
800-CALL-UND
www.und.edu

President: Mark Kennedy, MBA
Nickname: Fighting Hawks

Mission

The University of North Dakota, as a member of NDUS, serves the state, the country, and the world community through teaching, research, creative activities, and service. State-assisted, the university's work depends also on federal, private, and corporate sources. With other research universities, the university shares a distinctive responsibility for the discovery, development, preservation, and dissemination of knowledge. Through its sponsorship and encouragement of basic and applied research, scholarship, and creative endeavor, the university contributes to the public well-being.

The university maintains its original mission in liberal arts, business, education, law, medicine, and engineering and mines and has also developed special missions in nursing, fine arts, aerospace, energy, human resources, and international studies. It provides a wide range of challenging academic programs for undergraduate, professional, and graduate students through the doctoral level. The university encourages students to make informed choices, to communicate effectively, to be intellectually curious and creative, to commit themselves to lifelong learning and the service of others, and to share responsibility both for their own communities and for the world. The university promotes cultural diversity among its students, staff, and faculty.

In addition to its on-campus instructional and research programs, the University of North Dakota separately and cooperatively provides extensive continuing education and public service programs for all areas of the state and region.

Vision

Exceptional UND is the vision roadmap that outlines the university's five strategic priorities that build on and support our mission of teaching, research, and service.

History

An act of the 1883 Dakota Territory legislature created the University of North Dakota (the first use of the name "North Dakota") six years before statehood was achieved. Unlike most state institutions of higher education west of the Mississippi, the University of North Dakota did not begin as an agricultural school or only as a teachers' college. Instead, it was organized as a College of Arts & Sciences with a Normal School for the education of teachers. The first classes met in September 1884 when the first building was completed. The university's location at Grand Forks was recognized in North Dakota's 1889 Constitution.

Valley City State University

101 College Street Southwest
Valley City, ND 58072
800-532-8641
www.vcsu.edu

VALLEY CITY
STATE UNIVERSITY

President: Dr. Tisa Mason
Nickname: Vikings

Mission

Valley City State University is a public, regional university offering exceptional programs in an active, learner-centered community that promotes meaningful scholarship, ethical service, and the skilled use of technology. As an important knowledge resource, the university offers programs and outreach that enrich the quality of life in North Dakota and beyond. Through flexible, accessible, and innovative baccalaureate and master's programs, Valley City State University prepares students to succeed as educators, leaders, and engaged citizens in an increasingly complex and diverse society.

Vision

Valley City State University will be nationally recognized for advancing important collaboration, fostering innovative engagement, and promoting noteworthy transformation. Through effective use of best practices in technology, teaching, and learning, Valley City State University will be a destination university for students in North Dakota and throughout the region, extending its reach and influence beyond the campus boundaries.

History

The 1889 State Constitution located a normal school at Valley City, and the school was established by the 1890 Legislature. Valley City Normal School opened in October 1890 above a downtown business and occupied its first building in December 1892. In 1921, the school began granting a bachelor of arts degree in education and changed its name to State Teachers College in Valley City. The name was changed to Valley City State College (1963); State University of North Dakota-Valley City (January 1, 1987); and, finally, to Valley City State University (April 27, 1987). The university has been a leader in applying technology to enhance learning. In 1996, it was the second university in the nation to become a laptop university, which means that every full-time student has access to their own laptop computer, provided by Valley City State University. In 2005, the university was authorized to offer its first master's degree program, a master of education.

NDUS Two-Year Institutions

Bismarck State College

P.O. Box 5587
1500 Edwards Avenue
Bismarck, ND 58506
701-224-5400
800-445-5073
www.bismarckstate.edu

President: Dr. Larry C. Skogen
Nickname: Mystics

Mission

Bismarck State College, an innovative community college, offers high quality education, workforce training, and enrichment programs reaching local and global communities.

Vision

A national model for innovative education and workforce training.

History

Created in 1939 in response to a community need for a local college, Bismarck State College was originally known as Bismarck Junior College. Classes began on September 4, 1939, on the third floor of Bismarck High School. By the late 1940s, a new location became urgent as college enrollments soared with returning GIs. In 1951, the Legislature granted the college 15 acres on the Capitol grounds, and Bismarck Junior College moved into its own building at 900 Boulevard Avenue in 1955. The college quickly outgrew the site. In 1959, Harold Schafer, local entrepreneur and founder of the successful Gold Seal Company, offered the college land overlooking the Missouri River at the northwest edge of Bismarck. Classes began on the new campus in the fall of 1961. Part of the Bismarck Public Schools for many years, the college became part of NDUS in 1984. The college's name was changed to Bismarck State Community College on January 1, 1987, and then to Bismarck State College on April 27, 1987.

Dakota College at Bottineau

105 Simrall Boulevard
Bottineau, ND 58318
800-542-6866
701-228-5488
www.dakotacollege.edu

President: Dr. Steven Shirley
Campus Dean: Dr. Jerry Migler
Nickname: Lumberjacks and Ladyjacks

Mission

Dakota College at Bottineau provides students with a quality education in a caring environment. The institution values diversity and personal enrichment by promoting engaged learning for employment and university transfer. With the help of a supportive community, Dakota College at Bottineau emphasizes nature and technology to accomplish its mission through an array of curricula, programs, and services.

- Liberal arts education provides students the knowledge and tools to continue their education, to serve as good stewards of the environment, and to function as responsible citizens.
- Career/technical education provides students with the knowledge and skills required to succeed by utilizing natural, human, and technological resources.
- Distance delivery provides students increased access to education and career opportunities.
- Community education provides diverse lifelong learning experiences.
- Support services provide opportunities for individual growth and success.
- Campus activities provide for interpersonal development.
- Campus outreach provides area schools and groups access to college resources.
- Workforce training and development provides the human resources for economic development.
- All programs provide a greater understanding of human diversity.

Dakota College at Bottineau's curricula, programs, and services take students *beyond nature and technology* and leave them with an ethic of concern and care for the natural world.

Vision

Dakota College at Bottineau is rooted in the past and grows towards the future by combining the best from the *Past, Present, and Future* to provide students with innovative educational opportunities. The campus will emphasize a knowledge and appreciation of *Nature,* implement a rapidly changing *Technology,* and prepare students to go *Beyond* and improve the quality of life.

History

The 1889 constitution located a School of Forestry within the counties of McHenry, Ward, Bottineau, or Rolette; a popular vote in November 1894 placed it at Bottineau. The 1897 Legislature formally established the North Dakota School of Forestry, although the school did not begin operations until 1907. The school closed briefly during 1923-1925 when the Legislature refused to provide funding and reopened primarily as a junior college. In 1968, the school was attached to North Dakota State University for administrative purposes and is now administratively attached to Minot State University. Effective August 1, 2009, the college's name was changed to Dakota College at Bottineau. The Minot State University president oversees operations at both sites, and the chief executive officer at the college is the campus dean. The campus is located on the north side of Bottineau, a city near the Turtle Mountains in north-central North Dakota.

Lake Region State College

1801 College Drive North
Devils Lake, ND 58301
701-662-1600
800-443-1313
www.lrsc.edu

President: Dr. Doug Darling
Nickname: Royals

Mission

We enhance lives and community vitality through quality education.

- Academic Education: Provides academic courses and programs that lead to an associate in arts degree, meeting the NDUS general education requirements, and allows for seamless transfer to baccalaureate-granting institutions.
- Vocational/Technical Training: Provides courses and programs in vocational and technical career training that lead to a certificate of completion, a diploma, or an associate in applied science degree preparing students for an immediate career, advancement in specific occupations, or transfer to an articulated technical baccalaureate program.
- Workforce Training: Develops linkages with businesses, industry, and organizations to encourage economic development.
- Educational Outreach Opportunities: Provides educational outreach opportunities for individuals who are time and/or place bound.
- Lifelong Learning: Provides opportunities for continuing and lifelong learning in the form of cultural, educational, occupational, social, athletic, and vocational programs, courses, workshops, and institutes. The college is committed to being a responsive diverse institution, which prepares students for successful living and citizenship in a rapidly changing local, national, and world community.

History

In July 1941, Devils Lake residents voted to create Devils Lake Junior College and Business School, a two-year college to operate as an extension of the public school system. Classes began in September 1941 in a former high school building, and the college moved to its present 35-acre campus in 1966. In 1963, the name was changed to Lake Region Junior College, and in 1981, to Lake Region Community College. On July 1, 1984, the college joined NDUS, with administrative supervision transferred to the North Dakota State College of Science in Wahpeton in 1985 for a two-year transition period. The college became affiliated with the University of North Dakota in 1987, operating as a branch campus under the name UND-Lake Region. On July 1, 1999, the college attained independent status within NDUS as Lake Region State College.

North Dakota State College of Science

800 6th Street North, Wahpeton, ND 58076
1305 19th Avenue North, Fargo, ND 58102
800-342-4325
www.ndscs.edu

President: Dr. John Richman
Nickname: Wildcats

Mission

The North Dakota State College of Science (NDSCS) is a comprehensive, associate degree-granting college founded on a tradition of quality and integrity. We deliver learner-focused education through a unique and evolving collegiate experience. Using innovative delivery strategies, NDSCS anticipates and responds to statewide and regional needs by providing access to occupational/technical programs, transfer programs, and workforce training.

Vision Statement

To enrich people's lives through responsive lifelong learning in a dynamic educational and technological environment.

History

The 1889 constitution directed that a state scientific school be located at Wahpeton. The Legislature ratified this action in 1890 and again in 1903, creating the North Dakota Academy of Science. The first classes met in 1903. In 1905, the school took over the building of Red River Valley University, a Methodist college. North Dakota State School of Science changed its name to North Dakota State College of Science in 1987. In 1997, NDSCS established the Skills and Technology Training Center as a regional workforce training center located in Fargo. In 2005, the Center for Nanoscience Technology was established at NDSCS-Fargo and the welding technology program was also expanded to NDSCS-Fargo. The 125-acre campus is located on the north side of Wahpeton.

Williston State College

1410 University Avenue
Williston, ND 58801
701-774-4200
888-863-9455
www.willistonstate.edu

Acting President: Dr. John S. Miller
Nickname: Tetons

Mission

Williston State College, "Where the People Make the Difference," is to provide accessible, affordable, life-changing, and lifelong educational pathways to residents of North Dakota, the Upper Plains, and beyond.

Vision

We are committed to student excellence. We embrace quality student experiences, open communication, and actionable data that enrich personal relationships among our college, faculty, and students. We believe that people make the difference; that the college is the heart of the communities we serve; that our facilities are a needed, neutral, and central community space; and that our faculty and staff serve multiple and diverse needs in a global environment. We strive for a strong student presence on-campus, expanded offerings, fiscal sustainability, modern facilities, current technologies, and continuous improvement as a result of both our master and strategic plans.

History

From its beginning as an extension center, Williston State College (WSC) now provides educational opportunities to the greater Williston area in northwest North Dakota. The University of North Dakota (UND) first offered extension classes in Williston during the fall of 1957. In 1961, WSC, then known as the UND Williston Center, founded its own resident campus, faculty, and curricula through a contractual arrangement between UND and Williston School District #1. This arrangement continued until July 1, 1984, when the North Dakota State Board of Higher Education assumed responsibility for the college, and the institution was renamed UND-Williston. In 1999, legislative action expanded the college's mission to include workforce training, and UND-Williston then became an autonomous campus renamed Williston State College.

Private Colleges and Universities

Trinity Bible College and Graduate School

TRINITY
BIBLE COLLEGE & GRADUATE SCHOOL

50 Sixth Avenue South
Ellendale, ND 58436
800-523-1603
www.trinitybiblecollege.edu

President: Dr. Paul Alexander
Nickname: Lions

Mission

Trinity Bible College and Graduate School is committed to training and educating people with theological reflection and missional passion, in order that people and communities everywhere will hear the good news of Jesus and see his love demonstrated.

History

This private school, operated by the Assemblies of God denomination, was founded in 1948 as Lakewood Park Bible School in Devils Lake. It moved to Aberdeen, South Dakota, in 1960, where it became Hub City Bible Institute. In the fall of 1967, it moved to the former Trinity Hospital in Jamestown and was renamed Trinity Bible Institute. When the University of North Dakota-Ellendale Branch (Ellendale State Teachers College) closed, Trinity moved to that facility and offered its first classes there in October 1972. The present name was adopted in 1983.

University of Jamestown

University of JAMESTOWN

Jamestown Campus
6000 College Lane
Jamestown, ND 58405
701-252-3467
www.uj.edu

President: Dr. Robert S. Badal
Nickname: Jimmie

Mission

University of Jamestown is a community dedicated to the development of wholeness in our students. We adhere to a curriculum of academic excellence which balances the ideals of the liberal arts tradition and sound professional preparation. Our Christian tradition encourages an atmosphere of self-discipline, responsibility, and concern for the continuing growth of the individual.

Vision Statement

University of Jamestown will be nationally recognized for preparing professional and community leaders through a total experience that is student-centered and character focused. Students will be engaged academically through close interaction with faculty in a curriculum that integrates the liberal arts with sound professional programs.

History

The University of Jamestown was founded as Jamestown College on October 31, 1883, by the Presbyterian Church. In September 1886, the college held its first classes at the North Side School House, a local public school building. The college was forced to close in spring 1893 because of hard financial times throughout the country. It reopened on September 22, 1909, when things improved. On August 21, 2013, the name was changed to University of Jamestown "to better reflect the breadth of its educational offerings at all levels – bachelor's, master's, and doctoral – and to recognize significant growth and change in its 130-year history."

University of Mary
7500 University Drive
Bismarck, ND 58504
701-355-8030
800-288-6279
www.umary.edu

President: Monsignor James Shea
Nickname: Marauders

Statement of Mission and Identity

The University of Mary exists to serve the religious, academic, and cultural needs of the people in this region and beyond. It takes its tone from the commitment of the Sisters of Annunciation Monastery. These sisters founded the university in 1959 and continue to sponsor it today. It is Christian, it is Catholic, and it is Benedictine.

History

The University of Mary was founded in 1955 as Mary College, a two-year institution, by the Roman Catholic Benedictine Sisters of Annunciation Priory. It became a four-year college in 1959 and achieved university status in 1986. The 150-acre campus is located on a site overlooking the Missouri River Valley southeast of Bismarck and is adjacent to the Annunciation Priory.

Chief Executive Officers of North Dakota's Colleges and Universities

Bismarck State College (Bismarck)
Dr. Larry C. Skogen, President
March 2007–June 30, 2013; July 1, 2015

Cankdeska Cikana Community College (Fort Totten)
Dr. Cynthia Lindquist Mala, President
October 2003

Dakota College at Bottineau (Bottineau)
Dr. Steven Shirley, President
July 2014

Dickinson State University (Dickinson)
Dr. Thomas Mitzel, President
December 21, 2015

Lake Region State College (Devils Lake)
Dr. Doug Darling, President
March 8, 2013

Mayville State University (Mayville)
Dr. Gary Hagen, President
July 1, 2007

Minot State University (Minot)
Dr. Steven Shirley, President
July 2014

North Dakota State College of Science (Wahpeton)
Dr. John Richman, President
July 1, 2007

North Dakota State University of Agricultural and Applied Science (Fargo)
Dr. Dean L. Bresciani, President
June 2010

Nueta Hidatsa Sahnish College
Dr. Twyla Baker-Demaray, President
October 2014

Sitting Bull College (Fort Yates)
Dr. Laurel Vermillion, President
May 1, 2006

Trinity Bible College (Ellendale)
Dr. Paul Alexander, President
June 1, 2012

Turtle Mountain Community College (Belcourt)
Dr. Jim L. Davis, President
2005

United Tribes Technical College (Bismarck)
Dr. Leander "Russ" McDonald
President
October 30, 2014

University of Jamestown (Jamestown)
Dr. Robert S. Badal, President
2002

University of Mary (Bismarck)
Monsignor James Patrick Shea
President
July 2009

University of North Dakota (Grand Forks)
Mark Kennedy, MBA, President
July 1, 2016

Valley City State University (Valley City)
Dr. Tisa Mason, President
October 30, 2014

Williston State College (Williston)
Dr. John S. Miller, Acting President
June 6, 2016

National Athletic Team Championships

North Dakota's college and university athletes have a history of success at regional and conference levels at both the individual and team levels.

Dakota College at Bottineau

- NJCAA, Men's Ice Hockey – 1986, 1991, 1998, 2003, 2007, 2008, 2009, 2010, 2016

Dickinson State University

- NAIA, Men's Outdoor Track & Field – 2004, 2005, 2006
- NAIA, Women's Volleyball – 2000

Minot State University

- NAIA, Men's Cross Country – 2002, 2003

North Dakota State University

- NCAA, FCS, Football – 2011, 2012, 2013, 2014, 2015
- NCAA, Division II, Football – 1983, 1985, 1986, 1988, 1990
- Football – 1965 (Pecan Bowl), 1968 (Pecan Bowl), 1969 (Camellia Bowl)
- NCAA, Division II, Women's Indoor Track and Field – 2002
- NCAA, Division II, Wrestling – 1988, 1998, 2000, 2001
- NCAA, Division II, Women's Softball – 2000
- NCAA, Division II, Women's Basketball – 1991, 1993, 1994, 1995, 1996
- NCAA, Division II, Men's Cross Country – 1972

Trinity Bible College

- NBCAA, Women's Volleyball – 1986, 1987, 1989

University of Mary

- NAIA, Division II, Women's Basketball – 2000

University of North Dakota

- NCAA, Division I, Men's Ice Hockey – 1959, 1963, 1980, 1982, 1987, 1997, 2000, 2016
- NCAA, Division II, Football – 2001
- NCAA, Division II, Women's Basketball – 1997, 1998, 1999

Williston State College

- NJCAA, Men's Ice Hockey – 2013, 2014

CHAPTER TEN

AGRICULTURE

Industrial Hemp Pilot Program

Hemp is an ancient plant that has been grown throughout the world for thousands of years. It was grown widely in the United States until it was criminalized due to its similarity to marijuana. Only recently has industrial hemp begun to take root again. North Dakota is one of 30 states that passed legislation related to industrial hemp and one of seven that had industrial hemp research crops in 2015.

In 2016, a select group of five North Dakota farmers grew a combined 70 acres of the state's first recorded commercial industrial hemp crop as part of the state's Industrial Hemp Pilot Program administered by the North Dakota Department of Agriculture.

History of Hemp in the United States

Hemp was a crop widely grown in the United States from colonial times through World War II. It was used for sailcloth and cordage on ships, as well as cloth, canvas, sacks, and paper. One of America's navy ships, the *USS Constitution* or "Old Ironsides," required more than 120,000 pounds of hemp fiber for lines, rigging, canvas sails, and caulking. The invention of steam ships eventually minimized the demand for hemp sailcloth and cordage.

Politics also played a role in the demise of hemp farming. In 1937, the federal government passed the Marihuana (sic) Tax Act, which regulated all varieties of cannabis and turned over the regulation of hemp production to the Department of Revenue. Farmers had to register their fields and purchase a tax stamp.

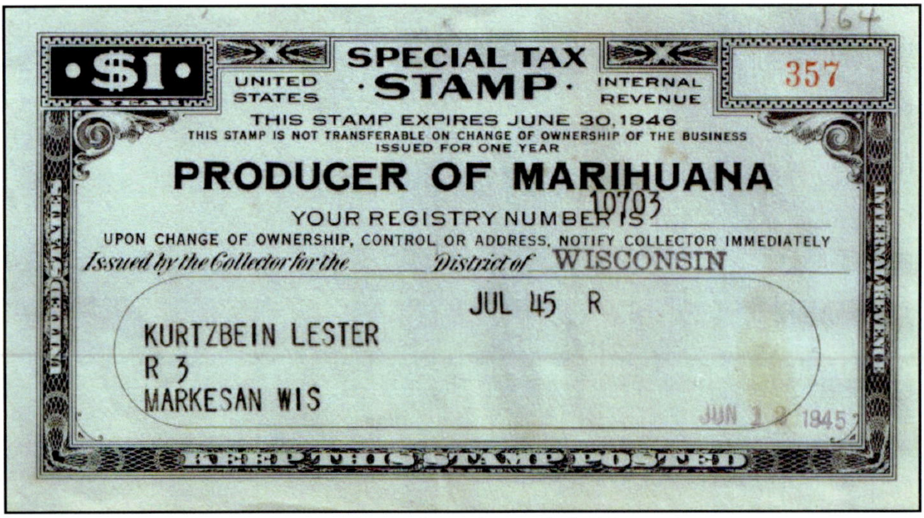

United States special tax stamp – producer of marihuana (sic), July 1945.

Hemp production got a small boost when the United States Department of Agriculture ran a "Hemp for Victory" campaign during World War II. More than 150,000 acres of hemp were cultivated in conjunction with the campaign for use in war materials.

Poster used during World War II.

In the 1950s, the availability of cheaper synthetic fibers diminished the industry. In 1970, industrial hemp was classified as a Schedule I drug under the Controlled Substances Act, and hemp farming in the United States became illegal. Since then, hemp has been imported from other countries.

Although a variety of the cannabis plant, industrial hemp has very low concentrations of THC (tetrahydrocannabinol), the high-producing compound found in marijuana. A provision in the Agricultural Act of 2014 (Farm Bill) gave authority to state departments of agriculture and institutions of higher education to cultivate industrial hemp for research purposes in states where it is legal.

Breaking Ground in North Dakota

The North Dakota Department of Agriculture (NDDA) created the Industrial Hemp Pilot Program to research the growth, cultivation, and marketing of industrial hemp in North Dakota. The goal was to increase the understanding of how industrial hemp fits into the current agricultural landscape and investigate how it may contribute to the economy of North Dakota.

In October 2015, applications were sought for the program. Seventeen producer applications were received and reviewed by a committee created by the agriculture commissioner. The commissioner deliberated on the committee recommendations and selected five pilot producers. Geographical spread, soil type, environmental conditions, and proximity to processing facilities were key considerations in the selection of the candidates.

The five growers planted a total of 70 acres of industrial hemp as part of the 2016 research program. Three hemp seed companies in the Canadian province of Manitoba supplied the four varieties planted (Table 1). The varieties selected were a mixture of high-yielding grain varieties and a type known to produce high oil content. Very tall hemp varieties suitable for fiber production were not chosen for the program, as there are no fiber processing facilities nearby. The objective was to select hemp types that yielded well under northern prairie conditions. The NDDA worked with the Manitoba Agriculture Department to determine the best seed varieties to secure, as Canada has been growing industrial hemp for both the seed and fiber markets since 1998.

Table 1 exhibits the historical yield expectations among the test varieties under Manitoba conditions. All varieties were plant variety protected (PVP) and pedigreed (certified or foundation grade). Canadian seed laws specify all hemp seed sold must be of a certified pedigree and tested by Canadian agencies to ensure a THC content below 0.3 percent on a dry weight basis. For instance, *cv Finola,* a variety bred for high oil content, generally produces the lowest grain yield relative to the other test varieties in nearly 20 years of Manitoba field trials. The other three varieties listed exhibited yields that were statistically equivalent over the same time period. This finding suggests there could be large swings in seed yields year over year. It is important to note growing industrial hemp carries considerable risk to the producer as it is not eligible for crop insurance, and markets and returns are not consistent year to year.

Long-term Agronomic Characteristics of Industrial Hemp Cultivars: 2016 NDDA Industrial Hemp Pilot Research Program (Table 1)

Cultivar	Seed Source	Flower Type	Use	Maturity (Days)	% Seed Yield* (% of Variety CRS-1)
CANDA	Parkland IHG Coop	Monoecious	Grain, Fiber	110	86
CFX-1	Hemp Genetics Int.	Dioecious	Grain, Fiber	105	106
CRS-1	Hemp Genetics Int.	Dioecious	Grain	110	100
FINOLA	Hemp Oil Canada Inc.	Dioecious	Grain, Oil	100	83**

*Manitoba Agriculture data, Check variety CRS-1 @ 1548 lb/A [averaged over 21 site years].
**Note: cv *Finola* seed yield was significantly lower compared to the other grain varieties in long-term yield trials in Manitoba. *Finola* is regarded as a high oil content low yielding variety.

The research focus varied according to producer interest (Table 2). Grower data was collected at each site and included their general agronomic practices, rainfall, observations of insect pests, weeds and diseases, crop establishment and development, and grain yield.

Research Details: 2016 NDDA Industrial Hemp Pilot Research Program (Table 2)

Trial County	Research Focus	Cultivar	Acres
LaMoure	Grain yield	CANDA	15
	Grain yield (comparison on two soil types)	CANDA	14 + 1
Grant	Grain yield	CRS-1	5
	Grain yield	CFX-1	5
Benson	Variety performance, grain yield	CFX-1	7.5
	Variety performance, grain yield	FINOLA	7.5
Foster	Variety performance, grain yield, processing, marketing	CANDA	7.5
	Variety performance, grain yield, processing, marketing	FINOLA	7.5

Though this was the first time individuals were able to grow industrial hemp in North Dakota, 12 varieties of hemp had been grown in research plots at North Dakota State University's (NDSU) Langdon Research Extension Center in 2015. NDSU planted research plots in Langdon again in 2016 to research the agronomic performance of nine different seed varieties. Unfortunately, excessively wet conditions following heavy rainfall events resulted in substantial plant stand losses, and the 2016 trials were abandoned.

North Dakota industrial hemp crop (2016). *(Photo 3)*

Industrial hemp pilot producer variety trial (Benson County July 2016). *(Photo 4)*
Note: Monoecious plants, white stalks (male flowers), can constitute 10–20 percent or more of the plant stand.

About Hemp

Hemp varieties are monoecious or dioecious. The former cultivars have both male and female flowers on the same plant and the latter cultivars maintain separate male and female plants (Photo 3). Plants tend to be 75 to 80 percent dioecious with the proportion of exclusively monoecious female plants being 10 to 15 percent and males about 10 percent (Photo 4). Under stressful conditions (hot/dry), the proportion of pure male plants can increase to 20 percent, reducing yield. Pilot producers in North Dakota observed that because hemp does not branch very well, there may be some benefit to boosting the planting density (above 10 to 12 plants per square foot) to improve yields. A side benefit to this practice likely benefits competition against weed growth. Future studies will be needed to investigate this phenomenon.

Materials and Methods

In May 2016, NDDA imported 2,175 pounds of industrial hemp seed through the three Manitoba suppliers.

Previous crops that had been planted on the pilot producers' sites were spring wheat, flax, corn, or soybeans. Site details for each producer are outlined in Table 3. There are no registered pesticides (insecticides, herbicides, fungicides, or seed treatments) for use in industrial hemp crops. With this being the case, producers were very cognizant to select their cleanest fields. In all cases, the growers pre-treated their fields with glyphosate to contain any early season weed growth. Hemp grows best under warmer soil conditions, so it is planted later than other commercial crops. This late planting may allow for an additional flush of weeds that can be eliminated by the pre-plant burn-off application of glyphosate. All fields were fertilized by the growers either in the previous fall or prior to planting.

Site Details: 2016 NDDA Industrial Hemp Pilot Research Program (Table 3)

County	Hemp Variety	Soil Type	Planting Depth (inches)	Planting Row Spacing (inches)	Final Plant Height (inches)
LaMoure 1	Canda	Svea Barnes Loam	.75 ± .25	6	60
LaMoure 2	Canda	Svea Barnes Loam	.75 ± .25	6	86
LaMoure 3	Canda	Svea Barnes Loam	.75 ± .25	6	63
Grant 1	CRS-1	Sandy Loam	.5-.75	10	84
Grant 2	CFX-1	Sandy Loam	1-1.25	10	84
Benson 1	CFX-1	Heimdal-Emrick Loam	.5-1	7	85.2
Benson 2	Finola	Heimdal-Emrick Loam	.5-1	7	56.4
Foster 1	Canda	Clay Loam	.75	7.5	78
Foster 2	Finola	Clay Loam	.75	7.5	48

Planting took place between May 24 and June 13, 2016. Growers used a range of newer and older planting equipment, and there were no apparent problems with seeding (Table 4). Planting density was set to achieve 10 to 12 live seeds per square foot. Planting took place once soils warmed and changed into a firm and moist seed bed. Hemp is highly photo sensitive, and planting later reduced the crop height but did not result in lower yields or later maturity. Early May plantings favor producing very tall plant stands (suitable for fiber production) but will not provide significant gains in earlier harvesting nor seed yields. Final plant heights were between 4 feet and 7.2 feet tall.

Planting Equipment Used by 2016 Pilot Program Producers

(Table 4)

County	Planting Equipment (May 24 to June 13)
LaMoure	Case 6200 double disc press drill
Grant	Concord hoe air drill with Dutch openers and disc closers
Benson	Haybuster 107 seed drill
Foster	JD 1990 air seeder

Sampling for THC Content

Industrial hemp has a very low level of delta-9 tetrahydrocannabinol (THC) of under 1 percent. THC levels in marijuana plants average about 10 percent. The Agricultural Act of 2014, North Dakota Century Code, and North Dakota Administrative Code define industrial hemp as having no more than 0.3 percent of THC on a dry-weight basis. As part of the program, the fields were sampled for THC content.

NDDA staff collected random samples from each hemp field to evaluate the THC content in the foliage and leaves of the hemp inflorescences (flowers). Sampling was timed when approximately half of the seeds were resistant to compression (Photo 5). The THC content in hemp is known to peak when the seeds begin to ripen. Seed forms quickly, usually about 10 days after the first flower.

Industrial hemp stage at sampling time for THC analysis (2016). *(Photo 5)*

Established Canadian hemp sampling protocols involved collecting the top 2 to 2.5 inches of 60 randomly selected industrial hemp inflorescences (flowers). The samples were evenly split into two 30-plant sets. Each set was bagged and labeled, and one set was couriered immediately to a federally accredited laboratory for THC analysis. The second duplicate sample set was retained as a backup. Standard published analytical methods were followed by the lab to determine the THC content. The results of the analyses are shown for each field in Table 5. In all cases, the THC content found in these plant parts were at trace levels and below the allowable limit.

Delta-9 THC in Industrial Hemp Samples at Seed Ripening Stage (Table 5)

Producer	Cultivar	% THC (dry weight)
LaMoure	CANDA	.002
	CANDA (2 fields)	.012 + .037
Grant	CRS-1	.007
	CFX-1	.007
Benson	CFX-1	.007
	FINOLA	.008
Foster	CANDA	.004
	FINOLA	.044

Pest Issues

No significant insect pest pressures were seen at any site. Cutworm, Bertha armyworm, corn borers (Photo 6a), Lygus bugs, aphids, and grasshoppers on occasion can be a problem. Bees were found to be very numerous at flowering time at several field locations, as were lady beetles.

Weed pressure was particularly light on all fields, except for some volunteer wheat at the Benson County location and at the Grant County location where there was a mixture of annual weeds in one field under a thin crop stand and an open canopy (Photo 6b). Sandy soil, with uneven and inconsistent planting depth, was attributed to the spotty emergence. Lack of significant rain through June resulted in a poor plant stand with significant weed issues and lower yields. The extra handling at harvest was necessary to remove the moist weeds and dry down the hemp seed to a safe level for storage (10 to 11 percent moisture content).

Both wheat and wild buckwheat (*Polygonum convulvulous*) are problematic as it is most difficult to separate out of hemp seed. Wheat also may cause issues with processors who hope to maintain gluten-free facilities.

Hemp is very competitive against weeds. It emerges very rapidly (three to four days) in warm and moist soils and can quickly shade and outcompete weeds. Growers commented on how quickly hemp develops.

European corn borer infesting a hemp stalk (Grant County 2016). *(Photo 6a)*

Thin canopy and dry conditions encouraged weed development (Grant County 2016). *(Photo 6b)*

No plant diseases were observed. Hemp is reported to be susceptible to some seedling diseases, such as *Pythium* and *Rhizoctonia*. *Sclerotinia* (white mold) and *Botrytis* are also said to be the most serious foliar diseases for hemp. The foliar diseases generally form at the top of the plant in the inflorescences.

Harvesting

Harvesting was completed in September 2016. Harvest equipment is listed in Table 6. The hemp crop was straight cut, and no difficulties were reported, other than the combine speed being run intentionally slow to avoid any potential plugging or wrapping issues with the volume of green material.

Some growers in Canada swath the crop; however, it is prone to sprout. Normally the seed moisture content at harvest should be 18 to 19 percent, and seed is considered dry and safe for storage at 10 percent moisture. Hemp plants may appear quite green at normal harvest time. The seed matures rapidly at this stage and may shell out readily during the harvest operation (Photo 7).

Harvesting Equipment Used by 2016 Pilot Program Producers

(Table 6)

County	Harvesting Equipment (Sept. 10-22)
LaMoure	JD5680 combine with JD 635 flex draper head
Grant	NH CR 940 twin rotor combine with NH 30 foot draper head
Benson	JD 9650 cylinder walker with 30 foot rigid head
Foster	JD 8770 with JD flex head

Harvesting industrial hemp (LaMoure County). *(Photo 7)*

Seed cleaning was required in all instances to reduce the amount of moist foreign material in the sample and lower the moisture content to a safe level for storage and processing.

Normal yields obtained in Manitoba are 800 to 1,200 pounds per acre. The pilot producers were pleased with the results and harvested between 895 to 1,266 pounds per acre – in line with Canadian yield expectations for these varieties. Unfortunately, the Grant County test site yielded only 219 pounds per acre due in part to a sparse plant stand and very dry conditions at the end of May into early July (Table 7). The May through August rainfall was only 4.8 inches at the Elgin NDSU Extension Station. The variability in yields should caution potential growers willing to grow hemp on stubble with low soil moisture reserves.

Monthly Rainfall Totals in Inches: 2016 Pilot Sites (Table 7)

	Foster	LaMoure	Grant	Benson
May	1.1	3.7	0.8	2.2
June	1.6	2.8	0.7	3.5
July	4.5	3.9	1.6	4.5
August	3.6	3.0	1.7	0.8
September	1.8	3.9	2.3	3.0
Totals	12.6	17.3	7.1	14.0

Because industrial hemp does appreciably branch or tiller, the stubble that remains is composed of long individual fibrous stocks that are tough to work down and generally moist, such that burning will not be very effective (Photo 8). Normally, the stubble is left standing over the winter and is then rolled in the spring to produce a dense soil cover to facilitate successful burning.

Post-harvest crop residue management (LaMoure County 2016). (*Photo 8*)

Industrial Hemp Processing

All grain was processed at Healthy Oilseeds LLC, located in Carrington, North Dakota. The grain was crushed to extract hemp oil; the remainder was milled to produce a finely-ground, high-protein flour and also extruded into pellets (Photo 9). Seed contains 30-35 percent oil of a desirable fatty acid profile, and flour contains around 25 percent protein. There are reliable foreign markets for these commodities. A grain dehuller is also being considered in the future as the markets for industrial hemp commodities increase. Dehulled hemp or "hemp hearts" are a high demand commodity. The fiber stalks remained in the field.

Processed industrial hemp commodities. *(Photo 9)*

Representative samples of each of the above commodities (Photo 9) have been sampled (Photos 10a, 10b) by NDDA staff, following a United States Drug Enforcement Administration (DEA) request, then couriered to a laboratory to analyze for cannabidiol (CBD) and THC. CBD is produced at higher levels than THC in hemp and is then extracted for its medicinal properties (i.e., anticonvulsive, anti-epileptic, and anti-microbial). As expected, the final analytical step of the processed commodities showed low THC content. This should result in unencumbered trade of the hemp commodities currently held by the pilot producer/growers.

Hemp meal sampling. *(Photo 10a)*

Hemp oil sampling. *(Photo 10b)*

In addition, samples of roasted grain will also be germination tested by the NDSU Seed Department to verify seed sterility prior to any sale or movement. Other uses for industrial hemp are shown (Table 8) and are anticipated as acres and processing capabilities increase.

Industrial Hemp Uses (Table 8)

Food Uses	Hemp Oil Product Uses	Hemp Fiber Product Uses
Confectionary Items	Cooking	Fabric
Beer	Salad Dressing	Insulation
Flour	Dietary Supplements	Carpeting
Feed	Body Care Products	Paneling
Dietary	Fuel	Pulp and Paper
Snacks	Detergents	Recycling Additive
Non-dairy Milk and Cheese	Spreads	Automobile Parts
Baking	Paint	Animal Bedding and Mulch

Economics of Industrial Hemp

All the grain was trucked to the sole processor, Healthy OilSeeds LLC. The proprieter provided an extra incentive to encourage grower delivery and paid a premium of $1 per pound. At the time of writing, the current market price was approximately $0.62 per pound in Canada, and typical industry returns range from $0.62 to $1 (all reported in U.S. dollars).

Each grower penciled out their individual costs to produce the hemp crop. Current seed cost is approximately $2.25 per pound (approximately $56/acre). Three of the four growers (Table 9) had decent returns. Only one grower had poor returns but will market his products separately to improve the bottom line.

Economic Analysis by Growers: Profitability of Industrial Hemp Under 2016 NDDA Industrial Hemp Pilot Research Program (Table 9)

Grower County	Acres Planted	Yield (pounds per acre)	Yield (bushels per acre)	Grower Costs Per Acre	Gross Return Per Pound	Net Profit Per Acre
LaMoure	30	1,266	28.8	$441.73	$1.00	$824.27
Foster	15	895	20.3	$387.27	$1.00	$507.53
Benson	15	1,171	26.6	$303.85	$1.00	$867.51
Grant	10	219	5.0	$330.35	Unknown	Unknown

Conclusions

Industrial hemp holds promise as a viable alternative crop for North Dakota producers. Based on the industrial hemp growers' experiences, the crop appears to be well adapted over most of North Dakota's agricultural conditions. Generally, the field trials had low weed pressures, good plant stands, and lacked significant diseases and other pests. The pilot program growers were comfortable growing the new crop and were able to plant, maintain, and harvest hemp without significant modifications to their current farming equipment and practices. Both the seed yields and economic returns were impressive for first-time growers.

Industrial hemp may also generate additional revenue streams in the development of supporting businesses such as grain and oil processing and distribution, mobile seed cleaning, honey production, and hemp fiber and fabric industries.

References

1. Anon. 2016. Manitoba Department of Agriculture, Industrial Hemp Production.
2. Johnson, Renee. 2015. "Hemp as an Agricultural Commodity: Congressional Research Service," CRS Report.
3. Leizer, Cary et. al. 2000. "The Composition of Hemp Seed Oil and Its Potential as an Important Source of Nutrition," Journal of Neutraceuticals, Functional and Medicinal Food.
4. Layton, Catharine and Wilhad, M. Reuter. 2015. Analysis of Cannabinoids in Hemp Seed Oils by PLC Using PDA Detection.
5. Hemp Genetics International (HGI). Hempgenetics.com/index.html
6. Will Ill, Oscar H. 2004. "The Forgotten History of Hemp Cultivation in America." *Farm Collector.* http://www.farmcollector.com/farm-life/strategic-fibers?pageid=1#PageContent1.
7. "Hemp for Victory – Full Feature Film – US Government asks Farmers to Grow Hemp!" *YouTube*, uploaded by Foods Alive Video Network, 5 July 2011, https://www.youtube.com/watch?v=XWLpLIP3g-w&feature=youtu.be.\

North Dakota's 70th State Dairy Princess

North Dakota's 70th State Dairy Princess is Heidi Jacob, daughter of Gerard and Lori Jacob of Linton. She was crowned June 19, 2017, during the Midwest Dairy Association North Dakota Division board meeting. In addition to the crown, Jacob received a $500 scholarship from the Midwest Dairy Association, which sponsors the princess program.

Jacob will spend her year serving as the official ambassador for the state's dairy farmers, advocating and educating on their behalf during public appearances that include media interviews, classroom appearances, dairy events, and fairs.

Jacob graduated from Linton High School in May 2017 and worked on her family's dairy farm near Linton during the summer. In fall 2017, she began attending Bismarck State College, studying secondary education.

At Linton High School, Jacob earned multiple honors in various activities, including Future Business Leaders of America; Family, Career, and Community Leaders of America; basketball; volleyball; choir; and National Honor Society. She was also selected to serve on the State Youth Advisory Council for North Dakota Farmers Union.

North Dakota's 2016 Rank Among the States

North Dakota's farmers and ranchers maintained the state's number one ranking in the production of dry edible, navy, and pinto beans, canola, flaxseed, sunflowers, and durum and spring wheat in 2016. North Dakota was also the leading producer of honey in the United States.

2016 U.S. Rank	Commodity	Percent of Nation's Production
#1	Beans, All Dry Edible	31%
	Beans, Navy	38%
	Beans, Pinto	60%
	Canola	87%
	Flaxseed	91%
	Honey	23%
	Peas, Dry Edible	44%
	Sunflower, All	43%
	Sunflower, Oil	45%
	Wheat, Durum	56%
	Wheat, Spring	50%
#2	Beans, Black	30%
	Beans, Great Northern	8%
	Lentils	30%
	Sunflower, Non-Oil	30%
	Wheat, All	14%
#3	Barley	22%
	Oats	11%
	Sugarbeets	17%
#4	Beans, Chickpeas	5%
#6	Potatoes, All	5%
	Safflower	5%
#9	Soybeans	6%
#10	Hay, Alfalfa	4%
#11	Corn for Grain	3%

Source: U.S. Department of Agriculture
National Agriculture Statistics Service
North Dakota Field Office
PO Box 3166
Fargo, ND 58108-3166

Agriculture: One of North Dakota's Leading Industries

- North Dakota agriculture reached $8.2 billion in market value in 2015.
- The total value of 2015 crop production in North Dakota was $6.9 billion.
- The largest sector in North Dakota's economy, production agriculture, makes up almost 25 percent of the state's economy.
- Nearly one-fourth of North Dakota's workforce is farmers or ranchers or those employed in agriculture-related businesses or industries.
- North Dakota's 29,800 farms and ranches occupy 39.1 million acres. The average farm size is 1,312 acres.

North Dakota's Agriculture Profile

Number of Farms	29,800
Land in Farms (acres)	39,100,000
Percent of Land in Farms	90%
Average Size of Farm in Acres	1,312
Average Age of Operator	57
Primary Occupation of Operator	
Farming	17,509
Other	13,452
Gender of Primary Operator	
Male	27,728
Female	3,233

Sources: 2012 Census of Agriculture and U.S. Department of Agriculture

Ag Production Facts

- It takes a combine nine seconds to harvest enough wheat to make 70 loaves of bread.
- A pig can run a seven-minute mile.
- An ear of corn contains approximately 800 kernels.
- More than 72 billion pounds of edible "surplus" food is thrown away in the United States each year.
- United States farmers and ranchers receive 15.6 cents of every dollar spent on food.
- Fifty cents of every food dollar is spent on food prepared outside the home.

2015 Food Dollar (nominal): Marketing Bill

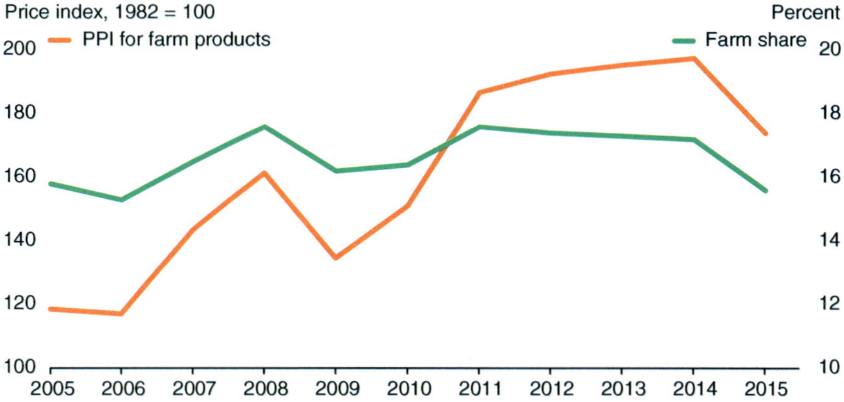

PPI = Producer Price Index
Source: USDA, Economic Research Service for the farm share and U.S. Bureau of Labor Statistics for the Producer Price Index.

North Dakota's Top Ag Exports 2015

	Rank Among States	Value (millions)
Wheat	1	$988.4
Oilseeds and Products*	1	$681.7
Soybeans	9	$862.9
Soybean Meal	9	$219.2
Feeds and Other Feed Grains**	12	$238.5
Total Exports	**9**	**$4,068.4**

*Oilseeds and products include peanuts (oilstock), other oil crops, corn meal, other oilcake and meal, protein substances, bran, and residues. **Feeds and other feed grains include processed feeds, fodder, barley, oats, rye, and sorghum.
Source: USDA-ERS State Fact Sheet 2015 Estimates

North Dakota's Top Producing Counties 2016

Four North Dakota counties are the largest producers in the nation of the following products:

County	Products
Williams	Durum Wheat
Cavalier	Canola
Cass	Soybeans
Ward	Flaxseed

Source: USDA – NASS North Dakota Field Office 2016

North Dakota's Organic Production 2014

Number of certified organic farms	94
North Dakota's rank in number of farms	32
Number of certified organic acres	134,632
North Dakota's rank in number of acres	4
Total value of all organic products sold in North Dakota	$27,279,000

Source: USDA-NASS Organic Survey 2014

North Dakota's Cash Receipts 2012-2015

2012	$9,188,953
2013	$8,840,653
2014	$8,672,533
2015	$7,108,250

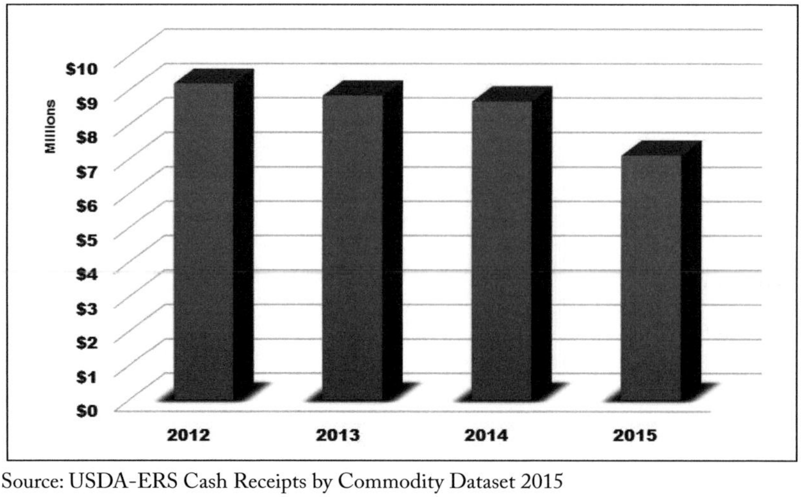

Source: USDA-ERS Cash Receipts by Commodity Dataset 2015

North Dakota's Leading Commodities 2015

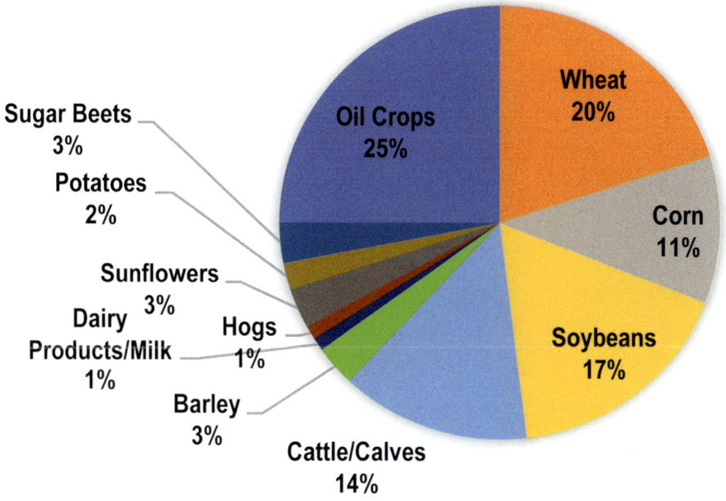

Commodity	Value of Receipts (in thousands of dollars)
All Commodities	$7,108,250
Crops	$5,757,777
Wheat	$1,654,528
Soybeans	$1,358,951
Livestock and Products	$1,350,473
Cattle and Calves	$1,102,292
Corn	$882,685
Canola	$355,391
Barley	$267,551
Sugarbeets	$233,405
Sunflowers	$222,861
Dry Beans	$219,465
Potatoes	$198,982

Source: USDA-ERS Farm Income and Wealth Statistics: Cash Receipts by Commodity 2010-2015; 2015 USDA – Census of Agriculture: State Data

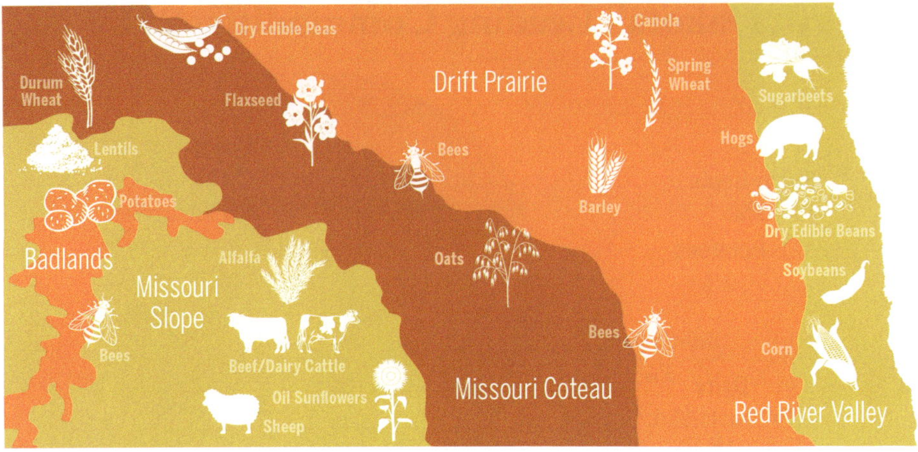

Source: USDA National Agricultural Statistics Service

Many commodities are produced across North Dakota. This map shows the highest concentrations throughout the state.

The Messer family of Beaver Creek Ranch is passing family farming traditions to the next generation.

Chapter Eleven

Natural Resources

Climate

Since North Dakota's settlement days, the state has experienced extreme weather patterns from the drought during the "Dirty Thirties" to the extended wet cycle that led to the rise of Devils Lake, beginning in 1993. More recently, the state has experienced record floods in 2009 and 2011 and an exceedingly dry year in 2012.

North Dakota spans a region that often swings from "too wet" to "too dry." This range of climate varies not only geographically, east to west, but over time as well. It is not uncommon for the state to experience extreme drought in one place and severe flooding in another – sometimes at the same time.

30 Year (1987 - 2016) Average Rainfall (April - September)

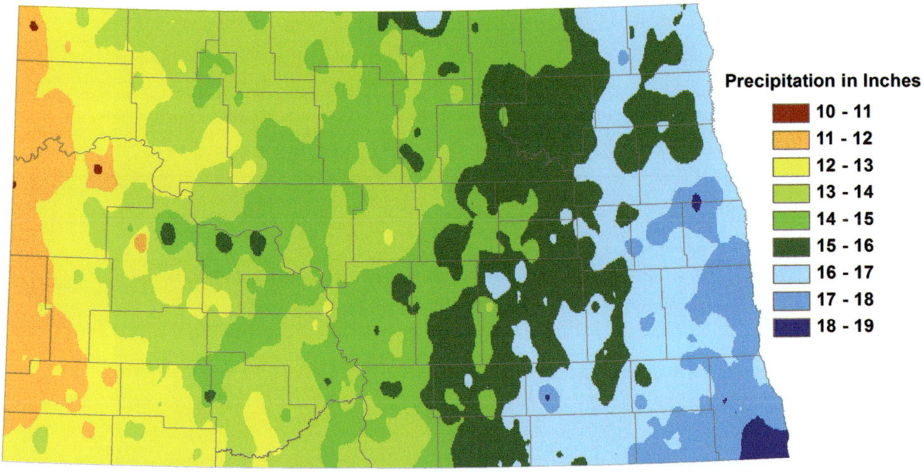

The state has experienced an extended wet cycle beginning in 1993 that has increased average annual precipitation statewide. (Courtesy NDARB)

The 100th Meridian line of longitude roughly splits the state in half. East of this line, there is generally more precipitation in the form of snow and rain than there is the uptake of water by plants and evaporation. West of the 100th Meridian, water loss generally exceeds precipitation. Recent fluctuations in climate have shown this artificial boundary between wet and dry shifts slightly east or west, depending on larger climatic patterns. Geological evidence indicates this boundary can shift even more dramatically.

A Comparison of Precipitation Variety

July 2012 Percent of Normal Rainfall

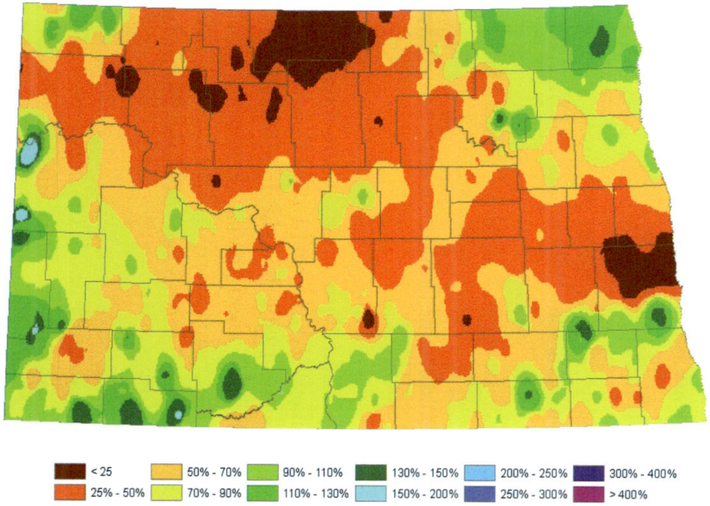

July 2016 Percent of Normal Rainfall

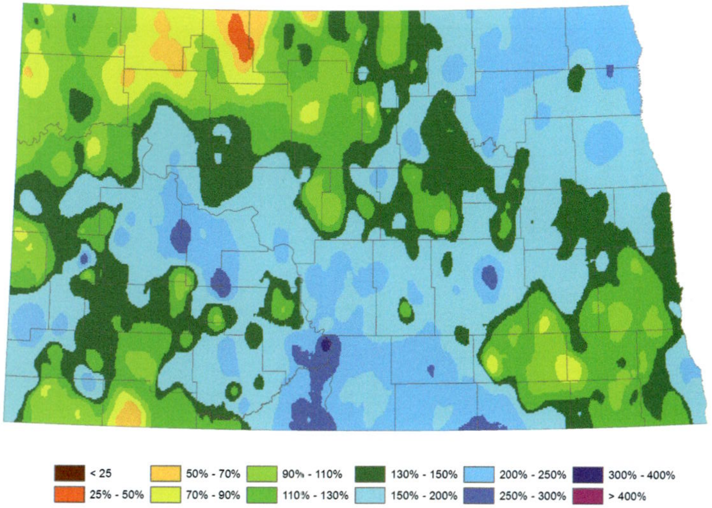

North Dakota experiences extremes in precipitation, as shown in these monthly precipitation maps for July in 2012 (a dry year) and 2016 (a wet year).

Source: NDARB Cooperative Observer Network

Drought

Drought has often been a defining aspect of climate in North Dakota, from the many problems caused by drought in the 1930s through several shorter dry cycles experienced as recently as 2012. Drought can cause crops to fail, stress municipal water supplies, impact recreation, and create challenges for anyone who makes their living from the land.

Drought certainly is not new to the region. The most severe dry periods recorded were in the 1930s and the 1980s. Studies of isolated lakebeds in several places in North Dakota show extreme fluctuations in the pattern of excessive precipitation and drought are normal. Studies found, in the case of lakes, a variation between wet cycles and dry cycles has existed for thousands of years. Lakebed records indicate, since the glaciers receded, droughts and wet cycles lasting more than 100 years have occurred.

While in an "average" year there is often sufficient precipitation, historical and paleoclimatological records indicate there will be periods of time when there is not nearly enough moisture.

Flooding

While droughts are common in the northern Great Plains, it is also true the region experiences wet cycles. Climatologists believe North Dakota is currently in a wet cycle that began in 1993, which has led to flooding throughout the state. It is useful to note, although the state is believed to be in a long-term wet cycle, mini-droughts can be experienced within this cycle. This has been the case in recent years, with drought afflicting western, and increasingly, eastern North Dakota.

Flooding in the Red River Valley in 1997 was one of the most severe in recorded history. Parts of the Red River Valley experienced a record-breaking 12 feet of snow, followed by a severe spring ice storm and rapid melt. These factors, along with ice jams in several key areas, led to the catastrophic flooding that most visibly impacted the city of Grand Forks. Partial records indicate a flood more severe than the 1997 event occurred prior to settlement.

With regard to the Devils Lake Basin, many in the state were concerned the fishery was in imminent danger of dying off in 1992 due to high salinity related to low lake levels caused by the late 1980s drought. In 1993, all of that changed and, with significant rainfall and snow runoff, the lake began to rise. The flooding of Devils Lake has been relentless, rising more than 30 feet in a little over 20 years, with only the drought of 2012 and the operations of the Devils Lake outlets causing appreciable reductions in lake levels.

Two significant and very damaging floods impacted most of the state in 2009 and 2011. Most of the major cities in the state were affected, with Minot and Bismarck especially impacted. In Minot, the 2011 flood impacted one-third of the city's homes.

Climate Trends

Several studies of lake sediment in North Dakota have demonstrated the state is subject to long-term climatic variation, alternating between extended wet and dry cycles. Evidence has shown the state does not really have a "normal" climate.

In recent years, climate change and global warming have gained greater attention. While the root causes of climate change, whether natural or human-induced, are still very much under debate, recent data does indicate global temperatures have increased slightly. If warming trends continue, it is uncertain what effects North Dakota will experience.

Climatological data inferred from lake core samples that provide a picture of climate in the region since the termination of the last ice age indicate when global temperatures are warmer, North Dakota's climate may not react in a predictable manner. With a wet cycle that has lasted for more than two decades and models indicating a likelihood that current patterns could persist for decades more, regular flooding may become the new normal for much of the state.

Weather Facts

- Highest temperature: 121 degrees, Steele, July 6, 1936.
- Lowest temperature: 60 degrees below zero, Parshall, February 15, 1936.
- Largest rainfall event in 24-hour period: 10.05 inches, Gilby, June 2000.
- Largest snowfall event in 24-hour period: 24.0 inches, Amidon, February 1998.
- The average first day of frost occurs in mid-September in northern parts of the state.
- The average last day of frost occurs in mid- to late-May.
- North Dakota receives a higher percentage of possible sunshine and more hours of sunshine annually than any other state along the Canadian border. On an annual basis, the state receives 58 to 62 percent of total possible sunshine.
- July is the sunniest month, when approximately three-quarters of possible sunshine is recorded.
- July and August will record about twice as many sunshine days as any other month of the year.
- Average yearly rainfall ranges from 24 inches in the southeastern portion of the state to 14 inches in the far west.
- When compared to the period from 1907-1992, average annual precipitation has increased during the "wet cycle" period of 1993-2016 by approximately 29 percent in Fargo, 28 percent in Bismarck, and 11 percent in Dickinson.
- North Dakota's greatest source of atmospheric moisture is the Gulf of Mexico.

North Dakota Drainage Basins

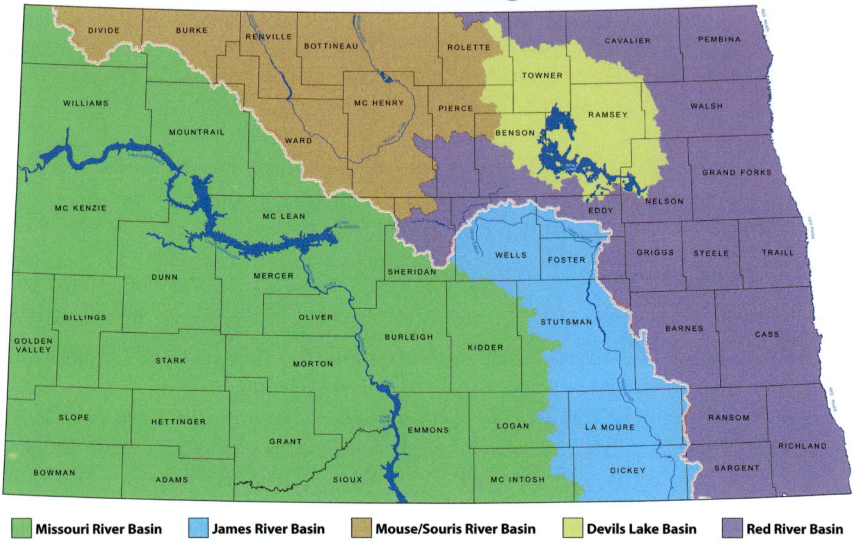

Water Resources

Surface Water Resources

North Dakota is separated by a continental divide running from the northwest to the southeast corners of the state. The northeastern portion of the state drains into Hudson Bay and includes the Mouse (Souris), Devils Lake, and Red River basins. The southwestern part is drained by the Missouri and James River basins to the Gulf of Mexico.

Flow in all North Dakota streams and rivers are seasonably and annually variable. Runoff is generally greatest in early spring as a result of snowmelt water and spring rainfall. Many smaller streams experience little or no flow for extended periods during summer months. Dramatic flow variations in river discharges can be caused by changes in weather patterns, isolated storm events, evaporation rates, and snow pack conditions.

In North Dakota in 2016, there were almost 715,967 acres of natural lakes and reservoirs (239,237 acres and 476,730 acres respectively) and about 3,206,820 acres of wetlands. In the state, there are 21,108 waterbodies of at least 10 acres or greater in size.

The state's four largest reservoirs (Sakakawea, Oahe, Audubon, and Ashtabula) comprise about 10 percent of North Dakota's total water surface acres, accounting for a surface area of 397,467 acres. The majority of these acres are contained within the two mainstem Missouri River reservoirs (Lake Sakakawea and Lake Oahe) at their normal operating pool elevations.

Ground Water Resources

Ground water underlies the land surface throughout the state and generally occurs in two major types of rock – unconsolidated deposits and bedrock.

Unconsolidated deposits are loose beds of gravel, sand, silt, or clay of glacial origin. Bedrock aquifers consist primarily of shale, sandstone, and lignite.

Aquifers of glacial origin are generally more productive than aquifers in the underlying bedrock. Bedrock aquifers underlie the entire state and tend to be more continuous and widespread than aquifers in the unconsolidated deposits.

It is estimated 60 million acre-feet of water are stored in major unconsolidated aquifers in the state. The amount of water available in the major bedrock aquifers is estimated to be approximately 435 million acre-feet.

In recent years, the development of technologies such as horizontal drilling and aquifer recharge and recovery (previously called artificial recharge) could also prove to be a vital tool in mitigating the boom-bust nature of precipitation the state frequently experiences.

Atmospheric Water Resources

Mean annual precipitation ranges from a maximum of nearly 24 inches in the southeast corner of the state to just over 14 inches in the extreme west. It is worth noting the maximum mean annual rainfall in southeast North Dakota has increased from just over 21 inches to 24 inches due to the extended wet cycle, which started in 1993 and continued through 2016.

During North Dakota's growing season (April-September), precipitation ranges from approximately 18 inches in the southeast part of the state to about 10 inches in the far west. This distribution results in generally adequate moisture for dry land farming in the east, but less reliable supplies in the semi-arid west.

Precipitation is largely dependent upon an adequate supply of airborne moisture, both visible (clouds) and invisible (water vapor). The primary atmospheric water source for North Dakota is the warm, humid air originating from the Gulf of Mexico.

While westerly flow from the Pacific Ocean does initially move atmospheric moisture toward the state, the repeated lifting and cooling of the air as it passes over the Rocky Mountains causes much of the moisture to precipitate from the air before it reaches the plains. Moisture from the Gulf of Mexico faces no such impediments.

The capacity of the atmosphere to hold moisture is largely governed by its temperature. Warm summer air can hold enough moisture to allow a thunderstorm to generate several inches of rainfall in a short period of time, whereas cold arctic air from the Canadian prairies can scarcely support any precipitation. As such, the warm season accounts for more than three-quarters of the state's total annual precipitation.

Depending on the season, the total water contained in the atmosphere above North Dakota ranges from approximately 350,000 acre-feet in the winter to 5.5 million acre-feet in the summer. Most of the water passes through the state borne by winds aloft. On any given day, nature converts a small fraction of the available water to clouds and sometimes precipitation.

Current and Historic Water Use

Water in North Dakota is used in a variety of ways. While the traditional uses of "mining, irrigating, and manufacturing" found in the North Dakota Constitution in Article XI, Section 3, still remain prevalent, new diverse uses and needs are continually being created.

2006-2015 Average Annual Total Water Use = 1,332,819 Acre-Feet

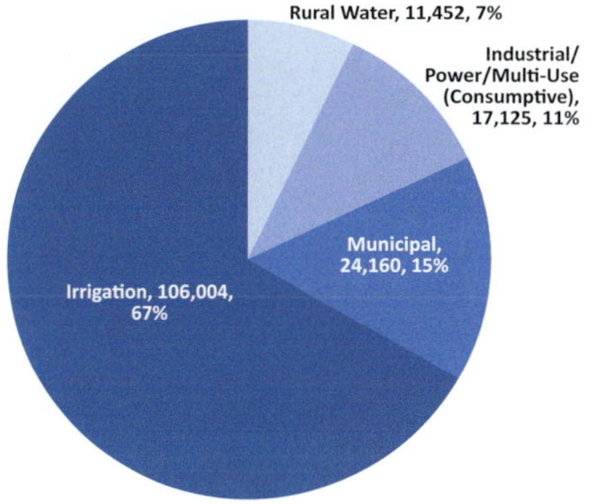

2006-2015 Ground Water Average Use (In Acre-Feet)
Total: 158,761

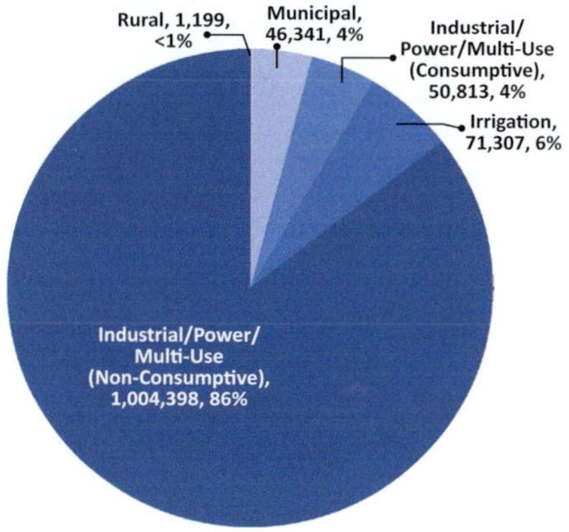

2006-2015 Surface Water Average Use (In Acre-Feet)
Total: 1,174,058

Historically, and through today, the greatest percentage of consumptive water use is for irrigation, and the greatest percentage of non-consumptive use is for power generation, such as Garrison Dam and coal power plants along the Missouri River. When comparing the state's consumptive water use to the rest of the states in the country, North Dakota ranks fifth lowest at 0.13 percent of total consumptive water use.

Hydrofracturing for oil, or "fracking," is a technology that began to see widespread use in the state in 2007. Although fracking water use has often been portrayed as representing a substantial portion of North Dakota's water use, all water use in oil production in 2015 accounted for only 24,757 acre-feet, or 7 percent of consumptive water use, out of the state's 10-year average of approximately 328,000 acre-feet.

Water Facts

- There are five major hydrologic subdivisions in North Dakota: the Missouri River Basin, the James River Basin, the Red River Basin, the Devils Lake Basin, and the Mouse River Basin.
- Lakes and reservoirs total about 863,000 acres.
- There are 54,373 total river miles.
- There are 427 river border miles.
- Total miles of rivers and streams by basin: Missouri River, 36,094; Red River (includes Devils Lake Basin) 11,881; Mouse River, 3,645; and James River, 2,753.
- The longest river completely within the state is the Sheyenne at 506 miles.
- There are about 2.5 million acres of wetlands.
- Average daily stream flow of the Missouri River at Bismarck is 22,680 cubic feet per second (cfs); the Red River at Drayton is 4,393 cfs; the Mouse River at Westhope is 269 cfs; and the James River at LaMoure is 163 cfs.
- The lowest elevation in the state is 750 feet above mean sea level (amsl) where the Red River crosses the border into Canada.
- Devils Lake is the largest natural lake in the state. At an elevation of 1,454 feet amsl, it covers about 205,000 acres, including Stump Lake.
- Lake Sakakawea is the largest reservoir and body of water in the state. At a maximum operating pool (elevation 1,854 feet amsl), it covers 380,000 acres.
- At its normal operating pool elevation of 1,837.5 feet amsl, Lake Sakakawea has more shoreline (1,340 miles) than California has coastline (840 miles).
- Garrison Dam is 210 feet high and 11,300 feet (2.1 miles) long.
- It is estimated 60 million acre-feet of ground water is stored in the major unconsolidated aquifers in the state.

Navigable Waters

"Navigable waters" are those waters that were navigable at the time of statehood. This means they were used, or were susceptible of being used, in their ordinary condition as highways for commerce, over which trade and travel were, or may have been, conducted in the customary modes of trade on water, such as a boat.

North Dakota considers the following waters navigable:

- Missouri River
- James River
- Sheyenne River
- Pembina River
- Mouse River
- Red River of the North
- Bois De Sioux
- Knife River
- Heart River
- Cannonball River
- Yellowstone River
- Devils Lake
- Lake Metigoshe
- Painted Woods Lake
- Sweetwater Lake
- Upper Des Lacs Lake
- Long Lake, Bottineau County

Sovereign Lands

North Dakota's sovereign lands are those areas, including the beds of waterbodies and islands, lying within the ordinary high watermark of navigable lakes and streams. The state engineer is responsible for administering the state's non-mineral interests in North Dakota's sovereign lands.

The state engineer is responsible under the Public Trust Doctrine to use prudent judgment in identifying all rivers and lakes throughout the state that should be included on the state's list of navigable waters.

The state of North Dakota has ownership to the ordinary high watermark of the state's navigable waters. The delineation of the ordinary high watermark is a critical component of sovereign land management because it identifies the specific areas in and around the state's navigable waters that are under the jurisdiction of the state engineer of the State Water Commission. The ordinary high watermark delineates the boundary between the uplands owned by the riparian landowners and the state-owned sovereign lands.

Threatened and Endangered Species

Since 2015, one species has been declared endangered in North Dakota and added to the list maintained by the U.S. Fish and Wildlife Service in accordance with the Endangered Species Act of 1973.

The Rusty Patched Bumble Bee (Bombus affinis) is endangered; it is a species of bumble bee that lives in colonies, including a single queen and female workers. In late summer, males are produced, and only males and workers have a rusty reddish patch on the back.

North Dakota does not have a state threatened or endangered species list. Only those species listed by the Endangered Species Act are considered threatened or endangered in North Dakota. A total of 12 species are currently listed in North Dakota, although not all species are known to have populations in the state. There are several species that have been petitioned to be listed, such as the monarch butterfly and moose, as well as two more bumble bee species. The process for determining if a listing is warranted can take several years.

The U.S. Fish and Wildlife Service has primary oversight of threatened and endangered species. For additional information, contact the North Dakota Ecological Services Field Office in Bismarck at 701-250-4481 or northdakotafieldoffice@fws.gov or visit http:ecos.fws.gov/ipac/.

Current List of Threatened or Endangered Species for North Dakota

Common Name	Scientific Name	Type	Status	Date Added to ESA List
Whooping Crane	*Grus americana*	Bird	Endangered	3/11/1967
Least Tern (Interior)	*Sterna antillarum*	Bird	Endangered	5/28/1985
Piping Plover	*Charadrius melodus*	Bird	Threatened	12/11/1985
Red Knot (Rufa)	*Calidris canutus rufa*	Bird	Threatened	1/12/2015
Black-footed Ferret	*Mustela nigripes*	Mammal	Endangered	3/11/1967
Northern Long-eared Bat	*Myotis septentrionalis*	Mammal	Threatened	5/4/2015
Gray Wolf	*Canis lupus*	Mammal	Endangered	3/9/1978
Pallid Sturgeon	*Scaphirhynchus albus*	Fish	Endangered	9/6/1990
Dakota Skipper	*Hesperia dacotae*	Insect	Threatened	11/24/2014
Poweshiek Skipperling	*Oarisma poweshiek*	Insect	Endangered	11/24/2014
Rusty Patched Bumble Bee	*Bombus affinis*	Insect	Endangered	3/21/2017
Western Prairie Fringed Orchid	*Platanthera praeclara*	Plant	Threatened	9/28/1989

Aquatic Nuisance Species

Aquatic nuisance species (ANS), whether they are animals, such as the zebra mussel or common carp, or plants, such as curly-leaf pondweed, threaten fishing, boating, swimming, and other water-based activities. In states where they have become established, ANS are expensive to combat and difficult or impossible to control or eliminate.

In 2015, adult zebra mussels were confirmed in the Red River for the first time. The current list of ANS that exist in North Dakota is as follows:

Animals	**Plants**
Zebra mussel	Curly-leaf pondweed
Silver carp	Eurasian water milfoil
Common carp	

Other ANS are found in nearby states, and numerous regulations are in place to help prevent their introduction into North Dakota waters.

Fishing and Hunting Licenses

Fishing License Increase

A record number of resident and nonresident anglers have fished in North Dakota from 2013-2016. Much of this increase in participation is due to a significant increase in the number of fishing waters, along with aggressive fish management in those waters, which are now providing excellent fishing opportunities in many places they did not exist historically.

At the end of 2016, North Dakota had more than 425 fishing waters, compared to less than 200 in 1993 when the current wet cycle started.

Hunting License Decline

North Dakota resident and nonresident hunting license sales have gradually declined since peaking in 2007. That decline is largely attributed to reduced opportunity due to loss of approximately 2 million acres of Conservation Reserve Program grassland acres since 2007, plus several difficult winters during the last decade, which set back resident pheasant and deer populations.

The pheasant harvest has declined by more than a third since 2007, and deer gun license availability fell from more than 140,000 to 49,000 in 2016.

North Dakota
Fishing License Sales

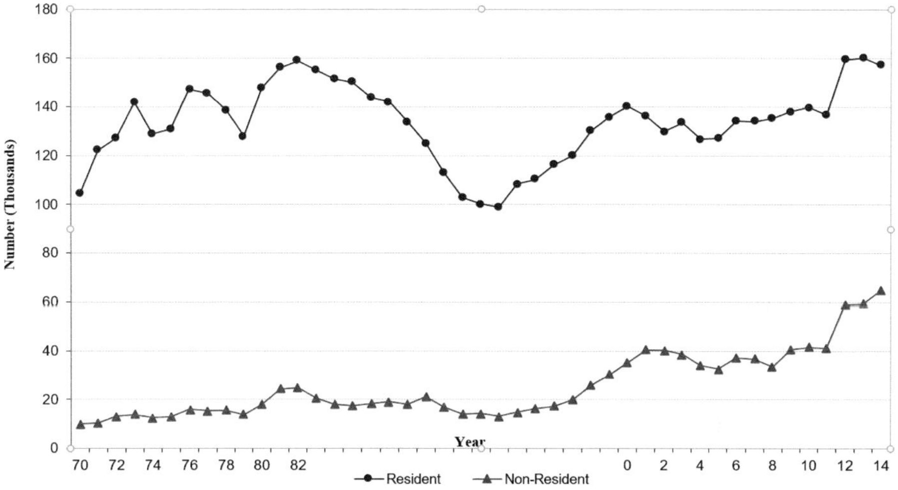

North Dakota
General Game License Sales

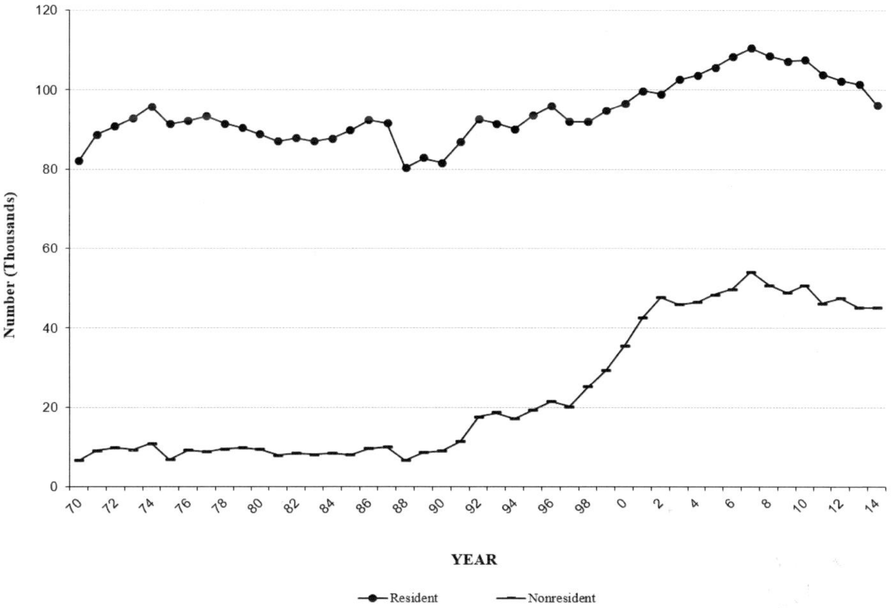

Fishing in North Dakota.

Hunting in North Dakota.

Chapter Twelve

Energy

Joseph Christain Leyendecker

Technologies at Work in the Oil Patch

Continual technological development drives the oil and gas industry, allowing companies to explore new sources and lower their production costs. These are some of the technologies that have advanced the oil and gas industry and established North Dakota as a major world player within it.

Up until the 1920s, it was widely believed well drilling yielded vertical boreholes. This belief was challenged by a build-up of evidence that indicated wells drilled on one property were sometimes crossing boundaries at depth and penetrating reservoirs on neighboring properties. Tools were developed to "survey" boreholes by taking repeated measurements of depth, inclination, and magnetic azimuth, and directional drilling was established as designs for down-hole equipment, which could bring a crooked hole back closer to vertical, were developed. The advent of directional drilling also created options to expose greater length of a wellbore to reservoirs by entering at an angle and made it possible to drill under water bodies or towns. However, for the next several decades, it remained a complicated process.

A major advance was seen in the 1970s as downhole drilling motors became common. These motors enable drill bits to continue rotating while the drill pipe remains stationary and allows for a bent sub, a short cylindrical device which deflects the motor off vertical, to be placed between the motor and the drill pipe without pulling out of the hole. As a result, horizontal drilling, where a vertical well is drilled down to a "kickoff point" from which it curves until it enters the targeted formation or zone horizontally, became more common. The horizontal laterals allow for even greater wellbore contact with the producing zone. The precision of directional drilling is further enhanced by the real-time geological information made available through mud logging, measurement while drilling (MWD), and logging while drilling (LWD) probes, which can operate in the hole while it is being drilled. Rather than drilling a well to reach fixed-spacial position, geosteering utilizes this real-time data in conjunction with well plans and models to control the direction of the wellbore and optimize its exposure to the reservoir. In the Bakken, this has led to laterals that have maintained position within thin primary targets for 90 percent or more of their length.

Once a well is drilled, it can be beneficial to stimulate oil and gas production by the process of hydraulic fracturing whereby a high-pressure injection of a fluid mix of water, sand, or ceramic proppant and thickening agents create and maintain fractures in the formation which allows oil, gas, and water to more easily flow through the rock and enter the wellbore. In unconventional resource plays, such as the Bakken, where tight formations greatly restrict the flow of oil and gas, slickwater fracking has emerged as a popular fracking option. Rather than using thickening agents to help carry the proppant into the cracks, slickwater fracks use fewer chemical additives and require greater water volumes and higher pressure. Some industry professionals believe this method also creates a more complex fracture network, which may

Putting flags out on an oil rig west of New Town.

increase production. Mechanical diverters physically block portions of a lateral to allow multiple frack stages to be completed.

Oil wells generally experience production declines with the passage of time. Within the first year, this decline can be quite steep. Processes have been developed that enable some older wells to regain higher rates of production or achieve greater initial production volumes for a new well. Refracture technology utilizing chemical diverters is being looked to as a means to re-stimulate wells. An acid stimulation treatment for wells in carbonate formations makes use of degradable fibers that temporarily block existing fractures, causing the acid to forge new paths into the rock. Hours later, the fiber blockages dissolve and restore permeability across the completion. In a similar fashion, chemical diverters are also being used in the initial fracture of shale formations like the Bakken in order to create more entry points into the formation and a more extensive fracture network. This also allows more sand to be delivered into the fracture network and distributes the sand more evenly among the perforation points.

Water flooding and enhanced oil recovery (EOR) are techniques that utilize injection wells within an oil field to displace residual oil within a formation and move it toward the producing wells. They are proven technologies that have long been used in conventional oil fields where primary recovery may be in the range of 15 to 20 percent of the total amount of oil in the formation. Water flooding can recover an additional 15 to 20 percent, after which EOR can add even more recovery. Due to the tight nature of the Bakken formation, the primary production of a well is closer to 4 to 6 percent of the total oil volume of the formation, and water flooding

Men working on a rig in the Bakken.

is generally not successful. EOR is being tested in the Bakken, using a CO_2 gas injection. The gas maintains reservoir pressures and improves oil displacement by reducing the tension between the oil and water. However, large volumes of CO_2 are necessary, imposing high costs on the technology until more cost-effective means of extracting CO_2 are developed.

EmPower North Dakota

Through the EmPower North Dakota Commission, leaders from all major energy industries in North Dakota meet regularly with one common goal: to be critical thinkers for the development of the state's energy resources. The strategic partnerships between North Dakota's long-standing and emerging energy industries enable all sectors of the industry to work together as they meet the state's and country's energy needs without government mandates. North Dakota is proactive and aggressive in addressing energy development. It serves as a model for America in fostering innovative, long-term energy strategies to meet the nation's growing energy demand and need for energy security in an environmentally responsible manner.

The state's diverse energy landscape celebrates many successes:

- North Dakota is the second largest oil-producing state in the nation and the fourth state to surpass production of 1 million barrels per day. The industry has more than 13,000 oil and gas producing wells.
- Utility companies produce 4,000 megawatts of lignite and other coal generation at seven locations, which provide low-cost and reliable electric power to two million customers in North Dakota, South Dakota, Minnesota, Montana, and Iowa. North Dakota is one of the country's top 10 coal-producing states, mining approximately 30 million tons every year since 1988, which results in an annual economic impact of $3 billion.
- North Dakota leads the nation in the production of 10 different agricultural commodities, including two commodities used for liquid fuels. Several additional crops provide feedstock for successful and developing bio-refining industries in North Dakota.
- North Dakota's five ethanol plants have an annual production capacity of 500 million gallons per year – a more than tenfold increase since 2005. The industry contributes more than $625 million annually to the economy and supports more than 10,000 direct and indirect jobs. The state is a national leader in flex fuel pump infrastructure and has seen a 250 percent increase in flex fuel vehicles over the past five years.
- Twenty-eight natural gas processing plants operate in western North Dakota. Also, the oil and gas industry is investing more than $6 billion in infrastructure to capture natural gas.
- North Dakota has almost 3,000 megawatts of wind energy capacity installed throughout the state, consisting of more than 1,500 turbines. The North Dakota Public Service Commission has permitted more than 3,846 megawatts of wind generation.

Biofuel

Biofuel production has grown in North Dakota in recent years, with the addition of five biofuel facilities in the last 10 years. North Dakota corn-based ethanol facilities have the capacity to produce a combined total of 500 million gallons of ethanol each year. The North Dakota Ethanol Council estimates 156 million bushels of corn are utilized in the state each year to produce ethanol. North Dakota is also home to a canola-based biodiesel facility at Velva. This Archer Daniels Midland (ADM) facility has a production capacity of 85 million gallons of biodiesel per year. Strides are also being made in the development of the next generation of technologies and feedstocks for the biofuels industry. Researchers at North Dakota State University estimate bioenergy production could contribute an estimated $800 million in direct annual economic activity in the state. Biofuel producers are eligible for several state incentive programs, including the Ethanol Production Incentive Program and the Biofuels PACE Program.

Highlights include:

- North Dakota's five ethanol plants have an annual production capacity of 500 million gallons per year.
- The state's ethanol industry generates nearly $625 million in economic activity each year and directly employs almost 225 workers across the state with an average annual wage of $64,000.
- Approximately 10 percent of the ethanol produced annually in North Dakota is blended with gasoline and sold within the state. The remaining 90 percent is shipped primarily to the east or west coasts.
- In a modern ethanol facility, one bushel of corn produces 2.8 gallons of ethanol, 18 pounds of livestock feed (DDGs), 18 pounds of carbon dioxide, and up to one pound of corn oil.

Dakota Spirit AgEnergy Ethanol Plant located in Spiritwood.

Biomass

North Dakota is an agricultural state, and much of our land area is in working farms and ranches. There are many opportunities in the area of agriculture-related energy production on the horizon. The federal Oak Ridge National Laboratory ranks North Dakota first in the nation in the potential to produce perennial energy crops. Utilizing biomass for energy production may have many benefits, including improved national security, increased economic growth, and broad-based environmental benefits. Biomass is simply all plant and animal matter on the earth's surface. Harvested biomass may be used to generate various forms of energy, such as heat, electricity, biofuels, and other biobased products. Examples of biomass include wood waste, energy crops, crop residues, and other forms of organic waste.

Highlights include:

- North Dakota State University (NDSU) estimates a direct economic impact of more than $180 million annually from a 50-million gallon biorefinery that is converting wheat straw to ethanol. Researchers at NDSU and the University of North Dakota's (UND) Energy & Environmental Research Center are actively engaged in biomass research.
- Dakota Spirit AgEnergy operates a 65-million gallon per year biorefinery next to Great River Energy's Spiritwood Station power plant.

Energy Efficiency

Energy efficiency continues to be a high priority in public buildings around the state and in North Dakota homes. More than 11,000 energy efficiency and renewable energy rebates were given to North Dakota residents and businesses, resulting in $3.4 million in energy cost savings.

Highlights include:

- The Agricultural and Biosystems Engineering Department and NDSU Extension Service provided education and technical assistance on energy efficiency and conservation through programs such as Home Energy 101, home builders educational seminars, 4-H leader training on the importance of home energy, and energy savings opportunities related to grain drying.
- Energy conservation efforts helped weatherize 570 homes for low-income individuals across North Dakota in 2015.
- North Dakotans received 3,800 rebates (at $150 each) for ENERGY STAR refrigerators and will save approximately 2 million kilowatt hours annually.
- Approximately 164 local government buildings across the state have been retrofitted through the Energy Efficiency and Conservation Block Grant annually, saving more than $1.1 million.
- The state building code now encompasses the 2009 International Energy

Conservation Code and the International Residential Code energy efficiency requirements.
- More than 1,130 ground source heat pump systems have been installed in both residential and commercial buildings across North Dakota.

Ethanol

The ethanol industry contributes nearly $625 million annually to the state's economy and supports more than 10,000 jobs. North Dakota's ethanol plants employ nearly 225 workers directly in positions such as chemists, engineers, accountants, managers, and support staff. The average annual wage for an ethanol plant employee in North Dakota is approximately $64,000.

Highlights include:

- Each North Dakota ethanol plant is located in a community with a population of less than 2,500 and contributes an average of 49 jobs and an average annual payroll of $3.3 million to the community.
- North Dakota ethanol plants use approximately 160 million bushels of corn annually with more than 80 percent of the corn purchased from North Dakota farmers. Forty to sixty percent of North Dakota's total corn production annually is purchased by North Dakota ethanol plants.
- Approximately 10 percent of the 500 million gallons of ethanol produced annually in North Dakota is blended with gasoline and sold within the state.
- North Dakota is a national leader in the establishment of flex fuel pumps. The state also has 121,500 flex fuel vehicles.

A dragline at Falkirk Mine in Underwood.

Lignite

North Dakota's lignite industry is a vital part of the state's economy with an economic impact of more than $3 billion. The state supports 4,000 megawatts of lignite and other coal generation at seven locations, providing low-cost, reliable, and clean electric power to two million customers in North Dakota, South Dakota, Minnesota, Montana, and Iowa. North Dakota is one of the country's top 10 coal-producing states, mining approximately 30 million tons every year since 1988. Nearly 80 percent of the lignite coal mined annually is used to generate electricity; about 13 percent is used to make synthetic natural gas that is delivered to 400,000 homes and businesses in the eastern United States; and 7 percent is used to produce fertilizer products containing anhydrous ammonia and ammonium sulfate.

Highlights include:

- Great River Energy's Spiritwood Station is a combined heat and power plant that began operations in 2014. Its primary product is steam, which is sold to users at the Spiritwood Energy Park near Jamestown. The plant also produces some electricity for the regional grid.
- The Great Plains Synfuels Plant (Synfuels Plant), owned by Dakota Gasification Company (Dakota Gas), is the only commercial-scale coal gasification plant in the United States manufacturing natural gas. Average daily production of natural gas is about 170 million cubic feet, the majority of which is used in the eastern United States.
- The Synfuels Plant supplies carbon dioxide to the world's largest carbon capture and storage project in the world in Saskatchewan, Canada, for use in enhanced oil recovery. Dakota Gas currently captures 3 million metric tons of carbon dioxide (CO_2) per year.
- Dakota Gas exports about 152 million cubic feet per day of CO_2 to Canada, about 50 percent of the CO_2 produced when running at full rates.
- A portion of reclaimed land becomes devoted to public use, such as Harmony Lake, which is now used for hunting, fishing, photography, birding, canoeing, boating, and other outdoor activities.
- Currently, the Lignite Research Council is participating in 15 research and development projects worth approximately $170 million. Many of these projects focus on ways to reduce, capture, and store CO_2.

Natural Gas

North Dakota's natural gas industry has worked hard to connect more than 2,100 new wells to gas plants. There are 28 natural gas processing plants operating in western North Dakota. A challenge of the petroleum industry is capturing the natural gas co-produced with oil. As of December 2016, 13 percent of the natural gas produced in North Dakota was being burned off or "flared."

Highlights include:

- Natural gas liquids present many opportunities for value-added energy. Research and studies exploring these possibilities provide great opportunities for expansion of the economic benefits beyond the oil-producing region.
- The state's first liquefied natural gas plant is near Tioga. Liquefied natural gas is natural gas that has been converted to a liquid form for easier storage and transportation.
- The North Dakota Industrial Commission, through the Oil and Gas Research Program in partnership with private parties, has invested more than $2 million in research for new technologies to capture and use natural gas at well sites. The results are intended to encourage and promote the use of new technologies that have a positive economic and environmental impact on oil and gas exploration. Examples include:

    - An $873,300 grant awarded to Bakken Express LLC to use toward a $3 million natural gas capture initiative.
    - A $750,000 grant awarded to Energy & Environmental Research Center to use toward a $1.9 million natural gas capture initiative.
    - A $375,000 grant awarded to Blaise Energy Inc. to use toward a $7.475 million natural gas capture initiative.

A rig west of New Town.

Oil

North Dakota's oil industry generates more than $43 billion of economic activity and supports 55,000 direct workers and more than 65,000 indirect jobs across all sectors of the economy. The necessary job skills continue to broaden as industry moves from the exploration phase toward the development phase.

Highlights include:

- North Dakota is the second largest oil-producing state in the nation and among the top 20 producers in the world.
- As of December 2016, preliminary figures indicated there were 13,337 producing wells, with 86 percent of those in the Bakken Formation.
- In March 2017, North Dakota's Legacy Fund, which receives 30 percent of the oil tax revenue, had a balance of more than $3.8 billion.

Petroleum Marketing

North Dakota petroleum marketers are dedicated to providing quality product and great customer service and continue to be strong community leaders and supporters. Consumer demand always has and always will dictate what a petroleum retailer offers its customers. The unprecedented economic growth in the state has been very good for the retail petroleum industry. One of the major challenges amidst all the prosperity has been finding adequate supplies of diesel, gas, and even propane, particularly during peak demand seasons for the industrial and agricultural sectors. Workforce availability remains a major concern in the retail service arena with such strong, high-paying jobs developing across the state in all sectors of the economy.

Highlights include:

- There are roughly 500 petroleum marketers in North Dakota. There are also about 500 convenience stores/truck stops across the state. This number has grown significantly in the past few years as the state's economy continues to prosper and expand. These operations deal in every aspect of refined petroleum and renewable fuel products, ranging from wholesale and supply to the numerous retail outlets scattered across the state.
- North Dakota petroleum marketers continue to support research and development of renewable fuels as viable sources of alternate energy.

Refining

North Dakota's refining capacity continues to expand with the continued growth of Bakken oil production.

Highlights include:

- North Dakota's largest refinery is Tesoro Mandan Refinery, with a crude operating capacity of 71,000 barrels per day.
- Teroro Dickinson Refinery, formerly Dakota Prairie Refinery LLC, opened in December 2014 and started selling diesel fuel in June 2015. Tesoro Dickinson Refinery has a crude capacity of 20,000 barrels per day and produces 7,000 to 10,000 barrels per day of diesel and other byproducts. It is the first refinery built in the United States since 1976.

Solar, Geothermal, Hydrogen, and Hydro Power

North Dakota has invested in research for hydrogen, solar, and geothermal applications. This includes $2.5 million for a Centers of Excellence project at the Energy and Environmental Research Center's National Center for Hydrogen Technology, which is attracting hydrogen-based business to the state; funding for research at UND for commercial application of geothermal; and funding for solar energy research at NDSU.

Highlights include:

- Several electric cooperatives offer a program to help ranchers install solar-powered stock pond watering pumps in rural areas where it is uneconomical to construct electric transmission lines. As an example, Verendrye Electric Cooperative has provided support for more than 260 solar pumps and avoided building about 300 miles of distribution line at a savings of nearly $30,000 per mile.
- Whiting Petroleum uses solar PV systems at oil well sites to power pump jacks in isolated areas in which electrical service is not available.
- The Geothermal Laboratory at UND is conducting a geothermal power demonstration project in North Dakota in collaboration with the U.S. Department of Energy, Continental Resources Inc., Slope Electric Cooperative, and Access Energy LLC. The objective of the project is to demonstrate and test the technical and economic feasibility of generating electricity from non-conventional, low-temperature geothermal resources using Organic Rankine Cycle (ORC) technology.
- The Garrison Dam on the Missouri River, with a capacity of 583 megawatts, is North Dakota's fifth largest plant in electricity generation capacity.

Transmission

The development of new transmission in North Dakota continues as companies construct lines to support new load growth, as well as connect new generation to the electric grid. Studies to identify impacts of new load on existing transmission systems and identify new lines needed for the future continue at individual companies and at regional transmission planning entities.

Highlights include:

- The North Dakota Transmission Authority conducted a study of the impact of oil and gas development in the Williston Basin on electric load growth and transmission infrastructure.
- Minnkota Power Cooperative operates a 345-kV transmission line that stretches 250 miles from Center to Grand Forks.
- CapX2020 has now invested $1.85 billion in completing four high voltage transmission line projects totaling nearly 725 miles across Minnesota, North Dakota, South Dakota, and Wisconsin.

Wind

North Dakota is known for being windy, and the potential for wind energy is great. According to a study completed by the National Renewable Energy Laboratory and AWS Truepower, North Dakota is the sixth "windiest state."

Highlights include:

- North Dakota has almost 3,000 megawatts of wind energy capacity installed throughout the state, consisting of more than 1,500 wind turbines.
- North Dakota's wind resource for potential development is ranked sixth in the country, and the state ranks 11th for installed wind capacity, getting 21.5 percent of its net electricity generation from wind resources.

Wind turbines in a sunflower field near Wilton.

Chapter Thirteen

North Dakota during World War I

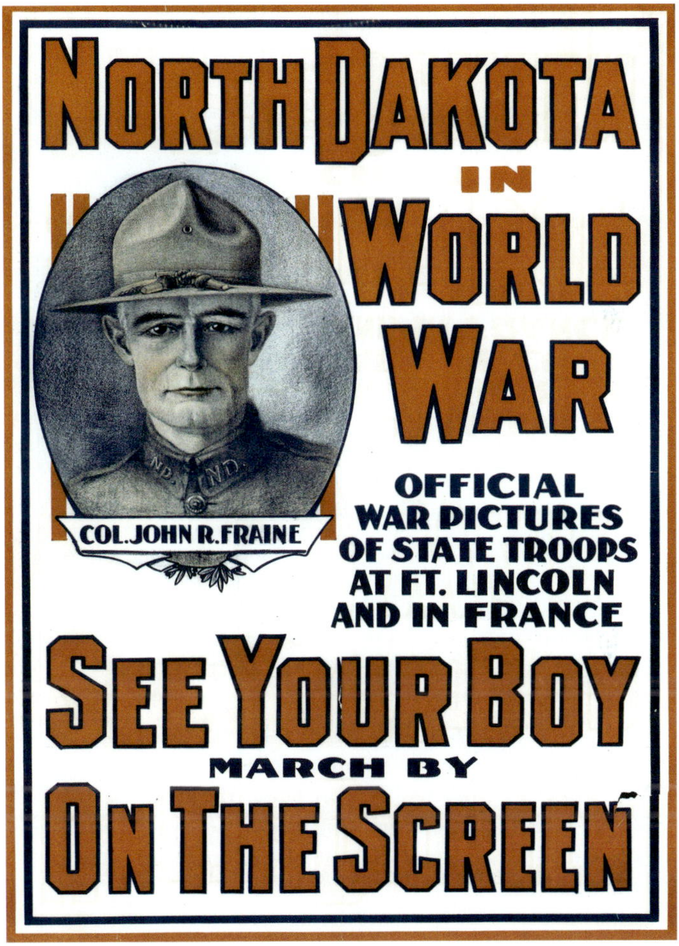

Pre-War in the United States

When World War I began in Europe in August 1914, many in the United States hoped America would not get involved. President Woodrow Wilson's view, and the official position, was that America should remain neutral. This position was not an easy one to maintain, and Wilson was often criticized from both sides. The overall consensus in North Dakota was to support Wilson in his efforts to stay neutral. With a large German-American population, many in North Dakota opposed American entry into the war against Germany. North Dakota's congressional delegation and its citizens were strong voices in the effort to remain neutral as war broke out overseas.

President Woodrow Wilson.

The war continued to be a pivotal issue in the nation. During the 1916 election, Wilson won representation for the Democratic Party at the Democratic convention in St. Louis. Part of his platform called for military preparedness and a world association of nations to maintain peace after the war in Europe ended. The greatest cheers came with the campaign slogan, "He Kept Us out of War." The argument was made that if one wanted peace, one needed to vote for Wilson, which resonated for many in North Dakota.

The election results were close, and it was not clear who won until two days later. Republican candidate Charles Evans Hughes lost the traditionally Democratic South and the progressive West. He also lost in a few key Midwestern states. Wilson won 49.4 percent (9,127,695) of the popular vote; Hughes captured 46.2 percent (8,533,507). The Electoral College ballot gave Wilson a narrow 23-vote margin (277 to 254). North Dakota was among those states that voted to re-elect President Wilson, a significant fact that made the headlines in *The New York Times*. North Dakota's five electoral votes were credited, along with other swing states, in helping Wilson win in the final tally.

The situation in Europe did not improve, and in 1917, America's neutrality was pushed toward the edge. German leadership decided to shift their style of battle from offense to defense, combined with unrestricted submarine warfare. Germany had more than 200 submarines, and they believed they could defeat the Allied forces within six months if they waged an unrestricted campaign against all shipping freight, including U.S. ships. On January 31, 1917, the German government informed the world that, beginning the next day, German U-boats would sink all vessels, neutral and Allied alike, without warning.

To further anger the United States, German Foreign Minister Arthur Zimmerman sent a telegram to the German ambassador to Mexico proposing that, in the event of war with the United States, Germany, and Mexico should join in an alliance. Zimmerman assured Mexico that Germany would aid them with financial assistance, and with a victory over America, Mexico could regain her lost territories of Texas, New Mexico, and Arizona. British intelligence intercepted this message and handed it over to President Wilson, as well as the American media and public. Although Mexico never accepted the alliance, the threat seemed valid as only six months earlier President Wilson and President Carranza were almost at the brink of war when General Pershing invaded Mexico territory. Congress, along with most of the nation, was shocked and angered by the Zimmerman telegram. Any hope of continued neutrality was shattered.

On February 3, 1917, Congress voted on President Wilson's resolution to break diplomatic ties with Germany. Representative Henry T. Helgesen and Senator Asle J. Gronna from North Dakota voted not to support the president.

Many in North Dakota were not yet ready to take the next step, as evident in the following comment by noted Bismarck author James W. Foley, who wrote the following which was published in the *Bismarck Tribune* on February 24:

> *"We have seen a little of war and some of our ancestors have served in all the wars from the Revolution, but we have had all we care for. My son, James, says he is ready and willing to go, but we will remain in the Bad Lands until Wilhelm [II] gets to Fryburg Hill."*

On April 2, President Wilson went before Congress and asked for a declaration of war. Wilson accused Germany of conducting "warfare against all mankind." He also stated the war was not just to defeat Germany, but it was a war for the principles of peace and justice. It was a war to make the world "safe for democracy."

Although declaration of war was inevitable at this time, those who wanted to take a last stand were allowed to state their views. On April 4, Senator Gronna reminded those in attendance that Europe now regretted the war they started in 1914 and was weary of it but could not end it because of "false national pride." North Dakota Senator Porter J. McCumber made a last effort plea that Germany be given a second chance and called for a delay in the declaration of war. Despite misgivings, Senator McCumber voted reluctantly for the resolution of war. Senator Gronna cast the first vote against the war. The vote was 82-6 in the Senate. On April 6, 1917, the House voted 373-50 in favor of the war declaration. The United States, joining its allies Britain, France, and Russia, was now at war.

North Dakota Enters the War

Following the declaration of war by the U.S. Congress, citizens across the country and in North Dakota began to rally. Although many in North Dakota had hoped to stay out of the war, once the United States entered into the conflict, many promptly prepared to support the war efforts. Various businesses and local groups began showing support for the war, while men and women began to look for ways to become involved. Those who remained hesitant or opposed were encouraged to join the wave of patriotism that demanded everything should aid the war efforts.

Yet, some U.S. citizens had already been supporting the war for the past few years. Even before America was officially in the war, some North Dakota men entered the war by serving in the Canadian services. For example, John Bridges, a young man who graduated from Valley High School in 1913 and then attended classes at the University of North Dakota, saw the front trenches before the United States joined the war efforts. After the *Lusitania* was sunk and America did not go to war, he went to Winnipeg in August 1915, where he enlisted in the Canadian Highlanders. After reaching the front, he volunteered to serve as company stretcher bearer. He was wounded by an enemy bomb in August 1916 while running forward to assist a wounded soldier. He died two days later.

Citizen Soldiers Over Here, Over There

The first men called to service were those in the Second Battalion of the North Dakota National Guard. The Second Battalion consisted of companies from Bismarck, Mandan, Jamestown, and Dickinson, along with eight men from the Hospital Corps out of Lisbon. Called into service on March 25, 1917, they were placed under the command of Major Dana Wright. Their immediate assignment was sending detachments to guard the Northern Pacific Railroad Bridge over the Missouri River at Bismarck, along with bridges at Jamestown, Valley City, and Fargo. On July 1, the battalion was relieved from this guard duty and sent to Fort Lincoln, near Bismarck, for mobilization. From there, those in the Second Battalion were sent to training for overseas duties.

Feeling the patriotic call to serve, other companies began to drill in local armories. Due to the high numbers of men in these companies, Governor Lynn Frazier authorized on June 30 the formation of the Second Regiment, which was placed under the command of Colonel Frank White.

President Wilson called the National Guard into federal service on July 3, 1917. North Dakota's regiments departed for Camp Greene in North Carolina. There they became part of the 41st, or Sunset Division, which was composed of National Guard units from North Dakota and several other western states, such as Montana, Idaho, and Oregon. It became a replacement division, its men widely scattered to serve with various regular Army units.

Governor Frazier (standing back center between middle flag and boy in white cap) with the North Dakota State Council of Defense No. 1 in Bismarck.

Of the nine infantry regiments assigned to the 41st Division, only four remained intact. One of these was the First North Dakota Regiment, which became the 164th due to necessary uniformity in the American Expeditionary Force. The men of the 164th were soon in training. However, it was not the desired six months of training; instead, they received nine days of target practice. Even that time was limited, with each man only shooting for two hours on the rifle range. The reality was basic order drills, lack of real equipment such as machine guns, and a shortage of uniforms, interrupted by epidemics.

The Second North Dakota Regiment did not remain together, experiencing military reorganization when they reached North Carolina, along with other state units. These officers and men were sent to the 41st auxiliary unit. This was a harsh reality for the men from North Dakota who had joined as a state unit. When broken up, they lost their own officers, as well as a sense of belonging with their fellow state volunteers.

On December 15, 1917, the 41st Division, including the 164th, sailed for Liverpool on the *Leviathan* after only a few weeks of training. General Headquarters used the division to provide replacement for other combat divisions upon its arrival in Europe in January 1918. As a replacement unit, North Dakota soldiers became even more widely scattered and, as a result, the men initially comprising the First and Second North Dakota Regiments participated in many diverse areas of combat. Men from North Dakota participated in the battles of Cantigny and Soissons, as well as the battles of Toul Sector, Chateau-Thierry, St. Mihiel, and the Argonne Forest, which was the high tide of American participation in the hardest theaters of combat.

The use of the 41st Division as a replacement division was not unusual but was also not well received by the 164th. In fact, it was a demoralizing blow. The North Dakota Guardsmen, these citizen soldiers, were now part of the anonymous armies in the Great War, and the old image of fighting as private citizens defending their state and country was lost. The breakup of the Second North Dakota Regiment and then later the splitting up of the 41st Division, including the North Dakotans of the 164th, created some resentment among the soldiers.

Many of the North Dakota Guardsmen were assigned noncombat duties. Most of the officers from North Dakota were relegated to the rear, working behind the lines. Such was the case for Colonel Frank White, former hero of the Philippines effort during the Spanish-American War and two-time governor of the state of North Dakota. Due to his advanced age, White was not sent to active duty. He himself acknowledged this and realized he could do plenty of work in back of the lines. He ended up working with the French civilian population and obtaining buildings for quartering troops. Later, he would receive the title of commanding officer in charge of renting, requisitions, and claims service. The mundane but essential job was an endless series of details and negotiations, such as setting rental rates and agreements and dealing with property damages and complaints. As important as this job may have been, as White wrote to his wife about this job none would want, "If I had a job that any one wanted, they would probably find some excuse to go after me."

Yet not all of the North Dakota Guardsmen were left out of the action behind the lines. The 164th lost 278 men in the war, with 166 deaths attributed to battle,

Soldiers in the trenches.

62 to wounds, and the rest to disease, mainly influenza. There were also nearly 650 men who suffered battle wounds. However, none of the casualties were attributed to the 164th, since these men officially served in the 41st Division. In all, 4,195 officers and men served in World War I as National Guardsmen; a few served in the state quartermaster detachment, and the majority went overseas.

North Dakota Dough Boys

The majority of North Dakota servicemen were not in the National Guard; they either enlisted as volunteers or were drafted through the Selective Service System. The Selective Service Act, which Congress passed and President Wilson signed in May 1917, required men between 21 and 35 years of age to register for the draft. In North Dakota, the first draft call came on September 2, 1917, and 1,582 men were called up.

A unique ethnic group of German-Russian citizens was among the men of service age in North Dakota. They were part of a migration of Germans who had first emigrated to Russia but had never integrated into Russian society, remaining an isolated people before migrating to America. A large number of these German-Russians came to the Dakotas. They maintained their traditions, kept to themselves, and rarely made an effort to learn English. These characteristics led to several instances where some of the German-Russians faced obstacles in their new communities, and in some cases, outright arrests. A few neglected to register or heed their draft notices; for some, this was because they could not read or write English. Others were sometimes forcibly prevented from doing so. For example, one father locked his two draft-age sons in the barn to prevent them from registering. The majority of the young men of German-Russian heritage did in fact register and comply with the law, and most men entered military service willingly. Many young women also volunteered for training as student nurses.

On March 29, 1918, the McIntosh County community, which was widely composed of this German-Russian population, had a two-day celebration to honor 50 young men on their way to Camp Dodge in Iowa. An estimated four thousand sent them off. On May 25, more than three thousand did the same for 38 young men going to Camp Lewis in Washington. The local papers ran stories, often with photos, of the young men in their uniforms, many of whom seemed to be enjoying the adventure and a bit of an escape. The men wrote letters home about showers and clean cloths, even beds with springs and mattresses. They also wrote about the good meals of meat and vegetables. One North Dakota soldier, Christian Kurle, wrote to his nephew that he was a soldier now, "and don't know if I ever will be a farmer."

The men from North Dakota who served in World War I were generally young, in the range of 18 to 24 years old, but that was not always the case, as is evident with Fred E. Smith. His family moved to Grand Forks in 1880 where he attended grade school and later took high school classes at the University of North Dakota preparatory

Burleigh County men gather in Bismarck enroute to training.

school. He moved on to the University of North Dakota where he took classes on military drill and tactics, receiving a bachelor's degree and rising to the rank of cadet captain after five years of military courses. Lt. Colonel Smith arrived in France on May 14, 1918, as part of the 308th Infantry and was soon at the front lines. Smith was awarded the Medal of Honor, the highest award for valor in action against an enemy force which can be bestowed upon an individual serving in the armed services of the United States. He received this honor for his extraordinary heroism on September 29, 1918, while serving at Binarville, France. In the citation by Major General Robert Alexander, he told of Colonel Smith's heroism and personal courage under fire, where he served in the most forward position directing operations personally. In addition, the French awarded Smith the bronze Croix De Guerre with one palm and later the French Legion d' Honneur (the French Legion of Honor Medal).

North Dakota's Native American Soldiers

More than 200 of the young men from North Dakota who served in the military were from Indian Country. Many, like Benjamin D. Cloud, enlisted in Headquarters Company, 1st Infantry, North Dakota National Guard. Several joined the war before America did by enlisting in the Canadian Expeditionary Forces, such as Joseph McCloud of Belcourt, who joined in Winnipeg on August 2, 1915. John Redbean, born in Fort Yates, also enlisted with the Canadian Expeditionary Forces in fall 1916, where he served for 11 months but never went to Europe. He returned to America and later was inducted at Fort Yates, along with 17 other men from the community, and then sent to Camp Dodge. Redbean eventually served with the 82nd, which was known as the All American Division.

Albert Grass, from Fort Yates, was the grandson of Chief John Grass and had been a student at the boarding school in Bismarck. He was among the first Native Americans from Standing Rock Reservation who joined the North Dakota National

Guard, enlisting in July 1917 and from there participating in the war efforts overseas. Private Grass was killed at the Battle of Soissons in July 1918, when he tried to get water for his fellow soldiers. In May 1921, the body of Grass was returned to Cannon Ball, where it was ceremoniously buried. The American Legion Post in Fort Yates was named in his honor.

Thomas Everett Rogers, also known as Charges Alone, enlisted in the North Dakota National Guard in August 1917. He was sent overseas, arriving in France in January 1918, where he served as a scout. Rogers ultimately returned home to North Dakota. After the war ended, Ferdinand Foch, the Marshal of France and Supreme Commander of the Allied Forces during WWI, visited the Bismarck-Mandan area on November 26, 1921. There was great excitement over his arrival, and many special ceremonies were planned. The *Bismarck Tribune* announced, "The city began to take on a real holiday air today as decorations in honor of the coming of Marshal Foch tomorrow began to multiply." Notably, Marshal Foch picked Rogers out of those who had gathered to see him. He announced, "Tom Rogers was the bravest soldier in France."

> "*Tom, who was a scout, was sent out every night to the German Front to get information as to what organization was there. His manner of getting the desired information was a novel one. A white lieutenant accompanied him as far as it was safe to go; Tom then went on alone to the front, creeping through the grass, bushes and weeds, and when a sentinel passed, captured him with his bare hands and took him back to the American camp, where he was questioned. In case the sentinel attempted to give the alarm Tom 'croaked' him and carried his coat to camp. In 90 nights he was on this service, he did not make a single failure to bring in his man or a coat. He brought 33 of the latter.*"

Foch was thrilled by the community's reception. Thousands attended a parade in his honor and his presentation at Bismarck's City Auditorium. Among the planned events was a special ceremony, in which Sioux Indians from the Standing Rock Reservation presented Foch with the pipe of peace and tobacco pouch at the conclusion of his speech.

Foch accepted the gift from Red Tomahawk. The pipe was made by one of the Indians at Standing Rock: 18 inches long with a small, red stone bowl, accompanied by a beautiful beaded tobacco pouch. Red Tomahawk said a prayer as he puffed the pipe of peace, then handed it to Marshal Foch, who also smoked it. Red Tomahawk then conferred the name of Charging Thunder on Marshal Foch, telling the Marshal that some of his young men and the Marshal's people had spilled blood together in France, and they now lay side by side, buried under the earth. Chief Tomahawk then exacted a promise from Marshal Foch to prevent any violation of their graves. Foch replied, "I know the record of the North American Indian in the war, and I have come here in part particularly to thank this nation for the splendid men they sent and the mothers of the Indian Soldiers. I am happy to receive this pipe."

The Red Cross

While men were drafted or enlisted to join the war efforts, many women joined the cause by working through the Red Cross. Women spent time making surgical dressings and rolling bandages to be used at military hospitals. Some of the volunteers knitted socks and mittens for soldiers. Even the Junior Red Cross worked to help supply troops with supplies, food, and clothing. Local chapters of the Red Cross also raised money to fund hospitals near the war front. Membership in the Red Cross by December 31, 1917, was an impressive 166,151 in North Dakota. These members took on vigorous duties of support, exceeding the production numbers for knitted sweaters as well as collections of reading material for the troops. All over the state, weekly sessions were held to cut and roll bandages, and many attended classes on subjects like hygiene, first aid, and food conservation.

Red Cross volunteers did not just serve at home. Through the American Red Cross Nursing Service Committee, women from North Dakota were allowed to fully participate in support of the war effort. During the war years, Red Cross nurses were either assigned stateside or overseas. Candidates were required to be 25 to 40 years of age, unmarried, and have proof of some training. One nurse who signed up was Ingeborg Dalborten of Grand Forks, who later stated, "Perhaps this was a bit of Viking spirit in me, for I had a love for the strange and unheard of adventures in seeing foreign countries."

The patriotic need to assist in the war effort was a factor as well. Minnie Hage from Fargo had instructed a class on knitting socks and sweaters and served as a Red Cross instructor of surgical dressings but was left unsatisfied: "So when the student nursing corps was organized, I enlisted in Fargo at once and was sent as a civilian employee in the Medical Department of the Army to the Base Hospital at Camp Lewis, Washington, in 1918."

For those who made the crossing overseas, the reality of the war was immediate. The front was divided into three zones. The first was the closest to the fighting. There, medical attention was in the form of initial treatment. The second zone was more mobile and could be shifted according to the dictates of the campaign. Field hospitals were set up there. The third zone was where evacuation hospitals and somewhat more permanent stations were set up. Army nurses served in all but the first zone, but the difference between the first and second zone could be fluid. Army nurses could thus be under fire.

It was a chaotic and hectic reality for all, including those nurses arriving from North Dakota. Lillian Blackwell wrote in her diary on July 29, 1918:

> *"Patients, patients – simply pouring in and lying all over the hillsides under the trees. They are so tired, many only slightly wounded, but how they sleep from sheer exhaustion! Over 1,100 were admitted to Evacuation VII last night: roads are*

lined with trucks. We had 8,100 in eight days for our 300 bed hospital, but 1,100 in one night."

When the war ended, many nurses remained in the Red Cross through the demobilization. Several even stayed in the military for a few years after the war. Most returned to their homes and families, taking a discharge of duty as soon as possible. For those who served overseas, many came home with memories of their time in France. One nurse named Norah Engen came home with a husband.

Dr. Eric P. Quain in uniform.

Both men and women served through the Red Cross. One North Dakotan who served overseas was Dr. Eric P. Quain, founder of the Quain and Ramstad Clinic in Bismarck. He organized a Red Cross hospital unit with doctors and nurses from Bismarck. This became a base hospital at Bazeilles-sur-Meuse, with Quain serving as chief of surgical services, as well as a director of operating teams in a number of hospitals in France.

Two-term Governor Louis B. Hanna (elected in 1912 and 1914), who served as the chairman of the Liberty Loan drives in 1917 and 1918, volunteered to go overseas for the Red Cross, along with seven other men, in 1918. Hanna served in France as a captain in the American Red Cross and was cited as an officer of the French Legion of Honor by the French government.

By the time of the Armistice, 148 North Dakota nurses and about 200 physicians had served with the U.S. Army Medical Corps.

North Dakota Home Front

North Dakotans, along with the rest of the country, helped the war effort from home. Even if they didn't volunteer with the Red Cross, citizens donated money or goods for the cause. Conservation of resources at home so soldiers overseas had better access to goods also helped. Many grew their own victory gardens, reducing pressure on the public food supply and allowing more of this food to go to the front lines.

In North Dakota, farmers experienced great growth and change in daily operations. The day after war was declared, Governor Lynn Frazier urged the state's farmers to plant every available acre to maximize food production. Land values rose 65 percent. At the same time, a modernization movement was occurring, with improvements made industrially in all areas of machinery. While farm sizes were in some ways expanding, there was a shortage of farm labor as thousands were joining

A Liberty Bond poster.

the military or leaving the state for war-related job opportunities. The circumstances led many farmers to trade in traditional horse-powered equipment for modern tractors and modernize their farms. It became a necessity, in order to assist in the expanded acreage, with less manpower available.

Some helped with the war effort by buying Liberty Bonds, a form of a loan to the government to finance the war that would be paid back with interest in the future. In total, there were five bonds issued. The last bond, the "Victory Bond," came in April 1919. In the end, Americans would purchase more than $23 billion of Liberty Bonds.

Each state was given a quota, and North Dakota oversubscribed every loan. Across the country, Americans bought 16 percent more bonds than expected. In North Dakota, the five bond drives resulted in oversubscribing by 24 percent. To help encourage the purchasing of Liberty Bonds, a great number of patriotic posters were created and placed around communities, encouraging all citizens to buy these bonds. There also were the so-called "Four Minute Men," volunteers who gave brief speeches wherever they could get an audience, from movie theaters to churches.

Various other agencies in the state also aided the war effort. For example, the YMCA called for volunteers, and more than 100 men and several women entered the war service through this means in North Dakota. Most of the men worked as secretaries, a few as drivers; most of the women were employed in the canteen service. Dozens served overseas as well as in home camps. The YWCA was also enlisted to aid the war stateside as hostesses at the University of North Dakota and North Dakota State University for members of the Student Army Training Corps at each respective university. Possibly the most difficult service was during the influenza epidemic, where some of the YWCA women cared for the mothers and sisters of the sick soldiers, as well as prepared food for the convalescents.

The Influenza Epidemic

As the events of the Great War were unfolding, a new concern surfaced: the influenza epidemic of 1918, often called the Spanish Flu, ravaged Americans domestically as well as in foreign posts. This particular strain often led to pneumonia, adding more complications and contributing to deaths from the disease.

By October 1918, influenza was found in all the military camps. Between September and November, 316,089 cases were reported throughout the military ranks. There were only 112,000 available hospital beds, so other resources, like empty buildings and churches, were used to meet the needs.

The Red Cross nurses from North Dakota and other locales were thrown into the midst of this epidemic, often with little preparation. When she arrived in Boston, Birdie Adair was told by her supervisor that, due to the shortage of nurses, recent arrivals were to be "capped" at once. Esther Teichmann left Bismarck to go to Camp

Dodge in Iowa, where the whole camp was in quarantine for six weeks. Her job was in a part of the camp referred to as "Siberia," where barracks were used as hospital wards due to the severe bed shortage. During Teichmann's six weeks in "Siberia," she "had 192 patients under my care, and I was the only nurse there at night."

Maybe one of the best examples of the toll the flu took on nurses was in the recollections of Dorothy Blodgett of Minot, who was working in Camp Custer in Michigan. She later recounted every ward in Camp Custer was filled to capacity. Even the corridors had cots on both sides. Many of the patients lived only two or three days. The highest death rate in one day reached almost 70 men.

Due to this epidemic and other diseases, not all servicemen died in combat, even if they did manage to get overseas. Captain Addison Bentley Falconer graduated from Bismarck High School in 1907 and later attended University of Wisconsin and the University of North Dakota. He enlisted on August 26, 1917, and was eventually promoted to captain. In October 1918, he embarked for overseas service on board the *USS Siboney*. The second day out, he became ill with influenza, which developed into pneumonia. By the time he reached France, he was so ill he was immediately taken to the hospital, where he died 12 days later on October 29. He was buried with military honors at the new American cemetery at Kerhoun; his was the first grave in the officer's row.

Five North Dakota servicewomen were also among the causalities of this pandemic. Effie Larson and Mable Christenson died working the cantonments in the United States. Three others, Florence Kimball, Sebra Hardy, and Nora Anderson, died overseas, all succumbing to the flu or its complications.

In North Dakota, the threat of influenza first arrived in the form of newspaper coverage that soon became a daily record of misery elsewhere, accompanied by the underlying fear that the disease could come to the state.

When it did arrive in North Dakota, the epidemic left its mark in community after community. The impact of the Spanish influenza hit at the basic core of daily life. On advice from the State Board of Health, Mandan authorities acted early, closing all theaters, churches, schools, and other places of public gatherings. The October 9, 1918, edition of the *Bismarck Tribune* noted the occasion on its front page, "Everything Is Closed Tight by the 'Flu.'" The community of Bismarck also shut down. Even the state prison was locked down with no visitors allowed inside. All services in Bismarck churches were stopped. However, it didn't prevent the virus from spreading. On October 14, the *Bismarck Tribune* reported the epidemic hit the state hard as five people died from the virus within a 48-hour time period. There were more ongoing difficulties to report:

"With 100 new cases of Spanish influenza reported in Fargo within the last 48 hours, eight deaths have occurred, making 23 deaths in ten days. The number of cases here is estimated at 2,000."

The reality of the epidemic hit the state when the Minot Normal School closed on October 16. The town of Steele was very much in the grip of the epidemic when their only resident doctor was confined to bed by the illness. Three deaths and no doctor prompted the dispatch of a replacement doctor, along with three trained nurses from the clinic of Quain and Ramstad in Bismarck. On October 25, Mandan reported the death of County Judge J.C. Johnson, along with six others who died in seven days in that city and its immediate vicinity. In Morton County, 13 deaths had been recorded.

The epidemic extracted a high toll on the state. In November, Dickinson was nearing the end of the city's ban on public meetings, which had lasted nearly a month. An estimated 80 percent of the community had suffered from Spanish flu. More than 40 individuals had died there by November 2; additional deaths occurred throughout the rest of the month and from a second smaller outbreak that occurred in December. The deaths included George Ulschak and his wife, who left their young son of nine months an orphan. After two months of the epidemic, the *Dickinson Press* estimated at least 75 city resident fatalities.

In Devils Lake, the hardships of the disease were even greater, as they had to care for the ill of nearby New Rockford, which was one of the towns in North Dakota that was hit earliest by the illness. Along with those who succumbed from the epidemic, several nursing staff died while caring for the ill, including Henrietta Waters Halliday, the chairman of the Ramsey County Red Cross Nursing Service Committee, and five other nurses in training and volunteers.

The impact of influenza in Grand Forks was hardest among the young men who were there because of the Students Army Training Corps program, which was located on the campus of the University of North Dakota. Twenty-nine of these young men died, not from enemy bullets or shells, but from an illness that had killed at minimum 1,378 citizens within the state.

As the epidemic drew to an end in Bismarck and schools prepared to be reopened, one editorial stated the flu epidemic was the most distressing chapter in Bismarck's history. The editorial continued that the next day's church services should include prayers of thankfulness that Bismarck's portion of woe was not greater, as compared to other cities in the state.

The actual number of those who died from influenza in North Dakota was not well-documented, as there was little effort to take accurate statistics. The nationwide death rate of 0.5 percent, when used on North Dakota's population, would indicate an estimated number of 3,235 dead.

Although the Spanish influenza still caused deaths among military populations and civilians for months to come, the numbers decreased after November 1918, becoming part of a natural life and death cycle of everyday life.

An Issue of Loyalty

The nation went to war on many levels and as patriotic emotions heightened, attacks broadened and intensified against specific targets within the United States. The spirit of prosecution extended to include those who opposed the war, including socialists, Mennonites, and labor parties. Those most affected were recent immigrants of German heritage and those with politically leftist views, both of whom were present in North Dakota.

Despite the large number of German-American immigrants settled in North Dakota, the anti-German fervor that was sweeping the nation did not skip the state. Around the country, these sentiments often proved to be extreme, irrational, and even comical in practice. Nationwide, people with German names were targets of prosecution. German language newspapers suffered under this general outpouring of super-patriotism in forms of both official and private harassment. Several such newspaper offices were raided, and several editors were arrested and interned. The anti-German attitude was so overwhelming it included the banning of German music. Beethoven was banned in Pittsburgh. Sauerkraut was even renamed liberty cabbage.

The anti-German fervor rose especially over use of the German language. In many areas, German was removed from the curriculum of school systems. In Montana and South Dakota, the abandonment of the German language was ordered in all public schools at the elementary, secondary, and college levels. In Montana, this mandate was extended to cover private and parochial schools as well.

The most effective means of prosecution was the Espionage Act of 1917 and the Sedition Act of 1918, which deemed what activities could be considered offensive and chargeable behavior. It could be an offense to say or do almost anything that might obstruct the sale of the U.S. Liberty Bonds or use language intended to incite resistance to the United States or promote the cause of its enemies. If convicted of this, individuals faced fines, imprisonment, or both.

The first prosecution under the Espionage Act in North Dakota was the federal indictment of socialist Kate Richards O'Hare. She was an avowed socialist of national standing from Kansas. Strongly opposed to American entry into World War I, O'Hare toured the nation presenting a speech entitled "Socialism and the War." On July 17, 1917, she addressed a crowd in Bowman. This was the 76th time she had given the address. In Bowman, however, O'Hare was arrested after her speech. During her Bismarck trial, the St. Louis native was charged with saying: "Any person who enlisted in the army of the United States for service in France would be used for fertilizer and that is all that he is good for and that the women of the United States were nothing more or less than brood sows to raise children to get into the army and be made into fertilizer."

O'Hare was charged with obstructing enlistment under the Espionage Act. The trial took place in Bismarck under Judge Martin Wade of South Dakota, who was sitting in for Judge Charles F. Amidon. She was judged guilty and sentenced to five years at the federal prison at Jeffersonville, Missouri, as well as fined for the costs of the trial. The *O'Hare* decision was the only case in North Dakota based on the Espionage Act not heard by Amidon.

Another such case was filed against the minster of a German Evangelical Church in New Salem. Reverend John Fontana was brought to trial under the Espionage Act. He was charged for not buying Liberty Bonds and not supporting the Red Cross, as well as with singing songs and offering prayers for German victory. He was also openly questioned over areas of national pride, such as the flag. Many charges were dismissed by Amidon as irrelevant, but he did allow the jury to consider whether Fontana had stated he was proud of the Germans and their fight, as well as whether or not he had stated America had no right to take up arms against the Germans and whether or not he had prayed for a German victory.

Testimony from witnesses against Fontana stated he would not buy a Liberty Bond because he didn't want to prolong the war, and that in his view, the Kaiser was a man of peace. There was also testimony Fontana had said the sinking of the *Lusitania* was a humane act on the part of Germany, due to the munitions aboard, which cost German lives. This testimony was damaging to Fontana, in spite of the fact that on cross-examination the witness said Fontana had said all of this at home, not in front of any crowds, eligible draftees, or in his church. However, Amidon charged the jury to determine whether the statements were made, and if so, whether they had been willfully and with purposes the Espionage Act forbade. The jury found Fontana guilty.

Judge Amidon refused the defense counsel's motions for a new trial. Amidon's examination of the defendant and comments about the judgment were strongly worded. He concluded that in taking citizenship, Fontana should have "set almost earnestly growing an American soul, and put away your German soul." Amidon felt Fontana had not done that, saying he had cherished everything German: "You have preached German, prayed German, read German, sung German. Every thought of your mind and every emotion of your heart through all these years has been to German."

Amidon expanded this judgment to include other Germans who had come before him during the trial, stating "as I looked at them and tried as best I could to understand them, there was written all over every one of them, 'made in Germany.'" Amidon continued with a lecture from the bench about how immigrants had excluded everything American and cherished everything foreign, and that from now on they should begin at once "to cherish American thought, American history, American ideals." Amidon continued in this vein with statements on how to achieve this goal by replacing foreign ideas and customs with American ones. To stifle American life and to make foreign life perpetual was, according to Judge Amidon, a form of disloyalty, and it was one of the objectives of the courts in his view to give notice that this must be stopped.

> *And the object of the sentence which I pronounce upon you today is not alone to punish you for the disloyalty of which you have been guilty, but to serve notice on all the groups of people in this district who have been cherishing foreigners, that the end of that regime has come. It is a call to every one of you to set about earnestly the growing of an American soul inside of you.*
>
> *The court finds and adjudges that you are guilty under each count of the indictment, and as a punishment therefore it is further adjudged that you be imprisoned in the federal penitentiary at Leavenworth for the term of three years.*

The opinion written by Amidon was widely read and quoted in North Dakota. The *Fargo Forum* ran almost the entire sentencing statement. It was even partially covered in the Sunday *New York Times*, printed under the headline, "Some Wholesome Truth."

The largest number of cases commenced under the Espionage Act per capita of any state in the union came from the office of North Dakota's U.S. Attorney Melvin A. Hildreth. By 1921, the District of North Dakota started 103 prosecutions under the Espionage and Sedition Acts, exceeded only by the more populous states of Texas, California, New York, and Illinois. All but one indictment by grand jury came in 1918. Fifty occurred in one month alone.

Significantly, a large number were terminated by federal actions. Out of the 103 indictments, only 16 were ever actually taken to the jury. Of this number, only seven defendants were found guilty; six were acquitted, two were dismissed due to a hung jury, and one defendant was acquitted by a directed verdict from the bench. The percentage of convictions under the Espionage and Sedition Acts in North Dakota was only 13 percent. In the neighboring states of South Dakota and Wisconsin, the rate of conviction was 57 percent, and in Minnesota, 41 percent. Only Montana had a lower rate at nine percent.

The End of the Great War

On November 11, 1918, an armistice was signed between the fighting parties, marking a victory for the Allied forces and a defeat for Germany, though it was not a formal surrender. A ceasefire was called at 11 a.m. Paris time. The fighting was over, although negotiations over the Treaty of Versailles continued for another six months.

Newspapers across the state reported on the new development. The *Bismarck Tribune* announced the big news in their daily edition, but later in the day published a second extra edition of their paper. This extra edition included more information and news about the Armistice and reported on celebrations in the city:

> *The news spread over the state like a wildfire. Only a few minutes after the official dispatches had been received by* The Tribune, *long distance telephone calls began coming in from out-lying points and finally from towns as far distant as Valley City. All were anxious to confirm the rumors which they had received, fearing that they might be hoaxed into a second premature celebration. They lost no time in ripping off the lid when informed that the report this time was official and of unquestioned authenticity.*

With the ceasefire in effect, citizens in North Dakota and across the country began to consider the safe return of their troops. Several long months would pass before many would return.

On March 6, 1919, the *Bismarck Tribune* announced the homecoming of many soldiers. An event was set up for those returning and those who had already returned and included a reception at the train, a dinner with hospitable Bismarck families where "prominent citizens" would vie with each other to honor the returning soldiers, a rally, and a dance.

The returning fragment of the First North Dakota Regiment numbered some 551 men. They arrived at Camp Dodge, where the units were mustered out within the next few days.

> *Of old Co. A, but 31 men are returning with the present contingent, but there are a number of Bismarck boys in the headquarters company and the sanitary detachment, and there will be at least fifty of the Fighting First in addition to those who have already returned from other branches of the service. The homecoming is to be given in honor of all the soldiers and sailors who have come back to Bismarck and vicinity.*

The homecoming was a great event, according to the *Tribune*, with almost 200 soldiers and guests. The streets were lined with relatives, friends, and admirers. The evening was filled with good company, and food and music flowed at the Masonic temple.

> *The guests included two Native American soldiers with their wives, Sioux volunteers from Standing Rock, and the spectators included at least one proud father and mother from the reservation, who watched the dancing and the feasting and saw their boy sitting among those most honored, and thoroughly enjoyed it. It was a touch which gave the evening a fitting climax.*

It was an occasion "never to be forgotten by those fortunate enough to enjoy it" but wasn't to be the last. There were still more soldiers to return, and more similar events would occur. The *Tribune* stated, "but last night's homecoming was a premiere, and it established a standard and set a precedent."

Throughout 1919, stories of memorial services or returning servicemen and others involved in the war efforts were told in every community around the state. In Grand Forks, a memorial service was held at the University of North Dakota for all members who fought in the war. The paper listed the names of alumni and former students who had died.

In appreciation for their service, the North Dakota Legislature passed the Returned Soldiers Fund program. The legislature declared a moratorium on their debts, and when the war was over, provided them a bonus of $25 for each month of service. North Dakota was the first state to give veterans a substantial bonus. By the end of 1928, the state had paid $8.8 million to 26,475 veterans.

Consequences of the Great War

War brought change to North Dakota, both positive and negative. Like other parts of the country, the fighting brought a heightened sense of patriotism and unity to the country, but also for some a sense of xenophobia. In this atmosphere of the war and post-war years, assimilation was affected by the attitude expressed by many during the war years.

Men and women alike had helped in whatever way they could, but the strain of the war drained resources from everywhere. The most obvious impact was the strain on the labor force. Especially in strong agricultural areas, this drain of young male workers brought about necessary change in farm machinery and equipment.

The war also changed the voting status for Native Americans, whose rights up to that time were limited. As a result of World War I, legislation passed in 1919 stated any American Indian veteran who wished to apply for U.S. citizenship would be granted it. Before that time, they had not been considered natural-born citizens of the United States. On June 2, 1924, Congress finally granted citizenship to all Native Americans born in the United States.

North Dakota had contributed a lot to the war efforts. According to a 1919 article in *The Quarterly Journal of the University of North Dakota,* North Dakota provided 27,253 men between April 2, 1917, to October 31, 1918. Of this, 18,595 men went into the national Army; 6,611 joined the Regular Army; 1,838 became part of the Navy; and 209 entered the Marine Corps. The article noted this did not represent the total of North Dakota's contribution to the armed forces, as it did not take into account those who had enlisted prior to April 2, 1917, or others who were at that time in the federal service. Adjutant General G. Angus Fraser approximated the total number in active service from North Dakota to be around 30,000 men.

Later, historian Elwyn Robinson set the number at 31,269 officers and men from North Dakota who served in the various branches of the armed forces during World War I in his book, *History of North Dakota*. Of those, 19,772 volunteered, 11,481 entered through the Selective Service System, and 16 were civilians attached to the armed forces. Robinson also listed the total number of deaths for men from North Dakota serving their nation at 1,305. Of these, 514 were killed in action, 149 died from wounds, and 642 died from disease, with a majority of these due to the influenza epidemic.

By the end of the war, 133 North Dakotans had won some form of decoration, including two Medals of Honor. In addition, they received 26 Distinguished Service Crosses, four Distinguished Service Medals, four Navy Crosses, and 97 decorations from America's Allied government.

Serving along with the volunteers and the drafted, almost 200 physicians and almost 148 nurses served with the U.S. Army Medical Corps. Many other citizens volunteered by working with the Red Cross, army libraries, and YMCA or YWCA.

North Dakotans responded by buying Liberty Bonds in record numbers, growing their own gardens, and sacrificing bread and meat products. Men and women of all ages played their part. Children joined in assisting the Junior Red Cross. Young women made surgical dressings, socks, and later, clothing for the children of war-torn Europe. Every effort was made to strengthen the home front.

In the end, North Dakota contributed much to the war effort, which influenced a wide variety of trends and changes in the state.

U.S. Cavalry on parade.

Soldiers from Sims, North Dakota.

Index

B

C

D

E

F

H

I

J

K

L

M

N

O

P

Q

R

S

T

W

Y

Z